W9-AHU-188

www.wadsworth.com

www.wadsworth.com is the World Wide Web site for Wadsworth and is your direct source to dozens of online resources.

At *www.wadsworth.com* you can find out about supplements, demonstration software, and student resources. You can also send email to many of our authors and preview new publications and exciting new technologies.

www.wadsworth.com
Changing the way the world learns®

Crime Types

A Text/Reader

DEAN A. DABNEY
Georgia State University

THOMSON
™
WADSWORTH

Australia • Canada • Mexico • Singapore • Spain
United Kingdom • United States

THOMSON
WADSWORTH

Senior Acquisitions Editor, Criminal Justice:
Sabra Horne
Editorial Assistant: *Elise Smith*
Marketing Manager: *Dory Schaeffer*
Advertising Project Manager: *Stacey Purviance*
Signing Representative: *Davene Staples*
Project Manager, Editorial Production:
Brenda Ginty

Print/Media Buyer: *Emma Claydon*
Permissions Editor: *Joohee Lee*
Production Service: *Peggy Francomb,*
Shepherd, Inc.
Copy Editor: *Carey Lang*
Cover Designer: *Reuter/Design-SF*
Text and Cover Printer: *Transcontinental*
Compositor: *Shepherd, Inc.*

For more information about our products,
contact us at:
Thomson Learning Academic Resource
Center
1-800-423-0563
For permission to use material from this text,
contact us by: **Phone:** 1-800-730-2214
Fax: 1-800-730-2215
Web: http://www.thomsonrights.com

Library of Congress Control Number:
2003112924
ISBN 0-534-59373-9

Wadsworth/Thomson Learning
10 Davis Drive
Belmont, CA 94002-3098
USA

Asia
Thomson Learning
5 Shenton Way #01-01
UIC Building
Singapore 068808

Australia/New Zealand
Thomson Learning
102 Dodds Street
Southbank, Victoria 3006
Australia

Canada
Nelson
1120 Birchmount Road
Toronto, Ontario M1K 5G4
Canada

Europe/Middle East/Africa
Thomson Learning
High Holborn House
50/51 Bedford Row
London WC1R 4LR
United Kingdom

Latin America
Thomson Learning
Seneca, 53
Colonia Polanco
11560 Mexico D.F.
Mexico

Spain/Portugal
Paraninfo
Calle/Magallanes, 25
28015 Madrid, Spain

Contents

CHAPTER 7

Public Order Crime   239

CHAPTER 8

Crime within Complex Organizations   307

CHAPTER 9

Patterns and Prospects   363

Preface

Over the years, the content of student evaluations and personal reflections regarding my teaching experience has gradually convinced me that there exists a noticeable hole in the academic textbook market. At present, academics in search of text resources for their classes are forced to choose between traditional textbooks and anthologies/readers. In an effort to be all things to all people, contemporary textbooks have adopted an "everything but the kitchen sink" approach when it comes to content selection—each new edition packs in more information at the expense of readability and real-life flavor. This forces the instructor to make hard decisions about what materials to cover in a set 10- or 15-week term and leaves students both unstimulated and feeling like they wasted their money since some appreciable portion of the book's content was never discussed in class. This state of affairs has led many to turn to readers as an alternative or supplement to traditional textbooks. When used as a primary text, readers generally stimulate student interest in the class, but force the instructor to do much more work in the way of filling in the substantive gaps in the material. When used as a supplemental text, anthologies arouse student interest but do so at the added financial expense of the student.

It is time for a change; namely, the academic book market is in need of a hybrid template: the text-reader. Structurally speaking, the present book seeks to bring together the comprehensive overview of a textbook with the real-life feel of a anthology/reader. Such a cost-effective alternative allows the instructor the flexibility to cover a wide range of material, both in an overview and application sense, while at the same time holding the students' interest.

Substantively speaking, this book focuses on criminal behavior. The subject matter is divided into seven meaningful categories: homicide and assault, violent sex crimes, robbery, burglary, common property crime (i.e., larceny and auto theft), public order crime (i.e., drugs and prostitution), and crimes within complex organizations (i.e., employee, corporate, state, and governmental crime). Each of these seven chapters contains a concise overview discussion that reviews the existing data about patterns of offending, victimization, situations, and societal responses to the criminal event in question. Moreover, readers are presented with engaging research articles that report back from ground zero about the nature and dynamics of the players and their actions. Each article is preceded by a brief editor's note that touches upon its major conceptual highlights. Moreover, each chapter contains a series of discussion questions that serve to move student thinking and class conversations to a higher conceptual level. These questions force the reader to think about broader causal and prevention issues. There also is a companion website for this book. The website provides a host of supplemental readings and web-based resources for those who wish to see more data or discussion on a given form of crime. Such a resource is invaluable for those looking to write term papers or continue their discussion on a given type of crime.

The materials contained in this text/reader are a valuable resource for introductory criminology or deviance classes. It provides students with a comprehensive, yet engaging overview of what we know about crime and criminals. Students are exposed to the latest statistics and theory on a wide host of criminal behaviors. What is more, the book's twenty-one articles bring criminals, victims, situations and social control agents to life and show the reader how crime really plays itself out on a daily basis. There is simply no substitute for these rich descriptions when it comes to better appreciating life on the streets or in the suites; crime at ground zero.

This text/reader serves a broader substantive role. The first chapter maps out a typologies approach to crime. This perspective suggests that one consider moving away from thinking about crime as a generic conceptual entity and become more sensitive to the subtle differences that exist across types of crime. For example, the offender, victim, and situational aspect of homicide are very different from those observed for the crime of burglary. Chapter 1 of the present text provides brief overview of the typologies approach to crime and then maps out four part conceptual framework that allows students to better appreciate the nature and dynamics of a criminal event. Discussion centers on the behavioral, cognitive, and cultural dimensions of crime as well as the resulting societal reaction. Each of the subsequent seven chapters expound upon the behavioral, cognitive, cultural, and societal reactions germane to the type of crime in question. In this regard, the present text exposes readers to a more hands-on approach to crime, one that considers the idiosyncracies and similarities that exist across and within different types of crime. The final chapter of the text seeks to illustrate similarities and differences that exist within and between crime types, thus tying the discussion together. It is hoped that readers will better appreciate the criminological enterprise and emerge more ready and willing to think critically and respond to broad and/or specific crime problems.

Crime Types

A Text/Reader

CHAPTER 1

A Typology Approach
to Crime

Criminal behavior is a topic that captures the attention of the average American. There is simply something about the darker side of human behavior that peaks our interest. Consider the familiarity of the following scenarios.

While involved in a manic run of high-speed channel surfing, an image of Charles Manson or Osama bin Laden suddenly flashes across the television screen. The image is gone as fast as it arrived and your eyes adjust to the next channel. Almost instinctively, you find yourself flipping back to the previous channel and you proceed to fixate upon what is being said about these monsters of modern time.

You are sitting alone in a public place. Suddenly, you hear a nearby voice telling a friend how he broke the law the past weekend but presumes that he was lucky enough to evade suspicion. . . . perhaps the person is describing how he filed a false tax return or got into fisticuffs at the local pub the night before. Your ears quickly perk up as you anxiously eavesdrop on the crime-related confessional.

These anecdotes speak to the armchair criminologist that seems to exist in all of us. When we see or hear about criminal behavior, we want to know more. When the topic comes up in conversation, we are always willing to add our proverbial two cents.

Americans clearly have a healthy appetite for crime. Day in and day out, television viewers have a long list of reality-based network television shows (e.g., *Cops, America's Most Wanted, Judge Judy*), crime dramas (e.g., *CSI, Law & Order*), or cable station documentaries (e.g., Court TV, The Discovery Channel, A&E) from which to choose, as network executives scramble to quench our thirst for crime-related subject matter. What is more, it is rare to find a front page of a newspaper or popular magazine that does not flaunt a crime-related story prominently in the headlines. Even mainstream lifestyle magazines, such as women's *Cosmopolitan* and *Glamour* or their male equivalents, GQ and *Maxim,* now include regular features on "true crime."

Having established that crime sells, the obvious question becomes, Why? The answer is simple—we are feverishly attracted to that which we do not fully understand. Like a puppy chasing its tail, we spin around and around searching for the ever-elusive answers. The average citizen is not alone in this ongoing quest for enlightenment. Year in and year out, legions of scholars, criminal justice practitioners, and politicians spend billions of dollars, kill millions of trees, and exhaust countless hours trying to understand, explain, and prevent the exorbitant amount of criminal behavior that exists in today's society. Just think about how much written and spoken commentary has been directed toward understanding the behavior and mindset of modern terrorists such as Timothy McVeigh or Osama bin Laden!

Efforts to describe and explain crime and criminality overload shelves with books, journals, and reports that detail various theoretical and policy initiatives. What is the net gain of this sustained investigation? Or, have we made any substantial progress toward solving this problem? The harsh reality is that we as "learned professionals" have not made nearly as much progress as we would like; and we certainly have not made anywhere near as much progress as the general public *expects.*

This textbook represents a necessary first step toward remedying this situation. The remainder of this first chapter introduces the reader to an organizational approach that can be used to better structure one's learning and appreciation of crime and criminal behavior. Chapters 2 through 8 go about applying this conceptual framework to a host of conceptually meaningful categories of crime, instilling the reader with up-to-date data and research on the behavioral, cognitive, and contextual (i.e., societal reactions) aspects of the actions and actors in question.

PARAMETERS OF THE DISCUSSION
AND APPROACH

Part of the problem with the criminological enterprise is that it is difficult to come to grips with the parameters of our substantive discussion and approach. First, one must address two fundamental questions: *(1) What is the subject matter that we should be studying? (2) What is the best way to study it?* Let us start with the first question. Surely, coming up with an acceptable definition of crime should be simple enough. After all, crime is a routine topic in our daily conversations, it is a mainstay in media reports, and serves as a popular topic for books. However, upon closer examination, we see that "crime" is a relatively slippery concept. By crime do we mean all those acts or omissions of acts that are defined by the criminal law? Many sociologists consider this sort of legally bound definition of crime to be overly constraining. Becker (1963) points out that the "collective conscience" of society can be far more offended by non-criminal acts of deviance (i.e., social norm transgressions) than it is by some violations of the law. For example, although it may not be illegal to shout racial slurs in public, there tends to be a much more resounding public outcry against this form of behavior than there is when a minor law violation such as speeding or littering takes place.

Many scholars acknowledge this point, but opt instead to pursue the path of least resistance—they contend that the subject matter in question should include only violations of the criminal law. This definitional parameter is convenient because it immediately limits the discussion to a much more identifiable and manageable set of behaviors. More importantly, violations of the criminal law (i.e., **criminal acts**) are subject to formal, state-imposed sanctions, while violations of customs or norms (i.e., **deviant acts**) are subject to informal, peer-imposed reprimands. This difference in the nature and process of social control efforts has long been seen as a critical issue that separates crime from deviance.

The laws of the land are passed by a legislative body and recorded for dexterity purposes in a document known as the **criminal code.** This is the document that police officers and prosecutors use to guide their daily activities. One must recognize, however, that a definition of "crime" that is based solely on existing criminal codes will still produce an *exceedingly* long list of offenses. At the most basic level, one must contend with the fact that there exists no single, definitive criminal code. Instead, each jurisdiction, ranging from the federal to the state to the thousands of local jurisdictions, has in place a slightly different criminal code that it calls its own. As such, an effort to compile an exhaustive list of every law violation that is currently "on the books" would result in a truly massive, unmanageable, and often conflicting list of criminal statutes.

So let us assume that you could settle on a single criminal code, one from the federal, state, or local jurisdiction of your choice. Such a code would include high-profile offenses such as murder, rape, robbery, and theft. However, the complete list would be far more expansive, including thousands of law violations—everything from jaywalking to murder. In addition, criminal codes routinely contain a host of obscure, outdated, and rarely enforced statutes. Seuling (1975) provides a long list of the more ridiculous examples, including:

> In Kansas City, Missouri, it is illegal for children to buy cap pistols, but not shotguns.
>
> Killing an animal with "malicious intent" can result in first-degree murder charges in Oklahoma.
>
> It is illegal to have a bathtub in your house in Virginia.

Few people are willing to afford equal weight to all of the behaviors detailed in a given criminal code. Instead, one is inclined to set aside the "petty" and "outdated" offenses and focus the discussion on the more "serious" categories of crime. Most scholars follow suit. Some turn to the Federal Bureau of Investigation's **Uniform Crime Reports (UCR)** (FBI, 2002) for direction. The UCR is an annual effort to document the number of reported and cleared (i.e., a perpetrator has been identified) cases (and arrests) of murder, sexual assault, aggravated assault, robbery, burglary, larceny, auto theft, and arson that are encountered by the various law enforcement agencies across the United States. These eight offense types are called Part I offenses. The FBI asks all law enforcement agencies to provide a host of offense and offender data that are then used to generate descriptive crime statistics (e.g., demographic profiles and crime rates).

TYPOLOGIES SCHOLARS

Some scholars applaud the persistent data collection efforts of the FBI, but nonetheless see the Part I offense classification scheme as too restrictive. Such a parameter is said to exclude a number of prevalent and pressing forms of criminal behavior (e.g., white-collar crime, public order crime). These criminologists contend that the parameters for our "crime" discussion are best set somewhere between the all-inclusive criminal code and the narrow list of the UCR's Part I offenses. They seek a middle ground, one that yields an efficient categorization scheme capable of providing scholars and practitioners alike with a focused understanding of how and why people commit different varieties of criminal behavior. This tact also provides insight into what can be done to remedy the situation. It is commonly said that these scholars adopt a **crime typology** or **criminal behavior system** approach to crime.[1]

Typology scholars rely on logic-based conceptual frameworks to categorize and theorize about crime. There are two mutually dependent facets to a viable typology of crime. First, the scholar must organize the subject matter into a clearly delineated set of conceptual categories. In short, they must answer question 1 above (What is the subject matter that we should be studying?) by generating a list of **crime types,** detailing which offenses fit in each conceptual category. These categories, however, must be based on some requisite logic. This means that the scholar must engage in a second task wherein he or she articulates a set of **underlying dimensions** or **framework,** descriptive criteria that guide his or her offense categorization scheme. This clearly stated set of definitions and descriptions then addresses question 2 (What is the best way to study our agreed upon subject matter?) and provides the reader with a full understanding of the logic behind the classification scheme. More important, these underlying dimensions represent those factors that the scholar sees as the proverbial "ground zero" of criminal behavior systems. They are the core behavioral and motivational aspects of criminal behavior that serve to organize our understanding of this complex subject matter.

The classification scheme and the underlying dimensions work hand in hand for the typologies scholar. In effect, he or she constructs and defines a set of underlying dimensions that allows him or her to justify and substantiate a given typology of crime. Keep in mind that the differences or similarities on any or all of the theoretical dimensions need not be complete. Instead, it is tacitly implied that partial or conditional similarities or differences can exist across or within the framework of the typology. It is argued that this more focused approach to the study of criminal behavior affords us a fuller understanding of the patterns and dynamics of criminal behavior. It allows us to speak to the unique factors associated with a given category of crime. At the same time, we can identify similarities that exist between homicide and aggravated assault, rape, or even burglary.

Building upon the tenets of the crime typology tradition, this textbook employs a dual-level analysis of the crime problem. On the surface, the discussion centers on grouping the criminal into a series of meaningful categories. Just beneath the surface, however, there exists the requisite, multitrait conceptual framework that serves as the basis and/or justification (the glue, if you will) for this ordered classification scheme. To this end, the goal of this textbook is to provide readers with a broad yet deep appreciation for the social phenomenon that we know as criminal behavior.

A MANAGEABLE AND MEANINGFUL LIST OF CRIME TYPES

This textbook will showcase the following seven categories of criminal behavior.

Homicide and assault

Violent sex crimes

Robbery

Burglary

Common property crime

Public order crime

Crime within complex organizations

Some of these categories are less complex than others. For example, most would agree that robbery includes a streamlined set of behaviors and motivations. On the other hand, public order crime includes a far more diverse set of criminal activities (e.g., drug use, drug dealing, prostitution, vagrancy, gambling). Even with this broad conceptual focus, this textbook will expose the reader to only a fraction of what is known about each of these variants of public order crime. Nonetheless, by applying the underlying dimensions of the typology framework, this textbook occupies an important pedagogical space as it highlights the differences and similarities in offenders, victims, and situational elements that exist across this genre of crime.

THE CRIMINAL EVENT AND ITS UNDERLYING DIMENSIONS

When speaking of criminal behavior systems, it is useful to adopt the **criminal event** as the unit of analysis. The criminal event is the social context in which the crime occurs, with every criminal event being comprised of an offender, a victim (or target), and a setting. By way of example, the average date rape involves a male offender and a female victim, and takes place in a leisure setting such as the offender's house. Too often, typology scholars focus exclusively on the offender (criminal) or offense (crime) and lose sight of the meaningful roles that the victim and/or contextual norms of a given setting play in the criminal outcome. This textbook adopts a more inclusive orientation that is sensitive to all three.

Criminal events are best understood when viewed in light of four organizing principles or sensitizing concepts: *behavioral aspects, cognitive aspects, cultural aspects,* and *societal reactions.* These sensitizing concepts specifically direct the readers' attention toward common themes or criteria by which he or she can compare and contrast offender, victim, and setting roles across different types of crime and thus serve as the underlying dimensions of the present seven-part classification scheme. In other words, these organizing principles stress the multifaceted aspects of the criminal event (i.e., the offender, victim, situation, and legal distinctions) and allow for a more complete appreciation for the category or type of crime in question.

Behavioral Aspects of the Criminal Event

Human beings have a knack for patterning and regimenting their behavior over time. Crime is no different. Much like the common behavioral components to swimming, there are common behavioral aspects to homicide. Swimming involves the act of propelling one's self through water, whereas a homicide manifests itself as the unlawful killing of a human being. Likewise, there are different techniques, patterns, and skills that delineate the various swimming strokes (e.g., breaststroke, backstroke). There are also different techniques, patterns, and skills associated with different subtypes of homicide (e.g., stranger homicide, intimate homicide, serial homicide).

The concepts of crime and criminal behavior have their humble beginnings in the **legal definitions,** or necessary conditions that are set forth by the criminal code. Most fundamentally, a crime is defined as an act committed or omitted in violation of a law or statute that expressly forbids or commands it and is accompanied by some form of state-sanctioned punishment. In order for the state to establish that said crime has occurred, it must be shown that the event in question satisfies the ***actus reus*** (guilty act) and the ***mens reus*** (guilty mind) aspects of a particular criminal statute. These two critical components detail the behavioral and mental states required for an event to be defined as criminal. For example, most jurisdictions define burglary as the unlawful entry of a structure (actus reus) with the intent to commit a felony or theft (mens reus). Each subsequent chapter will present the legal definition for the crimes under consideration. These concepts are then reinforced in the multiple articles provided in each chapter. For example, Chapter 3 contains an article by Bergen that reviews the legal intricacies of wife rape. Similarly, a selection in Chapter 8 by Matthews and Kauzlarich uses the events of the crash of ValuJet flight 592 as a vehicle for discussion on the criminal statutes for fraud and homicide as they apply to corporate entities.

The behavioral aspects of a given type of crime also encompass the **skills and techniques** that are used by offenders. In the case of homicide, this means that one must speak to the manner in which the offender brings about the death of the victim (e.g., strangulation, blunt-force trauma, gunshot wound). Many crimes oblige or even require the offender to master the use of various mechanisms or tools that serve to assist in the commission of the offense. The "tools of the trade" for a murderer might include a wide variety of weapons (e.g., guns, knives, toxins, bare hands). This fact will be stressed in detail as it applies to hired hitmen in the Levi article that appears in Chapter 2. Conversely, the article in Chapter 5 by Decker, Wright, Redfern, and Smith will describe how burglars are often obliged to use deception or disguises, enlist the assistance of various power tools, or simply peer through windows en route to gaining entry into a targeted residence. Collectively, the patterned skills, techniques, and tools of the trade make up the "nuts and bolts" of how offenders effectively yet efficiently perpetrate their criminal acts.

A thorough discussion of the behavioral aspects of a crime should also take into account the patterned aspects of the **criminal transaction.** Recall the previous assertion that all criminal events are comprised of an offender, a victim, and a setting. Criminal events do not occur when these three elements spontaneously combust. Instead, they occur in a transactional manner whereby the offender, victim, and audience members negotiate the criminal outcome. This point will be stressed in a reading in Chapter 2, in which Luckenbill conceives of homicide events as "situated transactions" in which the pressure, volatility, and eventual lethal violence progresses through a series of interactional stages that are collectively negotiated by the offender, victim, and audience members.

Criminal transactions often take on a given "form." For example, some transactions involve a lone offender and a lone victim in an isolated environment. This solitary existence is captured well in Scully and Marolla's article on stranger rapists that appears in Chapter 3. Others transactions involve multiple offenders, multiple victims, and interactive audience members. Examples of more complex transactional forms are shown in the Decker article on gang violence that appears in Chapter 2. A full understanding of the patterned form of the criminal transaction is necessary if one is to comprehend the behavioral aspects of a given offense type.

There also exists a patterned "process" to criminal transactions whereby stable actions and roles emerge among the offender, victim, and audience members. For example, an article in Chapter 5 by Walsh and Chappell highlights the patterned interactions that exist between burglars, illegitimate pawn shop operators (i.e., fences), and pawn shop customers.

The behavioral aspects of criminal offending are patterned on yet another, more broadly defined level. Namely, offenders tend to progress through what is called a **criminal career.** Criminal careers are measured in terms of recidivism rates (rates of re-offending) as well as career trajectories (offending routines that emerge as individuals enter into, persist through, and exit their criminal lifestyles). Criminals can specialize in a given type of crime or behave as generalists who engage in a wide variety of criminal behaviors. Both of these career variations are described in detail in an article by Decker and associates in Chapter 5. In particular, the research shows how female burglars tend to focus their offending in a select few offense categories, while their male counterparts tend to be less discriminatory and adopt more of a "jack of all trades" orientation.

The severity of an offender's wrongdoings may remain relatively stable or they may intensify. Similarly, a criminal career can be short and erratic or it can be long and tightly routinized. The individuals may have frequent contact with the criminal justice system or might be able to allude suspicion and apprehension for extended periods of time. Past research suggests that there tends to be a patterned aspect of criminal career trajectory within a given criminal behavior system. This idea of focused offending is a point well emphasized in Dabney and Hollinger's article on drug abusing pharmacists in Chapter 8. A more sporadically focused orientation to offending is captured in Faupel and Klockars's discussion of heroin addicts in Chapter 7.

Cognitive Aspects of the Criminal Event

There is much more to understanding criminal behavior than simply mapping out the patterned aspects of the behaviors in question. For starters, one must consider the thoughts and cognitions that underlie the behaviors. Appreciating how different criminals think is anything but an exact science. After all, we are talking about trying to figuratively crawl inside the heads of criminals in an effort to tap their state of mind and decision-making processes. This is not an easy task with any one individual, and the waters are even muddier when we try to talk about patterned thought processes across whole categories of offenders. Nonetheless, there are important issues that must be considered. First, one must tackle the issue of **criminal motivation.** As mentioned, criminal definitions expressly indicate that the criteria must be satisfied before an act can be considered a crime. For the legal scholar, criminal motivation is a relatively simple concept referring narrowly to the individual's state of mind (mens reus) at the time of the crime. For the criminologist who seeks to better understand criminal behavior, criminal motivation is a broad and complex concept that speaks to the totality of an offender's mental state, in that time period preceding the crime, during the actual commission of the crime, and in the post-offense aftermath.

Criminal motivation must thus be approached as a complex, situationally based phenomenon in need of careful consideration. Moreover, a full treatment of this concept must also take into account the ways that expected victim and setting roles can shape the mindset of the offender. For example, the issue of criminal motivation, as it applies to the mindset of street thugs (i.e., stickup artists), will be belabored in depth by Jacobs and Wright in an article in Chapter 4.

Criminal planning is yet another important part of the criminal thought process. Once the prospective criminal decides that it is beneficial to commit an offense, the individual must settle on what constitutes the most effective and efficient set of behavioral processes to achieve said act. Planning refers to the rational decision-making processes that map out target selection and the way in which the individual(s) intend to commit the crime. The articles in Chapter 5 illustrate how a burglary crew often implements a system of planning that includes a clearly established division of labor, event simulations, and contingency plans. Conversely, Fleming's entry on juvenile car thieves (Chapter 6) depicts limited amounts of pre-event planning with offenders engaging more haphazard target selection methods and operating with little concern for police intervention.

Having a clear conscience is a hallmark of the contemporary human psyche. We as Americans have developed a near instinctual desire or need to think of ourselves as good people. In effect, there appears to be no wrongful behavior that the human mind is unable to cognitively reconstitute as normal or acceptable. **Normative neutralizations** are part and parcel to the cognitive dimension of crime. When their behavior is called into question by themselves or others, criminals are compelled to generate a cognitive neutralization that excuses or justifies their actions. In effect, when persons do wrong, they feel the need to convince themselves and others that it was not so bad. Several readings contained in this book speak directly to this issue. Among other applications, the reader will be confronted with how victims of domestic assault come to grips with their abusive situation (Ferraro and Johnson entry in Chapter 2), how rapists vilify their victims and downplay personal wrongdoing (Scully and Marolla article in Chapter 3), and how prostitutes come to think and talk about their careers and clients (Phoenix article in Chapter 7).

Cultural Aspects of the Criminal Event

All criminal events are social phenomena. As mentioned, they occur in a given social situation or what is termed a "situated criminal transaction." It was further pointed out that the form of that transaction is often patterned for any given offense and may even appear to be scripted. While the habitual interactions of victims and audience members is worthy of notice, criminologists are also interested in the routinized behavior of the offender. We have come to realize that the patterning of offender attitudes, beliefs, and behaviors can be a by-product of the behavior and sentiments that exist in the larger **criminal subculture.** In a noncriminological context, we acknowledge that cultural-based learning is a force to be reckoned with. Few would question the influence that a place of employment, say a law firm, has on the attitudes, beliefs, and behaviors of, say, a new attorney who seeks partner status. The same can be said of criminal sub-culture. A large part of a criminal's normative and behavioral makeup can be fostered through interactions with fellow offenders. Significant relationships and scripted roles can be developed and these relationships often play a significant role in the way that the offenders think and behave. For example, the article by Inciardi, O'Connell, and Saum that appears in Chapter 7 illustrates the complex web of roles and relationships that exist within the Miami sex-for-crack market.

It is useful to conceive of a criminal subculture as having two central features: organizational alignment and socialization scripts. **Organizational alignment** refers to the networking or structuring of interactions that shape a given criminal subculture. Best and Luckenbill (1994) speak at length about the importance that membership roles and positions play in criminal outcomes. These authors argue that criminals carry out their misdeeds within the context of one of the following organizational forms: loners, colleagues, peers, teams, and formal organizations. **Loners** work alone, relying on no one to assist them in their misdeeds. They manipulate and/or adapt the behavioral and cognitive aspects of their legitimate (noncriminal) worlds as a means of developing and refining their criminal repertoire. The Dabney and Hollinger selection in Chapter 8 uses the term "therapeutic self-medicators" to describe pharmacists who misappropriate their pharmacological expertise en route to developing their own private drug abuse patterns. These insolent professionals use drugs alone and slowly manipulate their legitimate training and professional roles until they have in effect taught themselves how to think and act as a drug addict. Dabney and Hollinger term other drug-using pharmacists "recreational abusers." These individuals often operate within a **colleague**-based organizational alignment. Colleagues offend alone but look to the misdeeds and rationalizations of other deviants to shape the thoughts and behaviors associated with their illicit behavior. Those organizational alignments that fit into the peer category take on a slightly different social form.

Peers take on co-offenders and openly interact with other perpetrators in a loose and transient social setting (Best and Luckenbill, 1994). For example, in the Chapter 7 article by Faupel and Klockars, hard-core heroin addicts comingle and draw upon the collective experiences of the junkie subculture to refine their drug-related skills and attitudes.

Criminal subcultures can also take on an organizational alignment that Best and Luckenbill (1994) refer to as **teams.** A team structure is defined by its consistent and patterned interactions. Here, the offender comes to interact and offend with the same group of individuals. Consistent relationships are seen as mutually beneficial, as offenders gain proficiency from a patterned division of labor and loosely structured mentoring. For example, the Chapter 7 article by Hafley and Tewksbury will expose readers to the loose social organization of marijuana growers in Kentucky blue grass country and how the growth and distribution system is held together by informal norms and behaviors.

The most advanced of criminal subcultures manifest itself as what Best and Luckenbill (1994) term **formal organizations.** By operating in a membership-like format, these criminals serve fixed roles, with some sort of formal or informal mentoring system to recruit and retain the membership base. Organized crime "families" are the best example of this organizational form. Readers will be exposed to a different variant in Chapter 8, when Zukier maps out the way in which Adolf Hitler used the Nazi regime to carry out the Holocaust.

Organizational alignment represents the structural dimension of a criminal subculture as it describes the context in which criminal interactions occur. This structural, dimension gives way to a process-oriented aspect of criminal subcultures termed **socialization scripts.** Here, the actual content of subcultural messages and interactions is placed center stage as we seek to ascertain the process through which criminal learning occurs. For example, in Chapter 3, an article by O'Sullivan provides evidence of how the cultural messages and cues within our nation's universities can serve to shape the motives and behaviors of college men to engage in gang rape. This discussion will illuminate the way that the content and dynamics of the learning process come to produce a socialization script that is somewhat unique to gang rapists.

Societal Reaction to the Criminal Event

Criminal acts are, by definition, prohibited by law, and the laws of this democratic country are supposed to represent the collective conscious of the populous. As such, in theory, that which is defined as a potential harm or offense to the state should be defined as a potential harm or offense to the average citizen. Reactions to criminal behaviors can take on one of two forms: formal or informal. **Formal reactions** to criminal events take the shape of institutional responses. In most cases, the institution in question is the criminal justice system (i.e., law enforcement, courts, and corrections). When a mother openly beats a child in public, law enforcement officials are quick to reference existing criminal statutes and cite the mother with child abuse. This matter is then forwarded to the court system where the courtroom workgroup (i.e., prosecutor, defense attorney, judge) sets out to determine if in fact a crime has been committed and, if so, what should be the appropriate punishment. Once a sentence has been handed down, members of the correctional system impose the prescribed punishment. To this end, a full understanding of crime begs consideration of the way that institutions such as law enforcement, the courts, and our correctional system respond to the various types of criminal offenses.

Institutional (formal) contacts are not the only form of societal reaction that can potentially shape the thoughts and behaviors of those involved in the criminal event. **Informal reactions** are also important. These are the perceived or real responses from audience members and/or valued relations that help shape criminal events. On a most fundamental level, audience members may intervene or choose not to intervene in a criminal event, thereby altering its existence. In fact, the mere existence of an audience changes the nature of the offense. The sexual assault readings from Chapter 3 do well to illustrate this point. O'Sullivan's article shows how the group dynamic plays an important role in the occurrence of gang rape on university campuses. A second article by Bergen shows how the one-on-one dynamic of marital rape produces a significantly different series of events.

Informal reactions also serve as important precursors to a criminal event. Namely, the perceived responses of valued relations (i.e., friends, family members, role models) can and do effect both the decision to commit a crime and the accounts and justifications that are constructed once the event has transpired. Scholars once again observe that these perceptions often become patterned for a given type of crime. The Chapter 2 entry by Luckenbill drives this point home well as it applies to audience roles in the murder event.

ORGANIZATION OF THE BOOK

This book is intended to serve as an instructional device that will provide novice criminologists and sociologists more with a baseline appreciation of the who, what, when, and where of crime than with the question of why. To this end, each chapter introduction will provide a cursory discussion of how the four underlying dimensions (i.e., behavioral aspects, cognitive aspects, cultural aspects, and societal reactions) generally apply to the crime type under consideration. This exercise serves to illustrate the patterned factors of the criminal event and to get the reader thinking about the defining aspects of that crime type. Each chapter then provides a series of articles that present data and observation on the criminal behaviors under consideration. The number of articles vary from two to five per chapter, depending on the complexity of the crime type at hand. These articles were chosen first and foremost because they provide cutting-edge research on the behavioral, cognitive, and cultural aspects of crime. However, the list also was shaped by a desire to present the reader with an overview of the broad spectrum of behaviors that can fall under one generic offense category. In most cases, the articles have been edited from their original published form. Introductory editor's notes are provided to summarize the overall conceptual focus, research methodology, and findings of each article. Discussion questions appear at the end of each chapter to help stimulate higher order thought processes in the reader. The textbook also comes with a companion Web site (located at http://cj.wadsworth.com/dabney_crimetypes/ that is designed to further broaden the reader's understanding and appreciation for crime and criminal behavior. Among other things, this user-friendly website provides readers with quick access to the following supplemental resources: additional printed and online books, chapters, and reports; potential research topics for each of the chapters; contact information for relevant advocacy groups; and hotlinks to the original government data, tables, and reports that are cited in the textbook.

NOTE

1. The idea that individual varieties or groupings of crime take on unique characteristics was first proposed by Edwin Sutherland (1939). He was the first to use the term "criminal behavior systems" to refer to conceptual

groupings of offenses. Sutherland urged scholars to develop logically derived classifications systems, based on real-world behavioral and cognitive factors, to help better organize and orient to crime. Sutherland's observations were later supplemented by Merton's (1957) recommendation that scholars be more open to "theories of the middle-range" that might be intentionally tailored to a given type of crime or criminality (as opposed to treating crime as a generic, unidimensional construct). During the second half of the twentieth century, scholars such as Roebuck (1966), Gibbons (1992), Farr and Gibbons (1990), Clinard, Quinney, and Wildeman (1994), Miethe and McCorkle (1998), and Tittle and Paternoster (2000) began to substitute the term *crime typologies* for *criminal behavior systems* and expand the work in this area.

KEY TERMS

actus reus	criminal planning	normative neutralizations
colleagues	criminal subculture	organizational alignment
crime types	criminal transaction	peers
crime typology	deviant act	skills and techniques
criminal act	formal organizations	socialization scripts
criminal behavior system	formal reactions	teams
criminal career	informal reactions	underlying (dimensions) framework
criminal code	legal definition	
criminal event	loners	Uniform Crime Reports (UCR)
criminal motivation	mens reus	

DISCUSSION QUESTIONS

1. Despite ever-increasing resources and efforts, experts make little progress toward predicting and controlling crime. What principle factors lead many observers to say that there is not much light at the end of the tunnel in this regard?

2. How do law enforcement officials benefit or suffer from pursuing a typologies approach to the prevention of violent crime?

3. Criminologists have long found inquiries into the cognitive aspects of crime to be particularly frustrating. Why is this the case and what can be done to ease these frustrations?

4. Criminal learning often occurs within a criminal subculture. What types of social control efforts can be taken to crack the borders of these learning networks and thus limit their impact on individuals?

5. Scholars agree that informal social control efforts have the potential to pay far greater dividends than formal social control efforts. Choose a form of crime and formulate three community-based initiatives that might help reduce the incidence of this behavior.

CHAPTER 2

Homicide and Assault

Disagreement is a cornerstone of human interaction. In most cases, disputes are resolved calmly and civilly with little more than heated emotions and words being exchanged. However, this is not always the case. In some instances, there is a breakdown in verbal problem solving and a violent physical altercation occurs. Research shows that the outcome severity of these violent confrontations (i.e., lethal versus nonlethal) can hinge on everything from luck to the level of emotion and force that are present in the situation. Most lethal altercations do not start out with death as an intended outcome. Instead, most murders manifest themselves as assaults gone awry wherein an unintended fatality results from an overly efficient weapon, an errant blow, or the blind rage of the moment (Warley, Crimmins, Ryder, and Brownstein, 1998). As such, it is best to think of the crimes of assault and murder as comprising a single conceptual category wherein varied degrees of negative consequences are possible (i.e., injury versus death).

CRIMINAL HOMICIDE
AND ASSAULT DEFINED

According to the Model Penal Code (American Law Institute, 1962, p. 125), a person is guilty of **criminal homicide** if he or she "purposely, knowingly, recklessly, or negligently causes the death of another human being." Most jurisdictions distinguish between three grades of homicide: murder, manslaughter, and negligent homicide (although the labels may vary). These gradations are shaped by the element of criminal intent, with **murder** referring to a purposeful or knowing material state, **manslaughter** referring to a condition of recklessness, and **negligent homicide** encompassing those acts committed under a state of unjustifiable risk or "negligence." This three-pronged definition leaves room for noncriminal homicides, as in the case of a state-sanctioned killing (i.e., capital punishment, wartime killings, or lethal force on the part of a law enforcement officer). The law also recognizes a private citizen's right to use deadly force against another person where it can be shown that failure to do so would likely result in his or her own death (i.e., self-defense). Involuntary intoxication and insanity are legal defenses that speak to a private citizen's inability or lack of capacity to form criminal intent and thus, in extreme cases, have been used as a criminal homicide defense (Samaha, 1999).

Lawmakers have also long frowned upon nonlethal means of physical problem solving. As far back as the ninth century, judges are known to have sanctioned instances of battery (defined as unjustified offensive touching) and assault (defined as attempted or threatened offensive touching) among the populous. Over time, these two legal categories grew together into what is today commonly referred to in criminal codes as **criminal assault** or **assault and battery** (Samaha, 1999). In most jurisdictions, one is guilty of assault and battery (shortened hereafter to assault) if he or she purposely, knowingly, recklessly, or negligently engages or threatens to engage in an act of offensive touching against another. Criminal statutes differentiate between simple and aggravated assault as a way of allowing the state to factor in the amount of harm that is caused by a given attack. The Model Penal Code (American Law Institute, 1962, p. 134) defines **simple assault** as any attempted, threatened, or completed act whereby an individual knowingly, purposely, recklessly, or negligently causes bodily harm to another. This statutory provision is generally invoked in response to minor fights or fisticuffs. Conversely, the Model Penal Code states that the more serious criminal offense of **aggravated assault** occurs when a perpetrator purposely, knowingly, or recklessly seeks to "cause serious bodily injury" to another. Central to this more flagrant offense category is the presence of a deadly weapon or any violent behavior that demonstrates an "extreme indifference to the value of human life." Practically speaking, a charge of aggravated assault is usually reserved for potentially lethal violent encounters or those requiring medical attention.

HOMICIDE AND ASSAULT TRENDS

Each year, the federal government conducts the **National Crime Victimization Survey (NCVS)**. This study uses a complex sampling strategy to query tens of thousands of households about their victimization experiences over the past year. The survey asks about a wide variety of violent and property offenses and is used to generate victimization estimates (raw numbers and rates) for the

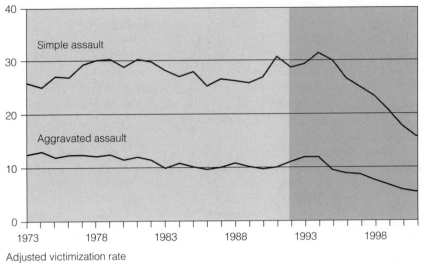

Adjusted victimization rate
per 1,000 persons age 12 and over

Figure 2.1   Assault rates.

Source: http://www.ojp.usdoj.gov/bjs/

entire U.S. population. Data from the 2001 NCVS suggest that nearly 4.9 million assaults (3.7 million simple assaults and 1.2 million aggravated assaults) took place in America that year. All total, these two offense categories constitute 20% of the estimated 24.2 million total criminal victimizations and 82% of the violent victimizations (i.e., robbery, rape, and assault) that occurred that year. This translates into a victimization rate of 27.4 assaults per 1,000 persons or households. No other form of violent crime registers a victimization rate this high and theft and burglary are the only other forms of major crime to post higher victimization rates. Put a different way, data suggest that one in every fifty-five Americans was the victim of a criminal assault in 2001 (NCVS, 2003). The FBI estimates that an aggravated assault occurred every 34.8 seconds that year (FBI, 2002).

Figure 2.1 provides a graphic representation of assault victimization rates over a recent 28-year time period (1973–2001). Notice a general stability in both aggravated and simple assault rates during the 1970s and 1980s. After peaking in the early 1990s (12.0 per 1,000 persons/households for aggravated assault in 1993 and 31.5 simple assaults per 1,000 persons/households in 1994), we observe both rates tapering off consistently through the latter half of the decade. These same victimization reports are of little help when it comes time to assess the scope of the homicide problem—dead individuals cannot tell tales. Our best source of homicide data is the Uniform Crime Reports (UCR). Figure 2.2 plots these law enforcement–generated homicide rates over the last half of the twentieth century. Notice that rates generally increased through the 1960s, and 1970s (reaching an all-time high of 11.6 per 100,000 persons in 1980), and homicide rates have decreased rather steadily over three decades to

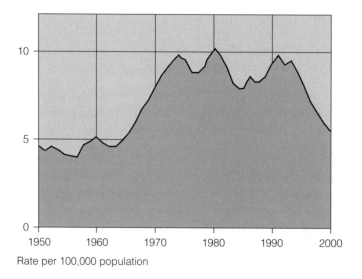

Figure 2.2   Homicide victimization, 1950–2000.

Source: http://www.ojp.usdoj.gov/bjs/

5.5 per 100,000 in 2000 (Fox and Zawitz, 2002). The Centers for Disease Control and Prevention (CDC, 1995) states that U.S. residents face a one in 154 chance of being the victim of a homicide during their lifetime. In general, one can expect somewhere between 15,000 and 20,000 homicides to occur each year in this country (15,980 were reported to police in 2001). Thus, unlike assault, homicide is a relatively rare criminal event comprising 1% to 2% of the roughly 1.5 to 2 million violent crimes that are reported to police annually.

Homicide and assaults have long been largely urban phenomena with the highest rates reported in major metropolitan areas. For example, 80% of the homicides in 2001 took place in locales with a population exceeding 50,000 persons (FBI, 2002). From 1976 to 1998, more than one half (57.3%) of all homicides occurred in cities with a population exceeding 100,000. Nearly half of these, or almost one quarter of all U.S. homicides during this period, occurred in cities with a population exceeding 1 million—the 1999 murder rate for the sixty-six largest urban centers stood at nearly 3 times the national average at 113.2 per 100,000 (FBI, 2000). Similar trends are observed for assault. The major metropolitan areas with the highest murder rates in 1999 were Washington, D.C. (46.4), followed by Detroit (42.6), St. Louis (38.1), Atlanta (34.8), and New Orleans (33.9). These cities also rank at or near the top in terms of assault rates (Maguire and Pastore, 2001).

America continues to lead in murder and assault rates. According to the International Police Organization (Interpol, 1999), America's 1998 homicide rate of 6.3 per 100,000 persons ranked atop the list of industrialized countries. That year, our aggravated assault rate of 382 per 100,000 was surpassed only by that of Australia (713.3). The rest of our sister nations experienced markedly lower murder and assault rates—Italy (4.4 and 46.4), Canada (4.3 and 142.3),

France (3.7 and 148.4), Germany (3.5 and 134.4), Spain (2.6 and 23.9), England and Wales (2.8 and 405.2), Israel (2.4 and 463.0), and Japan (1.1 and 15.4).

Beckett and Sasson (2000) attribute our nation's sizable murder and assault rates to four principle factors: the proliferation of guns, high levels of economic and racial inequality, the proliferation of the illegal drug trade, and a culture of violence that is clearly manifest from a "code of the streets." The National Rifle Association uses the slogan, "Guns don't kill people—people kill people," to downplay the guns–crime relationship. Beckett and Sasson endorse an alternative viewpoint. They see the presence of 200 million guns (70 million of which are handguns) in the hands of Americans, one fourth of all households being armed, a vast proliferation of concealed weapons among juveniles (15% of high school students report recently carrying a gun), and the fact that there are more federally licensed gun dealers in this country than there are gas stations as overwhelming evidence that a guns–violent crime relationship does exist.

Beckett and Sasson (2000) suggest that social inequality can effect levels of homicide and assault. They observe that the strongest democracies and wealthiest countries have traditionally experienced the highest homicide rates. Moreover, they cite factors such as poverty, chronic stress and frustration, and relative deprivation as contributing to the high homicide rates that are experienced in our inner-city, minority neighborhoods.

Beckett and Sasson (2000) also identify the illegal drug market as contributing to our nation's high rates of interpersonal violence. They depict drug deals and competition over drug markets as adding to a culture of lethality. The authors note that over 50% of the murders that occurred in New York City and Washington, D.C., are directly linked to the cities' illegal drug trade.

These authors further contend that factors such as rising poverty rates and the proliferation of the drug markets (especially crack cocaine) have led to the emergence of a code of the streets in most urban areas. They observe that blocked opportunities and mounting frustrations have slowly led to the emergence of alternative core beliefs and values. Many inner-city youth no longer view earning potential and educational attainment as viable sources of social capital. Instead, a steadfast willingness to engage in violence or a menacing public presence becomes the primary source of self-respect and cultural capital for these youth.

THE TECHNIQUES OF MURDER
AND ASSAULT

Contrary to public perception and television portrayals, interpersonal violence—be it murder or assault—is generally not associated with high levels of skill and precision. *Most homicides and assaults are spontaneous acts of rage. Most assaults take shape as low skill, low tech confrontations.* More often than not, offenders enlist their bare hands to inflict their injuries. For example, the 2001 NCVS documents an absence of weaponry in 70% of all assaults—6.4% involved a firearm, 5.6% a knife or sharp object, and 4.6% a blunt object. A decidedly different portrait emerges among those assaults during which serious bodily injury was incurred (i.e., aggravated assaults). Here, victims reported that a weapon was present 93.5% of the time. Guns were the tools of the trade in 26.6% of these cases, knives or sharp objects were present 23.3% of the time, and blunt objects in 19.2% of the cases (NCVS, 2003).

The presence of a weapon also increases the potential lethality of the confrontation. This is best illustrated by the fact that nearly two thirds (65%) of the homicides occurring in 2000 were committed using a firearm, and nearly eight in ten (78%) of these cases involved a handgun. The remaining homicides were committed using knives or cutting objects (13%); one's hands, fists, or feet (8%); or some blunt object such as a club or hammer (5%) (Fox and Zawitz, 2002).

THE HOMICIDE AND ASSAULT
TRANSACTION

Chapter 1 introduced the reader to the idea that criminal events take on a transactional (give-and-take) nature. It was argued that the "form" and "content" of these exchanges can vary across different types of crime. *Homicide and assault transactions generally take on the form of a one-on-one, heated interaction between acquaintances.* According to Fox and Zawitz's (2002) analysis of Supplementary Homicide Reports,[1] the vast majority of homicide incidents that were reported to police in 2000 were known to involve a lone assailant and a lone victim. Only 17% were known to involve more than two offenders and 4% involved multiple victims.[2] Similarly, victimization reports indicate that multiple offenders were present in only 23.5% of the assault cases occurring during 2001 (NCVS, 2003).

Turning to the nature of relationship, about one half of all murder and/or assault victims are known to be related or acquainted with their attacker.[3] Moreover, roughly one in ten of these incidents are categorized as cases of intimate violence wherein the combatants are either intimates or are linked via a blood or marital relationship. An analysis of the circumstances surrounding murder reveal that nearly one third of all homicides begin as a simple argument, while less than one in five are committed in conjunction with another felony offense (Fox and Zawitz, 2002; NCVS, 2003).

Homicides and assaults occur disproportionately in loose social settings. Most often, violent exchanges take place at night and on weekends in locations where acquaintances are accustomed to interacting with one another (Harries, 1997). These types of familiar settings are governed by relaxed social norms that allow individuals to more freely express their emotions. For example, Harries (1997) found that 55% of all homicide cases in her sample occurred in residences, while 9% occur in or near bars. Only 18% were found to occur in the more impersonal setting of a street or public park. Felson (1998) takes the discussion to the next level and reports that most violent predators commit their crimes in close proximity to their residence.

The majority of homicide and assault transactions involve individuals of the same age, race, and gender groups (Fox and Zawitz, 2002). From 1976 to 2000, people between the ages of 18 and 34 years made up the bulk of homicide offenders and victims—nearly two thirds of all homicide offenders and one half of all victims fell in this age range. In 2000, the average homicide offender was 28.5 years of age and the average victim was 32.2 years of age. That same year, individuals between the ages of 18 and 24 committed murder at a rate of 27.3 per 100,000. This figure was more than five times larger than the homicide rate of the 35- to 49-year-old age group (4.9) and nearly twenty times higher than for persons over the age of 50 (1.5).

The same type of trend is observable in the victimization rates. Take for example the crime of assault. In 2001, the reported assault victimization rate for individuals between the ages of 12 and 24 years exceeded forty per 1,000 persons or households. This is almost double the rate in the overall population (21.2) and more than twenty times the rate reported among persons over the age of 65 (1.80). A similar trend can be observed with regard to the age of the offender. Most victims of assaultive behavior estimate that at least one of their attackers was under the age of 30—this was the case in 56.9% of the single offender assaults and 91.1% of the multiple offender assaults (NCVS, 2003). Murder is no different. In fact, the CDC (1995) ranked homicide as the No. 2 cause of death among 18- to 25-year-olds. Only unintentional injuries accounted for more deaths among members of this age group.

It is clear that murder and assault take on an **intra-aged** transactional form, meaning that offenders and victims come from similar age groups. In the case of assault, nearly three fourths of all victims between the ages of 12 and 20 estimate that their attacker comes from this same age group. Similar patterns are observed in the 30+ age bracket.

Race is another telling indicator in homicide and assault transactions. The 2001 NCVS reveals that assault rates among blacks (26.4 per 1,000) were significantly higher than those observed among whites (20.8) and Hispanics (23.1). This trend is further reflected in the 2001 UCR arrest data—despite comprising only 12% of the overall population, blacks accounted for one third (34.8%) of the aggravated assault arrests that year.

The picture becomes even more disturbing when we focus solely on murder. The CDC (1995) states that a black person faces a one in forty-four chance of becoming a homicide victim at some point in his or her life, compared to a one in 253 chance among whites. African Americans represented 51.5% of the known homicide offenders and 46.7% of the known homicide victims between 1976 and 2000. These data translate to offender (32.4 per 100,000) and victimization (forty per 100,000) rates that far surpassed the national average (8.3 and 9.2, respectively).

Homicide and assault take form as a markedly **intraracial** crime (occurring within the same racial group). For example, between 1976 and 2000, 86% of white victims were killed by white perpetrators and 94% of blacks were killed by other blacks. A close examination reveals that most **interracial** (across races) murders involve younger perpetrators victimizing strangers (Fox and Zawitz, 2002). Shifting to the crime of assault, 78.5% of white assault victims claim that their attackers were of the same race and 82.7% of black assault victims claim that they were attacked by a fellow African American.[4] It appears that even offenders behave in an intraracial capacity—only one in ten assault victims who was attacked by more than one offender claims that the attackers were of mixed races (NCVS, 2003).

Homicide events traditionally involve male participants. For example, from 1976 to 2000, males accounted for 87.9% of the known homicide offenders and 76.4% of the homicide victims. In 2000, males were almost 10 times more likely than females to be a murder offender and more than three times more likely to be a victim. Most homicide events take shape as **intragendered** (male on male or female on female) transactions—from 1976 to 2000, nearly two thirds of the known homicides involved all male participants (Fox and Zawitz, 2002).

A slightly different portrait emerges for assault. Here again, males account for the majority of the offender and victim pools. In 2001, 79.9% of the individuals who were arrested for aggravated assault (FBI, 2002) and 55.4% of the pool of assault victims (NCVS, 2003) were men. The fact that men account for only a slight majority of the victim population but a considerably larger majority of the offender pool suggests that many of these assaults manifest themselves as male-on-female or **intergendered** transactions. In most cases, this male-on-female violence takes its form as intimate partner violence (i.e., domestic violence or spousal abuse). A recent survey of representative samples of 8,000 men and women found that 22.1% of the women versus 7.4% of the men had been the victim of domestic assault at least once in their lives. The authors estimate that a total of 22,254,037 women who are alive today will at some point be physically assaulted by an intimate partner—at a rate of 1,300,000 per year (Tjaden and Thoennes, 2000).

Murder and assault rates become particularly problematic when the age, gender, and race variables are included in the same equation. This observation is best illustrated via a close consideration of data from the Supplementary Homicide Reports. In 2000, the overall reported U.S. homicide offending rate was 6.1 and the victimization rate was 5.5 per 100,000 population. For black males between the ages of 18 and 24, those rates ballooned to 205.8 and 100.2, respectively. Conversely, the homicide offending and victimization rates among white females 25 years or older was 0.8 and 2.0, respectively, that year. Census data indicate that black males between the ages of 18 and 24 make up 1.1% of the U.S. population but accounted for a staggering 26% of all known homicide offenders and 13% of all homicide victims in 2000.

The process of the homicide and/or assault transaction is typically marked by brevity and intensity. Most murders and/or assaults last only a few seconds. In the case of murder, the short amount of time required of the act can be attributed to the fact that firearms are present in nearly two thirds of all homicide cases (Fox and Zawitz, 2002). Guns also add to the intensity of the situation. This is well evidenced by the fact that 26.6% of aggravated assault victims in 2001 claimed that their attacker carried a gun, compared to 6.4% for the overall pool of assault victimizations. When asked why they carried guns, one fourth of violent felons claimed that they intended to kill or injure their victim(s), while one half claimed that the gun was originally intended as a scare tactic (Dobrin, Wiersma, Loftin and McDowall, 1996). Intentions aside, one cannot underestimate the tendency for a gun to "up the ante" in any potentially violent situation.

Murders and assaults take on an undeniably interactive and escalating flavor. The upcoming article by Luckenbill breaks the homicide transaction into six distinct phases. He describes most homicides as disputes and/or potential assaults that have gone terribly wrong. They are situations in which factors such as ego, reputation, and irreversible moments of misinterpretation regrettably come together to produce lethal consequences. This observation was confirmed and expanded to the crime of assault by Warley, et al. (1998).

CRIMINAL CAREER

Given our society's propensity for physical problem solving, it should come as no surprise that murder and assault offenders generally develop pronounced criminal careers. These individuals tend to possess a proverbial short fuse and are not shy about resorting to physical means to resolve life's problems. For example, one third of all individuals who faced a felony assault charge and 58% of all murder defendants during 1996 were found to have at least one prior felony arrest. More than one in five murder defendants had a rap sheet that included five or more prior felony arrests, while one in five assault defendants had at least ten prior felony arrests. Additionally, better than one in four (26%) assault defendants and one in three (37%) murder defendants in the sample were still serving out some existing criminal sentence (Hart and Reaves, 1999).

Langan and Levin (2002) conducted a recidivism study in which they tracked a sample of more than 272,000 inmates released from state prisons in 1994. The data show that 40.7% of all released murderers and 65.1% of all assault releasees were charged with another criminal offense within three years of leaving prison. Most of these arrests resulted in a second conviction and follow-up term of incarceration.

There is some evidence of escalation and specialization in the career trajectories of homicide and assault offenders. For example, Langan and Levin (2002) found that 22% of those who served time for assault were picked up for yet another assault charge within three years of their release. In addition, a full 11.9% had graduated to murder by the end of that three-year window of time. Polk (1994) provides a plausible explanation for these high levels of recidivism. He notes that the average murderer is a confrontational male with a long history of violent rehearsals. Repeated involvement in physical violence tends to produce increasing intensity and severity in one's actions. While most murderers do not involve themselves exclusively in homicide, an analysis of criminal history data reveals that they have a tendency to concentrate their offending in the area of violent crime. This is substantiated by Langan and Levin (2002) who found that 16.7% of the murderers and 31.4% of the assault releasees faced a new violent felony arrest within 3 years.

COGNITIVE ASPECTS OF HOMICIDE

There exists a great deal of conjecture and assumption about what goes on inside the mind of the violent offender. Media outlets are more than willing to produce fictional and nonfictional accounts of the thought processes of homicide or assault offenders. As entertaining as the depictions may be, the public is provided little accurate information about the mindset of the average murderer.

For starters, most scholars agree that there is nothing innate or inborn about human violence. Goldstein (1986) points to contrasted levels of societal violence (approaching zero in some primitive and/or non-Western cultures) to refute the contention that humans are instinctively aggressive. He attributes the high levels of U.S. violence to our long-standing cultural norms and propensity for misunderstanding. He observes that (1) parents allow or even encourage aggressive behavior in children, especially boys; (2) all individuals are exposed to gratuitous levels of violence in the print and television media; and (3) we are exposed to displays of aggression on a daily basis in our work and social lives. These three factors come together to produce a culturally based acceptance of violence. While no one of the above sources actually causes violence in a given individual, they can come together to produce a broad-based tolerance for violent problem solving, especially in pockets of society where frustration and violence is more pervasive.

Goldstein (1986, p. 19) observes that "the antecedents of violent crimes are reported by offenders themselves have always impressed me as extraordinarily petty." Unfortunately, some individuals choose to bestow offensive or threatening meanings to the seemingly innocuous comments, gestures, or actions of another. Too frequently, this flawed assessment is followed by a mental exercise to overcome one's inhibitions against conflict (i.e., a mental stamp of approval) and then an intense physical response.

The volatility of these situations is exacerbated by the fact that most violent combatants commit their crimes while under the influence of drugs and/or alcohol. Surveys of incarcerated persons (Mumola, 1999) reveal that more than one half of all murders and assaults occur while the offender is under the influence of drugs and/or alcohol—roughly 40% report being impaired by alcohol and roughly 30% report being impaired by some other form of illegal drug. It is worth noting that burglary, theft, and robbery are the only index crimes that exhibit higher levels of drug and/or alcohol usage at the time of the offense. These substances can significantly numb an individual's reasoning and motor skills. This is illustrated by Spunt, Goldstein, Brownstein, Fendrich, and Langley (1994) who conducted interviews with 268 convicted murderers and concluded that drug and/or alcohol impairment was often the determining factor that turned a simple argument or fist fight into a homicide.

Murderous and/or assaultive behavior can be supported by both expressive and instrumental motives. **Expressive motivation** is associated with emotional states in which the individual strikes out spontaneously in a crime of passion. **Instrumental motivation** is used to describe a more calculated mental state in which the offender is driven by the will to achieve a predetermined goal. Scholars have long belabored the issue of violent motivation. Most stress the emotional and seemingly nonsensical nature of violence. It is particularly popular to interpret gang or "ghetto" violence in this manner. Katz (1988) offers a competing interpretation. He contends that violence occupies a more central role in the normative culture of inner-city America. Katz asserts that all violence is bound to the situation or surroundings within which it occurs and that one simply *must* understand the underlying cultural text of the environment if he or she wishes to unravel the meanings and intentions behind a given act. In the case of "ghetto" violence, Katz argues that street thugs use overt acts of force as a means of enhancing their social status on the streets (somewhat equivalent to accumulating monetary wealth in middle- and upper-class American culture). The previous observations lead to a somewhat muddled explanation of assaultive and murderous motives. On one hand, the physical outburst represents a situationally bound overflowing of expressive motions. At the same time, this eruption of emotional energy is not mindless, but takes on an instrumental quality as it is generally guided toward solving some tangible problem. In short, the emotions serve as the means of accomplishing what the individual sees as a rational end.

Cooney (1998) provides some clarity in his discussion of murder. He distinguishes between **predatory** and **moralistic murder.** He observes that the public is most familiar with and intrigued by the predatory variety—those cases that involve a serial or habitually murderous offender stalking victims in a methodical, blood-thirsty manner. This brand of killer is showcased in the upcoming article on contract killers by Levi. Like modern-day gang members, these predatory offenders stalk their impersonal prey and commit what we see as cold, calculated acts of violence. Cooney (1998) observes that most murderers do not fit this stereotypical image. Instead, he claims they are moralistic offenders. This brand of killer commits crimes in a loosely structured, sometimes disoriented state of rage. Cooney's two-part taxonomy drives home the point that although a small minority of murderers chronically commit predatory homicides with instrumental motives, most killers are novices of the moralistic variety who possess expressive motives that are bound to the uncertainty of the moment.[5] We often refer to the moralistic homicides as crimes of passion.

It follows that noticeable levels of criminal planning tend to be observable among predatory murderers, whereas moralistic murders take on a more haphazard quality. Habitual murderers are likely to develop set patterns, rituals, and methods to their madness, whereas the spontaneous and emotional nature of moralistic homicide usually precludes the likelihood of structured planning on the part of the offender. Conversely, planning generally occupies a notoriously small role in a moralistic or assaultive transaction. The spontaneous and emotional nature of these acts leaves little time for conscious aforethought. Although these individuals may plan the dynamics of an aggressive response, their heightened emotional state rules out the possibility for them to ponder or preconceive the volatility of the transaction.

Normative neutralizations play an important part in the cognitive dimension of murder and assault. Despite all the cultural messages that subtly reinforce violence as an alternative means of problem solving, would-be offenders must still redefine the situation. Individuals quickly overcome existing inhibitions against violence by convincing themselves that violence is an acceptable or appropriate course of action. In the case of a mundane assault, this usually involves a preoccupation with the severity of the victim's actions. In other cases, the offender will draw mental parallels to past experiences in which violence served a viable alternative. Homicide offenders are also known to develop and refine stable normative neutralizations. In fact, the upcoming Levi article will illustrate how even the most vicious murderer (i.e., mafia hitman) becomes adept at recasting his actions in a positive, self-righteous light.

CULTURE OF MURDER

There is near universal agreement that violent messages permeate nearly every aspect of social life in this country, as we live in a society that implicitly and/or explicitly exposes individuals to heavy doses of violent imagery and ideals. Our movies and television programs are hyperviolent. Our sporting events and other leisure activities tend to revolve around violent themes. Even our children's cartoons and video games are inundated with violence. Although no direct, causal relationship exists, social commentators tend to agree that this pervasive **subculture of violence** serves to reinforce individual-level thoughts and behaviors. The actual assaultive or homicidal transactions generally do not hinge upon recent or heightened levels of exposure to these violent stimuli; however, this type of social climate does make physical problem solving appear to be a more acceptable and realistic course of action.

Murderers have been known to interact or network with other known killers, taking on everything from a collegial to a formal organizational format. *However, when it comes to the issue of organizational alignment, most murderers fit the description of what Best and Luckenbill (1994) call loners.* Namely, they choose to work alone and go to great lengths to keep their offending a secret. While some perpetrators of criminal assaultive operate as loners (abusive parents or domestic partners), *the average assaulter (the male combatant who is prone to street or barroom fights) operates within a colleague or peerlike existence.* In extreme cases, such as gang violence, offenders are known to interact as part of a team or formal organization. Here, the violence takes on a collective form with fellow combatants passing along normative and behavioral guidance to one another. Sometimes, we even see active recruitment and apprenticeships within these collectives.

The average offender learns violent ways by mutating or exaggerating existing social-ization scripts. They tend to be persons with a history and proficiency in physical problem solving. Faced with emotionally charged situations, these individuals allow the situation to get out of hand to such a degree that a would-be assault becomes an assault or murder.

SOCIETAL REACTION
TO CRIMINAL HOMICIDE

Society's formal social control agents clearly take a hardline orientation toward the crimes of homicide and assault. Law enforcement hits the ground running when these crimes occur. In 2001, 62.4% of all known homicides and 56.1% of all aggravated assaults were cleared by arrest. No other form of violent or property crime enjoys a clearance rate that approaches this level (FBI, 2002).

Statutory provisions allow for the serious charges to be levied against these arrested individuals. For example, The Model Penal Code (American Law Insti-tute, 1962, p. 125) assigns a felony status to all three grades of criminal homi-cides. Murder is treated as a **first degree felony** which means that, in most jurisdictions, it is punishable by a 1- to 20 year prison term. Where aggravating circumstances are present, someone convicted of murder may be sentenced to life in prison or even death. The Model Penal Code defines manslaughter to be a **second degree felony.** If convicted on this charge, the defendant can be sen-tenced to 1 to 10 years in prison. Finally, the Model Penal Code classifies neg-ligent homicide as a **third degree felony.** A person convicted on this charge must contend with a 1- to 5-year prison sentence.

The Model Penal Code (American Law Institute, 1962) classifies aggravated assaults (those committed with a deadly weapon or against a peace officer) as a felony in the second degree. Such an offense is punishable by 1 to 10 years of prison. Simple assault is assigned a graded offense designation. Most simple assaults receive a generic **misdemeanor** designation, punishable by a fine and/or jail term of less than 1 year. When evidence of mutual consent (i.e., a fight) is present, the offense may be downgraded to a **petty misdemeanor.** This grade of offense is punishable by a fine and/or jail term of up to 6 months.

Murder and assault cases receive close scrutiny from the court system. Hart and Reaves (1999) note that nearly two thirds of all homicide defendants and one third of the assault defendants remain in jail while they await trial. They state that, in 1996, the average bail amount for a murderer was set at $133,000 while most assault defendants faced a bail amount of less than $10,000. These researchers found that 64% of the homicide defendants and 53% of the assault defendants in their study were eventually convicted.

Once convicted, Hart and Reaves (1999) found that the vast majority of homicide and assault defendants were subject to extreme sanctions. Over 90% of the murderers were sentenced to incarceration with a median prison sentence of 30 years. Only 8% of the murderers were sentenced to less than 10 years in prison and nearly one fourth of all murder cases that year resulted in a life sentence. The data show that nearly three fourths of all assault defendants were sentenced to prison with the average sentence set at 69 months.

Maguire and Pastore (2000) report that, nationwide, there were 3,452 murderers awaiting death sentences in 1998. This means that there was one individual on death row in the United States for every five homicides that were committed that year.

Surprisingly, informal reactions to homicide and assault offenders and offenses vary across different situations. Cooney (1998) contends that the presence of third parties can alter the process of a homicide transactions in a number of ways. They can avoid involvement, negotiate further escalation, intervene in the dispute, or simply tolerate the violence as an impartial observer. Staged experiments show that citizens are wary to intervene in physical disputes that they witness (Barofsky, Stollak, and Masse, 1971; Shotland and Straw, 1976). This holds true even when the attacker is a man and the victim is a woman. Cooney (1998) argues that onlookers are particularly hesitant about intervening in disputes when they do not have social ties (i.e., friendships, family ties, group affiliation) to the combatants. Conversely, when third parties know one or more of the combatants, these allegiances are more likely to inspire them to join the fight. Unfortunately, this involvement usually serves to exacerbate, not defuse, the level of violence. The complex and unpredictable nature of third-party responses lead scholars (Cooney, 1998; Felson and Steadman, 1983) to conclude that their presence rarely takes on a noticeable informal social control function.

NOTES

1. The FBI relies on two standardized forms to collect homicide data from state and local law enforcement authorities. The UCR form asks the law enforcement agency to report a monthly tally of the number of known murders and nonnegligent manslaughters. The second form, known as Supplementary Homicide Reports (SHR), queries agency representatives about the victim, offender, and circumstance characteristics of each known homicide. The data show that SHRs are completed and returned for 95% of all known criminal homicides. This comprehensive database is maintained by the University of Michigan's Inter-university Consortium for Political and Social Research (Dobrin et al., 1996).

2. Due to a lack of arrest or incomplete SHR information, police are often unable to determine whether there are multiple offenders or victims present at a given homicide event. This was the case in 28% of the homicides that were reported to police in 2000.

3. Due to a lack of arrest or incomplete information, police are often unable to determine the nature of the offender–victim relationship. This was the case in 40% of the homicide incidents that were reported to police in 2000.

4. These data apply only to single offender assaults and exclude the more than 800,000 multiple offender assaults that occurred in 2001.

5. Cooney's two-part typology is readily applicable to criminal assault.

KEY TERMS

aggravated assault

assault and battery

criminal assault

criminal homicide

expressive motivation

first degree felony

instrumental motivation

intergendered

interracial

intra-aged

intragendered

intraracial

manslaughter

misdemeanor

moralistic murder

murder

National Crime Victimization Survey (NCVS)

negligent homicide

petty misdemeanor

predatory murder

second degree felony

simple assault

subculture of violence

third degree felony

DISCUSSION QUESTIONS

1. It is often observed that criminal homicide and criminal assault have much in common. This being said, what types of prevention initiatives are best suited for both, and what types of prevention initiatives are best kept separate?

2. When thinking and talking about homicide and assault, most people have trouble getting past the barbaric interpersonal aspects of the crimes. They tend to fixate on the cold-blooded nature of the offender's actions and the innocent qualities of the victim. Beckett and Sasson (2000), however, shift our attention to the way that structural aspects of American society (proliferation of guns, economic and racial inequality, the drug trade, and a code of the streets) contribute to the thousands of lethal exchanges that

occur each year. How, if at all, is American culture responsible for the high levels of homicide that presently exist in this country?

3. Many public interest groups have called for the criminal justice system to involve itself more in the various forms of interpersonal violence that occur within the context of organized sports. Is there a need for further involvement in this area and, if so, what form should it take on?

4. It has become popular to blame the media for our country's subculture of violence, claiming that youth transform messages from the big and small screen into violent tendencies. What role does the popular media play in this subculture of violence and how can or should this institution be altered?

1

Criminal Homicide as a
Situated Transaction

DAVID F. LUCKENBILL
University of California

In this article, Luckenbill seeks to provide the reader with an inside view into the homicide event. To accomplish this goal, he conducted a content analysis of all official documents that existed in conjunction with seventy-one criminal homicides that were processed by the criminal justice authorities of a California county from 1963 to 1972. He referenced all sides of the story to reconstruct a summary account of the "situated homicide transaction," systematically mapping out the actions and reactions of the offender, victim, and audience members. The author observes that the vast majority of the altercations occurred between individuals who were known to one another (family members, friends, enemies, or acquaintances) and most had engaged in some sort of less serious violent rehearsal in the past. Luckenbill distills the basic structure and development of the homicide transactions down a time-ordered, six-stage model. Central to the onset of the process was an offense of face or character challenge on the part of one participant. This perceived affront leads to a return challenge in an effort to preserve their dignity in the eyes of onlookers. This sort of stalemate produced a pressure-cooker-type situation with a swift and lethal exchange right around the corner. After a brief battle, the offender and audience members negotiated an appropriate response and the situation was handed over to the authorities. This article delves into the dynamic, interactive nature of the homicide transaction. It stresses the relatively static roles and exchanges that are played out by the offenders, victims, and audience members who are present at the time that a homicide occurs.

By definition, criminal homicide is a collective transaction. An offender, victim, and possibly an audience engage in an interchange which leaves the victim dead. Furthermore, these transactions are typically situated, for participants interact in a common physical territory (Wolfgang, 1958: 203–205; Wallace, 1965). As with other situated transactions, it is expected that the participants develop particular roles, each shaped by the others and instrumental in some way to the fatal outcome (cf. Shibutani, 1961: 32–37, 64–93; Blumer, 1969: 16–18). However, research, with few exceptions, has failed critically to examine the situated transaction eventuating in murder (Banitt et al., 1970;

©1977 by The Society for the Study of Social Problems. Reprinted from *Social Problems*, Vol. 25, No. 2 (December 1977), pp. 176–186, by permission of the University of California Press.

Shoham et al., 1973). At most, studies have shown that many victims either directly precipitate their destruction, by throwing the first punch or firing the first shot, or contribute to the escalation of some conflict which concludes in their demise (Wolfgang, 1958: 245–265; Schafer, 1968: 79–83; Goode, 1969: 965; Toch, 1969; Moran, 1972). But how transactions of murder are organized and how they develop remain puzzles. What are the typical roles developed by the offender, victim, and possible bystanders? In what ways do these roles intersect to produce the fatal outcome? Are there certain regularities of interaction which characterize all transactions of murder, or do patterns of interaction vary among transactions in a haphazard fashion? Making the situated transaction the unit of investigation, this paper will address these questions by examining the character of the transaction in full.

THE SOCIAL OCCASION
OF CRIMINAL HOMICIDE

Criminal homicide is the culmination of an intense interchange between an offender and victim. Transactions resulting in murder involved the joint contribution of the offender and victim to the escalation of a "character contest," a confrontation in which at least one, but usually both, attempt to establish or save face at the other's expense by standing steady in the face of adversity (Goffman, 1967: 218–219, 238–257). Such transactions additionally involved a consensus among participants that violence was a suitable if not required means for settling the contest.

DYNAMICS OF THE SITUATED
PERFORMANCE

These are the occasions in which situated transactions resulted in violent death. But examination of the development of these situated interchanges is not to argue that such transactions have no historical roots. In almost half the cases there had previously occurred what might be termed rehearsals between the offender and victim. These involved transactions which included the escalation of hostilities and, sometimes, physical violence. In twenty-six percent of these cases, the offender and, sometimes, victim entered the present occasion on the assumption that another hostile confrontation would transpire.

Whether or not murderous episodes had such rehearsals, an examination of all cases brings to light a conception of the transaction resembling what Lyman and Scott (1970: 37–43) term a "face game." The offender and victim, at times with the assistance of bystanders, make "moves" on the basis of the other's moves and the position of their audience (cf. Goffman, 1967: 239–258; 1969: 107–812). While these moves are not always of the same precise content or degree, it was possible to derive as set of time-ordered stages of which each shares certain basic properties.

Stage I The opening move in the transaction was an event performed by the victim and subsequently defined by the offender as an offense to "face," that image of self a person claims during a particular occasion or social contact (Goffman, 1967: 5). What constitutes the real or actual beginning of this or any other type of transaction is often quite problematic for the researcher. The victim's activity, however, appeared as a pivotal event which separated the previous occasioned activity of the offender and victim from their subsequent violent confrontation. Such a disparaging and interactionally disrupting event constitutes the initial move.

While the form and content of the victim's move varied, three basic types of events cover all cases. In the first, found in over forty-one percent of the cases, the victim made some direct, verbal expression which the offender subsequently interpreted as offensive. This class of events was obviously quite broad. Included were everything from insults levied at some particular attribute of the offender's self, family, or friends to verbal tirades which disparaged the overall character of the offender:

> *Case 34* The offender, victim, and two friends were driving toward the country where they could consume their wine. En route, the victim turned to the offender, both of whom were located in the back seat, and stated: "You know, you really got some good parents. You know, you're really a son-of-a-bitch. You're a leech. The whole time you were out of a job, you were living with them, and weren't even paying. The car you have should be your father's. He's the one who made the payments. Any time your dad goes to the store, you're the first in line to sponge off him. Why don't you grow up and stop being a leech?" The offender swore at him, and told him to shut up. But the victim continued, "Someone ought to come along and really fuck you up."

A second type, found in thirty-four percent of the cases, involved the victim's refusal to cooperate or comply with the requests of the offender. The offender subsequently interpreted the victim's action as a denial of his ability or right to command obedience. This was illustrated in transactions where parents murdered their children. When the parent's request that the child eat dinner, stop screaming, or take a bath went unheeded, the parent subsequently interpreted the child's activity as a challenge to rightful authority.

The third type of event, found in twenty-five percent of the cases, involved some physical or nonverbal gesture which the offender subsequently defined as personally offensive. Often this gesture entailed an insult to the offender's sexual prowess, and took the form of affairs or flirtation:

> *Case 10* When the victim finally came home, the offender told her to sit down; they had to talk. He asked her if she was "fooling around" with other men. She stated that she had, and her boyfriends pleased her more than the offender. The offender later stated that "this was like a hot iron in my gut." He ripped her clothes off and examined her body, finding scars and bruises. She said that her boyfriends liked to beat her. His anger magnified.

Although the content and the initial production of these events varied, each served to disrupt the social order of the occasion. Each marked the opening of a transformation process in which pre-homicide transactions of pleasurable, or serious yet tranquil, order came to be transactions involving an argumentative "character contest."

Stage II In all cases ending in murder the offender interpreted the victim's previous move as personally offensive. In some cases the victim was intentionally offensive. But it is plausible that in other cases the victim was unwitting. In Case forty-three, for instance, the victim, a five-week old boy, started crying early in the morning. The offender, the boy's father, ordered the victim to stop crying. The victim's crying, however, only heightened in intensity. The victim was too young to understand the offender's verbal order, and persistent crying may have been oriented not toward challenging his father's authority, but toward acquiring food or a change of diapers. Whatever the motive for crying, the child's father defined it as purposive and offensive. What the victim intends may be inconsequential. What the offender interprets as intentional, however, may have consequences for the organization of subsequent activity.

In sixty percent of the cases, the offender learned the meaning of the victim's move from inquiries made of victim or audience. In reply, the offender received statements suggesting the victim's action was insulting and intentional. In thirty-nine percent of the cases, the offender ascertained the meaning of the impropriety directly from the victim:

> *Case 28* As the offender entered the back door of the house his wife said to her lover, the victim, "There's _____." The victim jumped to his feet and started dressing hurriedly. The offender, having called to his wife without avail, entered the bedroom. He found his wife nude and the victim clad in underwear. The startled offender asked the victim, "Why?" The victim replied, "Haven't you ever been in love? We love each other." The offender later stated, "If they were drunk or something, I could see it. I mean, I've done it myself. But when he said they loved each other, well that did it."

In another twenty-one percent of the cases, however, the offender made his assessment from statements of interested bystanders:

> *Case 20* The offender and his friend were sitting in a booth at a tavern drinking beer. The offender's friend told him that the offender's girlfriend was "playing" with another man (victim) at the other end of the bar. The offender looked at them and asked his friend if he thought something was going on. The friend responded, "I wouldn't let that guy fool around with [her] if she was mine." The offender agreed, and suggested to his friend that his girlfriend and the victim be shot for their actions. His friend said that only the victim should be shot, not the girlfriend.

In the remaining forty percent of the cases the offender imputed meaning to the event on the basis of rehearsals in which the victim had engaged a similar role. The incessant screaming of the infant, the unremitting aggressions of a drunken spouse, and the never-ending flirtation by the lover or spouse were activities which offenders had previously encountered and assessed as pointed and deliberate aspersions. Such previous activities and their consequences served the offender as an interpretive scheme for immediately making sense of the present event.

Stage III The apparent affront could have evoked different responses. The offender could have excused the violation because the victim was judged to be drunk, crazy, or joking. He could have fled the scene and avoided further interaction with the victim by moving into interaction with other occasioned participants or dealt with the impropriety through a retaliatory move aimed at restoring face and demonstrating strong character. The latter move was utilized in all cases.

In countering the impropriety, the offender attempted to restore the occasioned order and reaffirm face by standing his or her ground. To have used another alternative was to confirm questions of face and self raised by the victim. The offender's plight, then, was "problematic" and "consequential" (Goffman, 1967: 214–239). He could have chosen from several options, each of which had important consequences both to the face he situationally claimed and to his general reputation. Thus, the offender was faced with a dilemma: either deal with the impropriety by demonstrating strength of character, or verify questions of face by demonstrating weakness (Goffman, 1969: 168–169).

In retaliating, the offender issued an expression of anger and contempt which signified his opinion of the victim as an unworthy person. Two basic patterns of retaliation were found. In eighty-six percent of the cases, the offender issued a verbal or physical challenge to the victim. In the remaining cases, the offender physically retaliated, killing the victim.

For the latter pattern, this third move marked the battle ending the victim's life:

> *Case 12* The offender, victim, and group of bystanders were observing a fight between a barroom bouncer and a drunk patron on the street outside the tavern. The offender was cheering for the bouncer, and the victim was cheering for the patron, who was losing the battle. The victim, angered by the offender's disposition toward the fight, turned to the offender and said, "You'd really like to see the little guy have the shit kicked out of him, wouldn't you big man?" The offender turned toward the victim and asked, "What did you say? You want the same thing, punk?" The victim moved toward the offender and reared back. The offender responded, "OK buddy." He struck the victim with a single right cross. The victim crashed to the pavement, and died a week later.

Such cases seem to suggest that the event is a one-sided affair, with the unwitting victim engaging a passive, non-contributory role. But in these cases the third stage was preceded by the victim's impropriety, the offender's inquiry of the victim or audience, and a response affirming the victim's intent to be censorious. On assessing the event as one of insult and challenge, the offender elicited a statement indicating to participants, including himself, his intended line of action, secured a weapon, positioned it, and dropped the victim in a single motion.

While ten cases witness the victim's demise during this stage, the typical case consists of various verbal and physically nonlethal moves. The most common type of retaliation was a verbal challenge, occurring in forty-three percent of the cases. These took the form of an ultimatum: either apologize, flee the situation, or discontinue the inappropriate conduct, or face physical harm or death.

In about twenty-two percent of the cases, the offender's retaliation took the form of physical violence short of real damage or incapacitation.

In another ten percent, retaliation came by way of countering the victim's impropriety with similar insults or degrading gestures. This response entailed a name-calling, action-matching set of expressions resembling that which would be found between boys in the midst of a playground argument or "playing the dozens" (cf. Berdie, 1947).

The remaining cases, some eleven percent of the sample, were evenly divided. On the one hand, offenders issued specific commands, tinged with hostility and backed with an aggressive posture, calling for their victims to back down. On the other hand, offenders "called out" or invited their victims to fight physically.

This third stage is the offender's opening move in salvaging face and honor. In retaliating by verbal and physically nonlethal means, the offender appeared to suggest to the victim a definition of the situation as one in which violence was suitable in settling questions of face and reputation.

Stage IV Except for cases in which the victim has been eliminated, the offender's preceding move placed the victim in a problematic and consequential position: either stand up to the challenge and demonstrate strength of character, or apologize, discontinue the inappropriate conduct, or flee the situation and thus withdraw questions of the offender's face while placing one's own in jeopardy. Just as the offender could have dismissed the impropriety, fled the scene, or avoided further contact with the victim, so too did the victim have similar alternatives. Rather than break the escalation in a manner demonstrating weakness, all victims in the remaining sample came into a "working" agreement with the proffered definition of the situation as one suited for violence. In the majority of cases, the victim's move appeared as an agreement that violence was suitable to the transaction. In some cases, though, the offender interpreted, sometimes incorrectly, the victim's move as implicit agreement to violence. A working agreement was struck in several ways.

The most prominent response, found in forty-one percent of the cases, involved noncompliance with the offender's challenge or command, and the continued performance of activities deemed offensive:

Case 54 The victim continued ridiculing the offender before friends. The offender finally shouted, "I said shut up. If you don't shut up and stop it, I'm going to kill you and I mean it." The victim continued his abusive line of conduct. The offender proceeded to the kitchen, secured a knife, and returned to the living room. She repeated her warning. The victim rose from his chair, swore at the offender's stupidity, and continued laughing at her. She thrust the knife deep into his chest.

Similarly, a spouse or lover's refusal, under threat of violence, to conciliate a failing marriage or relationship served as tacit acceptance that violence was suitable to the present transaction.

Whether the victim's noncompliance was intentional or not, the offender *interpreted* the move as intentional. Take, for example, the killing of children at the hands of parents. In an earlier illustration, the first move found the parent demanding obedience and backed by a hostile, combative stance. In several of these cases, the child was too young to understand what the parent demanded and the specific consequences for noncompliance. Nevertheless, the child's failure to eat dinner or stop screaming was interpreted by the parent as a voluntary protest, an intentional challenge to authority. Consequently, the unwitting activities of victims may contribute to what offenders define as very real character contests demanding very real lines of opposition.

A second response, occurring in thirty percent of the cases, found victims physically retaliating against their offenders by hitting, kicking, and pushing—responses short of mortal injury:

> *Case 42* The offender and a friend were passing by a local tavern and noticed the victim, a co-worker at a food-processing plant, sitting at the bar. The offender entered the tavern and asked the victim to repay a loan. The victim was angered by the request and refused to pay. The offender then pushed the victim from his stool. Before the victim could react, the bartender asked them to take their fight outside. The victim followed the offender out the door and, from behind, hit the offender with a brick he grabbed from a trash can immediately outside the door. The offender turned and warned the victim that he would beat the victim if he wouldn't pay up and continued his aggressions. The victim then struck the offender in the mouth, knocking out a tooth.

In the remaining cases, victims issued counter-challenges, moves made when offenders' previous moves involved threats and challenges. In some cases, this move came in the form of calling the offender's bluff. In other cases, the counter came in the form of a direct challenge or threat to the offender, a move no different from the ultimatum given victims by offenders.

Unlike simple noncompliance, physical retaliation against offenders and issuance of counter-challenges signify an explicit acceptance of violence as a suitable means for demonstrating character and maintaining or salvaging face.

Just as the victim contributed to the escalation toward violence, so too did the audience to the transaction. Seventy percent of all cases were performed before an audience. In these cases, onlookers generally engaged one or two roles. In fifty-seven percent of these cases, interested members of the audience intervened in the transaction, and actively encouraged the use of violence by means of indicating to opponents the initial improprieties, cheering them toward violent action, blocking the encounter from outside interference, or providing lethal weapons:

> *Case 23* The offender's wife moved toward the victim, and hit him in the back of the head with an empty beer bottle stating, "That'll teach you to [molest] my boy. I ought to cut your balls off, you motherfucker." She went over to the bar to get another bottle. The victim pushed himself from the table and rose. He then reached into his pocket to secure something which some bystanders thought was a weapon. One of the bystanders gave the offender an axe handle and suggested that he stop the victim before the victim attacked his wife. The offender moved toward the victim.

In the remaining cases, onlookers were neutral. They were neither encouraging nor discouraging. While neutrality may have been due to fear, civil inattention, or whatever reason, the point is that inaction within a strategic interchange can be interpreted by the opponents as a move favoring the use of violence (cf. Goffman, 1967: 115). Consider the statement of the offender in the following case:

> *Case 48* Police officer: Don't you think it was wrong to beat [your daughter] when her hands were tied behind her back? [Her hands and feet were bound to keep her from scratching.]
> Offender: Well, I guess so. But I really didn't think so then, or [my wife] would have said something to stop me.

Stage V On forging a working agreement, the offender and, in many cases, victim appeared committed to battle. They contributed to and invested in the development of a fateful transaction, one which was problematic and consequential to their face and wider reputation. They placed their character on the line, and alternative methods for assessing character focused on a working agreement that violence was appropriate. Because opponents appeared to fear displaying weakness in character and consequent loss of face, and because resolution of the contest was situationally bound, demanding an immediacy of response, they appeared committed to following through with expressed or implied intentions.

Commitment to battle was additionally enhanced by the availability of weapons to support verbal threats and challenges. Prior to victory, the offender often sought out and secured weapons capable of overcoming the victim. In about thirty-six percent of the cases, offenders carried hand guns or knives into the setting. In only thirteen percent of these cases did offenders bring hand guns or knives into the situation on the assumption that they might be needed if the victims were confronted. In the remainder of these cases such weapons were brought in as a matter of everyday routine. In either event, to inflict the fatal blow required the mere mobilization of the weapon for action. In sixty-four percent of the cases, the offender either left the situation temporarily to secure a hand gun, rifle, or knife, or transformed the status of some existing situational prop, such as a pillow, telephone cord, kitchen knife, beer mug, or baseball bat, into a lethal weapon. The possession of weapons makes battle possible, and, in situations defined as calling for violence, probable.

The particular dynamics of the physical interchange are quite varied. In many cases, the battle was brief and precise. In approximately fifty-four percent of the cases, the offender secured the weapon and dropped the victim in a single shot, stab, or rally of blows. In the remaining cases, the battle was two-sided. One or both secured a weapon and exchanged a series of blows, with one falling in defeat.

Stage VI Once the victim had fallen, the offender made one of three moves which marked the termination of the transaction. In over fifty-eight percent of the cases, the offender fled the scene. In about thirty-two percent of the cases, the offender voluntarily remained on the scene for the police. In the remaining cases, the offender was involuntarily held for the police by members of the audience.

These alternatives seemed prompted by two lines of influence: the relationship of the offender and victim and the position of the audience vis-a-vis the offense. When there is no audience, the offender appeared to act on the basis of his relationship to the victim. When the offender and victim were intimately related, the offender typically remained on the scene and notified the police. Sometimes these offenders waited for minutes or hours before reporting the event, stating they needed time to think, check the victim's condition, and make arrangements on financial matters, the children, and work before arrest. In contrast, when victims were acquaintances or enemies, offenders typically fled the scene. Moreover, these offenders often attempted to dispose of their victims and incriminating evidence.

Seventy percent of the cases, however, occurred before an audience, and offenders' moves seemed related to audience reactions to the offense. Bystanders seemed to replace the victim as the primary interactant, serving the offender as the pivotal reference for his exiting orientations. The audience assumed one of three roles: hostile, neutral, or supportive. In the hostile role, accounting for nearly thirty-five percent of the cases, bystanders moved to apprehend the offender, assist the victim, and immediately notify police. Such audiences were generally comprised of persons who either supported the victim or were neutral during the pre-battle escalation. In several of these cases, bystanders suggested, without use of force, that the offender assist the victim, call the police, and so forth. These audiences were comprised of the offender's intimates, and he followed their advice without question. In either case, hostile bystanders forced or suggested the offender's compliance in remaining at the scene for police.

In almost seventeen percent of the cases, the audience was neutral. These people appeared as shocked bystanders. Having witnessed the killing, they stood numb as the offender escaped and the victim expired.

In the remainder of the cases, the audience was supportive of the offender. These audiences were usually comprised of persons who encouraged the offender during the pre-battle stages. Supportive bystanders rendered assistance to the offender in his escape, destroyed incriminating evidence, and maintained ignorance of the event when questioned by the police, breaking down only in later stages of interrogation. Thus, while a hostile audience directs the offender to remain at the scene, the supportive audience permits or directs his flight.

CONCLUSION

On the basis of this research, criminal homicide does not appear as a one-sided event with an unwitting victim assuming a passive, non-contributory role. Rather, murder is the outcome of a dynamic interchange between an offender, victim, and, in many cases, bystanders. The offender and victim develop lines of action shaped in part by the actions of the other and focused toward saving or maintaining face and reputation and demonstrating character. Participants develop a working agreement, sometimes implicit, often explicit, that violence is a useful tool for resolving questions of face and character. In some settings, where very small children are murdered, the extent of their participation cannot be great. But generally these patterns characterized all cases irrespective of such variables as age, sex, race, time and place, use of alcohol, and proffered motive.

2

Becoming a Hit Man

Neutralization in a Very Deviant Career

KEN LEVI

University of Texas at San Antonio

While conducting an interview-based study of murder among convicted murderers in Detroit, Ken Levi got a sense that one of his respondents was more well versed in lethal violence than the others. Levi suspected that he was dealing with a professional and used a series of seven in-depth, confidential interview sessions with "Pete" (often speaking in the 3rd person) to explore the behavioral and cognitive aspects of contract killing. This article provides a rare glimpse into the "nuts and bolts" of contract killing. More importantly, the author shows how even a solitary and heinous criminal actor such as this is able to develop and refine a set of normative neutralizations. The presence of identifiable justifications and excuses within the psyche of such a solitary and habitually violent type of criminal speaks to the resiliency of this cognitive dimension of deviant behavior. The discussion maps out the process through which the hitman was able to adeptly negotiate the cognitive dissonance that he experienced

Ken Levi, *Journal of Contemporary Ethnography* (formerly *Urban Life*), Vol. 10, No. 1 (April 1981), pp. 47–49, 52–63, copyright © 1981 by Sage Publications, Inc. Reprinted by permission of Sage Publications, Inc.

in conjunction with his crimes. By adopting a sense of pride in his work, minimizing his emotional attachment to the victims, and focusing on his own skills, he was gradually able to reconceptualize killing as an acceptable and rewarding business profession.

Our knowledge about deviance management is based primarily on behavior that is easily mitigated. The literature dwells on unwed fathers (Pfuhl, 1978), and childless mothers (Veevers, 1975), pilfering bread salesmen (Ditton, 1977), and conniving shoe salesmen (Friedman, 1974), bridge pros (Holtz, 1975), and poker pros (Hayano, 1977), marijuana smokers (Langer, 1976), massage parlor prostitutes (Verlarde, 1975), and other minor offenders (see, for example, Berk, 1977; Farrell and Nelson, 1976; Gross, 1977). There is a dearth of deviance management articles at all about one of the (legally) most serious offenders of all, the professional murderer. Drift may be possible for the minor offender exploiting society's *ambivalence* toward his relatively unserious behavior (Sykes and Matza, 1957). However, excuses for the more inexcusable forms of deviant behavior are, by definition, less easily come by, and the very serious offender may enter his career with few of the usual defenses.

This article will focus on ways that one type of serious offender, the professional hit man, neutralizes stigma in the early stages of his career. As we shall see, the social organization of the "profession" provides "neutralizers" which distance its members from the shameful aspects of their careers. But for the novice, without professional insulation, the problem is more acute. With very little outside help, he must negate his feelings, neutralize them, and adopt a "framework" (Goffman, 1974) appropriate to his chosen career. This process, called "reframing," is the main focus of the present article. Cognitively, the novice must *reframe his experience* in order to enter his profession.

THE SOCIAL ORGANIZATION OF MURDER

Murder, the unlawful killing of a person, is considered a serious criminal offense in the United States, and it is punished by extreme penalties. In addition, most Americans do not feel that the penalties are extreme enough (Reid, 1976: 482). In overcoming the intense stigma associated with murder, the hit man lacks the supports available to more ordinary types of killers.

Some cultures allow special circumstances or sanction special organizations wherein people who kill are insulated from the taint of murder. Soldiers at war, or police in the line of duty, or citizens protecting their property operate under what are considered justifiable or excusable conditions.

Individuals acting on their own, who kill in a spontaneous, "irrational" outburst of violence, can also mitigate the stigma of their behavior.

> I mean, people will go ape for a one minute and shoot, but there are very few people who are capable of thinking about, planning, and then doing it [Joey, 1974: 56].

Individuals who kill in a hot-blooded burst of passion can retrospectively draw comfort from the law which provides a lighter ban against killings performed without premeditation or malice or intent (Lester and Lester, 1975: 35). At one extreme, the spontaneous killing may seem the result of a mental disease (Lester and Lester, 1975: 39) or dissociative reaction (Tanay, 1972), and excused entirely as insanity.

But when an individual who generally shares society's ban against murder, is fully aware that his act of homicide is (1) unlawful, (2) self-serving, and (3) intentional, he does not have the usual defenses to fall back on. How does such an individual manage to *overcome his inhibitions* and *avoid serious damage to his self-image* (assuming that he does share society's ban)? This is the special dilemma of the professional hit man who hires himself out for murder.

THE SOCIAL ORGANIZATION
OF PROFESSIONAL MURDER

There are two types of professional murderers: the organized and the independent. The killer who belongs to an organized syndicate does not usually get paid on a contract basis, and performs his job out of loyalty and obedience to the organization (Maas, 1968: 81). The independent professional killer is a free-lance agent who hires himself out for a fee (Pete). It is the career organization of the second type of killer that will be discussed.

The organized killer can mitigate his behavior through an "appeal to higher loyalties" (Sykes and Matza, 1957). He also can view his victim as an enemy of the group and then choose from a variety of techniques available for neutralizing an offense against an enemy (see, for example, Hirschi, 1969; Rogers and Buffalo, 1974). But the independent professional murderer lacks most of these defenses. Nevertheless, built into his role are certain structural features that help him avoid deviance ascription. These features include:

(1) *Contract.* A contract is an unwritten agreement to provide a sum of money to a second party who agrees, in return, to commit a designated murder (Joey, 1974: 9). It is most often arranged over the phone, between people who have never had personal contact. And the victim, or "hit," is usually unknown to the killer (Gage, 1972: 57; Joey, 1974: 61–62). This arrangement is meant to protect both parties from the law. But it also helps the killer "deny the victim" (Sykes and Matza, 1957) by keeping him relatively anonymous.

In arranging the contract, the hired killer will try to find out the difficulty of the hit and how much the customer wants the killing done. According to Pete, these considerations determine his price. He does not ask about the motive for the killing, treating it as none of his concern. Not knowing the motive may hamper the killer from morally justifying his behavior, but it also enables him to further deny the victim by maintaining his distance and reserve. Finally, the contract is backed up by a further understanding. If the killer fails to live up to his part of the bargain, the penalties could be extreme (Gage, 1972: 53; Joey, 1974: 9). This has the ironic effect that after the contract is arranged, the killer can somewhat "deny responsibility" (Sykes and Matza, 1957), by pleading self-defense.

(2) *Reputation and Money.* Reputation is especially important in an area where killers are unknown to their customers, and where the less written, the better (Joey, 1974: 58). Reputation, in turn, reflects how much money the hit man has commanded in the past. Pete, who could not recall the exact number of people he had killed, did, like other hit men, keep an accounting of his highest fees (Joey, 1974: 58, 62). To him big money meant not only a way to earn a living, but also a way to maintain his professional reputation.

People who accept low fees can also find work as hired killers. Heroin addicts are the usual example. But, as Pete says, they often receive a bullet for their pains. It is believed that people who would kill for so little would also require little persuasion to make them talk to the police (Joey, 1974: 63). This further reinforces the single-minded emphasis on making big money. As a result, killing is conceptualized as a "business" or as "just a job." Framing the hit in a normal businesslike context enables the hit man to deny wrongfulness, or "deny injury" (Sykes and Matza, 1957).

In addition to the economic motive, Pete, and hit men discussed by other authors, refer to excitement, fun, game-playing, power, and impressing women as incentives for murder (Joey, 1974: 81–82). However, none of these motives are mentioned by all sources. None are as necessary to the career as money. And, after a while, these other motives diminish and killing becomes only "just a job" (Joey, 1974: 20). The primacy of the economic motive has been aptly expressed in the case of another deviant profession.

> Women who enjoy sex with their customers do not make good prostitutes, according to those who are acquainted with this institution first hand. Instead of thinking about the most effective way of making money at the job, they would be doing things for their own pleasure and enjoyment [Goode, 1978: 342].

(3) *Skill.* Most of the hit man's training focuses on acquiring skill in the use of weapons.

> Then, he met these two guys, these two white guys . . . them two, them two was the best. And but they stayed around over there and they got together, and Pete told [them] that he really wanted to be good. He said, if [I] got to do something, I want to be good at it. So, they got together, showed him, showed him *how to shoot.* . . . And gradually, he became good. . . . Like he told me, like when he shoots somebody, he always goes for the head; he said, that's about the best shot. I mean, if you want him dead then and there. . . . And these two guys showed him, and to him, I mean, hey, I mean, he don't believe nobody could really outshoot these two guys, you know what I mean. *They know everything you want to know about guns, knives, and stuff like that* [Pete].

The hit man's reputation, and the amount of money he makes depend on his skill, his effective ability to serve as a means to *someone else's ends.* The result is a focus on technique.

Like in anything you do, when you do it, you want to do it just right.
. . . On your target and you hit it, how you feel: I hit it! I hit it! [Pete].

This focus on technique, on means, helps the hit man to "deny responsibility" and intent (Sykes and Matza, 1957). In frame-analytic terms, the hit man separates his morally responsible, or "principal" self from the rest of himself, and performs the killing mainly as a "strategist" (Goffman, 1974: 523). In other words, he sees himself as a "hired gun." The saying, "If I didn't do it, they'd find someone else who would," reflects this narrowly technical orientation.

To sum up thus far, the contract, based as it is on the hit man's reputation for profit and skill, provides the hit man with opportunities for denying the victim, denying injury, and denying responsibility. But this is not enough. To point out the defenses of the professional hit man is one thing, but it is unlikely that the *novice* hit man would have a totally professional attitude so early in his career. The novice is at a point where he both lacks the conventional defense against the stigma of murder, *and* he has not yet fully acquired the exceptional defenses of the professional. How, then, does he cope?

The First Time: Negative Experience

Goffman defines "negative experience" as a feeling of disorientation.

Expecting to take up a position in a well-framed realm, he finds that no particular frame is immediately applicable, or the frame that he thought was applicable no longer seems to be, or he cannot bind himself within the frame that does apparently apply. He loses command over the formulation of viable response. He flounders. Experience, the meld of what the current scene brings to him and what he brings to it—meant to settle into a form even while it is beginning, finds no form and is therefore no experience. Reality anomically flutters. He has a "negative experience"—negative in the sense that it takes its character from what it is not, and what it is not is an organized and organizationally affirmed response [1974: 387–379].

Negative experience can occur when a person finds himself lapsing into an old understanding of a situation, only to suddenly awaken to the fact that it no longer applies. In this regard, we should expect negative experience to be a special problem for the novice. For example, the first time he killed a man for money, Pete supposedly became violently ill:

When he [Pete], you know, hit the guy, when he shot the guy, the guy said, 'You killed me' . . . something like that, cause he struck him all up here. And what he said, it was just, I mean, *the look right in the guy's eye,* you know. I mean he looked like: *Why me?* Yeah? And then he said that at night-time he'll start thinking about the guy: like he shouldn't have looked at him like that. . . . I mean actually [Pete] was sick. . . . He couldn't keep his food down, I mean, or nothing like that. . . . [It lasted] I'd say about two months. . . .

Pete's account conforms to the definition of negative experience. He had never killed anyone for money before. It started when a member of the Detroit drug world had spotted Pete in a knife fight outside an inner city bar, was apparently impressed with the young man's style, and offered him fifty dollars to do a "job." Pete accepted. He wanted the money. But when the first hit came about, Pete of course knew that he was doing it for money, but yet his orientation was: revenge. Thus, he stared his victim in the *face,* a characteristic gesture of people who kill enemies for revenge (Levi, 1975: 190). Expecting to see defiance turn into a look of defeat, they attempt to gain "face" at the loser's expense.

But when Pete stared his victim in the face, he saw not an enemy, but an innocent man. He saw a look of: "Why me?" And this *discordant* image is what remained in his mind during the weeks and months to follow and made him sick. As Pete says, "He shouldn't have looked at him like that." The victim's look of innocence brought about what Goffman (1974: 347) refers to as a "frame break":

> Given that the frame applied to an activity is expected to enable us to come to terms with all events in that activity (informing and regulating many of them), it is understandable that the unmanageable might occur, an occurrence which cannot be effectively ignored and to which the frame cannot be applied, with resulting bewilderment and chagrin on the part of the participants. In brief, a break can occur in the applicability of the frame, a break in its governance.

When such a frame break occurs, it produces negative experience. Pete's extremely uncomfortable disorientation may reflect the extreme dissonance between the revenge frame, that he expected to apply, and the unexpected look of innocence that he encountered and continued to recall.

SUBSEQUENT TIME: REFRAMING THE HIT

According to Goffman (1974: 319), a structural feature in frames of experience is that they are divided into different "tracks" or types of information. These include, "a main track or story line and ancillary tracks of various kinds." The ancillary tracks are the directional track, the overlay track, the concealment track and the disattend track. The disattend track contains the information that is perceived but supposed to be *ignored*. For example, the prostitute manages the distasteful necessity of having sex with "tricks" by remaining "absolutely . . . detached. Removed. Miles and miles away" (1978: 344). The existence of different tracks allows an individual to define and redefine his experience by the strategic placement of information.

Sometimes, the individual receives outside help. For example, when Milgram in 1963 placed a barrier between people, administering electric shocks, and the bogus "subjects" who were supposedly receiving the shocks, he made it easier for the shockers to "disattend" signs of human distress from their hapless victims.

In other cases help can come from guides who direct the novice on what to experience and what to block out. Beginning marijuana smokers are cautioned to ignore feelings of nausea (Becker, 1953: 240). On the other hand, novice hit men like Pete are reluctant to share their "experience" with any one else. It would be a sign of weakness.

In still other cases, however, it is possible that the subject can do the reframing *on his own*. And this is what appears to have happened to Pete.

> And when the second one [the second hit] came up, [Pete] was still thinking about the first one. . . . Yeah, when he got ready to go, he was thinking about it. *Something changed*. I don't know how to put it right. Up to the moment that he killed the second guy now, he waited, you know. Going through his mind was the first guy he killed. He still seeing him, still see the *expression on his face*. Soon, the second guy walked up; I mean, it was like just his mind just *blanked out* for a minute, everything just blanked out. . . . Next thing he know, he had killed the second guy. . . . *He knew what he was doing,* but what I mean, he just didn't have nothing on his mind. Everything was wiped out [Pete].

When the second victim approached, Pete says that he noticed the victim's approach, he was aware of the man's presence. But he noticed none of the victim's personal features. He did not see the victim's face or its expression. Thus, he did not see the very thing that gave him so much trouble the first time. It is as if Pete had *negatively conditioned* himself to avoid certain cues. Since he shot the victim in the head, it is probable that Pete saw him in one sense; this is not the same kind of experience as a "dissociative reaction," which has been likened to sleep-walking (Tanay, 1972). Pete says that, "he knew what he was doing." But he either did not pay attention to his victim's personal features at the time of the killing, or he blocked them out immediately afterward, so that now the only aspect of his victim he recalls is the victim's approach (if we are to believe him).

After that, Pete says that killing became *routine*. He learned to view his victims as "targets," rather than as people. Thus, he believes that the second experience is the crucial one, and that the disattendance of the victim's personal features made it so.

Support from other accounts of hit men is scant, due to a lack of data. Furthermore, not everything in Pete's account supports the "reframing" hypothesis. In talking about later killings, it is clear that he not only attends to his victims' personal features, on occasion, but he also derives a certain grim pleasure in doing so.

> [the victim was] a nice looking woman. . . . She started weeping, and [she cried], 'I ain't did this, I ain't did that'. . . . and [Pete] said that he shot her. Like it wasn't nothing . . . he didn't feel nothing. It was just money [Pete].

It may be that this evidence contradicts what I have said about reframing; but perhaps another interpretation is possible. Reframing may play a more crucial role in the original redefinition of an experience than in the continued maintenance of that redefinition. Once Pete has accustomed himself to viewing his victims as merely targets, as "just money," then it may be less threatening to look upon them as persons, once again. Once the "main story line" has been established, discordant information can be presented in the "overlay track" (Goffman, 1974: 215), without doing too much damage. Indeed, this seems to be *the point* that both hit men are trying to make in the above excerpts.

THE HEART OF THE HIT MAN

For what I have been referring to as "disattendance" Pete used the term "heart," which he defined as a "coldness." When asked what he would look for in an aspiring hit man, Pete replied,

> See if he's got a whole lot of heart . . . you got to be cold . . . you got to build a coldness in yourself. It's not something that comes automatically. Cause, see, I don't care who he is, first, you've got feelings [Pete].

However, the "made rather than born" thesis does explain one perplexing feature of hit men and other "evil" men whose banality has sometimes seemed discordant. In other aspects of their lives they all seem perfectly capable of feeling ordinary human emotions. Their inhumanity, their coldness, seems narrowly restricted to their jobs. Pete, for example, talked about his "love" for little children. Examples of human warmth indicate that the cold heart of the hit man may be less a characteristic of the killer's individual personality, than a feature of the professional framework of experience which the hit man has learned to adapt himself to, when he is on the job.

DISCUSSION

This article is meant as a contribution to the study of deviance neutralization. The freelance hit man is an example of an individual who, relatively alone, must deal with a profound and unambiguous stigma in order to enter his career. Both Pete and Joey emphasize "heart" as a determining factor in becoming a professional. And Pete's experience, after the first hit, further indicates that the inhibitions against murder-for-money are real.

In this article "heart"—or the ability to adapt to rationalized framework for killing—has been portrayed as the outcome of an initial process of reframing, in addition to other neturalization techniques established during the further stages of professionalization. As several theorists (see, for example, Becker, 1953; Douglas, 1977; Matza, 1969) have noted, people often enter into deviant acts first, and then develop rationales for their behavior later on. This was also the case with Pete, who began his career by first, (1) "being willing" (Matza, 1969), (2) encountering a frame-break, (3) undergoing negative experience, (4) being willing to try again (also known as "getting back on the horse"), (5) reframing

the experience and (6) having future, routine experiences wherein his professionalization increasingly enabled him to "deny the victim," "deny injury,"
and "deny responsibility." Through the process of reframing, the experience of
victim-as-target emerged as the "main story line," and the experience of
victim-as-person was downgraded from the main track to the disattend track
to the overlay track. Ironically, the intensity of the negative experience seemed
to make the process all the more successful. Thus, it may be possible for a person with "ordinary human feelings" to both pass through the novice stage, and
to continue "normal relations" thereafter. The reframing hypothesis has implications for other people who knowingly perform stigmatized behaviors. It may
be particularly useful in explaining a personal conversion experience that
occurs despite the relative absence of deviant peer groups, deviant norms,
extenuating circumstances, and neutralization rationales.

3

Collective and Normative Features of Gang Violence

SCOTT H. DECKER
University of Missouri–St. Louis

*The author shows how the normative and behavioral aspects of a street gang collective serve
to shape and routinize the violent ways of its members. Decker defines a gang as an "aggregated peer group that exhibits permanence, engages in criminal activity, and has symbolic
representations of membership." With the help of a street ethnographer who himself was
an ex-gangster, Decker identified and interviewed ninety-nine active gang members. All
interviewees were seasoned veterans in the St. Louis gang scene. The interviews reveal that
violence serves a critical, symbolic purpose within the gang subculture. Violent themes permeate all aspects of gang life. All gang members seek to develop and maintain a threatening physical presence. Violence is incorporated into the entry rituals, social gatherings, and
story-telling of the group. An overdeveloped sense of urgency and "threat" produces a contagion of violence, a hallmark of which is a never-ending cycle of preemptive and retalia-*

Excerpted with permission from *Justice Quarterly*, Vol. 13, No. 2, (June 1996),
© 1996 Academy of Criminal Justice Sciences.

tory violence among and between rival gangs. In this regard, Decker provides valuable insight into the behavioral cognitive, and cultural aspects of collective violence.

In 1927 Frederic Thrasher observed that gangs shared many of the properties of mobs, crowds, and other collectives, and engaged in many forms of collective behavior. Despite the prominent role of his work in gang research, few attempts have been made to link the behavior of gangs to theories of collective behavior. This omission is noteworthy because, despite disagreements about most other criteria—turf, symbols, organizational structure, permanence, criminality—all gang researchers include "group" as a part of their definition of gangs. Gang members are individuals with diverse motives, behaviors, and socialization experiences. Their *group* membership, behavior, and values, however, make them interesting to criminologists who study gangs.

In this paper we explore the mechanisms and processes that result in the spread and escalation of gang violence. In particular, we focus on contagion as an aspect of collective behavior that produces expressive gang violence. Collective behavior explanations provide insights into gang processes, particularly the escalation of violence, the spread of gangs from one community to another, and increases in gang membership in specific communities.

GANG VIOLENCE

Violence is integral to life in the gang, as Klein and Maxson (1989) observed, and gang members engage in more violence than other youths. Thrasher (1927) noted that gangs developed through strife and flourish on conflict. According to Klein (1971: 85), violence is a "predominant 'myth system' " among gang members and is constantly present.

Our analysis of gang violence focuses on the role of *threat,* actual or perceived, in explaining the functions and consequences of gang violence. We define threat as the potential for transgressions against or physical harm to the gang, represented by the acts or presence of a rival group. Threats of violence are important because they have consequences for future violence. Threat plays a role in the origin and growth of gangs, their daily activities, and their belief systems. In a sense, it helps to define them to rival gangs, to the community, and to social institutions.

Katz (1988) argues that gangs are set apart from other groups by their ability to create "dread," a direct consequence of involvement in and willingness to use violence. Dread elevates these individuals to street elites through community members' perceptions of gang members as violent. In many neighborhoods, groups form for protection against the threat of outside groups (Suttles, 1972). Sometimes these groups are established along ethnic lines, though territorial concerns often guide their formation. Both Suttles (1972: 98) and

Sullivan (1989) underscored the natural progression from a neighborhood group to a gang, particularly in the face of "adversarial relations" with outside groups. The emergence of many splinter gangs can be traced to the escalation of violence within larger gangs, and to the corresponding threat that the larger gang comes to represent to certain territorial or age-graded subgroups.

Threat also may contribute to the growth of gangs. This mechanism works in two ways: through building cohesiveness and through contagion. Threats of physical violence increase the solidarity or cohesiveness of gangs within neighborhoods as well as across neighborhoods. Klein (1971) identified the source of cohesion in gangs as primarily external—the results of intergang conflict; Hagedorn (1988) also made this observation. According to Klein, cohesion within the gang grows in proportion to the perceived threat represented by rival gangs. Padilla (1992) reported a similar finding, noting that threat maintains gang boundaries by strengthening the ties among gang members and increasing their commitment to each other, thus enabling them to overcome any initial reluctance about staying in the gang and ultimately engaging in violence. Thus the threat of a gang in a geographically proximate neighborhood increases the solidarity of the gang, motivates more young men to join their neighborhood gang (see Vigil, 1988), and enables them to engage in acts of violence that they might not have committed otherwise.

The growth of gangs and gang violence contains elements of what Loftin (1985) calls "contagion." In this context, contagion refers to subsequent acts of violence caused by an initial act; such acts typically take the form of retaliation. Violence—or its threat—is the mechanism that spreads gang from one neighborhood to another, as well as contributing to their growth.

The threat of attack by a group of organized youths from another neighborhood is part of the gang "myth" or belief system, and helps to create the need for protection as well as to generate unity in a previously unorganized group of neighborhood youths. The origin and spread of such beliefs explain, among other things, the viability of the gang. Threat performs an additional function: it enhances the mythic nature of violence in the gang by increasing the talk about violence and preparedness for violent engagements.

The threat of violence also "enables" gang members to engage in violent acts (especially retaliatory violence) that they might not have chosen under other circumstances. The need to respond effectively to rival gang violence escalates weaponry and increases the "tension" that often precedes violent encounters between gangs.

Threat has an additional function, however. As gangs and gang members engage in acts of violence and create "dread" (Katz, 1988: 135), they are viewed as threatening by other (gang and non-gang) groups and individuals. Also, over time, the threats that gang members face and pose isolate them from legitimate social institutions such as schools, families, and the labor market. This isolation, in turn, prevents them from engaging in the very activities and relationships that might reintegrate them into legitimate roles and reduce their criminal involvement. It weakens their ties to the socialization power and the controlling norms of such mainstream institutions, and frees them to commit acts of violence.

COLLECTIVE BEHAVIOR

Collective behavior and social organizations such as gangs share many common elements, including group behavior, collective processes, and group structure. Thus it is productive to view collective behavior on a continuum with social organizations rather than regarding them as separate topics of study. Thrasher (1927) observed that collective behavior processes operated within the gang, and could be used to account for the emergence of collective violence. Such processes included games, fights, meetings, and defining common enemies. His theoretical formulation, and the supporting distinctions between gangs and other forms of social organizations (e.g., groups, mobs, crowds, publics) make clear the role that he perceived for collective behavior explanations of gang activity.

We adopt our definition of collective behavior from McPhail (1991), who identified three elements of collective behavior: (1) group, (2) behavior, and (3) common actions that vary on one or more dimensions such as purpose, organization, or duration. McPhail observed that gang violence is a form of collective behavior because it emerges from a group process involving common actions that have a defined purpose.

COLLECTIVE VIOLENCE PROCESSES
WITHIN THE GANG

Gang violence includes a number of acts and is most likely to involve assaults and the use of weapons. Although the motives for these acts are diverse, much gang violence (as discussed above) is retaliatory. This quality is evident in the disproportionate number of assaults and shootings committed in response to the acts of other gangs. This finding is similar to those of other gang researchers including Hagedorn (1988), Klein and Maxson (1989), Maxson, Gordon, and Klein (1985), Moore (1978), Sanders (1993), and Vigil (1988). Initial interviews made clear that a number of violent acts were committed by gang members outside the gang. It would be inappropriate to classify these acts as gang-related, even though they were committed by gang members. Our classification of gang violence included only those acts committed by gang members which were organized by gang members and motivated by gang concerns, especially revenge, retaliation, reputation, and representation of membership. This classification corresponds to the more restrictive of the two definitions applied by Maxson and Klein (1990).

The centrality of violence to gang life was illustrated by counts of the times a topic was mentioned during an interview. Except for drugs (which were mentioned more than 2,000 times), our subjects mentioned violence more often than any other topic. They referred to violence 1,681 times, including hundreds of references to specific acts such as killing or murder (246), assault (148), and robbery (71). As further evidence of the importance of violence, nine of our ninety-nine subjects have been killed since the study began in 1990; several showed us bullet wounds during the interview. As stated earlier, this group had extensive arrest histories: 80 percent had been arrested at least once, the mean number of arrests per subject was eight, and one third reported that their most recent arrest was for assault or weapons violations.

Other incidents also illustrate the salience of violence in the lives of gang members. One day three gang members were sitting on their front porch, waiting for the field ethnographer to pick up one of them for an interview. As he drove up their street, he heard shots and saw the three subjects being shot in a drive-by. Their wounds were superficial, but this incident underscored the daily potential for violence as well as our ability to observe it firsthand. During the course of our research, several gang members offered to demonstrate their ability to use violence, typically by inviting us to accompany them on a drive-by shooting or to drop them off in rival territory and watch them shoot a rival gang member. We declined all such invitations, but they are not uncommon in field research (Wright and Decker, 1994). On a few occasions during interviews, gang members displayed a firearm when asked whether they possessed a gun. Most subjects reported beginning their life in the gang with a violent encounter; usually they were "beaten in" by members of the gang they were joining. The process of leaving the gang was also described in violent terms: by being "beaten out," leaving through fear of violence, suffering serious injury, or death.

The research reported here attempts to provide a framework for understanding the peaks and valleys of gang violence. As Short and Strodtbeck (1974) observed, efforts to understand gang violence must focus both on process variables (such as interactions) and on situational characteristics (such as neighborhood structure, age, race, and sex). For these reasons we concentrate on stages in the gang process that illustrate important aspects of gang violence, and we examine such violence in the context of five spheres of gang activity: (1) the role of violence in defining life in the gang, (2) the role of violence in the process of joining the gang, (3) the use of violence by the gang, (4) staging grounds for violence, and (5) gang members' recommendations for ending their gang.

The Role of Violence in Defining Life in the Gang

A fundamental way to demonstrate the centrality of violence to life in the gang is to examine how gang members defined a gang. Most answers to this question included some mention of violence. Our subjects were able to distinguish between violence within the gang and that which was unrelated to the gang.

> **INT:** What is a gang to you?
> **007:** A gang is, I don't know, just a gang where people hang out together and get into fights. A lot of members of your group will help you fight.
> **INT:** So if you just got into a fight with another girl because you didn't like her?
> **007:** Then it would be a one-on-one fight, but then like if somebody else jump in, then somebody would come from my side.

INT: Why do you call the group you belong to a gang?

047: Violence, I guess. There is more violence than a family. With a gang it's like fighting all the time, killing, shooting.

INT: What kind of things do members of your organization do together?

085: We have drive-bys, shootings, go to parties, we even go to the mall. Most of the things we do together is dealing with fighting.

Most often the violence was protective, reflecting the belief that belonging to a gang at least would reduce the chance of being attacked.

INT: Are you claiming a gang now?

046: I'm cool with a gang, real cool.

INT: What does that mean to be cool?

046: You don't got to worry about nobody jumping you. You don't got to worry about getting beat up.

Other subjects found the violence in their gang an attractive feature of membership. These individuals were attracted not so much by protection as by the opportunity to engage in violence.

INT: Why did you start to call that group a gang?

009: It's good to be in a gang cause there's a lot of violence and stuff.

INT: So the reason you call it a gang is basically why?

101: Because I beat up on folks and shoot them. The last person I shot I was in jail for five years.

INT: What's good about being in a gang?

101: You can get to fight whoever you want and shoot whoever you want. To me, it's kind of fun. Then again, it's not . . . because you have to go to jail for that shit. But other than that, being down for who you want to be with, it's kind of fun.

INT: What's the most important reason to be in the gang?

057: Beating Crabs. If it wasn't for beating Crabs, I don't think I would be in a gang right now.

Whether for protection or for the opportunity to engage in violence, the members of our sample attached considerable importance to the role of violence in their definition of a gang. Many of the comments evoke what Klein (1971) termed "mythic violence"—discussions of violent activities between gangs that reinforce the ties of membership and maintain boundaries between neighborhood gangs and those in "rival" neighborhoods. In this sense, violence is a central feature of the normative system of the gang; it is the defining feature and the central value of gang life.

Violence in Joining the Gang

Most gangs require an initiation process that includes participation in violent activities. This ritual fulfills a number of important functions. First, it determines whether a prospective member is tough enough to endure the level of violence he or she will face as a gang member. Equally important, the gang must learn how tough a potential member is because they may have to count on this individual for support in fights or shootings. The initiation serves other purposes as well. Most important, it increases solidarity among gang members by engaging them in a collective ritual. The initiation reminds active members of their earlier status, and gives the new member something in common with other gang members. In addition, a violent initiation provides a rehearsal for a prospective member for life in the gang. In short, it demonstrates the central-ity of violence to gang life.

Three-quarters of our subjects were initiated into their gangs through the process known as "beating in." This ritual took many forms; in its most common version a prospective gang member walked between lines of gang members or stood inside a circle of gang members who beat the initiate with their fists.

> **020:** I had to stand in a circle and there was about ten of them. Out of these ten there was just me standing in the circle. I had to take six to the chest by all ten of them. Or I can try to go to the weakest one and get out. If you don't get out, they are going to keep beating you. I said "I will take the circle."

One leader, who reported that he had been in charge of several initiations, described the typical form:

> **001:** They had to get jumped on.
> **INT:** How many guys jump on em?
> **001:** Ten.
> **INT:** And then how long do they go?
> **001:** Until I tell em to stop.
> **INT:** When do you tell em to stop?
> **001:** I just let em beat em for bout two or three minutes to see if they can take a punishment.

Other gang members reported that they had the choice of either being beaten in or "going on a mission." On a mission, a prospective member had to engage in an act of violence, usually against a rival gang member on rival turf. Initiates often were required to confront a rival gang member face-to-face.

> **041:** You have to fly your colors through enemy territory. Some step to you; you have to take care of them by yourself; you don't get no help.
> **084:** To be a Crip, you have to put your blue rag on your head and wear all blue and go in a Blood neighborhood—that is the hardest of all of them—and walk through the Blood neighborhood and fight Bloods. If you come out without getting killed, that's the way you get initiated.

Every gang member we interviewed reported that his or her initiation involved participating in some form of violence. This violence was rarely directed against members of other gangs; most often it took place within the gang. Then in each successive initiation, recently initiated members participated in "beating in" new members. Such violence always has a group context and a normative purpose: to reinforce the ties between members while reminding them that violence lies at the core of life in the gang.

The Use of Gang Violence

To understand gang violence more clearly, it is critical to know when such violence is used. In the four following situations, gang members did not regard themselves as initiating violence; rather, because its purpose was to respond to the violent activities of a rival gang. Retaliatory violence corresponds to the concept of contagion (Loftin, 1984) as well as to the principle of crime as social control (Black, 1983). According to this view, gang violence is an attempt to enact private justice for wrongs committed against the gang, one of its members, or a symbol of the gang. These wrongs may be actual or perceived; often the perceived threat of impending violence is as powerful a motivator as violence itself.

This view of gang violence helps to explain the rapid escalation of intergang hostilities that lead to assaults, drive-by shootings, or murders between gangs. Such actions reflect the collective behavior processes at work, in which acts of violence against the gang serve as the catalyst that brings together subgroups within the gang and unites them against a common enemy. Such violent events are rare, but are important in gang culture. Collective violence is one of the few activities involving the majority of gang members, including fringe members. The precipitation of such activities pulls fringe members into the gang and increases cohesion.

When Violence Comes to the Gang We asked gang members when they used violence. Typically they claimed that violence was seldom initiated by the gang itself, but was a response to "trouble" that was "brought" to them. In these instances, the object of violence was loosely defined and was rarely identified; it represented a symbolic enemy against whom violence would be used. These statements, however, indicate an attempt to provide justifications for gang violence.

> **INT:** How often do gang members use violence?
> **005:** When trouble comes to them.
> **INT:** When do you guys use violence?
> **018:** When people start bringing violence to us. They bring it to us and set it up. We take it from there.
> **INT:** When do members of the gang use violence?
> **037:** When somebody approaches us. We don't go out looking for trouble. We let trouble come to us.
> **INT:** When do you guys use violence?

042: Only when it's called for. We don't start trouble. That's the secret of our success.

The view of gang members passively sitting back and waiting for violence to come to them is inconsistent with much of what we know about gang life. After all, many gang members reported that they joined the gang expressly for the opportunity to engage in violence; many lived in neighborhoods where acts of violence occurred several times each day; and most had engaged in violence before joining the gang. Even so, unprovoked violence against another gang is difficult to justify; retaliatory actions against parties that wronged them can be justified more easily. Also, such actions are consistent with the view of the gang as a legitimate social organization serving the legitimate purpose of protecting its members—a central value in the gang's normative structure.

Retaliation A number of gang members told us that they used violence to even the score with a specific group or individual. Unlike the subjects above, who reported generalized responses, these individuals identified a specific target for their violence: someone who had committed a violent act against them or their gang in the past.

> **002:** I had on a blue rag and he say what's up cuz, what's up blood, and I say uh, what's up cuz, just like that, and then me and him got to arguin' and everything, and teachers would stop it, and then me and him met up one day when nobody was round. We got to fightin. Naw, cause I told Ron, my cousin, my cousin and em came up to the school and beat em up. And the next day when he seen me, he gonna ask me where my cousin and em at. I say I don't need my cousin and em for you. They just came up there cause they heard you was a Blood. And they whooped em. Then me and him had a fight the next day, yeah. And then I had to fight some other dudes that was his friends and I beat em up. Then he brought some boys up to the school and they, uh, pulled out a gun on me and I ran up in the school. And then I brought my boys up the next day and we beat on em.

Specific examples of retaliation against rival gangs were mentioned less frequently than was general gang violence. This point underscores the important symbolic function of gang violence, a value that members must be ready to support. The idea that rival gangs will "bring violence" to the gang is an important part of the gang belief system; it is pivotal in increasing cohesion among members of otherwise loosely confederated organizations.

Graffiti A third type of gang violence occurred in response to defacing gang graffiti. Organizational symbols are important to all groups, and perhaps more so to those whose members are adolescents. The significance of graffiti to gangs has been documented by a number of observers in a variety of circumstances (Block and Block, 1993; Hagedorn, 1988; Moore, 1978; Vigil, 1988). In particular, graffiti identify gang territory, and maintaining territory is an important feature of gang activity in St. Louis and other cities. As Block and Block observed in Chicago, battles over turf often originated in attempts by rival gangs to "strike out" graffiti. Several gang members told us that attempts to paint over their graffiti by rival gangs were met with a violent response, but no gang members could recall a specific instance. Claiming to use violence in response to such insults again reflects the mythic character of gang violence; it emphasizes the symbolic importance of violence for group processes such as cohesion, boundary maintenance, and identity. Further, such responses underscore the threat represented by rivals who would encroach on gang territory to strike out gang graffiti.

> **INT:** What does the removal of graffiti mean?
> **043:** That's a person that we have to go kill. We put our enemies up on the wall. If there is a certain person, we "X" that out and know who to kill.
> **INT:** What if somebody comes and paints a pitchfork or paints over your graffiti? What does that mean to your gang?
> **046:** First time we just paint it back up there, no sweat. Next time they come do it, we go find out who did it and go paint over theirs. If they come back a third time, it's like three times you out. Obviously that means something if they keep painting over us. They telling us they ready to fight.

Territory Most gang members continued to live in the neighborhood where their gang started. Even for those who had moved away, it retained a symbolic value. Protecting gang turf is viewed as an important responsibility, which extends well beyond its symbolic importance as the site where the gang began. Our subjects' allegiance to the neighborhood was deeply embedded in the history of neighborhood friendship groups that evolved into gangs. Thus, turf protection was an important value.

When we asked gang members about defending their turf, we received some generalized responses about their willingness to use violence to do so.

> **INT:** If someone from another gang comes to your turf, what does your gang do?
> **019:** First try to tell him to leave.
> **INT:** If he don't leave?
> **019:** He'll leave one way or the other—carry him out in a Hefty bag.

In other instances, however, the responses identified an individual or an incident in which the gang used violence to protect its turf.

> **INT:** What kind of things does the gang have to do to defend its turf?
> **013:** Kill. That's all it is, kill.
> **INT:** Tell me about your most recent turf defense. What happened, a guy came in?
> **013:** A guy came in, he had the wrong colors on, he got to move out. He got his head split open with a sledgehammer, he got two ribs broken, he got his face torn up.

INT: Did he die from that?

013: I don't know. We dropped him off on the other side of town. If he did die, it was on the other side of town.

Staging Grounds for Violence

Gang members expect that when they go to certain locations they will be the targets of violence from other gangs or will be expected by members of their own gang to engage in violence. In some cases, large-scale violence will occur. Other encounters result only in "face-offs." These encounters highlight the role of situational characteristics in gang violence. Most often the staging grounds are public places such as a restaurant.

INT: Do they ever bring weapons to school?

011: No, cause we really don't have no trouble. We mainly fight up at the White Castle. That's where our trouble starts, at the White Castle.

The expectation of violence at certain locations was so strong that some members avoided going to those places.

INT: Do you go to dances or parties?

047: I don't. I stay away from house parties. Too many fights come out of there.

According to another gang member, violence at house parties had reached such a level that many hosts searched their guests for weapons.

074: Sometimes people wait until they get out of the party and start shooting. Now at these parties they have people at the door searching people, even at house parties.

In general, gang members reported that they "hung out" in small cliques or subgroups and that it was rare for the entire gang to be together. This reflects the general character of social organization in the gangs we studied. An external threat—usually from another gang—was needed to strengthen cohesion among gang members and to bring the larger gang together. Many members of our sample reported that they did not go skating, to the mall, or to dances alone or in small groups because they knew that gang violence was likely to erupt at such locations. Thus the gang went *en masse* to these locations, prepared to start or respond to violence. These expectations contributed to the eventual use of violence. In this way, the gang's belief system contributed to the likelihood of violent encounters.

Ending Gangs

When we asked for gang members' perspectives on the best way to end gangs, we expected to find a variety of recommendations targeted at fundamental causes (racism, unemployment, education) as well as more proximate solutions (detached workers, recreation centers, job training). Instead the modal response reflected the centrality of violence in the gang. Twenty-five of our 99 subjects told us that the only way to get rid of their gang would be to use violence to get rid of the members. This response was confirmed by gang members in their conversations with the field ethnographer. For many gang members, life in the gang had become synonymous with violence; for one respondent, even job offers were not sufficient to end the gang.

> **INT:** What would be the best way to get rid of your gang, the Rolling Sixties?
> **033:** Smoke us all.
> **INT:** Kill you all?
> **033:** Yeah.
> **INT:** We couldn't give you guys jobs?
> **033:** No, just smoke us.

Others recommended using extreme violence to get rid of their gang.

> **INT:** What would it take to get rid of your gang?
> **035:** Whole lot of machine guns. Kill us all. We just going to multiply anyway cause the Pee Wees gonna take over.
> **INT:** What would be the best way to get rid of the Sixties?
> **042:** Kill us all at once. Put them in one place and blow them up.

Violence is so central a part of gang culture that even the members' recommendations about ending gangs include elements of violence.

The Process of Gang Violence

The analysis above suggests a model that accounts for the escalation of gang violence and is consistent with the nature of gang process and normative structure: it reflects the lack of strong leadership, structure, and group goals. The key element is the collective identification of threat, a process that unites the gang and overcomes the general lack of unity by increasing cohesion. This occurred in response to threats against the gang, either real or perceived, by rival gangs. The role of mythic violence is particularly important in this context; it is the agent through which talk about violence most frequently unites gang members.

We suggest that a seven-step process accounts for the peaks and valleys of gang violence. The key to understanding violence is the nature of organization within gangs. Most gangs originate as neighborhood groups and are characterized by loose ties between their members and the larger gang. These groups generally lack effective leadership; cohesion in small cliques is stronger than the ties to the larger gang. Against this backdrop, symbolic enemies are identified when subgroups interact with other gangs near them. Threats from those groups—whether real or perceived—expand the number of participants, and may increase cohesion among members and heighten their willingness to use violence. Violence between gangs is most often the result of a mobilizing event that pushes a ready and willing group beyond the constraints against violence. Such events may include the deployment of gang members to protect or attack certain locations, to engage in actions in cars, or simply to act "loco." Violent encounters typically are short-lived and de-escalate rapidly. This de-escalation, however, may be only a respite before the next retaliation. The process moves through the following seven steps:

1. Loose bonds to the gang;
2. Collective identification of threat from a rival gang (through rumors, symbolic shows of force, cruising, and mythic violence), reinforcing the centrality of violence that expands the number of participants and increases cohesion;
3. A mobilizing event possibly, but not necessarily, violence;
4. Escalation of activity;
5. Violent event;
6. Rapid de-escalation;
7. Retaliation.

CONCLUSION

Gang violence, like other gang activities, reflects the gang's organizational and normative structure. Such violence, especially retaliatory violence, is an outgrowth of a collective process that reflects the loose organizational structure of gangs with diffuse goals, little allegiance among members, and few leaders.

If gangs are composed of diffuse subgroups, how is violence organized? Our answer to this question is "Not very well and not very often," because most gang violence serves important symbolic purposes within the gang. In addition, most gang violence is retaliatory, a response to violence—real or perceived—against the gang.

Gang violence serves many functions in the life of the gang. First, and most important, it produces more violence through the processes of threat and contagion. These mechanisms strongly reflect elements of collective behavior. Second, it temporarily increases the solidarity of gang members, uniting them against a common enemy by heightening their dependence on each other. When gang violence exceeds tolerable limits, a third function may be evident: the splintering of gangs into subgroups and the decision by some individuals to leave the gang.

4

Motivations for Gun Possession and Carrying Among Serious Juvenile Offenders

JOSEPH F. SHELEY
Tulane University

JAMES D. WRIGHT
University of Massachusetts

Scholars, lobbyists, and policy makers have long argued over the role that guns play in the thoughts and behaviors of young violent offenders. This article grabs the issue of juvenile gun crime by the horns as it relies on interviews with incarcerated juvenile offenders to illustrate why youths carry guns and what role they play in their criminal activities. The authors gained access to 835 young male offenders who were being housed in six different maximum security juvenile detention centers located in four different states (California, New Jersey, Illinois, and Louisiana). The vast majority (83%) of the youths report owning a gun in the days before they were incarcerated. All shapes (handguns, rifles, shotguns) and forms (single-action, semiautomatic, automatic) of gun ownership were will represented in the sample. Guns appeared to be a common part of these youth's daily lives, as most said that they routinely carried these weapons when they were outside of their own homes. A strong relationship between guns and crime is observed as many youths claimed to have fired their weapons at someone, used it in a robbery, or bought the gun for the expressed purpose of committing a crime. Surprisingly, self-preservation emerged as the primary reason for carrying and using a gun. The data show that these youths live in a violence-prone world and thus see a very real need to arm themselves as a means of surviving and thriving in this environment. The authors argue that this perceived need to be armed poses a formidable stumbling block for policy makers who seek to reduce gun-related violence on our city streets.

A number of recent investigations reflect a growing concern with the prevalence of gun possession among juveniles, though it is important to note that these studies pertain to relatively average rather than to more seriously criminal youth. A 1987 survey of 390 high school students in Baltimore, for example, found that almost half of the males had carried a gun to school at least once (Hackett, Sandza, Gibney, and Gareiss, 1988). Three percent of the males in a 1987

From *Behavioral Sciences and the Law*, Vol. 11, pp. 375–388. Reproduced by permission of John Wiley & Sons Limited.

survey of 11,000 eighth- and tenth-grade students in 20 states reported bringing a handgun to school during the year preceding the survey (National School Safety Center, 1989). Four percent of a 1990 nationally representative sample of 11,631 students (21% of the black males) in grades 9 through 12 reported carrying a gun at least once within the 30 days prior to being surveyed (US Department of Health and Human Services, 1991). A 1990 survey of 11th grade students in Seattle found that 11% of the males reported owning a handgun; 6% had carried a gun to school sometime in the past (Callahan and Rivara, 1992). Focusing only on inner-city youth, a 1991 multi-state study found that one in three male and one in ten female high school students had carried a gun on the streets (Sheley, McGee, and Wright, 1992). Presumably, these figures, pertaining as they do to relatively standard student populations, would inflate to the extent they reflected the firearm-possession patterns of more criminally active youth.

Though the prevalence problem is now fairly well grounded empirically, little research has examined juveniles' reasons for possessing and carrying guns beyond noting that juveniles who report robbery and assaultive behavior have higher rates of gun and other weapon possession than do non-violent juveniles (Callahan and Rivara, 1992; Fagan, Piper, and Moore, 1986). However, without indicting the logic of the guns and crime equation, it is also fair to say that it reflects the worries of actual and potential victims of crime more than their thoughtful analysis of the many roles firearms might play in the lives of youth. For example, two percent of the students in one national-level study had carried a weapon (including, but not limited to, guns) to school for *protection* at least once during a six-month period (Bastion and Taylor, 1991; see also Asmussen, 1992). In a second national-level study, one in five high school students reported carrying a weapon (including, but not limited to, guns; also not limited to weapon-carrying in schools) during the past 30 days for *protection* or *use in a fight* (U.S. Department of Health and Human Services, 1991). The issue of motivation for possession and carrying of firearms remains open for the present.

THE PRESENT STUDY

To what ends are guns carried by youth—self-protection, intimidation, crime, status enhancement? The present study examines the question of motivation behind gun possession and carrying by criminally-inclined youths through analysis of survey data collected from juveniles incarcerated in maximum security reformatories. The research questionnaire contained primarily forced-choice items pertaining to firearms possession and carrying, use of firearms in criminal activity, and reasons for carrying a gun generally and during commission of a crime. Importantly, the present study is the only one to date to provide information not only on firearms in general, but on specific *types* of firearms (revolvers, semiautomatic and automatic handguns, sawed-off shotguns, etc.). Measurement of specific variables is described throughout this article on a topic-by-topic basis.

While clearly not representative of all juvenile offenders, youths of the sort found in the present sample likely are responsible for a very high percentage of the serious crime committed by juveniles and are far more criminal than the most criminal of non-incarcerated youth (see Cernkovich, Giordano, and Pugh, 1985). Most were apprehended and incarcerated because they committed so many serious crimes that the odds caught up with them. To the extent firearms activity is pervasive among juveniles, it should be so among this population. The issue is whether or not criminal activity represents the motivating factor in gun possession and carrying by youths like these; if not, then it is not likely to be the motivating factor among less seriously offending youths. In this light, the motivation issue becomes particularly important for policy makers, especially for those relying upon gun control and "get tough" legislation as an anticrime strategy.

FINDINGS

Guns and Crime

Possession, Carrying, and Offending To assess firearm possession, respondents were asked to check, from a list of firearms, those they owned or possessed immediately prior to incarceration. Types of guns included (a) revolvers, (b) automatic or semiautomatic handguns, (c) regular shotguns, (d) sawed-off shotguns, and (e) "other." Automatic and semiautomatic firearms (rifles and handguns that automatically place a new round into the firing chamber) were treated in combination because the aim was simply to distinguish rapid-fire from more traditional guns. The carrying of guns was measured in terms of the frequency with which the respondent carried a gun during the year or two prior to incarceration, "outside your home (including in your car)." *Routine* gun-carrying was operationalized as carrying "all" or "most" of the time (as opposed to "only now and then" or "never").

Crime-related behaviors were measured in terms of whether or not the respondent had ever (a) obtained a gun "specifically to use in committing crimes"; (b) "committed a crime with a gun"; (c) "fired a gun during a crime"; (d) "actually fired a gun at somebody"; or (e) committed armed robbery ("stuck up stores or people"—though not specifically with a gun).

Table 1 provides findings regarding both the gun- and the crime-related activities of the inmate respondents. Eighty-three percent possessed a gun of some kind. Handguns were the most commonly owned firearms, followed closely by sawed-off shotguns. Regular shotguns and automatic and semiautomatic rifles, clearly more cumbersome weapons, were less favored. Fifty-five of the inmates carried guns routinely prior to incarceration. Nearly half of the sample had committed armed robbery. Though only 40% had ever procured a gun specifically for a crime, 55% had fired a gun during a crime. Seventy-six percent of the respondents had actually fired a gun at someone. In short, the popular fear concerning victimization by armed juveniles is not wholly unfounded, though the findings that only four in ten respondents had procured a gun specifically for use in crime and that three in four respondents had fired at someone point to multiple needs and uses for guns among the respondents.

Table 1 Inmates' Involvement in Gun- and Crime-Related Activities

Activity	Percent	N
Gun possession	83	823
Gun type:		
Revolver	58	823
Auto/semiauto handgun	55	823
Auto/semiauto rifle	35	823
Regular shotgun	39	823
Sawed-off shotgun	51	823
Other	25	823
Carried gun routinely	55	802
Procured gun for crime	40	762
Fired gun during crime	55	800
Fired gun at someone	76	801
Committed armed robbery	49	811

Relationship of Guns to Violent Crime Although an immediate task was to gain some sense of patterns of violent criminality by respondents who reported having possessed firearms, it is important to note the problem of causal direction regarding the gun-crime relationship. It may well be that predators seek out guns or certain types of guns; it may as easily be that persons with guns or certain types of gun are more likely to rob or kill. The former possibility is, of course, a relative truism given that the crimes examined in this study are directly firearm-related. As expected, current respondents involved in violence were indeed significantly more likely than those who were not to own every kind of gun of interest here and to carry firearms routinely, though it is noteworthy that reasonably high percentages of those who did not engage in crimes of violence owned and carried firearms. Involvement in crime was particularly associated with possession of handguns and sawed-off shotguns, less so with possession of regular shotguns and automatic and semiautomatic rifles.

While these findings may not surprise, those displayed in Table 2 may—at least in terms of the *strength* of the associations found between types of guns owned and involvement in violent crime. Ownership of any given type of firearm and the routine carrying of a gun are both significantly and strongly related to violent activity.

The findings suggest that, at least for the type of juvenile confined in a maximum security reformatory, it is as likely that gun possession leads to violent crime as it is that violent crime promotes gun possession. More likely still, the findings point less to a *causal* possibility than to an environment characterized by both firearms and crime. Firearms are carried for numerous reasons; they are also useful in the commission of crimes, most of which would be attempted even if firearms were not available. This is suggested particularly by the findings in the last column of Table 2: possession and carrying of guns are

Table 2 Inmates' Involvement in Violent Activity by Gun Ownership and Carrying

Own/Carry Firearm	Violent Activity			
	Armed Robbery	Procured Gun for Crime	Fired Gun During Crime	Fired Gun at Someone
Revolver				
% yes/no	57/37	48/26	65/40	89/57
(N)	(802)	(754)	(698)	(789)
Auto/semiauto handgun				
% yes/no	59/36	49/27	68/38	90/58
(N)	(802)	(754)	(698)	(789)
Auto/semiauto rifle				
% yes/no	56/44	56/30	43/25	93/67
(N)	(802)	(754)	(698)	(789)
Regular shotgun				
% yes/no	58/42	53/24	71/36	93/58
(N)	(802)	(754)	(698)	(789)
Sawed-off shotgun				
% yes/no	61/35	53/24	71/36	93/58
(N)	(802)	(754)	(698)	(789)
Carried guns routinely				
% yes/no	61/35	55/21	74/31	94/53
(N)	(780)	(777)	(685)	(745)

more strongly linked to generally having fired at someone than to having engaged in the predatory offenses indexed in the table (first three columns).

Use of Guns in Crime Why do juveniles carry or use firearms in the commission of crimes? Some research attention has been devoted to possession of guns by criminals as "tools of the trade." Cook (1976) argues, for example, that robbers prefer guns because they permit robbery of more lucrative targets; others point to guns as highly intimidating and, thus, more facilitative of robbery. Injury to victims is inversely related to the use of a gun as the robber's weapon (Cook, 1980; Skogan, 1978). Wright and Rossi (1986) argue that much of gun use in predatory crimes is motivated by the felon's perceived need to protect himself from the potentially aggressive victim. Much regarding choice and use of weapons by criminals likely depends upon whether or not the offenders are "professionals" or "career" offenders (Conklin, 1972; Greenwood, 1980). The motivations for firearm use in crimes by juveniles—not yet "career" offenders—have yet to be identified.

Table 3 presents the percentage of armed-crime inmates who considered a given reason to carry a weapon during a crime "very important." Two items touched on the intimidating effect of a weapon used in a crime: 45% felt a

Table 3 "Very Important" Reasons for Carrying a Weapon During a Crime—Inmates Who Routinely Carried Guns During Crime (N=393)

Reasons for Carrying a Gun During Crime	Percent Very Important
Have to be ready to defend self	80
Chance victim would be armed	58
Might need weapon to escape crime scene	49
Victim won't put up a fight	45
People don't "Mess With" armed offender	42

Routinely carrying guns refers to the practice of "always" or "usually" arming oneself for crime.

weapon decreased the odds that a victim would resist the offender, and 42% reasoned that people do not "mess with" someone with a weapon. Important though it seemed to be for the type of juvenile studied here, intimidation with a weapon took a back seat to self-protection in the decision to arm oneself to commit a crime. The two reasons considered most important by the offenders in question related to the offender's sense of risk of harm associated with the crime. Eighty percent considered it very important to be ready to defend oneself in a crime, and 58% expressed concern that a victim might be armed. In a related vein, 49% thought a weapon might facilitate an escape from a crime scene.

The perception of risk to the offender in a crime situation likely is not groundless. A juvenile in the process of deciding to commit a crime contemplates a range of risks and benefits. The benefits consist of financial or other gains. The costs include the possibility of being caught and imprisoned as well as being shot (or otherwise injured) in the course of the crime either by the victim, a bystander, or the police. The probability of encountering a victim who possesses a firearm is by no means trivial. Many private citizens claim to own guns for self-defense (Wright, Rossi, and Daly, 1983). Indeed, 36% of the respondents in this study reported having decided at least "a few times" not to commit a crime because they believed the potential victim was armed. Seventy percent of the respondents reported having been "scared off, shot at, wounded, or captured by an armed crime victim."

Guns as Status Symbols

As aspects of the preceding results suggest, to determine that criminal violence and gun ownership and carrying are related is not necessarily to find that the reason (or, at least, the primary reason) juveniles own and carry guns is to commit crimes. Indeed, as noted above, the percentage of inmates who had procured a gun specifically for use in a crime (40%) was considerably less than the percentage of inmates who had committed gun-related crimes (63%). It is possible then that crimes often were committed with guns that were obtained or carried routinely with other ends in mind. According to some media reviews of the issue, "respect" is a major element in the decision to carry a gun (Hackett et al., 1988; *New Orleans Times Picayune,* 1993). In this view, the gun is principally a symbolic totem that displays "toughness" or "machismo" and serves primarily to make an impression on one's peers.

Inmate respondents were asked to agree strongly, agree, disagree, or disagree strongly, "I'm my crowd, if you don't have a gun people don't respect you." Eighty-six percent of the inmates *rejected* this statement, most of them strongly. They were also asked to agree or disagree (strongly or otherwise) that "My friends would look down on me if I did not carry a gun." Eighty-nine percent of the inmates also *disagreed* with this statement (most, again, strongly). These findings hold as well for inmates who had carried guns. It thus appears that the "symbolism" or "status" hypothesis may be dismissed with a great deal of confidence, at least for the sample studied here.

A similar conclusion is evident from the findings presented in Table 4. Inmates who said they carried guns at least occasionally, but not "all of the time," were asked about the circumstances in which they were most likely to carry a gun. The question is, of course, meaningless for those who never carried and for those who carried all, the time. The *least* likely circumstance in which inmates would carry guns was when they were "out raising hell," presumably a peer-linked activity. They were also relatively unlikely to carry guns when they were "hanging out with friends" or when they were with friends who were themselves carrying guns. If it were simply a matter of status of reputation, one would expect these to be the *most* (not the least) likely circumstances in which they would carry. These findings pertain not only to the larger sample of inmates but to subsamples of those who had committed armed robbery and those who "always" or "usually" were armed when committing a crime.

Guns as Protection

Rather than signalling a concern with status, the responses summarized in Table 4 are dominated—overwhelmingly—by themes of self-protection and self-preservation. Inmates who carried guns did so most frequently when they were in a strange area (72%), when they were out at night (58%), and whenever they thought they might face a need for self-protection (75%). The same themes emerged in responses by subsamples of robbers and armed offenders. Likewise, the results indicate that, for any of the three types of guns purchased by inmates, use in crime or to "get someone" was very important for no more than 43% of those purchasing guns and no more than 52% of gun purchasers who were involved in armed offenses. Here too, the desire for protection and the need to arm oneself against enemies were the primary reasons to obtain a gun, easily outpacing all other motivations.

The theme of self-protection is again evident, though less clearly so, in the circumstances in which the inmate respondents had actually *fired* their guns (Table 5). Here the most frequent circumstance was "when hanging out with friends" (one of the less frequent reasons for carrying a gun; see Table 4), regardless of whether or not the respondents had committed violent crimes. The second most frequent circumstance involved self-defense; this also held true regardless of respondent's involvement in violent crime. Sixty-nine percent of the inmates had fired a gun in what they considered self-defense. More

Table 4 When Were Inmates Likely to Carry Guns? (Respondents Who Had Carried Guns "Now and Then" or "Most of the Time")

How Likely Were You to Carry a Gun When:		% "Very Likely"		
		Whole Sample	Armed Robbers*	Armed Criminals**
	(N=)	**(477)**	**(416)**	**(427)**
Doing a drug deal		50	57	71
Raising hell		32	39	43
In a strange area		72	79	86
At night		58	64	74
Hanging out with friends		38	43	49
Friends were carrying guns		39	42	47
Needing protection		75	78	82
Planning to do a crime		37	50	61

* Inmates who had committed armed robbery.

** Inmates who "always" or "usually" were armed with a gun when committing a crime.

Table 5 When Inmates Fire Their Guns

		Armed Robbers*	
Circumstance	Whole Sample	%Fired (N)	Armed Criminals**
In self defense	69 (718)	81 (352)	87 (318)
During a crime	55 (704)	76 (356)	79 (320)
During drug deals	53 (697)	66 (342)	76 (318)
While hanging out with friends	75 (711)	89 (358)	89 (324)
While high or drunk	54 (691)	71 (346)	69 (314)
While fleeing from police	35 (682)	48 (340)	53 (312)
During a fight	61 (709)	75 (351)	80 (321)
To scare someone	66 (720)	80 (359)	76 (325)

*Inmates who had committed armed robbery.
**Inmates who "always" or "usually" were armed with a gun when committing a crime.

than eight in ten of those who had committed armed robbery, or more generally were armed when committing crimes, had fired in self-defense as well. Aside from the low percentage of inmates who had fired while fleeing from the police, most of the other circumstances examined here drew similar, relatively high percentages across inmate categories: shooting during a crime, firing to scare someone, and firing during drug deals and fights.

The earlier findings regarding reasons for the purchase and carrying of firearms pointed clearly to a perceived need for self-protection. The findings in Table 5 suggest a complex of reasons why the inmates (serious offenders who would be expected to have fired guns during crimes) might shoot a gun. That same complex suggest that these juveniles, both by design and by fate, find themselves in circumstances that, in their judgment, require gunfire. It is likely that, in their view, the distinction between victim and perpetrator is often vague. Most of these inmate respondents had used guns to intimidate others and had had guns used against them. Much of the self-protection they sought, in short, was likely protection against one another.

CONCLUSION

All the evidence reviewed here suggests that, among the juveniles studied, the odds of surviving in a hostile environment were seen as better if one were armed. Exceptional rates of crime, violence, and gun activity appeared to characterize the social environments from which these respondents were drawn. Most regularly experienced threats of violence and violence itself. Eighty-four percent reported that they had been threatened with a gun or shot at during their lives. Half had been stabbed with a knife. More than eight in ten (82%) had been beaten.

Not surprisingly given this climate, significant percentages of respondents felt that shooting another person was justified under circumstances that conventional society would not deem appropriate. Thirty-five percent agreed or strongly agreed that "it is okay to shoot a person if that is what it takes to get something you want." Twenty-nine percent agreed or strongly agreed that it was "okay to shoot some guy who doesn't belong in your neighborhood."

Elements of insult and injury inevitably increased the perceived acceptance of violent responses. It was considered "okay [agree or strongly agree] to shoot someone who hurts or insults you" by 61% of the inmates. If one's family was the target of the insult or injury, the percentage agreeing rose to 74, 24% agreeing and 50% agreeing strongly. Thus, if their enemies and even perfect strangers possessed the weapons and mentality that allowed them to take a life quickly and easily from a distance, the present respondents likely reasoned that arming themselves was necessary.

It is difficult to label the juvenile's use of a gun in crime as peripheral to the possession of a gun, since so many of the inmate respondents had used guns for crime. Instead, it is likely that any gun procured principally for protection (or status) is also viewed as *potentially* instrumental in committing crimes. Unfortunately, the implications of these results are not encouraging. The perception that one's very survival depends on being armed makes a weapon a necessity at nearly any cost. Attempts to reduce juvenile gun-related crime through threat of criminal justice sanctions can hardly be expected to produce results if a juvenile "must" have a gun to survive, and crimes are committed with guns because they happen to be in the youth's possession. Gun-related crime (though not necessarily all weapon-related crime), then, will likely decrease only when juveniles are convinced that they do not have to carry guns for protection.

5

How Women Experience Battering: The Process of Victimization

KATHLEEN J. FERRARO
JOHN M. JOHNSON
Arizona State University

The authors undertook this study in the late 1970s, a time when society was just com-
ing to grips about the realities of intimate partner violence. Ferraro and Johnson draw
upon their experiences as participant observers at a shelter for battered women to shed
light on how these women cope with their habitual abuse. By working with fellow staff
members and fostering relationships with 120 women who passed through the shelter
over a 14-month period, they were able to generate a series of generic observations about
how women experience and think about their abusive relationships. The victimization
process is divided into three parts. As the violence begins, the data show that the women
struggle to make sense of their situations by drawing upon one of six rationalization
frameworks. Here, thoughts and behaviors serve to accentuate the positive aspects of the
relationship while simultaneously downplaying the negatives. These cognitive devices
temporarily inhibit the individual's sense of rage and deter her from leaving her abusive
spouse. As time goes by and the intensity of the abuse increases, the woman experiences
a mental transformation. In this second stage of the process, the woman enlists the use of
a "catalyst for change" to reorient her world view, thus empowering her to leave the abu-
sive situation. Upon departure, the woman embarks upon a third stage in which she
slowly rebuilds her self-confidence and reflects upon her past situation. This article is
somewhat unique in that it takes on the issue of criminal assault from the perspective of
the victim.

Although the existence of violence against women is now publicly acknowledged, the experience of being battered is poorly understood. Research aimed at discovering the incidence and related social variables has been based on an operational definition of battering which focuses on the violent act. The Conflict Tactic Scales (CTS) developed by Straus

© 1982 by The Society for the Study of Social Problems. Reprinted from *Social Problems,*
Vol. 30, No. 3 (February 1983), pp. 325–339, by permission of the University of
California Press.

(1979), for example, is based on the techniques used to resolve family conflicts. The Violence Scale of the CTS ranks eight violent behaviors, ranging in severity from throwing something at the other person to using a knife or gun (Straus, 1979). The scale is not designed to explore the context of violent actions, or their meanings for the victim or perpetrator. With notable exceptions (Dobash and Dobash, 1979), the bulk of sociological research on battered women has focused on quantifiable variables (Gelles, 1974, 1976; O'Brien, 1971; Steinmetz, 1978; Straus, 1978).

Interviews with battered women make it apparent that the experience of violence inflicted by a husband or lover is shocking and confusing. Battering is rarely perceived as an unambiguous assault demanding immediate action to ensure future safety. In fact, battered women often remain in violent relationships for years (Pagelow, 1981).

Why do battered women stay in abusive relationships? Some observers answer facilely that they must like it. The masochism thesis was the predominant response of psychiatrists writing about battering in the 1960s (Saul, 1972; Snell et al., 1964). More sympathetic studies of the problem have revealed the difficulties of disentangling oneself from a violent relationship (Hilberman, 1980; Martin, 1976; Walker, 1979). These studies point to the social and cultural expectations of women and their status within the nuclear family as reasons for the reluctance of battered women to flee the relationship. The socialization of women emphasizes the primary value of being a good wife and mother, at the expense of personal achievement in other spheres of life. The patriarchal ordering of society assigns a secondary status to women, and provides men with ultimate authority, both within and outside the family unit. Economic conditions contribute to the dependency of women on men; in 1978 U.S. women earned, on the average, 58 percent of what men earned (U.S. Department of Labor, 1980). In sum, the position of women in U.S. society makes it extremely difficult for them to reject the authority of men and develop independent lives free of marital violence (Dobash and Dobash, 1979; Pagelow, 1981).

Material and cultural conditions are the background in which personal interpretations of events are developed. Women who depend on their husbands for practical support also depend on them as sources of self-esteem, emotional support, and continuity. This paper looks at how women make sense of their victimization within the context of these dependencies. Without dismissing the importance of the macro forces of gender politics, we focus on inter- and intrapersonal responses to violence. We first describe six techniques of rationalization used by women who are in relationships where battering has occurred. We then turn to catalysts which may serve as forces to reevaluate rationalizations and to initiate serious attempts at escape. Various physical and emotional responses to battering are described, and finally, we outline the consequences of leaving or attempting to leave a violent relationship.

The term battered woman is used in this paper to describe women who are battered repeatedly by men with whom they live as lovers. Marriage is not a prerequisite for being a battered woman. Many of the women who entered the shelter we studied were living with, but were not legally married to, the men who abused them.

RATIONALIZING VIOLENCE

Marriages and their unofficial counterparts develop through the efforts of each partner to maintain feelings of love and intimacy. In modern, Western cultures, the value placed on marriage is high; individuals invest a great amount of emotion in their spouses, and expect a return on that investment. The majority of women who marry still adopt the roles of wives and mothers as primary identities, even when they work outside the home, and thus have a strong motivation to succeed in their domestic roles. Married women remain economically dependent on their husbands. In 1978, married men in the United States earned an average of $293 a week, while married women earned $167 a week (U.S. Department of Labor, 1980). Given these high expectations and dependencies, the costs of recognizing failures and dissolving marriages are significant. Divorce is an increasingly common phenomenon in the United States, but it is still labeled a social problem and is seldom undertaken without serious deliberations and emotional upheavals (Bohannan, 1971). Levels of commitment vary widely, but some degree of commitment is implicit in the marriage contract.

When marital conflicts emerge there is usually some effort to negotiate an agreement or bargain, to ensure the continuity of the relationship (Scanzoni, 1972). Couples employ a variety of strategies, depending on the nature and extent of resources available to them, to resolve conflicts without dissolving relationships. It is thus possible for marriages to continue for years, surviving the inevitable conflicts that occur (Sprey, 1971).

In describing conflict-management, Spiegel (1968) distinguishes between "role induction" and "role modification." Role induction refers to conflict in which "one or the other parties to the conflict agrees, submits, goes along with, becomes convinced, or is persuaded in some way" (1968: 402). Role modification, on the other hand, involves adaptations by both partners. Role induction seems particularly applicable to battered women who accommodate their husbands' abuse. Rather than seeking help or escaping, as people typically do when attacked by strangers, battered women often rationalize violence from their husbands, at least initially. Although remaining with a violent man does not indicate that a woman views violence as an acceptable aspect of the relationship, the length of time that a woman stays in the marriage after abuse begins is a rough index of her efforts to accommodate the situation. In a U.S. study of 350 battered women, Pagelow (1981) found the median length of stay after violence began was four years; some left in less than one year, others stayed as long as 42 years.

Battered women have good reasons to rationalize violence. There are few institutional, legal, or cultural supports for women fleeing violent marriages.

In Roy's (1977: 32) survey of 150 battered women, 90% said they "thought of leaving and would have done so had the resources been available to them." Eighty percent of Pagelow's (1981) sample indicated previous, failed attempts to leave their husbands. Despite the development of the international shelter movement, changes in police practices, and legislation to protect battered women since 1975, it remains extraordinarily difficult for a battered woman to escape a violent husband determined to maintain his control. At least one woman, Mary Parziale, has been murdered by an abusive husband while residing in a shelter (Beverly, 1978); others have been murdered after leaving shelters to establish new, independent homes (Garcia, 1978). When these practical and social constraints are combined with love for and commitment to an abuser, it is obvious that there is a strong incentive—often a practical necessity—to rationalize violence.

Previous research on the rationalizations of deviant offenders has revealed a typology of "techniques of neutralization," which allow offenders to view their actions as normal, acceptable, or at least justifiable (Sykes and Matza, 1957). A similar typology can be constructed for victims. Extending the concepts developed by Sykes and Matza, we assigned the responses of battered women we interviewed to one of six categories of rationalization: (1) the appeal to the salvation ethic; (2) the denial of the victimizer; (3) the denial of injury; (4) the denial of victimization; (5) the denial of options; and (6) the appeal to higher loyalties. The women usually employed at least one of these techniques to make sense of their situations; often they employed two or more, simultaneously or over time.

(1) *The appeal to the salvation ethic:* This rationalization is grounded in a woman's desire to be of service to others. Abusing husbands are viewed as deeply troubled, perhaps "sick," individuals, dependent on their wives nurturance for survival. Battered women place their own safety and happiness below their commitment to "saving my man" from whatever malady they perceive as the source of their husbands' problems (Ferraro, 1979a). The appeal to the salvation ethic is a common response to an alcoholic or drug-dependent abuser. The battered partners of substance-abusers frequently describe the charming, charismatic personality of their sober mates, viewing this appealing personality as the "real man" being destroyed by disease. They then assume responsibility for helping their partners to overcome their problems, viewing the batterings they receive as an index of their partners' pathology. Abuse must be endured while helping the man return to his "normal" self. One woman said:

> I thought I was going to be Florence Nightingale. He had so much potential; I could see how good he really was, and I was going to 'save' him. I thought I was the only thing keeping him going, and that if I left he'd lose his job and wind up in jail. I'd make excuses to everybody for him. I'd call work and lie when he was drunk, saying he was sick. I never criticized him, because he needed my approval.

(2) *The denial of the victimizer:* This technique is similar to the salvation ethic, except that victims do not assume responsibility for solving their abusers' problems. Women perceive battering as an event beyond the control of both spouses, and blame it on some external force. The violence is judged situational and temporary, because it is linked to unusual circumstances or a sickness which can be cured. Pressures at work, the loss of a job, or legal problems are all situations which battered women assume as the causes of their partners' violence. Mental illness, alcoholism, and drug addiction are also viewed as external, uncontrollable afflictions by many battered women who accept the medical perspective on such problems. By focusing on factors beyond the control of their abuser, women deny their husbands' intent to do them harm, and thus rationalize violent episodes.

> He's sick. He didn't used to be this way, but he can't handle alcohol. It's
> really like a disease, being an alcoholic. . . . I think too that this is what
> he saw at home, his father is a very violent man, and alcoholic too, so it's
> really not his fault, because this is all he has ever known.

(3) *The denial of injury:* For some women, the experience of being battered by a spouse is so discordant with their expectations that they simply refuse to acknowledge it. When hospitalization is not required—and it seldom is for most cases of battering—routines quickly return to normal. Meals are served, jobs and schools are attended, and daily chores completed. Even with lingering pain, bruises, and cuts, the normality of everyday life overrides the strange, confusing memory of the attack. When husbands refuse to discuss or acknowledge the event, in some cases even accusing their wives of insanity, women sometimes come to believe the violence never occurred. The denial of injury does not mean that women feel no pain. They know they are hurt, but define the hurt as tolerable or normal. Just as individuals tolerate a wide range of physical discomfort before seeking medical help, battered women tolerate a wide range of physical abuse before defining it as an injurious assault. One woman explained her disbelief at her first battering:

> I laid in bed and cried all night. I could not believe it had happened, and I
> didn't want to believe it. We had only been married a year, and I was
> pregnant and excited about starting a family. Then all of a sudden, this!
> The next morning he told me he was sorry and it wouldn't happen again,
> and I gladly kissed and made up. I wanted to forget the whole thing, and
> wouldn't let myself worry about what it meant for us.

(4) *The denial of victimization:* Victims often blame themselves for the violence, thereby neutralizing the responsibility of the spouse. Pagelow (1981) found that 99.4 percent of battered women felt they did not deserve to be beaten, and 51 percent said they had done nothing to provoke an attack. The battered women in our sample did not believe violence against them was justified, but some felt it could have been avoided if they had been more passive and conciliatory. Both Pagelow's and our samples are biased in this area, because they were made up almost entirely of women who had already left their abusers, and thus would have been unlikely to feel major responsibility for the abuse they

received. Retrospective accounts of victimization in our sample, however, did reveal evidence that some women believed their right to leave violent men was restricted by their participation in the conflicts. One subject said:

> Well, I couldn't really do anything about it, because I did ask for it. I knew how to get at him, and I'd keep after it and keep after it until he got fed up and knocked me right out. I can't say I like it, but I shouldn't have nagged him like I did.

As Pagelow (1981) noted, there is a difference between provocation and justification. A battered woman's belief that her actions angered her spouse to the point of violence is not synonymous with the belief that violence was therefore *justified*. But belief in provocation may diminish a woman's capacity for retaliation or self-defense, because it blurs her concept of responsibility. A woman's acceptance of responsibility for the violent incident is encouraged by an abuser who continually denigrates her and makes unrealistic demands. Depending on the social supports available, and the personality of the battered woman, the man's accusations of inadequacy may assume the status of truth. Such beliefs of inferiority inhibit the development of a notion of victimization.

(5) *The denial of options:* This technique is composed of two elements: practical options and emotional options. Practical options, including alternative housing, source of income, and protection from an abuser, are clearly limited by the patriarchal structure of Western society. However, there are differences in the ways battered women respond to these obstacles, ranging from determined struggle to acquiescence. For a variety of reasons, some battered women do not take full advantage of the practical opportunities which are available to escape, and some return to abusers voluntarily even after establishing an independent lifestyle. Others ignore the most severe constraints in their efforts to escape their relationships. For example, one resident of the shelter we observed walked 30 miles in her bedroom slippers to get to the shelter, and required medical attention for blisters and cuts to her feet. On the other hand, a woman who had a full-time job, had rented an apartment, and had been given by the shelter all the clothes, furniture, and basics necessary to set up housekeeping, returned to her husband two weeks after leaving the shelter. Other women refused to go to job interviews, keep appointments with social workers, or move out of the state for their own protection (Ferraro, 1981b). Such actions are frightening for women who have led relatively isolated or protected lives, but failure to take action leaves few alternatives to a violent marriage. The belief of battered women that they will not be able to make it on their own—a belief often fueled by years of abuse and oppression—is a major impediment to acknowledge that one is a victim and taking action.

The denial of *emotional* options imposes still further restrictions. Battered women may feel that no one else can provide intimacy and companionship. While physical beating is painful and dangerous, the prospect of a lonely, celibate existence is often too frightening to risk. It is not uncommon for battered women to express the belief that their abuser is the only man they could love, thus severely limiting their opportunities to discover new, more supportive relationships. One woman said:

He's all I've got. My dad's gone, and my mother disowned me when
I married him. And he's really special. He understands me, and I
understand him. Nobody could take his place.

(6) *The appeal to higher loyalties:* This appeal involves enduring battering
for the sake of some higher commitment, either religious or traditional. The
Christian belief that women should serve their husbands as men serve God is
invoked as a rationalization to endure a husband's violence for later rewards in
the afterlife. Clergy may support this view by advising women to pray and try
harder to please their husbands (Davidson, 1978; McClinchey, 1981). Other
women have a strong commitment to the nuclear family, and find divorce
repugnant. They may believe that for their children's sake, any marriage is
better than no marriage. One woman we interviewed divorced her husband of
35 years after her last child left home. More commonly women who have survived violent relationships for that long do not have the desire or strength to
divorce and begin a new life. When the appeal to higher loyalties is employed
as a strategy to cope with battering, commitment to and involvement with an
ideal overshadows the mundane reality of violence.

CATALYSTS FOR CHANGE

Rationalization is a way of coping with a situation in which, for either practical
or emotional reasons, or both, a battered woman is stuck. For some women,
the situation and the beliefs that rationalize it, may continue for a lifetime.
For others, changes may occur within the relationship, within individuals, or in
available resources which serve as catalysts for redefining the violence. When
battered women reject prior rationalizations and begin to view themselves as
true victims of abuse, the victimization process begins.

There are a variety of catalysts for redefining abuse; we discuss six: (1) a
change in the level of violence; (2) a change in resources; (3) a change in the
relationship; (4) despair; (5) a change in the visibility of violence; and (6) external definitions of the relationship.

(1) *A change in the level of violence:* Although Gelles (1976) reports that the
severity of abuse is an important factor in women's decisions to leave violent
situations, Pagelow (1981) found no significant correlation between the number of years spent cohabiting with an abuser and the severity of abuse. On the
contrary: the longer women lived with an abuser, the more severe the violence
they endured, since violence increased in severity over time. What does seem
to serve as a catalyst is a sudden change in the relative level of violence. Women
who suddenly realize that battering may be fatal may reject rationalizations in
order to save their lives. One woman who had been severely beaten by an alcoholic husband for many years explained her decision to leave on the basis of a
direct threat to her life:

It was like a pendulum. He'd swing to the extremes both ways. He'd get drunk and beat me up, then he'd get sober and treat me like a queen. One day he put a gun to my head and pulled the trigger. It wasn't loaded. But that's when I decided I'd had it. I sued for separation of property. I knew what was coming again, so I got out. I didn't want to. I still loved the guy, but I knew I had to for my own sanity.

(2) *A change in resources:* Although some women rationalize cohabiting with an abuser by claiming they have no options, others begin reinterpreting violence when the resources necessary for escape become available. The emergence of safe homes or shelters since 1970 has produced a new resource for battered women. While not completely adequate or satisfactory, the mere existence of a place to go alters the situation in which battering is experienced (Johnson, 1981). Public support of shelters is a statement to battered women that abuse need not be tolerated. Conversely, political trends which limit resources available to women, such as cutbacks in government funding to social programs, increase fears that life outside a violent marriage is economically impossible. One 55-year-old woman discussed this catalyst:

I stayed with him because I didn't want my kids to have the same life I did. My parents were divorced, and I was always so ashamed of that. . . . Yes, they're all on their own now, so there's no reason left to stay.

(3) *A change in the relationship:* Walker (1979), in discussing the stages of a battering relationship, notes that violent incidents are usually followed by periods of remorse and solicitude. Such phases deepen the emotional bonds, and make rejection of an abuser more difficult. But as battering progresses, periods of remorse may shorten, or disappear, eliminating the basis for maintaining a positive outlook on the marriage. After a number of episodes of violence, a man may realize that this victim will not retaliate or escape, and thus feel no need to express remorse. Extended periods devoid of kindness or love may alter a woman's feelings toward her partner so much so that she eventually begins to define herself as a victim of abuse. One woman recalled:

At first, you know, we used to have so much fun together. He has kind've, you know, a magnetic personality; he can be really charming. But it isn't fun anymore. Since the baby came, it's changed completely. He just wants me to stay at home, while he goes out with his friends. He doesn't even talk to me, most of the time. . . . No, I don't really love him anymore, not like I did.

(4) *Despair:* Changes in the relationship may result in a loss of hope that "things will get better." When hope is destroyed and replaced by despair, rationalizations of violence may give way to the recognition of victimization. Feelings of hopelessness or despair are the basis for some efforts to assist battered women, such as Al-Anon. The director of an Al-Anon organized shelter explained the concept of "hitting bottom":

Before the Al-Anon program can really be of benefit, a woman has to hit bottom. When you hit bottom, you realize that all of your own efforts to control the situation have failed; you feel helpless and lost and worthless and completely disenchanted with the world. Women can't really be helped unless they're ready for it and want it. Some women come here when things get bad, but they aren't really ready to be committed to Al-Anon. Things haven't gotten bad enough for them, and they go right back. We see this all the time.

(5) *A change in the visibility of violence:* Creating a web of rationalizations to overlook violence is accomplished more easily if no intruders are present to question their validity. Since most violence between couples occurs in private, there are seldom conflicting interpretations of the event from outsiders. Only 7% of the respondents in Gelles (1979) study who discussed spatial location of violence indicated events which took place outside the home, but all reported incidents within the home. Others report similar findings (Pittman and Handy, 1964; Pokorny, 1965; Wolfgang, 1958). If violence does occur in the presence of others, it may trigger a reinterpretation process. Battering in private is degrading, but battering in public is humiliating, for it is a statement of subordination and powerlessness. Having others witness abuse may create intolerable feelings of shame which undermine prior rationalizations.

He never hit me in public before—it was always at home. But the Saturday I got back [returned to husband from shelter], we went Christmas shopping and he slapped me in the store because of some stupid joke I made. People saw it, I know, I felt so stupid, like, they must all think what a jerk I am, what a sick couple, and I thought, 'God, I must be crazy to let him do this.'

(6) *External definitions of the relationship:* A change in visibility is usually accomplished by the interjection of external definitions of abuse. External definitions vary depending on their source and the situation; they either reinforce or undermine rationalizations. Battered women who request help frequently find others—and especially officials—don't believe their story or are unsympathetic (Pagelow, 1981; Pizzey, 1974). Experimental research by Shotland and Straw (1976) supports these reports. Observers usually fail to respond when a woman is attacked by a man, and justify nonintervention on the grounds that they assumed the victim and offender were married. One young woman discussed how lack of support from her family left her without hope:

It wouldn't be so bad if my own family gave a damn about me. . . . Yeah, they know I'm here, and they don't care. They didn't care about me when I was a kid, so why should they care now? I got raped and beat as a kid, and now I get beat as an adult. Life is a big joke.

Clearly, such responses from family members contribute to the belief among battered women that there are no alternatives and that they just tolerate the abuse. However, when outsiders respond with unqualified support of the victim and condemnation of violent men, their definitions can be a potent catalyst toward victimization. Friends and relatives who show genuine concern for a woman's well-being may initiate an awareness of danger which contradicts previous rationalizations.

> My mother-in-law knew what was going on, but she wouldn't admit it. . . . I said, 'Mom, what do you think these bruises are?' and she said 'Well, some people just bruise easy. I do it all the time, bumping into things.' . . . And he just denied it, pretended like nothing happened, and if I'd said I wanted to talk about it, he'd say, 'life goes on, you can't just dwell on things.' . . . But this time, my neighbor *knew* what happened, she saw it, and when he denied it, she said, 'I can't believe it! You know that's not true!' . . . and I was so happy that finally, somebody else saw what was goin' on, and I just told him then that this time I wasn't gonna' come home!

Shelters for battered women serve not only as material resources, but as sources of external definitions which contribute to the victimization process. They offer refuge from a violent situation in which a woman may contemplate her circumstances and what she wants to do about them. Within a shelter, women meet counselors and other battered women who are familiar with rationalizations of violence and the reluctance to give up commitment to a spouse. In counseling sessions, and informal conversations with other residents, women hear horror stories from others who have already defined themselves as victims. They are supported for expressing anger and rejecting responsibility for their abuse (Ferraro, 1981a). The goal of many shelters is to overcome feelings of guilt and inadequacy so that women can make choices in their best interests. In this atmosphere, violent incidents are reexamined and redefined as assaults in which the woman was victimized.

The relevance of these catalysts to a woman's interpretation of violence vary with her own situation and personality. The process of rejecting rationalizations and becoming a victim is ambiguous, confusing, and emotional. We now turn to the feelings involved in victimization.

THE EMOTIONAL CAREER
OF VICTIMIZATION

As rationalizations give way to perceptions of victimization, of woman's feelings about herself, her spouse, and her situation change. These feelings are imbedded in a cultural, political, and interactional structure. Initially, abuse is contrary to a woman's cultural expectations of behavior between intimates, and therefore engenders feelings of betrayal. The husband has violated his wife's expectations of love and protection, and thus betrayed her confidence in him. The feeling of betrayal, however, is balanced by the husband's efforts to explain his behavior, and by the woman's reluctance to abandon faith. Additionally, the political dominance of men within and outside the family mediate women's ability to question the validity of their husband's actions.

At the interpersonal level, psychological abuse accompanying violence often invokes feelings of guilt and shame in the battered victim. Men define violence as a response to their wive's inadequacies or provocations, which leads battered women to feel that they have failed. Such character assaults are devastating, and create long-lasting feelings of inferiority.

The emotional career of battered women consists of movement from guilt, shame, and depression to fear and despair, to anger, exhilaration, and confusion. Women who escape violent relationships must deal with strong, sometimes conflicting, feelings in attempting to build new lives for themselves free of violence. The kind of response women receive when they seek help largely determines the effects these feelings have on subsequent decisions.

CONCLUSION

The process of victimization is not synonymous with experiencing violent attacks from a spouse. Rationalizing the violence inhibits a sense of outrage and efforts to escape abuse. Only after rationalizations are rejected, through the impact of one or more catalysts, does the victimization process begin. When previously rationalized violence is reinterpreted as dangerous, unjustified assault, battered women actively seek alternatives. The success of their efforts to seek help depends on available resources, external supports, reactions of husbands and children, and their own adaptation to the situation. Victimization includes not only cognitive interpretations, but feelings and physiological responses. Creating a satisfying, peaceful environment after being battered involves emotional confusion and ambiguity, as well as enormous practical and economic obstacles. It may take years of struggle and aborted attempts before a battered woman is able to establish a safe and stable lifestyle; for some, this goal is never achieved.

The victimization process which we have described refers to the interpretations of a specific set of violent events within a particular relationship. It is important to emphasize that this victimization is limited to those violent events, and does not encompass a more global perspective on the woman's life. Individuals working with battered women have pointed out the importance of helping battered women to distinguish between being a victim of an assault and assuming the identity of a victim (Ridington, 1978; Vaughan, 1979). The first involves rejecting the responsibility for being beaten; the second involves giving up the responsibility for one's life. The role of victim is contradictory to the assertive and creative action necessary to establish a life free of violence. To accomplish the latter goal, women must quickly overcome the feelings of helplessness and self-pity that accompany victimization. They must confidently assume responsibility for making decisions and working towards the goals they set, and reject identification with the role of victim.

CHAPTER 3

Violent Sex Crimes

It is well established that sexual assault has a significant effect on the daily thoughts and behaviors of American women. Let us begin with a sampling of the statistical evidence. The National Crime Victimization Survey (NCVS, 2003) estimates that 248,250 women fell victim to some form of unwanted sexual advance in 2001. It is estimated that some sort of sexually assaultive action is present in one of every ten violent crimes involving a female victim. As disconcerting as these numbers are, they do not tell the whole story. Women clearly live in fear of being raped and this preoccupation has a profound effect on their overall sense of personal security. Anxiety about being raped serves as the most direct and formidable predictor of a woman's overall fear of criminal victimization (Gordon and Riger, 1989). The first- and secondhand accounts of real-life sexual assaults go a long way to shape this perceived vulnerability. These are the stories of women who suffer long-lasting physical and psychological traumas, and they produce a broad-reaching impact. For this reason, the personal and societal impact of rape may exceed even that of murder. We as a society have slowly come to respect this orientation and have thus assigned a special status to violent sex crimes.

VIOLENT SEX CRIMES DEFINED

The criminal law has evolved from a limited treatment of sexual misconduct to a much more broad legal orientation. Early common law included only rape (forced heterosexual penetration) and **sodomy** (consensual homosexual conduct) under the heading of sex crimes. This conservative treatment prevailed well into the 1960s. For example, the Model Penal Code (American Law Institute, 1962) restricted the definition of rape to those acts of violent sexual penetration between a male offender and a female victim who were not presently married. Contemporary criminal codes take on a more gender and relationship neutral tone and thus include an expansive list of offenses, ranging from forced sexual intercourse to forms of sexual touching that are devoid of violence.

The present discussion turns to a contemporary source for an up-to-date legal definition of violent sex crimes. Samaha (1999) observes that most jurisdictions delineate three generic offense categories: rape, statutory rape, and sexual assault. An individual is guilty of **rape** if he or she specifically intends to achieve nonconsensual sexual penetration against another by force or the threatened use of force. This definition subsumes all forms of sexual penetration regardless of its duration or degree. **Statutory rape** encompasses all forms of sexual penetration committed against an individual under the specified age of consent (i.e., minors). The specified age of consent varies across jurisdictions, but the vast majority of states invoke a standard between 16 and 18 years of age. This age-graded offense is considered a strict liability offense and thus does not require that the *mens reus* (guilty mind) element of "intentional force" be present. **Sexual assault** is a broader offense category that covers all forms of forceful or coercive unwanted sexual contact.

VIOLENT SEX CRIME TRENDS

Aside from murder, the crimes of rape and sexual assault occur with less regularity than any other form of violent crime. In 2001, the NCVS data show that 146,240 attempted or completed rapes and 102,010 sexual assaults occurred in this country. This translates into a victimization rate of 0.6 per 1,000 individuals or households for rape and 0.4 for sexual assault. Collectively, rape and sexual assault offenses accounted for only a small fraction (4%) of the more than 5.9 million violent crime victimizations that occurred nationally that year (NCVS, 2003). Still, the FBI estimated that a new rape occurred every 5.8 minutes that year (FBI, 2002).

In 1996, the National Institute of Justice and the Centers for Disease Control co-sponsored the National Violence Against Women Survey (Tjaden and Thoennes, 2000). This interview-based study of 16,000 randomly selected adult men and women (8,000 of each sex) provides a wealth of information about the incidence and prevalence of sexualized violence. The researchers found that 18% of the female and 3% of the male respondents claimed to have been a victim of rape at some point during their lifetime. This led Tjaden and Thoennes to estimate that as many as 20 million Americans (1 in 6 women and 1 in 33 men) would become the victim of rape before they die.

Given the high levels of trauma and betrayal that often accompany a rape, it should come as no surprise that a considerable number of rapes go unreported to police. With only 90,491 rapes (excluding sexual assaults) being reported to law enforcement agencies during 2001, it is safe to say that this form of crime goes without official detection more often than any other type of violent

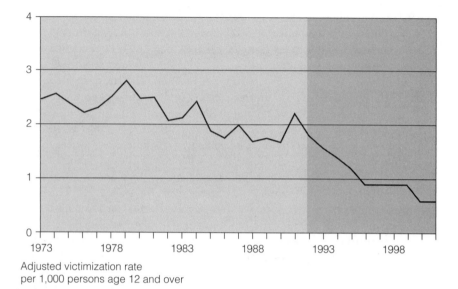

Adjusted victimization rate
per 1,000 persons age 12 and over

Figure 3.1   Rape rates

Source: http://www.ojp.usdoj.gov/bjs/

offense (FBI, 2002). We know from victim reports (NCVS, 2003) that a little over one third (38.6%) of the persons who were raped and/or sexually assaulted in 2001 chose to inform the police about the incident. Roughly 40% stated that they sustained physical injuries in the attack. A study of violence-related injuries treated at hospital emergency rooms during 1994 found that 63,800 rape or sexual assault victims received medical care that year (Rand, 1997).

Figure 3.1 provides a graphic representation of rape victimization rates for the final quarter of the twentieth century. *These data reveal that the latest rape rates are nearly 3 times lower than they were just over 25 years ago.* These gains were not realized overnight and the data show considerable ebbs and flows to the progress. During the last half of the 1990s, however, we witnessed rape rates remaining uncharacteristically stable at a rate of 0.9 victimizations per 1,000 persons or households.

The highest rates of rape and sexual assault victimization are experienced in the western and southern regions of the United States. Slightly lower rape/sexual assault rates have traditionally existed in the Midwest and Northeast. Uniform Crime Reports data from 1998 indicate that the offending rate (per 100,000 residents) for the crime of forcible rape was highest in Alaska (68.6), Delaware (67.1), New Mexico (55.1), Nevada (52.1), and Michigan (50.4). That same year, residents from Montana (17.8), Maine (18.1), West Virginia (18.7), Wisconsin (19.9), and New Jersey (20.0) exhibited the lowest offending rates.

Rape and sexual assault rates are clearly related to population density. The NCVS data from 2001 reveal a composite rape/sexual assault rate of 1.9 in urban environments. This figure is more than twice the victimization rates experienced in suburban and rural areas (0.9 and 0.5, respectively). Among the sixty-six cities with a population exceeding 250,000 residents in 1999, the highest rates of forcible rape (known offenses per 100,000 residents) were observed in Minneapolis (126.7), Memphis (112.8), Cleveland (101.6), Columbus (94.7), and Nashville (88). Conversely, 1999 UCR data rank New York City (22.9), Louisville (24.1), Virginia Beach (24.4), and San Francisco (25.5) as the most rape-free cities (Maguire and Pastore, 2001).

America appears to be the violent sex crime capitol of the world. The 1998 U.S. rape rate of 35.9 (per 100,000 inhabitants) was more than double that of its nearest rivals: Israel (14.3), England and Wales (14.7), and France (13.4). Moreover, U.S. rape rates were exponentially higher than those observed in Germany (9.6), Spain (3.2), and Japan (1.5) that year (Interpol, 1999). This raises the obvious question of why rape rates are so much higher in this country.

Baron and Strauss (1989) reviewed four relevant theoretical perspectives of rape that they believe provide some much needed insight in this area. They begin with their **gender inequality theory,** a favorite of many feminists. "Scholars who take this position believe that rape and the fear of rape enable men to assert their power over women and maintain the existing system of gender stratification" (Baron and Strauss, 1989, p. 61). These rape motivations need not be an overt and malicious feature of societal gender norms. Instead, more subtle forms of gender oppression, such as the objectification of women and sexist attitudes, are said to set the stage for increased levels of rape and sexual assault; these cultural undercurrents reinforce the notion that women are inferior to men and are misinterpreted by some violent individuals to indicate that sexualized violence is one way of protecting their manhood. The gender equality theory of rape predicts that rape rates will be highest in patriarchal societies where women are considered to be the sexual servants of men. The advertising imagery and gender biases that limit women's status attainment in contemporary America are held as evidence that the tenets of this theory are readily applicable to U.S. culture.

Other feminist scholars prefer to gravitate toward the **pornography theory.** These scholars contend that pornographic imagery depicting the domination and degradation of women sends the wrong cultural message—the images convey an implicit message that all women want sex and lead men to expect it from women. Repeated exposure to this imagery serves to reinforce and condone violent sexual behavior in men. Although the evidence of the pornography theory is inconclusive, Baron and Strauss (1989) report that rape rates were highest in those states that experienced the most sizable circulation rates for adult monthly periodicals such as *Playboy*, *Hustler*, and *Penthouse*.

Many mainstream sociologists endorse the **social disorganization theory** of rape. These scholars theorize that crime rates will increase as social disorganization increases and the institutional infrastructure of society breaks down. Factors such as widespread poverty, the collapse of the traditional nuclear family unit, racial tension, and decreased religiosity are thought to breed a sense of alienation and desperation among the effected parties. This, in turn, produces a frustration reaction. Criminal behavior in general, and rape in particular, are thus said to represent prime examples of the reaction formation concept. Clearly there is no shortage of these types of structural instabilities in contemporary American society. Baron and Strauss (1989) point to the fact that rape rates are highest in those states that experience elevated levels of social disorganization as one such measure of support for the theory.

The **legitimation of violence theory** offers a more social, psychologically oriented take on rape causation. Scholars who endorse this perspective view rape as little more than a specialized form of violent behavior. Forms of sexual violence are said to represent a "spillover effect" in cultures that glorify or condone the use of physical problem solving. Baron and Strauss (1989) found that the legitimation of violence seems to work hand in hand with gender inequality to produce higher rates of sexual violence. Namely, states with a volatile mix of high gender inequality and an established culture of violence consistently experience the highest rape rates.

TECHNIQUES OF VIOLENT SEX CRIME

In general, violent sex crimes take shape as unskilled, technically simple acts. Victimization data indicate that nearly 70% of all rapes and sexual assaults are committed by someone who is known to the offender (acquaintance, intimate partner, family member). These forms of violent betrayals are referred to under the heading of **acquaintance** or **date rape.** Warshaw (1994) and Russell (1984) found that coercion, intimidation, and brute strength—more so than weaponry or props (rope, handcuffs, tape, etc.)—serve as the tools of the trade for the average date rapist. The term **stranger rape** is used to describe those acts where the offender and victim have no previous relationship. The cold and calculating nature of this rape dynamic oftentimes translates into a heightened reliance on weapons and props on the part of the offender. Victims report that weapons were present in 7.6% of all rapes and sexual assaults occurring in 2001 (NCVS, 2003).

SEXUAL ASSAULT TRANSACTION

The overwhelming majority of rape/sexual assault offenses involve a single acquaintance forcing him or herself sexually onto a single unwilling victim. Victims' reports indicate that almost all (97.5%) rape/sexual assault incidents involve a lone victim. Similarly, 91.8% of the cases involve a single perpetrator (NCVS, 2003). We use the term **gang rape** to describe rape events with three or more perpetrators present. When multiple offenders are present, the crime tends to take place within some organizational context and oftentimes involves perverse and prolonged forms of sexual deviance. Multiple offenders are often the hallmark of prison rapes (Weis, 1974), athlete-perpetrated offenses (Benedict, 1998), and fraternity rapes (Sanday, 1990). Gang rape cases account for only about 1% of all violent sex crimes reported by victims each year. The O'Sullivan article that appears later in this chapter provides the reader with a thorough treatment of gang rape as it manifests itself on college campuses.

In addition to being crimes of violence, most rapes/sexual assaults incorporate an element of betrayal. Roughly 70% of all single-offender rape/sexual assaults occurring in 2001 were committed by an individual who was known to the victim. A full

31.7% of victims described their attackers to be close friends. An additional 27.9% of the attackers were said to be casual acquaintances. Almost one in twenty said that their attacker was a spouse or blood relative. No other form of violent crime involves such high proportions of offenders who were related to or acquainted with the victim (NCVS, 2003).

The presence of drugs and/or alcohol seem to play an important part in the violent sexual transaction. Victim reports from the 2001 NCVS indicate that nearly one half (43.6%) of all rape/sexual assault victims believed that their attacker was under the influence of drugs or alcohol at the time of the offense. This figure corresponds closely with the percentages that are derived from self-report studies involving convicted rapists. A full 45.2% of the state prison inmates surveyed (Beck et al., 1993) admit that they were using drugs or alcohol in the hours preceding their violent sex offense. A new trend has emerged whereby rapists enlist the help of potent prescription medicines (e.g., Rohypnol, GHB), termed "date rape drugs," to unknowingly intoxicate and incapacitate their victims (Fitzgerald and Riley, 2000).

Most violent sexual attacks occur at night in private settings. The majority take place after 6 P.M. Furthermore, victim reports indicate that nearly two thirds of the transgressions occur in or near a private residence. No other form of crime posts such high numbers in this regard. The remainder of violent sex crimes occur in commercial establishments or open-air, public environments (NCVS, 2003).

Rapes and sexual assault are principally committed by young, white men while the victims are disproportionately young, minority women. Gender is the most telling variable in the rape/sexual assault equation. Almost all violent sex crimes are intergendered (i.e., male on female) offenses. Nearly 99% of the individuals arrested on rape charges in 2001 were men (FBI, 2002). That same year, victim reports indicated that 90% of the rape and sexual assault victims were women and more than 93% of the offenders were men. This translates into a female rape/sexual assault victimization rate that is ten times the rate that is observed among males (NCVS, 2003).

Age is another noteworthy variable in the rape and sexual assault equation. Better than four in ten (45.4%) individuals arrested for forcible rape in 2001 were under the age of 25 (FBI, 2002). Victim accounts support this claim, as 57% of rape victims that year estimated that their attacker(s) were under the age of 30 (NCVS, 2003). Young people are clearly at the highest risk of experiencing a violent sexual attack. This makes rape an intra-aged crime. In 2001, the victimization rate for individuals under the age of 25 was five times greater than that experienced among individuals above this age threshold.

It is well established that the majority of rape/sexual assault offenders are white. A full 62.7% of the individuals who were arrested on forcible rape charges in 2001 were white (FBI, 2002). Almost identical percentages of whites were observed in that year's victimization reports (NCVS, 2003). Things are not so cut and dried for the African American population. While African Americans comprised more than one third of all rape arrests in 2001, victims attributed only slightly more than one fifth of the rapes that year to black perpetrators.

In 2001, the victimization rate for African Americans was 1.1 per 1,000 persons or households. This was similar to the rates experienced by Hispanics and whites (1.1 and 1.0, respectively). Collectively, the data suggest an intraracial patterning of violent sex crimes.

Certain demographic segments of the U.S. population can face vastly increased chances of being the target of a violent sex crime. Take, for example, data from the 1999 NCVS. That year, the average U.S. adult faced a rape/sexual assault victimization rate of 1.7 per 1,000 persons or households. However, the victimization rate for black women (4.6) was nearly twice that of white or Hispanic women (2.7 and 2.5, respectively). These figures are significantly higher than the Hispanic male (1.3), white male (0.4) and black male (0.2) victimization rates (NCVS, 2001). Note that these pronounced racial/gender disparities have subsided in recent years (NCVS, 2003).

Noticeable fluctuations can be observed when the age/race/gender analysis is further specified. The 2001 rape/sexual assault victimization rate was observed to be 1.1 per 1,000. Noticeably high victimization rates are observed for African Americans between the ages of 12 and 15 (3.4), whites ages 16 to 19 (4.0), and African Americans ages 20 to 24 (3.9). Females in the 12 to 15 (3.5) and 20 to 24 (4.2) age groups also face noticeably high victimization rates. Still, no other segment of the American population is at more risk than 16- to 19-year-old females—this particular group's 2001 victimization rate was 6 times the national average or 6.9 per 1,000 persons or households (NCVS, 2001).

The disturbing age/race/gender-based trends have prompted the systematic study of rape victimization among college-aged women. The findings are even more disheartening. Fisher, Cullen, and Turner (2000) found that nearly 3% of the 4,000+ college women that they surveyed had been the victim of an attempted or completed rape during the previous school year. This translates to a victimization rate of 27.7 per 1,000 women attending U.S. colleges that year.

Most violent criminal events take on an unmistakably fast and furious quality. Rape and sexual assault offenses are somewhat different. *While intense levels of violence are generally a cornerstone of the rape event, the assault and corresponding struggle takes some time to run its course.* Interview-based accounts (Amir, 1974; Brownmiller, 1975; Scully, 1994) reveal that rape victims are subject to prolonged trauma as the offender uses a forceful and drawn out sex act as a vehicle for power, degradation, and dominance.

The onset of the rape transaction generally leaves little room for misinterpretation on the part of the victim. Faced with the reality that they are about to be forced into a prolonged and nonconsensual sex act, rape victims almost always seek to resist the aggressive advances of the attacker. Recent NCVS data show that seven of ten rape/sexual assault victims take self-protective measures against their attackers. Most women try to flee, while some opt to fight back. The majority of victims contend that their countermeasures served to improve the situation. A study by Kleck and Sayles (1990) reveals that resistance, especially violent forms of resistance, serves as effective means of (1) preventing rape completion, and (2) reducing the level of injuries sustained by the victim.

THE CRIMINAL CAREER
OF THE VIOLENT SEX OFFENDER

The criminal career of the rapist is decidedly different than it is for other violent offenders. While other violent predators are known for their propensity to accumulate long, diverse criminal histories, the violent sex offender tends to stay more focused. *Compared to other violent offenders, convicted rapists and sexual assaulters tend to amass shorter rap sheets and post lower violent and property recidivism rates* (Greenfeld, 1997). Hart and Reaves's (1996) criminal history study found that 42% of the rape defendants in their sample had a prior felony arrest record, 21% had been felony arrested five or more times, and 29% had a prior felony conviction.

Turning to prison recidivism potential, Langan and Levin (2002) note that 42% of the released rapists that they tracked were rearrested within 3 years. As alarming as this number may be, it is worth noting that only murders posted lower overall recidivism rates. The bad news is that, relative to other types of offenders, rapists return to sex crimes at a disproportionate rate. A recidivism study by Beck and Shipley (1989) estimates that one in ten rapists will be rearrested for a similar charge at some time in the future. Langan and Levin (2002, p. 10) extrapolate further, stating that "a released rapist's odds of committing a new rape are 3.2 times greater than a non-rapist's odds of rape." This level of specialized recidivism is unusual among criminals. This observation has prompted many local and state jurisdictions to mandate that convicted serial sex offenders register with local law enforcement agencies upon moving into a neighborhood (Zevitz and Farkas, 2000). In fact, efforts are well underway to develop a national database to allow for the cross-jurisdictional monitoring of convicted serial sex offenders (Finn, 1997). Repeat sex offending takes on one of two forms. Some rapists, commonly referred to as **serial rapists**, target numerous victims over an extended period of time (Stevens, 1999). Other habitual rapists repeatedly assault the same individual. This pattern almost exclusively manifests itself in established intimate relationships. Tjaden and Thoennes (2000) found that 8% of the 8,000 randomly sampled respondents surveyed had been raped by an intimate partner at least once in their lifetime. Repeat victimization was common among these cases.

COGNITIVE ASPECTS
OF VIOLENT SEX CRIMES

Scholars have repeatedly attempted to dissect the cognitive aspects of rape and sexual assault. The most frequently employed means of accomplishing this goal has been to ask convicted rapists about their past offending patterns. The forthcoming article by Scully and Marolla (1985) represents one of the most comprehensive and respected of these offender-based inquiries. *This offender-based research reveals that most rapists are driven by a will to degrade or dominate their victims, not by a quest for sexual gratification.* In short, the sex act is characterized as a convenient and especially effective way to assert control or revenge over a particular individual or class of individuals (Amir, 1971; Brownmiller, 1975; Groth, 1979; Stevens, 1999).

At the same time, rapists can sometimes be driven by instrumental motives. A violent sex act can be used as a way of settling a score or satisfying an elusive sexual desire. Clearly, the use of such extreme forms of conflict resolution are not condoned or pursued by most individuals. However, in the mind of a sexually aggressive individual, the wrong set of situational and cognitive variables can make rape take on acceptable or even desirable qualities.

Planning does not seem to be a well-defined component of most violent sex crimes. In the case of acquaintance or intimate rape, the violent sex act may spontaneously surface as a form of frustration reaction; perhaps the perpetrator expected more sexual interaction with his date or a husband becomes upset with the way his wife acted while they were out that night. Regardless of the catalyst, most acquaintance rapes spontaneously emerge out of a dangerous combination of cognitive, cultural, and social factors and there exists little time for mindful planning. The serial rapist stands as the noticeable exception to this rule. Stevens (1999) notes that these predators often exhibit highly routinized predatory habits. They are known to operate in a selective environment and/or to target specific types of victims.

Normative neutralizations occupy an important role in the rapist's mental repertoire. Like other criminals, the rapist sees a need to justify or rationalize his or her aberrant behavior. Most scholars agree that the key to this mental mechanism lays in the offender's view of what constitutes acceptably social or intimate relations. Greenfeld (1997) observes that many rape offenders are exposed to emotional or physical trauma (often sexual in nature) early in their lives. In the pages that follow, Scully and Marolla will argue that these traumas, when mixed with patriarchal gender norms, provide a convenient cognitive canvas for the male rapist to work with. The perpetrator's anger thus allows him to distort cultural messages about intimate relationships and women in general in such a way that rape becomes an acceptable means of problem solving. The male rapists that Scully and Marolla interviewed offered up a host of excuses ranging from revenge, to adventurous sex, to sexual fetishes to account for their violent sexual acts. In almost every case, these offenders attributed the blame for the act onto the victim or some external forces beyond their control.

THE CULTURE OF RAPE
AND SEXUAL ASSAULT

Scholars acknowledge that societal gender norms play an important role in the rape equation (Abbey, 1991; Barnat, Calhoun and Adams, 1999; Jackson, 1995; Warshaw and Parrot, 1991). LeMoncheck (1999) organizes the cognitive and behavioral aspects of intimate relations on what she terms a **continuum of sexual behavior.** At one end of the continuum, she locates healthy sexual behavior that serves to empower and liberate both men and women. She positions acts of sexual violence at the other end of the continuum. Between these two extremes, there exists a whole range of sexual behaviors. The closer one gets to the rape end of the continuum, the more deviant and oppressive the sexual norms and behaviors become.

LeMoncheck's (1999) conceptual model provides us with an important departure point. For most men, exposure to domineering sex scripts has little effect. Given the fact that they are normatively grounded toward the nonrape end of the continuum, they reject these messages as deviant. However, an oppressive or overly patriarchal upbringing can leave an individual firmly entrenched in a location closer to the pro-rape end of the continuum. This person becomes receptive to violent sexual messages and is thus more likely to act and think in ways that represent the psychological and behavioral environments with which he or she is most familiar and comfortable.

Most rapists operate as what Best and Luckenbill (1994) would call colleagues. Although they commit their crimes without the assistance of other offenders, they maintain frequent contacts with the sexual underworld. They are often habitual consumers of pornographic materials and may exhibit peculiar sexual tastes and fantasies. *Routinized contacts with other sexual deviants provide the rapist with vicarious reinforcement (i.e., socialization scripts) for the sexually aggressive ideas and behaviors.* These contacts do not replace the types of mundane socialization contacts that were previously mentioned. Instead, they represent supplements to the biased gender norms and traumatic life events that are part and parcel of these individuals' social worlds.

SOCIETAL REACTIONS TO RAPE
AND SEXUAL ASSAULT

Violent sex crimes generally elicit a harsh response from the criminal justice system. Rape is granted a two-tiered offense categorization in most jurisdictions. Those rapes in which nonconsensual sexual penetration occurs, but the victim incurs minimal physical injuries, are generally graded as a second degree felony. If convicted, the perpetrator faces the prospect of 1 to 10 years in prison; however, the court may choose to upgrade this type of rape to a felony in the first degree if there is evidence that the offender inflicted serious bodily harm to the victim. In these more severe cases, the offender faces a sentence ranging from 1 year to life in prison. Most jurisdictions classify statutory rape as a first degree felony. Sexual assault or those less serious instances that involve the forceful or coercive unwanted sexual touching of another are generally classified as misdemeanors and carry a sentence of up to 1 year in prison. Some courts have leeway to upgrade a sexual assault case to a second or third degree felony charge (Samaha, 1999).

Police have a difficult time combatting violent sex crimes. A total of 90,491 forcible rapes were reported to law enforcement agencies in 2001. Less than

50% of these cases were cleared for arrest. This translated to an arrest rate of 9.6 per 100,000 inhabitants. This clearance rate is significantly less than the 60% to 70% levels that were realized that year for the crimes of murder and aggravated assault (FBI, 2002).

Once arrested, violent sex offenders receive heavy-handed treatment from the U.S. court system. Greenfeld (1997) observed that rape cases represent only about 5% of all felony cases processed through state courts each year; however, the available data indicate that these cases are subject to close scrutiny. Hart and Reaves (1999) found that eight in ten rape defendants in their sample had their bail amount set in excess of $10,000 (average = $63,500) and 12% were denied bail entirely. These high dollar amounts led to nearly half of all rape defendants that year being held in custody from the point of arrest to final disposition.

Hart and Reaves (1999) state that rape defendants face a 50/50 chance of being convicted and sentenced to some term of imprisonment (jail or prison). When the prosecution is able to secure a guilty verdict or plea, they generally waste no time getting the person off the streets. Levin, Langan, and Brown (1999) report that 82% of the state-level rape and sexual assault trial convictions in 1996 resulted in a prison term. The average sentence was nearly 10 years (median length of 6 years), with 2% receiving a life term. It is estimated that a convicted rapist will serve 5 years, or roughly half of their prison sentence. At year-end 2000, convicted rapists comprised 2.6% of the total state prison population and 5.4% subpopulation of persons serving time for a violent crime.

While we as society are taking a relatively strong formal stance toward rape and sexual assault, our informal social control efforts are lacking. Studies of high school and college students (Abbey, 1991; DeKeseredy and Schwartz, 1994; Koss, 1989; Mills and Granoff, 1992) reveal that boys and girls alike feel ill-equipped to deal with aggressive sexual behavior in relationships. These studies suggest that young males often misinterpret the sexual desires of women and that young women tend to do a poor job in communicating their displeasure with progressively intrusive sexual acts. In these cases, there appears to be a breakdown in dating relationships that opens the door for increasingly problematic levels of unwanted sexual contact.

KEY TERMS

acquaintance (date) rape

continuum of sexual behavior

gang rape

gender inequality theory

legitimation of violence theory

pornography theory

rape

serial rape

sexual assault

social disorganization theory

sodomy

statutory rape

stranger rape

DISCUSSION QUESTIONS

1. Many scholars contend that the long-term social and emotional costs of rape outweigh that of any other form of violent crime. This would suggest that violent sex crimes warrant an especially stringent societal response. Apart from traditional imprisonment options, what other forms of innovative sanctions might we pursue in response to rape and sexual assault?

2. Feminist scholars have focused a great deal of attention on the way that conventional gender norms serve to implicitly reinforce pro-rape messages. At the same time, a sizable portion of American women are content with the sexual politics of the day and oppose significant changes to the way males and females interact in the courtship process. What can and should be done to resolve this structural impediment to gender norm revisions?

3. We hear so little about male rape—the forced penetration of a male victim. Why is this such a rarely reported phenomenon and what can be learned from this indisputable reality?

4. It is commonly held that some maladjusted men revert to rape as an extreme manifestation of gender socialization gone awry. In effect, the average rapist is portrayed as suffering from a dangerous mix of psychological trauma and hypermacho cognition. Is there a female equivalent to the male rapist? That is, do you get the same extreme deviant manifestation when you mix a hyperfeminine upbringing with serious psychological trauma? If so, what are the societal costs?

6

"Riding the Bull at Gilley's": Convicted Rapists Describe the Rewards of Rape

DIANA SCULLY
JOSEPH MAROLLA
Virginia Commonwealth University

Scully and Marolla conducted in-depth, face-to-face interviews with a snowball sample of 114 incarcerated rapists in hopes of determining the motivations that existed at the time of their sex crimes. While the respondents were given considerable opportunity to "tell their side of the story," the authors referenced each inmate's case file to establish that their accounts were factually accurate. The authors uncovered six motivational themes among the rapists. Some respondents claimed that they committed their crimes out of revenge or as an act of punishment. Others committed rape in conjunction with another felony offense—faced with one pending violation they viewed their sex crimes as an "added bonus." A third manifestation saw individuals using rape as a means of sexual access or a way to fulfill wild fetishes or fantasies. The fourth motivational category had men using the rape act as an impersonal means of establishing or regaining self-esteem or power over the other sex. Still other rapists emphasized the recreational or adventurous aspects of the rape act, insisting that it provided them with a sense of excitement or challenge. Finally, some men used rape as a simple source of self-gratification, claiming that the act represented an emotional or physical release. The consistent presence of rational, self-gratification-oriented motivations leads the authors to conclude that gender norms play a critical role in the impetus and proliferation of male-on-female sexual violence.

Over the past several decades, rape has become a "medicalized" social problem. That is to say, the theories used to explain rape are predicated on psychopathological models. They have been generated from clinical experiences with small samples of rapists, often the therapists' own clients. Although these psychiatric explanations are most appropriately applied to the atypical rapist, they have been generalized to all men who rape and have come to inform the public's view on the topic.

Two assumptions are at the core of the psychopathological model: that rape is the result of idiosyncratic mental disease and that it often includes an uncontrollable sexual impulse (Scully and Marolla, 1985). For example, the presumption of psychopathology is evident in the often cited work of Nicholas Groth (1979). While Groth emphasizes the nonsexual nature of rape (power, anger, sadism), he also concludes, "Rape is always a symptom of some psychological dysfunction, either temporary and transient or chronic and repetitive" (Groth, 1979:5). Thus, in the psychopathological view, rapists lack the ability to control their behavior: they are "sick" individuals from the "lunatic fringe" of society.

In contradiction to this model, empirical research has repeatedly failed to find a consistent pattern of personality type or character disorder that reliably discriminates rapists from other groups of men (Fisher and Rivlin, 1971; Hammer and Jacks, 1955; Rada, 1978). Indeed, other research has found that fewer than 5 percent of men were psychotic when they raped (Abel et al., 1980).

Evidence indicates that rape is not a behavior confined to a few "sick" men but many men have the attitudes and beliefs necessary to commit a sexually aggressive act. In research conducted at a midwestern university, Koss and her coworkers reported that 85 percent of men defined as highly sexually aggressive had victimized women with whom they were romantically involved (Koss and Leonard, 1984). A recent survey quoted in *The Chronicle of Higher Education* estimates that more than 20 percent of college women are the victims of rape and attempted rape (Meyer, 1984). These findings mirror research published several decades earlier which also concluded that sexual aggression was commonplace in dating relationships (Kanin, 1957, 1965, 1967, 1969; Kirkpatrick and Kanin, 1957). In their study of 53 college males, Malamuth, Haber and Feshback (1980) found that 51 percent indicated a likelihood that they, themselves, would rape if assured of not being punished.

In addition, the frequency of rape in the United States makes it unlikely that responsibility rests solely with a small lunatic fringe of psychopathic men. Johnson (1980), calculating the lifetime risk of rape to girls and women aged twelve and over, makes a similar observation. Using Law Enforcement Assistance Association and Bureau of Census Crime Victimization Studies, he calculated that, excluding sexual abuse in marriage and assuming equal risk to all women, 20 to 30 percent of girls now 12 years old will suffer a violent sexual attack during the remainder of their lives. Interestingly, the lack of empirical support for the psychopathological model has not resulted in the de-medicalization of rape, nor does it appear to have diminished the belief that rapists are "sick" aberrations in their own culture. This is significant because of the implications and consequences of the model.

A central assumption in the psychopathological model is that male sexual aggression is unusual or strange. This assumption removes rape from the realm of the everyday or "normal" world and places it in the category of "special" or "sick" behavior. As a consequence, men who rape are cast in the role of outsider and a connection with normative male behavior is avoided. Since, in this view, the source of the behavior is thought to be within the psychology of the individual, attention is diverted away from culture or social structure as contributing factors. Thus, the psychopathological model ignores evidence which links sexual aggression to environmental variables and which suggests that rape, like all behavior, is learned.

CULTURAL FACTORS IN RAPE

Culture is a factor in rape, but the precise nature of the relationship between culture and sexual violence remains a topic of discussion. Ethnographic data from pre-industrial societies show the existence of rape-free cultures (Broude and Green, 1976; Sanday, 1979), though explanations for the phenomena differ. Sanday (1979) relates sexual violence to contempt for female qualities and suggests that rape is part of a culture of violence and an expression of male dominance. In contrast, Blumberg (1979) argues than in pre-industrial societies women are more likely to lack important life options and to be physically and politically oppressed where they lack economic power relative to men. That is, in pre-industrial societies relative economic power enables women to win some immunity from men's use of force against them.

Among modern societies, the frequency of rape varies dramatically, and the United States is among the most rape-prone of all. In 1980, for example, the rate of reported rape and attempted rape for the United States was eighteen times higher than the corresponding rate for England and Wales (West, 1983). Spurred by the Women's Movement, feminists have generated an impressive body of theory regarding the cultural etiology of rape in the United States. Representative of the feminist view, Griffin (1971) called rape "The All American Crime."

The feminist perspective views rape as an act of violence and social control which functions to "keep women in their place" (Brownmiller, 1975; Kasinsky, 1975; Russell, 1975). Feminists see rape as an extension of normative male behavior, the result of conformity or overconformity to the values and prerogatives which define the traditional male sex role. That is, traditional socialization encourages males to associate power, dominance, strength, virility, and superiority with masculinity, and submissiveness, passivity, weakness, and inferiority with femininity. Furthermore, males are taught to have expectations about their level of sexual needs and expectations for corresponding female accessibility which function to justify forcing sexual access. The justification for forced sexual access is buttressed by legal, social, and religious definitions of women as male property and sex as an exchange of goods (Bart, 1979). Socialization prepares women to be "legitimate" victims and men to be potential offenders (Weis and Borges, 1973). Herman (1984) concludes that the United States is a rape culture because both genders are socialized to regard male aggression as a natural and normal part of sexual intercourse.

Feminists view pornography as an important element in a larger system of sexual violence; they see pornography as an expression of a rape-prone culture where women are seen as objects available for use by men (Morgan, 1980; Wheeler, 1985). Based on his content analysis of 428 "adults only" books, Smith (1976) makes a similar observation. He notes that, not only is rape presented as part of normal male/female sexual relations, but the woman, despite her terror, is always depicted as sexually aroused to the point of cooperation. In the end, she is ashamed but physically gratified. The message—women desire and enjoy rape—has more potential for damage than the image of the violence *per se*.

The fusion of these themes—sex as an impersonal act, the victim's uncontrollable orgasm, and the violent infliction of pain—is commonplace in the actual accounts of rapist. Scully and Marolla (1984) demonstrated that many convicted rapists denied their crime and attempted to justify their rapes by arguing that their victim had enjoyed herself despite the use of a weapon and the infliction of serious injuries, or even death. In fact, many argued, they had been instrumental in making *her* fantasy come true.

The images projected in pornography contribute to a vocabulary of motive which trivializes and neutralizes rape and which might lessen the internal controls that otherwise would prevent sexually aggressive behavior. Men who rape use this culturally acquired vocabulary to justify their sexual violence.

Black's (1983) approach is helpful in understanding rape because it forces one to examine the goals that some men have learned to achieve through sexually violent means. Thus, one approach to understanding why some men rape is to shift attention from individual psychopathology to the important question of what rapists gain from sexual aggression and violence in a culture seemingly prone to rape.

In this paper, we address this question using data from interviews conducted with 114 convicted, incarcerated rapists. Elsewhere, we discussed the
vocabulary of motive, consisting of excuses and justifications, that these convicted rapists used to explain themselves and their crime (Scully and Marolla,
1984). The use of these culturally derived excuses and justifications allowed
them to view their behavior as either idiosyncratic or situationally appropriate
and thus it reduced their sense of moral responsibility for their actions. Having
disavowed deviance, these men revealed how they had used rape to achieve a
number of objectives. We find that some men used rape for revenge or punishment while, for others, it was an "added bonus"—a last minute decision
made while committing another crime. In still other cases, rape was used to
gain sexual access to women who were unwilling or unavailable, and for some
it was a source of power and sex without any personal feelings. Rape was also
a form of recreation, a diversion or an adventure and, finally, it was something
that made these men "feel good."

HOW OFFENDERS VIEW
THE REWARDS OF RAPE

Revenge and Punishment

As noted earlier, Black's (1983) perspective suggests that a rapist might see his
act as a legitimized form of revenge or punishment. Additionally, he asserts that
the idea of "collective liability" accounts for much seemingly random violence.
"Collective liability" suggests that all people in a particular category are held
accountable for the conduct of each of their counterparts. Thus, the victim of
a violent act may merely represent the category of individual being punished.

These factors—revenge, punishment, and the collective liability of
women—can be used to explain a number of rapes in our research. Several
cases will illustrate the ways in which these factors combined in various types
of rape. Revenge-rapes were among the most brutal and often included beatings, serious injuries and, even murder.

Typically, revenge-rapes included the element of collective liability. This is,
from the rapist's perspective, the victim was a substitute for the woman they
wanted to avenge. As explained elsewhere, (Scully and Marolla, 1984), an upset-
ting event, involving a woman, preceded a significant number of rapes. When
they raped, these men were angry because of a perceived indiscretion, typically
related to a rigid, moralistic standard of sexual conduct, which they required
from "their woman" but, in most cases, did not abide by themselves. Over and
over these rapists talked about using rape "to get even" with their wives or other
significant woman. Typical is a young man who, prior to the rape, had a violent
argument with his wife over what eventually proved to be her misdiagnosed
case of venereal disease. She assumed the disease had been contracted through
him, an accusation that infuriated him. After fighting with his wife, he
explained that he drove around "thinking about hurting someone." He

encountered his victim, a stranger, on the road where her car had broken down. It appears she accepted his offered ride because her car was out of commission. When she realized that rape was pending, she called him "a son of a bitch," and attempted to resist. He reported flying into a rage and beating her, and he confided.

> I have never felt that much anger before. If she had resisted, I would have killed her . . . The rape was for revenge. I didn't have an orgasm. She was there to get my hostile feelings off on.

Although not the most common form of revenge rape, sexual assault continues to be used in retaliation against the victim's male partner. In one such case, the offender, angry because the victim's husband owed him money, went to the victim's home to collect. He confided, "I was going to get it one way or another." Finding the victim alone, he explained, they started to argue about the money and,

> I grabbed her and started beating the hell out of her. Then I committed the act. I knew what I was doing. I was mad. I could have stopped but I didn't. I did it to get even with her and her husband.

Griffin (1971:33) points out that when women are viewed as commodities, "In raping another man's woman, a man may aggrandize his own manhood and concurrently reduce that of another man."

Revenge-rapes often contained an element of punishment. In some cases, while the victim was not the initial object of the revenge, the intent was to punish her because of something that transpired after the decision to rape had been made or during the course of the rape itself. This was the case with a young man whose wife had recently left him. Although they were in the process of reconciliation, he remained angry and upset over the separation. The night of the rape, he met the victim and her friend in a bar where he had gone to watch a fight on TV. The two women apparently accepted a ride from him but, after taking her friend home, he drove the victim to his apartment. At his apartment, he found a note from his wife indicating she had stopped by to watch the fight with him. This increased his anger because he preferred his wife's company. Inside his apartment, the victim allegedly remarked that she was sexually interested in his dog, which he reported, put him in a rage. In the ensuing attack, he raped and pistol-whipped the victim. Then he forced a vacuum cleaner hose, switched on suction, into her vagina and bit her breast, severing the nipple. He stated:

> I hated at the time, but I don't know if it was her (the victim). (Who could it have been?) My wife? Even though we were getting back together, I still didn't trust her.

During his interview, it became clear that this offender, like many of the men, believed men have the right to discipline and punish women. In fact, he argued that most of the men he knew would also have beaten the victim because "that kind of thing (referring to the dog) is not acceptable among my friends."

Finally, in some rapes, both revenge and punishment were directed at victims because they represented women whom these offenders perceived as collectively responsible and liable for their problems. Rape was used "to put women in their place" and as a method of proving their "manhood" by displaying dominance over a female. For example, one multiple rapist believed his actions were related to the feeling that women thought they were better than he was.

> Rape was a feeling of total dominance. Before the rapes, I would always get a feeling of power and anger. I would degrade women so I could feel there was a person of less worth than me.

An Added Bonus

Burglary and robbery commonly accompany rape. Among our sample, 39 percent of rapists had also been convicted of one or the other of these crimes committed in connection with rape. In some cases, the original intent was rape and robbery was an after-thought. However, a number of the men indicated that the reverse was true in their situation. That is, the decision to rape was made subsequent to their original intent which was burglary or robbery.

This was the case with a young offender who stated that he originally intended only to rob the store in which the victim happened to be working. He explained that when he found the victim alone,

> I decided to rape her to prove I had guts. She was just there. It could have been anybody.

Similarly, another offender indicated that he initially broke into his victim's home to burglarize it. When he discovered the victim asleep, he decided to seize the opportunity "to satisfy an urge to go to bed with a white woman, to see if it was different." Indeed, a number of men indicated that the decision to rape had been made after they realized they were in control of the situation.

The attitude of these men toward rape was similar to their attitude toward burglary and robbery. Quite simply, if the situation is right, "why not." From the perspective of these rapists, rape was just another part of the crime—an added bonus.

Sexual Access

In an effort to change public attitudes that are damaging to the victims of rape and to reform laws seemingly premised on the assumption that women both ask for and enjoy rape, many writers emphasize the violent and aggressive character of rape. Often such arguments appear to discount the part that sex plays in the crime. The data clearly indicate that from the rapists' point of view rape is in part sexually motivated. Indeed, it is the sexual aspect of rape that distinguishes it from other forms of assault.

Groth (1979) emphasizes the psychodynamic function of sex in rape arguing that rapists' aggressive needs are expressed through sexuality. In other words, rape is a means to an end. We argue, however, that rapists view the act as an end in itself and that sexual access most obviously demonstrates the link between sex and rape. Rape as a means of sexual access also shows the deliberate nature of this crime. When a woman is unwilling or seems unavailable for sex, the rapist can seize what isn't volunteered. In discussing his decision to rape, one man made this clear.

> All the guys wanted to fuck her . . . a real fox, beautiful shape. She was a beautiful woman and I wanted to see what she had.

The attitude that sex is a male entitlement suggests that when a woman says "no," rape is suitable method of conquering the "offending" object. If, for example, a woman is picked up at a party or in a bar or while hitchhiking (behavior which a number of the rapists saw as a signal of sexual availability), and the woman later resists sexual advances, rape is presumed to be justified. The same justification operates in what is popularly called "date rape." The belief that sex was their just compensation compelled a number of rapists to insist they had not raped. Such was the case of an offender who raped and seriously beat his victim when, on their second date, she refused his sexual advances.

> I think I was really pissed off at her because it didn't go as planned. I could have been with someone else. She led me on but wouldn't deliver . . .
> I have a male ego that must be fed.

The purpose of such rapes was conquest, to seize what was not offered.

Despite the cultural belief that young women are the most sexually desirable, several rapes involved the deliberate choice of a victim relatively older than the assailant. Since the rapists were themselves rather young (26 to 30 years of age on the average), they were expressing a preference for sexually experienced, rather than elderly, women. Men who chose victims older than themselves often said they did so because they believed that sexually experienced women were more desirable partners. They raped because they also believed that these women would not be sexually attracted to them.

Finally, sexual access emerged as a factor in the accounts of black men who consciously chose to rape white women. The majority of rapes in the United States today are intraracial. However, for the past 20 years, according to national data based on reported rapes as well as victimization studies, which include unreported rapes, the rate of black on white (B/W) rape has significantly exceeded the rate of white on black (W/B) rape (La Free, 1982). Indeed, we may be experiencing a historical anomaly, since, as Brownmiller (1975) has documented, white men have freely raped women of color in the past. The current structure of interracial rape, however, reflects contemporary racism and race relations in several ways.

First, the status of black women in the United States today is relatively lower than the status of white women. Further, prejudice, segregation and other factors continue to militate against interracial coupling. Thus, the desire for sexual access to higher status, unavailable women, an important function in B/W rape, does not motivate white men to rape black women. Equally important, demographic and geographic barriers interact to lower the incidence of W/B rape. Segregation as well as the poverty expected in black neighborhoods undoubtedly discourages many whites from choosing such areas as a target for house-breaking or robbery. Thus, the number of rapes that would occur in conjunction with these crimes is reduced.

Reflecting in part the standards of sexual desirability set by the dominant white society, a number of black rapists indicated they had been curious about white women. Blocked by racial barriers from legitimate sexual relations with white women, they raped to gain access to them. They described raping white women as "the ultimate experience" and "high status among my friends. It gave me a feeling of status, power, macho." For another man, raping a white woman had a special appeal because it violated a "known taboo," making it more dangerous and, thus more exciting, to him than raping a black woman.

Impersonal Sex and Power

The idea that rape is an impersonal rather than an intimate or mutual experience appealed to a number of rapists, some of whom suggested it was their preferred form of sex. The fact that rape allowed them to control rather than care encouraged some to act on this preference. For example, one man explained,

> Rape gave me the power to do what I wanted to do without feeling I had to please a partner or respond to a partner. I felt in control, dominant. Rape was the ability to have sex without caring about the woman's response. I was totally dominant.

Another rapist commented:

> Seeing them laying there helpless gave me the confidence that I could do it . . . With rape, I felt totally in charge. I'm bashful, timid. When a woman wanted to give in normal sex, I was intimidated. In the rapes, I was totally in command, she totally submissive.

Perhaps we should note here that the appeal of impersonal sex is not limited to convicted rapists. The amount of male sexual activity that occurs in homosexual meeting places as well as the widespread use of prostitutes suggests that avoidance of intimacy appeals to a large segment of the male population. Through rape men can experience power and avoid the emotions related to intimacy and tenderness. Further, the popularity of violent pornography suggests that a wide variety of men in this culture have learned to be aroused by sex fused with violence (Smith, 1976). Consistent with this observation, recent experimental research conducted by Malamuth et al., (1980) demonstrates that men are aroused by images that depict women as orgasmic under conditions of violence and pain. They found that for female students, arousal was high when the victim experienced an orgasm and *no* pain, whereas male students were highly aroused where the victim experienced an orgasm and pain. On the basis of their results, Malamuth et al., (1980) suggest that forcing a woman to climax despite her pain and abhorrence of the assailant makes the rapist feel powerful, he has gained control over the only source of power historically associated with women, their bodies. In the final analysis, dominance was the objective of most rapists.

Recreation and Adventure

Among gang rapists, most of whom were in their late teens or early twenties when convicted, rape represented recreation and adventure, another form of delinquent activity. Part of rape's appeal was the sense of male camaraderie engendered by participating collectively in a dangerous activity. To prove one's self capable of "performing" under these circumstances was a substantial challenge and also a source of reward. One gang rapist articulated this feeling very clearly,

> We felt powerful, we were in control. I wanted sex and there was peer pressure. She wasn't like a person, no personality, just domination on my part. Just to show I could do it—you know, macho.

Our research revealed several forms of gang rape. A common pattern was hitchhike-abduction rape. In these cases, the gang, cruising an area, "looking for girls," picked up a female hitchhiker for the purpose of having sex. Though the intent was rape, a number of men did not view it as such because they were convinced that women hitchhiked primarily to signal sexual availability and only secondarily as a form of transportation. In these cases, the unsuspecting victim was driven to a deserted area, raped, and in the majority of cases physically injured. Sometimes, the victim was not hitchhiking; she was abducted at knife or gun point from the street usually at night. Some of these men did not view this type of attack as rape either because they believed a woman walking alone at night to be a prostitute. In addition, they were often convinced "she enjoyed it."

"Gang date" rape was another popular variation. In this pattern, one member of the gang would make a date with the victim. Then, without her knowledge or consent, she would be driven to a predetermined location and forcibly raped by each member of the group. One young man revealed this practice was so much a part of his group's recreational routine, they had rented a house for the purpose. From his perspective, the rape was justified because "usually the girl had a bad reputation, or we knew it was what she liked."

Solitary rapists also used terms like "exciting," "a challenge," "an adventure," to describe their feelings about rape. Like the gang rapists, these men found the element of danger made rape all the more exciting. Typifying this attitude was one man who described his rape as intentional. He reported:

> It was exciting to get away with it (rape), just being able to beat the system, not women. It was like doing something illegal and getting away with it.

Another rapist confided that for him "rape was just more exciting and compelling" than a normal sexual encounter because it involved forcing a stranger. A multiple rapist asserted, "it was the excitement and fear and the drama that made rape a big kick."

Feeling Good

At the time of their interviews, many of the rapists expressed regret for their crime and had empirically low self-esteem ratings. The experience of being convicted, sentenced, and incarcerated for rape undoubtedly produced many, if not most, of these feelings. What is clear is that, in contrast to the well-documented severity of the immediate impact, and in some cases, the long-term trauma experienced by the victims of sexual violence, the immediate emotional impact on the rapists is slight.

When the men were asked to recall their feelings immediately following the rape, only eight percent indicated that guilt or feeling bad was part of their emotional response. The majority said they felt good, relieved or simply nothing at all. Some indicated they had been afraid of being caught or felt sorry for themselves. Only two men out of 114 expressed any concern or feeling for the victim. Feeling good or nothing at all about raping women is not an aberration limited to men in prison. Smithyman (1978), in his study of "undetected rapists"—rapists outside of prison—found that raping women had no impact on their lives nor did it have a negative effect on their self-image.

Significantly a number of men volunteered the information that raping had a positive impact on their feelings. For some the satisfaction was in revenge. For example, the man who had raped and murdered five women:

> It seems like so much bitterness and tension had built up and this released it. I felt like I had just climbed a mountain and now I could look back.

Another offender characterized rape as habit forming: "Rape is like smoking. You can't stop once you start." Finally one man expressed the sentiments of many rapists when he stated,

> After rape, I always felt like I had just conquered something, like I had just ridden the bull at Gilley's.

CONCLUSIONS

This paper has explored rape from the perspective of a group of convicted, incarcerated rapists. The purpose was to discover how these men viewed sexual violence and what they gained from their behavior.

We found that rape was frequently a means of revenge and punishment. Implicit in revenge-rapes was the notion that women were collectively liable for the rapists' problems. In some cases, victims were substitutes for significant women on whom the men desired to take revenge. In other cases, victims were thought to represent all women, and rape was used to punish, humiliate, and "put them in their place." In both cases women were seen as a class, a category, not as individuals. For some men, rape was almost an after-thought, a bonus added to burglary or robbery. Other men gained access to sexually unavailable or unwilling women through rape. For this group of men, rape was a fantasy come true, a particularly exciting form of impersonal sex which enabled them to dominate and control women, by exercising a singularly male form of power. These rapists talked of the pleasures of raping—how for them it was a challenge, an adventure, a dangerous and "ultimate" experience. Rape made them feel good and, in some cases, even elevated their self image.

The pleasure these men derived from raping reveals the extreme to which they objectified women. Women were seen as sexual commodities to be used or conquered rather than as human beings with rights and feelings. One young man expressed the extreme of the contemptful view of women when he confided to the female researcher.

Rape is a man's right. If a women doesn't want to give it, the man should take it. Women have no right to say no. Women are made to have sex. It's all they are good for. Some women would rather take a beating, but they always give in; it's what they are for.

This man murdered his victim because she wouldn't "give in."

Undoubtedly, some rapes, like some of all crimes, are idiopathic. However, it is not necessary to resort to pathological motives to account for all rape or other acts of sexual violence. Indeed, we find that men who rape have something to teach us about the cultural roots of sexual aggression. They force us to acknowledge that rape is more than an idiosyncratic act committed by a few "sick" men. Rather, rape can be viewed as the end point in a continuum of sexually aggressive behaviors that reward men and victimize women. In the way that the motives for committing any criminal act can be rationally determined, reasons for rape can also be determined. Our data demonstrate that some men rape because they have learned that in this culture sexual violence is rewarding. Significantly, the overwhelming majority of these rapists indicated they never thought they would go to prison for what they did. Some did not fear imprisonment because they did not define their behavior as rape. Others knew that women frequently do not report rape and of those cases that are reported, conviction rates are low, and therefore they felt secure. These men perceived rape as a rewarding, low risk act. Understanding that otherwise normal men can and do rape is critical to the development of strategies for prevention.

7

Acquaintance Gang Rape
on Campus

CHRIS S. O'SULLIVAN
Michigan State University

Gang rape represents a rare but conceptually unique phenomenon. Unlike the vast majority of rapes where a lone male forces himself on a lone female, gang rapes involve multiple offenders in a collective criminal transaction. Moreover, these crimes often occur on college campuses and are committed by groups of male assailants who are well known to the victim. O'Sullivan references the group psychology literature in an effort to shed light on the mindset and behaviors of college gang rapists. Several critical concepts are brought to bear from the literature. First, the author observes that the rapes are often committed by individuals who share a membership to some sort of cohesive formal organization (i.e., a fraternity or sports team). Perpetrators often occupy an elevated or privileged status in the university community. He establishes that the organizations in question tend to be known for their partying and objectification of women. The author points to the concepts of diffused responsibility, deindividuation, and modeling to explain how seemingly harmless group interactions can get out of hand. Finally, O'Sullivan notes that the attacks usually take place in conjunction with coed social events where alcohol or drug use by the victims and offenders almost always seems to be present.

I n the Spring of 1984, two "gang rape" trials were in progress. One received a great deal of national publicity. Six men were charged with aggravated rape of a woman at Big Dan's Tavern in New Bedford, Massachusetts. Four were convicted. The other trial received only local attention and sent a different message. Seven college students were tried for third-degree sexual assault of a 17-year-old Michigan State University (MSU) student in a dormitory. After a three-week trial, in the course of which the five defense lawyers each displayed the victim's jeans and football jersey before the court and asked her why she wasn't wearing a bra when she went to the midnight dorm party, the students were acquitted. Questioned about the verdict, an MSU senior was quoted in the local paper as saying, "I don't believe she was raped . . . I believe they ran a train on her" (Pierson, 1984, p. 1B). A notable similarity between the two trials—and others—was the community support given to the defendants.

In New Bedford, over 6,000 citizens gathered outside the City Hall to protest the conviction of four of the men (Chancer, 1987). In a similar demonstration, when five Kentucky State University students were arrested on charges of raping and sodomizing a fellow student, 200 students held an angry rally in their support. In both instances, the protesters not only defended the men but also attacked the woman, maintaining she should be punished. This pattern of sympathy suggests that such sexual behavior is acceptable for men.

As further evidence that such behavior is tolerated in "decent" young men, the character witnesses for the Michigan State defendants included a minister and a girlfriend who testified that the men were incapable of rape. The defense argument was that the woman had consented or had not clearly expressed her objection. Because the defendants in these cases did not deny having sex with the same woman sequentially or simultaneously, the testimony of the character witnesses and community support for the defendants implied that exemplary moral character is consistent with having sex with a young woman in tandem with several buddies.

The thesis of this review is that group sexual assault is considered normal behavior for some groups of young men in our society. I will attempt to provide some preliminary answers to the fundamental questions of what the practice is, how often it occurs, who does it, to whom, and why.

THE GANG RAPE PHENOMENON

Although considerable attention has been devoted to rape in psychological and sociological literature over the past decade, group rape has rarely been discussed as a distinct phenomenon. While the existing literature is extremely helpful in understanding the sociocultural context that supports sexual aggression, there may be important differences between single- and multiple-perpetrator rape, especially in regard to motivation and situational characteristics. Others differences may include offender characteristics and psychological consequences for victims. The primary focus here is on perpetrators rather than victims.

To term it "gang rape" when many men have sex with same woman and the men deny coercion, is to prejudice the issue. Many of the cases discussed in this chapter as instances of gang rape were not determined to be rapes in judicial proceedings. Aside from the fact that many rapists and their victims do not recognize the crime that has been committed, difficulties of proving rape charges are compounded when there are multiple perpetrators. Because prosecutions and convictions are so rare, any case in which a woman alleged that her participation in sex with a group of men was involuntary is considered an instance of group rape for purposes of this discussion. Cases in which we do not know the woman's view of the incident and there are no allegations of force will be termed "trains," in the common vernacular of the subcultures in which such sex is practiced.

A group is considered here to consist of three or more men. There are two reasons for adopting this criterion. First, although two persons are often considered a group in social psychology, most of the group dynamics relevant to gang rape are not activated unless there are at least three group members. Second, several female college students in my samples reported soliciting sex with two men, preferring it to sex with one man, but none reported voluntarily engaging in or enjoying sexual encounters with more than two men. The mean number of male participants in the cases I have studied is five.

Campus gang rapes are emphasized here. That street gangs (Amir, 1971) or motorcycle gangs (Fort, 1971) have sex with a single female ritualistically, for example, as an initiation rite, is known and is typically accounted for by the social deviance of these groups. That group rapes may be a common practice among college students is the basis of the claim that they are normative and of the hypothesis that they are an outgrowth of conventional sex roles. Campus gang rapes are also usually acquaintance rapes, occurring during social get-togethers.

INCIDENCE OF GROUP SEXUAL ASSAULTS
ON COLLEGE CAMPUSES

Because there have been no systematic attempts to collect data on the incidence and prevalence of gang rapes in particular, estimates of their occurrence must be extrapolated from the rape literature or from anecdotal evidence and media reports.

Koss (1987), in a study of the national incidence of acquaintance rape among college students, found that 15% of the women (as victims) and 4% of the men (as perpetrators) had been involved in forced intercourse. The mean number of rapes reported by these subjects was above two. Five percent of the women who reported having been raped and 16% of the men who reported having raped said that their most serious incident involved more than one offender. Thus, in Koss's sample, nearly 1% of the men and women at colleges across the United States identified their most serious experience with sexual aggression as involving two or more men and one woman. These data may provide an underestimate of the occurrence of gang rapes because subjects were asked to report the number of men involved in only their single most serious experience. On the other hand, Koss's data may provide an overestimate because cases involving two men are included but do not meet the criterion for group rape here.

Using a more restricted sample, Rivera and Regoli (1987) mailed surveys to 400 randomly selected sorority women at a southwestern university. Two percent of their 174 respondents reported having been raped by two or more men while at the university. Drawing on a different population, Amir's (1971) study of rape in Philadelphia showed a much higher percentage of gang rape: 26% of the 646 rapes he identified were perpetrated by three or more men, and 55% of the rapists were involved in group rapes. Similarly, of the 81,030 rapes in 1986 on which the Bureau of Justice Statistics had data, 25% involved group rape offenders (Flanagan and Jamieson, 1988).

Anecdotal evidence of collegiate gang rapes is consistent with the frequency level suggested by Koss's data. Bernice Sandler of the Association of American Colleges reported that she had been told of 80 cases of group sexual assaults at colleges across the country (personal communication, May 16, 1988). She described the phenomenon as occurring among students at all types of institutions, from private religious colleges to large state universities and Ivy League colleges (Ehrhart and Sandler, 1985).

CHARACTERISTICS OF ASSAILANTS

Those most likely to rape or be raped, respectively, are men and women 20 to 24 years old; the next most likely group is 16 to 19-year-olds (Russell, 1982). Thus, sexual assault is most commonly committed by college-age men against women of college age. In their study of men convicted of sexual assault of adults, Groth and Birnbaum (1979) reported that the majority of the gang rapes were peer rapes between young adults; the mean age of the rapists was 23 and of the victims, 22.

Although some researchers (Amir, 1971; Schwendinger and Schwendinger, 1983) contended that the tendency to be sexually aggressive is associated with social deviance and low socioeconomic status (SES), Smith and Bennett (1985) maintained that sexual aggression is predicted by conflict between the sexes, across class and economic lines. As with other forms of criminal behavior, particularly abuse within relationships (child and spouse abuse), it may be that low SES individuals are more likely to be detected, prosecuted, and convicted than high SES perpetrators.

In fact, in parallel to the groupthink phenomenon (Janis, 1982), membership in a *privileged* group may protect a perpetrator from doubts about the propriety of his behavior, as well as from the perception of criminality by others. Janis proposed the concept of groupthink to explain disastrous decisions by elite groups, such as the decision by Kennedy's cabinet to invade Cuba. Impressed by each other, Janis suggested, members of such high status groups become convinced of the group's moral superiority, invulnerability, and consensus.

Cohesive Groups

Of the 24 documented cases of alleged gang rape by college students in the past 10 years, 13 were perpetrated by fraternity men, four by groups of basketball players, four by groups of football players, one by lacrosse players, and only two by men unaffiliated with a formal organization. Fraternities have houses where they can have unsupervised parties, serve alcohol, and enjoy privacy from nonmembers in their bedrooms and living rooms. College football and basketball players often live in their own dormitory and have motel rooms when on the road (the University of Minnesota basketball players assaulted their victim in a motel). Thus, these groups are more likely than others on college campuses to have facilities and opportunities for illicit activities.

Their living situation may facilitate gang rape, but other evidence suggests that the cohesiveness of these groups is an equally important factor. First, several of the known gang rapes by college athletes and fraternity brothers have taken place not in reserved residences but in regular campus housing. Second, other tightly knit groups of men, such as members of a rock band (Blakely, 1984), have been implicated in gang rapes. Although only two of the prosecuted campus gang rapes did not involve football or basketball players or fraternity members, a participant in one of these incidents referred to his codefendants as "the other members," although they did not belong to any known organization. That is, the assault was perpetrated by such a tightly knit group of friends that they saw themselves as "members." Often, some of the team members who rape together come from the same hometown and grew up together.

Another group that has been identified as having participated in group sexual assaults are soldiers in combat. Brownmiller (1975) reported that gang rapes were committed in World War II by German soldiers as they marched through France and Belgium, by Japanese soldiers in China, by Moroccan soldiers in Italy, and by American soldiers in France and Germany. She provided vivid second-hand accounts of repeated group sexual assaults followed by murder and mutilation of their victims by Americans fighting in Vietnam. Combat soldiers tend to fall into the same age range as college students or street gang members, and belong to a formal single-sex organization.

Differential association theory (DeFleur and Quinney, 1966) is helpful in formulating predictions. This theory postulates that criminal behavior is learned through symbolic interactions within intimate social groups. Which segments of the populations of American men aged 16 to 24 are likely to participate in group sexual assaults? The theory suggests that fraternity members and members of athletic teams may participate in group assaults not only because they have the facilities and are already organized, but also because the behavior is *learned* within these primary groups and is passed down along with other traditions. In some cases, there seems to be a ritualistic aspect to the assaults.

Research on campus rape also shows that athletes and fraternity men are more likely to be sexually aggressive individually than other college students. Garrett-Gooding and Senter (1987) found that more fraternity men (35%) reported having forced intercourse than did members of other organizations, such as student government (9%), or men not affiliated with any organization (11%). A *Philadelphia Daily News* investigation (Hoffman, 1986) reported:

> Football and basketball players representing NCAA-affiliated schools were reported to police for sexual assault approximately 38% more often than the average male on a college campus, as measured by an FBI survey.
>
> (p. 104)

Furthermore, men who would *not* rape alone may become rapists in the company of their sexually aggressive buddies. Groth and Birnbaum (1979) noted that the majority of those convicted of group rape in their sample, whom they identified as "followers" rather than instigators, had raped only in groups prior to their conviction. One of the Kentucky State defendants told police that he left the woman alone when he found her partially clothed in his room because she was unwilling to have sex with him. When he returned and found his friends assaulting her, he joined in.

MOTIVATIONS FOR
GROUP SEXUAL ASSAULT

One of the most interesting aspects of group sexual assault is that it is a *group* activity, implying that the discussion of motivation must take into account the fact that there is, in some sense, an audience and that something is being shared. One source of hypotheses about motives is Scully and Marolla's (1985) study of convicted rapists' accounts of the rewards of rape, with particular attention to the responses of gang rapists, who were mostly in their late teens or early twenties. Brownmiller's (1975) review of gang rape provided confirmation of the motives identified by Scully and Marolla (1985), and Farr's (1988) study of "Good Old Boys Sociability groups" (GOBS), men who maintained a group affiliation from adolescence into adulthood, provided a helpful picture of the activities of middle-class "gangs."

Excitement and Belonging

The most common description of the rewards of rape by the incarcerated gang rapists interviewed by Scully and Marolla (1985) fell into the category of recreation and adventure. Farr (1988) stated that "fun and trouble enjoy a symbiotic relationship as sociability themes" (p. 271). One activity that fits this description, Farr continued, is fooling around with a "bad woman," defined as any woman who is not the wife or girlfriend of a member.

A unique reward of gang rape described by Scully and Marolla's (1985) respondents was the camaraderie among the men. A reporter interviewed by Brownmiller (1975, p. 98) believed that American soldiers, unlike South Vietnamese soldiers, preferred gang rape to solitary rape because our soldiers were trained in the buddy system. I would suggest that the fact that American soldiers did not share a language with their victims, who resembled the enemy, also provided a motive for sharing the rape with friends. Similarly, Groth and Birnbaum (1979) listed rapport, fellowship, and cooperation as unique benefits of gang rape.

Also viewed positively, by Scully and Marolla's respondents and American soldiers (Brownmiller, 1975, p. 107), was the challenge of performing in the group situation. Farr (1988) noted that, just as fun and trouble go hand-in-hand, so are competition and camaraderie intertwined in male sociability groups. Geis (1971) also maintained that a primary motive in group sexual assault, especially for group leaders, is to sustain an image with the group. For followers, Groth and Birnbaum (1979) added, participation seems to stem in part from indebtedness to or emotional dependency on the leader.

In part, then, participation in a group sexual assault is motivated by the relationship among the men, for the purpose of maintaining or creating images and roles within the group. Certainly, providing a woman to the group, as in several of the documented campus cases where a college student offered his date to his friends, falls in the category of motives related to intragroup acceptance. An intriguing possibility is suggested by the presence in both the Florida State and Michigan State cases of a visiting friend from another college. Does an outsider intensify the competition and need to create a masculine image?

Sex

It appears that part of the appeal is the shared experience with one's buddies. Earlier studies of gang rape posited that the men were latent homosexuals and sharing the woman was a way of sharing sex covertly. The same authors (e.g., Blanchard, 1959) often alleged at the same time that women wanted to be raped. We reject the latter reading of the unconscious, and contemporary social science has rejected the former as requiring unnecessary and unsupported assumptions. The men are sharing an experience of heterosexual sex. That does say something about their social and emotional relationships with their own sex, but does not in itself inform us that they would rather have sex with each other. Groth and Birnbaum (1979) concurred: "Men do not rape women out of sexual desire for other men, but they may rape women, in part, as a way to relate to men" (p. 116). To further this point, these authors used the analogy of two men robbing a store together: they are not covertly expressing a desire to rob each other.

One motive that should not be overlooked in this age group, however, is simply the opportunity to have heterosexual intercourse. One offender who was interviewed by Scully and Marolla (1985) had been involved in 20–30 group rapes. He stated that he had participated in gang rapes because his driver's license had been revoked, depriving him of the opportunity to take women out alone. A college student interviewed by Gianturco and Smith (1974) about his participation in a "train" during Spring break in Florida seemed to be delighted by the unusual sexual availability of college women. He did not know the other men, thus apparently relations among the men played little or no role in his participation.

A related enticement of group rape for young men who are unable to make relationships with women on their own is that it allows for sexual intercourse without responsibility toward the sexual partner. Solitary rapists sometimes seek reassurance from their victims that they were also sexually satisfied, as Brownmiller (1975, p. 196) and Russell (1974, p. 111) noted. Conversely, Scully and Marolla (1985) were told that a reward of group rape was that no individual had to be concerned about or relate to the woman.

AGGRESSION IN GROUPS

It is well-established that individuals are more aggressive in groups than they would be when acting along. Such group processes are probably what participants in group sexual assaults and their defenders have in mind when they attempt to deflect blame by explaining, "Things got out of hand" (as several "enlightened" male students have confided to me about group sexual assaults). Three factors identified by social psychologists to explain why groups are so easily ignited to aggression can be applied to gang rape.

An individual in a group is less likely to behave altruistically and more likely to harm others than if the same individual were alone. One reason for these tendencies is that responsibility for the welfare of a victim is diluted by the presence of others, who share the blame. The term *diffusion of responsibility* is applied to situations in which the presence of others acting in a similar fashion diminishes the feeling of responsibility any individual feels for the harmful consequences of his or her own behavior.

A slightly different concept, *deindividuation*, refers to a state of loss of self-awareness, including awareness of one's beliefs, attitudes, and self-standards. (In contrast, diffusion of responsibility does not entail forgetting oneself or what one considers proper behavior, but only feeling it is not one's job to uphold these standards all alone. Deindividuation connotes irrationality.) This loss of self is sometimes encouraged to promote group spirit, as in a pep rally, or to facilitate behavior that is otherwise unacceptable. For example, soldiers' uniforms are deindividuating in that they remove signs of individuality and are thought to make it easier for them to adopt the alien role of killer. Alcohol promotes deindividuation by allowing escape from one's conscience and self-consciousness. Group cohesion and loyalty can produce deindividuation by substituting a group identity, with a group history and mores, for individual identities with unique, personal histories and beliefs.

Finally, in a group setting, particularly when group identity produces conformity, *modeling* of aggression also occurs. Not only would watching peers rape and sadomize a woman indicate the appropriateness of such behavior, it would also demonstrate how it is done.

Medea and Thompson (1974), reporting an incident in which up to forty fraternity brothers raped and sexually humiliated a woman who was developmentally disabled, speculated about the men's motivation. They attributed the students' behavior to group membership, illustrating how diffusion of responsibility, deindividuation, and modeling might come together to render a grotesque act not only tolerable but pleasurable:

> Who can doubt that these same young men would . . . have had considerable qualms about doing these things to a woman by themselves? They would probably have felt that what they were doing was perverse and shameful. It was the presence of other men that made the act acceptable; in fact, it was probably the presence of the other men that made it attractive . . . it was the sort of appeal that baiting a dog, or watching a hanging holds.
>
> (p. 35)

SOCIAL FOUNDATIONS OF GANG RAPE

The victims of the majority of gang rapes by students are women. This behavior simply cannot be understood—although the volumes of commentary and analysis generated about the Central Park gang rape case in the Spring of 1989 (O'Sullivan, 1990) have attempted to do so—without consideration of the perpetrators' attitudes toward women and of women's roles in the society and subcultures in which group sexual assaults are practiced and tolerated.

Attitudes

A large number of recent studies of college students have identified the relationship between traditional sex-role attitudes and the prevalence of rape. Hall, Howard, and Boezio (1986) found sexist attitudes to be more strongly correlated than antisocial personality with tolerance of rape. Berger, Searles, Salem, and Pierce (1986) concluded from a review of recent literature that traditional gender-role orientations are associated with rape-tolerant attitudes, and traditional attitudes toward female sexuality are associated with higher levels of sexual aggression. Garrett-Gooding and Senter (1987) suggested that their finding that fraternity men are more sexually aggressive than other college men was due to a combination of selections (fraternities disproportionately select men with traditional sex-role attitudes) and socialization.

Cultural Correlates

Perhaps more helpful in explaining group sexual assault as normative was an anthropological study by Sanday (1981), who reviewed anthropological records to classify 156 tribal societies as rape-free or rape-prone. Most of the rape-prone cultures she described had prescriptions for gang rape, rather than individual rape. A few of the correlations she identified as uniquely characterizing rape-prone cultures seem especially applicable to the population under consideration here.

One cultural characteristic that was strongly associated with the prevalence of rape was having special places for men and special places for women (Sanday, 1981). Among the Mundurucu of Brazil, for example, each village has a men's house, where all the men live together; women and children live in separate dwellings (Murphy, 1959). Thus, it is postulated here that group sexual assaults are most likely to occur in sex-segregated men's housing on college campuses. Perhaps recognition of this pattern motivated Bowdoin College to require admission of women to fraternities ("Bowdoin Fraternities Assailed," 1988), to reduce aggressive and antisocial behavior.

In rape-prone societies, the sexes are separated not only physically but also by rigid sex-role differentiation in which the male role is more valued. Thus, we might expect gang rapes to be most common among men who not only live apart from women but also perform roles closed to women (e.g., football players and fraternity members).

In such societies, which Sanday (1981) labeled male-dominated, a woman's violation of her prescribed sex role may be punished by rape or the threat of rape. One of these prescriptions is that women are supposed to be sexually naive and inexperienced. Gang rape is a punishment for promiscuity and can be seen as a means of controlling women's sexuality. Adulterous or promiscuous women are punished with gang rape among the Cheyenne, Omaha, and Mundurucu. According to Mead, as cited by Webster (1978), cultures must discipline female receptivity to maintain the family structure.

Parallels may be seen in accounts of gang rape in our own culture. A male student attempted to explain to me why a woman who charged several football players with rape and assault had not in fact been raped. His explanation was that, by dating two of the men who were close friends and having sex with each, she had hurt their feelings. They were angry at her for being sexually indiscriminate and, joined by other players, "ganged up" on her in revenge when she came to visit. The norm is that women are supposed to be sexually selective. If they are not, they may be "fair game," or worse. A student at another college told me of plans his fraternity made for "running a train." The woman was selected weeks in advance. They believed she was sexually promiscuous and therefore wouldn't "mind." Such beliefs bear a resemblance to those of the Canela in Brazil. If a young unmarried woman in Canela society takes a lover, she is supposed to be available to all men. If she refuses, she will be gang raped (Webster, 1978).

Characteristics of Gang-Rape Victims

The mean age of the victims in the 24 cases of campus gang rapes discussed in this view was 18; usually they were first-year students who were inexperienced with campus life. Victims of group assaults by acquaintances at fraternities and men's dorms tend to have two characteristics: They are naive, but they have somehow gained a reputation among the men for being promiscuous. A "perfect victim," from that point of view, was the complaining witness in the Kentucky State case. At the age of 20, she was divorcing the man she had dated from the age of 14; she had been at the university for a few weeks. To the 18- and 19-year-old men she accused, she seemed a racy character. Not only was she older and a divorcée, but also she had sneaked into the men's dorm on a prior occasion. One man told the others, as they rode a bus to a football game, that he had had sex with her that first evening, within hours of meeting her. (She denied it.)

Generally, women who habitually socialize with a group of men, and therefore are more often available to them, are no more likely to be victims of a group sexual assault than social outsiders are (Garrett-Gooding and Senter, 1987). The reason seems to be that social insiders are cognizant of the group mores. Sorority women learn from their sisters what different behaviors "mean" within the system. For example, they learn not to go upstairs to the bathroom at a fraternity party unless accompanied by another woman (Ehrhart and Sandler, 1985) and that getting drunk is taken by the men as a signal of availability. Women who are not part of the same social set as the men may be ignorant of such rules. Consequently, they miscommunicate their intentions by violating the norms or may unknowingly take risks, and become targets of sexual assault. Despite their knowledge of these rules, several of the victims in the 24 cases were girlfriends or long-term friends of the perpetrators who were lulled into trust, thought they were protected in violating the rules, and found themselves betrayed.

CONCLUSION

This review suggests that the measures being taken on college campuses to reduce the frequency of sexual assault may not ameliorate the problem of acquaintance gang rapes. Such measures include having separate dorms for men and women, restricting visitation, and having better campus lighting (Carmody, 1989; Herzog, 1989). These policies and practices admittedly are designed to prevent sexual interactions among college students altogether

(Herzog, 1989) or are oriented toward reducing the incidence of stranger rape. The cultural and attitudinal correlates of group sexual assault and the conditions under which campus gang rapes have occurred demonstrate that restricted access between the sexes will not remedy the problem. Profound attitude change is necessary.

With a few notable exceptions, educational efforts to reduce rape are primarily directed at or attended by college women rather than men. Although such education may help women to recognize when they have been raped, it will be less effective in reducing group assault than would educating those who have a choice about engaging in it. Prevention must begin with education of young men, particularly those who belong to male groups.

Attitude change in two areas will be necessary for men in groups to desist from joining in sexual assaults. The first such needed change is in attitudes toward women and understanding of women's sexuality. It seems to be particularly important to convey that a woman who chooses to be sexual, perhaps with several different individuals, is still sexually selective and is not available to the population at large. A related misconception common among college men is revealed by responses to Burt's (1980) Rape Myth Scale: Any woman who dresses or behaves "provocatively" is thought to be directing her seduction at all men who happen to see her and not at a particular man.

An even more difficult area of change that would effectively reduce sexual assault is men's attitudes toward themselves and their own sexuality. It is instructive to consider how men involved in group sexual assaults or "trains" may differ from those who find the practice unappealing and would not participate. My interviews have yielded two characteristic attitudes of men who are repulsed by the notion. They feel that sex is private (they reject sex as an arena for "cooperation and competition"); and they feel that sex is intimate (they reject sex without caring about their partner).

Although attitude change at the individual level might reduce the campus acquaintance rape rate, it does not address the problem of group norms and group pressure. Yet, attempts to educate the groups as such will probably succeed only when the perspective presented is endorsed by highly regarded group members. In the absence of such leadership, an alternative is to diminish group cohesion and decrease opportunities for group assaults by dispersing members throughout campus residences. Comparing practical strategies, breaking up male groups would probably be more effective in reducing group assault than attempting to keep women out of men's dorms.

8

Understanding Women's
Experiences of Wife Rape

RAQUEL KENNEDY BERGEN
St. Joseph's University

Bergen turns our attention to yet another most disturbing manifestation of rape—those instances in which a husband forces himself sexually upon his wife. The discussion begins with a history lesson in which the author observes that, until only recently, wife rape stood as a legal impossibility—most jurisdictions observed a marital clause through which the sanctity of marriage protected a husband from the allegation of rape. Bergen used service providers to locate and interview a snowball sample of forty women who report being raped at least once by their husbands. She categorizes the behavioral and psychological features of the offenders using a three-part typology. Force-only rapists use fear and intimidation to gain sexual submission. For the battering rapist, the unwanted sex act represents a simple extension of a violent physical assault upon his wife. The sadistic rapist combines physical force and perverse sexual motivations to degrade and demean his wife. Bergen theorizes about the causes of wife rape and details the emotional pain and coping strategies of the victims. She paints a picture of an evolving cycle of violence and self-reflection in which the women grapple with the painful realization that they are being sexually victimized by their most intimate companion. This emotional betrayal leads to a series of emotional and behavioral countermeasures that enable the victims to compartmentalize their troubled marital relations.

The goal of this chapter is to develop a more comprehensive understanding of women's experiences of wife rape by focusing on the nature of this type of sexual violence and how women cope with it. How victims of domestic violence respond to the violence in their relationships has been studied by many researchers including Ferraro and Johnson (1983), Mills (1985), Pagelow (1992), and Walker (1979). Frieze (1983) found that women who are raped by their husbands are more likely than battered women to file legal charges and to try to leave their partners; Russell (1990) analyzed how raped wives end the violence. However, there is no research to date that systematically documents the coping strategies of wife rape survivors. As Kelly (1988) argues, women's coping strategies must be considered if we are to acknowledge the

From *Wife Rape: Understanding the Response of Survivors and Service Providers* by Raquel Kennedy Bergen, pp. 11–36, copyright ©1996 by Sage Publications, Inc. Reprinted by permission of Sage Publications, Inc.

complexity of women's experiences of sexual violence and the impact of that violence on their lives. Furthermore, by exploring how women manage wife rape, we see that they "are not passive victims at the time of assault nor are [they] passive victims in relation to the consequences of abuse" (Kelly, 1988, p. 159).

WOMEN'S EXPERIENCES OF WIFE RAPE

Within the larger society, wife rape is often understood as a relatively innocuous incident in which a husband wants to have sex, his wife rejects him, and he holds her down on the bed and has intercourse with her. Although a few of the women in this sample experienced this type of sexual assault, this scenario was far from the norm. Indeed, the women I interviewed described a wide range of experiences, from assaults that were relatively quick in duration and involved little physical force to sadistic, torturous episodes that lasted for hours.

Based on their interviews with 50 women, Finkelhor and Yllö (1985) identified three types of wife rape. Incidents in which women were not battered but experienced "only as much force as necessary to coerce their wives into sex" (p. 38) were characterized as *force-only rapes. Battering rapes* were identified as "forced sex combined with beating" (p. 37) and accounted for the largest number of cases. The third category, which applied to about half a dozen women in their sample and largely involved men who used pornography, was defined as *obsessive rapes.* Finkelhor and Yllö characterized obsessive rapes as those incidents in which physical force was combined with "the strange and the perverse" (p. 50). This category closely resembles what Nicholas Groth (1979) calls *sadistic rapes,* in which assaults typically involve bondage and torture. In this study I too will refer to these rapes as sadistic rapes.

Like Russell (1990) and Finkelhor and Yllö (1985), I suspect that there are many other types of wife rape. Furthermore, the type of violence women experienced often changed over the course of the relationship. However, these classifications reflect how women themselves talked about their experiences of sexual violence—from being coerced to have sex when they really didn't want to, to being terrorized with sadistic acts involving torture. Thus, I find Finkelhor and Yllö's categorizations useful for beginning to discuss the nature of the violence these women faced.

Force-Only Rape

In my study, 10 of the women described force-only rapes. Although they were all physically battered at other times during their relationship, the sexual abuse was generally not characterized by physical violence. For example, Abigail told me,

> He shoved me down on the bed very forcefully, and I said, "What are you doing? . . . No, I don't want this." And there [were] no preliminaries and no tenderness. Nothing. And he entered me and it was painful and I just remember being so repulsed.

The women in the force-only category described incidents of sexual abuse devoid of excessive physical violence. However, they talked about their fear of physical violence if they resisted their partners' sexual advances. As Cory told me, "If I resisted, he would beat me up, so I learned not to resist and I just gave in."

Several other women in this force-only category experienced severe physical violence at other times during their relationship, and their fear of the physical repercussions is what motivated many of them not to resist their partners' sexual advances. However, it is significant to note that these women were not freely consenting to have intercourse; they only acquiesced out of fear that physical violence would occur if they did not. Other women, although not freely choosing to have sex, did so out of a sense of obligation. Kayla said, "I thought I had to. Nobody ever told me I had the right to say no. I knew it was yucky and I dreaded it, but I thought I had to do it." Paula described her reasons:

> He always wanted to have sex. He was jealous, and if he didn't have sex with me every single day, that meant that I was with another guy and that was his theory. From the time I was 18, I had sex every single day for the first year we were married, and maybe I had 2 days off when I had my period. But we did it every day because he wanted to and I thought I had to.

Supporting findings by Finkelhor and Yllö (1985), these women were no less upset or humiliated than other wife rape survivors, simply because these incidents were devoid of excess force. Indeed, Lisa told me that after each rape, "I was real upset and I would cry afterwards. I felt so terrible and it didn't even bother him. He didn't care." Noelle, who had been raped by an acquaintance when she was a teenager, was particularly traumatized by her husband's attack. She said,

> That's [rape] the worst thing he could have done knowing my background and knowing how I felt about the issue—it's a violation of trust and commitment and the whole bit and compound it with knowing my background, and it was the worst thing he could have done to me.

Thus, we see that the women in this sample who experienced force-only rape suffered serious emotional consequences from being raped by their partners even though they did not suffer from excessive physical violence.

Battering Rape

All of the women in this sample experienced physical violence at some point during their relationships, and several were severely battered by their partners. Again, this is probably the result of my sample, which was drawn largely from a battered woman's shelter. Russell (1990) argues that not all women who are raped by their partners are battered wives. However, researchers such as Browne (1993), Campbell (1989), and Shields and Hanneke (1983) have noted that wife rape is more likely to occur in marriages characterized by extreme physical violence.

In this study, women who had been severely battered talked about common injuries, such as black eyes, broken bones, blood clots in their heads, and knife wounds. In a particularly violent incident, Nina described how her partner (who was angered by her pregnancy) dragged her into the woods, where he beat and raped her and then used a knife to slice open her abdomen. While not all of the women in my sample were subjected to such extreme forms of physical violence, about 70% of them experienced battering rapes at some point.

For some, the physical violence regularly accompanied the sexual abuse. For example, Barbara told me,

> He would fight me and then he would always rip all of my clothes off me. I don't have hardly any clothes left because he always ripped off my clothes, and I was naked. Then he would try to lay on me and put it in. Sometimes I was able to fight him off, and I would fight like wild, and he wouldn't be able to get it in. But usually he would [succeed in penetrating her], and he put me in the hospital a lot. He broke my nose and my jaw and cut my wrists.

For many women, like Karen, the rape followed on the heels of the physical abuse when their partners were attempting to reconcile. For example, Jen said, "He sexually assaulted me a couple of times and always after he beat me up. He would want sex, and he would actually think in his own mind that he really hadn't done anything." Melissa told me,

> He would beat me and then take it. He would choke me. He put his elbow in my throat and choked me. He would throw anything he could get his hands on—ashtrays, or whatever, he broke my fingers and hands. He was real violent. He threw knives at me, and he would throw me naked into the street and pour cold water on me and make me stay out there in the winter . . . then he would make me have sex and then go and eat a sandwich. I never understood how he could do that. How can you do that to somebody?

Other women in this sample experienced battering rapes frequently, but not necessarily all the time. For example, Sonya experienced both force-only rapes and battering rapes at various times in her relationship. She said,

> Sometimes we would go to bed, and he would push my legs aside and force sex on me. Or he would grab my head and force me [to give him oral sex]. . . . Other times he would beat the crap out of me in bed or hold a gun to my head to force me.

Sadistic Rape

The third type of wife rape, sadistic rape, was experienced by a total of nine of the women in this sample at some point in their relationships. These women characterized their experiences not only as physically violent but also as involving "perverse" acts or torture. Seven women experienced both battering rapes and sadistic rapes. However, two were always sadistically raped—for both this occurred more than 20 times during the course of their relationships. For example, Tanya was regularly choked to the point of passing out and then raped by her partner. She told me,

> He was really into watching porno movies, and he tried to make me do all sorts of things. And I [didn't] like it. He hurt my stomach so bad because I was pregnant, and he was making me do these things. I think he's a sadist—he pulls my hair and punches me and slaps me and makes me pass out.

For several of the women in this study, bondage was a usual occurrence in their experiences of sexual violence. Lorraine, who was regularly sadistically raped, remembered

> just waking up and being tied to the bed by my arms and legs, and the thing that woke me up was him touching me [vaginally] with a feather and me waking up in shock. And he had this thing about taking pictures of it all and trying to open me up [vaginally]. So he would use his fist and other objects and then make me do exercises on the toilet to tighten [my vagina] up again.

The women who described sadistic incidents of sexual assault suffered particularly severe physical and emotional trauma as a result of the violence. This is likely the result of both the terroristic nature of the assaults they experienced and the great frequency with which they were raped by their partners.

Frequency of Wife Rape

The experiences of women who were raped by their partners differed not only by the type of violence they suffered but also in terms of the frequency of the incidents. For a few women in this sample, rape was a relatively rare occurrence. For example, Abigail was married to her partner for 25 years and was raped once early in the relationship. Other women were raped so frequently they lost count. Debbie was raped as often as three times a day over a period of 8 years. We see from Table 2.1 that most women (55%) were raped frequently—more than twenty times during the course of their relationships. Finkelhor and Yllö (1985) also found that 50% of the women in their sample were raped more than twenty times. Although there is a wide range of experiences represented in this sample, rape was not an infrequent occurrence but the norm for most women.

Table 2.1 Frequency of Wife Rape

Frequency	Number of Women	Percentage (*n* = 40)
Once	7	17
Twice	3	8
3–10 times	6	15
11–20 times	2	5
20 times or more	22	55

Types of Forced Sexual Behavior

Women who are raped by their husbands experience not only vaginal penetration but a variety of unwanted, forced sexual acts. In fact, Peacock (1995) writes that marital rape survivors are more likely to experience unwanted oral and anal intercourse than women who are raped by acquaintances. About 57% of the women in my sample were vaginally raped by their partners. However, 40% of the women reported at least one incident of anal rape, and 33% had been forced to perform oral sex on their partners. Thus, we see considerable variation in the type of sexual violence women experienced and the frequency with which they were raped by their partners.

CAUSES OF WIFE RAPE

The women in this sample offered many explanations for the rapes inflicted on them by their partners. However, it is significant to note that these explanations were offered after they had ended the violence.

While the relationships were ongoing, many of the women said, they blamed themselves for the violence. In retrospect, they were more likely to hold their husbands responsible for sexually abusing them.

Entitlement to Sex

One of the most popular explanations women offered was that their partner believed that he had the right to sexual intercourse on demand; when refused, he had the right to take it. Such thinking is created and perpetuated by the traditional patriarchal family structure defined by men's domination and women's subordination. As Finkelhor and Yllö (1985) note, the ideal of sex as a conjugal right is particularly evident among men who rape their wives. Their research reveals that many men feel a sense of entitlement to their wives' bodies and thus do not regard forced sex as rape.

The majority of women in this sample indicated that their husbands felt a sense of ownership that gave them the sexual rights to their wives' bodies at all times. For example, Wanda remembered that her husband told her repeatedly, "That's my body—my ass, my tits, my body. You gave that to me when you married me and that belongs to me." Similarly, Emily recalled that on the night her husband raped her, "he was saying something like I'm his wife and I'm supposed to have sex with him and by law I was his or something like that—his possession."

When several of the women in this study informed their partners that the act they had committed was rape, the men still adamantly denied this because of their sense of sexual entitlement. For example, Rhonda's husband told her, "You're my wife—this ain't rape." When Terri confronted her partner, he said, "Girl, I didn't rape you. How can I rape my own woman?" Even after eight of the women in this sample filed criminal charges against their partners for sexual assault, the majority of the men continued to deny that their actions could legally be rape.

Several women in this study said that when they were forbidden, for medical reasons, to have sex with their partners, their risk of being raped increased because their partners' sense of entitlement was challenged. In one of the most brutal examples in my study, Stacey returned home from having a cesarean section to have this encounter with her husband, who was a physician:

> I told him [my husband] I couldn't have intercourse, and he told me "Skin heals in 72 hours." I'll never forget that. Then he kneeled with a knee on either side of my shoulders and smacked his penis across my face and said, "You suck me, bitch."

Stacey's husband reasserted "his rights" by forcing her to have a oral intercourse, after which he sodomized her.

This sense of entitlement often lasts even after the couple is separated or divorced, as was the case with 20% of the women in this sample. For example, after she was separated, Lisa was raped frequently by her partner when he showed up to give her his child support payments. She said, "I dreaded the weekends. It was like clockwork, and he would just make me do it, and I knew it was coming and that made it worse."

As the research of Finkelhor and Yllö (1985), Frieze (1983), and Russell (1990) reveals, women are particularly at risk of being raped when they are separated or divorced, because despite the dissolution of the marital bond, this sense of entitlement and the belief that their (ex) wives are their property live on.

Rape as Punishment

Several of the women in my sample believed that the sexual abuse was their partners' attempt to punish either their loved ones or the women themselves. For example, Sally recalled the following exchange that occurred one night, just before her husband raped her:

> I think he thought that I was his wife, and he could do anything to me, and if he wanted sex, he got sex. And he could do anything and do no wrong and I belonged to him. Like one night when my daughter came back from her date, he flipped because the boy didn't shake his hand, and he screamed, "She's never going out with him again." And he went on and on and said, "Now it's time for you to pay. It's time to pay up like you did the other night."

Sally was punished for the actions of her daughter's boyfriend. Other women were raped as punishment for their own "sins," as Natalie described here:

> A lot of times it [rape] happened because he was so jealous. He always thought that I was looking at other men. Like the time my brother and his friend—who I grew up with—were over, and he thought I was looking at his friend, and he was really mad. He started hitting me and then forced me to have sex.

Tanya remembered a similar linkage between punishment and rape:

> He [her partner] would try to choke me, and then I would pass out. Then he would rape me. He would put me to sleep and then rape me. Sometimes when we were out somewhere, and he didn't like something I did, he would say "You wanna go to sleep?" and laugh like it was real funny. It was like a punishment.

Like Natalie and Tanya, several women in this study recalled that their partners forced them "to pay" sexually as punishment. Ultimately, these women perceived the assaults as their partners' attempt to control their behavior.

Rape as a Form of Control

The majority of women in this sample saw the sexual violence as their partners' way to assert power and control over them. As Pam told me,

> The more control he thought he was losing, the worse it got. If I got a job or I was doing good, he would take it away. He would beat me up and force me up and force me [to have sex] just to get that control back.

Nine of the women told me that their partners, in an ultimate attempt at control, raped them in order to impregnate them so that they would not leave the relationship. In five cases, their partners' efforts were successful. For example, Annabel said, "We had five children. I think he raped me to keep me pregnant all the time because he knew I would never leave the kids."

Whereas some partners used pregnancy to control their wives, several women told me that their husbands were angered by their pregnancies, possibly because this represented a loss of control over them. Indeed, three women in this study talked about their partners' attempts to make them "lose the baby" through increased violence and/or coerced abortions because they believed that their wives had been unfaithful to them. For example, Wanda recalled that her husband

> tried to force me to have an abortion because he didn't believe it was his child. . . . When I refused to get an abortion, he took me to [the] women's clinic, and I was on the table and I was far enough along that the doctor said he couldn't do it.

Although he was not successful in forcing his wife to have an abortion, her husband continued to sexually and physically abuse her throughout her pregnancy, Wanda said, possibly with the hope that she would lose the baby.

In this sample, pregnancy was a factor that appeared to place women at a higher risk of being both physically and sexually abused. Researchers such as Browne (1992), Campbell, Poland, Waller, and Ager (1992), and Gells (1988) have noted the correlation between battering and pregnancy. Campbell (1989) found that women who were sexually abused by their partners were also more likely to be abused during pregnancy. One third of the women in my sample spoke about the increase in physical and sexual violence they experienced during pregnancy.

The women who were raped during their pregnancies were traumatized, not only by the sexual assaults but also by the fear of how their unborn children might be affected by their partners' violent behavior. However, most of the women felt that there was little they could do to stop the sexual abuse and their husbands' attempts to dominate them in this way.

In conclusion, we see that there are a variety of explanations offered by women to explain the sexual violence in their lives. Furthermore, it is clear that the sexual violence the women in this sample experienced varied greatly. Indeed, no stereotypical depiction of the "average wife rape" emerges from their descriptions.

Despite individual differences among the participants' experiences, there were similarities in how these women managed the sexual violence. Let us now turn to a central question of this book: How do women cope with their experiences of wife rape?

COPING WITH WIFE RAPE

Trudy Mill's (1985) research on battered women reveals that women implement a variety of coping strategies to deal with the violence in their lives and protect themselves from harm. Mills (1995) argues that women who are abused by their husbands must manage the violence and that this involves

> the attachment of meaning to the violence and the development of strategies to cope with it. The meanings the woman attaches to the violence and the resources she believes she has shape strategies for living with, or ending, the violence. (p.107)

In her analysis of the impact of sexual violence on the lives of women, Liz Kelly (1988) explores how women cope with sexual violence. She defines coping as

> the actions taken to avoid or control distress. Women's coping responses are active, constructive adoptions to the experiences of abuse. The responses of any particular woman will depend on how she defines her experience, the context within which it occurs, and the resources which are available to her at the time and subsequently. (p. 160)

Just as battered women and other survivors of repeated acts of violence learn to manage the violence, my research indicates that wife rape survivors too develop strategies to cope with their experiences of sexual abuse, beginning with the first incident.

The First Incident

For the majority of women in this study, the first forced sexual experience was merely one in a long line of abuses to come. Indeed, only seven women were able to escape the relationship after having been raped only once. Six of these women terminated their relationships immediately after the first incident of rape. Those women were either separated or seriously considering separation from their partners at the time of the rape, and several had the economic resources to survive on their own. For example, Rhonda and her husband were separated at the time of the incident but maintained an amicable relationship. On the night of the rape, he entered her house, which was not unusual, and then, she says, "It was like something just snapped in him. He grabbed me and said, 'We gonna have sex, I need to fuck.' " Rhonda was raped for 7 hours before her husband finally left. At the time of the rape, Rhonda owned her own home, had a job, and was already separated from her assailant, so the decision to remove herself from any further contact with her husband was easy to make.

Whereas Rhonda's circumstances allowed her to immediately end all contact with her husband, most of the women in this study were not in a position to do this. For example, although Karen also identified her first experience as rape, it took her 2 months to save money and finalize her plans to leave. She was raped 11 more times during this period.

The vast majority of women in this sample did not leave the relationship after the first incident but instead tried to manage the violence. After the first incident, all of the women reported feeling a similar sense of shock that the assault was happening to them and a general feeling of disbelief that someone they loved was responsible for their pain. Debbie is typical in her response to the first rape:

> The first time, I thought, "I don't believe this is happening, I just don't believe it." I was in shock—totally numb—and I don't know how I ever got over being that numb. It just blew me out, and I thought this can't be happening to me.

Most of the women reported that they thought the first assault was an aberrant incident that would never happen again. Frieze and Bulman (1983) report that shock, confusion, anxiety, fear, helplessness, and a belief that this will only happen once are common psychological responses to victimization. Indeed, for most victims of haphazard crimes, this coping mechanism of treating the incident as a single occurrence may suffice. However, many survivors of wife rape (more than 80% of women in this sample) learn that the first incident is not aberrant but an ongoing problem. Thus, after the initial shock has ceased, survivors of wife rape are forced either to develop strategies to manage the violence or end the relationship.

MANAGING THE VIOLENCE

Mills (1985) argues that the two fundamental goals in managing violence are protecting oneself from injury and justifying the continuation of the relationship. During the course of the relationship, a woman's coping strategies often change as it becomes clear to her that she will or will not be able to avoid an assault. My interviews revealed that a variety of strategies were employed by women to protect themselves, including minimizing the risk of violence, diminishing injuries once the violence had begun, and emotionally surviving the violence.

Minimizing the Risk of Violence

A primary way women in this sample tried to cope with being raped by their partners was to minimize the risk that violence would occur. As Sally told me,

> You know what's gonna happen, and you're trying to think in your brain, how can I stop this without getting hurt? And you don't know how to stop it without angering him because you know you're going to get killed, and it's like looking a murderer straight in the eye, and they have this cold-blooded look, and you know you're dead unless you can do something.

There were several strategies implemented by women to minimize the risk that they would be sexually assaulted.

Active Resistance Most women in this sample attempted, on at least one occasion, to minimize the risk of violence by physically resisting their partners. Like the women in Finkelhor and Yllö's (1985) study, one quarter of the women in this sample were successful at least once in resisting their husbands' attempts to rape them. For example, Erica physically resisted to the point where her husband grew tired and gave up. On one occasion, Samantha was able to kick her husband in the groin and escape. Several other women used weapons, such as guns or knives, to deter their partners; Terri stabbed her partner in the arm with a kitchen knife. Clearly these women were courageous and creative in their attempts to resist their partners' attacks. However, most of the women in this sample said they learned not to resist but merely to "give in." Debbie recalled how she quickly learned not to resist her husband:

> I live in an apartment where you go up the steps to get in, and do you know how many times I've been dragged up the stairs? Get away? It just doesn't happen. So I learned quick, and then I never fought back or anything because it would just prolong the agony. It's over quicker if I just give in.

Avoidance Most of the women in this sample found that a more successful strategy than active resistance was simple avoidance. Indeed, several women tried a tactic similar to Natalie's: "He would come home from work angry over something and take it out on me. So I would try to stay out of his way." Danielle knew that she was particularly at risk for being sexually assaulted after her husband watched pornographic movies, so she made extra efforts to avoid him at these times.

Many women avoided the bedroom, feigned sleep, or went to bed only after they were certain their partners were asleep.

Other women in this sample used more direct tactics to avoid their husbands. For example, Debbie particularly feared her husband when he had been drinking.

When he came home drunk, she regularly took advantage of his ulcer by putting tabasco sauce into his food. The result was that he became very thirsty and continued to drink more beer, not realizing why he was so thirsty. Debbie says that "if I was lucky, he would pass out and leave me alone." Otherwise, Debbie was forced to have sexual intercourse until he passed out from sheer exhaustion.

Placating Their Husbands   The most popular tactic for minimizing the risk of assault was for women to placate their husbands. Placation took many forms, including not seeing close friends of whom their husbands did not approve, quitting jobs, distancing themselves from their families, maintaining a clean home, having dinner ready at specific times, and keeping the children quiet at all times. These were all components of what these women perceived as their roles as "good wives," and they tried actively to meet their husbands' expectations in order to avoid violent episodes. The majority of women told stories similar to this account by Annabel, who remained with her husband for 29 years: "I felt if I could just be what he wanted—a good wife—and stay at home, then he would stop." Cory remembered thinking, "OK, I can play housewife, I can do that."

Like many battered women, most of the women in this sample understood that if they could fulfill their partners' expectations about being a good wife and mother, they would reduce their risk of experiencing violence. However, it should be emphasized that these women were not merely passive in their acceptance of their husbands' demands and gender role expectations; placating their partners was an active coping strategy used to minimize their risk of being abused (Kelly, 1988).

Minimizing Injuries Once the Violence Had Begun

Although most of the women went to great lengths to please their husbands, they all learned that they could not manipulate every situation and avoid being sexually assaulted. Thus, they tried to minimize their injuries as a way of maintaining some form of control over the violence. Stacey said, "I would try to manipulate him during the sex, not for my own needs or orgasms, but to control his anger and try to reduce it so I wouldn't get really hurt." Many of the women tried to appease their husbands sexually in order to minimize their risk of harm. For example, Annabel knew that she had to "service him [her husband] to keep the peace." Natalie told me, "I would fake it (orgasm)—I was the best damn actress—I could have won an award. I even did things to him when there were tears in my eyes."

One quarter of the women in this sample said they sometimes performed oral sex on their husbands, although they despised this act, so that the abuse would end quickly. This was particularly difficult for several of the women, who were incest survivors and recalled being forced to engage in fellatio with their assailants when they were children.

Other women in this sample recalled engaging in what they referred to as "perverse" activities, such as anal intercourse and bondage, to reduce their risk of injury. Although she despised having anal intercourse, Lorraine remembered that she allowed her husband to do this so that he would not severely batter her in front of their children.

Emotionally Surviving Wife Rape

When rape appeared inevitable, these women had little choice but to focus their energy on limiting their injury and emotionally surviving the attack. All of the women who experienced more than one assault described mechanisms that allowed them to survive the actual rape. As Judith Herman (1981) found in her work with incest survivors, many victims of sexual assault resort to psychological measures to minimize the trauma. Some women find their time perception and sensory perception altered as they disassociate themselves from the experience or treat it as if it is happening to somebody else (Hawkins, 1991). Kelly (1988) defines this process of "cutting off" as not just a coping strategy but also an act of resistance. In doing this, a woman refuses to let her partner control her mind and feelings.

One of the most prevalent survival strategies was best described by Debbie as "orbing out." She recalled,

> He would be all over me, and then I just went out in my mind—I just wasn't there anymore. I took myself somewhere else, and I found out later that I had done that a lot. Even growing up and all, if anything hurts me, I orb out—I get totally numb.

Although this strategy was consistently employed, particularly by the one quarter of the women in this study who were survivors of incest, some women reported out-of-body experiences only during certain episodes. For example, Karen described having "out-of-body experiences—like I was watching from a corner of the room because I couldn't feel anything"—only during the sexual assaults but not during the physical assaults.

Several other women said they coped with the actual rape by focusing their thoughts ironically on the happy days of their marriages or on other aspects of their lives. For example, Kayla recalled, "I would lay there and pretend it's not happening to me. I would think of shopping or the kids or whatever else I had to do." Others, such as Rebecca and Wanda, repeated the same phrase continually in their minds in order to distract themselves from what was happening and help them to cope with the assaults.

All of these mechanisms enabled the survivors to cope during the actual time of crisis and to minimize emotional trauma.

EMOTIONAL SURVIVAL AFTER WIFE RAPE

My interviews with wife rape survivors revealed that women not only developed strategies for coping during the actual sexual assaults, but they also developed strategies for emotional survival after each incident of sexual abuse. Kelly (1988) defines emotional survival as "the extent to which women are able to reconstruct their lives so that the experience of sexual violence does not have an overwhelming and continuing negative impact on their lives" (p. 163).

Following their experiences of wife rape, the women in this sample, like other sexual assault survivors, worked not only to exist but also to put back together the pieces of their lives. Six women in this study began to do this by terminating their relationships with their partners immediately following their first experience of wife rape. Thus, as I indicated earlier, they did not take steps to manage the violence. They emotionally survived the assault by distancing themselves from their partners, seeking the help of service providers and turning to friends.

Gwenn was raped once by her partner after she returned home from having major surgery. Following the rape, she remembered getting dressed and leaving the house in a daze:

> I wound up at the police department, and then I found out husbands can rape their wives, so they sent me to a doctor for a rape test [kit] and then . . . I signed a criminal complaint and called [a rape crisis center] the next day.

However, the majority of women in this sample were raped multiple times by their partners. These women developed strategies to cope after each assault. Kayla typifies the reaction of many women in this sample. She recalled what happened one time after she was raped:

> He fell asleep and I got up and cleaned myself up and then I pretended that nothing happened. I thought about the kids coming over, and I just didn't deal with it [the rape]. I thought to myself, it wasn't that bad.

Kayla's recollection reveals the complex process of coping after sexual abuse and indicates several of the strategies women I interviewed used to put their lives back together again—cleaning themselves up, forgetting about the incident, justifying the assault, and minimizing the effects of the violence.

Like other survivors of sexual assault, most of the women I interviewed felt the need to "be clean" following their experiences of rape. For example, Sally told me,

> I went into the shower and I washed myself and scrubbed myself. I did everything a rape victim would do. Everything. It was like you knew what had been done to you and that this was something all rape victims do. And you knew you had to heal yourself because if you didn't heal yourself, nobody else would.

After each sexual assault, Sara said she would "take shower after shower because I felt so dirty and I couldn't get clean."

Two other strategies women used were to rationalize the violence and minimize the severity of the assault. As Russell (1990) notes, it is important for women who decide to stay in the relationship, either because they do not want to leave or are unable to leave the marriage, to discount the trauma of the rape. Similarly, Kelly (1988) notes that minimizing the effects of sexual violence allows women to define the violence in a way in which they do not have to immediately act, possibly because they see no other available options or because they fear the consequences of their actions. Thus, for most women to be able to remain in the marriage, they must "work" on their emotions, transforming the social reality of their situation, so that they do not see themselves as victims or their husbands as rapists.

Rationalizing the Violence

Many abused wives reconstruct their experiences by holding themselves, rather than their husbands, responsible (Ferraro & Johnson, 1983; Mills, 1985). Although self-blame is a characteristic more commonly associated with wives who are battered than with those who are raped, a significant number of raped wives (estimates range from 6% to 20%) engage in self-blame (Finkelhor & Yllö, 1985; Frieze, 1983; Russell, 1990). Studies by Finkelhor and Yllö (1985) and Frieze (1983) indicate that the length of time a women remains in the violent relationship and the extent to which she holds traditional ideals about the family are directly related to self-blame.

In this sample, one third of the women initially blamed themselves to some extent for their husband's actions. Many of these women felt they had failed in their roles as wives so they were able to rationalize that it was their own fault that the forced sex occurred. For example, both Sonya and Cory were incest survivors who were generally not interested in having sexual intercourse with their partners. They felt their unresponsiveness was the cause of the sexual abuse. Sonya said,

> I wouldn't let him touch me for the first 2 months after we got married because of what I went through with my father . . . and I was afraid he was going to go and get an annulment, and I feel like part of the problem of our marriage is because I can't. It's like I want to have sex with him, but I keep having flashbacks about what happened to me, and I just can't handle it. And I know he's my husband.

These women viewed sex as their marital obligation and felt their husbands were being neglected because they were unable to fulfill their duties. Thus, they did not, at least initially, blame their husbands for raping them.

Three other women I interviewed did not blame their husbands for assaulting them but instead blamed drug or alcohol use for triggering the attacks. Crack cocaine was one substance that several women blamed for changing their partners from loving individuals into sexually and physically abusive men.

These examples indicate that rather than viewing their husbands as assailants, these women perceived them as the victims in some way. By constructing the violence in this way, their husbands were free from blame, and they were able to remain in their relationships and cope with the sexual abuse.

Minimizing the Severity of the Violence

In her research, Kelly (1990) found that it was not uncommon for victims of rape to minimize or "limit the impact of incidents that they defined as abusive to some degree" (p. 126). Many of the women in this sample also minimized the extent of the sexual violence they had suffered. For example, after each rape, Debbie would tell herself, "That wasn't that bad. I got through that one so I'll get through another." Similarly, Becky thought, "I love him and I know he really loves me, so it [the abuse] wasn't so bad."

These women were hesitant to acknowledge the severity of their experiences because for a variety of reasons, including emotional and economic ties, they were not in a position to leave. Thus, rather than leave the relationship, they redefined their experiences in ways that were acceptable to them and developed elaborate coping strategies allowing them to survive from day to day. However, eventually all of these women reached a point where they were unable to cope with the violence any longer and ended their relationships.

CHAPTER 4

Robbery

Every individual can relate to skirmishes with friends or family members in which they wrestled the television remote control or the last Eggo waffle away from his or her wanton adversary. If you are coming up short on material, embark on an afternoon visit to your local playground or daycare center and you are sure to find dozens of examples of children using force to gain exclusive rights to their favorite toy. These are mundane and seemingly harmless instances of people using force to get what they want. This chapter considers the most extreme manifestations of forcible taking, thefts that often involve weapons and produce serious bodily harm.

ROBBERY DEFINED

According to the Model Penal Code (American Law Institute, 1962), an individual is guilty of **robbery** when he or she inflicts or threatens to inflict serious bodily injury upon another while in the course of committing a theft. The legal notion of what constitutes "in the course of committing a theft" includes those behaviors associated with the individual's attempt to take the item as well as the flight (escape) efforts that follow. In addition, most jurisdictions specify that the assailant need not be armed with a weapon. Any aggressive action on top of the minimal effort required to extract and carry the targeted item away is generally enough to satisfy the force requirement of the robbery statute.

Robbery poses a quandary for scholars who prefer to classify crimes as either violent, property, or public order offenses. A robbery is not a simple theft, nor is it a simple act of interpersonal violence. Instead, a robber combines elements of property theft and violence into a single criminal transaction. This prompts some to treat robbery as a unique conceptual entity—Samaha (1999, p. 496) prefers the term **aggravated property crime.** On a more practical level, the unpredictable and multifaceted nature of the crime means that a given offense may allow for criminal justice authorities to pursue multiple charges against a single perpetrator—it is not uncommon for perpetrators to have charges of theft, fraud, assault, possession of stolen property, burglary, and/or weapons possession stacked on top of a robbery rap.

ROBBERY TRENDS

The NCVS treats robbery as a form of violent crime. An estimated 630,690 attempted or completed robberies occurred in the United States in 2001. This figure represents 11% of the total number of violent offenses that year (second only to assault). This translates into a victimization rate of 2.8 robberies per 1,000 persons or households (NCVS, 2003).

Police are never made aware of a considerable portion of the robberies that occur each year. Data from the 2001 NCVS indicate that roughly 40% of robbery victims choose not to notify law enforcement authorities. According to the Uniform Crime Reports (FBI, 2002), the police were made aware of 422,921 robberies in 2001. This translates into a known offense rate of 148.5 robberies per 100,000 persons (or roughly 1.5 per 1,000).

Considerable physical, emotional, and financial losses stem from robberies. Simon, Mercy, and Perkins (2001) analyzed victimization data from 1992 through 1998 to assess the extent of physical injuries that are generated through violent crime incidents. Nearly one-third of the robberies (almost 350,000 annually) were shown to produce some form of injury. Of these injuries, 81% were described as minor (i.e., bruises, cuts, scratches) while 19% were deemed severe (i.e., flesh wound, broken bones, loss of consciousness, internal bleeding). More than one-half (52.7%) of the injuries required medical treatment and one in four resulted in an emergency room visit. Surveys of our nation's hospitals reveal that emergency room personnel administer care to well over 20,000 robbery victims annually (Rand, 1997).

The financial costs of robbery are also sizable. The FBI (2002) states that $532 million in property losses were produced by the more than 400,000 robberies that were investigated by police in 2001. This translates to an average dollar loss per incident of $1,258. Given the large numbers of robberies that go unreported to police, one can reasonably assume that somewhere in the neighborhood of $1 billion in property is lost to robbery offenders each year.

Figure 4.1 offers a graphic representation of robbery victimization rates over the final quarter of the twentieth century. The good news is that we have realized

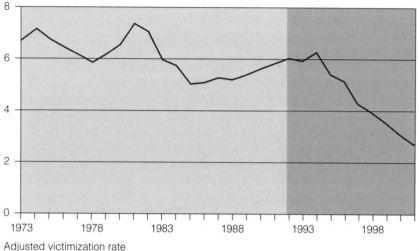

Adjusted victimization rate
per 1,000 persons age 12 and over

Figure 4.1 Robbery rates

Source: http://www.ojp.usdoj.gov/bjs/

a 50% reduction in robbery rates during that period (a rate of 2.8 in 2001 compared to 6.7 in 1973). The bad news is that these advances did not come
overnight or without periods of instability. Most notably, robbery victimization
rates reached an all-time high of 7.4 per 1,000 persons or households in 1981.

Robbery victimization rates are traditionally higher in the western and
southern regions of the United States. In 2001, victimization rates in the Midwest and Northeast (2.1 and 2.7, respectively) were noticeably lower than in
the West and South (3.1 and 3.0 per 1,000, respectively). Recent UCR data
suggest that law enforcement officers in the District of Columbia, Maryland,
New York, Nevada, and Illinois are most burdened by robbery calls. Conversely,
Vermont, North Dakota, Wyoming, Montana, and South Dakota weigh in at
the bottom of the UCR's 1999 state-level rankings (FBI, 2000).

As is the case with all forms of violent crime, increased population density
yields significantly higher robbery victimization rates. City dwellers experienced a robbery victimization rate of 4.9 per 1,000 persons or households in
2001. This compares to reported rates of 2.2 in suburban areas and 1.4 in rural
locales (NCVS, 2003). Of our major cities, the FBI lists Atlanta (990.1),
Newark (906.3), and Miami (823.7) as having the highest robbery rates. At the
other end of the spectrum, the 1999 UCR identifies San Jose (82.9), Mesa
(100.4), and El Paso (114.6) as having major cities with the lowest robbery rates
(Maguire and Pastore, 2001).

U.S. robbery rates tend to exceed those experienced in other developed
nations. Our 1998 official robbery rate was 165.4 per 100,000 persons. This
was surpassed only by Spain which posted a rate of 168.9 that year. Significantly lower robbery rates were experienced in France (144.1), England and

Wales (128.5), Australia (127.6), Canada (95.6), Germany (78.5), Israel (28.5), and Japan (2.7) (Interpol, 1999).

THE "ARMED" ROBBER

Robbery is a classic example of an unskilled crime where the offender enlists fear and intimidation tactics to achieve his or her goals. As the familiar heading of this section indicates, weaponry and robbery often go hand in hand—roughly half of all robbery victims recently claimed that their assailant was armed: 29.9% of attackers were said to carry a gun, 13.6% a knife or sharp object, and 4.6% relied on a blunt object (i.e., club, pipe, baseball bat). At the same time, almost four in every ten attacks took the form of "strong arm robberies" in which the offender relied only on the threat or use of brute force (NCVS, 2003).

Alternative sources of data suggest that the numbers of gun-toting robbers may be significantly higher. Take for example the 2001 UCR data: A full 42% of the robberies that police investigated that year were found to involve some sort of firearm. Similarly, a survey of state prison inmates (Beck et al., 1993) found that 36% of robbery offenders commit their offenses while carrying a firearm. Luckily, less than 10% of the inmate sample reported firing shots. In 2000, the FBI estimated a robbery-by-firearm rate of 59.5 per 100,000 (FBI, 2000).

Gun control advocates often attribute our high robbery rates to this country's fascination with firearms. Zawitz (1995) reports that an estimated 223 million firearms were circulating throughout the United States in 1994. Add to that roughly 4 million new firearms that are purchased each year and another 300,000 or so that get reported stolen, and it becomes abundantly clear that there are plenty of guns to go around. Some have argued that rigorous gun control measures would significantly reduce our robbery rates. This suggestion prompted criminologists Gary Kleck and Karen McElrath (1991) to conduct an in-depth analysis into the relationship between weapons and violent crime. They found that injuries occurred far less frequently in robberies involving a gun than they did when a knife, club, or no weapon was present. As the perceived lethality of the situation decreased (i.e., knives were less threatening than guns), robbery victims exhibited a greater willingness to resist or challenge their attackers. Both good news and bad news flow from these findings. Resisting seems to increases the chances that the victim will remain in control of his or her valuables. However, this course of action increases the likelihood that the attacker will turn to a weapon of choice as an equalizer. In the case of a gun, this generally results in dire consequences for the victim.

THE ROBBERY TRANSACTION

Most other violent transactions (i.e., murder, assault, and rape) take shape as one-on-one conflicts between known acquaintances. This is not generally the case with robbery. *The vast majority of robbery offenders and victims have no prior relationship.* More than 75% of robbery victims describe their attackers as strangers. Men, African Americans, and the elderly are almost never attacked by known assailants. Furthermore, unlike other violent crimes, only 5% of all robberies occur between individuals who are related to one another by blood or marriage (NCVS, 2003).

Almost all robbery transactions involve a lone victim; however, it is not uncommon for multiple perpetrators to join in the attack. Victim reports reveal that 94.5% of the persons who were robbed in 2001 were alone at the time of the attack. The offender dynamic is somewhat different. In 2001, 42.8% of all robbery victims claimed that they were attacked by multiple assailants. No other form of violent crime experiences this level of group offending (NCVS, 2003).

A number of observations can be made about the setting of the average robbery event. One, robberies are equally distributed across daytime and nighttime hours. Two, victim reports suggest that robberies take place in a variety of locales; about half of the robbery victimizations take place in open-air venues (e.g., in streets, parks) and another 30% take place at or near the victim's home (NCVS, 2003). Keep in mind that the NCVS data focus largely on personal victimizations. Those offenders who target commercial establishments are largely omitted from these data. Fortunately, the FBI's Uniform Crime Reports solicits information on the robbery setting. While these data show that public streets remain the favorite setting for robbery (a little less than 50% of known cases), commercial and/or financial establishments are targeted in roughly 25% of the cases, and private residences comprise another 13% of the cases. Given the risks and complexities that go along with pulling off a robbing in an institutional setting, one might expect that robbers would target the most lucrative businesses. This is not the case. Only a small fraction of these robberies occur at banking establishments (average yield in 2001 = $4,587) while a surprising majority transpire in "low budget" convenience stores (average yield in 2001 = $618).

The participants in the robbery transaction are disproportionately young, black men. In 2001, individuals between the ages of 12 and 24 experienced a robbery victimization rate that exceeded five per 1,000 persons or households. That victimization rate was roughly double the one for persons between the ages of 25 and 49 and nearly five times the rate for persons 50 years or older. A similar age pattern emerges among the offender population. Roughly three in ten robbery victims estimate that their attacker(s) were under the age of 20 and an estimated six in ten claim that they were attacked by a person(s) under the age of 30 (NCVS, 2003). These data indicate that robbery is an intra-aged crime.

The majority of robbery victims and offenders are men. Males accounted for two thirds of the robbery victims in 2001. This translated into victimization rates for men (3.8 per 1,000) that more than doubled that for women (1.7). Most robbery victims claim that they were attacked by male assailants—a man was present in 99.2% of all multiple-offender robberies and 93.9% of all single-offender robberies that occurred in 2001 (NCVS, 2003).

Clear racial disparities exist among robbery offenders and victims. The 2001 NCVS data suggest that 80% of the robbery victims were white and 16% black. A full 21% identify themselves as Hispanic. When one factors in relative representation in the U.S. population, the following robbery victimization rates emerge: 5.3 (per 1,000) for Hispanics, 3.6 for African Americans, and 2.6 for whites (NCVS, 2003). A more extreme picture emerges among the offender group. African Americans accounted for more than half (53.8%) of the robbery arrests that were reported by law enforcement authorities in 2001. This means that the robbery arrest rate for blacks is more than 6 times that of whites (FBI, 2003).

The robbery victimization rate for the average American was estimated to be 2.8 per 1,000 persons or households in 2001 (NCVS, 2003). That same year, Hispanic males experienced a victimization rate of 7.9; for black males, it was 6.4. In addition, black males between the ages of 16 and 19 were victimized at a rate of 27.6 per 1,000 persons or households.

Most robberies unfold as extremely abrupt, but unmistakably volatile exchanges. Regardless of whether the attack takes form as a street mugging or a bank robbery, it is in the offender's best interests to move quickly and purposefully. Research (Katz, 1988; Letkeman, 1973; Luckenbill, 1981; Wright and Decker, 1997) has shown that most robberies follow a set chronology of events. First, the attacker must get the victim's undivided attention and clearly state his or her intentions—eight in ten (83.1%) robbery victims report that their attackers introduced some unprovoked threat or act of force into the equation (NCVS, 2003). Katz (1988) calls this defining moment the declaration of stick-up and notes that it can take on a variety of shapes, ranging from a verbal statement to the passing of a note to a bank teller. This initiating step is forceful, direct, and seeks to place the offender in complete control of the victim's emotions and behavior. Next, the robber must go about his or her efforts to collect the desired money and/or valuables from the victim. This is clearly the most unpredictable stage of the game. Here, the attacker hopes that his or her threats and posturing will produce unwavering compliance from the victim. The available NCVS data tell us that this is seldom without complication—only one third of all robbery victims simply submit to their attackers' wishes. Once the robbery offender has successfully or unsuccessfully confiscated the victim's valuables, he or she then goes about closing out the interaction. In addition to physically fleeing the scene, Luckenbill (1981) reports that most offenders try to obscure their identity for any potential onlookers.

CRIMINAL CAREER

Robbery offenders tend to have long, pronounced criminal careers. Criminal history checks conducted by Hart and Reaves (1999) revealed that 62% of the accused robbers had a prior felony rap sheet. Nearly one in three (29%) had at least five felony arrests to his or her credit. A full 40% of the robbers in the sample had been convicted of a prior felony. Langan and Levin (2002) found that 70.2% of the released robbers in their recidivism study had been rearrested within 3 years. No other category of violent offenders lead such active criminal careers.

It is tempting to think of robbers as offense specialists (i.e., deal exclusively in robbery or similar offenses). This is not an unrealistic suggestion given that would-be thieves have a host of targets from which to choose. There are clearly enough potential persons and financial institutions to keep a person busy in a one-dimensional criminal career. Beck and Shipley's (1989) recidivism study provides some credence to the specialization hypothesis, as one in five robbers who were released from prison in 1983 had been rearrested on another robbery by 1986. However, interviews with known robbery offenders reveal the presence of a much broader criminal repertoire. As the upcoming article by Jacobs and Wright indicates, most robbers describe themselves as opportunists— persons who will pursue any course of action that is likely to yield desired ends. The drugs/crime connection serves to further solidify these individuals' commitment to a diversified criminal portfolio. A survey of state prison inmates (Beck et al., 1993) found that 27% claimed to have committed their most recent offense in an effort to get money to buy drugs. *On the whole, the available data suggest that most robbers are criminal generalists.* They are individuals who grow accustomed to a certain way of life; a life that includes fast living, heavy spending, and habitual drug use. This worldview requires offenders to seek a constant flow of cash that can be sustained only by a diversified and highly active commitment to crime.

COGNITIVE ASPECTS OF ROBBERY

Few would disagree that there are instrumental motives present in the mindset of the average robber. The most immediate goal of this type of offense is to deprive the victims of their valuables for personal consumption. Nonetheless, news reports are full of stories in which thieves expose themselves to high levels of risk in order to collect on very small sums of money. Convenience store robberies and/or the taxicab stick-ups are prime examples. *The growing presence of these high-risk, low-yield robberies has led numerous researchers to conclude that expressive motives also play an important part in the cognitive aspect of robbery* (Jacobs and Wright, 1999; Katz, 1988). For example, many robbers allege that they commit their crimes for emotional gratification or revenge. More importantly, these researchers have shown that inner-city street norms bestow a great deal of status onto individuals who are willing to live by the "survival of the fittest" credo. The concept of robbery motivation receives a full treatment in the upcoming article by Jacobs and Wright.

Many robbers commit their crimes while under the influence of drugs and/or alcohol. Nearly one in three persons robbed in 1999 had reason to believe that the assailant(s) was under the influence of drugs or alcohol at the time of the attack (NCVS, 2000). Not surprisingly, the accounts of known offenders suggest that the actual percentages may be somewhat higher. Interviews with a sample of imprisoned robbers revealed that 38% were under the influence of drugs or alcohol when they committed the violent theft that led to their incarceration (Beck et al., 1993). This impairment can limit the offenders' ability to make sound and reasoned decisions. This speaks further to the drugs/crime connection that impacts robbery.

Planning does not appear to play a large role in most robberies. As we will see in the Topalli and Wright article that appears later in this chapter, most violent thieves operate as **alert opportunists**—when in need of cash, they head out into the streets with the necessary weaponry and a behavioral script for how they would like to see the robbery event unfold. At the same time, they may have learned from past experience that most robberies are unpredictable, and thus view meticulous planning as a waste of time (Katz, 1988).

Interviews with habitual robbers reveal that even the most seasoned thieves feel a need to invoke some sort of normative neutralization to help set themselves and others at ease about their behavior (Feeney, 1986; Katz, 1988; Miller, 1998; Sommers and Baskin, 1993; Wright and Decker, 1997). These conversations show that robbers often blame the victim, claiming that the naive fool had it coming. Others adopt a "survival of the fittest" mentality, asserting that they are simply doing what must be done to get by in life. Still others speak of a "natural order on the streets," in which robbery is just another way of making a living. Regardless of the content, the message is clear: Robbers negotiate their identities like any other person.

CULTURAL COMPONENTS OF ROBBERY

Very few robbers operate in a lonerlike capacity. Instead, they interact with other members of the criminal element, rubbing shoulders, jointly partaking in illicit underground markets (e.g., drugs, stolen property systems), and exchanging communications. *This attachment to a criminal subculture means that many robbers operate in a colleague-like fashion* (Best and Luckenbill, 1994). The same cannot be said about those robbers who work in groups. These individuals internalize the "safety in numbers" motto and choose to gang up on their prey. More often that not, conspirators rely on a loose network of fellow thieves, switching on and off between collaborators as theft opportunities present themselves. *In this regard, the social organization of most conspiratorial robbers is best described as peerlike*—they do not get too cozy with one another but are willing to work together to achieve a mutually beneficial end (Best and Luckenbill, 1994). There is, however, a select minority of the offender population that interact in a much more stable and collaborative capacity. Movies such as *Heat* or *Point Break* depict robbery crews that forge long-term criminal associations with a clear set of roles and a well-defined division of labor. McCluskey and Wardle (1999) as well as Letkeman (1973) have shown that a teamlike social organization exists among some robbery specialists, particularly bank robbers.

Those robbers who are active participants in the criminal subculture (i.e., colleagues, peers, and teams) are provided ample opportunity to draw upon a host of socialization scripts that serve to shape and advance their criminal agenda. For example, the upcoming Jacobs and Wright article will outline the conduct norms of the street culture and then demonstrate how implicit and explicit messages serve to reinforce robbery as an acceptable means of survival. Katz (1988, p. 80) observes that street thugs are not explicitly tutored in "the ways of the badass," but rather come to internalize these norms and behaviors through imitation and street-level informal interactions.

SOCIETAL REACTION TO ROBBERY

Robbery generally receives a firm formal response from the criminal justice system. The Model Penal Code (American Law Institute, 1962) classifies robbery as a second degree felony. If convicted, the perpetrator shall be sentenced to 1 to 10 years in prison. When the offender threatens or achieves "serious bodily harm," he or she is likely to see the charge elevated to a first degree felony. In most jurisdictions, an armed robbery, especially one involving a firearm, will result in this more severe statutory designation. A person charged with a first degree felony faces anywhere from 1 year to life in prison.

A robber must first be apprehended before facing these stiff penalties. *Unfortunately, most offenders get away with their crimes.* In 2001, law enforcement authorities reported a meager 24.9% clearance rate for the crime of robbery (FBI, 2002). That means that roughly 75% of all robberies that are reported to police go unsolved. The 2001 Uniform Crime Reports reveal that law enforcement authorities made 108,400 robbery arrests that year, which translates into a per capita arrest rate of 39.8 per 100,000 persons (FBI, 2002).

When called upon to hear robbery cases, our nation's court system responds with considerable care. Hart and Reaves (1999) determined that robbery cases comprised 7% of the total court dockets that they studied. They found that the vast majority of the accused robbery offenders (87%) were offered some sort of pretrial release option (e.g., bail), with the median bail amount observed at $25,000. Despite these release options, only 39% of robbery defendants were able to gain release prior to the final disposition of their case. Of those released, roughly one third (34%) violated the conditions of their release order and 22% were rearrested before their original case could be resolved. This is particularly disturbing when one considers that two thirds of the cases were resolved in less than 6 months.

A review of the available adjudication data suggest that courts follow through a relatively hardline stance toward robbery offenders. Hart and Reaves (1999) found that 70% of the robbery defendants in their sample were eventually convicted. A full 90% of convicted robbers face some sort of incarceration. While the median sentence was 5 years, nearly one in five were sentenced to more than 10 years in prison. Among all felony offenses, only murder and rape experience higher felony conviction rates and/or longer median sentences (Hart and Reaves, 1999). Levin et al. (1999) report that, on average, an imprisoned robber can expect to serve a little less than one half of his or her sentence behind bars before being paroled.

It appears that informal social control plays a large part in the dynamics of robbery. Interviews with known offenders reveal that many stick-up artists specifically target other members of the criminal underworld. Some are even targeted for repeat victimization (Gill and Pease, 1998). These can include drug dealers (i.e., drug robbery), pimps, prostitutes, or the run-of-the-mill street thug. These persons tend to have money or valuables (i.e., cars, clothes, jewelry, drugs) in their possession and, more importantly, are not inclined to report their victimizations to the police. This sets the stage for "street justice" or vigilantism. As we will see in the upcoming article by Topalli and Wright, a single robbery victimization can set in motion a **contagion of violence** in which escalating vendetta cycles get played out over extended periods of time. The origin of these cycles of violence go largely undetected by police and usually spill over to other community members (Jacobs, Topalli, and Wright, 2000).

KEY TERMS

aggravated property crime   contagion of violence

alert opportunism   robbery

DISCUSSION QUESTIONS

1. What kind of realistic policy initiatives can be undertaken to help sever the pronounced relationship between robbery and the illicit drug market?

2. Despite the violent nature of the crimes, at present, less than one half of all robberies get reported to police and just over one third of these reported crimes are solved by police (i.e., lead to an arrest). Why is it so difficult for police to first identify and then solve robbery cases?

3. Our courts have come to adopt a simple, yet predictable approach toward robbery cases. At present, most accused robbers can expect to be convicted of some sort of violent felony and then be sentenced to considerable time behind bars. Recidivism data suggest that this long-standing approach has little impact on the person's willingness to return to violent crime once their sentence has ended. Formulate alternative strategies for the adjudication and sentencing of accused robbers that might help reduce the present recidivism rates.

9

Stick-up, Street Culture,
and Offender Motivation

BRUCE A. JACOBS
RICHARD WRIGHT
Universtiy of Missouri–St. Louis

The authors contend that much lip service has been paid to the criminal motivation, yet very little systematic understanding has emerged on the topic. This study draws upon interviews with a snowball sample of eighty-six active armed robbers in an effort to illustrate the processes and mechanisms by which an individual becomes inclined to enter into a robbery transaction. All respondents were recruited through a seasoned "street ethnographer" who specifically targeted persons who were known on the streets to be active thieves and were found to have perpetrated a robbery in the recent past. A need for money served as the primary and most immediate motivation for their crimes. However, the researchers contend that the unwritten conduct norms of the street serve as the critical secondary motivator for these habitual offenders. In short, a constant flow of cash is needed to finance a carefree lifestyle that includes new clothes, endless partying, and the never-ending ability to impress themselves and others. Over time, the cyclical pursuit of money and free spending transforms robbery into a central feature of the person's everyday life. These observations thus provide valuable insight into both the proximate (day-to-day) and distal (long-term) aspects of robbery motivation and behavior.

Motivation is the central, yet arguably the most assumed, causal variable in the etiology of criminal behavior. Obviously, persons commit crimes because they are motivated to do so, and virtually no offense can occur in the absence of motivation. Though the concept inheres implicitly or explicitly in every influential theory of crime, this is far from saying that its treatment has been comprehensive, exhaustive, or precise (but see Tittle, 1995). In many ways, motivation is criminology's dirty little secret—manifest yet murky, presupposed but elusive, everywhere and nowhere. If there is a bogeyman lurking in our discipline's theoretical shadows, motivation may well be it.

Much of the reason for this can be located in the time-honored, positivistic tradition of finding the one factor, or set of factors, that accounts for it. Causality has been called criminology's "Holy Grail" (Groves and Lynch, 1990: 360),

From Criminology, 37: 1, pp. 149–150, 154–163, 165–173. Excerpts used with permission from American Society of Criminology.

the quest for which makes other disciplinary pursuits seem tangential, sometimes inconsequential. The search typically revolves around identification of background risk factors (Katz, 1988)—behavioral correlates—that establish nonspurious relationships with criminal behavior (Groves and Lynch, 1990: 358). A panoply of such factors have been implicated over many decades of research—spanning multiple levels, as well as units, of analyses. They include, among other things, anomie, blocked opportunities, deviant self-identity, status frustration, weak social bonds, low self-control, social disorganization, structural oppression, unemployment, age, gender, class, race, deviant peer relations, marital status, body type, IQ, and personality (see e.g., Akers, 1985; Becker, 1963; Chambliss and Seidman, 1971; Cloward and Ohlin, 1960; Cohen, 1955; Cornish and Clarke, 1986; Felson, 1987; Hirschi, 1969; Merton, 1938; Miller, 1958; Quinney, 1970; Sampson and Laub, 1992; Shaw and McKay, 1942; Sutherland, 1947).

Common to all such factors, however, is their independent status from the "foreground" of criminal decision making—the immediate phenomenological context in which decisions to offend are activated (see also Groves and Lynch, 1990; Katz, 1988). Though background factors may predispose persons to crime, they fail to explain why two individuals with identical risk factor profiles do not offend equally (see e.g., Colvin and Pauly, 1983), why persons with particular risk factors go long periods of time without offending, why individuals without the implicated risk factors offend, why persons offend but not in the particular way a theory directs them to, or why persons who are not determined to commit a crime one moment become determined to do so the next (see Katz, 1988: 3–4; see also Tittle, 1995, on "theoretical precision"). Decisions to offend, like all social action, do not take place in a vacuum. Rather, they are bathed in an "ongoing process of human existence" (Bottoms and Wiles, 1992: 19) and mediated by prevailing situational and subcultural conditions.

In this article we attend to these important foreground dynamics, exploring the decision-making processes of active armed robbers in real life settings and circumstances. Our aim is to understand how and why these offenders move from an unmotivated state to one in which they are determined to commit robbery. We argue that while the decision to commit robbery stems most directly from a perceived need for fast cash, this decision is activated, mediated, and channeled by participation in street culture. Street culture, and its constituent conduct norms, represents an essential intervening variable linking criminal motivation to background risk factors and subjective foreground conditions.

MONEY, MOTIVATION, AND STREET CULTURE

Fast Cash

With few exceptions, the decision to commit a robbery arises in the face of what offenders perceive to be pressing need for fast cash (see also Conklin, 1972; Feeney, 1986; Gabor et al., 1987; Tunnell, 1992). Eighty of 81 offenders who spoke directly to the issue of motivation said that they did robberies simply because they needed money. Many lurched from one financial crisis to the next, the frequency with which they committed robbery being governed largely by the amount of money—or lack of it—in their pockets:

> [The idea of committing a robbery] comes into your mind when your pockets are low; it speaks very loudly when you need things and you are not able to get what you need. It's not a want, it's things that you need, . . . things that if you don't have the money, you have the artillery to go and get it. That's the first thing on my mind; concentrate on how I can get some more money.
>
> I don't think there is any one factor that precipitates the commission of a crime, . . . I think it's just the conditions. I think the primary factor is being without. Rent is coming up. A few months ago, the landlord was gonna put us out, rent due, you know. Can't get no money no way else; ask family and friends, you might try a few other ways of getting the money and, as a last resort, I can go get some money [by committing a robbery].

Many offenders appeared to give little thought to the offense until they found themselves unable to meet current expenses.

> [I commit a robbery] about every few months. There's no set pattern, but I guess it's really based on the need. If there is a period of time where there is no need of money . . . , then it's not necessary to go out and rob. It's not like I do [robberies] for fun.

The above claims conjure up an image of reluctant criminals doing the best they can to survive in circumstances not of their own making. In one sense, this image is not so far off the mark. Of the 59 offenders who specified a particular use for the proceeds of their crimes, 19 claimed that they needed the cash for basic necessities, such as food or shelter. For them, robbery allegedly was a matter of day-to-day survival. At the same time, the notion that these offenders were driven by conditions entirely beyond their control strains credulity. Reports of "opportunistic" robberies confirm this, that is, offenses motivated by serendipity rather than basic human need:

> If I had $5,000, I wouldn't do [a robbery] like tomorrow. But [i]f I got $5,000 today and I seen you walkin' down the street and you look like you got some money in your pocket, I'm gonna take a chance and see. It's just natural. . . . If you see an opportunity, you take that opportunity. . . . It doesn't matter if I have $5,000 in my pocket, if I see you walkin' and no one else around and it look like you done went in the store and bought somethin' and pulled some money out of your pocket and me or one of my partners has peeped this, we gonna approach you. That's just the way it goes.

Need and opportunity, however, cannot be considered outside the open ended quest for excitement and sensory stimulation that shaped much of the offenders' daily activities. Perhaps the most central of pursuits in street culture, "life as party" revolves around "the enjoyment of 'good times' with minimal concern for obligations and commitments that are external to the . . . immediate social setting" (Shover and Honaker, 1992: 283).

While the offenders often referred to such activities as partying, there is a danger in accepting their comments at face value. Many gambled, used drugs, and drank alcohol as if there were no tomorrow; they pursued these activities with an intensity and grim determination that suggested something far more serious was at stake. Illicit street action is no party, at least not in the conventional sense of the term. Offenders typically demonstrate little or no inclination to exercise personal restraint. Why should they? Instant gratification and hedonistic sensation seeking are quite functional for those seeking pleasure in what may objectively be viewed as a largely pleasureless world.

The offenders are easily seduced by life as party, at least in part because they view their future prospects as bleak and see little point in long-range planning. As such, there is no mileage to be gained by deferred gratification:

> I really don't dwell on [the future]. One day I might not wake up. I don't even think about what's important to me. What's important to me is getting mine [now].

The offenders' general lack of social stability an absence of conventional sources of support only fueled such a mindset. The majority called the streets home for extended periods of time; a significant number of offenders claimed to seldom sleep at the same address for more than a few nights in a row (see also Fleisher, 1995). Moving from place to place as the mood struck them, these offenders essentially were urban nomads in a perpetual search for good times. The volatile streets and alleyways that criss-crossed St. Louis's crime-ridden central city neighborhoods provided their conduit (see also Stein and McCall, 1994).

Keeping Up Appearances

The open-ended pursuit of sensory stimulation was but one way these offenders enacted the imperatives of street culture. No less important was the fetishized consumption of personal, nonessential, status-enhancing items. Shover and Honaker (1992: 283) have argued that the unchecked pursuit of such items—like anomic participation in illicit street action—emerges directly from conduct norms of street culture. The code of the streets (Anderson, 1990) calls for the bold display of the latest status symbol clothing and accessories, a look that loudly proclaims the wearer to be someone who has overcome, if only temporarily, the financial difficulties faced by others on the street corner (see e.g., Katz, 1988). To be seen as "with it," one must flaunt the material trappings of success. The quest is both symbolic and real; such purchases serve as self-enclosed and highly efficient referent systems that assert one's essential character (Shover, 1996) in no uncertain terms.

> You ever notice that some people want to be like other people . . . ? They might want to dress like this person, like dope dealers and stuff like that. They go out there [on the street corner] in diamond jewelry and

stuff. "Man, I wish I was like him!" You got to make some kind of money [to look like that], so you want to make a quick hustle.

The functionality of offenders' purchases was tangential, perhaps irrelevant. The overriding goal was to project an image of "cool transcendence," (Katz, 1988) that, in the minds of offenders, knighted them members of a mythic street aristocracy.

Obviously, the relentless pursuit of high living quickly becomes expensive. Offenders seldom had enough cash in their pockets to sustain this lifestyle for long. Even when they did make the occasional "big score," their disdain for long-range planning and desire to live for the moment encouraged spending with reckless abandon. That money earned illegally holds "less intrinsic value" than cash secured through legitimate work only fueled their spendthrift ways (Walters, 1990: 147). The way money is obtained, after all, is a "powerful determinant of how it is defined, husbanded, and spent" (Shover, 1996: 140). Some researchers have gone so far as to suggest that through carefree spending, persistent criminals seek to establish the very conditions that drive them back to crime (Katz, 1988). Whether offenders spend money in a deliberate attempt to create these conditions is open to question; the respondents in our sample gave no indication of doing so. No matter, offenders were under almost constant pressure to generate funds. To the extent that robbery alleviated this stress, it nurtured a tendency for them to view the offense as a reliable method for dealing with similar pressures in the future. A self-enclosed cycle of reinforcing behavior was thereby triggered (see also Lemert, 1953).

WHY ROBBERY?

The decision to commit robbery, then, is motivated by a perceived need for cash. Why does this need express itself as robbery? Presumably the offenders have other means of obtaining money. Why do they choose robbery over legal work? Why do they decide to commit robbery rather than borrow money from friends or relatives? Most important, why do they select robbery to the exclusion of other income-generating crimes?

Legal Work

That the decision to commit robbery typically emerges in the course of illicit street action suggests that legitimate employment is not a realistic solution. Typically, the offenders' need for cash is so pressing and immediate that legal work, as a viable money-making strategy, is untenable: Payment and effort are separated in space and time and these offenders will not, or cannot, wait. Moreover, the jobs realistically available to them—almost all of whom were unskilled and poorly educated—pay wages that fall far short of the funds required to support a cash-intensive lifestyle:

> Education-wise, I fell late on the education. I just think it's too late for that. They say it's never too late, but I'm too far gone for that . . . I've thought about [getting a job], but I'm too far gone I guess . . . I done seen more money come out of [doing stick-ups] than I see working.

Legitimate employment also was perceived to be overly restrictive. Working a normal job requires one to take orders, conform to a schedule, minimize informal peer interaction, show up sober and alert, and limit one's freedom of movement for a given period of time.

The "conspicuous display of independence" is a bedrock value on which street-corner culture rests (Shover and Honaker, 1992: 284): To be seen as cool one must do as one pleases. This ethos clearly conflicts with the demands of legitimate employment. Indeed, robbery appealed to a number of offenders precisely because it allowed them to flaunt their independence and escape from the rigors of legal work.

This is not to say that every offender summarily dismissed the prospect of gainful employment. Twenty-five of the 75 unemployed respondents claimed they would stop robbing if someone gave them a "good job"—the emphasis being on good:

> My desire is to be gainfully employed in the right kind of job . . . If I had a union job making $16 or $17 [an hour], something that I could really take care of my family with, I think that I could become cool with that. Years ago I worked at one of the [local] car factories; I really wanted to be in there. It was the kind of job I'd been looking for. Unfortunately, as soon as I got in there they had a big layoff.

Others alleged that, while a job may not eliminate their offending altogether, it might well slow them down:

> [If a job were to stop me from committing robberies], it would have to be a straight up good paying job. I ain't talkin' about no $6 an hour . . . I'm talkin' like $10 to $11 an hour, something like that. But as far as $5 or $6 an hour, no! I would have to get like $10 or $11 an hour, full-time. Now something like that, I would probably quit doing it [robbery]. I would be working, making money, I don't think I would do it [robbery] no more . . . I don't think I would quit [offending] altogether. It would probably slow down and then eventually I'll stop. I think [my offending] would slow down.

Even if the offenders were able to land a high-paying job, it is doubtful they would keep it for long. The relentless pursuit of street action—especially hard drug use—has a powerful tendency to undermine any commitment to conventional activities (Shover and Honaker, 1992). Life as party ensnares street-culture participants, enticing them to neglect the demands of legitimate employment in favor of enjoying the moment. Though functional in lightening the burdensome present, gambling, drinking, and drugging—for those on the street—become the proverbial "padlock on the exit door" (Davis, 1995) and fertilize the foreground in which the decision to rob becomes rooted.

Borrowing

In theory, the offenders could have borrowed cash from a friend or relative rather than resorting to crime. In practice, this was not feasible. Unemployed, unskilled, and uneducated persons caught in the throes of chronically self-defeating behavior cannot, and often do not, expect to solve their fiscal troubles by borrowing. Borrowing is a short-term solution, and loans granted must be repaid. This in itself could trigger robberies. As one offender explained, "I have people that will loan me money, [but] they will loan me money because of the work [robbery] that I do; they know they gonna get their money [back] one way or another." Asking for money also was perceived by a number of offenders to be emasculating. Given their belief that men should be self-sufficient, the mere prospect of borrowing was repugnant:

> I don't like always asking my girl for nothing because I want to let her
> keep her own money . . . I'm gonna go out here and get some money.

The possibility of borrowing may be moot for the vast majority of offenders anyway. Most had long ago exhausted the patience and goodwill of helpful others; not even their closest friends or family members were willing to proffer additional cash:

> I can't borrow the money. Who gonna loan me some money? Ain't
> nobody gonna loan me no money. Shit, [I use] drugs and they know [that]
> and I rob and everything else. Ain't nobody gonna loan me no money. If
> they give you some money, they just give it to you; they know you ain't
> giving it back.

When confronted with an immediate need for money, then, the offenders perceived themselves as having little hope of securing cash quickly and legally. But this does not explain why the respondents decided to do robbery rather than some other crime. Most of them had committed a wide range of income-generating offenses in the past, and some continued to be quite versatile. Why, then, robbery?

For many, this question was irrelevant; robbery was their "main line" and alternative crimes were not considered when the pressing need for cash arose:

> I have never been able to steal, even when I was little and they would
> tell me just to be the watch-out man . . . Shit, I watch out,
> everybody gets busted. I can't steal, but give me a pistol and I'll go get
> some money. . . . [Robbery is] just something I just got attached to.

Some of the offenders who favored robbery over other crimes maintained that it was safer than burglary or dope dealing:

> I feel more safer doing a robbery because doing a burglary, I got a fear of
> breaking into somebody's house not knowing who might be up in there.
> I got that fear about house burglary . . . On robbery I can select my
> victims, I can select my place of business. I can watch and see who all

work in there or I can rob a person and pull them around in the alley or push them up in a doorway and rob them. You don't got [that] fear of who . . . in that bedroom or somewhere in another part of the house.

A couple of offenders reported steering clear of dope selling because their strong craving for drugs made it too difficult for them to resist their own merchandise. Being one's own best customer is a sure formula for disaster (Waldorf, 1993), something the following respondent seemed to understand well:

A dope fiend can't be selling dope because he be his best customer. I couldn't sell dope [nowadays]. I could sell a little weed or something cause I don't smoke too much of it. But selling rock [cocaine] or heroin, I couldn't do that cause I mess around and smoke it myself. [I would] smoke it all up!

Without doubt, some of the offenders were prepared to commit crimes other than robbery; in dire straits one cannot afford to be choosy. More often than not, robbery emerged as the "most proximate and performable" (Lofland, 1969: 61) offense available. The universe of money-making crimes from which these offenders realistically could pick was limited. By and large, they did not hold jobs that would allow them to violate even a low-level position of financial trust. Nor did they possess the technical know-how to commit lucrative commercial break-ins, or the interpersonal skills needed to perpetrate successful frauds. Even street-corner dope dealing was unavailable to many; most lacked the financial wherewithal to purchase baseline inventories—inventories many offenders would undoubtedly have smoked up.

The bottom line is that the offenders, when faced with a pressing need for cash, tend to resort to robbery because they know of no other course of action, legal or illegal, that offers as quick and easy a way out of their financial difficulties.

DISCUSSION

The overall picture that emerges from our research is that of offenders caught up in a cycle of expensive, self-indulgent habits (e.g., gambling, drug use, and heavy drinking) that feed on themselves and constantly call for more of the same (Lemert, 1953). It would be a mistake to conclude that these offenders are being driven to crime by genuine financial hardship; few of them are doing robberies to buy the proverbial loaf of bread to feed their children. Yet, most of their crimes are economically motivated. The offenders perceive themselves as needing money and robbery is a response to that perception.

Though background risk factors, such as pressing financial need, predispose persons to criminality, they fail to provide comprehensive, precise, and deep explanations of the situational pushes, urges, and impulses that energize actual criminal conduct (Tittle, 1995). Nor do such factors identify the "necessary and sufficient" conditions for criminal motivation to eventuate in criminal behavior. Focusing on the foreground attends to these problems. A foreground analytic approach identifies the immediate, situational factors that catalyze criminal motivation and transforms offenders from an indifferent state to one in which they are determined to commit crime.

Although the streets were a prime focus of much early criminological work, the strong influence of street culture on offender motivation has largely been overlooked since (but see Baron and Hartnagel, 1997; Fleisher, 1995; Hagan and McCarthy, 1992, 1997). Below, we attempt a conceptual refocusing by exploring the criminogenic influence of street culture and its constituent conduct norms on offender decision making (see also Hagan and McCarthy, 1997). In doing so, we do not wish to make a Katzian attempt to "outgun positivism" with a sensually deterministic portrait of crime (see Groves and Lynch, 1990: 366). Our goal rather is to highlight the explanatory power and conceptual efficiency of street culture participation as a mediating foreground factor in the etiology of armed robbery.

Street culture subsumes a number of powerful conduct norms, including but not limited to, the hedonistic pursuit of sensory stimulation, disdain for conventional living, lack of future orientation, and persistent eschewal of responsibility (see Fleisher, 1995: 213–214). Street culture puts tremendous emphasis on virtues of spontaneity; it dismisses "rationality and long-range planning . . . in favor of enjoying the moment" (Shover and Honaker, 1992: 283). Offenders typically live life as if there is no tomorrow, confident that tomorrow will somehow take care of itself. On the streets, "every night is a Saturday night" (Hodgson, 1997), and the self-indulgent pursuit of trendy consumerism and open-ended street action becomes a means to this end.

The pursuit of fast living is more than symbolic or dramaturgical, it cuts to the very core of offenders' perceptions of self-identity. To be cool, hip, and "in," one must constantly prove it through conspicuous outlays of cash. The fetishized world of street-corner capitalism dictates that fiscal responsibility be jettisoned and money burned on material objects and illicit action that assert in no uncertain terms one's place in the street hierarchy. Carefree spending creates the "impression of affluence" (Wright and Decker, 1994: 44) by which offenders are judged; it serves to demonstrate that they have indeed "made it"—at least for the time. On the streets, the image one projects is not everything, it is the only thing (see Anderson, 1990). To not buy into such an approach is to abandon a source of recognition offenders can get nowhere else (see Liebow, 1967) or, worse, to stare failure full in the face. It is not hard to fathom why many offenders in our sample regarded a lack of funds as an immediate threat to their social standing.

The problem becomes one of sustenance; the reputational advantages of cash-intensive living can be appreciated and enjoyed to their fullest "only if participants moderate their involvement in it" (Shover and Honaker, 1992: 286). This requires intermittent and disciplined spending, an anomalous and ultimately untenable proposition. Offenders effectively become ensnared by their own self-indulgent habit—habits that feed on themselves and constantly call for more of

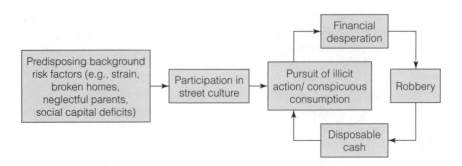

Figure 4.2   Etiological Cycle of Robbery

the same (Lemert, 1953; Shover, 1996). These habits are expensive and create a pressing and pervasive need for cash—a need remedied through robbery but only temporarily, since the proceeds of any given robbery merely "enable" more action (Shover, 1996). The seductive attractions of street life appear to take on a powerful logic of their own (Hagan and McCarthy, 1997); offenders burn money only to create (albeit inadvertently) the conditions that spark their next decision to rob. This self-enclosed cycle of reinforcing behavior (see also Lemart, 1953) is depicted schematically in Figure 4.2. Predisposing background risk factors also are represented (see Hagan and McCarthy, 1997, for a comprehensive discussion of these factors as they relate to street-culture participation).

As much as these offenders sought liberation through the hedonistic, open-ended pursuit of sensory stimulation, such a quest ultimately is both self-defeating and subordinating. Those hooked on street action may never see it this way, but objective assessments of reality are difficult to render when rationality is as severely bounded (Walsh, 1986) as it is here. Suffice it to say that, for those in our sample, the "choice" to rob occurs in a context in which rationality not only is sharply bounded, it barely exists. If one takes the influence of context seriously, most offenders "decide" to commit robbery in a social and psychological terrain bereft of realistic alternatives (Shover, 1996). Street-culture participation effectively obliterates, or at least severely circumscribes, the range of objectively available options, so much so as to be almost deterministic. Offenders typically are overwhelmed by their own predicament—emotional, financial, pharmacological, and otherwise—and see robbery as the only way out. Chronic isolation from conventional others and lifestyles only reinforces their insularity (Baron and Hartnagel, 1997: 413–414), driving them deeper and deeper into a "downward life trajectory" of ever-increasing criminal embeddedness (see Hagan and McCarthy, 1997; see also Ekland-Olson et al., 1984, on "role engulfment").

Being a street robber is more than a series of offenses that allow one to meet some arbitrarily specified inclusion criteria: it is a way of behaving, a way of thinking, an approach to life (see e.g., Fleisher, 1995: 253). Stopping such criminals exogenously—in the absence of lengthy incapacitation—is not likely to be successful. Getting offenders to "go straight" is analogous to telling a lawful citizen to "relinquish his history, companions, thoughts, feelings, and fears, and replace them with [something] else" (Fleisher, 1995:240). Self-directed going-straight talk on the part of offenders more often than not is insincere—akin to young children talking about what they're going to be when they grow up: "Young storytellers and . . . criminals . . . don't care about the [reality]; the pleasure comes in saying the words, the verbal ritual itself brings pleasure" (Fleisher, 1995: 259). Gifting offenders money, in the hopes they will reduce or stop their offending (Farrington, 1993), is similarly misguided. It is but twisted enabling and only likely to set off another round of illicit action that plunges offenders deeper into the abyss of desperation that drives them back to their next crime.

10

Dubs and Dees, Beats and Rims: Carjackers and Urban Violence

VOLKAN TOPALLI

Georgia State University

RICHARD WRIGHT

University of Missouri–St. Louis

Carjacking is defined as the theft of an automobile by force or threat of force. Despite its growing reputation, little is known about the thoughts and behaviors of persons who turn to this hybrid form of violent crime. To this end, the authors draw upon interviews with twenty-eight active offenders to illustrate how they engage in the planning, enactment, and aftermath of carjacking events. Offenders are described as opportunists who rely on carjacking as a source of reputation enhancement and income. The data show that stolen cars are sometimes used for short-term transportation but eventually get converted to cash through the use of a third party (i.e., chop shops) or by personally selling off in-demand accessories (i.e., rims, stereo components) on the street. A variety of internal and external pressures are shown to shape carjacking motivations. Offenders may choose to engage in the crime in response to peer pressure, boredom, or a perceived need for money, drugs, or transportation. The authors use the term "alert opportunism" to refer to those thefts in

Unpublished paper prepared especially for this reader. Reprinted with permission.

which the offenders do not actively seek to steal a car but rather take advantage of a soft target. Conversely, the term "motivated opportunism" is used to describe a predatory state in which the offender actively seeks out potential targets. These findings demonstrate a loose rationality behind carjacking, one that is fueled by an ongoing need for cash and status, and leads to a number of patterned behaviors.

With the exception of homicide, probably no offense is more symbolic of contemporary urban violence than carjacking. Carjacking, the taking of a motor vehicle by force or threat of force, has attained almost mythical status in the annals of urban violence and has played an undeniable role in fueling the fear of crime that keeps urban residents off of their own streets. What is more, carjacking has increased dramatically in recent years. According to a recent study (BJS 1999), an average of 49,000 carjackings were attempted each year between 1992–96, with about half of those attempts being successful. This is up from an average of 35,000 attempted and completed carjacking between 1987–92—a 40 percent increase.

Although carjacking has been practiced for decades, the offense first made national headlines in 1992 when a badly botched carjacking in suburban Washington, D.C., ended in homicide. Pamela Basu was dropping her 22 month old daughter at pre-school when two men commandeered her BMW at a stop sign. In full view of neighborhood residents, municipal workers, and a school bus driver, the two men tossed her daughter (still strapped to her car seat) from the vehicle and attempted to drive off with Basu's arm tangled in the car seat belt. She was dragged over a mile to her death. This incident focused a nationwide spotlight on carjacking and legislative action soon followed with the passing of the Anti Car Theft Act of 1992. Carjacking was made a federal crime punishable by up to a 25-year term in prison or—if the victim is killed—by death.

Like other forms of robbery, carjacking bridges property and violent crimes. Although a manifestly violent activity, it appears often to retain elements of planning and calculation typically associated with instrumental property crimes such as burglary. Unlike most robberies, however, carjacking apparently is directed at an object rather than a subject.

Most of the research on carjackings is based on official police reports or large pre-existing data sets such as the National Crime Victimization Survey. From this research, we know that carjackings are highly concentrated in space and time, occurring in limited areas and at particular hours (Friday and Wellford, 1994). These studies also indicate that carjackers tend to target individuals comparable to themselves across demographic characteristics such as race, gender, and age (Friday and Wellford, 1994; Armstrong, 1994). We know that weapons are used in 66–78 percent of carjackings, and that weapon usage increases the chance that an offense will be successful (BJS 1999; Donahue, McLaughlin, and Damm, 1994; Fisher, 1995; Rand, 1994). Finally, these studies suggest that carjacking is often a violent offense; approximately 24–38 percent of victims are injured during carjacking (BJS 1999; Fisher, 1995; Rand, 1994).

Despite these studies, much about carjacking remains poorly understood. By their very large-scale nature, such studies are incapable of providing insight into the interaction between motivational and situational characteristics that govern carjacking at the individual level. What is more, they overrepresent incidents in which the offenders and victims are strangers. Recent literature on the nature of acquaintance robbery (e.g., Felson, Baumer, and Messner, in press) and drug robbery (see Jacobs, Topalli, and Wright, 2000; Topalli, Wright, and Fornango, 2002) suggests that this limitation may represent a crucial gap in our understanding of the social and perceptual dynamics associated with carjacking. If, for example, offenders target victims who they know or "know of," the chance of serious injury or death may increase because within-offense resistance and post-offense retaliation both are more likely.

We conducted a field-based study of active carjackers, focusing on the situational and interactional factors (opportunities, risks, rewards) that carjackers take into account when contemplating and carrying out their crimes. Drawing on a tried and tested research strategy (Jacobs, Topalli, and Wright, 2000; Jacobs, 1999; Wright and Decker, 1994, 1997), we recruited 28 active offenders (with three asked back to participate in follow-ups) from the streets of St. Louis, Missouri, and interviewed them at length about their day-to-day activities, focusing on the motivations, planning, execution, and aftermath of carjackings. This methodological strategy allowed us to examine the perceptual links between offenders' lifestyles and the immediate situational context in which decisions to offend emerge, illuminating the contextual uses that mediate the carjacking decision. Interviews focused on two broad issues: (1) motivation to carjack and vehicle/victim target selection, and (2) aftermath of carjacking offenses (including vehicle disposal, formal and informal sanction risk management, use of cash, etc.). The issue of how carjacking occurs (i.e., offense enactment) is covered across the discussion of these two broader themes, because enactment represents a behavioral bridge that unites them. Thus, the procedural characteristics of carjacking naturally emanated from discourse regarding motivation, target selection, and aftermath.

MOTIVATION AND TARGET SELECTION

In the area of motivation, our interviews focused on the situational and interactional factors that underlie the decision to commit a carjacking, and the transition from unmotivated states to those in which offenses are being contemplated. On its face carjacking seems risky. Why risk a personal confrontation with the vehicle owner when one could steal a parked car off the street? Respondents felt that car theft was more dangerous because they never knew if the vehicle's owner or law enforcement might surprise them.

> **Low-Down:** I done did that a couple of times too, but that ain't nothing I really want to do 'cause I might get in a car [parked on] the street and the motherfucker [the owner of the vehicle] might be sitting

there and then it [might not] be running [any] ways. I done got caught like that before, got locked up, so I don't do that no more. I can't risk no motherfucking life just to get into a car and then the car don't start. That's a waste of time. I would rather catch somebody at a light [or] a restaurant drive-thru or something like that.

Throughout the interviews, two global factors emerged as governing motivation, planning, and target selection: the nature of a given carjacking *opportunity* (that is, its potential risks and rewards) and the level of *situational inducements* (such as peer pressure, need for cash or drugs, or revenge). When these factors, in some combination, reached a critical minimal level, the decision to carjack became certain.

INTERNAL AND EXTERNAL PRESSURES: SITUATIONAL INDUCEMENTS AND CARJACKING

Many of the offenders we spoke to indicated that their carjackings were guided by the power of immediate situational inducements. Such inducements could be internal (e.g., money, drugs, the avoidance of drug withdrawal, need to display a certain status level, desire for revenge, jealousy) or external (objective or subjective strains, such as pressure from family members to put food on the table, the need to have a vehicle for use in a subsequent crime). Situational inducements could be intensely compelling, pressing offenders to engage in carjacking even under unfavorable circumstances, where the risk of arrest, injury, or death was high or the potential reward was low. Here, the individuals' increased desperation caused them to target a vehicle or victim they would not otherwise consider (such as a substandard car, or one occupied by several passengers), initiate an offense at a time or location that was inherently more hazardous (e.g., day-time, at a busy intersection), or attempt a carjacking with no planning whatsoever.

Internal situational inducements usually were linked to the immediate need for cash. Most street offenders (including carjackers) are notoriously poor planners. They lead cash-intensive lifestyles in which money is spent as quickly as it is obtained (due to routine drug use, street gambling, acquisition of the latest fashions, heavy partying; see e.g., Jacobs, 1999; Wright and Decker, 1994, 1997; Shover, 1996). As a result, they rapidly run out of money, creating pressing fiscal crises, which then produce other internal situational inducements such as the need to feed oneself or to avoid drug withdrawal.

The sale of stolen vehicles and parts can be a lucrative endeavor. Experienced carjackers sometimes stripped the vehicles themselves (in an abandoned alley or remote lot) and sold the items on the street corner or delivered them to a chop shop owner with whom they had a working relationship. Of particular value were "portable" after-market items, such as gold or silver plated rims, hub caps, and expensive stereo components. Across our 28 respondents, profits from carjacking per offense ranged anywhere from $200 to $5,000, with the average running at $1,750. The cash obtained from carjacking served to alleviate ever emergent financial needs.

Little Rag, a diminutive teen-aged gang-banger, indicated that without cash the prospect of heroin withdrawal loomed ahead.

INT: So, why did you do that? Why did you jack that car?

Little Rag: For real? 'Cause it's the high, it's the way I live. I was broke. I was fiending [needed drugs]. I had to get off my scene real quick [wanted to get back on my feet]. I sold crack but I'd fallen off [ran out of money] and I had to go and get another lick [tempting crime target] or something to get back on the top. I blow it on weed, clothes, shoes, shit like that. Yeah, I truly fuck money up.

The need for drugs was a frequent topic in our discussions with carjackers. Even the youngest offenders had built up such tolerances to drugs like heroin and crack that they required fixes on a daily basis. Many were involved in drug dealing and had fallen into a well known trap; using their own supply. Whether they sold for themselves or in the service of someone else, the need for cash to replenish the supply or feed the habit was a powerful internal motivator. L-Dawg, a young drug dealer from the north side of St. Louis also had developed a strong addiction to heroin. Only two days before his interview with us, he had taken a car from a man leaving a local night club.

L-Dawg: I didn't have no money and I was sick and due some heroin so I knew I had to do something. I was at my auntie's house [and] my stomach started cramping. I just had to kill this sickness, 'cause I can't stay sick. If I'd stayed sick I would [have to] do something worse. The worse I get sick, to me, the worse I'm going to do. That's how I feel. If I've got to wait on it a long time, the worse the crime may be. If it hadn't been him then I probably would have done a robbery. One way or another I was going to get me some money to take me off this sickness. I just seen him and I got it.

External situational inducements could be just as compelling. Pressures from friends, family, other criminal acquaintances, or even the threat of injury or death were capable of pushing offenders to carjacking. For example, C-Low described an incident that occurred while he was with a friend in New Orleans. The two were waiting in the reception room of a neighborhood dentist when a group of men hostile to C-Low's friend walked into the office.

C-Low: They knew him. I didn't know them. It was something about some fake dope. I think it was some heroin. He got caught.
We weren't strapped [armed] at the time. We booked out. We left. We just left 'cause he know this person's gonna be strapped, and I didn't know this. So my partner was like, "Man, just burn out man, just leave." So we was leaving and they was coming up behind us [and started] popping [shooting] at us just like that, popping at my partner, just started shooting at him, so my partner he was wounded.

We had no car or nothing so we were running through and the guy was popping at us. So, there was a lady getting out of her car, and he stole it. We had to take her car because we had no ride. She worked at the [dentist's]. She like a nurse or something. It was a nice little brand new car. Brand new, not the kind you sort of sport off in like. She saw I was running. She heard the gun shots. I know she heard them, but she didn't see the guy that was shooting at us though. She had the keys in her hand. She was getting out her car, locking her door, yeah. She had her purse and everything. [My partner] just came on her blind side, just grabbed her, hit her. She just looked like she was shocked, she was in a state of shock. She was really scared. And [we] took her car and we left. We could've got her purse and everything, but we were just trying to get away from the scene 'cause we had no strap and they were all shooting at us. We just burnt on out of there. Got away. But then [later that day] he got caught though . . . somebody snitched on him and they told them [the police] that he had the car. He gave me the car but he got caught for it, they couldn't find the car 'cause I'd taken it to the chop shop. I sold the car for like twenty-seven hundred bucks and about 2 ounces of weed.

Similarly, Nicole, a seasoned car thief and sometimes carjacker, described a harrowing spur-of-the-moment episode. She and a friend had been following a young couple from the drive-in, casually discussing the prospect of robbing them, when her partner suddenly stopped their vehicle, jumped out and initiated a carjacking without warning. Nicole was instantly drawn into abetting her partner in the commission of the offense.

Nicole: My partner just jumped out of the car. He jumped out of the car and right then when I seen him with the gun I [realized] what was happening. I had to move. Once he got the guy out of the car he told me, "Come get the car." The girl was already out of the car screaming, "Please don't kill me, please don't kill me!" She was afraid because [she could see] I was high. You do things [when] you high. She's running so I'm in the car waiting on him. He's saying, "Run bitch and don't look back." She just started running . . . across the parking lot. [At] the same time he made the guy get up and run, "Nigger you do something, you look back, I'm gonna kill your motherfucking ass." As he got up and ran he shot him any ways.

RISKS AND REWARDS: HOW
OPPORTUNITY DRIVES CARJACKING

Need was not the only factor implicated in carjacking. Some carjackers indicated that they were influenced by the appeal of targets that represented effortless or unique opportunities (e.g., isolated or weak victims, vehicles with exceptionally desirable options). Here, risks were so low or potential rewards so great that, even in the absence of substantive internal or external situational inducements, they decided to commit a carjacking. Such opportunities were simply too good to pass up.

Po-Po (short for "Piss Off the POlice") descirbed just such an opportunity-driven incident. She and her brother had spent the day successfully pickpocketing individuals at Union Station, a St. Louis mall complex. On their way out, she noticed an easy target, an isolated woman in the parking lot, preoccupied with the lock on her car door.

> **Po-Po:** It was a fancy little car. I don't know too much about names of cars, I just know what I like. A little sporty little car like a Mercedes Benz like car. It was black and it was shiny and it looked good. I just had to joy ride it. She was a white lady. It looked like she worked for [a news station] or somebody. We just already pick pocket[ed] people down at Union Station, but fuck. So we just walked down stairs and [I] said, "You want to steal a car? Come on dude, let me get this car." I didn't have a gun on me. I just made her think I had a gun. I had a stick and I just ran up there to her and told her, "Don't move, don't breathe, don't do nothing. Give me the keys and ease your ass away from the car." I said, " You make one sound I'm going to blow your motherfucker head off and I'm not playing with you!" I said, "Just go on around the car, just scoot on around the car." Threw the keys to my little brother and told him go on and open the door. And she stood around there at the building like she waiting on the bus until we zoomed off. We got away real slow and easy.

Likewise, Kow, an older carjacker and sometimes street robber, was on his way to a friend's house to complete a potentially lucrative drug deal when he happened on an easy situation—a man sitting in a parked car, talking to someone on a pay phone at 2 A.M.

> **INT:** What drew you to this guy? What were you doing? Why did you decide to do this guy?
>
> **Kow:** Man, it ain't be no, "What you be doing?," [it's] just the thought that cross your mind be like, you need whatever it is you see, so you get it, you just get it. I was going to do something totally different [a drug deal] but along the way something totally different popped up so I just take it as it comes. I was like, "Whew! Get that!" I don't know man, your mind is a hell of thing. On our way to this other thing. It just something that just hit you, you know what I'm saying? Plus, [he looked like] a bitch. I don't know, it's just something, he look like a bitch, just like we could whip him, like a bitch, you know what I'm saying? Easy.

Not all irresistible opportunities were driven solely by the prospect of monetary gain. In a city the size of St. Louis, offenders run into one another all the time, at restaurants, malls, movie theaters and night-clubs. As a result, individuals with shared histories often encounter unique chances for retaliation or personal satisfaction. Goldie emphasized how such opportunities could pop up at a moment's notice. While cruising the north side of St. Louis, he spotted an individual who had sexually assaulted one of his girlfriends.

> **Goldie:** I did it on the humbug [spontaneously]. I peeped this dude, [saw that] he [was] pulling up at the liquor store. I'm tripping [excited] you know what I'm saying, [as I'm] walking there [towards the target]. You know, peep him out, you dig? He [was] reaching in the door to open the door. His handle outside must have been broke cause he had to reach in [the window] to open the door. And I just came around you know what I'm saying. [I] put it [the gun] to his head, "You want to give me them keys, brother?" He's like, "No, I'm not givin' you these keys." I'm like, "You gonna give me them keys, brother. It's as simple as that!" Man, he's like, "Take these, motherfucker, fuck you and this car. Fuck you." I'm like, "Man, just go on and get your ass home." [Then I] kicked him in his ass, you know what I'm saying, and I was like, "Fuck that, as a matter of fact get on your knees. Get on your knees, motherfucker . . ." Then I seen this old lady right, that I know from around this neighborhood. I was like "Fuck!," jumped on in the car [and] rolled by. I wanted to hit him but she was just standing there, just looking. That's the only thing what made me don't shoot him, know what I'm saying? 'Cause he's fucking with one of my little gals. 'Cause he fucked one of my little gals. Well, she was saying that he didn't really fuck her, you know, he took the pussy, you know what I'm saying? He got killed the next week so I didn't have to worry about him. Motherfuckers said they found him dead in the basement in a vacant house.

ALERT AND MOTIVATED OPPORTUNISM

Offenses motivated purely by either irresistible opportunities or overwhelming situational inducements are relatively rare. Most carjackings occur between these extremes, where situational inducements merge with potential opportunities to create circumstances ripe for offending. What follows are descriptions of offenses spurred by the combination of internal or external situational inducements and acceptable (or near acceptable) levels of risk and reward. The degree to which a given situation was comprised of rewards and risk on the one hand and internal and external pressures on the other varied, but when the combination reached a certain critical level, a carjacking resulted.

Offenders often described situation in which inducements were present, but *not* pressing, where they had *some* money or *some* drugs on them, but realized that the supply of either or both was limited and would soon run out. In such cases, the carjackers engaged in a state of what Bennett and Wright (1984; see also, Feeney, 1986) refer to as *alert opportunism*. In other words, offenders are not desperate, but they anticipate need in the near term and become increasingly open to opportunities that may present themselves during the course of their day-to-day activities. Here, would-be carjacking prowled neighborhoods, monitoring their surroundings for good opportunities, allowing potential victims to present themselves.

Corleone, a sixteen year-old with over a dozen carjacking under his belt, had been committing such offenses with his cousin since the age of 13. The two were walking the streets of St. Louis one afternoon looking for opportunities for quick cash when they saw a man walking out of a barbershop toward his parked car, keys in hand. Motivated by the obliviousness of their prey and the lightness of their wallets, they decided to take his car.

> **Corleone:** it was down in the city on St. Louis Avenue. We was just walking around, you know. We just look for things to happen you see just to get money. We just walk around and just see something that's gonna make us money. We just happened to be going to the China-man [a restaurant] to get something to eat. [We had] about five or six dollars in our pocket which ain't nothing. It was this man driving a blue Cutlass. It has some chrome wheels on there. He just drove up and we was going to the Chinaman and . . . my cousin was like, "Look at that car, man, that's tough [nice]. I'm getting that. I want that." [I was] like, "Straight up, you want to do it?" He was like, "Yeah." He was all G[ood] for it. Then he [the victim] came out the barbershop. It was kind of crowded and we just did what we had to do. There was this little spot where [my cousin] stash[es] his money, drugs and all that type of stuff and then he got the gun [from the stash]. He got around the corner. He say, "Hey, hey." I asked him for a cigarette so he went to the passenger's side [of the vehicle to get one]. I ran on the driver's side with a gun. Put it to his head and told him to get out the car.

> **INT:** Did you know that you were going to do carjacking or . . .?

> **Corleone:** No. Not necessarily. But since that was what came up, that's what we did.

No matter how alert one is, however, good opportunities do not always present themselves. Over the course of time, situational inducements mount (that is, supplies of money and drugs inevitably dry up), and the option of waiting for ideal opportunities correspondingly diminishes. Such conditions cause offenders to move from a "passive" state of alert opportunism to an "active" state of what could be referred to as *motivated opportunism* (creating opportunities where none previously existed or modifying existing non-optimal opportunities to make them less hazardous or more rewarding). Here, attention and openness to possibilities expands to allow offenders to tolerate more risk. Situations that previously seemed unsuitable start to look better.

Binge, a 45 year old veteran offender who had engaged in burglary, robbery, and carjacking for over 20 years, discussed his most recent decision to get a car on a wintry January day. He had been carrying a weapon (a 9mm Glock) since that morning, looking to commit a home invasion. After prowling the streets for hours and encountering few reasonable prospects, he happened on an easy opportunity—a man sitting parked in a car, its engine running, at a Metrolink (trolley) station.

> **Binge:** Well, I was out hustling, trying to get me a little money and I was walking around. I was cold. I was frustrated. I couldn't get in [any] house[s] or nothing, so I say [to myself], "Well I'll try and get me a little car, and you know, just jam off the heat and shit that he [the vehicle's owner] got," you know? I was strapped [carrying a firearm] and all that, you know and I was worried about the police catching me, trying to pull my pistol off, and I see this guy. Well, he was at the Metrolink you know, nodding [falling asleep] in his car. So, I went up to the window. I just think that I just peeped it on [happened on the situation]. I was at the Metrolink you know, I was standing at the bus station trying to keep warm and so I just walked around with no houses to rob, and I seen this dude you know sitting in his car, you know, with the car running. And I said "Ah man, if I can get a wag at this [take advantage of this opportunity]," you know. It wasn't just an idea to keep warm or nothing like that. I was cold and worried, and it just crossed my mind and I thought I can get away with it, and I just did it. I'd do anything man, I'd do anything. If I want something and I see I can get away with it I'm gonna do it. That's what I'm saying. That night I saw an opportunity and I took it, you know. It just occurred to me.

Just as compelling were instances where third parties placed demands on offenders. A number of our respondents indicated that they engaged in carjacking to fulfill specific orders or requests from chop shop owners or other individuals interested in a particular make and model of car or certain valuable car parts. The desire to fulfill such orders quickly created conditions ripe for motivated opportunism.

Goldie, for instance, was experiencing strong internal situational pressures (the need for cash) and external pressures (the demand for a particular vehicle by some of his criminal associates) combined with a moderately favorable opportunity (inside information on the driver of the wanted vehicle and its location):

> **Goldie:** He's from my neighborhood. He's called Mucho. He's from the same neighborhood but like two streets over. Them two streets don't come over on our street. You know, we not allowed to go over on they street. It was a nice car. The paint, the sound system in it, and the rims. [It] had some beats, rims. Rims cost about $3,000, some chrome Daytons. 100 spokes platinums.
>
> **INT:** OK. That's a lot of money to be putting on a car. What does he do for a living?
>
> **Goldie:** I don't know. I don't ask. What they told me was they wanted this car and they are going to give me a certain amount of money.
>
> **INT:** You say they told you they wanted this car. You mean they told you they wanted his car or they wanted a car like that?

Goldie: His car. His car. They want [Mucho's] car. They said, "I need one of these, can you get it for me?" And they knew this guy. So now, I need that car. That car.

Low-Down also specialized in taking orders from chop shops,

Low-Down: What I do, I basically have me a customer before I even go do it. I ask a few guys that I know that fix up cars, you know what I'm saying. I ask them what they need then I take the car. But see, I basically really got a customer. I'm talking about this guy over in East St. Louis. Me and Bob, we real cool. He buy 'em cause he break 'em down, the whole car down and he got an autobody shop. He sell parts. He'll take the car and strip it down to the nitty gritty and sell the parts. He get more money out of selling it part by part than selling the car. And, before I get it I already set the price.

He also had a drug habit:

Low-Down: The main reason basically why I did it was I be messing with heroin, you know what I'm saying. I be using buttons [heroin housed in pill-form]. I be snorting some, but I be snorting too much, you know? I got a habit for snorting cause I be snorting too much at a time, that's how I call it a habit. I probably drop about 5 or 6 [buttons] down first [thing in the morning]. [So] I was basically really sick and my daughter needed shoes and shit like that and my girlfriend was pressuring me about getting her some shoes. She had been pressing me about two or three days. Baby food and stuff like that. But the money I had, I had been trying to satisfy my habit with it. Basically I just thought it was a good thing to do. It was a good opportunity.

AFTERMATH

The second portion of our interviews with carjackers dealt with the aftermath of carjackings. Here, we were concerned with basic questions: What did they do with the vehicles? What did they do with their money? Given the propensity of many carjackers to target other offenders, how did they manage the threat of retaliation? The majority of our respondents immediately disposed of the vehicle, liquidating it for cash. As Corleone put it, "there's a possibility they report[ed] the car stolen and while I'm driving around the police [could] pull me over. I ain't got time to hop out [of the vehicle] and run with no gun. I just want to get the money that I wanted."

Although most of our respondents immediately delivered the vehicle to a chop shop or dismantled it themselves, a fair number of them chose to drive the vehicle around first, showing it off or "flossing" to other neighborhood residents and associates. Despite the possibility that the vehicle's owner or the police might catch up with them, they chose to floss.

INT: What do you like to do after a carjacking?

Binge: Well, what I like to do is just like to, see my friends. They don't give a damn either, I just go pick them up and ride around, smoke a little bit [of] weed, and get some gals, and to partying or something like that you know. I know it's taking a chance but, you know like I say, they don't give a damn.

INT: Is that what did you did with the car that you took off the guy at the Metrolink?

Binge: Yeah. I was just riding around listening to the music, picked up a couple of friends of mine. We rode around. I told them it was a stolen car. It was a nice little car too. Black with a kind of rag top with the three windows on the side. The front and back ones had a little mirror and another window right in the roof. Oh yeah, oh yeah—[it had] nice sounds. I was chilling man, I was chilling, you know? I was driving along with the music playing up loud. Ha ha. You know I wasn't even worried. I was just feeling good. 'Cause I'm not used to driving that much you know 'cause I don't have a car you know. That's why when I do a carjacking I just play it off to the tee, run all the gas off, keep the sounds up as loud as I can, keep the heat on, you know just abuse the car you know. That's all about carjacking like that.

C-Low described his desire to floss as having to do with the ability to gain status in his neighborhood.

C-Low: Put it this way, you got people you know that's driving around. We just wanna know how it feels. We're young and we ain't doing shit else. So they [people from the neighbourhood] see you driving the car, they gonna say, "Hey, there's C-Low!" and such and such. That makes us feel good 'cause we're riding, and then when we're done riding we wreck the car or give it to somebody else and let him ride. We took the car and drove around the hood, flossing everything. And then we wrecked it on purpose, We ran it into a ditch. I don't know, we were fucked up high, we were high man, just wild! Wrecked the thing.

But even for offenders like these, the prospect of getting caught and losing profits eventually began to outweigh the benefits of showing off.

INT: So how long did you drive around in the [Chevrolet] Suburban before you stripped it?

Loco: Oh, we was rolling that. We drove for a good thirty minutes, then I said that I want[ed] to get up out of it because they might report it stolen. We was [still driving] right there [near] the scene [of the crime] and they [the police] would have probably tried to flag me [pull me over]. And if they tried to flag me, I would [have to] have taken them through a high-speed chase. Fuck that.

Sleezee-E informed us (as did other respondents) that disposing of the vehicle quickly was the key to getting away with a carjacking. Indeed, almost all respondents were aware of the police department's "hot sheet" for stolen vehicles (although their estimations of how long it took for a vehicle to show up on the hot-sheet varied greatly, from as soon as the vehicle was reported stolen to 24 hours or even longer afterwards).

> **Sleezee-E:** [People think that] the cops will wait 24 hours just to see what you are going to do with the car. Because some idiots, when they jack a car, they just drive it around and then they leave it someplace. I don't do that. That's how you get caught. Driving it around. You take that car right to the chop shop and let them cut that sucker up.

Once the vehicle was stripped, most carjackers disposed of the vehicle by destroying it somehow.

> **Littlerag:** 'Cause it was hot man! It was too hot. All I [wanted] was to take the rims, take the beats, the equalizer, the detachable face. Got all that off, then I just pour gas on it and burnt that motherfucker up. I had fingerprints [on it]. I didn't have no gloves on. I had my own hands on the steering wheel. I left my fingerprints.

Nicole and a boyfriend chose a less conventional method of getting rid of their stolen vehicle.

> **Nicole:** We got rid of the car first. We drove the car two blocks and went back down a ways to the park. We drove the car up there, we parked right there and sat for about ten minutes, made sure how many cars come down this street before we can push it over there. It's a pond, like it's a lake out there with ducks and geeses in it.

CASH FOR CARS: LIFE AS PARTY

While a few respondents reported that they used the proceeds from carjacking to pay for necessities or bills, the overwhelming majority indicated that they blew their cash indiscriminately on drugs, women, and gambling.

We had interviewed Tone on a number of previous occasions for his involvement in strong-arm drug robbery. Although robbery was his preferred crime, he engaged in carjacking occasionally (about once every two months) when easy opportunities presented themselves. During his most recent offense, he and three of his associates took a Cadillac from a neighborhood drug dealer and made $6000. When we asked what he did with his portion, he indicated that he, ". . . spent that shit in like, two days."

> **INT:** You can go through $1500 in two days?

> **Tone:** Shit, it probably wasn't even two days, it probably was a day, shit.

INT: What did you spend fifteen hundred on?

Tone: It ain't shit that you really want. Just got the money to blow so fuck it, blow it. Whatever, it don't even matter. Whatever you see you get, fuck it. Spend that shit. It wasn't yours from the getty-up, you know what I'm saying? You didn't have it from the jump so. . . . Can't act like you careful with it, it wasn't yours to care for. Easy come, easy go. The easy it came, it go even easier. Fuck that, fuck all that. I ain't trying to think about keeping nothing. You can get it again.

INT: So what does money mean to you?

Tone: What money mean? Shit, money just some shit everybody need, that's all. I mean, it ain't jack shit.

INT: Ok, so it's not really important to you?

Tone: Fuck no. Cause I told you, easy come, easy go.

Mo had taken a Monte Carlo from two men residing in another neighborhood. He had planned the offense over the course of a month and finally, posing as a street window cleaner, carjacked them as they exited a local restaurant. The vehicle's after-market items netted $5000 in cash.

INT: I'm just kind of curious how you spend like $5,000!

Mo: Just get high, get high. I just blow money. Money is not something that is going to achieve for nobody, you know what I'm saying? So everyday, there's not a promise that there'll be another [day] so I just spend it, you know what I'm saying? It ain't mine, you know what I'm saying, I just got it, it's just in my possession. This is mine now, so I'm gonna do what I've got to do. It's a lot of fun. At a job you've got to work a lot for it, you know what I'm saying? You got to punch the clock, do what somebody else tells you. I ain't got time for that. Oh yeah, there ain't nothing like gettin' high on $5000!

Binge and others confirmed that the proceeds from their illegal activities went to support this form of conspicuous consumption.

Binge: I just blowed it man. With the money me and my girlfriend went and did a bit of shopping, stuff for Christmas. But, the money I got from his wallet? I just blowed that, drinking and smoking marijuana.

For Corleone, the motivation to carjack was directly related to his desire to manage the impressions of others in his social milieu. His remarks served as a poignant comment on sociocultural and peer pressures experienced by many inner city youths. The purpose of carjacking was to obtain the money he needed to purchase clothing and items that would improve his stature in the neighborhood.

Corleone: [$1500 is] a lot. [I bought] shoes, shoes, everything you need. Guys be styling around our neighborhood. The brand you wear, shoes cost $150 in my size. Air Jordans, everybody want those. Everybody have them. I see everybody wearing those in the neighborhood. I mean come on, let's go get a car. I'm getting those, too.

INT: How many pairs of sneakers have you got?

Corleone: Millions. I got, I got, I got a lot of shoes. Clothes, gotta get jackets.

INT: Well, why do you have to look good, what's so big about looking good?

Corleone: It's for the projects, man. You can't be dressing like no bum. I mean you can't, you can't go ask for no job looking like anything.

INT: So you're saying like if you don't look good, you can't get girls, if you don't have the nicest shoes?

Corleone: You can't. Not nowadays, not where I'm from. You try to walk up to a girl, boy, you got on some raggedy tore up, cut up shoes they're gonna spit on you or something. Look at you like you crazy. Let's say you walking with me. I got on creased up pants, nice shoes, nice shirt and you looking like a bum. Got on old jeans. And that dude, that dude, he clean as a motherfucker and you look like a bum.

INT: So you're competing with each other, too?

Corleone: Something like that. Something like a popularity contest.

INT: Well, you know, you can look nice and clean and not have to spend $150 bucks on shoes, you know.

Corleone: It's just this thing, it's a black thing. You ain't going [to] understand, you don't come from the projects.

THE HAZARDS OF CARJACKING: RETALIATION AND THE SPREAD OF VIOLENCE

Interestingly, a sizeable proportion of our respondents purposely targeted people who themselves were involved in crime. Such individuals make excellent targets. Their participation in street culture encourages the acquisition of vehicles most prized by carjackers (those with valuable, if often gaudy, after-market items). And, because they are involved in a number of illegal activities (such as drug selling), they cannot go to the police. As Mr. Dee put it;

Mr. Dee: You can't go to no police when you selling drugs to buy that car with your drug money. So, I wasn't really worried about that. If he would have went to the police he would have went to jail automatically 'cuz they would have been like, "Where'd you get this thousand dollar car from?" He put about $4,000 into the car. So, he ain't got no job, he ain't doin it like that bro. He'd be goin' to the police station lookin' like a fool tellin' his story. I [could] see if he's workin' or something . . . and slinging. It'd be different 'cause he could show them his check stub from work.

However, there is a considerable danger associated with targeting such individuals because, unable to report the robbery of illegal goods to the police, they have a strong incentive to engage in retaliation—those who fail to do so risk being perceived as soft or easy (see e.g., Topalli, Wright, and Fornango, 2002). This introduces the possibility that incidents of carjacking likely are substantially higher than officially reported.

When asked about the possibility of retaliation many of the carjackers, displaying typical street offender bravado, indicated that they had no fear. The need to see oneself as capable and tough was essential to respondents. Such self-beliefs served to create a sense of invulnerability that allowed carjackers to continue to engage in a crime considered by many to be hazardous. As Playboy put it, "It [can't be] a fear thing. If you're gonna be scared then you shouldn't even go through with stuff like that [carjacking people]."

Likewise, Big-Mix expressed an almost complete disregard for the consequences of his actions. His comments confirm the short-term thinking characteristic of many street offenders, "I don't give a damn. I don't care what happens really. I don't care. That's how it always is. Whether they kill us or whether we kill them, same damn shit. Whatever. I don't fucking care." Pacman, a younger carjacker who worked exclusively with his brother-in-law, indicated that thinking about the possible negative consequences was detrimental to one's ability to execute an offense. When asked if he was worried about retaliation, he was dismissive.

Pacman: Yeah, you be pretty pissed. But like I say, I'm not looking over my back, you know what I'm saying? Because, I wouldn't be here for sure. I couldn't [keep carjacking]. I definitely wouldn't last man. I wouldn't have lasted as long as I lasted. Because it would be too many motherfuckers [that I've victimized], you know what I'm saying, [for me to look] over my shoulder all the time. When I look what the fuck could I do anyhow? I could get a few of them, but it would take a lot of motherfucking looking over my shoulder. I try to avoid that altogether. I'm going to avoid all that.

Other carjackers relied on hypervigilance (obsessive attention to one's surroundings and to the behavior of others), or anonymity maintenance (e.g., targeting strangers, not talking about the crime, using of disguises, carjacking in areas away from one's home ground; see Jacobs, Topalli, and Wright, 2000; Jacobs, 2001) to minimize the possibility of pay-back. Sexy-Diva, a female carjacker who worked with Sleezee-E, often spent hours with potential victims at night clubs before taking their cars, "I just disguises myself. I change my hair . . . my clothes. I change whatever location I was at. And then I don't even go to that area no more. They can't find me. No way, no how."

Nukie sacrificed a great deal of his day-to-day freedom by engaging in behaviors designed to anticipate and neutralize the threat of retaliation.

Nukie: That's why I don't go out. If I go somewhere to get me a beer, if I'm gonna get me some bud [marijuana] or something, I stay in the hood. I don't go to the clubs. There's too many people going there at night, you know what I'm saying? I don't need to be spotted like that. That's why I keep on the DL [down-low, out of sight]. You see, I stay in the hood. [If] I be riding [in a car], while I'm riding I might have my cats [friends] with me. You know, no motherfucker's gonna try to fuck with us like that. Yeah, I be with some motherfucker most of the time. If we're [going] to do something, go get blowed [high]—see, we get blowed everyday—I be with people, shit.

Pookie choose to employ similar preemptive tactics, but also emphasized the need to be proactive when dealing with the threat of retaliation, predicated on the philosophy that, "the best defense is a good offense."

Pookie: Well, you know the best thing [to deal] with retaliation like this here, you know, in order for you to get some action you got to bring some action. If I see you coming at me and you don't look right, then this is another story here. If you doing it like you're reaching for something, I'm gonna tear the top of your head off real quick, you know. I'm gonna be near you, where you're at because they ain't nothing but some punk-ass tires and rims that I took from you, that's all it is. What you gotta understand is that you worked hard for it, and I just came along and just took them, you know. You go back and get yourself another set son, 'cause if I like them then I'm gonna take them again.

In the end, there were no guarantees. No matter how many steps a carjacker took to prevent retaliation, the possibility of payback remained. As self-confidence bred the perception of security, so too did it breed over-confidence. This was true in the case of Goldie, whose motivation to carjack a known drug dealer named Mucho was described above. His attempt did not go as planned.

Goldie: He was going to put up a fight trying to spin off with [the car], I jumped in and threw it in park so now I'm tussling with him, "Give me this motherfucker!" He's trying to speed off. He got like in the middle of the intersection. I dropped my gun on the seat and he grabbed me like around here [the neck], trying to hold me down in the car, and throw it back in Drive, with me in the car, you dig? You know, I'm like no, I ain't going for that shit. I had my feet up on the gear [shift], you know what I'm saying? He ain't tripping off the gun. He trying to hold me, "Nigger motherfucker, you ain't going to get this car! Punk-ass nigger! What the fuck wrong with you? What the fuck do you want my car for?" [I said], "Look boy, I don't want that punk ass shit dude! I'm getting this car. This is mine. Fuck you!" The gun flew on the passenger's seat. So I grabbed the gun and put it to his throat, "So what you gonna to do? Is you gonna die or give up this car?" [He replied], "Motherfucker, you're going to have to do what you are going to have to do." He don't want to give up his car, right? So I cocked it one time, you know, just to let him know I wasn't playing, you dig? But I ain't shoot him on his head, put it on his thigh. Boom! Shot him on his leg. He got to screaming and shit hollering, you know what I'm saying, "You shot me! You shot me! You shot me!" like a motherfucker gonna hear him or something. Cars just steady drive past and shit, you know what I'm saying. By this time I opened up the door, "Fuck you!" Forced his ass on up out of there. He laying on the ground talking about, "This motherfucker shot me! Help, help!" Hollering for help and shit. But before I drove off I backed up, ran over him I think on the ankles like. While he was laying on the street, after I shot him. Ran over his bottom of his feet or whatever, you know what I'm saying. Oh, yeah. I felt that. Yeah. Boom, boom. "Aaaah!" scream. I hear bones break, like all this down here was just crushed. I didn't give a fuck though. Sped off. Went and flossed for a minute.

INT: I don't know—two streets over and he sounds like he's pretty scandalous. You're not worried about him coming up on you for this?

Goldie: No. I pretty much left him not walking. And he don't know who I am. [Later on] I heard about that. [People were saying], "Motherfucker Mucho, he got knocked [attacked], motherfucker tried to knock him, took his car, you know what I'm saying, on the block." I'm like, "Yeah, I heard about that. You know what I'm saying. I wonder who did this shit." You know what I'm saying?

Three months later, we spoke to Goldie from his hospital bed. Mucho had tracked him down and shot him in the back and stomach as he crossed the street to buy some marijuana.

Goldie: I call them a bad day . . . I got shot. I saw him [Mucho] drive by but I didn't think he seen me. He caught up to me later. [I got shot] in the abdomen (pointing at his stomach) . . . here's where they sewed me up. I had twenty staples.

INT: How did it go down?

Goldie: I wanted [to] stop on the North[side] and get me a bag of grass, grab me a bag of weed or something. So, [we were] going around to the set [the dealer's home turf] and I'm getting out, I see [Mucho's] car parked this time. He wasn't in it. I'm thinking in my mind like you know, "That's that puss ass." So I'm like, "Damn I'm having bad vibes already." So I instantly just turned around like, "Fuck it. I'll go somewhere else to get some grass." I'm walking [back] to [my] car and hear a gunshot. Jump in the car. You know . . . you [don't] feel it for a minute. [Then,] my side just start hurting, hurting bad you know what I'm saying? I'm like damn. Looked down, I'm in a puddle of blood, you know. She freaking out and screaming, "You shot! You shot!" and shit. [She] jumped out the car like she almost should be done with me, you know what I'm saying? So I had to immediately take myself to the hospital. [They] stuffed this tube all the way down my dick all the way to my stomach . . . fucking with my side, pushing all of it aside. [I was there] about a good week. I done lost about 15 or 20 pounds. That probably wouldn't have happened if I wouldn't have to go do that. Wanted some more grass. At the wrong spot at the wrong time.

Goldie made it clear during the interview that he felt the need to counter-retaliate to protect himself from future attack by maintaing a tough reputation, a valuable mechanism of deterrence.

INT: You don't feel like you all are even now? You shot him—he shot you. Why go after him?

Goldie: It's [about] retaliation. When I feel good is when he taken care of . . . and I don't have to worry about him no more. I mean my little BG's [Baby Gangsters, younger criminal protégées] look up to me. Me getting shot and not going and do [something about, it they would say], "Ah [Goldie's] a bitch. Aw, he's a fag." Now down there [in the neighborhood], when they hit you, you hit them back. You know, if someone shoot you, you gotta shoot them back. That's how it is down there or you'll be a bitch. Everybody will shoot you up, whoop your ass. Know what I'm saying? Treat you like a punk. It's just I got to do what I have to do, you know what I'm saying.

Many carjackers echoed such sentiments, indicating a common belief in the importance of following unwritten rules of conduct and behavior related to street offending, especially when they refer to matters of honor or reputation (see Anderson, 1999; Katz, 1988).

CONCLUSION

This chapter has demonstrated that the decision to commit a carjacking is governed by two things: perceived situational inducements and perceived opportunity (see Hepburn, 1984; Lofland, 1969). Situational inducements involve immediate pressures on the would-be offender to act. They can be internal (e.g., the need for money or desire for revenge) or external (e.g., the peer pressure of co-offenders). Opportunities refer to risks and rewards ties to a particular crime target in its particular environmental setting. Figure 4.3 outlines how these forces lead individuals to decide to initiate a carjacking.

Carjackings occur when perceived situational inducements and a perceived opportunity, alone or in combination, reach a critical level, thereby triggering that criminogenic moment when an individual commits to the offense. It is important to reiterate that either a perceived opportunity or perceived situational inducement on its own may be sufficient to entice an individual to

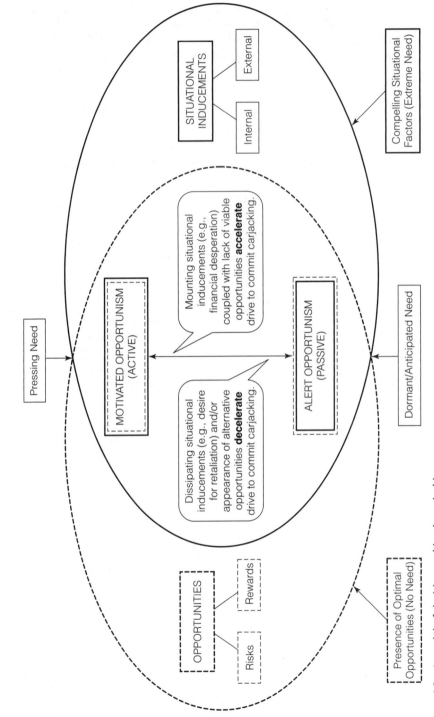

Figure 4.3 A model of decision-making in carjacking

commit a carjacking (see Hepburn, 1984). Numerous examples of this have been detailed throughout the first part of the chapter. It is also important to note that background and foreground factors (such as membership in a criminogenic street culture) can increase the chance that a carjacker will go after a vehicle by lowering his/her capacity to resist the temptation to offend.

More often, carjackings were motivated through the combined influence of opportunity and inducement. The carjackers' responses indicate that offenses triggered by *pure* opportunity or *pure* need are relatively rare. Most carjackings occur between the extremes, where opportunities and situational inducements overlap.

Owing to their precarious day-to-day existence—conditioned by risk factors such as persistent poverty, and exacerbated by "boom and bust" cycles of free-spending when money *is* available—carjackers are always under some degree of pressure and thus are encouraged to maintain a general openness to offending. During a "boom" period, carjackers anticipate future needs, but are not desperate to offend. This encourages Bennett and Wright's (1984) previously described notion of alert opportunism—a general willingness to offend if a particularly good opportunity presents itself.

But as time passes and no acceptable opportunities emerge, situational pressures to offend begin to mount in the face of diminishing resources. Approaching "bust" periods increasingly promote an active willingness to offend, driven by heightened situational inducements. Dormant or anticipated needs become pressing ones, moving carjackers from a state of alert opportunism to a state of motivated opportunism. As they continue to become more situationally desperate, their openness to offending expands to include opportunities perceived to have greater risk or lower reward (see Lofland, 1969). Targets that previously seemed unsuitable become increasingly attractive and permissible. The logical outcome is a carjacking triggered almost exclusively by pressing needs.

It is also possible for carjackers to move from a state of motivated opportunism to the lower state of alert opportunism, especially where the decision to commit such an offense is a driven desire for revenge. Retaliatory urges tend to be high initially, and then to dissipate over time. This is not to say however, that an offended party has necessarily forgiven the offending party. They may simply be getting on with their lives, even as they keep their eyes open for the object of their wrath.

Although infrequent when compared to strong-arm robbery or drug robbery, carjacking's proportional impact on the spread of violence is probably more significant than has been suspected. When offenders themselves are targeted carjacking, like other forms of violent crime, can produce retaliatory behavior patterns that serve to perpetuate and proliferate cycles of violence on the streets. In addition, their sensationalist nature increases the public's general fear of crime when law-abiding citizens are victimized. In either case, the preceding evidence and discussion indicate that carjacking is a unique and dynamic form of crime that probably deserves its own categorization (separate from robbery or auto theft) or, at the very least, further study and attention by those interested in criminal decision-making.

CHAPTER 5

Burglary

Recent victimization data suggest that crimes against property account for more than three fourths of all criminal victimizations that occur annually in the United States (NCVS, 2003). Roughly one in every six property crimes takes the shape as a household burglary. It takes very little to conjure up an image of a burglar crawling through an unlocked second-story window or jimmying the lock of a hotel room. This abstract imagery is reinforced by television series such as *Cops,* wherein nearly every episode includes at least one call-for-service to the scene of a burglary. Americans clearly view burglary as a serious crime that carries with it a potential to disrupt the lives of the citizenry as well as overburden the criminal justice system.

BURGLARY DEFINED

Laypersons have a tendency to interchange the terms *robbery, burglary,* and *larceny.* This is poor practice as there are distinct differences between these three types of crime. The previous chapter defined robbery as an act of force or threatened force occurring during the course of a theft. The clear emphasis on physical force leads to robbery being classified as a crime of violence. Larceny, as we will see in the next chapter, is defined as a simple act of taking without force and irrespective of where the theft occurs. This makes larceny a classic example of a property crime as the act is directed specifically toward depriving someone of his or her property. Burglary, on the other hand, is not so cut and dried. According to the Model Penal Code (American Law Institute, 1962), a **burglary** occurs when a person enters a building or occupied structure with the purpose of committing a crime therein. There are three important components of this definition: the entry (usually referred to as breaking and entering or remaining), the dwelling, and the intent to offend while inside.[1] Most scholarly sources (including the National Crime Victimization Survey and the Uniform Crime Reports) tacitly assume that the contents of a dwelling are the target of the crime and thus classify burglary as a property offense. However, since damage or deprivation of property need not occur, Samaha (1999) maintains that burglary is more aptly described a **crime of intrusion** or a **crime against habitation.**

BURGLARY TRENDS

Estimates suggest that 3,139,700 households were burglarized in 2001. This number represents 13% of total number of criminal victimizations that were reported that year and translates into a victimization rate of 28.7 burglaries per 1,000 households. The burglary rate that year was greater than the rate for all violent crimes combined. Of the dozens of criminal offenses that are tracked via the NCVS, only larceny and assault occurred at a higher rate and/or with greater frequency than burglary (NCVS, 2003).

The NCVS queries respondents exclusively on the topic of **residential burglary**—those offenses that target homes. This data source provides us no information about the prevalence of **nonresidential burglary**—those that occur in offices, stores, warehouses. The Uniform Crime Reports are considered our best source of data in this regard. Of the 2,109,767 burglaries that were reported to police in 2001, a full 734,199 (roughly one third) targeted nonresidential structures (FBI, 2002). A pooling of the NCVS data on residential burglary and the UCR data on nonresidential burglary suggests that roughly 4 million burglaries (residential and nonresidential) occurred in this country during 2001.[2]

Victims of burglary routinely complain about the sense of violation and perceived invasion of privacy that goes along with having their homes burglarized. However, there are usually monetary losses that accompany the emotional trauma. A full 86.5% of the household burglaries occurring in 2001 were said to result in a monetary loss due to theft or property damage. Where a theft is committed in conjunction with a break-in, burglars appear willing to direct their thievery toward a wide array of valuables—jewelry, household furnishings, tools, firearms and cash were among the most frequently stolen items. The price tag that goes along with these losses can be quite substantial. Roughly one in four burglary victims set losses in excess of $1,000 with the median dollar loss for 2001 reported to be $300. All total, victims of burglary suffered $2.9 billion in economic losses that year (NCVS, 2003). The loss figures grow substantially when more costly nonresidential burglaries are factored into the equation.

The historical data in Figure 5.1 provide encouraging news about the incidence of residential burglary. With the exception of a brief and minor upward turn during the early 1980s, our nation's victimization rates steadily declined

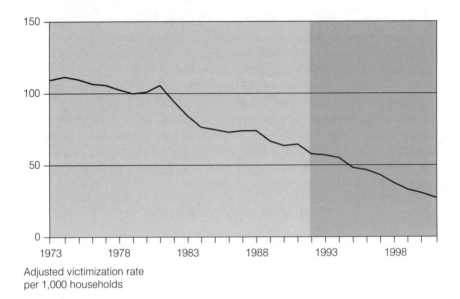

Adjusted victimization rate
per 1,000 households

Figure 5.1   Burglary rates

Source: http://www.ojp.usdoj.gov/bjs/

over the final quarter of the twentieth century. In fact, the burglary victimization rate for 2001 (28.7 per 1,000 households) represented nearly a 75%
decrease over the rate (110 per 1,000) that was observed in 1973.

Victimization data (NCVS, 2003) suggest that residential burglary rates are
relatively stable across the U.S. South (29.7), Midwest (33.6), and West (30.2).
The notable exception to this trend is seen in the Northeast, where the 2001
victimization rate was significantly lower at 18.7 per 1,000 households. Turning to state-level data from the 1999 Uniform Crime Reports, one notes that
North Carolina, New Mexico, Florida, Louisiana, and Mississippi posted the
highest burglary rates that year. At the other end of the continuum, New
Hampshire, North Dakota, Montana, South Dakota, and Pennsylvania were
shown to have the lowest burglary rates in 1999 (FBI, 2000).

A somewhat unconventional relationship exists between population density and burglary victimization rates. As expected, the 2001 NCVS data indicate that urban areas experience the highest residential burglary rate (37.3 per
1,000 households). What is somewhat unexpected is the fact that the aggregate
burglary rate for rural areas (26.7) is higher than the corresponding rate for
suburban areas (24.3). In light of this anomaly, several research projects have
sought to isolate the intricacies of suburban burglary (Maguire and Bennett,
1982; Mawby, 2001; Morgan, 2001; Rengert and Wasilchick, 2000; Reppetto,
1974). These studies show that burglary patterns often vary considerably across
and within suburban locales. Factors such as an effective police presence, active
neighborhood watch programs, and prevention-friendly residential design
(strategic landscaping and street layout) are found to have a significant impact
on the level of burglary activity in a suburb.

Burglary is one of the few crimes for which the United States fares well in comparison to other developed nations. Official reports made available by police agencies in the United States establish the 1998 nationwide offense rate for burglary at 862.0 per 100,000 inhabitants (FBI, 1999). By comparison, Australia (2,338.4), England and Wales (1,832.7), Germany (1,507.1), and Canada (1,155.7) experienced higher burglary rates that year. Lower rates were observed in countries such as France (676.9), Spain (570.2), and Japan (187.9) (Interpol, 1999).

TOOLS OF THE TRADE

Entry into an occupied dwelling is one of the critical components of the legal definition of burglary. *Contrary to popular belief, burglars tend to be an unsophisticated lot who rely on soft targets and brute force to accomplish their crimes.* Offender-based research (Cromwell, Olson, and Avary, 1991; Maguire and Bennett, 1982; Rengert and Wasilchick, 2000; Reppetto, 1974; Shover, 1996; Wright and Decker, 1994) shows that a surprising number of these unlawful entries are accomplished by the burglar simply passing through an open door or window. Habitual offenders learn that they cannot always count on this type of open invitation and thus come prepared with a variety of tools and/or strategies to assist them in defeating locks, windows, and doors. This is perhaps best evidenced by the fact that roughly two thirds of known burglaries involve some form of forced entry (FBI, 2002). Forced entry is often accomplished through the use of crowbars, screwdrivers, or hammers. A burglar may also become adept at popping sliding glass doors off their tracks, identifying alarms, or efficiently defeating deadbolt locks. For the most part, however, these skills and tools are best described as rudimentary in nature.

THE BURGLARY TRANSACTION

Burglary activities are shaped by a number of factors. The time of day and occupancy status of the dwelling stand as two clear examples. Law enforcement reports indicate that 60% of all residential burglaries occur during the day while roughly 60% of nonresidential burglaries take place at night (FBI, 2002). Occupancy appears to be the driving factor behind these statistics—residential dwellings are more likely to be unoccupied during the day; commercial dwellings are most susceptible to burglary at night when they are closed to business. Burglars clearly prefer unoccupied homes or businesses, as this situation allows them more freedom to enter and exit without being detected (Cromwell et al., 1991; Wright and Decker, 1994).

Residential burglars disproportionately come calling on multiunit rental properties. Multiunit dwellings are significantly more likely to be burglarized than single-family structures. In the same vein, rental properties generally experience higher victimization rates than do properties that are owned (NCVS, 2003). The transience and anonymity of these types of dwellings allow the burglar to move about without being noticed. The significance of this "transience effect" is further highlighted by recent victimization reports showing that a newly occupied residence (less than 6 months) faces more than three times the risk of burglary than a home that has been occupied for 5 or more years.

Residences that are occupied by young, poor, minority persons face the greatest risk of being burglarized. First, recent victimization data (NCVS, 2003) reveal a direct relationship between the age of the person who serves as the head of the household and the likelihood that the home will be burglarized. The burglary rate for homes in which the head of household is under 20 years of age (66.9) was more than 4 times that of homes in which the head of household is over the age of 65 (16.6). Victimization rates for African American–headed households (42.8) were significantly higher than for Hispanic or white–headed households (33.0 and 26.6, respectively). There also exists a clear negative relationship between burglary victimization rates and family income—homes with an annual family income of less than $7,500 experienced a burglary rate that more than doubled that of homes with a family income in excess $75,000 (58.0 versus 22.7).

A residence that has been burglarized once faces a higher risk of future victimization than a home that has never been targeted (Clarke, Perkins, and Smith, 2001; Kleemans, 2001; Morgan, 2001; Mawby, 2001). Repeat victimization is due, in part, to repeat offending—either the offender views the dwelling as a soft target or he or she returns to obtain goods that could not be removed during the first offense. There also seems to be a "neighborhood effect" underlying repeat victimization, wherein habitual offenders prefer to travel short distances from where they live and frequent those areas with appealing physical layouts (e.g., ready access to escape routes, poor lighting, minimal foot traffic). The offender–victim relationship also appears to play a role in initial and repeat burglary victimizations. Interviews with active offenders (Cromwell et al., 1991; Wright and Decker, 1994) reveal that burglars sometimes target the homes of acquaintances. Existing relationships afford the offender knowledge about the layout and contents of the home as well as the daily routines of the occupants. While few offenders report ripping off their close friends or relatives, they cannot pass up a casual acquaintance's home if it is a soft target.

Given the covert nature of the crime, we cannot rely on victimization reports to inform us about the characteristics of burglary offenders. Here we must turn to arrest data.[3] The 2001 Uniform Crime Reports (FBI, 2002) provides the following profile of the burglary offender. Nearly nine out of ten (86%) arrestees were men. Almost one third of the persons arrested were under the age of 18 and roughly six in ten were under 25. African Americans are overrepresented, comprising 29% of the arrestee population. While precise data are not available, it is safe to conclude that young, black males are overrepresented in the population of persons arrested.

Most burglaries take on a hit-and-run quality. Offenders claim that they try to spend as little time as possible getting in and getting out of the dwellings that they burglarize (Cromwell et al., 1991; Wright and Decker, 1994). This haste often means that broken windows, clues to their identity, and/or overlooked valuables are left behind.

Once a theft-related burglary is completed, the offender is left with the task of converting the stolen goods into cash. One option has the offender serving an entrepreneurial role and selling or trading the goods (for drugs or other desired commodities). In most urban communities, there exists what Henry (1978) terms an **underground economy.** This is the informal market economy that allows thieves to sell their booty to residents (from the seediest drug dealer to the most law-abiding blue-collar employee) who are more than happy to buy "warm" or even clearly "hot" goods if the price is right. These transactions run the gamut from a quick sale by the burglar out of the trunk of his or her car to a seasoned fence who stocks an entire warehouse or pawn shop with stolen goods. This entrepreneurial course of action requires time and effort on the part of the burglar. Many offenders choose to avoid these hassles by passing the stolen goods along to a fence. A **fence** is an individual who specializes in the buying and selling of stolen goods. Several case studies have been published about the "life and crimes" of persons who make a living from buying and selling of stolen goods (Cromwell et al., 1993; Gibbs and Shelly, 1982; Klockars, 1974; Steffensmeier, 1986). The Walsh and Chappell article that appears later in this chapter details the fence's role in the context of what the authors call the broader **stolen property system.** This concept refers to the various players (i.e., burglar, fence, buyer) and roles (extraction, repackaging, marketing, and sale) that come together to sustain a market for stolen property.

CRIMINAL CAREER

Burglary offenders generally exhibit pronounced criminal careers. The Hart and Reaves (1999) study of felony defendants from our nation's seventy-five largest counties provides a host of data to support this observation. Only 32% of the 4,000+ defendants who stood before the courts on felony burglary charge were without a prior felony arrest record. One third had a rap sheet containing ten or more arrests. Moreover, half had a prior felony criminal conviction under their belt and 10% had been convicted five or more times in the past. Four of ten burglary defendants were in an active criminal justice status (i.e., on probation, parole, or pretrial release) at the time that they were arrested for the burglary offense in question. Hart and Reaves conclude that the criminal history patterns of the burglary defendants were more pronounced than any other type of defendant.

Research on active burglars suggests that they engage in only limited specialization of offense (Cromwell et al., 1991; Reppetto, 1974; Shover, 1996; Wright and Decker, 1994). Most live a lifestyle that is build around immediate gratification (drug or drinking habits and frivolous spending) and are thus almost constantly in need of cash. They are not picky about the exact source of the funds and tend to pursue a host of illicit income-generating avenues (e.g., motor vehicle theft, robbery, larceny, fraud, drug sales). Langan and Levin's (2002) recidivism study provides indirect support for these claims. While nearly 74% of the burglars in their sample got in trouble with the law within 3 years of release into the community, only 23% were rearrested on a new burglary charge.

When specialization does occur among burglars, it tends to take on a "short term" quality (Maguire and Bennet, 1982, p. 80). This point is detailed at length in the article by Decker, Wright, Redfern, and Smith that appears later in this chapter. Their interviews with 105 active urban residential burglars found that better than 1 in 3 had restricted their criminal activities solely to the crime of burglary during the past 6 months. This finding suggests that some habitual street offenders may fall into a groove and rely exclusively on burglary to support their drug use or fast-paced lifestyle. Over time, factors such as an opportunistic introduction to other criminal outlet, increased perceived risk, or a saturation of "desirable" targets will inevitably lead them astray from their **short-term specialization.**

COGNITIVE ASPECTS OF BURGLARY

Burglary is a crime that is principally guided by shallow instrumental motives. Most would-be offenders are drawn to the crime because of its monetary payoff. Habitual offenders describe burglary as a low-risk, high-yield form of crime (Cromwell et al., 1991; Shover, 1996; Wright and Decker, 1994). These risk perceptions are shaped by several factors. First, by implementing a minimal level of vigilance and commonsense, most offenders know that they can get in and out of a home or business without being identified. Second, they know that in lieu of physical evidence or eyewitness testimony, burglary offenses are difficult for police to solve. Third, seasoned offenders know that urban burglary victims (especially repeat victims) tend to have little faith in the police department's ability to remedy their property losses or effect an arrest and thus may not be inclined to pursue the matter with the authorities. Finally, criminals know that burglary offenses are a low priority for law enforcement—numerous urban police forces now funnel burglary calls for service into an automated phone system that does little more than generate a police report for home owner's insurance purposes.

Most burglars become accustomed to a fast-paced lifestyle and/or are addicted to drugs and thus continue to commit burglaries in the face of increasing risks and diminished rewards (Maguire and Bennet, 1982; Walsh, 1980, and 1986; Wright and Decker, 1994). In rare instances, burglars are known to exhibit expressive motivations. Inquiries such as the ones conducted by Wright and Decker (1994), Cromwell et al. (1991), Reppetto (1974), and even Rengert and Wasilchick (2000) reveal that burglars sometimes commit their crimes for excitement, revenge, or while in a drug- or alcohol-induced stupor.

Issues of planning and target selection are critical to the burglar's decision-making process. Planning refers to any preevent preparations that the burglar might put in place to aid him or her in more smoothly accomplishing goals.

These preparations might include recruiting of accomplices with specific skills, "casing" the targeted establishment, or arranging for transportation. *Research indicates that most burglars engage in only minimal preevent planning* (Wright and Decker, 1994; Rengert and Wasilchick, 2000). They see no need to spend a lot of time thinking through the how, when, and where of their offending. Instead, they tend to operate in a somewhat spontaneous fashion, exploiting opportunities as they arise. For example, a motivated offender may come to burglarize a house with an accomplice, but he or she is apt to do so more because the associate is equally willing to take down an easy mark than the fact that they were recruited in advance. Bennett and Wright (1984) use the term **opportunistic planning** to refer to the more spontaneous breed of burglar who identifies break-in opportunities as they arise and quickly formulates and implements a plan of attack.

Alternatively, Bennett and Wright (1984) observe that seasoned professionals often engage in **search planning,** whereby they are willing to spend considerable time looking for lucrative targets or wait for tipsters to supply them with such locations. These burglars might even limit their offending to specific types of dwellings (supermarkets, hotels). Once a target is acquired, the offender(s) will formulate a predetermined division of labor, become familiar with the dwelling, and map out contingency-based extraction and escape scenarios. Interview data reveal that these meticulous prowlers view planning as the cornerstone of a low-risk, high-yield approach to the trade (Maguire and Bennet, 1982; Shover, 1996).

Target selection refers to the strategic criteria that attract or repel a would-be offender from a given dwelling. Oftentimes, offenders wait for someone else to direct them toward desirable targets. More precisely, they may rely on **inside information** from someone who is familiar with the dwelling (Cromwell et al., 1991). For example, an acquaintance, employee, subcontractor (pest control worker, landscaper, maid, cable guy, etc.), or pizza delivery driver might identify a given home or business as being particularly susceptible to a break-in. These informants sometimes go so far as to leave doors or windows unlocked or provide the location and type of valuables that are available for the taking. Such tips are invaluable to the burglar and usually result in some form of pay-off for the informant before or after the crime is committed (Shover, 1996; Wright and Decker, 1994).

Much of what we know about offender decision-making processes comes from a series of innovative studies specifically undertaken to assess the "in-the-field" thought processes of active burglars (Cromwell et al., 1991; Reppetto, 1974; Wright and Decker, 1994; Wright, Logie, and Decker, 1995). Collectively, these studies suggest that burglars are sensitive to the physical space and architectural design. These characteristics play an important role in whether they follow through on a desire to victimize a given home or business. Cromwell et al. (1991) distill offenders' target selection processes down into three categories: occupancy probes, surveillability cues, and accessibility cues. **Occupancy cues** allow the offender to determine if the dwelling is currently vacant. Empty homes or businesses are ideal because they minimize the likelihood that the assailant will be observed, interrupted, or reported while engaging in the crime. Burglars, therefore, become well versed at scanning the environment for signs of occupancy. Cues such as cars in the driveway/garage, silhouettes in the windows, or the sound of voices tell them that someone is home and that they are wise to keep moving along their way. A burglar might go so far as to look for newspapers on the stoop or a mailbox full of mail. Some will even knock on the door or call on the phone to see if anyone is inside. The most seasoned burglars will take a few days to study the daily routines of the occupants and even the neighbors.

Surveillability cues direct attention to the perimeter of a potential target. Here, the offenders seeks to determine whether they will be able to get into and out of an unoccupied structure without drawing the attention of neighbors or passers by. Ideal targets are poorly lit, secluded, fenced-in locations with minimal traffic and easily accessed entry and escape points. Conversely, nosey or nearby neighbors, significant foot traffic, neighbors with dogs, and the absence of shrubbery or fencing can encourage a burglar to move along their way. Cromwell et al. (1991) found that some burglars seek to blend into the environment by wearing uniforms or driving service vehicles that deflect attention.

Accessibility cues focus on the issue of entry. Here, the assailants seek out soft targets with unsophisticated or inoperable security devices. Unlocked doors or windows are appealing, while **target hardening devices** such as deadbolt locks, burglar alarms, burglar bars, or dogs serve as deterrents. Cromwell et al. (1991) found that some burglars claim to have knowledge or skills regarding how to defeat sophisticated locks or alarm systems but, in practice, almost always chose to avoid undertaking the task. It appears that offenders are pragmatic on these issues; namely, they see no reason to take on a challenging target when they can bank on the fact that a "soft" one exists somewhere nearby.

Drug and alcohol use appears to have an important impact on the thought processes of burglary offenders. Mumola's (1999) survey of federal and state prison inmates found that the majority (56%) of incarcerated burglars were under the influence of drugs or alcohol at the time of their most recent offense. Urinalysis testing of arrestees suggests that the actual level of offense-related substance use may be even higher—nearly 80% of the burglars who were tested via the Arrestee Drug Abuse Monitoring (ADAM) program were shown to have drugs or alcohol in their system (National Institute of Justice, 1998). These alarming statistics have led some to look more closely at the relationship between substance use and burglary (i.e., drugs/crime relationship). Cromwell, Olson, Avary, and Marks (1991) interviewed thirty active burglars with established drug habits. Several significant trends were revealed. As expected, these offenders explained that they relied on burglary as a primary source of money to support their drug habit (i.e., instrumental motive source). Somewhat unexpectedly, drug use was said to facilitate the actual commission of burglars. That is, the burglars claimed that they routinely used drugs to enhance their skills (alertness, steadiness, etc.) or to calm their nerves just prior to offending. Respondents described a tenuous relationship between burglary and drug use—they recognized that some drugs such as cocaine or other stimulants will predictably yield poor decision making and increased risks.

Burglars appear to rely on simple and pragmatic normative neutralizations to account for their criminal indiscretions. Most burglars attach a sense of necessity to their crimes (Cromwell et al., 1991; Maguire and Bennett, 1982; Rengert and Wasilchick, 2000; Reppetto, 1974; Shover, 1996; Waller and Okihiro, 1978; Wright and Decker, 1994). For those with substance abuse problems, burglary is viewed as a primary means by which they can feed the habit and thus avoid withdrawal. For the nonaddicted offenders that Wright and Decker (1994) interviewed, burglary represented a reliable source of illegitimate income (along with robbery, theft, and drug dealing) by which they could solve pressing financial crises and/or sustain their free-wheeling lifestyle and delicate social status.

CULTURAL COMPONENTS OF BURGLARY

Given that burglars are disproportionately young, poor, city-dwellers, they tend to have frequent contacts with other habitual offenders. The upcoming Walsh and Chappell article speaks directly to this issue, as it will outline the various structures and processes that go along with the "stolen property system"—the underground market through which in-demand goods are stolen, housed, marketed, and resold on the streets of America.

Burglary is a crime that is marked by varied levels of social organization (Best and Luckenbilll, 1994). Only on rare occasions do we find burglars who work as loners or within formal organizations. More often, burglars will operate as colleagues—the offender commits the crime alone but relies on other members of the criminal subculture to supply him or her with inside information or to assist in converting stolen property into cash. Burglars who take the situation to the next level and enlist help in the actual break-in follow a more peerlike existence. Here, loose partnerships are maintained and invoked when a burglary opportunity presents itself. A primitive example of the peer model would be two or three drug users who randomly stumble upon an unlocked home or unsupervised business and decide to work together to take it down. In some cases, burglary offenders will align themselves in what Best and Luckenbill (1994) term a teamlike format. These offenders invoke a division of labor with each participant serving a own predetermined role and duties. One person might be assigned a lookout/driver role. Another might serve as the entry specialist, defeating any lock and alarms that are confronted. Still another person can take on the "muscle" role, responsible for doing the heavy lifting.

Socialization scripts play an important part in how and why burglars commit their crimes. Interview-based research suggests that novice or occasional burglars often rely on the tutelage of more seasoned offenders as a way of learning the proverbial ropes of burglary. Novices receive advice and instruction on issues such as target selection, how to foster informants, how to defeat burglary countermeasures, and how best to convert stolen goods into cash (Cromwell et al., 1991; Cromwell, Olson, and Avary, 1993; Reppetto, 1974; Shover, 1996; Wright and Decker, 1994). This socialization generally takes shape as informal street corner conversations or jailhouse bravado.

SOCIETAL REACTION TO BURGLARY

On paper, burglary appears to receive serious treatment from the criminal justice system. The Model Penal Code (American Law Institute, 1962) classifies burglary as a felony in the third degree. In most jurisdictions, such an offense is subject to 1 to 5 years in prison. If the burglar is armed or threatens or inflicts bodily harm on another while unlawfully within a dwelling, that individual might see the charges elevated to second degree felony.

In practice, however, burglary receives mixed levels of formal response from the various components of the criminal justice system. First, let us consider the response of law enforcement authorities. Police agencies were able to effect an arrest for only 13% of the nearly 2.1 million burglaries that were reported to them in 2001 (FBI, 2002). No other form of index crime yields such a dismal clearance rate. Some of this slippage can be attributed to the covert nature of the crime—police often have no witnesses and minimal clues to guide the investigation. However, these low clearance rates are also impacted by the fact that many police officers and police agencies afford a low priority to burglary cases (Cordner, Greene, and Bynum, 1983; Rubenstein, 1974).

Court data reveal a different trend in terms of the veracity with which burglary cases are adjudicated. Durose, Levin, and Langan (2001) observed that U.S. courts produced nearly 90,000 felony burglary convictions in 1998. This figure represents 10% of all felony convictions that year. Hart and Reaves (1999) found that 68% of the burglary cases that were tried resulted in a conviction for the same offense and only 24% avoided some sort of conviction. The researchers found that burglary defendants do not receive a reprieve from the courts when it comes time for sentencing. A full 74% of the convicted burglars were sentenced to time behind bars. This rate was surpassed only by murder, robbery, drug trafficking, and driving-related offenses. While the median prison sentence for a convicted burglar was 41 months, nearly 10% received sentences in excess of 10 years.

Our correctional system does not appear to be particularly forgiving to persons who are convicted of burglary. Durose et al. (2001) estimate that, on average, burglary offenders can expect to serve almost half of their sentence—roughly 2 years. These time-served figures are on par with those of other property offenses (theft, fraud, and motor vehicle theft) but somewhat lower than that observed for violent (54%) and weapon-related offenses (60%).

Accounts from known burglars clearly suggest that informal social control efforts go a long way to deter and/or displace burglary activity (Cromwell et al., 1991; Maguire and Bennet, 1982; Rengert and Wasilchick, 2000; Wright and Decker, 1994). For instance, Cromwell and his colleagues (1999) contend that a minimal amount of vigilance on the part of homeowners can go a long way. They state:

> Measures designed to combat the relatively small population of high incidence "professional" burglars tend to overemphasize the skill and determination of most burglars. They are expensive, complex, and require long term commitment at many levels. . . . In fact, most burglars are young, unskilled, and opportunistic. This suggests that emphasis should be directed at such factors as surveillability, occupancy, and accessibility.

More specifically, dogs, good locks, and alarm systems deter most burglars (Cromwell et al., 1999, p. 195).

Community-level informal social control can also play an important role in burglary prevention. Cromwell et al.'s (1991) discussion of surveillability cues suggests that burglars tend to avoid neighborhoods with a lot of foot traffic or active neighborhood watches. This implies that observant or even nosy neighbors can have a measurable impact on burglary. However, as Wright and Decker (1994) observe, these types of collective efforts are difficult to enact and maintain in the areas that burglars most prefer—urban neighborhoods.

If nothing else, research by Waller and Okihiro (1978) and Rengert and Wasilchick (2000) suggest that the tenets of "crime prevention through environmental design" (Jeffrey, 1977) should be considered at a neighborhood level. These researchers found that simple environmental characteristics such as cul-de-sac street design, high levels of lighting, and well pruned landscaping that minimizes unobservable entry and exit points can have a significant impact on burglary victimization levels in a given community.

The aforementioned informal social control efforts represent examples of target hardening strategies aimed at deterring would-be burglars from victimizing a given house or displacing offenders from a given community. Wright and Decker (1994) see target hardening measures as short-sighted and potentially ineffective means of social control. These authors endorse a more fundamental measure of informal social control. Namely, they suggest that measures be designed and implemented that aim to undermine offenders' strong attachment to street culture. They offer expanded employment opportunities as one possible, but foreboding avenue to lure the offenders out of street life.

There exist even more simple and realistic measures that might effect change in this area. For example, Gillham (1992) details a coordinated burglary prevention program that was implemented in a midsize U.S. city during the early 1980s. He found that community activism and community involvement (i.e., block meetings, neighborhood cleanups, and raised awareness of vulnerabilities and potential offenders) showed promise for reducing burglary. In short, if community members care about the condition of their neighborhood and are willing to take steps to clean it up and exercise vigilance over problem people and places, there is hope for reducing burglary and other forms of street crime.

NOTES

1. Many jurisdictions impose a fourth requirement, namely, that the crime occur during nighttime.

2. A close examination of NCVS and UCR data suggests that 50% to 60% of all residential burglaries go unreported. The figure reported here was derived by adding the NCVS data on residential burglaries to an adjusted estimate of nonresidential burglaries that were reported in the UCR—one that factors a 60% nonreporting rate.

3. These data must be viewed with caution because 50% to 60% of all burglaries go unreported to police and only 14% of these lead to an arrest.

KEY TERMS

accessibility cues	inside information	search planning
burglary	nonresidential burglary	stolen property system
crime against habitation	occupancy cues	surveillability cues
crime of intrusion	opportunistic planning	target hardening devices
fence	residential burglary	underground economy

DISCUSSION QUESTIONS

1. Over time, the crime of burglary has slowly slipped down the list of crime fighting priorities. At present, less than half of all burglaries get reported to police, and only 13% of those result in an arrest. What kinds of social and legal factors have contributed to this present level of empathy when it comes to the formal and informal social control of burglary?

2. Adjudication data suggest that accused burglars face a high certainty of being convicted and sentenced to prison. This should send a message to police that burglary is a high priority for our nation's prosecutors and judges. Still, burglary investigation and arrest efforts remain lukewarm at best. What kinds of factors contribute to police officers' attitudes and behaviors regarding burglary patrol and enforcement?

3. Considerable evidence suggests that burglars refine strategies and cues that help them identify soft and potentially lucrative targets. Does this mean that burglars are more rational and planful than other types of criminals?

11

A Woman's Place Is in the Home: Females and Residential Burglary

SCOTT DECKER,
RICHARD WRIGHT,
ALLISON REDFERN,
AND DIETRICH SMITH
University of Missouri–St. Louis

These authors forward a gender-based analysis of residential burglary. The study is based on interviews with 105 active residential burglars, 87 of whom were males and 18 were females. The project employed a snowball sampling strategy in which an ex-offender

Excerpted with permission from *Justice Quarterly*, Vol. 10, No. 1 (March 1996), pp. 143–162,
© 1993 Academy of Criminal Justice Sciences.

recruited known burglars who were presently operating in a Midwestern city. They present their findings in two parts. First, they provide the reader with a comparison of male and female offending patterns. This includes consideration of overall and gender-based break-downs of demographics, frequency of offending, longevity of offending, offending styles, drug and alcohol usage, and arrest and adjudication information. The second part of the article uses the interview data from the female offenders to formulate a typology of female burglars. The gender-based comparison suggests that, in many ways, female burglars resemble their male counterparts. For example, both groups display long criminal histories that span a variety of property, violent, and public order offense categories. Both groups accumulate long, diverse substance abuse histories that overlap with and contribute to their involvements in burglary. At the same time, the gender-based comparisons reveal several differences. Female burglars begin offending at a later age, are more likely to co-offend, and have less contact with authorities. The authors' typology of female burglars describes offenders as either accomplices or partners. Factors of motivation, levels of target selection and planning, and patterned work roles serve to differentiate these two conceptual categories. The authors' gender-based comparisons do well to touch upon many of the behavioral dimensions of burglary, while the formulation and articulation of the authors' typology of female burglars speaks in depth about the cognitive and cultural dimensions of burglary.

D espite growing interest in female criminality, little is known about the *nature* of women's participation in crimes statistically dominated by males. Certainly that is the case for residential burglary, an offense labeled by Shover (1991) as an overwhelmingly male enterprise. For example, we hardly know how females become involved in such offenses or what roles they play. Are they tempted into these crimes, for instance, by the influence of delinquent peers or by the use of drugs? Because we lack detailed knowledge, we cannot assess the extent to which the processes underlying burglaries commited by females differ from those underlying burglaries by males. This lack also restricts our capacity to detect important differences among female burglars. An assessment of these differences, however, is crucial in formulating effective policy responses to female criminality and to developing theories of lawbreaking by women (Simpson, 1991).

Short of observing burglaries, perhaps the best way to acquire this information is to go to the offenders themselves. As Feeney (1986) noted, the first-hand perspective possessed by offenders is unique and must be taken into account in attempting to explain and prevent crime. In setting a research agenda for feminist criminology, Daly and Chesney-Lind make a similar point: "The most pressing need today is . . . to get our hands dirty [through observation and interviewing], and to plunge more deeply into the social worlds of girls and women" (1988: 518–19). Such a strategy, they observe, will allow researchers "to comprehend women's crime on its own terms."

This article, based on field interviews with currently active offenders, examines women's involvement in residential burglary by (1) comparing their characteristics to those of their male counterparts and (2) outlining a typology of female burglars which emphasizes the roles they play during offenses.

FINDINGS: COMPARISON OF MALE
AND FEMALE BURGLARS

We compared the male and female offenders in regard to their participation in crimes other than residential burglary, their offending "styles" (i.e., tendency to specialize, to co-offend, to use alcohol and drugs), their histories of offending, and their contact with the criminal justice system. Before reporting these comparisons, we must emphasize that any observed differences may be sampling artifacts. In addition, the small number of female burglars may introduce some instability into the comparisons.

Self-Reported Crimes

Often it is claimed that offenders are versatile and commit a wide range of offenses (see, for example, Gottfredson and Hirschi, 1990). This observation, however, is derived largely from studies of males conducted in criminal justice settings rather than on the street. During our interviews we asked the subjects whether they ever had committed other sorts of crimes beside residential burglary. We did so because we were concerned primarily with prevalence—that is, whether the subject ever had engaged in other kinds of offenses. The 11 crimes mentioned most often by our interviewees are presented in Table 5.1.

Stealing (which includes shoplifting and corresponds to the legal definition of this activity), auto theft, and assault were the offenses most commonly reported by the males. Stealing and assault were mentioned most frequently by the females; these offenses were comparable in rank of frequency to those reported by the males. Beyond these two offenses, however, little other criminality was reported by the females. The only meaningful difference between the men and the women for this measure was found in regard to auto theft. This crime was fairly common among the males, but unknown among the females. The explanation for this difference might reside in a strong cultural tradition linking masculinity to driving and car ownership. Alternatively, males may have "cornered the market" in auto theft; to be profitable, such a crime requires sophisticated connections with garage owners, junkyard employees, and car dealerships.

Styles of Offending

One important aspect of offending style concerns the degree of crime specialization—that is, the extent to which offenders concentrate on one particular type of offense. The results reported in Table 5.1 revealed considerable diversity among our respondents over time. A somewhat different picture emerged, however, when we asked the offenders whether they had been involved in crimes other than residential burglary during their most recent period of offending.

Thirty-four percent of the males and 42 percent of the females claimed that they had committed only residential burglaries during this period

Table 5.1 Percentages of Respondents Engaging in Criminal Acts

	Males % (N = 87)	Females % (N = 18)
Stealing (includes shoplifting)	27	33
Auto theft	26	0
Commercial burglary	6	0
Drug sales	5	0
Robbery	15	6
Weapons offenses	14	6
Assault	26	17
Prostitution	0	6
Public order offenses	14	6
Forgery	2	0
Murder, manslaughter	1	0

(roughly the last six months). This finding is consistent with a substantial body of previous research showing that offenders display considerable diversity over the course of their criminal careers, but may specialize in a particular "line" for short periods. Maguire and Bennett (1982: 80) labeled this phenomenon "short-term specialization" (also see Shover, 1991).

Another element of offending style concerns the inclinations to work with others in carrying out crimes. Previous research demonstrated that "more often than not, [burglary] is committed by two or more persons acting in concert" (Shover, 1991: 89). The results of our study bear this out: 79 percent of the males and *all* of the females reported that they had worked with others in the past. The males showed considerable variation in frequency of working with others: 39 percent said they "seldom" worked with others, while another 39 percent reported that they "always" did so. For the women, however, the picture was much clearer: an overwhelming 83 percent reported that they "always" worked with others, and the remaining 17 percent stated that they "usually" did so.

The final aspect of offending style that we examined here relates to drug and alcohol use among our respondents, as well as to their perceptions of the role played by intoxicants in leading them to commit such crimes. As Table 5.2 reveals, we found little difference between the males and the females in self-reported drug use.

When the drugs users were asked whether addiction had anything to do with their burglaries, 71 percent of the males and 82 percent of the females answered affirmatively. A majority of those in both groups said they committed burglaries to obtain the money they needed to buy more drugs. In addition, slightly more than three-quarters of the users in each group—76 percent of the males and 79 percent of the females—claimed that they used drugs *before* committing their burglaries. A higher percentage of females than of males stated that they "always" or "usually" used drugs beforehand. One explanation

Table 5.2 Drug and Alcohol Use

	Males (%) (N=87)	Females (%) (N=18)
No drug use	17	17
	(N=72)	(N=15)
Marijuana	72	73
Heroin	19	7
Cocaine	32	40
PCP	3	7
Other drugs	7	13
Do you consider yourself an addict?	37	47
Does your drug use have anything to do with your burglaries?	71	82
Do you use drugs before burglaries?	76	79
How often do you use drugs before committing burglaries?		
Seldom	32	9
Usually	41	55
Always	27	36
	(N=87)	(N=18)
Do you drink before your burglaries?	65	72
	(N=58)	(N=13)
Does your drinking have anything to do with your burglaries?	43	54
How often do you drink before committing burglaries?		
Seldom	40	31
Usually	25	31
Always	35	39

seems to be that many female burglaries arise from crack "runs." This point, however, is difficult to determine conclusively because (as noted above) use of the drug is heavily stigmatized.

History of Burglary Offending

We explored male-female difference on three dimensions designed to measure burglary offending histories: age at first burglary, total number of lifetime burglaries, and *lambda,* the mean number of annual burglaries.

The ages at which males and females committed their first residential burglary differed significantly: the males generally started much earlier in life. None of the female burglars had committed their first offense before age 12, but 22 percent of the males had done so. The modal category for males was the 13–16 age bracket, which accounted for 53 percent of the cases. Sixty-one percent of the females, on the other hand, were over 16 years old when they carried out their first burglary.

Given that the females started to commit burglaries later, on average, than their male counterparts, we are not surprised that a greater proportion of females had been involved in fewer than 20 residential burglaries in their lifetime. Perhaps more interesting, 39 percent of the females had committed more than 70 lifetime residential burglaries, a proportion roughly comparable to the males' figure of 41 percent. The bimodal distribution of the females' responses suggests that women are likely to engage in burglary at two very distinct levels, and perhaps to employ two different styles.

Contact with the Criminal Justice System

The males were more likely than the females to have had contact with the system for offenses of all types. This difference was most notable at the stage of the criminal justice process that resulted in incarceration. Over 90% of the respondents in each group had been arrested previously, but only one woman (6 percent) had been convicted and sentenced to a term of imprisonment. In contrast, 26 percent of the males had served time in the past. This difference may exist in part because the females began offending later and consequently had fewer "years at risk." Other factors, however, are probably at work as well, including (1) an assumption by the police that most burglars are male, which allows females to remain above suspicion (Horowitz and Pottieger, 1991), and (2) a tendency for those females who *are* arrested to receive preferential treatment in the courtroom (Simon, 1975). Certainly the women in our sample believe that their sex conferred a degree of protection from the law. Several expressed the belief that authorities would not take action against them simply because they were female.

FINDINGS: TYPES OF FEMALE BURGLARS

The data reported above suggest some of the ways in which female residential burglars may differ from their male counterparts. This information, however, tells us little about the nature of female participation in these crimes. Do female burglars, for example, tend to play "secondary roles" (Ward et al., 1979: 122) during offenses? To answer questions such as this, we constructed a typology of female residential burglars, using detailed descriptions of offenses provided by the women themselves.

In constructing our typology, we used the categories of *accomplice* and *partner* identified by Ward et al. (1979). (Our sample contained no *sole perpetrators*. By definition, *conspirators* were not included in the research because they did not participate directly in committing the offence.) We categorized six of the females in our study as *accomplices* because of their subservience to others—usually men—during their burglaries. (Not only females act as accomplices; a few of the males whom we interviewed also assumed this role. In no case, however, did a male respondent admit to being subservient to a woman during offenses.) We classified the 12 remaining females as *partners* because they participated as equals in their burglaries. Although some of these females co-offended with males, they did not take orders from them.

Partners could be distinguished form accomplices in a number of important ways, including (1) their motivation for committing the crimes, (2) their participation in target selection and planning, and (3) the work roles they adopted while committing the burglaries.

Motivation

The factors that the female burglars regarded as leading them to commit their crimes differentiated the partners clearly from the accomplices. Those who worked as partners, whether with other women, with men, or both, reported making an independent decision to commit their burglaries. They did not see themselves as drawn into offending against their will by other offenders or by the irresistible pressure of circumstances. The independence of such offenders is illustrated in the following quote:

> My partners ain't got to influence me. I just want to do it. I'm so used to doing it.

Women who carried out burglaries as partners often were motivated by material or instrumental concerns. Their responses reflected an affirmative commitment to burglary. Some, for example, saw the offense simply as an easy way of obtaining money. As one of them said,

> [Burglary's] a damn good way of getting over. It's like a white-collar crime. Hell, it's just fast money.

The women who worked as partners displayed considerable diversity in motives. Some reported engaging in burglary because they found it fun or enjoyable. These women derived a psychic reward from such offenses. One of the women said she committed burglaries for "the thrill," adding

> I get off on it. I do it for the enjoyment, 'cause I do truly enjoy it. It's a hobby; it's recreation to me.

The women who worked only as accomplices had a far different perspective. These offenders felt that they were caught up in circumstances beyond their control, which compelled them to commit burglaries. Often these circumstances arose in the context of an unequal relationship in which the females were reduced to carrying out the will of other, more dominant people. The dominant parties in such cases typically were males, though occasionally they were females. The woman quoted in the following passage expresses the belief that she was trapped by her companions' activities:

> [The burglaries] got worse when we moved and I started hanging with a different crowd. It wasn't too bad where I first did it. It's getting worse now, though, 'cause I'm with older guys and they go for bigger things,

and when they go, they got things planned—if somebody walks in before they are done, they would rather hurt them first.

Another entanglement for accomplices involved the lack of employment:

Sometimes I have to wonder myself why I [commit burglaries]. And I always come to the conclusion that my kids need things. I always go and fill out applications and everything like that, but they don't never seem to call back. Every time I want to go and finish school, something is always in my way.

Drugs also played a prominent role:

I got into this thing with cocaine with my friend, and she don't work or anything, and it ain't cheap. So I pretty much go out with the boys to get what we want. It is getting pretty deep.

Alcohol also was contributory factor. One woman explained that she and a male friend were enticed into burglaries by a third offender while they were intoxicated:

[Another offender would] always get us both either drinking alcohol, or [my friend] smoked marijuana a lot. I only smoked it two times in my life and I didn't like it and I don't do it, but he would get me drunk and say we need some more money. Then they would go to a house.

Target Selection and Planning

Females' participation in burglary can be examined with reference to their role in finding targets and planning offenses. The extent to which offenders participate in these tasks distinguishes partners clearly from accomplices. A number of the women with partner status played an important role in finding targets and planning offenses, as illustrated by the following quote:

Last time I took him. It was a real good, decent neighborhood, you know, like in the county. I mean, we just sit up and . . . spot them up, and I find what I find and he get what he get and we just go. It's like a sharing thing with us. He come to me and ask me what's up. I tell him nothing, but I know where we can get some money. We just come to each other. "I ain't doing nothing, what's happening?" "Well, I ain't got no money either, but I know where we can get some." He asked me if I been watching a house. "Yeah, I've been watching a house. There's some old people and they go to church every Sunday. Every Sunday they go. They be gone from like about four to five hours. They go to church in the morning, Sunday school then, you know, all of that. I had watched that one. They be old people. They be having good stuff."

Planning was crucial for many of the females who worked as partners in committing burglaries:

That's one reason why we got so many youngsters in jail today. I see this, so let's make a hit. No, no, no. If they see this and it looks good, then it's going to be there for a while. So the point is, you have to case it and make sure you know everything. I want to know what time you go to work, the time the children go to school. I know there's no one coming home for lunch. So plan it with somebody else. We'll take the new dishwasher, washing machine, and this other stuff. We just put it in the truck. Do you know when people rent a truck, nobody ever pays that any attention? They think you're moving [but] only if you rent a truck. Now if you bring it out of there and put it in the car, that's a horse of another color.

A few of the females classified as partners occasionally engaged in more spontaneous burglaries. The women who worked in this way, however, did not do so exclusively. These "spur-of-the-moment" burglaries emerged in the course of their day-to-day activities.

Women involved in burglaries as accomplices exercised much less control over the selection of targets and the planning of crimes. (In fact, some were unaware that a burglary was going to take place until they arrived at the site.) Other people invariably set up the burglaries:

He'll call me, you know. And he'll say "I don't think we're going out today." I'll say "OK." It's nothing really specific why he do it that way. He just stop for a little while and start back . . . [H]e'll pick them out. You can tell if it's a nice neighborhood or bad neighborhood. What areas we go in, he picks them out.

Work Roles

For the females who worked as partners, burglaries could involve a variety of tasks. Many of these tasks were indistinguishable from those traditionally associated with men, such as gaining entry, searching the house, carrying goods outside, and disposing of them. The following interview segment describes some of the tasks performed by a female acting as a partner. Although this was her first offense, she helped to find the transportation to reach the target (by stealing a truck) and took part in the actual break in:

Well, it wasn't up on me, somebody else who was in there different, not state, in a different county. He just came up and told me he knew about it, a rich guy that was gonna be gone for the weekend. He knew this person, knew who it was, and he knew about it. When he left that night about two or three in the morning, we went down there. We had stolen a truck, we had stolen my ex-boyfriend's father's truck, went down there. We tried to get in, but we couldn't get in. Everything was locked. Right. . . . We couldn't get in for nothing, so what we does was, we had some shit in back of the truck and we took some tape. Then we put it over the window real tight, then we busted it, and then we took the tape down and the window was shattered. It had no window in it. So—everybody used gloves of course—so we went in there, you know, and we knew, when we went, we knew nobody was gonna be home. There wasn't a house around for two blocks, each way you went. So . . . my first one was basically the easiest one.

As noted earlier, the target often was located by a female partner, who also took the lead in planning the offense. In these cases the woman had a substantial say in determining how the proceeds of the crime were divided:

> . . . whatever you chose to give to the other person. We tried to split everything equally. We were all good friends, you know, so I got the best deal out of it because of the fact that I needed the money more than everybody else. Me and my sister needed the money more than everybody did and . . . we were the ones that said hey, we pointed it out, we found a way to get in, we knew where everything was, we told them how, we had everything planned out down to the TV. This is where this is at and this is where that is at.

The roles played by female burglars are dynamic and can change over time. Many of the women who currently participate in offenses as partners started out as accomplices. The woman quoted below clearly has an equal relationship with her co-offenders, but this was not always the case:

> The first burglary I ever committed, I was in the house and I was smoking weed at the time. A friend came in and said "I want to go in this house." I said "Okay, it was around the corner. . . . what part am I going to play?" He says "All you got to do is watch the doors for me. The bags I bring down, take them out, and you also drive the car for me."

As should be obvious from the above, women who work as accomplices in burglary play much more limited roles. They seldom participate in planning the crime, and often do not even enter the dwelling. Some claimed to prefer working with others because they lacked the skills needed to be a successful burglar: "I can't do it all by myself . . . I haven't mastered that yet."

Others simply felt more comfortable when relying on a colleague's expertise; they were uncertain about their ability to work alone. In the following case, a woman reports that she deferred to her boyfriend's judgment in determining the suitability of a given target:

> He can look at them and tell. He's better at it than me. Sometimes I give him tips to go on, but he checks them out. I feel safer for him to check them out.

A common work assignment for accomplices was acting as a lookout or driver. Several of the women stated that driving was their primary job in burglaries:

> Well, see, me and my boyfriend had been together for a year, and he done them all the time. Well, not all the time, but it was no big deal, and all I had to do, all I ever do, is drive. I just go like he'll go, him and

his friend. He don't do 'em every week or anything like that. Like it's
not really 'cause we need the money or anything either. Like he'll go
during the day and he'll look at a house and he'll find one, and then
he'll tell me about where the house is . . . . all I have to do is drive to
the place and wait for them to start bringing out the stuff, and then
drive off.

Others said that they typically kept a lookout for their colleagues:

They came and picked me up with a stolen automobile. I didn't know
that it was stolen. We went out there to this house and they got out. I
just assumed—I didn't know what was going on at first. We got out and
they went in first, and then they came back out. One of the men came
back out and told me to come in and to keep an eye out to see if
anybody was there or anybody comes down the sidewalk or if anybody
drives down the street or anything.

In both of these cases the women, as accomplices, did not choose to perform
these secondary tasks. Instead the tasks were assigned to them by a dominant
co-offender.

CONCLUSION

What light does this quantitative and qualitative information shed on the
nature of female criminality? Our sample was not generated randomly; with
this fact in mind, the quantitative findings suggest that women involved in residential burglary do not differ significantly from their male counterparts on a
number of relevant dimensions (e.g., drug and alcohol use, degree of offense
specialization). Nevertheless, the results show that some important differences
may exist as well. Compared to the males, for example, the females (1) more
often committed burglaries with others, (2) began offending at a later age, and
(3) had less contact with the criminal justice system. Further examination of
these apparent differences is warranted.

The qualitative data demonstrate that women's involvement in residential
burglary is marked by diversity and that the debate about whether women play
a primary or a secondary role in the offense is probably a red herring. In fact,
as among males, some assume primary roles exclusively, some adopt secondary
roles exclusively, and other move from one type of role to another as they
become more experienced. This observation has important implications for
research into women's involvement in crimes committed more often by males.
To be sure, a much lower percentage of women than of men participate in residential burglary (Shover, 1991). Even so, our qualitative data reveal substantial
similarities between males and females. This fact suggests that the activities of
women who do engage in such offenses may be explained by some of the same
factors that explain men's participation.

12

Operational Parameters
in the Stolen Property System

MARILYN WALSH
DUNCAN CHAPPELL
Battelle Memorial Institute
Seattle, Washington

This article considers the way that the laws of supply and demand shape the stolen property system (SPS). This term refers to the loosely formed relationships that bring about the theft of property and the subsequent repackaging and resale of these goods via the "black market." The authors use contacts with law enforcement authorities to formulate a revised view of property crime. Instead of viewing burglaries as isolated incidents of theft, the authors argue that we should conceive of the acts and actors involved as spanning a more broadly defined set of roles and behaviors. They identify the thief, fence, and person who buys the stolen goods as key players in the SPS. They also identify multiple stages in the process: research and planning, extraction, exchange (i.e., conversion of the goods to money), marketing, redistribution/resale, and evaluation. Moreover, the roles and behaviors of the various players are said to be interchangeable and flexible. In the end, the authors urge us to reconsider the way that we think about property crime. They encourage us to be sensitive to the potential for business concepts such as division of labor, entrepreneurial spirit, supply and demand, and marketing to manifest themselves in the world of property theft. In doing so, the authors drive home the complexity and fluidity that can beset property crime events. Moreover, they illustrate how the criminal calculus can lead to mutually beneficial relationships and roles that allow the criminal subculture to expand and innovate.

A PROPERTY THEFT ORIENTATION

Perhaps no area of contemporary criminal activity holds more potential for improved understanding and successful intervention through analytical reorientation than does that of property theft. This area of crime is by no means new, a situation which may in fact constitute the greatest barrier to fresh

Reprinted from *Journal of Criminal Justice,* Vol. 2, © 1974, with permission from Elsevier Science.

thinking on the subject. Centuries of experience with thefts of property have given us a fairly strong conceptualization of this crime area, a conceptualization which centers almost exclusively on the thief. There is of course nothing illogical or erroneous about a concern for this individual; it is he after all who steals the property. What is argued here, however, is that an exclusive concentration on the thief yields a myopic view of the process of theft, a view which draws the boundaries of the crime too tightly around that individual. It is a view which tends therefore to consider each incident of theft as a unique event, determined and constrained by the motivations, needs, and skills of the perpetrator. This "conventional view of theft" (if we can use this phrase) prescribes a response to this crime which largely consists of a fairly sophisticated sorting process, linking one individual (or one group of individuals) with each event as it occurs.

Such an "individualistic" approach to crime and criminals is not, of course, confined to the property theft area. Cressey (1972:19), for example, suggests that it is the most prevalent approach to crime in general.

> Consistently, both the popular and scientific tendency is to view the criminal's behavior as a problem of individual maladjustment, not as a consequence of his participation in social systems. Perhaps it is for this reason that in criminology we have had thousands of studies that have sought some damaging trait in the personalities of individual criminals, but very few studies of the organizational arrangements among criminals who commit crimes in concert.

The tendency toward an individualistic interpretation of criminal behavior cannot be laid to the idiosyncracies of either the public or the scientist, but rather is undoubtedly influenced by the nature of the legal systems, with their concepts of individual responsibility an intent, upon which most democratic societies are based. But while such an interpretation may conform well to the needs of a legal system, it may have the additional effect of causing us to ignore some important dimensions of contemporary criminal behavior.

It is the perspective of this paper that property theft is one area of criminal behavior that has sorely suffered both conceptually and practically from a failure to probe "the relationships among criminals (and) . . . the structure and operations of illicit organizations." Perhaps the most glaring evidence of this failure concerns what the President's Crime Commission (1967:99) called the "little research . . . done on fencing," i.e., on the criminal receiver of stolen property. This crime figure, although tallying an impressive list of protestations to his importance over several centuries, (Colquhoun, 1806; Association of Grand Jurors of New York Country, 1928; Hall, 1968) has remained little explored, while his relationship with the thief has been virtually ignored by the criminologist. But if the popular and scientific tendency has been to overlook the fence, the police detective assigned the responsibility of dealing with property theft has not found it possible to do so. Instead, as the authors discovered in the course of an ongoing study of patterns of criminal receiving, police detectives possess a great deal of information about the fence. Other researchers have reported similar experiences (Mack, 1964 and 1970).

Because the police know about the fence does not imply that his activities are either successfully or efficiently interdicted, for the police agency is as influenced by an individualistic approach to crime as is the social scientist. Thus the bulk of enforcement resources and activity against theft is directed to the thief, and the situation in which police effort is devoted directly and *exclusively* to the fence appears to be rare indeed. The criminal receiver remains a curiosity to the criminal justice system, being infrequently arrested and even less often convicted.

The model of property theft employed here—the Stolen Property System— is an operationally based one, derived from the author's research into patterns of criminal receiving in a large urban area of the northeastern United States. As part of this study, access to police intelligence reports on the activities of burglars and fences has been obtained, as well as records of these activities maintained in a special investigative unit in the office of the district attorney. References to specific police reports, etc., found below are drawn primarily from these sources.

THE SCOPE AND DIMENSIONS
OF THE STOLEN PROPERTY SYSTEM

The Stolen Property System (hereafter SPS) is that set of individuals *and their interactions* which locates, plans, facilitates, and its transfer to a new owner. Ideally this system will have six functioning modes:

1. *Research and planning mode*—The determination of a demand for an item(s), its location, and how best it can be acquired.
2. *Extraction mode*—The actual separation of property from its owner (the theft).
3. *Exchange mode*—The transfer of the item from the extractor to the marketer (the person who will offer it for sale).
4. *Marketing mode*—This includes transportation and storage, demand analysis (marketing information subsystem), packaging and advertising (any necessary modification in property prior to resale).
5. *Redistribution mode*—The determination of where, when, and at what price the item will be resold.
6. *Evaluation model*—The analysis of the feedback to the system as to its performance.

In its simplest form, the SPS can consist of but a single individual as in the case of the thief peddling his own merchandise. In this situation, mode 3 would be combined with mode 2 into a single operation. At the uppermost level of complexity, the SPS can contain many individuals (the maximum number being indeterminate) as in the case of a truck hijacking. In this situation, the planning mode (mode 1) alone will require either the accurate forecasting of the behaviors of shipper, dispatcher, and driver, *or* the enlistment of the aid of one or all of these individuals. It is important to note that whether the SPS consists of one or a dozen individuals, *all* of its operations must be performed. If this is not done by those within the system, then it will be undertaken by its clients or by others in the environment. An abridged version of the SPS, then, does not imply a functional curtailment, but rather a combining of functions into fewer operational steps.

There is some evidence that the SPS in its simplest form does in fact occur. Eric Pace (1971) noted that the low prices which fences were offering to addicts for stolen property were forcing addicts to sell the merchandise themselves. It is clear, however, that the nature of the SPS is such that its most frequent manifestation consists of a division of labor between *at least two* individuals—the thief and the fence. Robert Earl Barnes explained it this way:

> A thief who steals merchandise is like bread without yeast, no good, just as yeast is an essential element in the making of good bread, the 'Fence' is the essential element in any accomplished act of thievery whenever merchandise is involved.

This basic division of labor between the thief and fence occurs roughly at mode 3, with modes 1 and 2 generally allocated to the thief and modes 4 through 6 to the fence. The relationship between the thief and the fence in mode 3, though little studied, is essential. It is also precisely that interaction which the conventional view of theft fails to recognize and account for.

The theoretical character of the relationship between thief and fence is best described by the mixed-motive bargaining situation. The thief is motivated to cooperate with the fence in order to divest himself of the stolen property, yet at the same time, he is motivated to compete with the fence in achieving the best price for the merchandise. The fence is in a similar situation. By the very nature of his role, he is in the market for stolen property (hence he will want to cooperate with the thief) and yet his profit margin depends upon how well he can compete with the thief for a favorable price on the goods. The pressures to cooperate are perhaps greater for the thief, since the consequences of failing to reach an agreement are likely to be more significant for him; i.e., the possibility of being caught with the goods in hand. The fence runs no risk, particularly in the short run, if a deal is not consummated. The consequences of protracted bargaining situations may, however, result in sharply decreasing his sources of supply as he gains the reputation of being an unfair bargainer. Dealings between thief and fence, as with all commercial dealings, are strengthened by *consistency* and *reliability*. Therefore, although fence and thief are motivated to compete with each other regarding the exchange value of stolen property, the clear bias for both is toward the establishment of cooperation. The thief-fence relationship is not unique in this respect for as Deutsch (1949) has explained, cooperative interests must be strong enough to overcome competitive interests if mixed-motive bargainers are to reach agreement.

The SPS is clearly able to foster the kind of cooperation necessary in the exchange mode (mode 3) to keep a continual supply of stolen goods flowing toward the fence. But were the exchange of goods the only dimension of the interaction between these two crime figures, the SPS model would be of little analytical value. In effect it would make it difficult to sustain the concept of the SPS as a total, integrated system, for the SPS could be regarded instead as the face-off of two stolen property mechanisms, one belonging to the thief and one to the fence. The relationship between thief and fence at mode 3, while essential, does not move us much beyond the individualistic tendencies of the conventional view of theft. If we are to appreciate instead the organizational quality of property theft crimes, it is necessary to explore further the interaction patterns of fences and thieves in other parts of the SPS.

FURTHER DIMENSIONS
OF THE STOLEN PROPERTY SYSTEM

In confining our attention to the thief-fence interaction at mode 3 (exchange) in the SPS, we stipulated that the system's division of labor allocated modes 1 and 2 to the thief and modes 4 through 6 to the fence. This is, of course, the most elementary form of that relationship, and while useful in elucidating some dimensions of the thief-fence interaction, it tends to shroud some of the more complex and more insightful relationships existing between these two individuals.

In order to understand more complex thief-fence relationships and to achieve a greater appreciation for the role of the criminal receiver, two important axioms regarding the SPS must be introduced:

A. *The effectiveness of the SPS does not require a single and specific division of labor to obtain.* That is, no particular allocation of the activities in the system is essential to its successful functioning.

B. *The functional integrity of the SPS is not disturbed by a nonsequential performance of its modes.* What this means is that although we have set down the logical progression of activities in the SPS in modes 1 through 6, this does not imply that they must be performed in that order.

These axioms emphasize at least two origins of *variety* in the SPS, and it is this variety which makes the system both interesting and analytically complex.

A. *Divisions of Labor*

We will begin our deeper analysis into the SPS by looking more closely at the questions raised by the first axiom. It should be noted here that although this axiom states that varying division-of-labor arrangements are possible in the SPS, it does not suggest that they are all equally likely. We will discuss three different modal allocations most descriptive both of what is and what is not likely to occur within the SPS. First, we will look at the division of labor between thief and fence in mode 1 (research and planning). Next we will look at the labor-sharing activities of these individuals at mode 2 (extraction). Finally, we will discuss the contributions of thief and fence in mode 4 (marketing).

1. *The division of labor between thief and fence in the planning of a theft.*
    To begin, it should be noted that the fence, as the buyer of the thief's produce, always has some *implicit* influence over the planning of a theft through his power to reward. Thus those items for which the fence is willing to pay more will be more often sought by the thief and this will, of course, affect his choice of target. The fence's patterns of reward mediation therefore becomes the "Invisible Hand" guiding the thief toward the selection of what property he will steal. This "guidance" is felt not only by the junkie but also by the professional thief.

ITEM 1: (interview with Greg, professional burglar)

I stole a beautiful pair of Imperial jade earrings one time and couldn't get rid of them. This just isn't a colored gem city (diamonds are biggest here) so a lot of fences won't touch things like rubies and saffires [sic], etc. Only Mr. A handled that sort of stuff. *Until I got connected with him,* there was no percentage in taking colored gems.

ITEM 3: (from statement of Joe, a semi-skilled burglar, to district attorney)

We could only get scrap prices from fences for stuff like silverware and tea sets, etc., so D (other burglar) said we were better off to steal the metals themselves. That's when we started working the warehouses and railroad yards.

A thief's selection of targets and items for theft is similarly influenced by the number of fences he knows and the degree of specialization in which they engage. Thus in item 1 Greg's acquaintance with Mr. A accrued to him rewards for property that had previously been unsalable. A burglar who only knows fences who handle TVs and clothing is likely to limit his thefts to those items.

The fence's "Invisible Hand" in mode 1, however, is not nearly always so invisible. Witness the following police activity report entries:

ITEM 4: (from police activity report)

Info that M (who fences from his auction house) is now selling insurance. What he does is visit older people who have money and antiques around and then fingers them for burglaries. Stuff all comes to him.

ITEM 6: (police activity report)

Info that Greg's gang (prof. burglars) is fencing stuff through X who works for a detective agency and gives the burglars floor plans and info on security devices.

In these items, we see the fence who, by virtue of his business or occupation, is in a position to know individuals who possess valuable property, the nature of that property, or something about their movements. By sharing this information with thieves, he becomes the engineer, the prime mover, of the theft. Implied in most of these arrangements, of course, is the agreement that he will receive the property once it has been stolen. The increased role of the fence as "set-up man" in mode 1 also increases his power vis a vis the thief since his control over valuable theft information has an impact upon the thief's livelihood and future. The thief who needs this information must be willing to accept completely the fence's terms. If he does not come to terms, the fence with complete knowledge of who committed the theft, is in an excellent position to "set-up" the thief as well. This is why some professional thieves prefer to rely on their own research and planning rather than risking an indenture (however brief) to the receiver.

2. *The division of labor between fence and thief in the extraction mode.*
Labor sharing between fence and thief in the actual theft can take two forms. The fence can actually participate in the theft or he can offer technical advice on its commission. The former arrangement is an extremely unlikely situation in the SPS.

ITEM 8: (interview with Greg, a professional thief)

I know the fence's job is a lot more lucrative and a lot safer (than that of the thief) because he never actually steals anything himself. But it just isn't as exciting.

Even though, then, the fence's participation in the theft's commission is highly unlikely, there is some evidence that he can assist in the offense in ways other than setting it up. He can, for example, instruct the thief as to techniques to use in avoiding suspicion and apprehension.

ITEM 10: (police activity report)

. . . word is that X tells burglars to sit on stuff till they call in and only to come to the store during regular hours.

Little evidence could be found of a more active role taken by the fence in the extraction mode. Instead his involvement here appears limited to the giving of advice or admonition to the thief. It is probably fair to say, therefore, that a division of labor in the SPS which allocates mode 2 to the fence is a highly unlikely arrangement and for all intents and purposes can be eliminated from consideration.

3. *The division of labor between fence and thief in the marketing mode.*

It is probably necessary to restate the activities which occur in the marketing mode of the SPS since it covers three general areas: an analysis of demand in the stolen property economy (a marketing information subsystem); activities related to the transportation and storage of property; and, finally, activities related to packaging and promotion (the modifications necessary in the preparation of stolen property for resale). As can be imagined, mode 4 is an extremely complex and comprehensive component of the SPS. This is in general the fence's milieu; and it is because of his skills in organizing and coordinating the various activities in this mode that he can command a lion's share of the rewards which the SPS has to offer. (Robert E. Bames suggests that he pays a " 'bucket of coal' for a bucket of diamonds.")

The quality of the demand analysis conducted by the fence will depend upon his individual business acumen. If he distributes stolen property through his own retail outlet, he must anticipate the future demands of his customers and determine what he needs to buy from his "suppliers." Similarly, he must decide what mix of stolen versus legitimate property he wants to maintain; this again will affect his buying habits. He will also need to analyze the market he serves to discover the different segments it contains and the varying tastes that he should satisfy in his product line. If the fence does not sell directly to the public but instead to other middlemen or to retail establishments, his demand analysis will follow the same general pattern as above but will depend as well upon the quality of the contacts he makes in the legitimate market place and the guidance they can provide. The fence, then, faces many of the same dilemmas as any legitimate marketer. There is no one formula for success, only the expertise which past success and failure teaches. (An accommodation to the difficulties in demand forecasting and analysis used in both legitimate and illegitimate market places will be discussed below when the nonsequential function of the SPS is considered.) There is little question, however, that the demand analysis function is an all-fence activity.

The other two activity areas in mode 4, though directed by the fence, can be shared with the thief. This is particularly true of the transportation and storage function where the evidence suggests that often an equal responsibility obtains. Consider the case in which the fence employs a "drop" where property is to be abandoned by the thief. The former pays for the storage facility while the latter must be responsible for transportation.

ITEM 11: (police activity report)

. . . what happens is that burglars are told to take stolen property to a drop at _____ St. and stash it in the garage until X (fence) can be called. He comes to the drop and if property is worth buying he opens his store for burglars to deliver it that night. Most of the stolen property is kept in a back room of the store and guarded by the police dog (kept mostly for protection against the police).

The "drop" is only one technique which the fence uses to facilitate the safe transport and storage of stolen property while at the same time insuring against his being found in "possession" of it. The rental of warehouse facilities serves a similar purpose.

It is clear that the storage function is the sole responsibility of the fence since the thief has at this point relinquished control over the property to him. Similarly, any further transportation that may be required is also the fence's concern. Some fences pursue occupations in the trucking and storage industries which are tremendous assets to their illegal business endeavors. Two individuals in the data base, for example, jointly own three moving and storage firms, with a dozen vans and numerous warehouses. Two of their legitimate businesses did a gross in 1969 of $96,000 and police won't attempt to estimate their profits from criminal receiving. These individuals also appear to provide transportation facilities for other fences in the city. Witness the following note from police files:

ITEM 15: (police activity report)

. . . suspicious activity at _____ Avenue re: building being used as warehouse for storage of stolen TVs and hi fis (foreign mfg.)— Detectives observed male get out of car and use key to gain entrance— car registered to Mr. C. who is suspected of being a fence. To add to suspicions, when TVs were moved across state to the present location at above-mentioned warehouse, the mover was X owner of _____ Moving and Storage (fencing outlet).

We have seen that activities related to transportation and storage in the SPS can be shared by fence and thief. The sharing of responsibility for these functions is not, however, haphazard nor random in nature. Instead it is determined by the degree of control which each is considered to exercise over the stolen property at a given point in time. Thus, any storage or transportation activities that are required, pursuant to an agreement reached in the exchange process (mode 3), are likely to be performed by the thief. Once this exchange agreement has been satisfied, any further need for transport or storage becomes the fence's responsibility. To require the thief to perform such functions beyond those pursuant to the exchange process would be to defeat his prime motivation for making an agreement with the fence, which is to divest himself of the stolen property. Similarly, to require the fence to perform these functions prior to an exchange agreement would force him to exercise control over property which he has not as yet decided to purchase. Both thief and fence recognize that their possession of (i.e., effective control over) stolen property requires the performance of certain activities; neither, however, will be willing or likely to assume responsibility for such activities once possession has been relinquished or before it has been undertaken.

The final activity area in mode 4 of the SPS is the preparation of property for resale. This is almost exclusively the province of the criminal receiver who, following the exchange with the thief, becomes the new *seller* of the merchandise. It is the fence who takes responsibility for decisions relating to modification of the goods prior to sale, in what quantities he will sell the goods, and in what manner he will present the items to potential customers. With some items, such as automobiles, the fence will find it important to remove or disguise identifying numbers while keeping the make and model apparent. In other cases, with fair-traded appliances for example, it may be more important to disguise make and model than identifying numbers. The type of customer which the fence serves, whether retail or wholesale, corporate or individual, knowledgeable or naive, will determine the quantities in which the merchandise is sold and the manner in which it is promoted. The planning and coordination of activities in the packaging and promotion area emphasize again the organizational know-how and financial base which a fence needs to operate efficiently. It also serves to explain why he may not be able to "afford" to reward the thief too generously for his efforts.

There are certain limited cases in which the thief shares responsibility for preparing stolen property for resale. One such case is that of the professional jewel thief.

ITEM 16: (interview with Greg, professional burglar)

As soon as we finished a job we always went back to my apartment. There I'd remove all the stones from their settings, weigh them, appraise them and put them in jeweler's paper to protect them.

Greg explained that this was done for two reasons: first, as a form of protection. Often the only identity possessed by a gem is its setting. By removing a gem from its setting, then, its identification becomes much more difficult so that even upon apprehension by the police he and his associates had a good chance of not being charged with anything. Second, Greg found that he could make better deals with fences with loose stones since he had saved them the trouble of removing the settings. In addition, the origins of the items could remain somewhat obscure protecting both of them.

The professional thief is probably one of the few classes of thieves who has sufficient skill or motivation to perform such preparatory activities. It is obvious that he does not perform them as a favor to the fence but out of his own self-interest. This activity area in mode 4, then, is similar to the area of transportation and storage where activities are performed by the individual in control of the property. Because of the nature of the packaging and promotion activities and the point in time in which they occur, it is the fence who in nearly all situations is in possession of the merchandise. Responsibility for these activities, therefore, falls primarily on him. From our review of mode 4 activity areas it also becomes quite clear that the fence is the prime mover in the marketing process of the SPS.

B. *Nonsequential activity performance*

The second axiom of the SPS relates to the nonsequential nature of the functioning modes. In order to demonstrate the sort of variety which this axiom suggests, we will discuss three modal configurations in the SPS: (1) the system beginning at mode 2 (extraction) and proceeding spontaneously; (2) the system beginning at mode 1 (planning), moving to mode 3 (exchange agreement) then to mode 2 (extraction) and finally proceeding to modes 4 and 5; (3) the system beginning at the mode 5 (redistribution) then moving to modes 1,3,2 and 4 in that order. Each of these configurations represents not only different degrees of *determinateness* in the SPS, but also different degrees of *integrative control* exhibited by the fence.

1. *The SPS beginning at the extraction mode 2, having eliminated a research and planning phase.*
   This configuration can be termed the "cheapest opportunity" model. It is likely to be initiated by the least skilled thief or the addict thief. Because of the lack of planning involved, it will also be the least determinate, least integrated and least efficient model in the SPS for one of two reasons. First, it is unlikely to yield property of great resale value since its targets must be those which can be attacked spontaneously and with a minimum effort. For example:

ITEM 17: (police radio message item)

B & E at pawnbroker's shop on _____ St. Window broken and two trays of jewelry removed. Assailant believed to be on foot.

In some cases, this model of the SPS will yield noting at all and instead will serve only to create a disturbance within the environment surrounding the system.

ITEM 18: (police activity report)

Alarm sounded at warehouse on _____ Avenue. Two w/m seen running from building. Would-be thieves didn't have time to get anything. Pct 2 will put a patrol car in the area in case they try again.

The second reason why the "cheapest opportunity" model is inefficient is that it fails to predetermine a demand for merchandise. For example, consider the luckless thieves below who managed to steal merchandise of some value but whose lack of planning rendered it not only valueless to them but also incriminating.

ITEM 19: (police activity report)

X and Y (thieves) were arrested this AM in the act of trying to peddle meat from the _____ warehouse. They did not have a refrigerated truck so most of it had already started to spoil when recovered.

This model, if it is to be effective at all, requires the existence of the generalist fence who is willing to handle a wide range of items of varying quality and indeterminate quantity. The SPS does of course provide for this sort of individual in the form of owners of secondhand and general merchandise outlets and used furniture and appliance stores. Fences who engage in this sort of trade do so because they can acquire property very cheaply from hard-pressed thieves whose lack of planning has put them in precarious possession of stolen property. If, then, the thefts initiated under this model are of the "cheapest opportunity" variety, they are also of the least rewarding variety to the thief. For the fence they also represent the "cheapest opportunity" since they comprise the best bargains he can get from any set of thieves.

If this model is to have any determinateness, it is the fence who must introduce it by manipulating the rewards offered in the exchange mode. By giving such direction to the thief's activities, the fence is not generating a planning process but only narrowing the range of products which he is likely to encounter. This can help make the thief a bit more predictable and the system a bit more determinate and efficient. This model of the SPS remains, however, the least integrated configuration.

2. *The SPS in the modal sequence of planning (mode 1), exchange (mode 3), extraction (mode 2), marketing (mode 4), and redistribution (mode 5).*
This is the "exchange-oriented" model of the system in which thefts are planned but not carried out until the terms of the exchange agreement and the responsibilities for activities pursuant to that agreement are determined. This model is significantly more determinate and efficient than is the "cheapest opportunity" model, although this is only true through the exchange-extraction processes. The marketing and redistribution modes retain an indeterminate quality in this model. The degree of integration in the "exchange-oriented" model depends upon who generates and plans the theft and who initiates the terms of the exchange agreement. Two basic situations are possible: the thief-generated pact, and the fence-generated pact.

The thief-generated pact is the situation in which the thief assures a market for the theft he envisions by making preliminary arrangements with a fence to buy the product of his activities. In some sense, then, it is the thief's insurance policy which he hopes will prevent him from being caught holding stolen property unnecessarily.

ITEM 20: (Robert E. Barnes)

one. . . must always remain conscious of the fact, it is impracticable
for the thief to steal what he cannot sell. What should be of vital
importance to law enforcement officials is the fact that semi and professional thieves *seldom steal before they sell,* thus proving the fact that all
major crimes whereas [sic] merchandise is involved would never
occur if there were no outlets for this merchandise.

In many cases the professional thief wants more than the assurance of a market, he may also want to make sure that his efforts will sufficiently rewarded before attempting a "big score."

Perhaps the most important element of the above statement is the fence's "if." It is clear that the professional thief can succeed in getting some assurances from the fence but it is unlikely that he can force any binding agreement upon the fence before he has seen the merchandise. Robert E. Barnes, for example, maintains that fences are notorious for promising to pay a certain price prior to thefts of goods and then reneging on the agreement later. The thief-generated pact under the exchange-centered model of the SPS, then, does not display very much integration. All it really does is assure the thief of a buyer and notify the fence as to the type of property he is likely to receive and when.

The fence-generated pact is somewhat different. Here a high degree of integration can be introduced into the system as the fence has the opportunity to *specifically* direct the activities of the thief and to positively determine the products he will acquire. The fence who plans the theft and who provides information important to its commission is also in a position to extract from the thief a *specific* exchange agreement. This makes for a highly rationalized extraction process which has been preplanned with an exchange phase that is predetermined. The integrative control of the fence over the exchange-extraction processes produces a more efficient and determinate model of SPS behavior.

3. *The SPS beginning at the redistribution phase (mode 5) and proceeding through mode 1 (planning), mode 3 (exchange), mode 2 (exchange), and mode 4 (marketing).*
This final modal configuration of the SPS is by far its most complex and sophisticated sequence. The most apt term for this configuration is the "production to order" model. What happens in this case is that no activities relating to a theft are initiated until and order for the merchandise has been received. Once this order is received, the theft is planned; an exchange agreement decided upon; the extraction carried out; and the marketing activities completed. And all of the above processes are coordinated and directed by the fence.

The "production to order" model is an accommodation made in the legitimate marketplace to avoid the stacking up of inventory surpluses and gluts in the marketing process. The fence uses the model for similar reasons but has the advantage over the legitimate marketer that his suppliers (thieves) are likely to produce goods quicker than is the legitimate manufacturer who supplies the legitimate businessman. The model, then, is likely to be much more effective within the SPS than it has been found to be in the legitimate marketplace.

The most frequently cited example of the "production to order" model in the SPS is the auto theft ring. Instances have been reported of automobiles being stolen to meet the exact specifications of buyers, with color and bogus engine numbers added before resale. Robert Earl Barnes suggests that the "production to order" model is not limited to the stolen auto area, being particularly prevalent in the hijacking and cargo theft arena (U.S. Senate, 1973: 162):

Prior to any hijacking, the merchandise has already been sold to underworld sources, and once the crime has been set-up, and carried out by the thieves, the merchandise is extremely difficult to recover, as it may go out for resale on the legitimate market to as many as 50 to 100 middle men.

Both the "cheapest opportunity" and "exchange-centered" models of the SPS require the fence to have increasing amounts of control over the forces of *supply* in the system. The "production to order" model requires of him the ability to generate the forces of *demand* as well. Demand control by the fence is somewhat more amorphous than is supply control. It will depend on such things as his individual abilities to forecast the desire of disparate customers; the kinds of contacts he has been able to cultivate at the wholesale and retail levels of the legitimate marketplace; and often upon his particular occupation. For example, the individual described below pursues a legitimate occupation of which generating orders for merchandise is an integral part. Their additional abilities to initiate an illegitimate supply process, allows them to operate a tight and effective stolen property distribution system.

ITEM 23: (police activity report)

Mr. S who owns a jewelry manufacturing company is alleged to be fencing for some of our better burglars. He supposedly has nationwide customers and contacts. Should be kept in mind whenever jewelry is taken in residence jobs.

The control which the fence has over the sequencing of events in the SPS under the "production to order" model makes it possible for him to bring the forces of demand and supply into a fairly stable equilibrium. This makes the model highly efficient and determinate. It also serves to protect all of the persons involved since by insuring that all aspects of the system are coordinated beforehand, stolen property can move swiftly to its final destination, minimizing the risk of either thief or fence being found in possession of it.

The limits upon the "production to order" model are of two orders. The model is limited, first, by the individual ability of the fence to generate demand (i.e., contacts and outlets to do business with him.) Second, the model hinges upon the amount of organizational and financial resources at the fence's disposal which can facilitate the completion of all activities based in mode 4, the marketing mode. This is perhaps the more important limitation since it defines the size and scope of his operation. No matter how organizationally skilled the fence, if he cannot command the use of storage and transport facilities—or cannot finance the performance of such activities by others—his business volume will remain small. The "production to order" model need not, then, be characterized by large scale operations. Instead this model describes a highly integrated, tightly controlled and finely precisioned model of the SPS in which the fence is both the orchestrator and the central character.

CHAPTER 6

Common Property Crime

U nfortunately, our country's ardent commitment to capitalism and the accumulation of wealth comes with a downside: Faced with the pressing need to obtain and expend monetary resources, untold scores of people simply take from their fellow citizens as a means of getting what they want. It is widely accepted that crimes against property account for the vast majority of criminal victimizations that occur annually in this country. However, these offenses tend to remain in the background of our discussions of crime, as society is much more concerned with the documentation and prevention of violent crime. This means that one must traverse a fragmented empirical and conceptual landscape when trying to piece together the nature and dynamics of what constitutes common property crime.

When it comes to shear incidence and law enforcement workload allocation, common property crimes collectively constitute a most menacing foe. Turning to the limited list of eight Part I index crimes, we see that property offenses (burglary, arson, larceny/theft, and motor vehicle theft) accounted for 88% of all offenses known to the police in 2001. That translated to an official property crime rate of 3,656 per 100,000 persons. These four offenses generated 1.6 million arrests in 2001, but this is only part of the picture (FBI, 2002). Several noteworthy forms of property crime are included on the supplemental list of Part II index offenses, namely, fraud, forgery and counterfeiting, embezzlement, receiving stolen property, and vandalism. When these offenses are added to the mix, we see that more than 2.5 million arrests for crimes against property occur each year in this country (Maguire and Pastore, 2001).

One could legitimately include a long list of offenses when trying to frame a discussion of what constitutes "common" property crime. The list might include such offenses as burglary, larceny-theft, motor vehicle theft, arson, fraud, forgery and counterfeiting, embezzlement, receiving stolen property, and vandalism. Given its unique status as a "crime of intrusion" (Samaha, 1999), burglary has been allocated its own separate discussion. Even with this significant paring, a full treatment of the remaining laundry list of property crimes is far beyond the scope of this textbook. Luckily, this sort of comprehensive discussion is not necessary because the similarities between these crimes far outweigh the differences. In the tradition of the typologies approach, this chapter will use discussion on the crimes of larceny-theft and motor vehicle theft to illustrate a single conceptual category that is termed *common property crime*. These two offenses were chosen for several reasons. First, they are among the most recognizable and pure forms of crimes against property. Second, their status as Part I index crimes means that comprehensive data are readily available on each. Third, they are consistently among the most prevalent forms of property crime. These two offenses comprise roughly 80% of known Part I property crimes each year and more than 50% of all Part I and II property crime arrests that are effected each year (Maguire and Pastore, 2001).

COMMON PROPERTY CRIMES DEFINED

The crime of **larceny** is steeped in a rich legal history. In common law times, the larceny statute was comprised of five essential parts: (1) an act of wrongful taking; (2) an act of carrying away; (3) a piece of property; (4) a rightful owner; and (5) the intent to permanently deprive the owner of possession (Samaha, 1999). As the nature of property and property relationships grew more complicated, so too did the larceny statute. In particular, the courts had to grapple with such complex issues as ownership versus possession, misappropriations that occur while a property owner has voluntarily relinquished possession to another for shipping or safekeeping, and what exactly constitutes "property." The result was the gradual emergence of a flexible and more amorphous legal definition of larceny that incorporates all acts of wrongful property misappropriation. Today, most jurisdictions follow the direction of the Model Penal Code (American Law Institute, 1962) and rely upon a **consolidated larceny–theft statute.** For example, the Uniform Crime Reports defines larceny-theft as any "unlawful taking, carrying, leading, or riding away of property from the possession or constructive possession of another" (FBI, 2002, p. 446). Note that this definition effectively incorporates all forms of property theft under a single heading, regardless of the means or motivations that lay behind the act. There are two important caveats that accompany the UCR's consolidated definition of larceny-theft. First, it does not apply to the theft of a motor vehicle. In particular, the theft or attempted theft of a self-propelled vehicle (i.e., any nonmanual, nonrail-running vehicle including cars, trucks, motorboats, construction equipment, airplane, or farming equipment) is in its own category named **motor vehicle theft.** Second, the UCR's consolidated definition does not apply to acts of theft or conversion that are accomplished by "false pretenses" (i.e., **fraud**), those thefts committed during the course of a contractual or work relationship (i.e., **embezzlement**), or other legal contexts that would allow for the act to be categorized under the heading of specialized form of property crime.

TRENDS IN COMMON PROPERTY THEFT

The National Crime Victimization Survey (NCVS) collapses all forms of theft by taking, regardless of their manifestation (i.e., by stealth or deceit) into one generic category—theft. Motor vehicle theft is afforded a separate offense designation. The NCVS classifies all nonviolent thefts from the body of a person under the heading of **purse snatchings** or **pocket pickings.** Approximately 14,135,090 thefts, 1,008,720 motor vehicle thefts, and 188,370 purse snatchings/pocket pickings occurred in 2001. Combined, generic thefts, motor vehicle thefts, and purse snatchings/pocket pickings accounted for almost two-thirds of the overall victimization tally from 2001 (NCVS, 2003).

These raw numbers produce some lofty victimization rates. For example, the 2001 theft rate was reported at 129 per 1,000 persons or households. This is more than 4 times higher than the rate of any other type of crime that is tracked by the NCVS (burglary is second with a rate of 28.7 per 1,000). The rate of 9.2 motor vehicle thefts per 1,000 persons or households was also among the highest crime-specific victimization rates that year (NCVS, 2003).

The public is hesitant to report most property crimes to the police. This trend is illustrated by the reporting rates of 30.1% and 35.2% that are observed for the larceny-theft and purse snatchings/pocket pickings offenses in the 2001 NCVS. Debriefings indicate that victims see little benefit from reporting property crimes, as police are thought to be too busy to attend to such minor crimes, thus making the recovery of their lost property unlikely.[1] Motor vehicle theft stands as a glaring exception to this rule. In 2001, 81.6% of all auto theft victims reported the incident to police. No other form of crime surpasses the 66% reporting level. This inordinately high reporting rate is driven primarily by insurance regulations that require victims to file police reports prior to having their automobiles replaced or repaired (NCVS, 2003).

In the aggregate, common property crimes generate a sizable price tag. Conventional victimization reports set the property losses due to larceny-thefts around $4 to $5 billion annually, with an average loss per incident of roughly $300. However, it is important to note that crimes against institutional or corporate entities are beyond the scope of the NCVS. This results in the exclusion of sizable numbers of shoplifting, employee theft, and embezzlement offenses that are perpetrated against businesses. Hollinger and Davis (2000) use data provided by retail loss security professionals to estimate that shoplifting alone costs retailers an estimated $10 billion each year. In light of this oversight, it

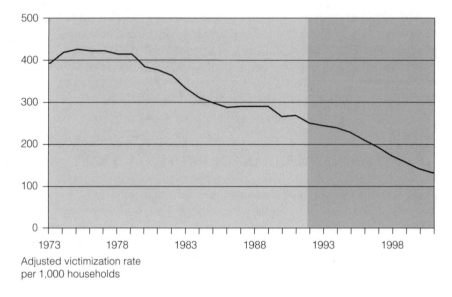

Adjusted victimization rate
per 1,000 households

Figure 6.1 Theft rates

Source: http://www.ojp.usdoj.gov/bjs/

seems reasonable to conclude that the actual dollar loss from larceny-theft
offenses is far larger than what is reported by the NCVS.

Equally disturbing dollar losses are attributed to motor vehicle theft. Victimization data suggest that the average auto theft victim experiences more
than $5,000 in losses. The overall price tag affixed to all reported auto theft vic-
timizations is $5 to $6 billion annually (NCVS, 2003).

Figure 6.1 shows how theft victimization rates have fluctuated over the past
three decades. Note the steady and precipitous decline in these numbers: The
theft rate in 1975 (424.1 per 1,000 persons or households) was more than
3 times the rate (129.0) reported in 2001. The data in Figure 6.2 depict a
slightly different trend for motor vehicle theft. As was the case with the theft
data, we observe a steady decline in motor vehicle theft victimization rates
from the early 1970s on through the early 1980s. After reversing course to
reach an all-time high of 22.2 in 1991, auto theft victimization rates experienced a precipitous decline, reaching a low of 8.6 in 2000.

There appears to be no clear-cut regional disparities for common property
crimes. Data from the Uniform Crime Reports show that, in 1999, theft-larceny
rates were highest in Utah, Florida, Arizona, New Mexico, and Louisiana. West
Virginia, Kentucky, Massachusetts, New Hampshire, and North Dakota were
found to have the lowest theft-larceny rates that year. Shifting our attention to
state-level rates of motor vehicle theft offending, we see that Arizona, Nevada,
Florida, Washington, and Michigan were at the top of the 50-state list. Officials

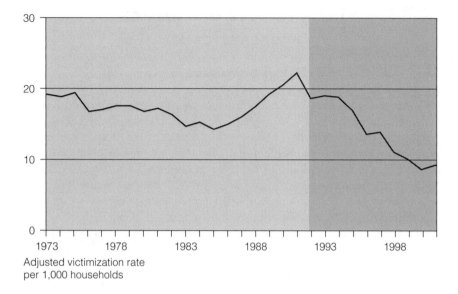

Figure 6.2   Motor vehicle theft rates

Source: http://www.ojp.usdoj.gov/bjs/

in New Hampshire, South Dakota, Wyoming, Maine, and Idaho reported the lowest rates of motor vehicle theft in 1999 (FBI, 2000).

Residents in densely populated, inner-city areas clearly experience a higher risk of property crime victimization than do their counterparts who live in more sparsely populated outlying areas. The 2001 NCVS data reveal an inverse relationship in theft rates across urban, suburban, and rural locales (rates of 160.4, 123.9, and 101.6, respectively). A similar trend is observed in the 2001 motor vehicle theft victimizations, where the rates in urban areas (15.1) exceed those of suburban (8.5) and rural (3.6) areas (NCVS, 2003). Critics observe that motor vehicle theft rates appear to be more a function of automobile density (measured either in terms of cars per square mile or per capita automobile registrations) than population density (Mayhew, 1990). A city-level analysis of UCR data reveals that New York, Chicago, Los Angeles, and Houston consistently rank among the top five most problematic locales in terms of larceny and motor vehicle theft rates (Morgan and Morgan, 2000).

The larceny-theft and motor vehicle theft rates in the United States compare favorably to those reported by other developed countries. In 1998, the United States experienced a larceny rate of 2,728.1 per 100,000 persons and an auto theft rate of 459.0 per 100,000. The official larceny and motor vehicle theft rates of our peer nations were as follows: England and Wales (3,460.2 and 753.0), Australia (3,033.7 and 706.2), France (2,527.5 and 546.1), Canada (2,431.0 and 547.1), Germany (2,406.3 and 137.4), Israel (2,149.0 and 694.1), Japan (1,198.1 and 28.4), and Spain (650.8 and 343.1) (Interpol, 1999).

INS AND OUTS OF COMMON
PROPERTY CRIME

There tends to be a decidedly unskilled dimension to property theft transactions, as thieves seem to prefer to keep things simple. Take, for example, auto theft. Karmen (1980) estimates that as many as 20% all auto thefts require little or no skill on the part of the offender as the offender gains entry through an unlocked door or takes advantage of the keys being left in the vehicle. If a would-be offender is not lucky enough to happen upon a defenseless automobile, then he or she needs only a minimal amount of expertise to close the deal. Very little skill is required to smash a window or gain access using a coat hanger or "slim jim" (a tool designed to assist tow truck drivers or police officers in opening unlocked doors). Once inside, the steering column can be easily broken with a hammer or crowbar and the car can be started in seconds with the turn of a screwdriver. Research also shows that auto thieves, especially seasoned violators, are well versed at defeating antitheft devices such as alarms and steering column locks (Clarke and Harris, 1992a; Mayhew, Clarke, Sturman and Hough, 1976; Tremblay, Clermont, and Cusson, 1994).

An observational study of shoplifters (Dabney, Dugan, and Hollinger, 2001) reveals further evidence of the unskilled nature of common property crime. Of the 105 persons observed stealing products in a retail drug store, less than 15% relied on anything more than their unmodified clothing to conceal the stolen merchandise. A sizable number of thieves (15%) made no effort whatsoever to conceal the merchandise and simply walked out of the store with the product(s) in hand.

PROPERTY THEFT TRANSACTIONS

Ecological factors play an important role in our understanding of property theft transactions. For starters, the setting plays an important role in the property theft equation. Victimization data (Hope, 1987; NCVS, 2003; NRMA Insurance, 1987) reveal that 40% to 50% of all auto thefts occur from areas immediately surrounding one's home (i.e., streets, parking lots, garages). Auto theft victimizations are also likely to be concentrated in certain places such as parking lots for railway stations (Liddy, 1987), shopping centers (Dabney and Hollinger, 1999; Florida Motor Vehicle Theft Prevention Authority, 1993), and select public parking lots (Eck and Spellman, 1993; Mancini and Jain, 1987). The hallmark of these auto theft "hot spots" is that they represent impersonal public venues with large numbers of unoccupied vehicles and low levels of guardianship. Research suggests that retail thieves also try to blend into their environment. Shoplifters seem to prefer a moderately crowded store wherein they can rely on employees to be busy with other customers while at the same time being able to access and conceal merchandise in a secluded location (Cameron, 1964; Cromwell,

Parker, and Mobley, 1999; Dabney, et al., 2001). Similarly, pickpockets seem to thrive in crowded streets or transit stations where they can operate with little fear of detection (Inciardi, 1975).

The offenders and victims of common property crime are disproportionately young, African American men. Recent NCVS data reveal an inverse relationship between age and property theft victimization rates. For example, in 2001, the motor vehicle theft victimization rate for a household headed by a person under the age of 20 (27.5 per 1,000) was more than 8 times the rate experienced by households headed by a person 65 years or older (3.3). A nearly identical pattern is observed in the offender pool. According to the 2001 Uniform Crime Reports (FBI, 2002), persons under the age of 25 accounted for 66% of all motor vehicle theft arrests and 56% of all larceny-theft arrests occurring that year. Conversely, only a small fraction of the arrests for these two offenses (4% of all larceny-theft arrests and 1% of all motor vehicle theft arrests that year) involved persons over the age of 50. Self-report data provide further evidence of juveniles' willingness to engage in common forms of property crime. Data from Johnson, Bachman, and O'Malley (1995) found that nearly one in three high school students admitted to shoplifting at least once in the past year. Sizable numbers of respondents also admitted to engaging in thefts in excess of $50 (12.5%) and motor vehicle theft (5.2%).

Race also appears to play an important role in the dynamics of common property crime. For example, data from the 2001 NCVS suggest that white households experience below average victimization rates for motor vehicle theft (8.2 per 1,000), whereas African American (16.1) and Hispanic (19.8) households experience victimization rates that far exceed the national average. Less pronounced race-based trends are observed in the theft victimization data. Shifting to offender-based data, African Americans comprised 31% of the larceny-theft arrests and 40% of the motor vehicle theft arrests in 2001 (FBI, 2002). This means that African Americans are overrepresented by a factor of 2 to 1 in the larceny-theft arrest figures and a factor of 3 to 1 with regard to motor vehicle theft arrests.

Next, we consider the way that gender manifests itself in the common property theft equation. Here we are at a bit of a disadvantage, as the NCVS does not provide data on the gender of property crime victims. However, UCR data shine some light on this subject. Males accounted for 64% of the larceny-theft arrests and 84% of the motor vehicle theft arrests occurring in 2001 (FBI, 2002). It is worth noting that no other form of crime posts female arrest percentages that even approach the 37% that is observed for the crime of larceny-theft. This anomaly is likely a function of women's high level involvements in shoplifting. Research by Dabney et al. (2001) found that 51% of persons who were secretly observed stealing from a chain drug store were women.

Most property crime transactions occur quickly, before the unsuspecting victim even knows what happened. Most offenders are able to perpetrate their crimes in a matter of minutes or even seconds without drawing much attention to themselves.

Offender-based research reveals that thieves are willing to conceal merchandise on their person within plain view of shoppers or even employees (Cromwell et al., 1999; Dabney et al., 2001).

CRIMINAL CAREER OF THE
COMMON PROPERTY OFFENDER

Property criminals tend to have relatively flat but drawn-out criminal careers. In other words, they tend to perpetrate numerous thefts over the course of their lives but the intensity of the violations remains predictably low. Hart and Reaves (1999) provide a host of data to support this contention. A full 60% of the persons charged with a theft-related felony (grand theft, grand larceny, or motor vehicle theft) had a prior felony arrest record. In fact, almost one in eight had a rap sheet containing ten or more prior felony arrests. Only burglary and drug defendants had more involved criminal histories. Over 40% of the felony theft defendants had a prior felony conviction on their record (10% had five or more) and 38% were in an active criminal justice status (i.e., on parole, probation, or pretrial release) at the time of their felony theft arrest.

A prison stay does not appear to deter common property criminals from future offending. Langan and Levin (2002) report that 78.8% of the auto thieves and 74.6% of the larceny inmates in their recidivism study were rearrested within 3 years of release. Perhaps more significant is the fact that one-third of the larceny-theft offenders and slightly more than one-tenth of the motor vehicle theft offenders found themselves under indictment for the exact same offense within 3 years. Interviews with known juvenile car thieves (Higgins and Albrecht, 1981; Light, Nee, and Ingham, 1993; Slobodian and Browne, 1997) speak further to the issue of offense specialization. It appears that a sizable portion of juvenile car thieves (approaching 50% according to Light et al., 1993) concentrate their illegal activities in the area of car crime. Those who stray outside the realm of auto theft tend to concentrate their offending in the areas of property and/or public order crime. Regardless of their level of specialization, a career portrait emerges in which individuals start out engaging in minor property and public order crime at an early age and then graduate to more serious types of crimes as they move into their late teens and early twenties. The career dimensions of youth auto crime are explored further in the upcoming article by Zachary Fleming.

Research by Shover (1983) and Tunnell (1992) suggests that most persistent property thieves begin their criminal careers while still in their early teen years. They tend to dabble in a variety of offenses, guided mostly by opportunity and peer pressure. The frequency and intensity reaches a peak during their twenties while their skill and comfort level with the crimes is at a high and the rigidity of their domestic and employment lives are at a low. Only a hardened few see their criminal careers persisting into the middle-age years.

COGNITIVE ASPECTS
OF COMMON PROPERTY CRIME

Research suggests that the motivational aspects of common property offending can vary significantly. For example, Moore (1984) proposes a five-part taxonomy of shoplifting offenders: impulse, occasional, episodic, amateur, and semiprofessional. Impulse shoplifters are spontaneous in their thefts and do so with little concern of the product's utility or the consequences of their actions. Their thefts are ritualistic in nature and often arise from some psychological malady (i.e., self-punishment, kleptomania, stress, depression). Occasional shoplifters steal inexpensive items for peer approval or to alleviate boredom. Episodic shoplifters are emotionally troubled thieves who steal specific items to satisfy bizarre rituals or perceived needs. Amateur shoplifters are opportunistic thieves who steal select items for which they do not want to pay. Finally, the semiprofessionals are habitual perpetrators who steal large quantities of goods for resale purposes. The motivational dimensions of this taxonomy mirror those discussed in the upcoming article by Cromwell, Curtis, and Withrow.

The literature on motor vehicle theft also highlights the presence of varied motivation. Challinger (1987) differentiates between profit motives, transportation motives, and recreational motives among auto thieves. The first of these categories takes on decidedly instrumental qualities while the second and third fit the description of expressive motivations. Most scholars agree that the motivational aspects of auto theft can be directly linked to the offender's intent. Those persons (usually youths) who steal cars for joyriding (recreational) purposes tend to exhibit expressive motives (i.e., status attainment) while those who intend to resell all or part of the car exhibit toward instrumental motives (Tremblay et al., 1994). The intricacies of auto theft motivations are discussed in detail in Fleming's article presented later in the chapter.

There appears to be a sense of situational rationality that goes into the planning and target selection aspects of common property crimes. Take shoplifting, for example. Weaver and Carroll (1985) accompanied known shoplifters through retail environments where they were asked to describe their thoughts and ideas about potential theft opportunities and preferences. The researchers used reported theft histories to categorize some subjects as "novices" and others as "experts." Novice shoplifters exhibited low levels of awareness of their surroundings and were not particularly concerned with store employees, the location of potential theft items, or the feasibility of their proposed theft. Expert or professional shoplifters were acutely aware of their surroundings and much more planful about their proposed theft opportunities, processing environmental cues more thoroughly and targeting small, expensive products.

Professional auto thieves (i.e., those who steal cars or their parts for resale purposes) are often meticulous in their planning and target selection. They may seek out specific makes and models of cars depending on their resale potential. Once an in-demand target has been acquired, they quickly scan the car to assess potential security and surveillance impediments before electing to break into it (Light et al., 1993; Tremblay et al., 1994). Oftentimes, they sell the cars to illegal chop shops that cut the car up and resell it for a profit.

A very different trend emerges among youthful car thieves. Most juveniles who steal cars for transportation (i.e., to get from point A to point B or to commit a crime) or recreation (i.e., to go cruising or show off) engage in little pretheft planning. We use the term joyrider to describe these offenders. In some cases, joyriders will steal the first soft target available. Other juveniles are more selective, seeking out luxury or sports car that fit their driving fancy (Clark and Harris, 1992b; Farrell, Phillips, and Pease, 1995; Higgins and Albrecht, 1981; Mayhew, 1990; McCaghy, Giordano, and Henson, 1977; Tremblay et al., 1994).

Drug and alcohol use appears to play a prominent role in the common property theft transaction. When asked to describe their state of mind, more than half of the larceny-theft and auto theft inmates that Mumola (1999) surveyed indicated that they were under the influence of some form of mind-altering substance at the time of their offense. Moreover, it appears that the financial demands of a drug habit often serve as the driving force behind routinized property offending. Interviews with seasoned property offenders establish a clear link between the frequency and intensity of drug use and the frequency and intensity of criminal activity (Inciardi, Horowitz, and Pottieger, 1993; Johnson et al., 1985).

Most common property thieves are quite unsympathetic about their victims' losses and unapologetic about their own behaviors. They tend to justify their actions and the resulting fallout on the basis of need. Persistent property thieves describe their victims as "suckers" or "easy marks" (Shover, 1996; Walsh, 1986). This sort of conceptualization allows offenders to downplay the wrongfulness of their actions at the same time as it puts them at ease about the degree of loss that they have brought upon their victims. For example, shoplifters will often reason that retail chains can afford minor losses or that they simply pass the losses on to paying customers in a "shoplifting tax" that amounts to mere pennies (Cameron, 1964; Johnson et al., 1985; Sullivan, 1989). Auto thieves have a tendency to emphasize insurance coverage or the temporary nature of a victim's losses (i.e., joyriding) as a way of rationalizing their behavior (Higgins and Albrecht, 1981; Light et al., 1993).

CULTURAL COMPONENTS
OF COMMON PROPERTY CRIME

The social organization of common property offending can take on a number of forms— offenders organize themselves as loners, colleagues, peers, or even teams (Best and Luckenbill, 1994). The loner variety often takes shape among amateur shoplifters (Moore, 1984), naive check forgers (Lemert, 1953), and auto thieves (Light et al., 1993). Here, the individual lives out a solitary existence, stealing as the opportunity or perceived need arises. Other property offenders operate under a colleague-like level of organization. For example, "systematic check forgers" (habitual offenders) choose to operate alone but are well aware of the other "paper hangers" that are at work in the same area (Lemert, 1967). Professional shoplifters (boosters) tend to organize as peers (Best and Luckenbill, 1994). Under this arrangement, we find offenders embarking upon collaborative theft activities in which short-term roles (i.e., lookout, diversionary, box man) are assumed to increase efficiency (Hayes, 1993). In the case of professional auto thieves, we often see the social organization of offending take on a teamlike format. In these instances, set roles and relationships emerge out of the need for steady business as chop shop owners need reliable in-house employees to cut up stolen cars and reliable thieves to target and deliver in-demand models (Tremblay, 1994).

Simplicity tends to be a hallmark of the socialization scripts that underlie common property offending. More often than not, learning takes place "on the fly" with a lone offender or collective of offenders reading and reacting to their surroundings. They tend to have considerable contacts with the criminal subculture but the lack of planning and pervasiveness of drug and/or alcohol use makes for a less than ideal learning scenario. Only in the case of peer or teamlike arrangements do we see point-by-point instruction taking place.

SOCIETAL REACTION TO COMMON PROPERTY CRIMES

In general, common property crimes do not receive a harsh treatment from the criminal justice system. This trend begins with the legal classification of the offenses. The Model Penal Code (American Law Institute, 1962) contains three-tiered offense grading for the crimes of larceny-theft and motor vehicle theft. The theft of a firearm, any motor vehicle, or any form of property valued in excess of $500 is deemed a felony in the third degree and thus subject to a potential sentence of 1 to 5 years in prison. A midlevel grading of misdemeanor is assigned to all thefts in which the targeted property is valued in excess of $50 but not more than $500. These offenses are punishable by up to 1 year in jail. Those thefts involving property valued at less than $50 are assigned a petty misdemeanor status, meaning that the perpetrator could be subject to a sanction ranging from a small fine to 6 months in jail.

Police are overwhelmed with property crime calls for service. In 2001, law enforcement officers made more than 1.3 million arrests on the charges of larceny-theft or motor vehicle theft. Unfortunately, more than 8 million of these crimes were reported to police agencies that same year. The clearance rate for crimes such as larceny-theft (17.6%) and motor vehicle theft (13.6%) were well below those of almost every type of crime, for example, the nearly 50% violent crime clearance rate that was recorded for murder, assault, rape, and robbery combined. In fact, burglary (12.7%) was the only form of index crime to post a lower clearance rate in 2001 (FBI, 2002). An arrest is not the only outcome that citizens hope for when they have been the victim of a common property crime. They also ask for the safe return of their valuables. Law enforcement data reveal that police are able to return roughly 60% of the stolen automobiles to their rightful owners (FBI, 2002). These data also show that the recovery of a stolen vehicle more than doubles the likelihood that an arrest will occur.

Given the shear volume of common property crime arrests that occur each year (larceny-theft cases alone accounted for 52% of the index crime arrests that were recorded by police in 2001), it should come as no surprise that court dockets are overflowing with these cases. Hart and Reaves (1999) report that common property offenders comprise roughly 20% of all felony defendants that are processed through the U.S. court system.

Hart and Reaves (1999) found that roughly 70% of property crime defendants in their study were able to obtain their release from jail while awaiting the final disposition of their case. A full one-third of the bailees engaged in at least one form of misconduct while under conditional release, and one in seven were rearrested before their pending case was even settled. Only 55% of the theft-related cases resulted in a felony conviction and sizable portions were resolved via a plea bargain to misdemeanor charges (15%) or a dismissal (29%).

Of all the offense types represented in the study, Hart and Reaves (1999) found that felony theft defendants were the least likely (22%) to be convicted and sentenced to prison. More often than not, a finding of guilt led to jail time (34%) or probation (34%). For those theft defendants who were unlucky enough to receive a term of imprisonment, the majority received a sentence of less than 2 years. Durose and his colleagues (2001) estimate that 1 in every 113 motor vehicle thefts that get reported to police result in an arrest and felony conviction. Moreover, they contend that slightly more than 1 in 10 of the motor vehicle thefts that produce an arrest will lead to a felony conviction and term of incarceration—with only 6% receiving a prison sentence.

The U.S. correctional system also appears to adopt a relatively relaxed approach to common property offenders. On average, these inmates serve less than half of their original sentence behind bars. Durose et al. (2001) report that a person who is imprisoned for felony larceny or fraud can expect to serve 17 months behind bars while a person imprisoned for felony auto theft will serve only 15 months in prison. These average time served figures are shorter than any other form of felony except felony drug possession.

The general public would be hypocritical to complain about the leniency that is afforded common property offenders by the agents of the criminal justice system. *There is a severe lack of effort when it comes to the informal social control of common property crime.* Take, for instance, the crime of shoplifting. Research has confirmed the long-feared assumption that shoppers are unwilling to intervene in the shoplifting event. For example, Klentz and Beaman (1981) found that few shoplifters come to the attention of store personnel as a result of customer-initiated action.

A series of quasi-experimental studies, known as staged shoplifting studies, were conducted to assess the thought processes behind this lack of informal social control (Felder and Pryor, 1984; Gelfand, Hartman, Walder, and Page, 1973; Steffensmeir and Terry, 1973; Steffensmeir and Steffensmeir, 1977). Gelfand and his associates (1973) found that only 28% of the persons who admitted to witnessing the theft reported the incident to store personnel.

Klemke's (1992) overview of this staged shoplifter research suggests that the race, gender, and perceived social class of the perpetrator play an important role in shoppers' decisions to intervene.

The findings of these staged shoplifter studies have spawned several efforts to get customers more involved in the social control of retail theft. Numerous public awareness efforts have been undertaken to raise levels of concern and intervention among the general public. These include the use of in-store signs, media campaigns, and ingenious school-based initiatives. Regardless of their form and process, Baumer and Rosenbaum's (1984) conclude that these efforts to mobilize citizen concern and action have been largely unsuccessful. In the final analysis, public opinion polls establish that the average citizen does not consider shoplifting to be a serious crime (Rossi, Waite, Bose, and Berk, 1974).

NOTES

1. Victims' concerns over a lack of police commitment seem to be justified in the case of common property crimes. Data from the 2001 NCVS indicate that only a fraction of these crimes produce forms of investigative police work (i.e., evidence gathering, seeking out and questioning suspects or witnesses, surveillance, pursuing arrest warrants) that move beyond simple report taking.

KEY TERMS

consolidated larceny-theft statute

embezzlement

fraud

larceny

motor vehicle theft

purse snatching/pocket picking

DISCUSSION QUESTIONS

1. One would think that a capitalist country such as the United States would have a low tolerance for the theft of personal capital. However, as the chapter suggests, we have long adopted weak formal and informal social control responses to crimes such as larceny and auto theft. Why is it that we as a country have been able to develop and maintain this seemingly conflicting set of ideals?

2. The available evidence suggests that auto thieves can be separated into two conceptual categories: profit-motivated professionals and recreational- or transportation-motivated joyriders. What kind of consequences does this two-part categorization pose for policy makers? What should be the characteristics of formal social control efforts directed toward both of these groups of offenders, and what should be the characteristics of programs that are directed specifically at one or the other type of offender?

3. It is commonly agreed that drug addiction plays an important part in the motivation of many chronic property

offenders. This has led some scholars to argue that the legalization of drugs might be expected to vastly reduce the occurrence of crimes such as theft and fraud. How feasible is this argument and how might one best approach the implementation and empirical assessment of this assertion?

13

The Dynamics of Petty Crime

An Analysis of Shoplifting

PAUL CROMWELL
JASON CURTIS
BRIAN WITHROW
Wichita State University

This study is based on a 9-year, four-phase data collection effort that spanned three states. In phase 1, "active" shoplifters from Texas were asked about the nature and dynamics of their shoplifting behavior. Phase 2 of the data collection effort enlisted the aid of heroin addicts in Miami to produce a snowball sample of 22 active, drug using shoplifters. In phase 3, the authors identified 141 shoplifters through a self-report study of criminal behavior among undergraduate students at the University of Miami. Follow-up efforts yielded additional self-report and in-depth interview data specific to their shoplifting activities. The final phase of the data collection saw the researchers accessing 137 known offenders from Kansas who completed a court-monitored diversionary program that was intended for "first-time" shoplifters. This last group of subjects were observed as they progressed through the 8-hour program and approached to be interviewed once it was complete. Collectively, these data afford the authors access to 320 known shoplifters, 115 of whom submitted to in-depth interview that are reviewed in this paper. The findings paint a complex and varied picture of shoplifting offenders. For starters, shoplifting motives varied within and across offenders. Most stole for financial reasons; however, heightened emo-

---

An earlier and expanded version of this paper appeared in Paul Cromwell (ed.) *In Their Own Words: Criminals on Crime,* 2nd Edition, © 1999 Roxbury, reprinted with permission of Paul Cromwell.

tions (stress, excitement), peer pressure, drug/alcohol impairment, and a host of other expressive motivations were also identified. Varied levels of planning, risk assessment, and skill were also observed within and across the shoplifters. These observations stress that shoplifting, like burglary and other forms of crime, is best understood as having diverse behavioral and cognitive manifestations.

Shoplifting may be the one crime that most people have committed at one time or another in their lives. It is perhaps the most commonly committed crime. It is widely distributed in the population and appears to cross racial, ethnic, gender, and class lines. Studies have shown that one in every 10–15 shoppers shoplifts (Lo, 1994; Russell, 1973; Turner and Cashdan, 1988). The Federal Bureau of Investigation estimates that shoplifting accounts for approximately 15 percent of all larcenies (Freeh, 1996). According to the *Monitoring the Future* data, shoplifting is the most prevalent and most frequent crime among high school seniors over time, with over 30 percent of respondents reporting having taken something from a store without paying on one or more occasions (Johnston, Bachman, and O'Malley, 1984–1995). And, a study by Ellen Nimick (1990) identified shoplifting as the most common offense for which youth under the age of 15 are referred to juvenile court. Estimates of losses attributable to shoplifting range from 12 to 30 billion dollars annually (Klemke, 1992; Nimick, 1990; Griffin, 1988). In her classic study, Mary Cameron (1964) wrote:

> Most people have been tempted to steal from stores, and many have been guilty (at least as children) of "snitching" an item or two from counter tops. With merchandise so attractively displayed in department stores and supermarkets, and much of it apparently there for the taking, one may ask why everyone isn't a thief (p. xi).

Yet, shoplifting is a relatively unstudied crime. There are few large scale studies yielding systematically collected data. Prior research on this subject tends to focus on small convenience or student populations (Katz, 1988; Turner and Cashdan, 1988; Moore, 1983), criminal justice or store security records (Cameron, 1964; Moore, 1984; Robin, 1963), special populations, such as the elderly (Feinberg, 1984), juveniles (Klemke, 1982; Hindelang, Hirschi, and Weis, 1981; Osgood O'Malley, Bachman, and Johnston, 1989) or psychiatric patients (Arboleda-Florez, Durie, and Costello, 1977), or involve a few questions about shoplifting as part of a larger more general survey (Johnston et al., 1984–1995). And, while there have been some large scale studies (e.g. Griffin, 1970, 1971; Fear, 1974; Won and Yamamoto, 1968), most of these have been conducted with apprehended shoplifters and have concentrated primarily on demographic data on the subjects.

The very fact that shoplifting is so widely distributed in the population enables us to see some things about the origin and motivation for crime that more serious offenses such as burglary and robbery may not. And, explaining why people shoplift may help explain why most of us at some time or another engage in deviant behavior and why some persist in such behavior where others do not.

If shoplifting is as prevalent as studies have shown and the losses attributed to shoplifting as great as estimates indicate, this criminal activity has major economic and social consequences and should be more widely and systematically studied.

The purpose of this study is to analyze the various motives that underlie shoplifting behavior.

RESULTS

The subjects expressed motivations ranging from pure greed to compulsive behavior over which they felt powerless. Most subjects reported more than one motive for their behavior. All the subjects were asked to explain their primary motivation for shoplifting. They were asked, "Why do you shoplift?" They were allowed to list as many reasons as they believed applied to them, but were asked to be specific about the "main reason you shoplift."

It was difficult to determine the *primary* motivation driving the shoplifting activity for most of the informants, as they shoplifted for different reasons at different times. Many reported multiple reasons for single shoplifting events. For example, one Wichita subject stated, "I wanted it. It's kind of a rush to take things, and I was mad at my mother at the time." When a subject expressed difficulty listing a primary motivation, the first motivation mentioned was considered primary. In the example above, the primary motive was recorded as "I wanted it." The subject was then asked if he/she had the money to pay for the item. If he/she said "yes" the motive was classified as "I wanted the item but did not want to pay for it." If he/she said, "no," the motive was classified as "I wanted the item but could not afford to pay for it."

A Miami student reported, "My girlfriend dared me to do it. It was real exciting—I was pumped." In this case, the motive was recorded as "peer pressure."

This finding of within-individual variation in motivation may be important as most of the literature in criminal decision making suggests a single, stable criminal calculus. However, it appears that many of the subjects in this study shoplifted for economic gain on some occasions and to satisfy some psychosocial need on others. Occasionally, the two motives were intertwined in a single offense.

In the following section each of the identified motives for shoplifting and representative statements by study subjects are presented.

"I Wanted the Item(s) but Didn't Want to Pay for It"

Eighty-two subjects listed this motive as primary. These shoplifters admit to having the money to pay for the items they steal, but prefer to steal the items anyway. Over sixty percent (64.6%) of males and only 47.5 percent of females reported this motivation as their primary reason for shoplifting. Many of these subjects also reported on occasion stealing for the thrill or rush, by impulse, or for some other "non-economic" reason. White respondents (42.6%) were more likely than black respondents (24.4%) or Hispanics (32.9%) to report this motivation. Some examples of their responses include:

> I did it because I didn't want to pay for anything. I've got better things to do with my money. (Wichita: 18 year old white male)
>
> I got two kids I gotta raise and I don't get no help from that shit of an ex-husband of mine. They like nice things and it makes me feel good seeing them dressed nice to go to school. It ain't hard to take stuff. I just take what I want, anytime I want it. I've got 3 televisions and 3 VCRs in my house. I took 'em all from Wal Mart. . . . I once went a whole year without washing clothes. Just threw them in the basement when they was dirty and "went shopping" for some more. (Wichita: 29 year old black female)

"It Was Peer Pressure"

Forty-nine (49) subjects reported peer pressure as the primary motivation for their shoplifting. Peer pressure—the second most cited motive in the present study—may be a highly rational motive for behavior, as perceived by the offender. Approval from peers is one of the most powerful motivators of youthful behavior. Robert Agnew writes, "This pressure might be direct, with respondents reporting that their friends explicitly encouraged them to commit the delinquent act. This pressure might also be indirect, with respondents stating that they were trying to impress their friends or simply act in conformity with them" (Agnew, 1990: 279).

Two-thirds of all the subjects reported shoplifting because of peer influences at one time or another in their life. However, only those subjects who were in the early stages of a shoplifting career or those who had shoplifted only a few times reported "peer influence" as the primary motivation for their current behavior. White respondents were 3–4 times more likely to report peer pressure as their main motive. Males were somewhat more likely than females to report peer pressure as a motive for their behavior. Many of the professional thieves reported shoplifting due to peer influence, but they seemed to be referring to their early experiences. Twenty-two Miami students (15 males and 7 females) and 27 Wichita informants (20 males and 7 females) listed peer influence as the primary motivation of their behavior.

> My mom is a shoplifter. Both my sisters do it. I got it from them. My oldest sister said, "Don't be stupid. Take what you want." (Wichita: 20 year old black female)
>
> I never stole anything in my life until I changed schools in the seventh grade. These girls had a sorority and to get in you had to shoplift something. They would tell you what to take. . . . I had to get a pair of earrings from a Woolworth store. Red ones. It was too easy. I still do it sometimes. (Miami student: 22 year old white female)

In some cases, need or greed supplied the primary motive, but peer pressure facilitated the actual offense. One Wichita subject stated:

> I had been wanting this CD and my friend started egging me on to steal it. I was afraid I'd get caught and stuff, but he just kept bugging me about it and finally I went in the store and put it down my pants and just walked out. I set off the alarm by the door and I just ran out. Now I can't ever go back in there 'cause they know what I look like. (Wichita: 19 year old female)

"I Steal for a Living"

These subjects shoplift for resale and much of their income is derived from shoplifting. Most, but not all, were or had been drug addicts with daily habits which ranged from $50 to $500. They engaged in a range of legal and illegal activities to support their habits. Most preferred shoplifting to other criminal activity because of the ease of committing the crime and the minimal sanctions associated with apprehension and conviction. Twenty of the Texas subjects (18 males and 2 females), 22 of the Miami drug clinic informants (21 males and 1 female), and four of the Wichita subjects (1 male and 3 females) were so categorized. In every case, these subjects looked on their shoplifting as "work." One subject in Wichita told the interviewer, "I'm a self-employed thief." Typical responses included:

> I changed from doing houses [burglary] to boosting cause it was getting too hot for me in Odessa. I couldn't go out of the house without being dragged down for some burglary I didn't commit. I've been down to TDC [Texas Department of Corrections] two times already and I could get the "bitch" [life imprisonment as a habitual criminal] next time so I went to boosting. It's a misdemeanor. Oughta have changed years ago. Boosting is easy and safer. [Y]ou steal a TV from a house and maybe you get $50 for it. I got a 19 inch Magnavox at Wal-Mart last week and sold it for half the sticker price. (Texas: 47 year old Hispanic male)
>
> I make more than you do [referring to the writer] just stealing from stores. Yesterday I rolled up 6 silk dresses inside my shirt and walked out of Dillard's [an upscale department store in Ft. Lauderdale]. They was worth over a thousand dollars and I sold 'em for $300. That was 30 minutes work. (Miami drug clinic: 39 year old white female)
>
> It's like it's my job. (Texas drug addict: 35 year old black female)

"I Wanted the Item(s) and Could Not Afford It"

Another common response to the motivation question was "I wanted [the item] and didn't have enough money, so I lifted it." This motivation was reported much more often by women (80%) than by men. Some of the women who reported this motivation were single parents with few financial resources. However, the majority simply coveted some item that they could not then afford to purchase. In many cases, this was one of the motivations for their first shoplifting experience. Five Miami student respondents (0 males and 5 females) and 36 Wichita subjects (8 males and 28 females) listed this as their primary motive for shoplifting. Typical responses included:

> I want nice things for my family but I can't afford to buy them. My husband and kids have the best wardrobe in town. My husband doesn't know, but I don't know how he doesn't. Where does he think all this stuff comes from? He never asks. Course, he doesn't know how much anything costs. (Wichita: 39 year old white female)
>
> My mom wouldn't buy me a pair of $30 jeans. . . . so I took 'em. (Wichita: 18 year old black female)

"I Don't Know Why. It Was Just an Impulse"

Many expressed the belief that their acts were impulsive, committed without thought or planning. Nine Miami college students (4 males and 5 females) and 28 Wichita subjects (10 males and 18 females) reported impulse as the primary motive for their shoplifting. Over one-half of all the subjects reported impulse as one of the motives for their shoplifting experiences. Typical responses included:

> I want to say "spur of the moment." It was a watch and I just wanted that watch then. The amazing thing was that I had the money in my pocket to pay for it. . . . I wish I could say that I had been drinking, but I can't. (Wichita: 33 year old black male)
>
> It was sort of an impulse. I didn't plan to do it. I'm really embarrassed by all this. (Wichita: 22 year old white female)

"I Was Under the Influence of Drugs or Alcohol"

Eleven of the subjects in the Wichita diversion sample (7 males and 4 females) and six in the Miami student sample (3 males and 3 females) reported shoplifting only when intoxicated or under the influence of drugs. Many stated that they never stole when sober and blamed the disinhibition of alcohol or drug use for their crimes. In most cases, they reported taking minor items such as beer, cigarettes, or candy. Subjects reported:

> Drinking causes it. I should stop altogether. Makes me impulsive. That's when I take things. Usually I'm too drunk to be a good thief. (Wichita: 40 year old black male)
>
> When I'm drunk or stoned, it's like I'm invisible. No, it's like I'm Superman. I ain't scared of nothing. Nobody can touch me. It seems like that's what always gets me in trouble. I'll just walk in and take something and walk out. (Wichita: 37 year old white male)

"I Enjoy the Thrill/Excitement/Rush/Danger"

Many informants viewed shoplifting as a challenge and a thrill. They enjoyed the risk taking and many discussed the "rush" they received from the act. Many of the subjects reported "excitement" or "rush" as one of the motivations for their illegal behavior; however, only 15 informants, six Miami students (6 males and 0 females) and nine Wichita subjects (7 males and 2 females), considered this motivation as primary.

> It's like an addiction. I like the feeling I get when I might get caught. Once you get in the car and you got away with it, it's like, wow, I did it. It's a buzz. An adrenaline buzz. I love that feeling—while I'm still in the store, my heart is pumping real loud and fast. It's so loud I know people can hear it. I'm really scared, but once I get away, I'm exhilarated. (Miami student: 21 year old white female)
>
> It's a thrill—the excitement, danger. Fear. Dude, my heart pounded like a drum. Like it was gonna come out of my chest. It made me feel alive. (Miami: 20 year old white male)

"I Can't Help Myself. It's Compulsive"

A few informants reported that their behavior was beyond their control. This category is differentiated from the "Impulse" category by the subject's assertion that they could not seem to stop. Many argued that they were addicted to shoplifting. There was significant crossover between those who reported compulsive behavior and those who reported shoplifting for thrill and excitement. Seven Miami students (0 males and 7 females) and six Wichita subjects (2 males and 4 females) reported that they could not easily control their shoplifting behavior. Typical responses include:

> I don't plan on stealing. I tell myself I'm not going to do it again and then I see something I want and I lift it. I already have it in my purse before I think about it. It's like, you know, automatic pilot. I'm addicted—that's all I know. (Miami student: 19 year old white female)
>
> I'm a kleptomanic. I steal anything I can get in my purse. The other day I stole a key chain—can you believe it? Took a chance on going to jail with a stupid key chain. (Wichita: 35 year old white female)

"I Was under a Lot of Stress"

A small number of subjects reported shoplifting as a response to stressful life situations. Five Wichita (2 males and 3 females) and five Miami students (0 males and 5 females) listed stress as the primary factor in their shoplifting behavior. Typical responses included:

> I was working long hours and not getting along with my wife and we had a lot of bills and some sickness. I don't know what happened to me. Next thing I know I'm stealing things. Books from Barnes and Noble, cigarettes, meat from [grocery store]. (Wichita: 40 year old white male)
>
> I get depressed. Things start to pile up and I start shoplifting. Sometimes it's at finals [final exams] or when I have a fight with my boyfriend. One

time when I thought I was pregnant. Who knows why. It's like I take out my feelings on them [the stores]. (Miami student: 24 year old white female)

CONCLUSIONS AND DISCUSSION

It is obvious, now, that to speak of shoplifting as having a simple causal dynamic, is to misunderstand the diversity and complexity of the behavior. When asked, "Why do you shoplift?", the 320 shoplifters in this study revealed motivations that ranged from purely economic to apparent manifestations of emotional maladjustment. Most of the subjects reported that they shoplifted for some economic benefit. These subjects chose to steal as a means of satisfying their material needs and desires. Others satisfied some emotional need by their shoplifting activity. Still others sought to avoid some unpleasant or painful encounter or activity. These behaviors—satisfying economic or emotional needs—may be seen as highly utilitarian and rational. Motivations in these categories included: (1) wanting the item but could not being able to afford it; (2) wanting the item but not wanting to pay for it; (3) pressure from peers; (4) stealing for a living; and (5) feeling of thrill, rush or danger. A small number of subjects reported that they stole to avoid the embarrassment of paying for condoms, to avoid long lines at the check-out station, to embarrass a spouse or parent, or to exact revenge on an employer or store where they perceived that they had been mistreated.

Of critical importance, however, was the finding that people who shoplift steal for different reasons at different times. In the 115 cases more extensively interviewed, there were few individuals who reported a single, stable criminal calculus. An otherwise "rational" shoplifter might occasionally act impulsively, stealing some item for which he or she had no need or purpose. The informants often expressed bewilderment over their motives in such cases. Of course, it is recognized that subjects may not have good insight into their own behavior or motives. Subjects may have reported their motive as "impulse," or "compulsive" because they could not articulate the dynamics of their behavior. Others may have reported stealing because of the disinhibition brought on by drugs or alcohol as a rationalization for behavior which they could not otherwise justify.

This points out the situational nature of offending. The motivation to shoplift is closely tied to the offender's current circumstances. In most instances offenders perceive the act as a means of satisfying some need. The "need" may be for cash, for some item(s) they wish to obtain for their personal use, or to satisfy some psychosocial need, such as revenge, self-esteem, peer approval, or for thrill and excitement. However, that same individual might also commit offenses without a clear motive. Several informants reported that they simply went along with friends who decided to shoplift during an otherwise legitimate shopping excursion. They joined in for no reason other than, as one informant said, "It seemed like a good idea at the time." Crozier and Friedberg (1977) argued that men seldom have clear objectives. They do not know exactly where they are going or what they want. Maurice Cusson (1983) notes that to imagine that people carry out only projects that are conceived in advance and act in terms that are clearly foreseen is "sheer idealism" (p. 19). A shoplifter may drift into crime on one day, following the lead of a friend or acquaintance, while on another occasion they may utilize a more thoughtful planning strategy before committing a crime. Wright and Decker (1994) argued that this type of offending is not the result of a thoughtful decision strategy, rather it "emerges out of the natural flow of events, seemingly coming out of nowhere" (p. 40). They conclude:

> [i]t is not so much that these actors consciously choose to commit crime, as they elect to get involved in situations that drive them toward lawbreaking (p. 40).

Some "otherwise rational" shoplifters reported that they occasionally took an item, not out of need or because they wanted it, but because they could do so without being observed. In these cases, the relative lack of risk appeared to be the major factor in the offender's calculus. They were individuals with a "readiness" to commit offenses if the circumstances were favorable, and they did so, even though they had no specific need for the item taken. Like the proverbial mountain that was climbed "because it was there," these shoplifters stole because they could.

Sixty informants reported occasionally committing offenses for what appeared to be nonrational motives. These included shoplifting as a response to stress, as a result of compulsion, impulse, anger, and alcohol or drug use. Such shoplifters often asserted that they did not know why they committed their acts or they did not understand their own behavior. The behavior was seldom obviously goal-oriented and it frequently did not have a significant acquisitive element. Many of these shoplifters took small, inexpensive items such as candy, cigarettes, and other nonsensical items such as key chains or small toys for which they had no use. However, upon closer examination, we found that all of these individuals recognized that they had a tendency to "compulsively" or "impulsively" shoplift, and yet they consciously entered places of business for that very purpose. Others appeared to attribute their shoplifting to forces over which they had no control as a means of maintaining their sense of self-worth or to impress the interviewer with their "basic goodness." One informant summed it up, stating, "I'm basically a good person. Sometimes I lift things and when it's over, I can't even tell you why. It's not like me at all." One college student reported that he never shoplifted unless he was drinking. Later, he admitted that he often had a few beers before going to a store in order to "get up his nerve" to commit the offense.

14

The Thrill of It All

Youthful Offenders and Auto Theft

ZACHARY FLEMING
Insurance Corporation of British Columbia

Fleming uses interviews with thirty-one youthful, incarcerated auto thieves to provide insight into the nature and dynamics of motor vehicle theft. Canadian correctional officials were used to identify youths with a history of auto theft offending. Prison visits across the British Columbia province of Canada allowed for lengthy face-to-face interviews with a broad array of youthful offenders. The respondents were described as active members of the lower-class street culture and were shown to have pronounced criminal histories that spanned a host of offense categories. Subjects' self-reported involvements in auto theft varied from three lifetime offenses to hundreds of offenses. Fleming describes some offenders as "acting out joyriders" who stole fast cars in order to vent their anger and immaturity through high-risk and high-speed driving behavior. Other study participants were labeled "thrill-seekers." These youth had pronounced substance abuse problems and used auto theft as a means of excitement or income to feed their drug habit. The remaining offenders were termed "instrumental offenders." These youth were more calculating in their behaviors and sought to use persistent auto theft and resale as a means of steady income. Levels of perceived risk and reward were found to vary across these three subgroups of offenders. Instrumental offenders may have committed thefts with greater frequency than thrill-seekers or joyriders, but they did so in a more guarded and planful manner. The conversations revealed that all of the offenders were unconcerned about the potential sanctions that were attached to their criminal activities.

I n contrast to decade-long national trends in both the United States and Canada which have seen auto theft levels rise and fall with other property crimes, the incidence of auto theft in the Canadian province of British Columbia increased over 200% during the past decade, outpacing the passenger vehicle fleet growth by a factor of 20, and greatly outdistancing the growth rates of other property crimes. Much of this increase came in two pronounced spurts. The first saw annual theft counts double between 1987 and 1991 before leveling off. Then in early 1995, monthly auto theft counts began a meteoric rise ending with an unprecedented 74% increase within a 12-month period before again leveling off.

From Paul Cromwell (ed.), *In Their Own Words: Criminals on Crime,* 2nd Edition, pp. 71–79.
© 1999 Roxbury, reprinted with permission of the publisher.

In response to the first rapid increase in auto theft, authorities undertook a province-wide study intended to triangulate information about offenders, victims, and vehicle characteristics, the auto theft event, and the justice system's response to the problem. These areas of interest were explored using multiple methods and data sources, including an examination of auto theft claims reported to one of the study's participants, the Insurance Corporation of British Columbia, which provides comprehensive automobile insurance coverage to three-quarters of the two million passenger vehicles licensed in the province. The availability of a very large sample of auto theft insurance claims information proved invaluable in the efforts to profile the nature of the auto theft problem.

AUTO THEFT MOTIVATIONS

Because the kinds of policies one would pursue to reduce the incidence of organized professional car theft differ significantly from those undertaken to thwart thrill-seeking youth, useful policy hinges on accurately profiling the nature of the auto theft problem in a given jurisdiction. Challinger's (1987) tripartite division of auto theft motivation adequately describes the sources of motivation uncovered in British Columbia:

I. *Profit motives*—including thefts for resale, chopping, stripping, and/or fraud;

II. *Transportation motives*—temporary appropriation for short-term or extended use, including use in the commission of other crimes; and

III. *Recreation motives*—temporary appropriation of automobiles for thrill and status-seeking by young persons (e.g., joyriding).

It is commonly believed that profit motives drive more or less organized, adult, "professional" offenders; recreation motives characterize disorganized juvenile offenders; and transportation motives underlie both juveniles and adults. Stolen automobiles not recovered or those recovered minus a significant percentage of their parts are thought to have been stolen because of the profit motive. Stolen autos that are recovered either intact, damaged, or vandalized are usually thought to have been stolen for recreation or out of need for temporary transportation.

During the past decade, 90–95% of all passenger vehicles stolen in British Columbia have been recovered. This high recovery rate existed even during periods when annual auto theft frequency counts increased greatly. Even among the small portion going unrecovered, very few have been the kinds of vehicles associated with professional auto thieves (e.g., late-year model German imports like BMW, Mercedes Benz, or Porsche; high-end luxury models such as Jaguar, Lexus, or Infiniti; or expensive sport utility models such as Toyota Landcruiser). Other analyses of auto theft insurance claims filed in recent years found that the vast majority of part replacement costs (other than door and ignition lock assemblies) stemmed from damage to vehicle body parts as opposed to systematic part stripping associated with organized offenders. Insurance data thus tend to point the finger at youth as the source of the rapid increase in auto theft.

In the late 1980s, police in British Columbia began seeing a growing number of stolen vehicles being intentionally damaged by new forms of reckless joyriding. Teenagers began stealing cars not merely to get to "bush" parties held in remote locations, but also for the expressed purpose of "trashing" them to entertain other partygoers. Police began to recover groups of totaled automobiles stolen to use in impromptu demolition derbies. By all accounts, auto stealing in British Columbia was becoming more thrill-focused.

The purpose of this study was to determine the motives and strategies underlying theft of automobiles by youthful offenders and to discover their perceptions of the deterrent effect of the criminal justice sanction.

FINDINGS

Rational choice perspectives argue for analytical distinctions between *criminal involvement* which entails long-term, multistaged decision making processes concerning initial involvement, continuance, and desistance in crime, and *criminal event* decisions which involve shorter processes in response to immediate circumstances and situations (Cornish and Clarke, 1986). In an effort to put their criminal event decisions in context, I begin with a look at how these young repeat offenders described their lives.

Lifestyle and Routine Activities

Ethnographic research on offender lifestyles has identified their involvement in crime as a means to obtain money in order to fulfill largely expressive needs (Rengert and Wasilchick, 1985; Clarke and Cornish, 1985; Cromwell et al., 1991; Shover and Honaker, 1996; Shover, 1996). The desire to live "life in the fast lane" was likewise true for many in this sample. Due to their ages, most of the respondents had few job experiences. More than half of the sample reported having no legitimate source of income, yet the reported average figure for reported monthly spending was roughly $1,750 (arrived at through itemizing weekly spending habits). Several offenders described spending sprees in the wake of obtaining money from crime in order to impress friends and show them a good time. Describing a three-day road trip where he put a group of friends up at an expensive hotel and took them all to an amusement park, a 17-year-old remarked:

> I probably spent about $5000, but it was worth it . . . easy come easy go. We partied hardy. That's the kind of stuff memories are made of.

Many expressed their disdain for the opposite of the fast life, the dullness of ordinary, unskilled work, what one subject referred to as being a "ham and egger":

> I worked as a busboy for a week once. It was like being a pig in everyone else's slop. Why should I put up with that shit? . . . Doing crime [referring to a smash and grab where he ran a truck through the front window of a Safeway store in order steal cigarettes] is a lot more fun and pays a lot better. (17-year-old)

Similar to the findings of other studies concerning the lifestyles of persistent property offenders (Cromwell et al., 1991; Shover and Honaker, 1996) many in this sample described patterns of offending as extensions to social activities with drinking and psychoactive drug use at the core. The most prevalent "recreational" activity reported by offenders was "hanging-out" with friends, and using drugs and alcohol. Fifty-five percent of the respondents said they used hallucinogens at least once a month; 23% said they did so between 12 and 20 times a month. Fifty-eight percent said they drank to intoxication at least twice a week; 20% did so five times a week. This latter 20% may well be on their way to severe adult drinking problems. On average, respondents used cocaine five times a month and marijuana almost daily. The majority of respondents indicated that they were motivated to steal cars when they were high on drugs and alcohol.

Most of those interviewed said they spend a considerable amount of time hanging around shopping malls. A few were cognizant of the effect frequent exposure to consumer goods played in motivating them to commit crime. Said one 14-year-old:

> I go to the mall almost every day and see stuff I want to buy. I do crime in order to buy nice stuff.

Auto Theft Involvement

It is likely true of most jurisdictions that the bulk of auto stealing can be attributed to transportation and recreation motives. Some portion of transportation motives involve the use of stolen vehicles for the anonymity they provide when doing other crime; however, this would probably account for a lesser proportion than the perceived need to steal a car simply to get somewhere. For the most part, auto theft appears by and large to be a crime against the property rights of others in the sense of unauthorized use.

Where youth are involved, motives for auto stealing are largely affective, and the heightened sense of risk-taking among today's youth has served to enlarge thrill- and status-seeking motives. The past decade has witnessed the cultivation of a daredevil ethic now rooted in popular culture and much of youth-focused product advertising. This growing desire to feel the "rush" of fear-induced adrenaline appears to have been the major driving force behind the massive increase in auto stealing in British Columbia.

Most in the sample described their auto stealing as thrill-seeking behavior from which they derive an "adrenaline rush" unmatched by legitimate thrill activities like skiing or snow boarding. "I got hooked on the thrill," said one 16-year-old reflecting on his commitment to auto theft. Seventy-one percent of the sample described themselves as thrill-seekers. The appeal of auto theft in this respect was threefold: (1) driving fast and recklessly; (2) the prospect of getting into a police pursuit; and (3) the prospect of getting caught. For many in the sample, thrill and status seeking were intertwined:

> I like to shock people, intimidate them, make them back down. We used to play tag with stolen cars and my friends couldn't believe the things I would do. (17-year-old)

I like crime. I like to get in police chases. I do crimes for the adrenaline rush. Car theft, B&E, smash and grab, whatever. (15-year-old)

Offenders with varying involvement in auto theft were interviewed. The most prolific in the sample claimed to have stolen hundreds of cars in recent years; the least active offender said he took three in his life. For the most part, differences in the level of auto theft involvement among offenders living in different regions of the province appear to be a function of urban versus rural living. The lack of anonymity perceived by youth in small towns appears to be a significant deterrent. All of the low-involvement offenders in this sample lived in small towns in the Interior or Northern regions of the province. The auto stealing they described was very opportunistic: they took vehicles left running in driveways on cold winter mornings. These offenders were inhibited both by a limited local street network and by the perceived likelihood of being caught if they drove the stolen car through towns where residents know each others' vehicles.

Juvenile Auto Thief Typologies

Of course each interviewed offender was uniquely motivated to steal automobiles; however, many described themselves and their motivations in ways that made it possible to draw some generalizations. What follows are profiles for the three most evident auto stealing personalities encountered in the interviews with young offenders:

Acting Out Joyrider

- most emotionally disturbed of the offenders interviewed—likes to convince his peers he's crazy
- engages in outrageous driving stunts—dangerous to pursue
- vents anger via car—responsible for large proportion of totaled and burned cars
- most committed to crime—irrational, immature
- least likely to be deterred—doesn't care what happens

Thrill-Seeker

- heavily into drugs—doing crime is a way to finance the habit—entices others to feel the "rush" of doing crime
- engages in car stunts and willful damage to cars, but also steals them for transportation and to use in other crimes
- steals parts for sale in a loosely structured friendship network
- likely to look for the "rush" elsewhere if autos become too difficult to steal—"rush" might be legitimately substituted

Instrumental Offender

- doing auto theft for the money—most active of the offenders but the smallest proportion of the sample—connected to organized theft operations

- rational, intelligent—does crimes with least risk—gravitated to auto theft from burglary—thinks about outcomes doing crime while young offender status affords them lenient treatment—indicate that they will quit crime at age 18

Even among this sample of multiple-offense, persistent young offenders, thrill-seeking motives were identified in more than half of their auto thefts. One variant of joyriding often incorporates deliberate destruction of the vehicles—68% indicated that they had stolen vehicles for the express purpose of "trashing" them.

> It's not your car: You can do whatever you want, beat it up, go as fast as you want, bake the tires, do jumps. (16-year-old)

Many offenders expressed the belief that this kind of activity did not really hurt anyone as the vehicles they typically stole to intentionally wreck were "old beaters" whose owners "probably got insurance money to buy a better one."

Profit-motivated auto stealing in this sample was evidenced in two areas: (1) vehicle acquisition for an adult-run theft ring; (2) haphazard stripping of parts for which a ready market existed. In stark contrast to the acting-out joyrider and thrill-seeker, instrumental offenders expressed little interest in adrenaline producing behavior. They took precautions to avoid police and usually worked alone. They possessed a reflective, business-like attitude about their crime of choice and this is what probably enabled them to find work with relatively rare organized theft rings.

> The newbies [younger kids just beginning their frequent involvement in auto stealing] are real heat scores [do things that attract police attention]. They wear the black Bulls [NBA team logo] skull caps and drive like idiots. If the guys I steal for ever saw one of them around, I'd never get another call. (17-year-old)

Target Selection and Acquisition

Perhaps the simplest way to dichotomize the targets of auto theft is to think in terms of supply and demand. Instrumental motives for auto stealing are driven by the *demand* for certain models sought in whole or for their parts. Why? People who like to drive fast and take risks much of the time (e.g., young males) are drawn to vehicles engineered and marketed for this "need for speed." They buy American "muscle cars" like Mustangs, Camaros, and Corvettes; European and Japanese sports coupes such as the Porsche 911 and Honda Prelude; or, if they are looking for off-road thrills, 4X4 pick-ups and sport utility vehicles.

One would expect that risk-taking drivers would crash with greater frequency, driving the demand for replacement parts. Because they are likely at fault in the majority of their crashes, drivers of these kinds of vehicles are greatly motivated to cover needed repairs outside the legitimate economy where they can stretch their repair dollar with stolen replacement parts. Relative to their fleet proportions, the kinds of models identified above are often over-represented in organized auto theft activities uncovered by police stings and task forces in many jurisdictions. The targets of instrumental theft, then, are in response to the demand for specific models.

On the affective motivation side, we would not expect to see much in the way of target specificity aside from general performance requirements—sporty cars that go fast and impress girls, or 4X4 trucks and sport utility vehicles sought for off-road thrill potential. A *supply* orientation should dominate this realm wherein largely opportunistic offenders steal whatever is most readily available.

A victimization survey done for the larger study found that 20% of vehicles were stolen with the owners' keys, roughly half of which were left in the ignition or elsewhere in the vehicle. As might be expected, no target specificity was exhibited amongst this subset of auto thefts—any car with the keys in it will do as far as most thrill or transportation seeking offenders are concerned. We did, however, find pronounced model specificity for the remainder serving to define the "path of least resistance" amongst the fleet of passenger vehicles.

Virtually all interviewed offenders identified older Japanese models as the targets of choice for thrill and transportation motives due to the relative ease with which their door and ignition locks could be defeated with ordinary objects such as scissors or screwdrivers. Simplistic, brute force techniques are the favored *modus operandi* of juvenile delinquents everywhere, and so it is with young car thieves.

We were able to quantify the degree of this target specificity by analyzing insurance claims data relative to the fleet of licensed passenger vehicles. When theft rates by vehicle make (e.g., Chevrolet, Ford, Mazda, etc.) were rank-ordered, we found Japanese nameplates occupying eight of the 10 makes most at risk of theft. Like many places in North America, Japanese makes are popular with British Columbians. In the early 1990s, they accounted for roughly one-quarter of the fleet; however, the 10-year-old models most at risk of theft made up a much smaller proportion.

Insurance claim data analyses replicated following the sharp auto theft increase witnessed between 1995 and 1996 found that passenger vehicles manufactured by the US conglomerate Chrysler, Plymouth, Dodge, Jeep, Eagle, Mitsubishi—makes exhibiting the lowest theft rates in the early 1990s—to be most disproportionately at risk of theft. Largely ignored in the first half of the decade, auto stealers in British Columbia learned in the intervening years that many older Chrysler, Plymouth, Dodge products were likewise vulnerable to their favored brute-force techniques. In 1996, 30 passenger vehicle models making up just 12% of the fleet accounted for more that a third of all auto thefts in the province.

The most obvious implication regarding the relative rarity of favorite targets has to do with offender search patterns. Motivated offenders would waste huge amounts of time if they settled on wandering about aimlessly in the hopes of finding the relatively few vehicles on which their limited theft skillset would likely work. This limited competence funnels them to places where they are apt to find their favorite prey—large parking lots. Conveniently, the large amounts of time young offenders spend in and around shopping malls provide a good match between their routine activities and a sufficiently large pool of easy-to-steal vehicles. Mall parking lots were noted as prime "hunting grounds." Roughly a third of the offenders thought underground parking lots the best place to steal vehicles.

Individual Theft Frequency

Two-thirds of the offenders interviewed could provide confident estimates of the number of vehicles they were stealing per week on average over the course of the year prior to being incarcerated. Excluding the three most prolific offenders and the four expressing minimal auto theft involvement, this sample of persistent young offenders claimed to have stolen almost three vehicles a week prior to their incarceration. These self-reported figures are consistent with other yearly auto stealing figures reported by high involvement offenders (e.g., Wilson and Abrahamse, 1992). If the total number of autos reported stolen by this small sample of juveniles were halved to allow for a good deal of bragging and lesser auto stealing levels for some portion of the year, it would still account for approximately 7% of the auto thefts known to police in British Columbia in 1992, or roughly $3 million in direct costs.

Offenders' Thoughts on Deterrence

Offenders' perceptions of deterrence was gauged in two areas—the prospects of target hardening (alarms, steering wheel and ignition locks, etc.) and how they viewed the criminal justice system's response to their offending. Notwithstanding the possibility of functional displacement in the form of "car-jacking," or displacement to less protected vehicles, target-hardening appears, on the basis of interviews with these offenders, the best prospect for reducing auto theft.

Three-quarters of the offenders said they avoid cars equipped with alarms and flee if an alarm goes off while attempting to steal a car. Few had encountered many mechanical anti-theft devices such as the "Club;" however, two-thirds said they would avoid a car equipped with such a device. Several offenders expressed their dislike of being encumbered with special tools needed to defeat anti-theft devices:

> It's easy to get a car [equipped] with a "club" . . . you can saw through the steering wheel in 30 seconds, but it's too big of a heat score carrying around a gym bag with a hacksaw. . . . Why go through all the hassle when you can just steal another one with a pen knife? (17-year-old)

The findings offer little encouragement for the deterrent value of the Combat Auto Theft (CAT) sticker program as intended. The CAT program attempts to assist police in the identification of stolen autos by having owners who do not routinely operate their vehicles between the hours of 1:00 and 5:00 AM place a brightly colored sticker on the inside of the rear window where it is visible to patrolling police officers. Among other things, the sticker grants police blanket permission to stop and search a vehicle bearing this sticker whenever it is observed in operation during the proscribed hours.

Only three offenders correctly identifying a CAT sticker said they would avoid a car so marked. The majority of offenders believed the sticker indicated the car was equipped with an alarm, so presumably, three-quarters of these young offenders would avoid cars marked with CAT stickers in order to avoid the assumed alarms. The rest of the offenders did not recognize the CAT sticker as a police signaling device and said the presence of the sticker on a car would not influence their auto stealing decisions. Because the majority of offenders believe the CAT sticker indicative of an alarmed car that most said they would avoid, it may be advantageous for the true nature of the CAT sticker to remain obscure. If more offenders knew what the sticker signifies, they might be more inclined to promptly peel them off once they gain entry to a vehicle so marked.

Offenders' Thoughts on the Criminal Justice System

On average, offenders in this sample stole their first vehicle at age 13, and were passengers in stolen cars an average of two and a half times prior to their first theft. Nearly a quarter of the sample identified auto theft as a "starter crime" leading to their involvement in other crimes. Sixteen percent indicated that they had curtailed burglary in favor of auto theft in the last year as "judges are getting tougher on B&Es." Several articulated a perception that they stood less chance of being incarcerated for auto theft:

> I told my friends they were stupid for doing robberies. . . . I'd make $500–$2000 a pop [for a stolen car]; they got chump change. . . . If I get caught I may get a month or two, they're gonna get 18. (15-year-old)

The deterrent value of existing sanctions were zealously assailed by offenders. They were confident about prevailing at nearly every stage of the process.

On Evading the Police Offenders were aware of the policy constraints under which police operate and expressed an eagerness to exploit them:

> [c]ops pull their guns out but I know they can't shoot at me for joyriding (14-year-old);
> We can drive anyway we want . . . up on the sidewalk, down a one-way street, cops have to obey the rules . . . police can't wreck cars so they won't follow you in the bush. (15-year-old)
> The heat [police] won't chase you during the day when there's a lot of traffic cause they'll get sued if they hit someone. (17-year-old)
> I never use the middle lane during rush hour because that where cops can box you in when you get stuck behind cars at a light. (17-year-old)
> It's easy to get away. You just jump out and leave it in drive. The cops have to go get it while you are running the other way. They can't use dogs on you if it is only a stolen car. (15-year-old)
> If they get you in the car they got you. If you get away from the scene they've got nothing. (16-year-old)

On Evading Punishment More than half of the sample was confident of prevailing in court once charged, and almost 60% said they did not worry about being punished by the court. Consistent with other findings regarding persistent property offenders' perceptions that offenses resulting in probation are "free crimes" (Cromwell et al., 1991), young offenders in this sample were nearly unanimous about the uselessness of probation. Virtually all the offenders characterized it is a "joke." They didn't abide by the conditions, especially the curfew imposed, and no one ever checked up on them:

> It's a joke! I'm going up for breach [probation violation] for the first time since age 12. . . . I never obeyed. (15-year-old)

Reflecting on his involvement in auto theft, another 15-year-old remarked:

> I think it's pretty much worth it. I've only spent two and a half months in jail and I have gotten away with hundreds [of auto thefts].

Many respondents identified the leniency of the juvenile system as a factor in their offending, though several expressed the view that a more punitive criminal justice system would not make a difference in their offending. While several offenders displayed an obvious lack of moral development, for example indicating that they thought it was great that lawyers work to get them off even when they committed the offense charged, most possessed a sense of the unique position in which the adolescent finds himself in Western society, hinting that they were involved in crime because they could do so without much repercussion:

> **Q:** Did you ever think about getting punished by the court?
> **A:** No, it was worth the risk . . . nothing happens . . . you get community hours or probation . . . I never abide by my curfew. (17-year old)
> **Q:** What do you think about getting probation?
> **A:** It's a joke . . . for four car thefts, a B&E and three breaches, I got seven days in closed custody, most charges were dropped. The juvenile system doesn't scare anyone, it just bores people to death . . . coming in here means nothing to me. (17-year-old)

Many of the young offenders in this study asserted that they did not consider the consequences of their actions, however this appears to be mostly situational. Based on our interviews, it becomes evident that many offenders do weigh the costs and benefits of their actions and conclude that crime is worth pursuing so long as their young offender status insulates them from what they themselves would see as meaningful sanctions.

The obvious conclusions to be drawn from these findings involve the use of (1) target hardening technology, including alarms, and steering wheel and ignition locks, and (2) increased likelihood and severity of punishment.

Consistent with the findings in the burglary study by Cromwell, Olson, and Avary (1991) the extra time and "hassle" required to overcome locks and alarms often discourages young, nonprofessional criminals. And, as many of the young offenders stated, the relative lack of punishment due to their status as juveniles encourages many to engage in offenses which they otherwise might not.

CHAPTER 7

Public Order Crime

To this point in the text, the discussion has focused on crimes against persons or property where there is an identifiable victim. Each of these crime types, ranging from homicide to burglary, fit under the heading of ***malum in se* offenses.** This Latin phase translates to "inherently bad or evil" acts. As Samaha (1999, p. 9) observes, "The serious felonies—murder, rape, robbery, burglary, arson, larceny—are classified as evil by their very nature. Killing another without justification or excuse, raping, robbing, burglarizing, and stealing are bad even if they were not crimes under the law." This chapter shifts the focus to those acts that fall under the heading of ***malum prohibitum* offenses**— acts that are deemed wrong by the law. These are the so-called victimless crimes that violate the norms or threaten the perceived moral well-being of society. Vice crime such as prostitution, drug abuse, and gambling tend to be consensual acts perpetrated by consenting adults and produce no immediate harm to anyone other than the active participants.

Clearly, conceptual schema such as vice crimes, public order crimes, or *malum prohibitum* offenses can include a broad and diverse array of law violations. Typologies scholars such as Miethe and McCorkle (2001) group drug abuse violations, prostitution, gambling, liquor-law violations, drunkenness, disorderly conduct, vandalism, and vagrancy together under the heading of public order crimes. Clinard, Quinney, and Wildeman (1994, p. 75) add homosexual acts, traffic offenses, and exhibitionism to their list. As was the case in the previous chapter, the current discussion assumes that there are more similarities than differences across these offenses. As such, this chapter provides a comprehensive treatment of the behavioral, cognitive, cultural, and societal reaction aspects of a select few variations of public order crime namely drug offenses and prostitution. This decision was again shaped by the fact that these are the most pervasive and well documented of the public order crimes and thus have accumulated the best systematic documentation from criminal justice experts.

PUBLIC ORDER CRIMES DEFINED

It is difficult to pinpoint uniform legal definitions of a given form of public order crime. Miethe and McCorkle (2001, p. 210) observe that "public standards regarding the criminality of public order offenses exhibit enormous variation across geographic areas." These authors point to instances of legalized prostitution or drug use (medicinal or personal use in small quantities) that exist within the United States or in other countries as evidence to this effect. Moreover, a sampling of the criminal codes of jurisdictions that criminalize vice offenses reveals that there exists a great deal of disagreement over what physical (*actus reus*) and mental (*mens reus*) criteria should comprise the legal definitions. As such, we find that traditional sources such as the Model Penal Code (American Law Institute, 1962) or criminal law textbooks (Samaha, 1999) provide us little guidance in defining the parameters of the discussion. The Uniform Crime Reports (FBI, 2000) provide some relief in this regard.

The data collection instrument for the UCR affords public order offenses a **Part II offense** designation. There are twenty plus offenses, ranging from weapons violations to public order crimes such as vandalism that are afforded such a designation. These crimes are deemed less serious than the Part I offenses but still worthy of systematic inquiry. The FBI provides law enforcement authorities with a generic set of legal definitions to assist them when categorizing their crime data. The definitions are intentionally vague but provide us with a sound departure point from which to proceed. **Prostitution** or commercialized vice is defined as "sex offenses of a commercial nature, such as prostitution, keeping a bawdy house, procuring, or transporting women for immoral purposes. Attempts are included" (FBI, 2002, p. 447). This definition encompasses acts or attempted acts of solicitation on the part of the prostitute and client (i.e., john), as well as the acts of pandering, transporting, and facilitation on the part of the pimp or madam. These acts can manifest themselves in several generic forms including street prostitution, bar ("b-girls") or hotel prostitution, illicit massage parlors, escort services, or brothel prostitution.

The UCR defines **drug abuse violations** as "state and/or local offenses relating to the unlawful possession, sale, use, growing, and manufacture of narcotic drugs. The following categories are specified: opium or cocaine and their derivatives (morphine, heroin, codeine); marijuana; synthetic narcotics—manufactured narcotics that can cause true addiction (demerol, methadone);

and dangerous nonnarcotic drugs (barbiturates, benzedrine)" (FBI, 2002, p. 447). For the purposes of this textbook, discussions will focus on the behaviors of drug manufacturers/smugglers, drug dealers, and drug users.

TRENDS IN PUBLIC ORDER OFFENDING

Given their consensual nature (i.e., victimless crimes), we cannot rely on victim reports (i.e., National Crime Victimization Survey) for accurate data on the occurrence of public order crimes. The UCR represents the only national-level source of data on these crimes; and even this data source has its shortcomings. The UCR treats all public order crimes as Part II offenses. These offenses are viewed as less serious than the Part I offenses (murder, rape, etc.) and result in the collection and release of far less detailed information—we are left with data on arrests and have no insight on the large number of reported offenses that go unsolved. This issue is particularly problematic for public order crimes because their consensual nature makes them prone to underreporting in the first place. Matters are further complicated by the fact that drug offenses are processed at the federal level and thus beyond the reach of the UCR data. For data on federal offenses, we must turn to the Bureau of Justice Statistics's annual report entitled, *Compendium of Federal Justice Statistics* (BJS, 2001b).

The UCR shows 80,854 prostitution arrests occurring in 2001 (FBI, 2002). Arrest trends reveal a sharp and steady increase from 1970 to 1983 (post WWII high of 125,600) and then steady decreases from that point through the end of the century. Given prostitution's folklore status as the "world's oldest profession," one must assume that the actual number of prostitution offenses is exponentially larger than indicated by arrests data. Reynolds (1986) estimates that there may be as many as 500,000 male and female prostitutes working in the United States in a given year. The actual number of offenses that are perpetrated by these sex workers is surely staggering given the fact that sexual exchanges represent a primary source of income for these individuals. This necessitates that they must engage in numerous sex acts each day to earn a livable wage. Lesieur and Welch's (1995) review of the prostitution literature leads them to conclude that as many as 1.5 million persons frequent prostitutes, spending an estimated $7 to $9 billion each year. There appears to be some hard data to support these figures. Survey research efforts show that 45% of non-college-educated men and 35% of college-educated males admit to paying for sex at least once in their lives (Hunt, 1974). Clearly, the prostitute and the client have a vested interest in avoiding law enforcement. By their own admission, law enforcement authorities often turn a blind eye to the problem (Janness, 1993; Miller, Romenesko, and Miller, 1989). Given the above facts and figures, it is entirely possible that tens of millions of acts of prostitution occur in this country each year.

The incidence numbers further balloon when one turns the attention to drug crime. In 2000, state and local law enforcement authorities recorded 1,579,600 arrests for the unlawful possession, sale, use, growth, and/or manufacture of illicit drugs (FBI, 2002). That year, federal law enforcement authorities recorded in excess of 32,000 drug arrests (BJS, 2002). No other form of crime results in more arrests, as these figures account for better than 1 in 10 arrests occurring each year. What's more, we can turn to numerous systematic data collection efforts to substantiate the assertion that the actual number of annual offenses far surpasses the nearly 2 million arrests mentioned previously.

The first source of data is the **National Household Survey on Drug Abuse (NHSDA).** This annual survey relies on sophisticated stratified, multi-stage area probability sample and door-to-door visits of tens of thousands of citizens. It provides population estimates of the nonmedicinal and/or illicit use of drugs, alcohol, and tobacco products for persons over the age of 12. The 2000 edition of the NHSDA estimates that 38.9% (nearly 87 million Americans) had engaged in at least one lifetime episode of illicit drug use.[1] Overall usage figures shrink to 11% (24.5 million) when the time interval is restricted to the past year and 6.3% (14 million) when it is restricted to the past month. In terms of marijuana use alone, the report estimates that 34.2%, or just under 77 million Americans, indicate at least one lifetime usage episode. What's more, 8.6% (19.1 million Americans) are estimated to have used marijuana at least once in 2000 and 4.8% or 10.7 million were said to have used it in the past month (NHSDA, 2001).

Drugs do not magically appear in the hands of wanton users. Instead, minor use and possession offenses are preceded by additional criminal acts (i.e., manufacturing, transporting, and sales offenses). This chapter's articles by Hafely and Tewksbury, Faupel and Klockars, and Inciardi, O'Connel, and Samm will provide readers with small-scale examples of how hyperactive the various transaction points (i.e., production, smuggling operations, street-level distribution, and usage patterns) in the illicit drug market can be. National estimates provide us a hint of how many illicit drug transactions take place on an annual basis. Take heroin, for example. The Office of National Drug Control Policy (ONDCP) estimates that there are roughly 977,000 hardcore heroin users in America.[2] The average street value of a "button" or bag (i.e., dose) of heroin is $10 to $20. The average hardcore user is said to spend $200 a week on heroin (i.e., five to ten bags). It is estimated that these persons account for 70% to 80% of all street-level heroin purchases or 8.6 to 9.8 metric tons of pure heroin each year. It is staggering to think of the number of production, smuggling, dealing, and use-related crimes that must occur to maintain the heroin supply chain. The numbers grow exponentially when one examines the cocaine problem where we find estimates of roughly 3 million hardcore cocaine users and 300 metric tons of cocaine consumed in the United States each year (ONDCP, 2000a).

Given their status as consensual and victimless crimes, we often overlook the social consequences that go along with public order crimes. At first glance, it would appear that these crimes produce no real social costs. On the surface, the prostitute, john, pimp, drug smuggler, drug dealer, and/or drug user victimizes no one but him or herself; however, the matter is not so simple. In addition to representing moral transgressions, these crimes often generate significant public health concerns (i.e., the spread of injury/disease, addictions, and violent crime).

Vast resources of the U.S. criminal justice system are deployed each year to pursue, apprehend, and punish public order offenders. Thus, when assessing the "social costs" of these crimes, officials often draw upon figures from the U.S. Departments of State, Treasury, Education, Justice, Health and Human Services, Veterans Affairs, and Transportation to broaden the scope of the issues to include the financial costs associated with the enforcement of laws, prevention and treatment efforts, and lost income. It is estimated that the collective national drug control budget for the 2002 fiscal year exceeded $19.2 billion. These figures only speak to government expenditures associated with the government's supply-reduction efforts ("war on drugs"). Additional estimates suggest that drugs cost the U.S. economy $98.5 billion in lost earnings, $88.9 billion in crime-related costs, and $12.9 billion in healthcare costs (ONDCP, 2002). In addition, it is estimated that drug users spend $60–70 billion on the purchase of illegal drugs each year (ONDCP, 2000a). An additional $70–80 billion annual price tag has been affixed to the morbidity and mortality costs assumed by the healthcare system due to the inappropriate dispensing and use of prescription drugs (Johnson and Bootman, 1995).

There are other more alarming problems that stem from these offenses, most notably their tendency to generate violence and injuries. A recently released governmental fact sheet states: "Research has long shown that the abuse of alcohol, tobacco, and illicit drugs is the single most serious health problem in the United States . . . contributing to the health problems and deaths of millions of Americans each year" (Ericson, 2001). A longitudinal study of heroin addicts revealed that nearly half had died before reaching the age of 60 (National Institute of Drug Abuse, 2001); and a study of intravenous drug users found one in five to be infected with HIV (Chitwood et al., 1991).

In 1999, hospital emergency room personnel treated 554,932 persons for drug-related episodes (e.g. overdoses, suicide attempts, unexpected reactions). This figure translates into a drug-related emergency room admissions rate of 243 per 100,000 persons and represents a 49% increase over the 1990 data (Substance Abuse and Mental Health Services Administration [SAMHSA], 2001). During a 10-month period in 1999, 139 medical examiners from forty cities attributed a total of 11,651 deaths to drug overdoses (ONDCP, 2000b). Rand (1997) notes that one in seven violence-related injuries that are treated in U.S. hospitals involves a person who had been using drugs. When focusing more narrowly on violent crime victims, research shows that 40% of the persons admitted into the hospital claim that their attacker was high on drugs or alcohol when the crime took place (Simon et al., 2001).

The situation is no better for prostitutes. Studies indicate that the violent victimizations are commonplace for street walkers (McKegney and Barnard, 1996; Miller, 1993). Even prostitutes who do not walk the streets are subject to a high level of violent victimization—Kinnell (1993) found that nearly half of the 115 call girls she surveyed had been victimized while on the job.

An analysis of arrest statistics reveals that vice arrests nearly tripled over the last 20 years of the twentieth century. In 1999, the average arrest rate for drug offenses was 614.5 and the rate for prostitution was 42.0 (per 100,000 persons).

State-level arrest rates reveal that Illinois (1,938.3), Kentucky (1,396.6), South Carolina (969.2), Florida (937.9), Mississippi (887.5), and California (768.3) posted the highest arrest rates for drug offenses in 1999. Shifting to prostitution arrest rates, the authors note that Nevada (251.3), Illinois (236.2), Kentucky (99.8), Florida (96.8), and Missouri (63.9) made the most per capita arrests in 1999 (Morgan and Morgan, 2000).

The Uniform Crime Reports (FBI, 2002) reveals that public order arrest rates are much higher in urban areas than in suburban or rural locales. For example, in 2001, the urban arrest rate for drug crime was 629.1 per 100,000 inhabitants. This compares to rates of 446 in suburban areas and 390.8 in rural counties. The urban arrest rate for prostitution was 42.2 compared to 6.2 in suburban areas and 0.9 in rural counties in 2001.

SKILLS AND TECHNIQUES
OF PUBLIC ORDER CRIMES

Most public order crimes require a baseline level of skill and organization. Upcoming articles by Faupel and Klockars as well as Inciardi and colleagues will depict street-level drug deals as simple, fast-hitting exchanges. Dealers and users develop simple routines such as keeping drugs separate from money, passing merchandise through slots in doors, or using pager/cell phones to help slow or hinder the efforts of law enforcement (Inciardi, 1993; Inciardi, Horowitz, and Pottieger, 1993; Jacobs, 1999; Murphy, Waldorf, and Reinarman, 1990; Sullivan, 1989; Williams, 1989). Growers and smugglers rely on a series of systematized practices (e.g. the use of chemistry and botany to refine purity levels at the production stage, disguising and moving large shipments at the smuggling stage, fronting drugs and money to a network of distributors) to minimize their risk of personal harm and maximize profits as they go about moving the drugs closer to their final street-level destinations (Adler, 1993; Jacobs, 1999). Drug dealers enlist the aid of scales, packaging materials, and substances with similar physical appearances as the drug to dilute (a.k.a. "cut" or "step on") the goods before they make them available for sale. Dealers also seek to maintain clear rules and sales schedules with a set of reliable users (Johnson et al., 1985; Murphy et al., 1990; Riley, 1997; Sullivan, 1989; Williams, 1989). Habitual drug users must become proficient in the use of drug paraphernalia and the skills that go along with preparing the drugs for use (e.g. cooking, cutting, copping) (Becker, 1953; Faupel, 1987, 1991; Inciardi et al., 1993; Preble and Casey, 1969; Taylor, 1993).

Similar tricks of the trade are observed in the sex industry. The clients of prostitution, also known as **johns,** employ strategies aimed at minimizing public contact, avoiding suspicion, minimizing health risks, and identifying desirable sex partners (McKegney and Barnard, 1996; McNamara, 1994). Prostitutes refine their craft by frequenting the same stretch of road, bar, or hotel (McKegney and Barnard, 1996; Prus and Irini, 1980; Weidner, 2001; Whelehan, 2001). They specialize their sex acts and seek to develop a steady set of clients (Hoigard and Finstad, 1986; Maher, 1997; McNamara, 1994). They maintain stashes of condoms, drugs, and weapons to help themselves cope with the job (Flowers, 2001; Inciardi, 1993, Maher, 1997). **Pimps** and **madams** (exploitive brokers located in between the prostitute and john) employ a series of techniques directed at the efficient recruitment and control of prostitutes and evading police intervention. Some of their favorite practices include the use of intimidation against rival sex brokers, false business fronts, bribes and payoffs, and total control over their employees' movements, appearance, and daily habits (Flowers, 2001; Hodson, 1997).

PUBLIC ORDER TRANSACTIONS

Most public order transactions take the form of one-on-one interactions between complete strangers or casual acquaintances. Prostitutes may recognize repeat customers and even be privy to their name and some personal details. However, these associations rarely progress beyond the business transaction. The same can be said about the relationships between actors in the illicit drug market (producers, smugglers, dealers, and users). These participants tacitly agree that a certain level of routinization and stable relations are good for business, but that too much of a good thing can and will produce problems. Getting too close to peers or clients exposes the individual to cognitive dissonance (i.e., psychological conflicts of interest), thus increasing the possibility that informant-based police practices will lead to brushes with the law (Adler, 1993; McKegney and Barnard, 1996; Phoenix, 1999a).

Most public order crimes occur in either open-air environments or private locales. In the case of prostitution, sex acts are generally performed by "call girls" or "house girls" in hotel rooms or private residences (Heyl, 1979; Inciardi, 1993). These crimes rarely see the light of day as the john solicits the prostitute via the phone or by dropping by the brothel in person. Street walkers, on the other hand, often negotiate their exchanges and even perform the sex acts in public places. Davis (1993) notes that street prostitutes used to be able to rely on cheap hotels or apartments for privacy. The popularity of urban renewal projects, however, has significantly reduced the prostitute's options in this regard. Where affordable shelter is not available, street walkers turn to secluded alleyways or automobiles as settings for their sex acts. The same pattern is observed with drug crime. Much of the actual drug dealing takes place on street corners, in seedy business establishments, or in alleyways. At the same time, some dealers work out of their homes. Most smugglers and midlevel distributors seek out private residences to conduct their more complex criminal exchanges (Adler, 1993; Jacobs, 1999; Williams, 1989).

It is difficult to accurately assess the age, sex, and racial composition of public order offenders, as the victimless/consensual nature of the offenses leaves us without reliable data sources in this regard. We are left with only arrest data at our disposal. The reliability of these data are dependent on the lofty assumption that police work is unbiased. This caveat aside, let us take a look at the demographic characteristics of public order arrestees. In 2001, state level drug crime arrestees were disproportionately young, male, minority members. A full 48.8% of persons arrested on drug charges were under the age of 25, 82.2% were males, and 34.5% were black (FBI, 2002). Although Hispanic representation is not provided in state- and local-level UCR data, federal arrest data reveal that 46% of the persons arrested on drug charges in 1999 were of Hispanic origin (Scalia, 2001). A different demographic profile emerges for the crime of prostitution. While there continue to be disproportionate numbers of African Americans in the arrest population (48.8% of total), markedly different age (only 21.3% were under 25 while roughly 35% were 25 to 34) and sex (66.6% were females) patterns are observed (FBI, 2002).

CRIMINAL CAREER
OF PUBLIC ORDER OFFENDERS

Public order offenders display some of the most pronounced criminal careers of any category of perpetrator. Drug crimes provide the best evidence to this effect. Hart and Reaves (1999) found that persons facing felony drug charges are likely to have long criminal histories. For example, 65% of the drug defendants in the sample had at least one prior felony arrest and 29% had a rap sheet containing five or more felony arrests. Shifting the focus to prior convictions, Hart and Reaves (1999) found that the 43% of drug defendants had at least one past felony conviction and nearly one in four (24%) had amassed a criminal resume that included five or more previous felony convictions. What's more, better than one in three (38%) were found to be in an active criminal justice status (i.e., out on pretrial release, probation, or parole) at the time of their arrest. Langan and Levin's (2002) longitudinal study of 272,000+ prison releasees further confirms the habitual nature of drug offenders' criminality; they found that two-thirds of the drug offenders were rearrested within 3 years.

Drug offenders exhibit considerable variation in their criminal activities, generally involving themselves in a variety of offenses. While Langan and Levin (2002) found that 41.2% of those released on a drug charge were arrested on a similar offense within 3 years, these offenders showed the greatest propensity to branch out and find themselves in trouble for some other form of crime as well.

These criminal career trends appear to hold true regardless of the type of drug-related offending engaged in. Small-scale studies of drug users (Boyum and Rocheleau, 1994; Inciardi et al., 1993; Riley, 1997), drug dealers (Jacobs, 1999; Williams, 1989), and drug smugglers (Adler, 1993) reveal a tendency for players in the drug underworld to carry out long and highly active criminal careers that span a wide variety of offense categories. Much of this activity and versatility are bi-products of their chosen lifestyle. If you are going to smuggle or deal drugs, you are bound to come into contact with violent persons and will need to engage in a number of property and public order offenses to maintain your "business." Conversely, habitual drug users find themselves drawn toward property and violent crimes as a means to feed their habits. Nearly one in five state prison inmates (17%) claim that they landed behind bars because they committed their chosen crime to get money to buy drugs (Beck et al., 1993). Interviews with known inner-city heroin (Boyum and Rocheleau, 1994) and cocaine users (Inciardi et al., 1993; Riley, 1997) also reveal that sizable portions, as many as one in four, rely entirely on illegal activities to fund their drug habits. This is startling when one considers that their drug habits can necessitate several hundreds or even thousands of dollars in funding each week.

COGNITIVE ASPECTS
OF PUBLIC ORDER CRIME

The pleasure principle tends to dominate the mindset of the public order offender. These persons are usually driven by short-term gratification and thus possess a self-interested and shortsighted outlook at the time of the offense. This observation is perhaps best evidenced by the high levels of drug and alcohol use that exist at the time of the offending. Mumola's (1999) survey of state prison inmates reveals that 53.9% of persons serving time on drug possession charges and 50.9% of persons incarcerated on drug trafficking charges admit to being under the influence of drugs or alcohol when they committed their crimes. High levels of substance use and abuse have also been observed in studies of prostitutes (Hoigard and Finstad, 1986; Maher, 1997; McNamara, 1994), johns (McKegney and Barnard, 1996; Sharpe, 1998), and pimps (Flowers, 2001; Hodson, 1997).

Public order offenders are driven by a host of instrumental and expressive motives. More often than not, persons of the production/distribution side of the public order crime equation are motivated by the promise of financial returns. Many drug dealers see legitimate jobs as being unattainable or even "sucker's work" and thus choose their illicit trade as a means of easy and free-flowing cash. This theme was well evidenced in Jacobs's interviews with crack dealers. As one respondent put it: "It's better money than everything. Make twenty dollars in one second, two seconds. It's better than robbery, it's better than everything. I done made three $100 sales in one minute one time" (Jacobs, 1999, p. 27).

Research on street pimps (Flowers, 2001; Hodson, 1997) and house madams (Heyl, 1979) indicates that these sex brokers are "in it for the money" and status (i.e., gender domination and "player" label) that goes with the job. Prostitutes, on the other hand, tend to exhibit a broader range of motivations. Most all prostitutes talk about the money that goes along with their trade; however, as we will see in the forthcoming article by Phoenix, prostitutes often use their involvements in the sex industry to fill an emotional (love) or psychological (pain, low self-esteem) void within themselves.

Persons who occupy the client role in public order offenses tend to be motivated by self-gratification or self-enrichment. These offenders seek the euphoria that comes from getting high or having sex. For example, Monto (2000) found pleasure pursuits such as being with an exotic or aggressive woman or fulfilling sexual fantasies to be primary motivational factors for persons who solicit prostitutes. The problem, however, is that these hedonistic pursuits have a propensity to get out of hand. Over time, individuals may become so dependent upon their chosen vice that survival or maintenance replaces what used to be the pursuit of pleasure.

Public order transactions tend to be preceded by rudimentary exercises in planning and target selection. While many of these processes are streamlined by the existence of mutual benefits between the distributor and client, perpetrators of public order crime must still contend with the fact that their vices are deemed illegal. This means that the transactions must take on a somewhat covert quality so that the participants' intentions and behaviors are not clearly evident to the public and members of law enforcement. Criminal exchanges are generally modeled in one of three ways: (1) the client and distributor can maintain a steady and private relationship; (2) the distributor can make him or herself available in a public location and then wait for the client to intermittently "cruise" by; or (3) the client may wait for the distributor to contact him or her directly when goods or services become available. Each category is preceded by its own form of planning and target selection process. Drug dealing is typically characterized by the first transactional exchange, wherein a single dealer serves as a main source for a given user. A recent study of drug users in six U.S. cities found that nearly half of the powder cocaine and heroin users relied on a single dealer to supply them with their drugs. Crack users were found to be less selective in their behaviors with just more than one-third saying that they maintained a steady source (Riley, 1997). A drug user who has a go-to source can often predict the quality of product that he or she will receive as well as the hours of operations, predictable location, and choice of substances that will be available. For the dealer, a steady roster of users helps to maintain a regular intake of cash, impose more rigid rules of operation, and limit the possibility of apprehension (Murphy et al., 1990). These factors serve to streamline the planning and target selection processes and enable the participants to pattern their relationship.

Street prostitution is often organized around a "cruising" model of exchange. Male (Calhoun, 1992; Luckenbill, 1986; McNamara, 1994) and female (Hubbard, 1999; Sharpe, 1998; Weidner, 2001) prostitutes alike are known to frequent the same stretch of road, commonly known as a "track," and make themselves visible to oncoming motorists in hopes of getting a "date." All the prostitute has to do is look the part, be available to clients, and avoid the attention of police. The john, on the other hand, must identify a suitable sex partner, negotiate a price, and avoid apprehension from undercover and uniformed police officers. Similar patterns of exchange and target selection have been observed in groups of drug dealers (Jacobs, 1999; Williams, 1989) call girls (Lever and Dolnick, 2000), hotel and bar prostitutes (i.e., b-girls) (Calhoun, 1992; Prus and Irini, 1980), and brothel prostitutes, pimps, and madams (Flowers, 2001; Heyl, 1979; Hodson, 1997). In each of these cases, a seemingly never-ending source of would-be clients seek out these service providers in a known location and then go about negotiating terms and consummating the exchange.

Much more rare are public order crime exchanges in which the distributor seeks out the would-be client. Drug producers (i.e., growers and manufacturers) and smugglers are prone to this model. Adler (1993) has documented scenarios in which a given drug smuggler will intermittently contact prospective dealers when he or she comes into possession of large quantities of a drug. This modality is also detailed in Hafley and Tewksbury's upcoming article on marijuana growers. On occasion, entrepreneurial pimps or prostitutes are known to drum up business by making their rounds at the local conventions or casinos (Hodson, 1997). Much of the planning and target selection that exists in these types of exchanges must come from the person in the distributor role.

Public order offenses get framed as relatively minor transgressions against the moral or righteous order of society. Drug use and prostitution are not framed so much as evil in their own right as they are indications of weak personal character. *This being the case, persons who engage in these acts usually invoke a series of normative neutralizations in an effort to protect or defend their moral standing.* Necessity is a common theme that emerges among public order offenders. Prostitutes, pimps, drug dealers, and other persons who occupy a distributor role in the public order equation tend to rely on these activities as a primary or secondary source of income. They involve themselves in the underground economy of vice because they see limited options in the legitimate economy. This gives way to a survivalist mentality in which conceptions of "right or wrong" take a backseat to making a livable wage.

Ironically, most of the proceeds from these illegal transactions do not go toward noble expenditures such as food and rent. Instead, the money tends to be spent on frivolous purchases (i.e., clothes or socializing) or gets used to finance some sort of addiction (i.e., drugs, alcohol, or gambling). When drug dealers and pimps spend foolishly and lavishly on leisure pursuits, they are apt to justify this spending (and the criminal activities that supported such spending) by protesting that they have earned it. In short, if the dealer has to put his or her life and freedom on the line to fill a void in the drug market, then surely, he or she is entitled to some just reward (Jacobs, 1999).

A somewhat different set of neutralizations are deployed by those who suffer from an addiction. This would include prostitutes, pimps, or drug dealers (i.e., distributors) who decide to spend their "hard earned" cash on drugs, alcohol, or other pleasure pursuits. This observation also extends to the clients (drug users or johns) who habitually purchase the illicit goods or services on the black market. These persons tend to distance themselves from responsibility and direct attention to the addictive state, not the crime itself. In short, they skirt personal responsibility by claiming that the addiction and/or "down and out" lifestyle that comes with long-term addiction left them without realistic options. This pattern is well evidenced in Phoenix's upcoming article on street prostitutes, as well as Faupel and Klockars's article on heroin users.

Regardless of their specific manifestations, public order criminals can become quite adept at deflecting blame and guilt for their actions. This is largely a bi-product of offenders who tend to exhibit long, drawn out deviant histories that afford them plenty of practice and reinforcement for their criminal thoughts and behaviors.

CULTURAL ASPECTS
OF PUBLIC ORDER CRIME

Public order crime shares a nearly inextricable bond with what we know as the criminal subculture. Sex and drug violations are illicit pleasure pursuits that take place on the proverbial underbelly of society. Given their sensual attractions and victim-less qualities, these crimes draw a healthy cadre of repeat customers. Over time, these widespread and routinized transactions become intertwined in the underground economy and criminal subculture. Cohen's (1980) research on street prostitutes, Prus and Irini's (1980) research on bar prostitutes, and Adler's (1993) study of upper-level drug smugglers reveal how isolated forms of public order crime (and their repeat offenders) are readily folded into the criminal subculture. These people share the same social space and go about their business with little concern for those around them.

Most all public order offending takes shape as what Best and Luckenbill (1994) call deviant exchanges. This entails two or more persons (usually a distributor and a client) engaging in illicit trades or sales as a means of exchanging goods or services. Often times, these exchanges become routinized to the point that we think of them as deviant markets. *The collective nature of this offending means that most offenders orient to one another as either peers, colleagues, or team members* (Best and Luckenbill, 1994). An example of a peer arrangement would be two drug users who share needles, dope, or a common "shooting gallery."

Still other public order offending gets organized along what Best and Luckenbill (1994) call a teamlike alignment. Routinized offending and a division of labor leads to set roles and cooperation among the offenders. Take, for example, drug dealers, pimps, or drug smugglers. These individuals will often work in concert with one another to maximize their profits and minimize risk of outside interference. Jacobs (1999) and Williams (1989) both have documented how small-time cocaine dealers prefer to operate in small collectives. One person might hold small, prepackaged units of the drugs on a street corner to perform the actual exchanges with drug users. Another serves as a street-level lookout who also holds the larger sums of money. A third person is located in a nearby apartment where he or she cuts and packages more drugs for sale. A fourth person serves as the runner who keeps a fresh supply of drugs moving from the apartment to the street corner.

There is a great deal of scripted interaction and socialization that takes place between the participants of public order crime. For example, prostitutes and their clients must develop and follow a scripted set of interactions that allow the participants to identify one another and negotiate the terms of a transaction while somehow not arousing the suspicions of those around them. Calhoun (1992) shows how male street prostitutes and their clients enact a series of verbal and nonverbal exchanges en route to agreeing on the terms of a sexual transaction. In fact, numerous scholars have documented rudimentary forms of socialization or tutelage occurring among parties to the public order crime transaction. For example, Heyl (1979) and others (Flowers, 2001; Hodson, 1997; Winick and Kinsie, 1971) have documented how pimps and madams recruit and even train (i.e., turn out) prostitutes, while others (Cohen, 1980; Feucht, 1993; Inciardi, 1993; Miller, 1995; Potterat et al., 1998) have shown how prostitutes develop agreed-upon rules that dictate where and when to do business and often shepherd one another into drug use.

SOCIETAL REACTION
TO PUBLIC ORDER CRIME

Public order crimes receive a mixed statutory response from the criminal justice system. Scalia (1999) observes that our nation's "war on drugs" has led criminal justice officials to reconsider their formal response to drug crimes. Crimes such as the possession of drugs or drug paraphernalia, possession with intent to distribute, and the manufacture or trafficking of illegal drugs were once afforded serious misdemeanor or minor felony distinctions under the law. Prior to the early 1980s, the vast majority of these offenses were dealt with by state or local authorities. This all changed under the Reagan administration, when the federal criminal code was revised. More severe, prescribed charges; and sentencing guidelines were enacted to allow for federal authorities to rigorously pursue and punish drug offenders. Crimes that used to be classified as state misdemeanors suddenly became class 1 felonies, subject to 20 years in federal prison. Moreover, broad, new criminal offenses such as "continuing criminal enterprise" and conspiracy offenses were added to the criminal code affording federal law enforcement officers and prosecutors a broader array of offense designations to direct toward drug offenders. Prosecutors began applying mandatory minimum sentencing and the principles of the Racketeer Influenced and Corrupt Organization Act (RICO) to drug offenders, further upping the statutory ante by treating drug dealers and smugglers as members of criminal syndicates. At present, drug dealers, as well as those who manufacture and smuggle the illicit drugs into and through the United States, face some of the most severe and vigilant criminal justice responses of modern times. For example, in 1999, the Federal Drug Control Budget was listed at $17.7 billion, there were 1.5 million drug arrests recorded, and 2.6 million pounds of drugs (marijuana, hashish, cocaine, and heroin) seized, drug cases made up one-third of all criminal court filings, and drug violators comprised more than one-third of our nation's total prison population (BJS, 2001c).

At the same time, other broad forms of vice such as gambling and prostitution are afforded petty misdemeanor status and draw little or no formal enforcement response from criminal justice officials at any jurisdictional level. For the most part, federal law enforcement and prosecutors refuse to be bothered by these "nuisance" offenses and direct the vast majority of their vice-related interdiction toward drug crime. In many cases, state and even local authorities adopt a similarly lukewarm response to these crimes. According to the *Compendium of Federal Criminal Justice Statistics* (BJS, 2002), there were a paltry 491 nonviolent sex offenses recorded by federal law enforcement authorities in 2000.

While exact figures are not available, scholars agree that the clearance rates for public order crimes are woefully low. Miethe and McCorkle (2001) identify several factors that contribute to low arrest numbers and clearance rates for prostitution and drug offenses. First, most of these crimes occur in private settings, outside of police and public view. Second, police must conduct clandestine investigations without the benefit of complaining witnesses due to the victimless nature of these offenses. Third, these crimes are viewed as minor offenses, meaning that beat cops are not pressured internally by their superiors or externally by the public to crack down on their occurrence in the same way that they are with more heinous offenses. Fourth, public opinion tends to be supportive or neutral toward these crimes, thus undermining potential deterrent effects.

Court officials clearly take drug offenses seriously.[3] An analysis of federal justice statistics reveals that, in 2001, nearly one-third (28.5%) of all U.S. attorney investigations were directed toward drug offenses. In addition, these federal prosecutors declined prosecution on only 17% of these cases—no other form of offense was pursued with this level of tenacity. Drug cases thus comprised 37% of the federal prosecutorial caseload that year (BJS, 2003). Hart and Reaves (1999) found that 37% of the felony cases that were processed in their state courts were drug cases. These researchers also found that nearly three in four state-level drug cases yielded a conviction of some sort, more often than not it was a felony conviction obtained through a plea arrangement. A similar trend is observed among federal drug defendants—89.3% of these cases produce convictions with 84.6% coming as the result of a plea bargain.

The available data suggest that sentencing hearings provide more bad news for convicted drug offenders. A full 72% of state-level convictions and 89% of federal convictions led to a term of incarceration for the guilty party. State-level convictions yielded an average prison sentence of 47 months while persons convicted in the federal system faced an average prison term of 74 months (Hart and Reaves, 1999; Scalia, 2001). Scalia (2001) found that the type and quantity of drug involved, the presence of an injured party, the use of a weapon, and the defendant's criminal history were all factors that contributed to longer federal prison sentences. Strict sentencing guidelines at the federal level means that offenders will end up serving better than 90% of these prescribed prison terms. Things are a bit more relaxed at the state level, where Durose et al. (2001) observe that, on average, drug offenders serve 49% of their original sentences behind bars.

At year end 2001, there were a total of 246,100 persons serving time in state prisons and 78,501 in federal prisons on drug charges. These figures represent 20% of the state inmate population and 55% of the federal inmate population and do not include the nearly 100,000 individuals housed in U.S. jails (Harrison and Beck, 2003). Drug offenders accounted for 14% of the growth in state inmate populations and 61% of the federal inmate population growth that occurred during the 1990s (Beck, 2001).

Society adopts a mixed message when it comes to the informal social control of public order crime. In the case of drug crime, it appears that we are mobilized in a broad antidrug initiative that approaches drug use and its accompanying criminal activities as a public health concern. Such an approach emphasizes the addiction issue and orients to the behaviors from an informal treatment and education perspective as opposed to a punishment one. For example, there were a total of 13,316 drug treatment facilities in operation on October 1, 1998, and these facilities were providing service to over 500,000 persons suffering from some form of drug abuse (Maguire and Pastore, 2000). These efforts are due, in large part, to $3.1 billion in health-related funding from the 1998 Federal Drug Control Budget. Moreover, local school districts working with justice officials converted $1.65 billion from the 1998 Federal Drug Control Budget into educational programs aimed at reducing demand among the future generations of potential users. Innovative school-based programs such as Drug Abuse Resistance Education (DARE) expose children in kindergarten through high school to a healthy dose of drug use prevention. These collaborative efforts between school administrators and local law enforcement personnel seek to instill school kids with the skills that they will need to resist the temptations of drug use and drug dealing. In 1995 alone, more than 5.5 million students in 250,000 classrooms nationwide received the core curriculum of the DARE program (BJS, 1995). This program serves to supplement other prevention programs such as "McGruff the Crime Dog."

At the same time, the public often takes an advocating position regarding vice crimes. There is a growing grassroots effort to legalize all or certain forms of drug use (Trebach and Inciardi, 1993). Several states have recently included referenda on their ballots to consider the medicinal use or limited recreational use of marijuana. Similarly, there is a well-organized effort underway to legalize prostitution. Since the 1970s, an organization named COYOTE (Call Off Your Tired Old Ethics) has been lobbying for a public health approach to prostitution, one that treats it as a legitimate occupation and injects a strong dose of regulation and disease prevention into the equation (Janness, 1993).

NOTES

1. This figure includes "any use of marijuana/hashish; cocaine, including crack; inhalants, hallucinogens, including LSD and PCP; heroin; and the nonmedical use of psychotherapeutics [prescription drugs], i.e., stimulants, sedatives, tranquilizers, and analgesics" (NHSDA, 2001, p. 7).

2. These data come from usage estimates for the years 1995–1998. Hardcore users are persons who use the drug at least once a week and occasional users are those who use less than once a week.

3. There exists no data that allows for a detailed analysis of the adjudication, sentencing, and correctional responses that are applied to prostitution, gambling or other public order offenses.

KEY TERMS

drug abuse violations

john

madam

malum in se offenses

malum prohibitum offenses

National Household Survey on Drug Abuse (NHSDA)

pimp

prostitution

UCR Part II offenses

DISCUSSION QUESTIONS

1. It has become increasingly popular to discuss the possibility of legalizing public order crimes such as prostitution and drug use. Assume that any one of these crimes were to be legalized and subject to some form of governmental regulation. What impact would this likely have on the behavioral, cognitive, cultural, and societal reactions to what was once a form of criminal behavior?

2. The United States spends billions of dollars each year trying to stop the flow of illegal drugs into this country. Still, no other country sees more drugs being used and sold on its streets. What is it about the American way of life that makes drug use so appealing and, hence, makes demand side programs so hard to effectively implement?

3. Prostitution is a crime that goes largely unsanctioned by police and prosecutors. When enforcement does occur, these efforts tend to focus much more energy on the female prostitutes than on the male clients. Feminists argue that this constitutes sex discrimination while others contend that is constitutes efficient supply reduction. Formulate several policy initiatives that might effectively and efficiently target male clients for demand reduction without seriously infringing upon citizen's civil rights.

15

Reefer Madness in Bluegrass County

Community Structure and Roles in the Rural Kentucky Marijuana Industry

SANDRA RIGGS HAFLEY
University of Cincinnati

RICHARD TEWKSBURY
University of Louisville

The authors use interviews with fifty-five members of a rural Kentucky community to highlight the normative and behavioral aspects of the marijuana growing industry that thrives in that part of the country. They paint a picture of an organized crime network in which the deviant behaviors of a minority of residents (i.e., growers) are disguised and facilitated by the structure and roles of the rest of the community. The article describes five types of marijuana growers: communal growers, hustlers, pragmatists, young punks, and entrepreneurs with considerable behavioral and motivational variation observed across the categories. The authors go on to elaborate on the roles of community members. This gives way to a seven-part typology of community members, each group having its own unique relationship with the marijuana growers. Next, they elaborate the roles that women community members play in the male-dominated world of the marijuana industry. They speak of "strumpets" who serve as the party girls or mistresses for the growers, "decent women" who bear their children and keep their homes, and the "women-in-between" who somehow carve out an egalitarian role in the patriarchal marijuana industry. This article covers considerable conceptual ground. It highlights the behavioral and cognitive aspects of drug manufacturing. Moreover, it provides a rare look inside the cultural aspects of this offense as well as the way that informal social control gets played out on a daily basis.

INTRODUCTION

Marijuana is often viewed as a harmful drug from which the public must be protected. In reality marijuana has been in use for at least 5000 years and is one of the oldest agricultural crops in existence (Schlosser, 1994a, 1994b). The negative image marijuana now possesses is largely a social construction,

From *Journal of Crime & Justice*, 19:1, excerpting from pp. 75–77, 79–94. © 1996 Anderson Publishing Co., and reprinted by permission.

created by moral entrepreneurs, not a product of concrete, scientific evidence attesting to the social and medical dangers of the drug. However, marijuana has served many purposes (in addition to being a recreational drug) over the years ranging from the manufacture of cloth and rope to medicinal applications. Despite its value, marijuana continues to maintain a negative image generating controversy whenever potential legalization is discussed in the United States (Szasz, 1992).

Despite the evolution of public disapproval and legal restrictions on the growth, distribution and use of marijuana, the marijuana industry continues unabated in Kentucky. During 1993, 645,232 plants worth perhaps $1 billion were confiscated and destroyed by law enforcement officials, making Kentucky the state with the most marijuana-related arrests, and the second most (behind Hawaii) number of cultivated plants confiscated (Associated Press, 1994; Nohlgren, 1994). It is widely believed that marijuana is the largest cash crop in the state of Kentucky. In 1991 nearly 905,000 marijuana plants were eradicated, worth over $1.3 billion (*Courier Journal,* 1992). In only eight months' of 1992 more than $985 million worth of marijuana was seized; the total value of the state's largest legal cash crop, tobacco, was estimated at between $820 million and $959 million (Bartlett, 1992; Kentucky Agricultural Statistics Service, 1993). Marijuana contributes a major portion of Kentucky's economy, yet is illegal. The purpose of this paper is to dispel the myth that such "crime" is an activity of a small minority of rural residents. Rather, our argument is that community and social structures, as exemplified by community members' social roles, function to facilitate this alternative (albeit illegal) industry.

TYPOLOGY OF MARIJUANA GROWERS

The typical rural Kentucky marijuana grower is a white male between the ages of 35 and 50, with a high school education (Weisheit, 1991b) who lives in deep or shallow rural areas of Kentucky. He is a member of the "We Poor Folk" social class (Davis, Gardner, and Gardner, 1941). He is almost always married, with at least one child. He is rarely a user of marijuana and is often a respected, church-going, community leader with no previous arrest record (Weisheit, 1991a; Hafley and Tewksbury, 1995). The typical marijuana grower, as is the case with nearly all community members, has strong, extensive kinship ties with roots in his community dating back to the first settlers.

Data about individuals involved in the marijuana industry and their culture and communities are relatively scarce in the academic literature. That which is available comes primarily from the work of Weisheit (1990a, 1990b, 1991a, 1991b, 1992, 1993; Weisheit, Falcone, and Wells, 1994; Weisheit, Smith, and Johnson, 1991) as well as Potter and Gaines (1992; also Potter, Gaines, and Holbrook, 1990) and the present authors (Hafley and Tewksbury, 1995). Weisheit, working in rural Illinois, has described the roles of marijuana industry participants, analyzed how the business of marijuana operates and discussed the influence of marijuana users and growers on society at large. In his work,

Weisheit has described three types of marijuana growers in Illinois: (1) the communal grower (2) the hustler, and (3) the pragmatist. The *communal grower* believes growing marijuana makes a social statement. Some purchase land with the intention of growing marijuana, others drift into marijuana production as a part of their lifestyle. In Kentucky, a similar motivation drives some marijuana growers who desire self-sufficiency and seek to earn additional money as a supplement to low paying jobs. Unlike the young, urban, outsiders who migrated into Kentucky for a short period of time, the rural resident is not retreating from society. He is trying to survive within his society and maintain his way of life.

The hustlers have both used and sold marijuana. They may grow a marijuana crop on land they own or they may purchase or rent land specifically for this purpose. Always adventuresome, the danger is an added appeal to the endeavor and allows the grower opportunities to match wits with law enforcement. When the excitement fades they may retire. These people might well be equally successful in a legitimate business. Many members of the "Country Boys," who dominate the Bluegrass County marijuana industry, fit in this category.

The pragmatist grows marijuana due to economic hardship. These individuals acknowledge that growing marijuana is morally and legally wrong, but feel that due to circumstances they have no better option. Most Kentucky marijuana growers fit into this variety of grower. While Weisheit's typology may appropriately explain the marijuana industry in Illinois, the unique cultural environment of rural Kentucky necessitates an expansion of this typology. In addition to Weisheit's three varieties, we argue that there must be two additional categories of participants in the rural marijuana industry: young punks and entrepreneurs.

The *young punk* is the marijuana wanna-be. These are young men between the ages of eighteen and thirty who are most likely without both older male relatives within the marijuana industry and a kinship network that is significantly tied to the marijuana industry. They do not own land or have the agricultural skills necessary to grow quality marijuana. True marijuana growers may use these young men as mules to transport their marijuana.

The *entrepreneur* most commonly begins as a hustler or pragmatist. In the beginning he grows marijuana out of economic necessity or he may view his actions simply as an alternative business venture. As time passes, he comes to enjoy devising new methods to elude detection. Even when he is financially secure, and no longer has an economic need to grow marijuana, he will continue to grow this crop and/or develop new ways of concealing and growing marijuana. Within this typology lies the primary reason why any attempts to eradicate marijuana growers from the hills of Kentucky have, and will likely continue to be next to impossible. The typical rural resident deeply resents interference from outsiders (Caudill, 1962; Montell, 1986; Pearce, 1994). Marijuana growers' attitudes towards outsiders is even more intense. Rural residents will not discuss illegal activities which occur within the community with outsiders.

It can be extremely difficult for the outsider to identify the marijuana industry participants within a rural Kentucky community. Marijuana growers are perceived as respectable citizens of the community and do not fit the stereotype of a "drug dealer" often portrayed in the media (Hafley and Tewksbury, 1995). The rural Kentucky resident knows who participates in the marijuana industry in the same way everyone in the community knows who is sleeping with whom and other community gossip.

THE MARIJUANA INDUSTRY IN KENTUCKY

Historically, illegal activities have been a part of rural Kentucky culture. Many marijuana growers are the descendants of moonshiners and bootleggers. Within rural Kentucky communities a culture exists which protects and shelters those engaging in illegal activities from the scrutiny of outsiders (Pearce, 1994; Potter and Gaines, 1992; Hafley and Tewksbury, 1995). These norms and values, coupled with the economic crises facing the agricultural industry in recent decades have pushed rural families to pursue off-farm income sources (Deseran, Falk, and Jenkins, 1984; Herbst and Hanson, 1971; Larson, 1976). However, rural Kentucky values encourage independence and self-reliance. One consequence of such values is a resistance to outside interference or attempts to control rural activities, including eradication of marijuana. The small rural community and the rural culture provide the necessary structure and stabilizing factors to successfully raise and sell marijuana. These communities provide safety for both small independent growers as well as those involved in the organized aspect of the industry.

The secrecy which surrounds marijuana growers (due to marijuana's illegal status) and the reluctance of the rural resident to discuss such activities with outsiders indicates an element of strong informal social control within the rural community. Such informal social control allows the marijuana industry to exist and flourish. Within the small rural community many expected social controls which are evident in mainstream society are not present. Thus, participants in illegal activities are allowed to function within the community without censor. Members of crime groups are not shunned, as would be expected if marijuana growers were perceived as deviants. Marijuana growers receive strong community support; the prevailing view in the community is that those involved in growing "alternative crops" have done nothing wrong.

Economic factors play a large part in the introduction of organized crime to rural Kentucky. Rural Americans have been entering off-farm employment in large numbers in the past three decades. By 1983 non-farm income accounted for over 70% of US farm family income (Pulver, 1986: 491–492). However, while farmers are increasingly relying on non-farm employment, in rural Kentucky high rates of unemployment lead many residents to the marijuana industry (Potter and Gaines, 1992; Voskull, 1993). In 1989 Kentucky had an unemployment rate of 6.2%, however Bluegrass County's unemployment rate was more than 30% higher at 8.3% overall and 9.7% for Bluegrass County males (Cabinet for Human Resources, 1990). Lacking plentiful employment opportunities, many rural Kentuckians are forced to migrate to cities. In an effort to retain their community, rural residents often remain silent or protect those involved in the marijuana industry and thereby keep residents in the community. Rural residents do not want their "kin" to migrate; consequently many rural citizens endure a long drive to and from the city rather than moving nearer their urban place of employment. Lacking well paying jobs, many rural males opt to grow marijuana to generate or supplement their incomes.

Residents of Bluegrass County regard outsiders with distrust, believing outsiders do not respect them. The example of a Bluegrass County resident being apprehended for trafficking in marijuana is tinged with resentment—not empathy or compassion—towards the resident outsider. Because he refused to heed their warnings, community insiders perceive him as remaining aloof and rejecting Bluegrass County residents as ignorant. However, despite the arrests, many community members continue to grow and sell marijuana. Joe Paul explains the persistence of the marijuana industry in Bluegrass County, saying:

"They's several that was bigger than Buford and them Country Boys ever thought about being. Hell they got him for organized crime. He ain't no big boss but they's others in Bluegrass County that are. The law's ignorant. They nailed Buford but they cover up their own screw-ups."

ROLES OF COMMUNITY MEMBERS

It would be erroneous to assume that rural Kentucky communities present universally supportive or even knowledgeable fronts regarding the marijuana industry. Rather, individuals in these communities can be identified as occupying one of seven primary roles. It is important to note, however, that these roles are primarily males' roles. (Women's roles will be discussed below.) The primary roles of community members are as ostriches, the fringe group, the in-the-knows, the profiteers, the part-timers, the retirees, and the active participants.

The Ostriches are aware that people in the community grow marijuana, but like myths about the flightless bird, stick their heads in the sand and pretend to not know anything about illegal activities. Consequently, these persons are the least informed about the nature and scope of the marijuana industry. Their constant denial serves to protect the marijuana grower from outside scrutiny. These people portray the marijuana grower as a deviant outsider and not one of "us" even when there is evidence to the contrary. This group attempts to project the image of a community of only good, law-abiding people. The role of the ostriches is to promote this image to outsiders and to reassure themselves of the goodness of the people within the community. For the most part they do not profit from the marijuana grower's enterprise. This is likely due to intimacy of community members and their awareness of the roles played by everyone in the community, including the ostriches.

The Fringe group is aware that the marijuana industry is a part of their community, but these people have no connection to kinship networks that participate in the marijuana industry. These individuals will acknowledge the industry's existence to others (while ostriches will not). However, they will rarely, if ever, inform law enforcement officials about such activity. The belief is that such knowledge should be contained within the community. They believe only insiders can and should exert social control over community and industry members.

The Fringe group persistently asserts that marijuana growers are a small deviant group within the community. This perspective, like that of the ostrich, offers the marijuana grower a degree of protection from outsiders. If organized crime is perceived as small and powerless, its members stand a better chance of avoiding detection and thereby enabling them to continue illegal activities (and presumably maintain community stability). For these reasons, those who disapprove of the marijuana grower facilitate his avoiding detection. Wearing the mantle of respectability, the grower is not recognized or acknowledged as a member of the marijuana industry (or, he is not recognized as a community member). In reality, the Fringe group's failure to publicly identify the scope of industry participation facilitates the invisibility enjoyed by many members, thus further entrenching the industry in the community fabric.

The In-The-Knows differ from the Fringe group because they have friends and relatives involved in growing and selling marijuana. These persons may be present and witness others' illegal activities or such activities may be discussed in their presence. This group is trusted by marijuana growers, and due to their strong kinship ties to those inside the marijuana industry, they never disclose information regarding illegal activities to law enforcement officials. Furthermore, kinship ties motivate these persons to protect industry participants whenever possible (Pearce, 1994). Most commonly this occurs via warnings of impending raids or investigations known to individuals because of their professional and personal access to such information. By protecting others from detection and apprehension these individuals promote community cohesion and continuation of current community structures and social/economic activities.

The Profiteers are those community members who, while not directly participating in the activities of the marijuana industry, indirectly benefit from the economic impact it has on the community. This group is made up of local business people who have knowledge of, and often support the marijuana growers. Marijuana is a major part of rural Kentucky communities' economies. Many businesses will accept cash for both large and small purchases. Large purchases, such as new cars, are not questioned when paid in cash (Weisheit, 1990b). The fact that a $20,000 vehicle is paid for in cash by someone whose home lacks indoor plumbing would draw attention from most, but not in a community that supports the rural marijuana industry.

Many members of organized growers, such as the Country Boys, are not full time participants. Some work in the marijuana industry for a short period of time, others move in and out of the group. Still others retire from the group but remain willing to help out when they are needed. All, however, remain fiercely loyal to the group. The Retiree is even more difficult to detect than the part-timer. He is no longer a participant, having retired due to advancing age (which may range from 60 to 80 years old). While no longer active in growing and selling, he is willing to teach other young men his trade and introduce them to his connections. On occasion retirement may be involuntary, a result of incarceration. Retirees may be extremely difficult for the outsider to identify. They are legitimate sector businessmen and professionals or literally almost anyone in the community. However, most community residents are keenly aware of these men's past activities.

It is rarely discussed, but community members know of these activities in the same way they know of the community's gossip. Wearing an air of respectability, the retiree may aid the active marijuana grower in laundering his money by introducing him to legitimate business opportunities and to those willing to accept cash for goods and services as well as finding markets for his product. The retiree has connections for the sale and safe transportation of marijuana, along with accumulated skills regarding efficient means to grow a crop. He may personally introduce novice growers within his kinship network to others who can provide information and resources. He may also teach the novice how to plant and grow marijuana or simply instruct him verbally about what is needed or how to correct problems. Retirees serve as an example to younger growers, modeling how to evade detection and achieve financial success. Those whose retirement is a result of imprisonment also serve as models, demonstrating that prison may be a part of doing business within the marijuana industry.

The final role available to community members encompasses all aspects of active, regular, involvement in growing and selling marijuana. These persons often have made the marijuana industry their career, and their primary source of income is generated by their marijuana crops. As noted above, active rural Kentucky marijuana participants are found in five forms: communal growers, hustlers, pragmatists, young punks, and entrepreneurs. Most of the active participants, like Weisheit's (1990b) pragmatist, have never been arrested and function on a limited scale. Others, such as members of the Country Boys, expand their operations and grow marijuana on a much larger scale. Most small growers do so because of perceived financial necessity. When so motivated, business operations are rarely expanded. The hustlers enjoy living on the edge and pursue their goals by increasing the size of their crops, (often venturing outside their communities to enlarge their illegal activities). This, of course, also means hustlers increase the likelihood of their detection, therefore putting the image and stability of the community in jeopardy. Young punks may be unable to obtain legitimate employment and so work as mules and tend the crops of the hustlers. As the economic underclass, young punks are cared for by those in the community who employ (exploit?) them.

The most obvious similarity across the varieties of active participants is that those involved are nearly all men. Women, however, do fulfill roles in the rural marijuana industry, but their roles are significantly different from men's roles. In order to complete our understanding of the culture of the rural Kentucky marijuana industry we now move to a discussion of women's roles.

WOMEN'S ROLES

Women in the male-dominated, rural culture of central and eastern Kentucky are often viewed as weak and passive. Growing up in a patriarchal society many such women outwardly display passivity when relating to men. They have been taught to submit to their fathers and husbands and bend to their will. However, while public displays often fit this mold, many women are in fact very strong and important contributors to their families, kinship networks and communities.

Just as there are certain types of male marijuana growers, there are also differing types of women associated with these men. Each of these varieties of women serves different roles in the business and life of the male marijuana grower. Women's functional roles include assisting in recruiting men into the industry and providing domestic and sexual services for isolated growers and aiding the men in growing, harvesting, transporting, and selling the crop. Females' roles, to an even greater extent than their male counterparts, in the marijuana industry are dependent upon social class membership. Women's degree of involvement ranges from passively assisting their husbands to playing highly active central roles. Theoretically more important though, is a view of women's cultural statuses in the communities of the rural marijuana industry. There are three distinct roles for women in these communities: Strumpets, Decent Women and the Women-in-Between.

The Strumpet is typically a young, uneducated and unmarried woman. Strumpets usually have one or more illegitimate children, are often substance abusers and therefore are perceived as being of loose morals. Additionally, or perhaps consequently, the strumpet rarely attends church, which is an important social function for the rural woman. The specific roles expected of the strumpet are to provide companionship, sexual services and to perform domestic chores for rural men, including marijuana growers. Unless she is fortunate enough to marry, as the strumpet ages she becomes increasingly expendable to the men in her life. In such a case, due to a lack of education and jobs available to women, the strumpet will live out the rest of her life in poverty, and be looked down upon by other, more respectable women. While marriage will not bring the strumpet the same degree of respectability afforded the decent woman, marriage will bring her relative financial security. These young women often associate with marijuana growers for personal gain. She receives clothing for herself and her children, is taken to restaurants and other places of entertainment, travels with her male associate and may receive additional money for her living expenses.

Strumpets display strong loyalty to the men of the marijuana industry. However, this loyalty does not extend to waiting for a grower after he is imprisoned, leaves the area or ends their relationship. She is typically a very pragmatic and self-interested person. Despite her avowed love for her man, she realizes that when he is no longer immediately available it is in her financial best interest to seek out another man. The rural male also recognizes this relationship as a practical arrangement. The strumpet fulfills very specific, and for him important, roles in his life. He does not expect the same loyalty from her that he does from his wife. The strumpet's role is to keep him sexually satisfied and to perform jobs decent women cannot and would not be asked to perform. Because including women in the growing operations would require living with other men, rural Kentucky males would never allow their wives or other female relatives to be involved. Those considered to be decent women would not consent to such an arrangement in any case (Halperin, 1990). When discussing the roles fulfilled by women in his organization, Buford described strumpets, saying:

"Most of us had girlfriends that we could trust with our lives . . . even though most of us were married at the time. These girls would go on some deals, more or less to keep us company. Also they kept the guys happy and content. . . . They didn't need to leave the marijuana farm for sex. We all loved women and always will."

Strumpets are not respected in their rural communities. As might be expected, such women receive especially strong disdain from female relatives of the men in the marijuana industry. However, even though a man's female kin will disapprove of a strumpet, because the culture is extremely patriarchal their disapproval need not drive him away from a relationship with a strumpet. The marijuana grower accepts the strumpet as a necessary, and sometimes valuable, part of his business. She is a commodity, valued only by the men with whom she couples.

The second type of female is quite different and much more respected. Decent Women are highly respected and very rarely placed in any jeopardy by rural men. Decent women include the majority of mothers, sisters, grandmothers, daughters, aunts and wives of the active participants in the marijuana industry (as well as many women with no connection to the industry). Although there are a few exceptions, these women do not generally grow, transport or in any way become involved with the activities of the marijuana industry. They are, for the most part, aware of illegal activities engaged in by the men in their lives, but they themselves rarely participate. Among decent women those most likely to express strong disapproval for marijuana-related activities are the mothers and grandmothers of the men involved. Country men show great respect, both real and ritual, for these women, displaying great deference to them. However, decent women's expressed disapproval does not lead the men to curtail their activities, for after all, they are "just women."

Living in a strictly patriarchal culture, the decent woman may be called upon by her male relatives to assist in recruiting new members of the marijuana industry. New participants, for the most part, are introduced into a kinship network involved in the marijuana industry by marriage to a decent woman. For the decent woman's husband to be incorporated into her kinship network of marijuana growers she must "indirectly" indicate her endorsement of her husband's involvement. It is her responsibility to communicate her husband's desire for inclusion. While she may (and probably will) voice her disapproval, in the end she will bow to her male relatives' wishes. Jolene, a decent woman, explains how her husband became involved in the marijuana industry by way of her male relatives:

"My husband and I was married about six years before he got in with the family. I kind of had an idea what my uncle was doing. My husband said he wanted some good pot . . . The only way my husband could be brought in was if I said the word . . . Finally, I mentioned it to my uncle in an off-hand sort of way. My uncle said for me to tell him to drop by, he might be able to help him out. I couldn't have gotten him in sooner. They had to see what he was like before inviting him in and then on my say-so."

Women-in-Between are distinct from, yet a combination of qualities found in, decent women and strumpets. They may be divorced and employed at the local factory. If unmarried they may frequent the local nightclubs in search of a new husband. They often meet and form intimate relationships with marijuana growers. Unlike strumpets, these women may insist upon a monogamous relationship of either marriage or at least living together. While more respected than the strumpet, they are still less respected than the decent woman. The woman-in-between is unique, she often has an active role in growing and distributing marijuana. Buford described the role of these women as a relatively recent development in rural culture.

The woman-in-between is a new social category in the world of marijuana growers. It is difficult to ascertain the full extent of her role in this culture partly because of her recent emergence and partly because of their status as a hidden member of the culture. Few of the women have been arrested and none has chosen to discuss her role. In this patriarchal society, she is apt to have been recruited and trained by male relatives, her husband or boyfriend. Her future in the marijuana industry remains to be seen. It appears women may be developing more egalitarian roles in the marijuana industry. It can also be speculated that as male marijuana growers are being imprisoned for longer periods of time the women are stepping in to replace them. It remains unclear, then, whether the emergence of women that is presently being seen is due to feminist politics or simple necessity. All three groups of women play significant roles in the marijuana industry. Some are respected in their community, others are not. They all reflect the culture in which they have been raised and have the same distrust of outsiders as their male counterparts.

CONCLUSION

The marijuana industry is a powerful economic and social force in the United States, especially in economically depressed, rural regions of the country. The growth and distribution of marijuana is not a randomly occurring, scattered endeavor, but rather is a structured industry that occupies an important cultural position in rural communities. Throughout this paper, we have argued that the organization of the rural Kentucky marijuana industry is composed of various identifiable roles, and includes all aspects of rural communities. Even those individuals who are not themselves actively involved in the industry play important roles in facilitating the industry's economic success and continued operation. Furthermore, within the organization of rural Kentucky communities there are structural factors that promote and support the marijuana industry. Due to cultural and economic factors of the region, the roles rural residents occupy in relation to the industry are focused on the maintenance of community and culture, not necessarily making the success of the industry itself the primary focus.

16

Drugs-Crime Connections

Elaborations from the Life Histories of Hard-Core Heroin Addicts

CHARLES E. FAUPEL

Auburn University

CARL B. KLOCKARS

University of Delaware

This article uses life history interviews with thirty-two hard-core heroin users to elaborate upon their criminal activities and drug use habits. Respondents were conveniently sampled from prison or the local drug scene, with most holding an active criminal justice status at the time of the interview. They were asked to talk about the family background, their initial encounters with drugs and crime, the evolution of their drug use and criminality, peak periods of drug use and criminality, their preferred criminal and drug use behaviors, their cognitive approach to these behaviors, as well as their perceptions and history of drug treatment. The interviews reveal pronounced careers of drug use and criminality. All persons reported heavy drug use and diverse criminal involvements, but the data did not reveal a clear causal relationship between these behaviors. Instead, there appeared to be fluidity and flexibility to these forms of deviance with the two alternatively feeding one another. The authors argue that levels of life structure and availability produce predictable patterns, periods, and stages in the addicts' deviant careers. Phase one of their model is characterized by low availability to drugs and high levels of life structure. They term these persons "occasional users" and stress the novice nature of their offending and drug use. From here, the respondents transition into the "stabilized junkie" phase. At this stage, the increased access

© 1987 by The Society for the Study of Social Problems. Reprinted from *Social Problems*, Vol. 34, No. 1 (February 1987), pp. 54–68, by permission of the University of California Press.

and appreciation for drugs along with steady life structure allows the addict to have the best of both worlds. Eventually, however, the drugs take control and the person slips into the "free-wheeling junkie" phase. Here, ever growing access to and mastery of the drug scene steadily erodes their conventional life structure. As time passes, they bottom out as "street junkies." Now degenerate addicts, the individual is left with little money, access to drugs, or respect in the drug scene. The authors argue that this career progression can be partial or complete and can take a short time period or be drawn out over years. Their research provides valuable insight into the drugs-crime connection and speaks in detail about the behavioral, cognitive, and cultural aspects of street-level drug use.

T he debate over the nature and extent of the relationship between heroin use and criminal activity is a long-standing one which has generated a voluminous literature. A 1980 survey (Gandossey et al., 1980) lists over 450 citations to books, articles, and research reports, which directly or indirectly bear upon the heroin-crime relationship. Since 1980 the study of this relationship has continued, and several large-scale quantitative studies (Anglin and Speckart, 1984; Ball et al., 1981, 1983; Collins et al., 1984, 1985; Johnson et al., 1985) generally support the thesis that an increase in criminality commonly occurs in conjunction with increased heroin use in the United States. These studies, together with a host of others preceding them (e.g. Ball and Snarr, 1969; Chein et al., 1964; Inciardi, 1979; McGlothlin et al., 1978; Nash, 1973; Weissman et al., 1974) have moved the focus of the debate from the empirical question of whether or not there is a heroin-crime connection to empirical and theoretical questions about the dynamics of that connection.

In particular, two hypotheses, neither of which is new, currently occupy center stage in the drugs-crime controversy. The first, stated by Tappan a quarter of a century ago, maintains that the "addict of lower socio-economic class is a criminal primarily because illicit narcotics are costly and because he can secure his daily requirements only by committing crimes that will pay for them" (1960: 65–66). This hypothesis maintains that heroin addict criminality is a consequence of addiction, albeit an indirect one. As physical dependence upon and tolerance for heroin increase, and the cost of progressively larger dosages of heroin increase proportionally, the addict is driven to criminal means to satisfy his or her habit. Empirically, this hypothesis predicts a linear increase in heroin consumption and a corresponding increase in criminal activity necessary to support it. In contrast, a second hypothesis maintains that the "principal explanation for the association between drug abuse and crime . . . is likely to be found in the subcultural attachment" (Goldman, 1981: 162) comprised of the criminal associations, identifications, and activities of those persons who eventually become addicted. The basis for this hypothesis can only be understood in the context of the contemporary socio-legal milieu in which narcotics use takes place. Since the criminalization of heroin in 1914, the social world of narcotics has become increasingly intertwined with the broader criminal subculture (Musto, 1973). Consequently, would-be narcotics users inevitably associate with other criminals in the highly criminal copping areas of inner cities, and, indeed, are often recruited from delinquent and criminal networks. Through these criminal associations, therefore, the individual is introduced to heroin, and both crime and heroin use are facilitated and maintained. Empirically, this second hypothesis predicts increases in heroin use following or coinciding with periods of criminal association and activity.

A shorthand title for the first hypothesis is "Drugs cause crimes"; for the second "Crimes cause drugs." Each, as we shall see below, is subject to a number of qualifications and reservations; but each, as we shall also see below, continues to mark a rather different approach to understanding the drugs-crime connection. Furthermore, each hypothesis has quite different policy implications associated with it.

METHODOLOGY

Our contribution to understanding the dynamics of the drugs-crime connection is based upon life-history interviews with 32 hard core heroin addicts in the Wilmington, Delaware area. We purposely selected the respondents on the basis of their extensive involvement in the heroin subculture. All of the respondents had extensive contact with the criminal justice system. At the time of interview, 24 of the 32 respondents were incarcerated or under some form of correctional authority supervision (e.g., supervised custody, work release, parole, or probation). While this places certain limits on the generalizations that can be made from these data, the focus of this study is the dynamics of addiction among heavily-involved street addicts. For example, controlled users or "chippers" will not have experienced many of the dynamics reported here. Similarly physicians, nurses, and middle class "prescription abusers" are not typically subject to many of the constraints experienced by lower-class street users. Hence, it is important to emphasize that the findings we report here are intended to describe "hard core" urban heroin addicts.

Women are slightly overrepresented, constituting 14 of the 32 respondents. Ethnically, the sample consists of 23 blacks and nine whites; Hispanics are not represented because there is not a sizable Hispanic drug-using population in the Wilmington area.

Respondents were paid five dollars per hour for their interview time, which undoubtedly contributed to the 100 percent response rate. The interviews ranged from 10 to 25 hours in length, with each interview session averaging between three and four hours. With a single exception, all of the interviews were tape recorded and transcribed. Respondents were promised confidentiality and, without exception, they spoke openly of their drug, crime, and life-history experience.

The incarcerated respondents and most of the street respondents were selected with the aid of treatment personnel who were carefully instructed regarding the goals of the research and selection criteria. This strategy proved invaluable for two reasons. First, by utilizing treatment personnel in the screening process, we were able to avoid the time-consuming task of establishing the "appropriateness" of respondents for the purposes of this research: the treatment personnel were already intimately familiar with the drug-using and criminal histories of the respondents. Second, the treatment personnel had an unusually positive relationship with Wilmington-area drug users. The treatment counselor in the prison system was regarded as an ally in the quest for better living conditions, appeals for early release, etc., and was regarded as highly trustworthy in the prison subculture. His frequent confrontations with prison authorities over prisoner rights and privileges enhanced his reputation among the inmates. Similarly, the treatment counselor who aided in the selection of street respondents was carefully selected on the basis of his positive involvement with street addicts. His relationship with area addicts is a long-standing and multifaceted one. His reputation among street addicts was firmly established when he successfully negotiated much needed reforms in one of the local treatment agencies. Because of the long-standing positive relationship they had with area addicts, this initial contact by treatment personnel greatly facilitated our establishing necessary rapport.

After a few initial interviews were completed, several broad focal areas emerged which formed the basis for future questioning. Respondents were interviewed regarding: (1) childhood and early adolescent experiences which may have served as *predisposing factors* for eventual drugs/criminal involvement: (2) *initial encounters* with various types of drugs and criminality; (3) the *evolution* of their drug and criminal careers; (4) their patterns of activity during *peak periods* of drug use and criminality, including descriptions of *typical days* during these periods; (5) their *preferences* for types of crimes and drugs; (6) the *structure of understanding* guiding drug use and criminal activity; and (7) their perceptions of the nature and effectiveness of *drug treatment*. Structuring the life-history interviews in this way insured that most relevant career phases were covered while at the same time it permitted the respondents a great deal of flexibility in interpreting their experiences.

DRUGS CAUSE CRIMES
VERSUS CRIMES CAUSE DRUGS

One of the earliest strategies for testing the Drugs-cause-crimes versus Crimes-cause-drugs hypotheses involved trying to establish a temporal sequence to drug use and criminal behavior. If it can be established that a pattern of regular or extensive criminal behavior typically precedes heroin addiction, that finding would tend to support the Crimes-cause-drugs hypothesis. Conversely, if a pattern of regular or extensive criminality tends to develop after the onset of heroin addiction, that finding would tend to support the Drugs-cause-crimes hypothesis. Previous research on this question is mixed, but mixed in a systematic way. Most of the early studies found little criminality before the onset of opiate addiction (Pescor, 1943; Terry and Pellens, 1928). Later studies, by contrast, have shown a high probability of criminality preceding heroin addiction

(Ball and Chambers, 1970; Chambers, 1974; Jacoby et al., 1973; Inciardi, 1979; O'Donnell, 1966; Robins and Murphy, 1967).

Our life-history interviews are consistent with the findings of the recent studies. All of our respondents reported some criminal activity prior to their first use of heroin. However, for nearly all of our respondents, both their criminal careers and their heroin-using careers began slowly. For the respondents in our study, a median of 3.5 years elapsed between their first serious criminal offense and subsequent involvement in criminal activity on a regular basis. Likewise, all of our respondents reported at least occasional use of other illicit drugs prior to their first experience with heroin. Moreover, many of our respondents indicated that they spent substantial periods of time—months and even years—using heroin on an occasional basis ("chipping" or "chippying"), either inhaling the powder ("sniffing" or "snorting"), injecting the prepared ("cooked") mixture subcutaneously ("skinpopping"), or receiving occasional intravenous injections from other users before becoming regular users themselves. Perhaps most importantly, virtually all of our respondents reported that they believed that their criminal and drug careers began independently of one another, although both careers became intimately interconnected as each evolved. In the earliest phases if their drug and crime careers, the decision to commit crimes and the decision to use drugs were choices which our respondents believe they freely chose to make and which they believe they could have discontinued before either choice became a way of life (also see Fields and Walters, 1985; Morris, 1985).

DRUG AND CRIME CAREER PATTERNS

From our interviews it appears that two very general factors shape and influence the drug and crime careers of our respondents, not only during the early stages of each career but as each career evolves through different stages. The first of these factors is the *availability* of heroin rather than the level of physical tolerance the user has developed. "The more you had the more you did," explains "Mona" a thirty-year-old female. "And if all you had was $10 than that's all you did. . . . But if you had $200 then you did that much." Addicts are able to adjust to periods of sharply decreased availability (e.g. "panic" periods when supplies of street heroin disappear) by reducing consumption or by using alternative drugs (e.g. methadone). They are also able to manipulate availability, increasing or decreasing it in ways and for reasons we discuss below.

As we use the term, availability also means something more than access to sellers of heroin who have quantities of the drug to sell. By availability we also mean the resources and opportunities to buy heroin or obtain it in other ways as well as the skills necessary to use it. In short, availability is understood to include considerations of all of those opportunities and obstacles which may influence a heroin user's success in introducing a quantity of the drug into his or her bloodstream.

The second general factor shaping the drugs and crime careers of our life-history interviewees is *life-structure*. By "life structure" we mean regularly occurring patterns of daily domestic, occupational, recreational, or criminal activity. Recent ethnographic accounts of heroin-using careers in several major cities reveal that, like their "straight" counterparts, most addicts maintain reasonably predictable daily routines (Beschner and Brower, 1985; Walters, 1985). Throughout their lives our respondents fulfilled, to one degree or another, conventional as well as criminal and other subcultural roles. In fact, during most periods of their crime and drug careers, our interviewees spent far more time engaged in conventional role activities than in criminal or deviant ones. Many worked conventional jobs. Women with children performed routine housekeeping and child-rearing duties. Many leisure-time activities did not differ from those of non-addicts. These hard core addicts spent time grocery shopping, tinkering with cars, visiting relatives, talking with friends, listening to records, and watching television in totally unremarkable fashion.

Life structure in the hard core criminal addict's life can be also provided by some rather stable forms of criminal activity. Burglars spend time staking out business establishments. Shoplifters typically establish "runs," more or less stable sequences of targeted stores from which to "boost" during late morning, noon, and early afternoon hours, saving the later afternoon for fencing what they have stolen. Prostitutes typically keep a regular evening and night-time schedule, which runs from 7 P.M to 3 A.M. Mornings are usually spent sleeping and afternoons are usually occupied with conventional duties.

It is within this structure of conventional and criminal roles that buying ("copping"), selling ("dealing"), and using ("shooting") heroin take place. For example, shoplifters typically structure their runs to allow times and places for all three activities. Likewise, prostitutes seek to manage their drug use so that neither withdrawal symptoms ("joneses") nor periods of heroin-induced drowsiness will interfere with their work. In order to meet the demands of criminal or conventional roles, addicts in our sample often used other drugs (e.g. marijuana, barbituates, alcohol, amphetamines, methadone) to alter their moods and motivations, saving heroin as a reward for successfully completing a job or meeting other obligations.

A Typology of Career Patterns

These two dimensions—*availability* and *life structure*—are critical to understanding the dynamics of addict careers. According to our respondents, differences in the ways addicts manage these functions and variations in these two dimensions that are beyond the control of addicts combine to produce fairly distinct patterns, periods, or stages in their careers. The interaction of availability and life structure may be understood to describe addict career phases that are familiar to participants or observers of the heroin scene.

In Figure 7.1, we identify four such familiar career phases, each of which is marked by a different interaction of heroin availability and life structure. It is important to note that while each denotes an addict type, none of the "types" imply a single career pattern. That is, throughout their drug-crime careers, addicts typically move through periods in which they may at one time be

Availability	Life Structure	
	High	*Low*
High	The Stabilized Junkie	The Free-Wheeling Junkie
Low	The Occasional User	The Street Junkie

Figure 7.1 A Typology of Heroin Use Career Phases.

described as one type and later as another. In our discussion of each type, we describe some of the ways in which transitions seem to occur.

The Occasional User—Low Availability/High Life Structure Initiates into the heroin-using subculture typically begin as occasional users. For the beginning heroin user, a variety of factors typically serve to limit the availability of heroin. The initiate has usually not spent enough time in the heroin subculture to develop extensive drug connections. In addition, the beginner must be taught how and where to buy heroin, and also must learn how to use it. Moreover, the typical beginning heroin user is unlikely to have sufficient income to maintain any substantial level of heroin consumption, and is most unlikely to have either the connections or the knowledge necessary to increase availability through low-level dealing or through shrewd buying and reselling as experienced addicts sometimes do.

In addition to these factors which tend to limit the availability of heroin to the beginning user and hold him or her to an occasional user role, a variety of factors related to life structure also tend to oblige the beginning heroin user to play an occasional user role, or at least to do so until that life structure can be modified to accommodate a higher level of heroin use. In many cases beginning heroin users are young, dependent, involved in school, and bear family roles and obligations which are not easily changed. Likewise, adult role obligations, such as a full-time employment, housekeeping, and child rearing, can be altered so as to be compatible with occasional patterns of heroin use, but not without considerable difficulty if those patterns include high or even moderately high levels of addiction.

One of our respondents, "Belle," explained how she and her husband, "Taps" maintained a very long period of occasional use, due largely to Taps' determination to keep his full-time job:

> I know of people that does half a bag generally. Do you understand what I'm saying? That they automatically live off of half a bag and got a jones. Like I Said, Taps waked—and he would shoot no more than half a bag of dope at any time he took off and wouldn't do no wrong. He would not do no wrong. He worked each and every day. And this is what I told you before—I said I don't know how he had a jones and worked, but he worked every day.

Moreover, Belle went on to explain that when the live structure Taps provided for her lapsed—and availability increased—she did not remain an occasional user:

> Taps had me limited a long, long time. I mean a long time limited to nothing but a half a bag of drugs, until he completely stopped hisself. Then when he stopped, I went "Phwee!"—because I didn't have anybody to guide me. I didn't have to take half a bag and divide it in half for him. And I went from one bag to more.

"Ron," another addict in our sample, played the role of "occasional user" without interruption for nearly eight years. During this period he consumed an average of $10–15 in street heroin per day, while holding down a full-time job and living with his mother, who refused to allow him to use drugs in her home. Toward the end of the eight-year period he became a "tester" for a local drug dealer, a role which increased the availability of heroin. At about the same time, he also lost his job and moved out of his mother's home. Having lost the support of the stable routine imposed by his job and living arrangements at the same time heroin became more readily available to him in his role of "tester," his drug use escalated dramatically within a very short time.

Interestingly, the low availability/high life structure pattern of occasional use, which typically marks the beginning addict's entrance into the drug-using world, is characteristic of many addicts' attempts to leave it. Many formal drug rehabilitation programs impose conditions of low (or no) heroin availability combined with high life structure upon addicts enrolled in their programs (Faupel, 1985). Likewise, as Biernacki (1986) and Waldorf (1983) have extensively demonstrated, addicts who attempt to quit on their own often seek to do so by limiting or eliminating altogether their contacts with addict friends, self-medicating with "street" methodone, and devoting themselves intensively to some highly demanding routine activity such as a full-time job or caring for young children.

The Stabilized Junkie—High Availability/High Life Structure For the occasional user to become a stabilized junkie, heroin must become increasingly available in large and regular quantities, and his or her daily structure must be modified to accommodate regular heroin use. Making heroin regularly available in sufficiently large quantities is not only a matter of gaining access to reliable sources of supply of the drug; it also involves learning new and more sophisticated techniques for using and obtaining it as well as getting enough money to be able to buy it regularly.

During the time beginning addicts play occasional user roles, they typically learn the fundamentals of copping, cooking, cutting, and spiking. These are all drug-using skills that take time to learn. It was not uncommon for the addicts in our sample to report that a sharp increase in their level of heroin use followed their learning to shoot themselves. When an occasional user learns to self-inject and no longer requires the more knowledgeable drug-using friends to "get off," this new level of skill and independence, in effect, increases the availability of heroin.

Likewise, copping skills and contacts which might have been sufficient to support occasional use require upgrading to support the needs of the stabilized junkie. The would-be stabilized junkie who must rely solely on low-quality, "street" heroin, who gets "ripped" by paying high prices for "bad dope," or who is totally dependent on what quality or quantity of heroin a single supplier happens to have available must seek to stabilize both the quantity and quality of regularly available heroin. Doing so seems to require extending and developing contacts in the drug subculture. In the words of one of our respondents:

> . . . you got to start associating with different people. You got to be in touch with different people for the simple reason that not just one person has it all the time. You got to go from one person to the other, find out who's got the best bag and who hasn't. . . . You want to go where the best bag is for your money, and especially for the money *you're* spending. You got to mingle with so many different people.

Making, developing, and maintaining the contacts that are helpful if not absolutely necessary to stable heroin use seem to invite natural opportunities for the most common modification in the stabilized junkie's life structure: dealing. From the point of view of the would be stabilized junkie, dealing has two major advantages over most other forms of routine daily activity. First, it can be carried on in the course of the stabilized junkie's search for his or her own supply of drugs and, second, it can be a source of money for the purchase of drugs or source of drugs itself. Dealing can be rather easily accommodated to the needs of both availability and life structure.

All of our respondents reported that at some time in their drug-using careers they had played the role of dealer, if only occasionally. Becoming an occasional dealer is almost an inevitable consequence of becoming a competent, regular user. A stabilized junkie will not only be approached to "cop" for occasional users and addicts whose suppliers are temporarily out of stock, but the stabilized junkie will come to recognize occasions on which especially "good dope" can be purchased and resold at a profit to drug-using friends.

Because the work of dealing drugs on a small scale does not require much more time or effort than that which goes into buying drugs regularly for one's own use, dealing also has another advantage which makes it an attractive activity for the stabilized junkie. Namely, it can be carried on as a source of drugs or income without undue interference with whatever other "hustle," if any, constitutes the stabilized junkie's additional source of support. This is particularly true if, in the course of carrying on the hustle—be it theft, shoplifting, pimping prostitution, bookmaking, or dealing in stolen property—the stabilized addict is likely to come into regular contact with other drug users.

The extent to which dealing can be carried on along with other hustles depends of course, both on the nature of that hustle and on the extent of the dealing. The stabilized junkie will tend to divide his or her hustling efforts between dealing and other hustles with an eye toward which one delivers the highest profit. However, dividing those efforts will also involve other considerations such as the stabilized junkie's personal preference for one type of work, life style and community reputation considerations, opportunities to practice one type of hustle or another, and the physical demands each type of hustle tends to require. Among female heroin users, a rather common accommodation to the profits and opportunities of dealing and those of other hustles is a live-together arrangement with a male user. In this division of labor each tries to conduct their outside hustle during hours when the other can be at home to handle dealing transactions. An important feature of this arrangement is that, if necessary, it can be structured so as to permit the stabilized female junkie to be at home for housekeeping and child-rearing duties as well as dealing.

The Free-Wheeling Junkie—High Availability/Low Life Structure
Although most heroin users spend some portion of their drug-using careers as stabilized junkies and many manage to live for years with high heroin availability and highly-structured daily routines, at least two properties of the stabilized junkie's situation tend to work against the maintenance of stability. One is the pharmacological property of heroin. It is a drug to which users tend to develop a tolerance rather rapidly, although as Zinberg (1984) has demonstrated, such tolerance is neither necessary nor universal. Moreover, as we have pointed out earlier, numerous factors in the social setting of heroin use mitigate the destabilizing effect of the drug. Work routines, household duties, and even subcultural roles all serve to structure drug consumption. However, in the absence of external structures of constraint, or when such routines are temporarily disrupted, the pharmalogical properties of heroin tend to destabilize the lifestyle of the addict further. In sum, contrary to popular belief, heroin use does not inevitably lead to a deterioration of lifestyle. Rather, the physiological dynamics of narcotics use tend to be most destabilizing under conditions where life structure is already weak and incapable of accommodating the physiological demands imposed by increased tolerance.

The other property of the stabilized junkie's life which tends to undermine stability is the hustle the junkie uses to finance his or her habit. According to our respondents, it is not hard times or difficulties in raising money through hustles which tend to destabilize the stabilized junkie's life. "You can adjust yourself to a certain amount of drugs a day," explained Belle, "that you don't have to have but just that much." In addition to reducing their drug consumption, stabilized junkies accommodate themselves to such lean periods by substituting other drugs for heroin, working longer and harder at their hustling, or changing the type of hustle they work.

On the contrary, it is the unusual success, the "big sting" or "big hit," that tends to destabilize the stabilized junkie's high degree of life structure. The "big sting" or "big hit" can come in many forms. One of our respondents—an armed robber who usually limited his robbing to street mugging, gas stations, and convenience stores—"hit" a bank, which to our respondent's surprise, produced a "take" of over $60,000. He increased his heroin consumption dramatically and, while doing so, abandoned virtually all the stabilizing routines which marked his life prior to his windfall take. In another instance, a relatively stable junkie dealer was "fronted" several thousand dollars of heroin on consignment.

Instead of selling it as he had agreed to do, he absconded with it to another state, shot up most of it himself, and gave the rest away. In still another case, a relatively low-level burglar/thief came across $10,000 in cash in the course of one of his burglaries. He took the money to New York where he intended to cop a "big piece" that he could bring back to the city in which he lived and sell for a nice profit. However, instead of selling it, he kept it for his own use and his habit rapidly increased from a stable three bags per day to nearly a "bundle"—25 bags per day.

Although the "big hit" or "big sting" appears to be the most common precipitator of the transition from the status of stabilized or occasional heroin user to the status of free-wheeling junkie, many other variants of similar destabilizing patterns are common. The stabilized junkie may not be the one who makes the big sting. It may be his or her spouse, roommate, paramour, addict friend, or regular trick who receives a windfall of drugs or money and invites the stabilized junkie to share in the benefits of good fortune. "Goody," a part-time street prostitute, moved in with a big-time drug dealer who provided her with all the heroin she wanted in exchange for domestic services, sexual favors, and some modest help in cutting and packaging drugs. Although her supply of drugs was virtually limitless, she took her child-raising obligations and responsibilities very seriously and they kept her to a modest level of use. However, after a year of domestic living she began to miss the "street" life and the friends she had there and to resent her total ("bag bitch") dependence on her dealer boyfriend. She returned to the street and used the money she earned from "hoing," and "ripping" her tricks to purchase drugs in addition to what she got at home for free. This behavior not only destabilized her drug use, but it also disrupted her home life to such an extent that she parted with her dealer and returned to the street full-time. Interestingly, this return to prostitution, theft, and robbery as her sole means of support forced her to develop a new life structure and abandon the free-wheeling pattern into which she had drifted when she had a dual source of supply.

Unless heroin addicts are disciplined by a life structure to which they are so committed and obligated that it effectively prevents them from doing so, they will expand their consumption of heroin to whatever level of use the availability of drugs or funds to buy them makes possible. What marks the career stage of the free-wheeling junkie is the almost total absence of structures of restraint. In the words of "Little Italy," who described a "free-wheeling" stage of his addict career:

> I can remember, I wouldn't be sick, I wouldn't need a shot. . . . And some of the guys might come around and get a few bags [and say] "Hey man, like I don't have enough money. Why don't you come down with me?" . . . I'm saying [to myself], "Oh-oh, here I go!" and I would shoot drugs I didn't even need to shoot. So I let it get out of control.

The problem for the first free-wheeling junkie is that the binge cannot last forever and is typically fairly short-lived. After a month or two of free-wheeling heroin use—during which time the free-wheeling junkie may have no idea of how much heroin he or she is consuming daily—not only is a modest usage level unsatisfying but the life structure within which he or she might support it is likely to have been completely abandoned or at least be in severe disrepair.

The Street Junkie—Low Availability/Low Life Structure At the point in a free-wheeling junkie's career when heroin availability drops precipitously and life structure does not provide the support necessary to stabilize heroin use, the free-wheeling junkie may manage to rebuild that life structure and accommodate to a new and lower level of availability. To the extent that this rebuilding and accommodation can be managed, the free-wheeling junkie may be able to return to the life of a stabilized junkie. However, if the rebuilding of life structure cannot be managed, the free-wheeling junkie may become a street junkie.

Street junkies most closely approximate the public stereotype of heroin addicts, if only because their way of life—both where and how they live— make them the most visible variety of heroin addict. Cut off from a stable source of quality heroin, not knowing from where his or her next "fix" or the money to pay for it will come, looking for any opportunity to make a buck, getting "sick" or "jonesing," being pathetically unkempt and unable to maintain even the most primitive routines of health or hygiene, the street junkie lives a very difficult, hand-to-mouth (or more precisely arm-to-arm) existence.

In terms of our typology, the street junkie's life may be understood as a continuous but typically unsuccessful effort to stabilize life structure and increase heroin availability. The two problems are intimately related in such a way that, unless the street junkie can solve both problems at once, neither problem will be solved at all. That is, unless the street junkie can establish a stable life structure, he or she will be unlikely to increase the availability of heroin. Likewise, unless the street junkie is able to increase the availability of heroin, he or she will be unlikely to establish a stable life structure.

To illustrate how this relationship works in less abstract terms, it is helpful to begin with a description of what low life structure means in the life of the street. Goldstein (1981: 69) captures the tenor of the street junkie's situation nicely when he observes that

> [if] any single word can describe the essence of how street opiate users
> "get over," that word is *opportunism*. Subjects were always alert to the
> smallest opportunity to earn a few dollars. The notion of opportunism is
> equally relevant to predatory criminality, nonpredatory criminality,
> employment, and miscellaneous hustling activities.

The cause of the street junkie's opportunism is his or her failure to establish a stable life structure which regularly produces enough income to support an addiction. Consequently, the street junkie's life is a series of short-term crimes, jobs, and hustles. Street junkies steal or rob when opportunities arise to do so. For a price or in exchange for heroin, they will "cop" for an out-oftowner, "taste" for a dealer, "tip" for a burglar, rent their "works" to another junkie, sell their "clinic meth" and food stamps, or share their "crib" accommodations with a junkie who needs a place to "get off" or a "hoe" who needs a room to take her "tricks." They will do odd jobs, wash cars, paint apartments, deliver circulars, move furniture, carry baggage, or snitch to the police. The problem is not only that this opportunistic crime, hustling, or legitimate work pays very little, but that none of it is stable. While one or more of these activities may produce enough income today, none of them may be counted on to do so tomorrow. Moreover, because typical street addict crimes pay so little, because such crimes must be repeated frequently to produce any sizable income, and because they are so unpredictably opportunistic, the chance that the street addict will be arrested sooner or later is very, very high. This was the unfortunate experience of Little Italy who after falling out with his supplier, was forced to discontinue drug sales as a major means of income and turned to armed robbery to support his use.

> I know today, I can say that if you don't have a plan you're gonna fuck up man. . . . Now those robberies weren't no plan. They didn't fit in nowhere . . . just by the spur of the moment, you know what I mean? I had to find something to take that place so that income would stand off properly, 'cause I didn't have a plan or didn't know anything about robbery . . .

As Little Italy's experience demonstrates, street junkies lives are further complicated by the fact that "big dealers"—vendors of quantities of good quality heroin—often refuse to sell to them. The reasons they refuse are directly related to the instability of street junkies' lives. Because street junkies can never be certain when and for how much they will "get over," they are frequently unable to afford to buy enough drugs to satisfy their "jones." In the face of such a shortage they will commonly beg drugs from anyone they know who might have them or have access to them, try to "cop short" (buy at less than the going rate), attempt to strike a deal to get drugs loaned or "fronted" (given on consignment) to them on a short-term basis, or, if necessary, engage in opportunistic hustling. Also, because street junkies are the type of addict most vulnerable to arrest they are also the most likely category of addict to be "flipped" by police into the role of an informant. Usually street junkies will be promised immunity from prosecution on the charge for which they were arrested if they "give up" somebody "big." Given the frequency with which street addicts "come up short," the relatively small amount of profit to be made in each individual transaction with them, and the higher than normal risk of police involvement, few "big dealers" are willing to put up with all of the attendant hassles and hustles that dealing with street junkies typically involves.

While there are exceptions—the most common being big dealers who are relatives of street junkies or their friends of long standing—street addicts are mainly limited to "street dope," heroin that has been repeatedly "stepped on" (diluted) as it is passed from the highest level of dealer to the lowest. In fact, some studies (Leveson and Weiss, 1976: 119) have shown that as much as 7 percent of street dope may have no heroin in it at all, while other studies (Smith, 1973) show a heroin concentration of from 3 to 10 percent in street dope as compared with an average concentration of nearly 30 percent in bags seized from "big dealers." The irony in this situation is that, as a consumer of "street dope," the street addict pays a higher per/unit price for heroin than any other person in the distribution chain. Furthermore, this very low and often unpredictable quality of heroin available to the street junkie serves to destabilize his or her life structure further.

17

The Miami Sex-for-Crack Market Revisited

JAMES A. INCIARDI
DANIEL J. O'CONNELL
CHRISTINE A. SAUM
University of Delaware

Inciardi and his colleagues draw upon field observations and interviews from the late 1980s and early 1990s to provide an up-close and personal look at the way prostitution and drug use come together on the inside of Miami's crack houses. The authors observe that some crack houses allow on-site drug use while others do not. Some tolerate sex acts, others do not. Some facilities produce and/or sell drugs and others do not. The first part of the article seeks to impose some order to this matter by forwarding a typology of crack houses. They describe the well-fortified and profit-oriented "castle." "Base houses" are described as the all-purpose 7–11 of the crack house world. They use the term "resort" to describe multiroom apartments that have been converted into efficient crack houses. They speak of "brothels" where sex is the order of the day and house girls, pimps, and crack users do business. A "residence house" is a private residence where the owner welcomes in partiers for extended drug and sexfests. "Graveyards" are described as free-for-all environments such as abandoned buildings and such. Finally, "organized crack houses" represent the most rule-oriented variation in which a highly present owner and staff members oversee drug sales and drug use in an orderly fashion. The second half of the article explores the life of the "crack whore." It highlights the intense sexual and drug use habits of this brand of prostitute and considers the accompanying health concerns. The authors also identify important differences that exist between crack whores and traditional street prostitutes. This article provides valuable insight into the nexus between drug use and prostitution.

Unpublished paper prepared especially for this reader.

It shows how crack cocaine has brought these two worlds dangerously close together, thus altering the behavioral and cultural aspects of the offending.

Crack was my pimp.

—A 28-YEAR-OLD MIAMI CHICKEN HEAD

W hen most people think of vice related crime, the two that come to mind are drugs and prostitution. Indeed, the two are intrinsically linked in both fictional and journalistic media accounts; prostitutes tend to be drug users (Maxwell and Maxwell, 2000) and many female drug users tend to be prostitutes (Inciardi, Lockwood, and Pottieger, 1993). What is less investigated are the ways in which particular patterns of drug usage affect patterns of prostitution. This article explores the relationship between crack cocaine and prostitution in Miami, Florida, in the late 1980s and early 1990s, with a particular focus on crack houses. First, we describe seven different kinds of crack houses and the method of crack sales and usage, as well as the type of prostitution practiced in each. Second, we describe the drug use and sexual histories of 52 men and women who sold sex for crack in Miami in 1989–1990, and the differences between those who sold sex "on the street," and those who did so in crack houses. Finally, a concluding comment suggests that those who sell (and buy) sex in crack houses are at extreme risk of contracting HIV, the virus that causes AIDS.

INSIDE SEVEN DIFFERENT CRACK HOUSES

The crack house is a carnival of vice. It is one hell of a nasty place where the kingrats and pay masters rule, where the gut buckets give slow necks for a penny, and where the freaks, rock monsters, and blood suckers will do anything for a hit on the stem.

—Miami kingrat

By 1989, the Drug Enforcement Administration estimated that there were no fewer than seven hundred operating crack houses in the greater Miami area (Drug Enforcement Administration, 1989). While the quote above may seem foreign to most of us, this use of slang is readily understandable among those in the crack world as they have fashioned their own argot or slang. In much the same way, the very term "crack house" and the physical characteristics that it represents can mean many different things—a place to use, a place to sell or do both, a place to manufacture and package crack—and the location may be a house, an apartment, a small shack at the back of an empty lot, an abandoned building, or even the rusting hulk of a discarded automobile. Close scrutiny reveals no fewer than seven distinct types of crack houses exist in the Miami area. The nature and dynamics of each is detailed below.

Castles

Reportedly few in number, castles are fortified structures where large quantities of crack are manufactured from powder cocaine, packaged in plastic bags or glass vials, and sold both wholesale and retail. Crack users (aka "rock monsters" or "base heads") are not permitted inside the walls of castles. Typical fortifications include barred windows, reinforced door and window frames, steel doors with heavy slide bolts, and walls reinforced from the inside with steel mesh and/or a layer of concrete blocks. Such heavy fortifications are for the purpose of making police raids difficult. An 18-year-old former lookout for a crack house reported in 1990:

> The whole idea [of the fortification] is to keep the cops off yer backs long enough to dump the stuff [crack] before they get in. This one rock castle I was in had all the doors and walls braced with steel bars drilled into the floor and ceiling. It had TV cameras lookin' up and down the street Nothin' could go down without them knowin' about it. The only time the DEA [Drug Enforcement Administration] got in was when they came with a tow truck to pull down the door and a battering ram to get past a concrete barrier. It took them fifteen minutes to get in, and by then we had the place clean [free of drugs].

In addition to fortifications, most castles are well armed, with workers typically carrying semiautomatic weapons at all times. Crack sales are accomplished with little or no interaction. In some houses of this type, exchanges are made through a slot or hole in the fortified door, with the money passed in and the crack passed out. In others, the transaction is accomplished by means of a basket or pail lowered from a second floor or attic window. Due to the fortifications and nature of drug transactions in castles, sex-for-crack trading is generally not practiced in these houses.

Base Houses

The base house seems to be an "all-purpose drug joint," as one informant put it. Base houses are used by many kinds of drug users, especially intravenous users. A variety of drugs are available, including crack. However, smoking crack is not the primary activity. Intravenous drug use (typically cocaine) is more commonly seen and accepted here than in other types of crack houses, but sex-for-drugs exchanges rarely occur. In this regard, a 35-year-old crack-using prostitute commented:

> You can go there and shoot drugs and she (the owner) shoot, but she didn't smoke crack. She'll let you smoke there as long as you . . . give her two dollars. If you was a smoker, a rock smoker, you can give her two dollars to smoke. If you was a cocaine shooter you give her cocaine to shoot or buy her some wine or something. The only thing she didn't let us do there is bring customers.

Another crack user offered a somewhat different description:

> OK, you go in there, and some people they have a syringe in their arm and a pipe in their mouth at the same time. You go in there and you buy crack and they rent a room or they go in the bathroom. You gotta pay fifteen dollars for this 'cause that's two different types of drugs that you get into your system. You can buy a syringe there too, but most times people bring their own syringes. And they go in there, and they shoots up first and they leave the needle in their arm and then they put the crack on top of the pipe and they tell somebody to hit them, you know, to keep the fire on the stem while they inhale it.

Resorts

The resort is one of the more customary types of crack house in Miami. The physical layout is that of a small apartment adapted for crack use. The kitchen is used for cooking rock, at least one bedroom is set aside for sex, and the living space is used for selling and smoking. As one crack user described the resort:

> It was just an apartment house where a lot of people that smoke crack come inside and just do drugs and smoke. One of them was his main room and the other two he would rent out, one for sexuals and one for just smoking. And sometimes there wouldn't be nobody smoking and they just come to have sex in both of them. Inside, candles burning, pillows on the floor; it wouldn't be very good for a person in his right mind.

The owners of these crack houses (aka "kingrats," "rock masters," or "house men") seem to be concerned about two things: money and crack. Many of them are addicted to crack and operate the houses to support their drug habits. Almost anything can happen in these crack houses. They were observed to be filthy, chaotic, and crowded. The crack smokers got into fights, attempted to steal each other's drugs, and exhibited extreme paranoia. A characteristic of the resort is easy access to crack, although each house has slightly different sales procedures. Some charge an entrance fee, and customers are free to smoke and have sex. Crack is usually on a table and purchases are informal. In other houses, the crack may not be on display, and customers pay a worker to bring them a rock. For example:

> They just have it there on the table, whatever you want, give them the money for it and go in the back and then if you want another you go right to the front and buy a nickel [five-dollar rock] and then you smoke that. You have to buy your stuff from them.
> There was one where you could bring your stuff, but you would have to pay, pay them to use their equipment.

In resorts, the bartering of sex and crack occurs between the prostitute (aka "head hunter," "gut bucket," "freak," "base whore," "crackie," "rock star," "skeeter head," or "skeezer") and her or his customer (aka "john" or "pay master"). The owner of the crack house receives a fee (crack or money) from the john for the use of the freak room. As such, the customer pays both the owner of the house and the prostitute. (The sexual activities that occur in resorts are described in greater length elsewhere in this chapter.)

And finally, the crack houses known locally as resorts are termed as such because of the variety of activities that occur there. A cocaine dealer reported in this regard:

> That they call it a "rock resort" has nothin' to do with music. Ha, ha. It's because you can really get into it there—drugs, sex, rock 'n roll, all three at once, whatever. You can smoke your brains out, fuck your brains out, get sexed any way you want, watch sex, get paranoid, fight, watch fights, cut somebody, get high, get killed, whatever the fuck you want.

Brothels

Although prostitution and trading sex for crack are among the primary activities of many crack houses, in the brothel the owner is a dealer/pimp and the sex-for-drugs exchange system is somewhat unique. The prostitute is a house girl and is not involved in the payment process. For the sexual services she provides, she receives payment from the houseman in the form of crack, room, and board.

Several respondents reported having actually lived in a crack house brothel, with many more having visited such establishments. A 26-year-old crack addict with a ten-year-career in drugs described her experience this way:

> Bein' that I been workin' the streets since I was eleven and don't really mind sexin' a lot of different guys, I thought it would be a real easy deal for gettin' all the cracks [more than one rock] that I needed. So this bondman [drug dealer] that I'd know'd real well takes me in. He says all it is givin' a lot a brains [oral sex]. Well man, I know'd a lot a brains. I probably done more *fellatio* [her emphasis] than any lady on the street.
>
> . . . I really got my self into somethin' bad. It wasn't just brains like he said. It was everything. There was guys pushin' their natures [genitals] everywhere—in my mouth, in my guts [vagina], up my ass; guys gettin' off [climaxing] in my face; one guy goin' down on me with five others watchin' and jerkin' off. Most of the time I just didn't care, 'cause I was gettin' all the rock I wanted. But times I just wanted to be left alone, but I couldn't. One time they raped me man; they raped me, cause I wouldn't fuck 'em just that minute. They held me down and beat me and did all kind of terrible things. . . .
>
> And I tried to leave but I was a prisoner there. After the rape I tried to leave, but the man at the door he's got his orders and I can't go. So when I try to get out he slapped me around and they rape me again. They raped me again real bad this time, fucking me in the cunt and the ass at the same time, slapping my face and pinching my tits, and one fuck pissed on me after he was done. An' then to teach me another lesson they hold back on the pipe. . . .

After a while I got sick, and I was all bruised and looked so bad, that they threw me out. They just threw me out like I was just some piece of shit.

In addition to the sexual services available in the brothels, some street prostitutes use them solely as places to have sex with their customers. For example, a 25-year-old woman who had been exchanging sex for money and drugs for eight years reported:

One of the rooms is for base [crack], the other three rooms are for tricking and one of the first rooms inside the door, that's where the dude sit, that's where the G-man [security man, bouncer] sit. When you come in the house he pat you down. They pat you down, and when you come in you say "date." That means pat you down and let you go and have a date. See anyone was allowed to bring a date, anyone was allowed to bring a trick. When you go in you can bring a date in from the outside and use the room and get money from him and you got to do what you gotta do—five dollars to use the room, five dollars one hour, they say an hour but they only give you forty-five minutes with that mother-fucker . . .

Residence Houses

Residence houses are quite numerous in the Miami area and are likely the most common form of crack house. They are houses or apartments where small groups of people gather regularly to smoke crack. The operators are reluctant to call these places "crack houses," because they are used as such only by their friends. However, the activities are the same as those in other crack houses, including sex-for-crack exchanges. The major differences revolve around the payment system. Crack is not sold in residence houses; it is only smoked there. In the more traditional crack house, such as a brothel or resort, payment for using the house can be made with money or crack, although money is preferred. In the residence house, payment is made only with crack. Visitors give crack or more often share crack with the owner of the house or apartment in return for having a place to smoke or turn a trick. There are usually fewer people in these crack houses than in others—five or six compared to fifteen or twenty. They are also the same five or six individuals, whereas in other types there is a greater turnover of people. Finally, whereas the visitors to other types of crack houses are "customers," only "friends" are invited to residence houses.

Graveyards

The designation graveyards, rooms in abandoned buildings, has an interesting genesis. At the comer of Northeast Second Avenue and Seventy-first Street in Miami stands a housing project, described by a local journalist in this way:

Sure, there always were problems. Its official name is Site 5, Project FL527-B, but residents began calling it The Graveyard years ago. Poverty breeds crime, and crime bred more of itself. But when a tidal wave of

cocaine rocks descended on the place two years ago, crime seemed to put
The Graveyard in a stranglehold. The pulse of the community grew faint.
Residents began moving out of The Graveyard and prospective tenants
refused to move in. So basers [crack users and dealers] claimed the vacant
apartments for themselves (Duke, 1987).

In time, The Graveyard's abandoned apartments became overrun by crack
dealers and users, so much so that the county government began boarding up
the project's vacant rooms (*Miami Herald,* 1987). But the name took on a life
of its own, and by the end of 1987 every abandoned building in Miami that
was used for smoking crack became known as a graveyard. A methadone client
and active crack user reported in 1988 that there were "lots of graveyards in
almost every part of the city—Liberty City, Overtown, Miami Beach, South
Miami—every neighborhood where there's empty buildings and lots of crack.
Crack, and lots of crack . . . that's what makes it a graveyard."

According to most informants, no one actually owns a particular graveyard,
although there do seem to be turf issues associated with their use, based on
squatters' rights. Crack users bring their own crack. Sex for money and/or
drugs is performed in these buildings. For example:

> It's an empty house, empty rooms. So somebody like go into this room,
> the first one there. They might put a board you know, you have cloth, you
> know, a bucket of water to bathe and shit. I did it myself. Put up those
> boards and shit, sometimes curtains hanging over the door, this room had
> no doors, no windows, nothing like that. I know'd this one place off
> Miami Avenue where this lady set up in a burned out house. She was sort
> of a whore/crack head/skeezer/bag lady who'd do anythin' for crack and
> for food for her trick baby [a prostitute's child fathered by a john], her
> base baby [a child conceived and gestated by a crack-using mother]. For a
> hit on the pipe or for some food or money or drugs or cigarettes she'd let
> you smoke in her digs and she'd suck your prick too.

And finally, somewhat related to graveyards are base cars—abandoned
automobiles that serve as places to smoke crack, to have sex, or to exchange
sex for crack.

Organized Crack Houses

Organized crack houses are reportedly few in number in Miami. The environment in these establishments is far more controlled than in any other type of
crack house, with the owners more visible and closely monitoring all activities.
Violence and general chaos are uncommon. The ambience is described as
calm, and children are not permitted. They have more workers than other crack
houses, most of whom maintain order inside or watch for police:

> They would have people outside, lookouts. Way up and down the street,
> like on the corner. And another guy sitting in the yard like he was
> cleaning the yard or something. There would be like a bouncer at the door

with a gun to watch to make sure no cops or anything would walk in. Or to make sure that there were no problems within the place itself. Just to make it secure for their sake.

Purchasing crack in organized houses is more structured than elsewhere. Several have specific hours of operation. Upon arrival, a customer is sold crack, seated with a pipe, and strict order is maintained. For example:

> You can't come in the house after 8:00. Other than that he passes it through the window. Before 8:00 you can come in and he lays them [crack and crack pipes] on the table and you can pick what you want. Sometimes you walk in and he's sifting it [cocaine hydrochloride] with the baking soda so he can cook it and tell you to come back in ten or fifteen minutes. When you walk in they have a person that pats you down to see if you got any weapons on you, and then you go through the doors then they have a person that brings you a torch. And they set you up to a table and OK when you first walk in the door it's goin; back a little bit you buy your rocks at the door. They have a little stand. They have all the rocks you want from five dollars all the way to a fifty-dollar rock. And you pick out which one you want, whatever your money can afford and then they have someone that escorts you back in the back, and that's where we smoke at. They give you a pipe, they give you a torch, and then you're on your own.
>
> It wasn't like these abandoned burned-out houses that you see here in the city. This house was very nice, very organized; he had house pipes, torches; he supplied lighters, screens, drugs; everything you needed was right there to prevent so much traffic. Once you get there if you have enough money, you can sit there and use the house pipes and everything. If you only came there to buy a nickel [five-dollar rock] or a dime [ten-dollar rock], you got it and left.

Finally, direct sex-for-crack exchanges do not occur in the organized houses. One prostitute noted that "they let the hookers and skeezers in the door only if they was going to buy crack. The house is for buying and smoking only. They let us cut deals there, you know, but you can't sex there. Got to go someplace else, usually out to the customer's car."

DRUG USE AND SEXUAL HISTORIES
OF MIAMI CRACK USERS

Crack is my keeper, my lover, my god.
—15-YEAR-OLD MIAMI CRACK WHORE

Interviews with 35 women and 17 men in Miami revealed a progression into the drug world that for some, especially the women, ended in virtual slavery to pimps and more importantly to crack. All of the fifty-two informants had long histories of drug use. For almost all of these subjects, alcohol and tobacco use preceded their illicit drug-using careers. Marijuana use began at a mean age of 14 years. A significant proportion of the group experimented with inhalants, hallucinogens, stimulants (uppers), and depressants (downers). Some 40 percent had histories of intravenous drug use, including cocaine, heroin, speed, and/or speedball (heroin mixed with cocaine). All of the men and all but one of the women had used cocaine (non-IV) during their teenage years, with 75 percent using the drug on a regular basis. Crack use began for both men and women by age 25.

In terms of current drug use, defined as any use during the thirty-day period prior to the interview, crack clearly predominated. Crack was smoked for as long as it was available and users had means to purchase it—with money or sex, stolen goods, or other drugs. It was rare that someone had just a single hit. It was typical that they spent fifty to one hundred dollars in one period, with binges lasting three or four days. During these smoking cycles, users neither ate nor slept. Some informants purchased crack over two hundred times in the thirty-day period prior to study recruitment.

While many of these crack users binged for several days in a row, over half (58 percent) used the drug on a daily basis. For every day they used crack, they were high from as few as three times to as many as fifty times. Moreover, once crack was tried, it was not long before it became a daily habit. One-third of the sample used crack daily immediately after first trying it. An additional 27 percent used it daily by the end of their first month.

For many of the women in this study, the craving for crack led eventually to prostitution. Once they ran out of money and things to sell, they found they could always sell themselves. The following quotation, drawn from the transcript of a 28-year-old black female crack user legally employed as a shipping clerk, clearly illustrates a characteristic aspect of the sex-for-crack phenomenon. She details her first exchange of sex for crack and how it came about.

> I had my last paycheck, that was $107. That day I went straight from there [work] with a friend guy and copped some drugs. I bought $25-five nickel rocks. We drunk a beer, we needed the can to smoke on. So we sat there and we smoked those five rocks and you know, like they say, one is too much and a thousand is never enough. And that's the truth. Those five rocks went like this [snaps fingers], and I had maybe about $80 left. I had intentions of takin' my grandmother some money home for the kids. But I had it in my mind you know I was, I was just sick. I wanted to continue to get high so push came to shove and I smoked up that whole day.
>
> OK all the money was gone, all the drugs was gone. About 9:00 we went and sat in the park. Usually when we set in the park, people will come over and they'll have drugs. I stayed out because I couldn't give an account for what I had did with the money. My grandmother done thought that I was goin' to pick up my check and comin' back. So I walked down this street— you know you got people that will pick you up. So this guy stopped, and I

got in the car, and I never did any prostituting but I wanted more drugs. So this guy, he asked me: "How much would you charge me for a head?" That's oral sex. And I told him $40. And so he say, how much would you charge me for two hours to have just sex not oral sex? And so I told him $40 so he say: "OK get in," and he took me to this hotel.

He had about six rocks. I didn't want sex. I wanted to get high, so we smoked the rocks and durin' the time I sexed with him. So after I sexed him, he gave me the money, and after the rocks was gone I still wanted to get high. So he gave me more money to go get more drugs. We went into another hotel. By that time it was maybe 6:00 in the morning. By that time I done spent all my $40. It wasn't nothing I had done wasted the money.

The individuals interviewed in this study had sexual histories that began early and involved many partners. The mean age of first sexual intercourse was 14 years, with the females initiating sex almost a year earlier than the males. The first sex-for-money exchange occurred at a mean age of 19.8 years and the first sex-for-drugs exchange occurred at a mean of 23.2 years.

During the thirty-day period prior to the interview, the sexual activities of the fifty-two informants were extensive. Among the seventeen male crack users, more than half had twenty-five or more male sex partners, and five of the seventeen had a hundred or more male partners. In addition, 60 percent of these male crack users had more than twenty-five female sex partners during the same period. Moreover, 42 percent participated in vaginal sex more than twenty-five times; 88 percent participated in oral sex more than twenty-five times, just under half participated in anal-insertive sex at least once; and 30 percent engaged in anal-receptive sex during this thirty-day period. Finally, 30 percent of these men masturbated other men ("hand jobs").

The women appeared to have many more sexual contacts than the men. Almost 90 percent of the women had a hundred or more male sex partners, and 11 percent had as many as twenty-five female partners. Some 39 percent of these women participated in vaginal sex more than fifty times, 57 percent engaged in oral sex more than fifty times, 20 percent participated in anal sex, and 29 percent provided men with hand jobs.

Respondents performed a wide array of sex acts. This might include generic oral sex (a "brain") or a specialized variation ("slow neck" involves sucking the penis slowly while "fast head" refers to a much faster motion and a "blood sucker" is a female who performs oral sex on a menstruating woman). Moreover, the majority of the respondents reported performing sexual acts that they would do only while on crack and/or for crack and doing so for a penny (one hit on a crack pipe) or less. For example, a 31-year-old male prostitute reported:

As a matter of fact, when you are high on crack you'll do almost anything. We [the respondent and his boyfriend] had sex in front of other people, and one male joined us. Usually I gave the other guy head while we had anal intercourse.

"Crack Whores" versus "Prostitutes"

There seem to be some interesting differences between women who exchange sex for crack in crack houses and those who hustle tricks on the street for money to buy crack. These latter women were not directly addressed in this chapter, chiefly due to their minimal representation in the sample. However, anecdotal data from interviews and observations suggest that they may be at lesser risk for HIV infection and transmission than their crack house counterparts. This inference is based on their frequency of sexual contacts and their attitudes and practices associated with condom use.

First, it appears that street prostitutes have fewer sex partners, and considerably less frequent sexual activity, than the so-called skeezers and chicken heads who exchange sex-for-crack in the smoking and freak rooms of neighborhood resorts, brothels, and base houses. Soliciting a trick on the street, negotiating a price, going to a place to have sex, engaging in sex, receiving payment, and then going back to the streets to purchase and smoke crack take time. To a considerable extent, this regulates a street prostitute's aggregate number of customers. Several of the street prostitutes in this study reported an average of three to six tricks each day that they worked, with most soliciting clients fifteen to thirty days during the month prior to interview. Although this, too, results in an inordinate number of sex partners during the course of a year, or even a month, the numbers may be considerably fewer than those of women who exchange sex exclusively in crack houses. Recall, for example, the remarks already mentioned by the women who spent much or all of the day in crack houses, smoking crack and participating in oral and vaginal sex.

Second, it appears that the street prostitutes in this study were more conscious of sexually transmitted diseases and more often insisted that their customers use condoms. The following comments are representative:

> If they don't want to use a condom, they don't go. I will not go, I will not do it. Most instances, there are very, very few where they don't even want to wear a condom, and very few refuse to wear them.
>
> I just tell them, "Hey, you know I'm afraid of getting AIDS. You don't know that you have it. I don't know if I have it, but you never can tell you know." You know I tell them if you want to make love to me or whatever, you have to put one on. If you don't you can't. And no oral sex either.

By contrast, based on observations and the reports of numerous informants, condoms are rarely used during the sexual activities that occur in crack house freak and smoking rooms. There are likely several reasons for this difference. There is a socialization process, for example, associated with becoming a prostitute. Would-be and neophyte prostitutes learn the appropriate techniques and safeguards through apprenticeships with pimps and/or more experienced prostitutes. In some cases, there is formal or informal training on how to protect oneself from theft, violence, or disease. For example, in one sociological analysis of prostitution as an occupation, it was found that the recognition of sexually transmitted disease was a specific topic of instruction for neophyte house prostitutes:

> Ann [the madam of a small house of prostitution] accompanies the turn-out [neophyte prostitute] and the client to the bedroom and begins teaching the woman how to check the man for any cuts or open sores on the genitals and for any signs of old or active venereal disease. She usually rechecks herself during the turn-out's first two weeks of work (Heyl, 1979).

Furthermore, however loose, unstructured, and transitory they may often be, those who work the streets or in organized houses of prostitution have friendships and peer relationships through which experiences are shared, techniques are traded, warnings are communicated, knowledge is reinforced.

Concern for cleanliness and signs of sexually transmitted disease were readily apparent among several of the street prostitute/informants in this investigation—for example:

> You know some of thems not clean, you know, like they haven't washed and before I even do something I check them out first. And if I see dirt I say, "No, you gotta wash up first." And even if I put my mouth to it and I can taste like it's not clean I just draw back from it. I say I don't want it, you know, and if I feel like if the taste is not right I give them their money back. Ain't no way any cock is goin' into any part of my body without me checkin' it twice. An' even after he pass inspection, then he got to put on a rubber [condom]. That's the rule I tell him. An' if he don't have a rubber I sell him one for a dollar. That's the way it been with me all along, even before AIDS. "Ya don't want to take anything home to yer ole lady," I say, "and I don't wanna take yer germs home to my old man." So now we both safe and sound.

There appears to be no such concern in crack houses. The women who trade sex for crack in crack houses are typically not experienced prostitutes who moved from the streets to the crack house. One street prostitute commented:

> I picked up a date in a crack house once and I didn't believe what I was seein' in there. She was a little girl—19, 18, maybe 17 that's all—doin' stuff like in a porno film. They be doin' anything and everything in front of anyone, and you could tell they were no bitches [street prostitutes]. . . . Yeah, I feel real sorry for 'em. They probably turned a trick now an' then, but they're not experienced girls [prostitutes]. If they was, they wouldn't be on their knees givin' heads all day in crack houses.

A second likely reason for the differences between skeezers and street prostitutes is the role that crack plays in their lives. For skeezers and house girls, crack is at the basis of their sex exchanges, as clearly evidenced in such comments as "I do it for crack" and "crack is my pimp." By contrast, although the use of crack and other drugs is the reason that many women engage in prostitution, their need for crack seems to be somewhat less pressing. For example, one prostitute remarked, "First I tend to business, you know, getting dates, getting money, saving for the rent, you know, and then I go buy a couple of rocks. If another date comes along, I wait to smoke." And associated with this is the prostitute's strong commitment to paying for her own crack. Prostitutes will exchange sex for money but not for a hit:

> If I had money I'd get my own drugs. I don't need nobody else. If I really wanted some more [crack] then I'd find someone to have sex with.
>
> The first time [sex was exchanged for crack] I'll tell you was about three years ago. And I made him pay me double in drugs as if it was money. And they did it, and I got it in my hand up front as payment as I would money. I don't do that very often, but it was the only way I was going to make anything and I was going to buy crack with my own money anyway and since I doubled the price of the cash that I wanted I went for it. And then I don't, very rarely do that [exchange sex for drugs rather than money].

The differences between prostitutes working the streets and those working in crack houses pose a differential risk for the HIV virus. The potential for transmission of HIV from women to men during vaginal intercourse in crack houses is related to one aspect of the cocaine/sexuality connection. Cocaine has long had a reputation as an aphrodisiac, although sexuality is notoriously a playground of legend, exaggeration, and rumor. In all likelihood, much of cocaine's reputation may be from the mental exhilaration and disinhibition it engenders, thus bringing about some heightened sexual pleasure during the early stages of use. At the same time, however, cocaine users have consistently reported over the years that the drug tends to delay the sexual climax and that after prolonged stimulation, an explosive orgasm occurs. Users also report that chronic use of the drug results in sexual dysfunction, with impotence and the inability to ejaculate the common complaints of male users and decreased desire for sex becoming the norm for both male and female users (Grinspoon and Bakaler, 1976; Weiss and Martin, 1987). What applies to powder cocaine with regard to sexual stimulation and functioning would also apply to crack cocaine. Male customers, as well as male and female providers, in the sex-for-crack exchange networks report the difficulties associated with ejaculating under the influence of crack. Some report that they can climax only through extremely vigorous masturbation. One house girl commented: "Some of these mens have trouble gettin' it up and keepin' it up, and it's hard to get a limp cock to come, although sometimes even that happens." Others similarly reported:

> The cracks causes problems for men. They can get a hard-on, but they don't come quick like when they're straight. So first they want heads, and when that don't work, they want pussy sex. Then it still takes 'em forever, pumpin' away until his cock gets sore, I get sore, and then I get pissed. But I can't say anything, because he already gave me the cracks.

It is within such a situation that the potential for female-to-male transmission of HIV exists. During vaginal intercourse, the friction of the penis against the clitoris, labia minora, and vaginal vestibule, opening, and canal causes stimulation that can generate copious amounts of vaginal secretions. And as noted, HIV has been isolated from vaginal and cervical secretions. Furthermore, since women who exchange sex for crack in crack houses do so with many different men during the course of a day or night, potentially HIV-infected semen from a previous customer can still be present in the vagina. Moreover, it was reported by one crack house prostitute that a customer ruptured the skin on his penis while having intercourse with her:

> One time this Hispanic dude was prongin' my pussy so long that he sees blood and starts yelling: "What the fuck's goin' on with you lady, you on the rag or something?" But it was him that was bleedin' in me. His cock was goin' in and out of me so long that he rubbed it raw.

Although vaginal and anal intercourse often occur, much of the sex that occurs in crack houses involves women performing oral sex on men. To date, however, evidence for an oral route of HIV has been unconvincing. In most of the investigations of homosexual practices where a full range of sexual activities were carefully considered, for example, the risk from either insertive or receptive orogenital contact was uncertain, although regarded to be quite low (Kaslow and Francis, 1989). The data concerning heterosexual spread of the virus by oral sex are also limited. For example, in one study of the spouses of AIDS patients, HIV seropositivity among spouses was higher for couples who practiced oral sex in addition to penile-vaginal sex, as compared with couples who practiced only penile-vaginal sex (Fischl et al., 1988).

There is another cofactor, however, apparent in crack house oral sex that may be affecting the spread of HIV: the open sores on the lips and tongues of crack users as the result of burns and other epidermal trauma caused by the heat in the crack pipe stem. Because most women who perform repeated acts of oral sex in crack houses refuse to swallow a customer's semen as it is ejaculated, the potential for HIV transmission from infected semen becomes apparent. For example, the 22-year-old who claimed to have engaged in more than thirty thousand episodes of oral sex commented:

> I may have swallowed a lot of cock in my time, but I don't swallow nobody's come [semen]. Ya can tell when the man is gonna come, so ya try to get his cock out of yer mouth so it ends up somewhere else. Most of the time it ends up on yer face, hair, chest. . . . Either that or he surprises me and I end up with a mouth full of gizz [semen]. So I wait 'til he's done pumpin' and then I let it out all at once. (This particular woman also reported having an open sore on the inside of her lower lip, which she assumed was from a crack pipe.)

Interestingly, and not surprisingly, street prostitutes not only disdain swallowing a customer's semen, but most of those interviewed in this study avoided having semen enter their mouths:

I don't like them to climax in my mouth. A man will push my head because they want it deeper. And I'll tell them, I'll give them one warning: "Get your hand off my head. I know my job, you know." I hate that, to push my head and I'll give them a warning and then I'll get out quick. They'll just come in your hand. I won't let them come in my mouth.

POSTSCRIPT

The use of crack and the existence of crack houses proliferated in Miami throughout the 1980s, and by the end of the decade, crack and crack house sex had become the community's major drug problems. But in the years hence, a number of things have changed. On the basis of focus groups conducted in 1999 and 2000, it would appear that crack continues to occupy a prominent place in the culture of drug-dependent women in Miami. In fact, informants often stated that crack has become "the common denominator in Miami's street drug scene." There is consensus, as well, that the drug is "the great equalizer on the street," in that it has forced crack-dependent women—regardless of age, race/ethnicity, occupation, religion, or family background—into sex trading or commercial sex work in order to support their drug-taking. The crack houses, on the other hand, have virtually disappeared, primarily because of vigorous law enforcement. Gone are the "house girls" and "freak rooms" and all of the specialized types of houses. What remains, however, are the many private houses and apartments where friends and acquaintances continue to gather to make crack, smoke crack, and exchange sex for crack.

18

An Analysis of Women's Involvement in Prostitution

JOANNA PHOENIX
University of Bath

Phoenix observes that there exists uncertainty about what possesses women to enter into and persist within the world of prostitution. Some scholars insist that prostitution is a form of gendered victimization whereby women's impoverished status in society forces them into

Unpublished paper prepared especially for this reader.

a life of prostitution and makes their exit unrealistic. Others view prostitution as a gendered survival strategy whereby entrepreneurial women utilize their involvements in the sex market as a means of achieving financial and personal independence. Phoenix uses lengthy interviews with twenty-one British streetwalkers to assess the legitimacy of these two competing orientations. These life histories reveal the presence of both gendered victimization and gendered survival strategies. Phoenix concludes that women experience their prostitution roles in contradictory ways; they see it as both a means of survival and a threat to their survival. Moreover, she documents a number of coping strategies that these women invoke en route to accommodating or making sense of this inherent contradiction. The prostitutes adopt a series of interchangeable identities. Sometimes they stress the financial aspects of their work and talk about "prostitutes-as-workers" or "prostitutes-as-commodified bodies." These mindsets construct men as sources of income that could be exploited via sex. When speaking about the pimp role, the women often invoke a "prostitution-as business-woman" or "prostitute-as-loving-partner" identity. These two competing world views construct men as a liability or expense, with the first rejecting the need for a pimp and the second rationalizing his presence in their lives. Still other times, the women invoke a "prostitute-as-victim" or "prostitute-as-survivor" mentality. These discussions frame men as a source of risk and stress that the prostitute must constantly confront or negotiate their antics. This article does well to capture the cognitive and behavioral aspects of street prostitution. It shows how these women act and think within a seemingly chaotic world, constantly struggling to impose and reimpose a sense of order or personal understanding to an inherently contradictory lifestyle.

INTRODUCTION

Centuries of prostitution-related research permit researchers to be fairly clear about one thing. Women who get and stay involved in prostitution tend to be women whose lives are torn apart by the aggregate effects of poverty and who often have been homeless, physically, sexually and emotionally abused by parents, partners or boyfriends, grew up in state care and in institutions and have had histories of absconding from foster placements and children's homes. Many have had drug and alcohol problems that compound the social and material adversity that they face (Carlen, 1996; Hoigard and Finstad, 1992). Others have already been in trouble with the law for petty property offences.

And yet research also tells another tale. Whilst poverty may drive women into prostitution, it is through prostitution that many women are able to secure a degree of control and stability within their personal and economic lives. Involvement in prostitution presents women with the opportunity to combine child care with full time work (i.e., prostitutes can choose their working hours, can work from home and can move in and out of work as they desire or need). It provides them with relatively higher amounts of income than they might otherwise have obtained. Hence it is that prostitutes have been talked about as "economic entrepreneurs" and prostitution as the resistance to relative poverty and economic dependency on men—situations created by women's exclusion from the labor market.

Of course, recognising both these research tales raises some very interesting questions. Chief amongst these are: what are the contradictions inherent in involvement in prostitution? What type of problems does sustained involvement in prostitution present to the women so involved? How are these problems and/or contradictions accommodated (i.e. made sense of)?

The following draws on research data that was collected in a large British city at the end of the millennium. The research project investigated and theorized the conditions in which it was possible for women's sustained involvement in prostitution. The story told here is both a condensed version of that larger story (Phoenix, 1999a) and a description of the various ways in which women experienced their involvement in prostitution and the symbolic landscape that helped them understand the choices they made. The argument of this article is very simple: women experience their involvement in prostitution in contradictory ways (i.e. as both a means of survival and a threat to their survival) and that contradiction is "accommodated" (i.e. made sense of) at the symbolic level via the ways in which the women understand themselves and the men around them. The article is broken into two main sections. Firstly, the contradictions of involvement in prostitution are discussed. Secondly, the symbolic landscape that the respondents of this study inhabited is described. Before beginning the analysis however, it is important to note that in the British context, selling sex is not illegal (although many prostitution-related activities are, such as loitering or soliciting, "living off the immoral earnings of a prostitute" and so on).

GENDERED SURVIVAL STRATEGY:
PROSTITUTION AS A WAY
TO A BETTER LIFE

Prostituting, as in the activity of selling sex, is above all else an economic activity: as with any economic activity, personal motivation is usually very clear—the desire for money. However, involvement in prostitution is much more than merely about money, if only because being involved in prostitution means being embroiled in activities that are potentially risky, quasi-legal and certainly criminalised. Most of the interviewees in this study discussed their involvement in prostitution as the opening of future possibilities for them *as women* in the face of ever-mounting social and material difficulties. Prostitution was seen as a way to survive: (i) poverty, (ii) housing difficulties, and (iii) violent relationships that were often the result of rejecting living a life that left them dependent on specific men (fathers, husbands or boyfriends) or on state welfare benefits.

In common with other working class women, the respondents had difficulty earning enough money to support themselves. They had few, if any educational qualifications, marketable skills or labor market experience. When they could find work (and only 14 had), they were employed in the low-paid unskilled service sector or unskilled retail sector. Thirteen women had excluded themselves from the labor market altogether. Many of the women simply stated: "no one would employ me." Removing oneself from the formal labor market or failing to maintain an "ordinary" working history can have profound effects. For these women, it left them with three choices: they could become dependent on state welfare benefits, dependent on particular men, or provide themselves with income in ways that are typically illegally criminogenic.

Independence and the rejection of dependency was the central theme in all interviews—especially when talking about violent relationships. Most women explained their involvement in prostitution as being bound up with their rejection of being dependent on husbands, fathers, boyfriends or state welfare benefits. Those women who grew up in Local Authority Care rejected dependence on a state-structured care system. Others attributed their involvement in prostitution to the need to "sort out" pressing financial problems, multiple debt and so on and when asked, it was precisely their rejection of being dependent on specific men (who were abusive or who did not provide economically or who exploited the women) that created the economic difficulties to which prostitution had become the answer, because it often precipitated an immediate financial crisis. In general, these women constructed the dependency they experienced in their childhood pasts or in their adult intimate relationships as *the cause* of the violent abuse, sexual abuse, neglect and/or restrictions that they experienced. By the women's own accounts, to be economically and socially independent was the means by which they could avoid any future abuse.

In short, the respondents talked about their involvement in prostitution as being a means of securing their future economic and social survival. As working class women, they lived within a social and material context where their survival was, generally, contingent on particular men, the state or casual part-time low-paid employment (Glendinning and Millar, 1992). Given that these specific women had also rejected ways of living that left them dependent on someone or something else, involvement in prostitution was seen not simply as an economic activity, but more importantly as a survival strategy that would enable them to live the lives they wanted to, to provide for themselves and any dependents they might have and to fashion a new better future for themselves in the face of ever decreasing legitimate opportunities in their present.

GENDERED VICTIMISATION:
PROSTITUTION AS A THREAT TO SURVIVAL

Involvement in prostitution also came to be seen by these women as a trap within which their survival was threatened. Each woman commented that being involved in prostitution had furthered her impoverishment, dramatically heightened her likelihood of being the victim of sexual and/or physical assault and increased her dependence on men (who, as pimps, were often violent).

The women discussed the tremendous economic risks inherent in engagement in prostitution regardless of whether they made the kind of money that allowed them to sort out their problems, sign off the social security register, obtain housing and leave their male partners. Specifically, they spoke of the great costs incurred through working such as the financial investments needed (for example, buying clothes and condoms, renting a flat, purchasing a mobile phone and paying for advertising). While it is true that many people have new expenditures when starting new work, for these women, the extra financial burdens involved in prostitution came at a time when their lives were already marked by extreme poverty and housing problems.

In addition, however, working from the streets brought with it its own unique financial problems and risks. All but two of the respondents had been convicted of a prostitution-related offence—typically loitering or soliciting. In most cases, the convictions had been punished with fines which became sentencing orthodoxy in 1983. This change in sentencing lead to an increase in the number of convictions and in the levels of fines which had the perverse result that *more,* not fewer, women were sent to prison not for prostitution-related offences, but for non-payment of fines (Matthews, 1986: 191).

Few of the interviewees could remember exactly how many times they had been arrested or the precise level of fines they either still had to pay or had paid in the course of their involvement in prostitution. However, my own observations in the court suggested fines tended to be in the region of £50–£100 (i.e. approximately $100–$200) per charge and that women often had three or more charges against them each time they went to court. Fining women involved in prostitution for their prostitution-related offences is paradoxical. Many of them simply did not have the financial resources to pay their fines. The obvious irony is that the criminal justice system, itself, created the conditions that both justified these women's continued involvement in prostitution as well as trapped them within it.

Perhaps the most dramatic way in which involvement in prostitution came to be understood as a form of gendered victimisation was in their experience of the practice of pimping—a practice which profoundly increased both their poverty, their homelessness and their likelihood of being victims of violence. All but two of the women had been pimped. Thirteen women recalled having most of their money taken from them under the threat of violence. They were left only with a "subsistence" allowance to get them through each day. Lois (aged 21) recalled being given only £2.50 (i.e. approximately $5.00) per day. Ruthie (aged 25) talked about having only £5.00 (i.e. approximately $10.00) each day in order to buy condoms and cigarettes.

In terms of violence, all of the women who had been pimped talked about regular episodes of violence. They recounted their fears of being murdered or of being punched, stabbed, raped or even shot by their pimps. One of the consequences was that the women believed that being pimped was inevitable and could not be escaped. All spoke of the impossibility of "just not giving him any more money." Too much was at stake. Threatened with violence, controlled through housing and debt, often cut off from family and friends, the women believed that resistance was futile. Katrina (aged 20) summarised the interconnections between these issues. "We're not getting no money out of it. The only way we're going to get money is if we hide it. And if we get found out—the beatings! We usually get found out."

Risk pervades the life of most prostitute and non-prostitute women in late-twentieth-century Britain. For prostitute women, however, the manner in which they negotiated the risks they encountered in their struggle to survive had led to their rejection of traditional modes of living and towards their involvement in prostitution. In this context, though, such involvement became highly contradictory. The contradiction between narrating involvement in prostitution as something that enables survival and while also threatening that survival is so acute as to raise the question of how the individual women can possibly make sense of their involvement. The next section examines the processes by which the contradictory narrations and effects of prostitution are rendered meaningful.

PROSTITUTE-IDENTITIES AND THE ACCOMMODATION OF CONTRADICTION

It is important to emphasize that the paradox of involvement in prostitution occurs because there is a fundamental discontinuity between the effects of engagement in prostitution that the women recalled and the stories that they told about such engagement. Hence, the women claimed that involvement in prostitution alleviated their poverty, provided them with housing, helped them to live independently and gave them a means to fashion better lives for themselves. Yet, they *also* claimed that involvement in prostitution created their poverty, generated their housing difficulties, made them more dependent on men and/or families and jeopardized their social and material survival. But, in their recollections, the women indicated that as they could see no alternative to their current lifestyle, they had to live within that contradiction (i.e. they had to make sense of their lives within prostitution). It is argued here that prostitution comes to make sense (i.e. is rendered plausible and coherent) by, and within, the construction of a specific "prostitute-identity" which is underpinned by a shifting set of meanings for men, money and violence.

There are six contingent elements of the "prostitute-identity." They have been characterized as contingent because each element was made possible by the social and material context in which the women inhabited. These six elements are described in contradictory pairs. Following these descriptions, the shifting set of meanings of "men," "money" and "violence" that underpin each pair is also outlined.

Prostitutes-as-Workers,
Prostitutes-as-Commodified Bodies

The first contingent element is the "prostitute-as-worker" identification in which all the respondents talked about themselves in relation to a generalised imaginary notion of "johns." Within this identification, prostitute-women were constructed primarily as rational economic agents pursuing monetary goals and, more specifically, as workers doing a job and getting paid for it. Prostitution was discussed as though it was a simple economic contract between prostitutes and their johns. This is evidenced in the euphemistic phrases used (i.e. "just making money," "doing business") and in the way the women described their involvement in prostitution, more generally. Lois (aged 21) said: "I'm doing a job. I was doing a job. Like any other person who goes out in the morning, goes to work, gets paid for it and goes home. That's what I do." Christina (aged 23) agreed: "It's a job. That's what you class it as—a job."

Interestingly, the identification of prostitutes-as-workers is also seen in the way that the women described their involvement in prostitution as having nothing to do with sex. The interviewees could make such statements because they denuded their involvement in prostitution of its social setting. Such decontextualisation permitted them to reduce their engagement in prostitution to only a set of episodic, economic moments in a series of individual exchanges between men and women. As Janet (aged 37) said: "You don't have sex with [johns]! Fuck no! That's not sex, you don't even think of it as sex. That's money. It's a job." Others, such as Jasmine (aged 30) and Ingrid (aged 44) put it more succinctly: "It's not sex, it's work" and "You don't think it's sex with [johns]. You don't think of *that* as sex."

The second element in the "prostitute-identity" is a "prostitute-as-commodified-body" identification (as evident in sixteen respondents narratives). In this identification, the women talked about themselves in relation to particular (and anonymous) johns and a notion of "pimp-as-owner" and defined their bodies (especially their vaginas) as rentable objects. This was a subtlety nuanced identification; the women also talked about both controlling and not controlling their rentable vaginas.

The prostitute-as-commodified-bodies identification occurred primarily in relation to an understanding of johns as anonymous men who were interested only in gratifying their own sexual desires and were willing to pay money to do so. This is in direct contrast to the prostitutes-as-workers identification where the respondents talked about themselves in relation to a generalised, imaginary and decontextualised notion of "johns" as one part of a simple economic exchange. The prostitutes-as-commodified-bodies identification was constructed within a specific definition of what was being sold to johns. Instead of selling skill, expertise, time or companionship, these women talked about themselves as being providers of rentable vaginas.

It hit me when I was 19 that I was actually a prostitute. I didn't really think about it before—it was just work. But then it hit me. I was actually selling myself. I was just a hole. I was nothing more than a body men paid to fuck. I was a prostitute. (Lois, aged 21)

The first nuance was in relation to a notion of owning and controlling the commodity (i.e. the rentable vaginas) which was possible through a symbolic separation of the women's bodies from their (assumed) selves. Other researchers have understood this separation as evidence of the emotional and psychological harm of involvement in prostitution (Hoigard and Finstad, 1992) and as specific strategies used by prostitutes to distance themselves from the socially stigmatised label "prostitutes" and thus refuse the negative personal characteristics associated with the label (McKeganey and Barnard, 1996). However, I argue that it is through the symbolic separation of their bodies and selves that the women were able to discuss themselves as owning and controlling (i.e. being ultimately able to dispose of) their rent-able vaginas. Ingrid (aged 44) and Patsy (aged 42) claimed, respectively: "The way I see it, there's me and my body and my body's just there to be sold" and "When I'm here, I'm me. But when I'm out there, I'm not there. I'm not there. I'm something else. I'm just a prostitute—I'm something I can sell."

The second nuance that occurred was in relation to a notion of owning, but not controlling their rentable vaginas. This second nuance was made possible by the *dissolution* of symbolic separation of body and self so that eight of the prostitute-women imagined that their selves had been lost to their continuously rented vaginas and via that, their johns had control over them. Witness Sammy's remarks: "In the end, you hate yourself for selling your body. They do what they want to you. Your body's an object and you've got no control over it."

The third nuance is noted in relation to a contextualised understanding of pimping practices. There was an unstated acceptance of one of the more "feudal" pimping practices—i.e. the buying and selling prostitutes between different pimps. Such an acceptance opened a space for four respondents in which they discussed themselves, in relation to a notion of pimps as owners. The fact that they had each been sold or traded at some point during their involvement in prostitution does not demonstrate this identification; nor do their comments that such practices were common place. But their reactions to and remarks about when they had been sold do. Each of the four women took issue, not with being treated like chattel property, but rather with how much money they had been sold for. The amount obtained represented to these women a symbolic measure of their worth as commodified bodies and rentable vaginas. As Barbara (aged 24) said: "Can you believe it? Kevin sold me to Steve for just fifty pounds! Fifty pounds!! I was worth more than that!"

Men as Money

Both the prostitute-as-worker and prostitute-as-commodified-body identifications were made possible by the fusing together of the meanings for "men" and "money." Men were constructed as both income (i.e. sources of money) and as income which could only be generated through exchanging sex for money. The construction of men as sources of money was an understanding of particular men (i.e. johns) which was applied to all men. This is most clearly seen in the women's repeated claims that "all men are johns." As Gail (aged 28) said: "To me, all men are [johns]. As far as I'm concerned I couldn't do it if it wasn't bought. And if it's not needed then why are we able to sell it."

Dominant discourses of male sexuality as a difficult to control, physical impulse provided the requisite ideological conditions in which the meanings for men and money could be fused together. The women portrayed male sexuality as a biologically driven, aggressive need, as "instrumental" rather than "expressive" and therefore they were able to characterise johns as any (and all) "normal" men doing only what "comes naturally." The john/prostitute relationship could, thus, be understood as though it was simply a routine economic exchange in which normal (i.e. ordinary, typical and not deviant) men buy "outlets" for their physical needs. Combined with this understanding of all men as johns was the women's belief that men as a group have easier access to and more money than women. This belief was most clear in the respondents' talk about men not having childcare problems and so having better access to legal and illegal ways of earning money.

Thus, the interviewees' identification as both workers *and* commodified-bodies was made possible by a reordering of the meanings of men and money whereby men came to represent income. Within such a symbolic landscape, the women were able to construct their prostituting as though it was nothing to do with sex and just routine economic exchange (with themselves in control of and the beneficiaries of that exchange) *and* as though it had everything to do with sex (with their rentable vaginas the object of that exchange). And, contradictorily, the same symbolic world permitted the women to tell stories in which men as johns (i.e. purchasers) and as pimps (i.e. owners) take control of prostitutes' commodified bodies. Hence, involvement in prostitution becomes a web of economic relationships over which the women believed they had control via ownership of their rentable bodies and absolutely no control or ownership as slaves to their pimps.

Prostitutes-as-Business-Women, Prostitutes-as-Loving-Partners

The identification of prostitutes-as-business-women occurred in seventeen of the twenty-one narratives. This identification was comprised of an understanding of prostitutes as being rational economic agents involved in weighing up the costs and benefits of particular courses of action, wherein individual women appraised themselves of, and in relation to, the respective financial and social costs accruing from being involved with men. This is an identification that is distinguished from the prostitute-as-worker identification for within the business woman identification the women talked about themselves as "smart." In common with Katz's (1988) "stick-up men" who deployed both rules and business metaphors when discussing the "business" of robbery, the women in this study positioned themselves as "smart women" working "the right way."

Such talk differed according to whether or not the women were being pimped at the time the interviews took place.

For the women who were not being pimped, being a business woman and working the "right way" meant maximizing income whilst reducing the possibility of exploitation. There were two fundamental rules: business women should not have any personal or intimate relationships with men; and, business women should not be naive about men. The women could demonstrate their business-like status by showing their willingness to accept these rules.

> I reckon if you work, you gotta stop being naive. You have to see men for what they are. [Do you mean johns?] No, I mean men. You have to be professional about how you see all men. They'll live off you if they can. (Olivia, aged 28)

In contrast, the women who were being pimped at the time of the interviews talked about a different rule. They said that working the right way meant minimizing the risk of violence that is associated with street work. The primary strategy used was to get a pimp. Hence, Anna (aged 36) made the following remark:

> The street's a dangerous place. If you're gonna be smart you have to have a man to protect ya and make sure no one kidnaps you or drives off with you. So what if you have to give him some money. (Anna, aged 36)

For these women, the pimp's dress and outward appearance were used to demonstrate their own business success:

> You want your [pimp] to look good, man. You want them to dress good, get nice cars and wicked gold. You give them your money so they can look good. I look at it as good advertising, you know? . . . If I were some stupid crackhead or something, I couldn't be earning the money I earn to make my man look good. (Katrina, aged 20)

In contrast, in nine of the twenty-one women's narratives was an identification of prostitutes-as-loving-partners making choices and taking courses of action based on the love they felt for the men they were involved with, rather than rules for business success. This identification was constructed in relation to the specific relationships the respondents had with men who financially exploited them (rather than within generalised notions of particular categories of men—i.e. "pimp," "partner," etc.). The women talked about themselves as willing to sacrifice their earnings, their safety and their security for their partners. The women were symbolically transforming their relationships with (often violent and) exploitative men from "business" relationships, or even abusive relationships, into intimate, loving, romantic and *above all else* non-prostitution related relationships (Phoenix, 1999b). Andrea's remarks below demonstrate the manner in which she erased the possibility of the violent relationship she experienced as being a relationship which was specific to her involvement in prostitution:

> I don't suppose he really was a [pimp] . . . I think he's the only person
> I ever really loved. Even now I sometimes get upset over it, coz I did love
> him. I was willing to give him everything I'd got—body soul,
> EVERYTHING. (Andrea, aged 27)

The prostitute-as-loving-partner identification was also made possible by the
way in which the women drew on dominant notions of how romantic love is
experienced by women as being a sublimation of their desires and a centraliz-
ing of their partner's desires (Person, 1988; Sayers, 1986).

> To tell you the truth, I was that besotted [i.e. in loved] with him that I'd
> give him everything. I'd give him the fucking world. I'd give him all my
> money and he'd beat me up. But I carried on giving him my money. You
> do, don't you when you love some one? (Ruthie, aged 25)

Men as Expense

The prostitutes-as-business-women and prostitutes-as-loving-partners identifications were made possible by a men-as-expense symbolic landscape where
men were defined in relation to money because involvement with them was
seen as necessitating payment in the form of "opportunity costs" (i.e. values
which must be given up in order to achieve something) and "hidden costs"
(i.e. values which are unknown at the time of calculation). The men-as-expense
symbolic nexus was a construction of involvement with men in general rather
than involvement with men in the context of engagement in prostitution.
Hence, Sophie (aged 28) made the comment: "If you get involved with a
man—ANY MAN—there's always a price to pay. There's always responsibility
to give him money or something. You never can get away with it for free."

Throughout all the respondents' talk there were differences drawn between
the actual opportunity cost incurred by relationships with different categories
of men. Involvement with pimps, boyfriends and the police were described as
necessitating an opportunity cost in that the women understood involvement
with all these men as providing them with "sanctuary" from prostitution or
protection from prostitution-related risks, but at different and specific prices.

Most of the women spoke about boyfriends with whom they were or had
been involved and who gave them sanctuary from prostitution through financially supporting them. But the women described such involvement as costing
them their independence and it was their unwillingness to pay this price that,
they believed, lead to the break up of those relationships. Similarly, involvement
with policemen was seen as offering the women protection from prostitution-
related violence, especially against violence from pimps. All but five respondents
said that policemen, *as men* who are not frightened of pimps, were the only people who could really provide the help the women needed. Indeed, two women
recalled that it was only after the intervention of the police that they were able
to leave their pimps. But here, the police did not arrest the pimps, rather they
arrested the women and took them to hostels or other helping agencies. The
price for this was understood as being both provision of information to the

police, and more importantly, being "indebted" to the particular policeman who provided the help. Lastly, in relation to pimps, more than half of the interviewees talked of making calculations about the quality of protection that pimps could offer them (against violence from johns or intimidation by other pimps) in exchange for the financial exploitation to which they would have to submit. This was most clearly seen in the women's discussions of "big, bad pimps."

> Once they know who you're working for and what status he's got—like who's the baddest, who's the hardest, who's got the gun and who hasn't. You have only to mention his name and that was that. People leave you alone. Other [pimps] and other girls just leave you be. They don't meddle because he's psychotic! He's notorious! He's one very sick and twisted individual. People are afraid of him. (Anna, aged 36)

Of course, the obvious irony is that, although the women understood involvement with their pimps as a form of opportunity cost, providing them with protection, in reality, these pimps provided them with little protection and, in fact, exposed to them further violence and certainly to further financial exploitation.

In contrast, involvement with men as partners was described by the women as incurring "hidden costs." In two cases, the hidden cost was initial entrance into prostitution. Both women talked about "having the knickers charmed off" them and being talked into engaging in prostitution. The cost was hidden because it only emerged after their relationships with these men were established. More commonly, however, was the women's understanding of the cost of *maintaining* their intimate relationships as being their *continued* involvement in prostitution. As Anna (aged 36) stated: "There's a lot of pressure. You have to do it, coz you need the money yourself. Then you get mixed up with someone and you have to do it again to help him, to keep a hold of him."

Prostitutes-as-Victims, Prostitutes-as-Survivors

In all but one of the respondents' narratives, and regardless of their specific prostitution-related experiences, was an identification of prostitutes-as-victims. Drawing on discourses of "victimhood" whereby victims are seen as being "blameless" and "not responsible" for the fate that befalls them (Walklate, 1989), these twenty interviewees talked about themselves as individuals who were unable to control the events of their lives and who were controlled by others that hurt, mistreated or injured them.

Most of the women discussed how past events (especially sexual and/or physical abuse) had "turned" them into prostitutes because, as a result of such events, all they now knew "was how to be used and abused." Witness Margie:

> I didn't have a clue then. All I knew was how to be raped, and how to be attacked and how to be beaten up and that's all I knew. By the time he put me on the game I was already a victim, I was just a born victim. (Margie, aged 37)

Their identification as victims was also seen in the way that the women recounted the injurious actions of others (usually their pimps) as displacing any agency they may have had. Barbara's comments exemplify this: "I did as I was told. You have to, otherwise you're dead. When they've got a gun pointed to your head, you do as you're told."

In contrast, in eighteen women's accounts there was also an identification of prostitutes-as-survivors in which the women talked about themselves as successfully surviving and negotiating the risks they encountered, as battling for control over their own money (in relation to pimps) and their own physical well-being (in relation to johns).

All but two of these eighteen women described themselves as "lucky" and such talk suggests their survivor-identity. Witness Georgie's characterisation of herself when she was being pimped by her last boyfriend: "I guess I was one of the lucky ones, I had clothes. I could pay my rent. I wasn't as bad off as some. I suppose I was lucky and because of that I've survived."

Interestingly, it was in their talk of luckiness and being survivors that the paradoxical nature of prostitution becomes especially clear.

> I get treated a lot better than most, as luck would have it. I keep some of my money, but only for the fact that he knows I've been to prison coz I killed someone. He knows what I'm capable of. And he knows I'll always make sure I survive. (Katrina, aged 21)
>
> There's two sorts of prostitutes. There's the ones that are out there for themselves, and there's the ones that are working for their guy. I'll give anyone credit for standing out on the streets, doing it for themselves, taking their money home. But I can't understand anyone that can stand out there and, then, give it all to some man. [But you were in that situation for over two years.] Yea. But at least I got out of it. I survived. In the end, I'm one of the lucky ones. I'm strong. (Lois, aged 21)

Both of these women (Lois and Katrina) were strident in presenting their engagement in prostitution as a trap threatening their physical, material and social survival. They both talked about being forced to prostitute through fear of death, about being pimped by men who were sadistic and brutal, who had battered and raped them. And yet, here, both women identified as being survivors.

Men as Risk

The prostitute-as-victim and prostitute-as-survivor identifications were made possible by the dissolving of the symbolic boundaries between "normal" and "abnormal" men so that all men with whom the respondents had (or might have) a relationship with became both (i) boyfriends *and* potential pimps; and (ii) ordinary men doing what comes naturally *and* abnormal dangerous men. The meanings for "men," "violence" and "danger" were fused together so that all men became "risky," "dangerous" (in the sense of individuals who threatened the women's overall social, material and, occasionally, physical safety) and/or "suspect" (in the sense of individuals could not be trusted). This meant that the women were unable to take anything in their relationships with men for granted, at the same time as necessarily having to recognise *and* ignore the potential threats and risks inherent in their relations with men in order to continue with their day-to-day lives. The conflation of men with danger is most evident in the women's talk about "pimps" who posed the specific threat of violence and financial exploitation. Earlier it was noted that the term "pimp" was used by the women in three distinct ways. Until this point, the term pimp has been used as a descriptive label. However, "pimps" also occupied a crucial and pivotal symbolic space in that the term was used in an imaginary fashion to represent the archetypal dangers of involvement in prostitution. At various points in all the narratives, the respondents separated "pimps" from boyfriends. "Pimps" were sadistically violent men who would rape, kidnap and entrap women, taking all their money and from whom there was no escape, no resistance no sanctuary. In the construction of this symbolic category, the women drew on discourses of criminal men which situated such men as "outsiders" in relation to ordinary morality (Katz, 1988) and on discourses of masculinity which essentialised male violence so that "pimps" were constructed as men who are always and already violent. Hence, Helena (aged 35) was able to comment: "Pimps are not like other men. They ain't got no heart. They only ever want money." Similarly, Anna (aged 36) stated:

> After I killed my [pimp], I realised that it weren't really his fault that he was like that. [Like what?] Well, raping me and beating up on me, making me have sex with dogs and shit, taking all my money. Some men are just like that. I think it's in their nature. The one thing I've learned is that you gotta steer clear of [pimps]. It's just too dangerous to get involved with them. (Anna, aged 36)

And yet, the distinction between "pimps" and other men (and especially other men as boyfriends) was also dissolved. Part of the set of meanings in which men represented "risk" was an understanding of men as being "suspect" (i.e. not trustworthy). Boyfriends were especially suspect because the women could never trust or be sure that the individual boyfriend they were involved with was not, in fact, a pimp. In other words, there was a notable construction of *all* partners with whom the women had relationships as being *also* (at least potentially) pimps. Witness the following:

> You gotta watch having boyfriends, coz he'll [pimp] ya if you're not careful. In the end you think, boyfriend, [pimp], boyfriend, [pimp], what's the difference? All boyfriends will [pimp] you in the end.
> (Barbara, aged 24)

Boyfriends became potential pimps, the respondents believed, because of the women's engagement in prostitution. The women believed that they turned their boyfriends into pimps by being willing to share their money with them.

> . . . it was my fault that he turned into my [pimp]. I'd give him money.
> I mean, he started getting violent, coz he started to want more and he was
> spending all my money on drink and drugs. I completely changed him.
> (Michelle, aged 33)

At the same time as dissolving the boundary between boyfriends and pimps,
the above extract (and others like it) demonstrate that the women also resur-
rected that boundary. Boyfriends became pimps when they got "greedy." Put
another way, for many interviewees, the difference between boyfriends and pimps
was not a matter of economics or economic exploitation because they understood all relationships as having an exchange of money (and not necessarily an
equal sharing of the total resources of the couple). Rather, the difference was
whether or not the women believed that their boyfriends were taking more
money then they were "due" (Phoenix, 1999b).

The simultaneously expressed prostitute-as-victim *and* prostitute-as-
survivor identifications were made possible by a restructuring of the meanings
of men and violence wherein men came to represent risk. Within such a symbolic landscape, the interviewees were able to construct their relationships with
johns, boyfriends and pimps as being risky and, therefore, were able to locate
themselves as victims *and* survivors of these relationships. Moreover, the men-
as-risk symbolic landscape permitted the women to tell contradictory stories
of engagement in prostitution as being both a specific form of victimisation
and a means to survive once the battle had been won.

CONCLUSION

This discussion has explored a different aspect of prostitution than that
explored within most of the previous 150 years of research. It has sought to
examine the interconnections between women's socio-economic position and
the stories they tell about being prostitutes in order to understand what that
involvement means to them. And, if this analysis can tell us anything, it tells us
that women's engagement in prostitution cannot be understood without a
recognition of their material conditions and how those conditions give shape
to a particular and necessary reordering of the meanings of men, money and
violence. When women's accounts are analyzed the question that arises is how
their stories, which appear to lack a coherent rationale, *can* make sense. To this
end, in describing the conditions in which engagement in prostitution becomes
possible, this chapter has argued at the symbolic level, the contradictions of
prostitution are resolved into a "calm unity of coherent thought" (Foucault,
1972: 155) via the symbolic strategies by which the women were located as
workers and commodified bodies, as business women and loving partners and
as victims and survivors (and the shifting meanings of men, money and violence that underpinned those strategies).

CHAPTER 8

Crime within Complex Organizations

With seemingly increasing regularity, we hear about instances in which formal organizations (or the individuals therein) engage in criminal acts. At times, these crimes are directed inward as is the case with acts of employee theft, embezzlement, or corporate or political espionage. Take, for example, Susan McDougal who was accused (but later acquitted) of bilking $150,000 from the failed Whitewater land deal that haunted the Clinton presidency. Robert Philip Hanssen also comes to mind, the FBI agent accused of selling over 6,000 pages of top-secret government materials to the Russians.

In other cases, the organizational crimes are directed outward toward specific clients, the competition, or the larger society. The Rodney King case or the assault on Abner Loima (i.e., the New York City man who was sodomized with a broomstick by members of the NYPD) stand as high-profile examples of police officers purposely and egregiously violating the human rights of a particular citizen. Another case involving the faulty tread design on Bridgetown/Firestone tires provides an example of how unsafe product manufacturing can result in the death of numerous unsuspecting consumers. Antitrust arrangements such as the alleged monopolization of the computer software industry by Microsoft's Windows program illustrate how free market competition can be stymied and businesses can be forced into an unfair market situation. Broader societal impacts are felt in instances when a government misrepresents itself or betrays the public to achieve military or economic goals. This was the case in the Nazi Holocaust and the Iran-Contra scandal. Similarly, a corporation or rogue employee (i.e., doctor or pharmacist) has the ability to enact a scheme that leads to broad-based economic or physical hardship for hundreds, thousands, or even millions of people. This was the case in the savings and loan scandal of the late 1980s, the Enron and World Com accounting fiascos, and the recent story of the Kansas City pharmacist who was diluting chemotherapy drugs for profit.

There is a common thread that runs through all of the above mentioned scenarios—they constitute breaches of trust that emanate from within an organizational entity. Crimes that are committed within the context of complex organizations represent a vexing conceptual category for criminologists. Traditionally, these acts have been aggregated under the heading of **white-collar crime,** a term that Edwin Sutherland coined in his 1939 presidential address to the American Society of Sociology. In his follow-up book, aptly entitled, *White Collar Crime,* Sutherland maintained that this concept "may be defined approximately as a crime committed by a person of respectability and high social status in the course of his occupation" (Sutherland, 1949, p. 9). In the 60 plus years since this statement, scholars have struggled in earnest to reach agreement over the conceptual and behavioral breadth that should be afforded to the white-collar crime rubric. Much of this apprehension results from the fact that the subject matter spreads like wild fire. As society advances, someone is always willing and able to exploit the situation through an act of criminal innovation. This means that, today, we must negotiate a host of governmental, corporate, and employee-perpetrated acts that simply did not exist 60 years ago.

Geis (2002) observes that criminologists and sociologist alike have repeatedly sought to refine or expand the conceptual landscape of white-collar crime. He notes that some have chosen to expand Sutherland's original definition to include the occupational offenses of lower status, blue-collar employees (Edelhertz, 1970). Others have enveloped any violent or property crime that is committed in the context of organizational influences (i.e., the role that organizational norms and directives have on individual actors) into the discussion (Ermann and Lundman, 1978). We have also seen the development of concepts such as "state crime" (Ross, 1995), "political crime" (Turk, 1982), or even the hybrid "state-corporate crime" (Kramer and Michalowski, 1990) to allow for a more complete treatment of governmental misconduct.

This textbook adopts its own unique conceptual stance. The term **crime within complex organizations** is meant to refer to any physical or nonphysical illegal act (i.e., violent or property offense) that is committed within an organizational context and seeks to further individual or organizational goals, regardless of the social status of that individual or organization. Such a definition subsumes occupational, corporate, organizational, political, and state-corporate crimes under a single conceptual rubric. It is a definition that stresses abuses of trust, not power or social status. This discussion centers most on the roles that organizational norms and opportunities play in shaping the cognitive and behavioral dimensions of criminal behavior. This definition stems from the central premise that all organizations are inherently corrupting. The norms and behaviors that become routinized in these structures can yield what Edward Gross (1979) calls a **criminogenic environment,** one in which the likelihood of a crime occurring is significantly different than it would be if the organizational dimension was removed. In short, the "organizational factor" is said to produce a new layer of analysis that warrants a special conceptual distinction and appreciation.

Green (1997) lays out a four-part typology that is particularly useful for organizing "crimes within complex organizations." He distinguishes between organizational occupational crime, state authority occupational crime, professional occupational crime, and individual occupational crime. **Organizational occupational crime** includes any crime that benefits the organizational initiatives. **State authority occupational crime** focuses on abuses of governmental authority that seek to achieve personal or political interests. **Professional occupational crime** encompasses all wrongdoing committed by persons who hold some sort of professional status. **Individual occupational crime** is concerned with garden variety employee thefts perpetrated by lone, nonsalaried perpetrators.

DEFINING CRIMES WITHIN
COMPLEX ORGANIZATIONS

As stated, the context in which the criminal act occurs, not the act itself, is the primary focus of this chapter. As such, any act (from murder to theft to drug abuse) would fall under this heading so long as it occurred in an organizational context and stemmed most directly from organization norms and opportunities. This notwithstanding, certain statutory provisions are unique to organizational settings. Coleman (1998) breaks down these statutes into four categories. First, are laws that seek to protect businesses. Beyond simple theft and pilferage statutes, embezzlement is the most noteworthy of these statutory provisions. **Embezzlement** occurs when an individual misappropriates property or money with which he or she has been entrusted. Legally speaking, the misappropriation is deemed a form of "conversion," not a "theft by taking," since the perpetrator has been voluntarily granted access to the materials as part of a trust agreement. In short, the *actus reus* is the conversion and the *mens reus* aspect of the crime is the intent to permanently deprive the rightful owner of possession (Samaha, 1999). For example, bank tellers are routinely entrusted with access to cash. If a teller permanently removes money from the bank, he or she is said to have illegally converted the funds and thus committed embezzlement.

Next, Coleman (1998) singles out laws that protect free market competition. Over the course of the past century or so, the U.S. Congress has crafted several legislative provisions that outlaw price-fixing, bid-rigging, monopolies, and other threats to fair business competition. Most notable was the Sherman Act of 1890. This piece of legislation criminalized any effort to prevent full and free competition, any business arrangements designed to artificially inflate prices, and/or any restraint on free trade. Congress has since passed the Clayton Act of 1914, and the Robinson-Patman Act and the Celler-Kefauver Act of

1950. Each of these pieces of legislation provides updates and specifications to the legal landscape that was outlined in the Sherman Act.

Coleman (1998) further delineates a series of laws that are designed to protect democracy. The most visible of these corruption statutes are bribery, perjury, and various tampering offenses. **Bribery** deems it illegal for any public official (e.g., judge, legislator, police officer) to offer, give, receive, or solicit anything of value to influence or alter an official outcome.[1] **Perjury** statutes make it illegal to make false statements while under oath (American Law Institute, 1962). This crime was thrust into the public arena when former President Clinton was accused of perjuring himself regarding the Monica Lewinski sex scandal. **Tampering** statutes make it illegal for an individual to alter or impede official proceedings or investigations.[2]

Political corruption can take on a wide variety of forms and the U.S. Congress has enacted numerous pieces of legislation to safeguard democracy. For example, the Federal Corrupt Practice Act of 1925 and the Federal Election Campaign Act of 1971 seek to regulate election processes and campaign contributions. Similarly, the Foreign Corrupt Practices Act of 1979 sought to put a stop to "international payoffs, bribes, kickbacks, gifts, and political contributions" that came to light in the Watergate scandal that rocked the Nixon administration (Boss and George, 2002, p. 37).

Coleman (1998) notes that there exists laws that seek to protect the public from being victimized by organizational entities. These include legal measures that safeguard consumers, workers, and the environment. Prosecutors often invoke fraud statutes to protect consumers against unsavory business entities. These efforts might target cases of consumer fraud (a bogus company or "ponzi or pyramid scheme" taking money from consumers for a substandard or nonexistent product or service), fraud in the professions (healthcare organizations or other professional entities overcharging clients), or financial fraud (banks or bankers making illegal loans or engaging in forbidden accounting practices).

Federal prosecutors have at their disposal specific legislative provisions and acts that they can use in their fight against organization-based fraud; for example, they can utilize provisions of the Consumer Product Safety Act of 1972 in cases involving product safety. They also have at their disposal specific pieces of legislation that have been enacted to protect the consumers of a particular type of good or service. For example, the Pure Food and Drug Act and the Meat Inspection Act of 1906 impose standards on the production, marketing, and preparation of food products and medications. Similarly, the Financial Institutions Reform, Recovery, and Enforcement Act of 1989, as well as the Crime Control Act of 1990, contains provisions that allow prosecutors to act against the illegal practices of banks and financial institutions. Another example would be the National Traffic and Motor Vehicle Safety Act of 1966, which imposes regulatory standards on the automobile industry. Similarly, Boss and George (2002) make note of the Insider Trading and Securities Fraud Enforcement Act which deems it illegal to compromise the fair value and trading of corporate stocks.

Resourceful federal prosecutors have even been known to use the 1970 Racketeering Influenced and Corrupt Organizations (RICO) Act to pursue white-collar criminals. Originally intended for use against organized crime, prosecutors have begun to exploit certain provisions in the statute. Namely, a person or organization can be subject to stiff RICO sanctions (25-year prison term per count and forfeiture of corrupt assets) if it can be shown that this person or organization used any form of enterprise to engage in a pattern of racketeering.[3] A pattern exists if two acts of racketeering are committed within a 10-year period. Boss and George (2002, p. 35) observe that there is a "laundry list of federal and state crimes that constitute racketeering, including such predicate crimes as murder, kidnaping, robbery, arson, extortion, obstruction of justice, mail and wire fraud, securities fraud, and (the recently added) financial institutions fraud."

The previous discussion provides a thumbnail sketch of the vast legal landscape which allows for criminal charges to be brought against persons or organizations that harm the public, democracy, or the free enterprise system. In addition to these sanctions, aggrieved parties are always given the option of seeking financial compensation via a civil action. This is often the preferred course of action, because most crimes within complex organizations, especially those of the corporate or organizational crime variety, pose a serious legal dilemma for the criminal court system. Most notably, one must establish that a criminal responsibility exists. In short, the question becomes: Can a corporation or complex organization commit a crime? Our legal system has traditionally thought of a "crime" to be an offense that occurs between two or perhaps three persons. Crimes that occur within complex organizations are often collective in nature (i.e., committed by the company or dozens of its employees) and do not make it easy for external authorities to identify a short list of suspects. Prosecutors are rarely able to convince judges and juries that corporate executives should be held criminally responsible for their behaviors. High-priced corporate lawyers and "happy capitalists" on the jury predictably produce acquittals for accused executives and corporations. This, in turn, leads to follow-up civil actions that seek to hit the executives and corporations in what stands as their only exposed legal area—their wallets.

TRENDS IN ORGANIZATIONAL OFFENDING

The Uniform Crime Reports collects data annually from law enforcement authorities on the crime of embezzlement. However, this crime is categorized as a Part II offense, which means that arrest data are disseminated to the public but data on the number of known offenses are not readily available. In 2001, state and local law enforcement authorities effected 20,157 embezzlement arrests (FBI, 2003). An additional 1,118 embezzlement arrests were reported that year by federal authorities (BJS, 2002). The UCR also tallies arrest data on fraud (deemed a Part II offense) but vague definitions leave us unable to separate those common property crimes that are committed by individuals from those that are perpetrated in an organizational context.

The painful reality is that there exists no reliable source of data on the incidence and/or prevalence of crimes within complex organizations. For one, the vast majority of these offenses never get reported—a recent national telephone survey of white-collar crime victimization found that less than 1 in 10 victimizations were reported to law enforcement or any other regulatory entity (Rebovich and Layne, 2000). It is widely reported that corporate victims of embezzlement or employee theft prefer to handle these matters in-house for fear that external involvement will bring negative publicity or unnecessary scrutiny, or even jeopardize proprietary information (i.e., trade secrets). When members of government (i.e., law makers or law enforcers) or corporate executives engage in economic or violent crimes against the public, they can usually rely on norms of secrecy or the threat of dire organizational sanctions to keep the matter from going public. Even if the public, media, or investigators begin suspecting foul play, corporate lawyers and the legal protections that are afforded to organizational entities will usually allow them to produce a formidable smoke screen. In the case of what Green (1997) calls "professional occupational crime" (i.e., crimes committed by members of a profession), perpetrators can readily hide behind the collective code of silence, structures of self-regulation, and privileged information clauses as a way of controlling the flow of damaging information. In light of these structural impediments, one must rely upon data from small-scale and narrowly focused research efforts to speak to the descriptive aspects of these criminal events.

Several studies have explored the topic of theft by employees. Hollinger and Clark (1983) conducted the most comprehensive study on this topic 30 years ago. These researchers distributed questionnaires and selective follow-up interviews with 9,175 retail, hospital, and manufacturing employees working in forty-seven corporations located across the United States. The authors differentiated between two types of employee misconduct: **property deviance** and **production deviance.** The former refers to the theft of hard assets (i.e., money, goods, raw materials) while the latter pertains to counterproductive behaviors such as the theft of time, the abuse of sick leave, on-the-job substance use, and engaging in intentionally slow and sloppy work. They found that one-third of the questionnaire respondents admitted to some form of property deviance and nearly two-thirds reported at least one instance of production deviance in the past year. A similar study involving restaurant employees found that 60% had engaged in at least one form of property deviance and a full 82% had engaged in production deviance in the preceding year (Hollinger, Slora, and Terris, 1992). Experts note that as much as 40% of all shoplifting that is experienced by retailers can be traced back to acts of collusion in which one or more dishonest employees chooses to aid the external thief in his or her crime (Bamfield, 1998).

Research on corporate-level violations reveals that companies engage in a good amount of offending as well. First, there were 6,558 white-collar crime cases involving 8,670 defendants tried by U.S. attorneys in 1999 (Maguire and Pastore, 2000, p. 412). There were an additional 6,332 persons investigated and 3,224 persons tried by U.S. attorneys' offices that year for violating federal regulatory statutes such as the Food and Drug Act or any one of the other special congressional provisions that were previously outlined (Maguire and Pastore,

2000, p. 435). In 2000, there were 901 antitrust cases brought before the U.S. district courts (90% were pursued as civil, rather than criminal cases). There is a general consensus that these numbers represent only a fraction of the actual corporate wrongdoing.

Numerous scholarly studies have attempted to more accurately estimate levels of corporate misconduct. Sutherland's (1949) pioneering study of court and administrative actions taken against the seventy largest U.S. corporations in the 1940s found widespread evidence of abuse. All seventy firms in the sample had at least one formal action brought against them. The average number of violations per company was fourteen. A full 60% of the firms had been convicted in criminal court. All total, these seventy firms accounted for 980 violations of the law. Goff and Reasons (1978) found similar offending trends among the fifty largest corporations in Canada. Clinard and Yeager's (1980) classic study of the universe of Fortune 500 companies found that nearly two-thirds had come under fire from one or more of twenty-four federal regulatory agencies for violating corporate law during a 1-year time period in the late 1970s.

Abuses of state authority also appear to be widespread. As of December 31, 1999, there were 1,134 elected or appointed U.S. officials facing some form of criminal indictment. That number is nearly double what it was 20 years earlier (Maguire and Pastore, 2000, p. 482). If nothing else, the impeachment of former President Clinton illustrates that these offenses are capable of permeating every level of government. Rosoff, Pontell, and Tillman (1998, p. 291) note: "Between 1970 and 1985, criminal indictments were brought against seven governors or former governors, more than 60 state legislators, nearly 50 mayors, as well as a considerable assortment of county officials."

Crimes by government agencies are yet another type of offense that must be assessed through targeted case studies. Rosoff et al. (1998) highlight several noteworthy examples. They point out that an estimated 63,000 developmentally disabled Americans were sterilized under eugenics statutes that were widely imposed across the South for the better part of the early 1900s. They also contend that the U.S. Public Health Service withheld treatment from more than 400 impoverished African Americans in the notorious "Tuskegee Syphilis Experiment."

The excessive use of force by police officers represents one of the most prevalent and "newsworthy" forms of state crime. Voluntary data provided by 100+ police agencies reveal 24,033 incidents of use-of-force occurring in these agencies during 1997. A broad-based survey of citizens made it known that as many as 1% of the 44.6 million police–public contacts that occurred in 1996 involved some form of force or threatened force on the part of the officer (Greenfield, Langan, and Smith, 1997). Research suggests that as many as 40% of all use-of-force incidents involve improper force tactics on the part of the officer(s) (Friedrich, 1980; Worden and Shepard, 1996). Taken on face value, these findings suggest that somewhere in the neighborhood of 180,000 abuses of police force occur each year in this country.

Crimes by persons of professional status are yet another form of crime for which we have little incidence and prevalence data. Members of the health-care community engage in a broad range of criminal behaviors. Estimates suggest that as many as 50% of all doctors, nurses, and pharmacists will engage in illegal prescription drug use at some point during their careers—5% to 10% will come to abuse these drugs (Dabney, 2001). Jesilow, Pontell, and Geis (1985) document widespread misconduct among physicians. For example, untold numbers of doctors are said to defraud Medicare and Medicaid through overbilling or retainer scams, engage in prescription violations, conduct illegal abortions, and take part in self-referral or fee-splitting schemes (i.e., providing kickbacks to other doctors for unnecessary or illegal referrals). Lanza-Kaduce (1980) estimates that as many as 15% of all elective surgeries are unnecessary; and Rosenthal (1995) and Inlander, Levin, and Weiner (1988) document considerable ineptitude and malpractice among doctors.

Other professional groups have also evidenced considerable levels of criminal and unethical behavior. Gartell et al. (1986) estimate that somewhere between 5% and 10% of all practicing psychotherapists have had a sexual relationship with a patient. Teich (1992) found that 27% of the university researchers that they surveyed admitted to having personal knowledge of research fraud or plagiarism on the part of one or more colleagues. Arnold and Hagan (1992) found that considerable numbers of lawyers have licensure complaints and criminal action filed against them.

The monetary and social costs that go along with crimes within complex organizations are staggering. The U.S. Chamber of Commerce estimates that American businesses suffer roughly $40 billion in lost revenues from employee theft each year (Green, 1997). A survey of retail loss prevention professionals suggests that employee theft cost the retail industry alone roughly $15 billion in 2001 (Tyco Interenational, 2001).

In assessing the losses due to corporate transgressions, Clinard and Yeager (1980, p. 126) state: "The Judiciary Subcommittee on Antitrust and Monopoly . . . estimated that faulty goods, monopolistic practices, and other violations annually cost consumers between $174 and $231 billion. A Department of Justice estimate put the total annual loss to taxpayers from reported and unreported violations of federal regulations by corporations at $10 to $20 billion, and the Internal Revenue Service estimated that about $1.2 billion goes unreported each year in corporate tax returns." Given the fact that these estimates are over 20 years old, one can safely assume that current estimates for each would be significantly larger.

Even more disturbing figures emerge when one shifts the focus to the physical harms perpetrated by corporate entities. For example, the Environmental Protection Agency (EPA) estimates that commercial entities are responsible for 90% of the more than 292 tons of toxic waste that are released into the environment each year (Coleman, 1998). These toxins produce untold levels of harm to the air, water, and land of this country. Routine exposure to these poisons can produce cancer or other fatal diseases. Stitt and Gia-copassi (1993) estimate that the heavily polluted air of Los Angeles produces 220 cancer deaths each year and that 240,000 persons will die from asbestos-related cancer over the next 30 years.

SKILLS AND TECHNIQUES
OF CRIMES COMMITTED
WITHIN ORGANIZATIONAL CONTEXTS

There exists variation in the skills and techniques that go along with crimes that are committed within an organizational context. *Organizational (i.e., corporate) and state-authority occupational crimes tend to take on relatively sophisticated forms.* For example, Calavita, Pontell, and Tillman (1997) found evidence of complex and collective offending in their analysis of the savings and loan scandal. They group these offenses into three categories: desperation dealing, collective embezzlement, and cover-ups. *Desperate dealing* took shape as a series of complicated, high-risk investment and loan actions employed by executives to save their sinking financial institutions. These practices included writing multiple loans to insolvent borrowers, inadequate loan underwriting practices, and other "go for broke" investment schemes. The term *collective embezzlement* refers to self-interested "looting" or unauthorized spending sprees that corporate executives pursued using investors' money. The authors contend that extravagant parties and high ticket purchases were the order of the day as executives sought to enjoy the last days of their sinking business enterprises. Once things began to come unglued, *cover-up* practices were used to keep their insolvent ships afloat. These scams ran the gamut from criminal accounting practices (i.e., misrepresenting capital reserves or capital-to-assets ratios) to money laundering, to hush money that was delivered to high-ranking state authorities and policy makers.

Crimes that are committed by state agencies or institutions also tend to take on an elaborate character. For example, numerous discussions (eg., Hilberg, 1985; Staub, 1989), including the upcoming one by Zukier, document how Nazi Germany and other rogue states have systematically embarked on genocidal plans to exterminate certain classes or creeds of people. Hitler's "final solution for the Jewish problem" included a concerted effort of persecution, mass murder, and cover-up. Similarly, the hearings of the Iran-Contra affair of the 1980s taught us that our own government is capable of hatching and carrying out some complex and especially devious criminal plans.

By comparison, acts of professional occupational crime or individual occupational crime tend to be much more simplistic. More often than not, the employee simply pockets the money or materials and makes little or no effort to cover his or her tracks (Ditton, 1977; Horning, 1970; Mars, 1982; Tathum, 1974). A similar trend has been observed among embezzlers (Benson, 1985; Cressey, 1953; Daly, 1989). The same can be said about most crimes that are perpetrated by professionals. For example, the upcoming article by Dabney and Hollinger will show how pharmacists who steal and use prescription drugs on the job tend to rely on simple and predictable routines.

ORGANIZATION-BASED CRIMINAL TRANSACTIONS

White-collar crime and criminals are spread throughout the landscape of the American industrial complex. No one type of business/industry, or even any one type of job role (secretaries versus executives), is disproportionately represented in the available samples of known offenders (Daly, 1989; Weisburd, Waring, and Chayet, 2001). In light of this observation, researchers have begun to adopt a more individual-level focus, targeting the role that occupational settings play in the spread of deviance. Vaughan (1985) observes that companies that operate in autonomous spaces, free of external social and regulatory control, will be more likely to engage in criminal behavior. This type of free-wheeling, self-regulatory work environment allows profit motives to blur the lines between acceptable and unacceptable "business practices." High levels of internal or external competition and cut-throat inner-office or industry-level politics appear to exacerbate matters.

 Organizational offenders are disproportionately white, middle-aged men who possess modest to high levels of social capital. Weisburd et al. (2001) conducted a detailed analysis of the case files of 968 white-collar offenders who were sentenced in seven U.S. district courts over a 3 year period.[4] The vast majority of the offenders were men. The sample was also lopsided in terms of race, as better than 75% of the subjects were white. The average offender was well into his thirties and several offense types (antitrust, securities, tax, and bribery offenses) were dominated by offenders over 40 years of age. The participant's elevated social capital was evident by the fact that most were salaried employees with modest financial assets. Most of the perpetrators were married homeowners with college degrees. Many occupied supervisory positions in their organizations.

CRIMINAL CAREER OF ORGANIZATIONAL OFFENDERS

Organizational offenders do not usually have squeaky clean pasts. Weisburd et al. (2001) found that 36% of the 965 white-collar criminals in their sample had at least one prior arrest and 67% had been arrested more than once in the previous 8 years. Of the repeat offenders, 33% recorded five or more arrests.

 The Weisburd study found little evidence of criminal specialization. Of the 465 repeat offenders, only 15% were exclusively arrested on white-collar charges. Repeat offenders tended to stay away from violent crimes, but they often drifted into property or public order offending. However, the longer the person's rap sheet, the more likely that he or she would face additional white-collar charges. Faced with comparisons to traditional street criminals, the authors conclude: "Using arrest as an indicator of offending, white-collar criminal careers begin and end later, and include smaller numbers of recorded criminal events, than do those of street criminals. However, they are similar to common crime careers in that they are unlikely to evidence a high degree of specialization, and that offenders seem to age out of crime" (Weisburd et al., 2001, p. 49). Moreover, they found the same variables that predict recidivism in street criminals (i.e., marital status, history of drug use, prior record, sex, employment status) to be predictive recidivism in white-collar offenders.

COGNITIVE ASPECTS OF CRIMES WITHIN COMPLEX ORGANIZATIONS

Criminal intent is a difficult concept to nail down in the case of most crimes committed within an organizational context. This is partly a result of the fact that there are so many cognitive and behavioral variations present in these criminal events. Mars's (1982) classic anthropological analysis of workplace argues that different jobs take on different cultural forms. For example, he used the term "hawk jobs" to refer to those work environments that stress entrepreneurial creativity. He claimed that persons working in this type of environment would be drawn toward innovative offenses directed toward enhancing their self-image among peers. He cited academics and business owners as examples of hawks. Next, he used the term "donkey jobs" to refer to those environments that are known for their "isolated subordination." He believed that deviance in this workplace would manifest itself as sabotage or resentment and would stem from low job satisfaction. Cashiers and nonunionized line workers provide good examples of donkeys. Mars coined the term "vulture jobs" to characterize occupations with loose work groups and high levels of individual-level decision-making power (e.g., outside salespeople). He argued that these persons would involve themselves in self-interested abuses intended to enhance their standing in the incentive-based reward system. Finally, "wolfpack jobs" were described as environments with tight work groups, for example, union employees and police officers. These persons, he suggested, would engage in habitual and collective forms of deviance intended to enhance group solidarity and camaraderie.

Instrumental motivation is a cornerstone of crimes that are committed within an organizational context. Regardless of whether the outcome is monetary or physical loss, most of these crimes can be traced back to greed or a thirst for power. Cressey (1953) was one of the first to elaborate on this issue. He found that the vast majority of the incarcerated embezzlers in his sample suffered from what he termed an "unsharable problem." This might include a self-imposed financial pinch resulting from promiscuous or seedy pursuits away from the job, sudden losses from a part-time business or investment venture, or the inability to finance an ever-increasing social status. Faced with the knowledge and skills of their jobs, these embezzlers came to exploit their position of trust as a means of alleviating the problem. Daly (1989) observed a slightly different motivational pattern among the female embezzlers that she studied; namely, the women tended to steal in order to provide for their families.

Analyses of corporate and/or state violators reveal that executives and politicians tend to commit their crimes to keep pace with the competition or to protect their own position within the organization. For example, most agree that former President Clinton committed perjury in an effort to avoid the political fallout associated with having extramarital sex in the White House. Regardless of the gender or organizational standing of the offender, these tend to be persons who commit their crimes because they see them as a way of alleviating some sort of specific threat.

It is difficult to assess the amount of planning that goes into the commission of organizational crimes, since most of them come about as exaggerations of normal operating procedures. In the end, onlookers have difficultly discerning where normal planning and implementation ends and where illegal and unethical cognition and behavior begins. Several scholars (Cressey, 1953; Horning, 1970; Hollinger, 1991) have found that persons who steal from their employers tend to construct their thefts as fringe benefits or simple extensions of normal business practices. For example, a bank embezzler might claim that they simply loaned him or herself the money. A person who steals scrap metal from a manufacturing plant might say that they were simply taking out the trash. By equating these thefts to everyday business, it is difficult to determine how much planning exists.

For decades, scholars have maintained that normative neutralizations play a central part in the initial and repeated offending that takes place among organizational offenders. More often than not, the source of these rationalizations and justifications can be found in the very workplace from which the offending emanates. For example, in his seminal study of embezzlers, Cressey (1953) used the term "vocabularies of adjustment" to describe how thieves routinely implied a sense of ownership or borrowing over the money that they stole as a means of denying their guilty mind. Benson (1985) found a similar pattern among the embezzlers that he studied.

Horning (1970) describes how manufacturing employees adhered to a "cognitive mapping of property." He found that most of the materials in the factory were afforded a status as either personal or company property and thus rarely subject to theft. However, other property was afforded a status as "property of uncertain ownership" and thus fair game for theft. The workers reasoned that taking scrap material or component parts was not the same as taking a coworker's wallet or an assembled television set in a box.

A tangential set of cognitive excuses has been uncovered among deviant professionals and corrupt state authorities. Blue ribbon commissions charged with investigating police misconduct have repeatedly unearthed evidence of a mindset in which habitual offenders deny criminal responsibility for their actions. The rogue officers claim that they were simply playing within the rules of aggressive crime fighting or explicitly following orders (Knapp Commission Report on Police Corruption, 1973; Rampart Independent Review Panel, 1999).

Dabney (1995) documents how workgroup norms centering around the need for effective and efficient patient care can lead nurses to excuse their repeated theft of hospital supplies and medications. Irrespective of the profession, we find that employees do not have to look long or far to find the normative definitions that they use to neutralize their acts of wrongdoing; more often than not, they are derived from established workgroup norms or accepted business practices.

CULTURAL ASPECTS
OF ORGANIZATIONAL OFFENDING

Most organizational offending takes on a loner, colleague, or peer format (Best and Luckenbill, 1994). For example, persons who engage in individual acts of crime and who work in environments with a weak work group dynamic (i.e., what Mars [1982] called hawk jobs) will tend to operate as loners. Embezzlers who steal cash from a bank, or academics who commit plagiarism or research fraud almost always seek to keep their crimes a secret. These offenders are willing to exploit opportunities that arise from associations with others but they rarely discuss their wrongdoings with others.

Other forms of organizational crime take on a more social character, fitting better into what Best and Luckenbill (1994) would call a colleague-like arrangement. This is the hallmark of offending that takes place in "vulture" or "donkey" jobs (Mars, 1982). Most salespeople who commit expense account fraud like to keep their offending to themselves, despite the fact that they know of coworkers who engage in similar misdeeds. The same type of pattern manifests itself among cashiers who steal from the till.

"Wolfpack" jobs (i.e., heavily rule-oriented, but group-centered workplaces) tend to produce yet another brand of organizational alignment. Here, strong group solidarity breeds peerlike associations and collective offending (Best and Luckenbill, 1994). For example, nurses (Dabney, 1995) and police officers (Kappeler, Sluder, and Alpert, 1998) are known to work together to refine and maintain their collective and continued workplace violations.

Regardless of the level of organizational alignment, it is safe to say that almost all organizational offending emerges from identifiable socialization scripts. The upcoming article by Zukier does a fine job of mapping out the way that even something as horrific as the Nazi Holocaust can be incorporated into the common flow of everyday life. All members of the Nazi party, German army, and German population did not conspire to kill millions of Jewish people. Instead, the Nazi leadership devised and implemented a gradual transformation of how the rest of the country thought and behaved toward the Jewish people. Zukier uses terms such as "metamorphosis," "soul murder," and "murder by installment" to describe the incremental move toward mass murder and the accompanying denial. The close-knit contacts within an organizational setting almost always provide ample opportunity for criminal tutelage to take place.

SOCIETAL REACTION TO CRIMES
WITHIN COMPLEX ORGANIZATIONS

By most accounts, the societal reaction to crimes that occur within organizational contexts is less severe than it is for street crime. This observation remains true even when the organizational crime in question is a violent or serious property offense. In the final analysis, Americans simply subject business relations to a more loose set of moral expectations than they do personal relations. If someone kills a friend during an argument, we are outraged. However, if someone dies because a profit-driven product was poorly designed or manufactured, we are likely to depict the situation as an unfortunate cost of doing business. Public apathy along with political denial or even complicity (i.e., pressure from lobbyists and/or campaign contributions) gives rise to relaxed formal social control processes at every stage in the game (i.e., enforcement, prosecution, and sentencing). Even when formal authorities want to get involved, they are forced to face the reality that these crimes are different. As Benson (2001, p. 381) observes: "Corporate offenses pose special investigatory and prosecutorial problems that make the successful application of the criminal law complicated and difficult."

The law enforcement response to crimes that occur within organizational contexts has long been notoriously weak. For starters, organizational crime draws spotty attention from members of the law enforcement community. Federal authorities who bear the brunt of the enforcement workload reported 10,477 fraud (individual and institution-based consumer fraud combined), 1,170 tax fraud, 1,118 embezzlement, 699 RICO (organizational and nonorganizational offenders included), 419 obstruction of justice, 400 generic regulatory offense, 381 bribery, 341 civil rights, 318 forgery, 141 food and drug violation, 24 antitrust, and 4 national defense arrests in 2000 (BJS, 2002). This total laundry list of corporate, occupational, state, and professional crimes barely produced 15,000 arrests that year.

Given the sheer number of employers and employees that exist in this country and the self-reported prevalence estimates that were provided here, it is seems quite reasonable to suggest that millions of organizational crimes go unreported to enforcement agencies each year. The question is why? Logic dictates the need for a multipart answer. First, many organizational offenses go undetected. Many of our nation's corporations are so big that even the loss of large sums of money may never come to the attention of supervisors. The situation is exacerbated by the fact that the finance departments of most American corporations are sadly lacking in auditing skills and implementation. As such, unless a financial transgression is painfully obvious, most accountants will pass over it (Wells, 1993).

In-house security personnel do little to improve this situation. In many cases, security departments are understaffed or underbudgeted. Take, for example, the retail industry. Hollinger and Davis (2000) report the average retail firm directs 0.79% of its total operating budget toward loss prevention and security.

Turning the attention to staffing, Hollinger and Davis report that the average firm employs 5.75 security employees for every $100 million in sales volume—the average firm deploys less than one security officer (0.85) per store location.

Oftentimes, corporate officials become aware of transgressions but choose not to report them to outsiders. Organizations are hesitant to report internal theft for fear that it will be perceived as a sign of financial ineptitude by stockholders or potential clients. For example, Hollinger and Davis (2000) report that company personnel choose to involve the police (i.e., press charges) in 36% of all employee theft cases but 79% of all shoplifting cases.

The news does not get much better when it comes to the prosecution of organizational offenders. According to the Bureau of Justice Statistics (2002), U.S. Attorneys declined to pursue a criminal indictment in 36% of the embezzlement, 52% of the bribery, 55% of the perjury, and 57% of the regulatory cases that were forwarded to them in 2000.

This is not to say that organizational offenders illicit no response from our federal prosecutors. A study (BJS, 1987) found that U.S. Attorneys brought criminal cases against 55% of the suspects that they investigated. This figure was nearly identical to that observed among non-white-collar suspects. When charges were filed, the federal prosecutors were said to pursue the cases with the same tenacity as they did violent, property, or public order offenses.

State-level Attorney Generals are the highest ranking state prosecutors with jurisdiction over organizational offenses. Ayers and Frank (1987) found that these officers of the court pursue individual violators with much greater frequency and tenacity than they do corporate or organizational entities. The researchers conclude that civil or administrative remedies were the preferred course of action when dealing with crime suspected white-collar crime.

It is fairly clear that prosecutors prefer to resolve white-collar crime cases via plea bargains. The average case is quite complex and defendants generally employ a very capable defense team. This makes for a long and expensive trial with no guarantee of a conviction. Albonetti (1994) reports that defendants will gladly plea bargain their case if they feel that the government has a strong case against them; namely, they will seek to cut a deal that allows them to avoid a term of incarceration. However, if the evidence is at all suspect, the defense team is likely to force the prosecutor into a trial. Weisburd, Wheeler, Waring, and Bode (1991) found that 20% of the federal white-collar defendants in their sample pled not guilty and forced a trial. This figure is 3 to 4 times the trial rate that is experienced for most conventional street crimes.

Cases involving corporations and/or their executives stand as a notable exception to the rule. Parker (1989) found that less than 1% of the 200,000+ organizational defendants in their sample saw their cases proceed to trial. Landmark criminal proceedings such as the Ford Pinto case reveal that it is very difficult to obtain a trial conviction in the case of corporate violence. In short, very few examples exist in which prosecutors have gone to trial alleging murder by a corporation or its executives and come away with a conviction. The resources that corporate entities can bring to bear are sizable and simply insurmountable.

The available literature suggests that white-collar individuals and organizations are treated less harshly than conventional offenders when it comes time for judges to impose sentencing (Coleman, 1998; Freidrichs, 1996a). Judicial empathy, a fear of the broad social consequences that go with harsh corporate sanctions, and the respectability of the offenders get offered up as possible explanations for the leniency. Reiman (1998) reports that convicted white-collar criminals face a 36% chance of going to prison. This compares to incarceration rates of 53% for those convicted of nonviolent street crimes and 80% among convicted violent offenders.

If convicted, white-collar offenders can generally expect to do less time than street offenders. Reiman (1998) cites statistics from the Federal Bureau of Prisons from 1986 that show the average time served for a robbery, larceny, and burglary was 46.5, 18.3, and 17.9 months, respectively. For fraud, embezzlement, and income tax evasion, the figures dropped to 13.6, 11.4, and 10.3 months, respectively. He notes that almost half of all white-collar defendants are sentenced to less than 1 year behind bars.

Governmental regulators and court officials often seek to levy fines and restitution as penalties against corporate and white-collar offenders. For example, Cohen (1989) found that 89% of the corporate defendants who were convicted in federal courts from 1984 through 1987 received some sort of fine. Another 16% were ordered to pay restitution, and 19% were ordered to make civil or some other sort of payment. Here again, however, corporate offenders are often able to sidestep the system by managing to have their cases subject to regulatory review as opposed to criminal prosecution. Mokhiber's (1998) review of thirty-six of the most notorious acts of corporate and governmental violence from the past century (everything from the Three Mile Island radiation leak to the Corvair and Pinto cases that plagued the automobile industry) reveals that, in the end, corporate violators almost always receive what can only be characterized as a slap on the wrist.

Civil litigation is the most frequently imposed form of formal social control that gets meted out against corporate, state, professional, and individual-level offenders. These cases can be brought to bear against violators by individuals, groups of individuals (i.e., class-action suits), governmental regulators, or other organizational entities. Coleman (1998) observes that, in almost every case, the plaintiff is severely outgunned by highly paid and knowledgeable corporate lawyers. More often than not, the defendant has vast resources and political power to mobilize on its behalf.

In light of this bleak picture, numerous scholars and policy makers have proposed alternative means of formal social control that might be directed toward organizational crimes and criminals. Loftquist (1993) has proposed a form of "organizational probation." Green (1997) proposes the use of "occupational incapacitation" in which convicted offenders would be removed from the corporate or market environment in which they habitually offended. He also calls for increased criminalization of corporate and individual-level misconduct. Albanese (1995) endorses the use of community service and point-by-point monitoring as a means of achieving "corporate rehabilitation."

Finally, Friedrichs (1996a) describes a proposed punishment called "corporate dissolution," whereby corporate entities would be held responsible for the crimes of their employees (if it could be shown that the corporation benefitted from or endorsed the crimes).

Informal social control efforts directed at crimes within complex organizations are diverse in nature but generally ineffectively implemented. We often allow corporations, industries, or professions to self-regulate themselves. This is generally accomplished through the development and use of codes of ethics and internal oversight entities (review boards, investigators, and the like). The sad reality is that profit motive and self-preservation usually get in the way of these efforts.

Braithwaite (1984) advocates the use of shame and embarrassment techniques as a means of informal social control. He encourages organizational entities to develop and maintain "corporate case law" that would allow them to counsel repeated offenders into compliance without having to rely on threatening and ineffective external sources of control. Glazer (1996) and Miethe (1999) advocate a structured transformation of organizations that would guide and encourage "whistleblowers" to come forward with information. Simon and Hagan (1999) suggest that we enlist the research capabilities of the newly formed National White Collar Crime Center (a hybrid academic-political agency) to study the diverse phenomena and formulate more effective alternative policies.

NOTES

1. Coleman (1998) notes that there also exist "commercial bribery" statutes that allow for the prosecution of private individuals or organizations that seek to curry such favor or unlawfully sway government outcomes or officials.

2. Most jurisdictions have in place specific statutory provisions that outlaw tampering with witnesses, informants, physical evidence, and/or public records or information (American Law Institute, 1962).

3. Racketeering statutes are also commonly used against organized crime entities and drug cartels.

4. Their analysis targeted all defendants from eight offense categories: embezzlement, mail fraud, false claims, credit fraud, bribery, tax violations, securities violations (SEC stock and bond violations), and antitrust cases.

KEY TERMS

bribery

crime within complex organizations

criminogenic environment

embezzlement

individual occupational crime

organizational occupational crime

perjury

production deviance

professional occupational crime

property deviance

state authority occupational crime

tampering

white-collar crime

DISCUSSION QUESTIONS

1. When asked to explain why our society reacts more severely to an individual act of murder than it does to a murder that results from corporate wrongdoing, many place the blame squarely on America's commitment to a capitalist economy. In short, they argue that we hold the economy in higher regard than we do any one individual. Is there any credence in this accusation and, if so, what will come of justice in the age of global capitalism?

2. In select instances, prosecutors have brought criminal charges against corporations and their executives when it appears that their actions (i.e., unsafe products) have led to wrongful deaths among consumers. What impact might the successful prosecution of such a case have on the way that corporations engage in product research and development, let alone the way they approach the market economy?

3. Research shows that the vast majority of American workers steal some sort of time or property from their places of employment. Most employers are aware of the offending but appear willing to tolerate occasional indiscretions. What are the factors that motivate this lack of response and what logic could possibly motivate an employer to adopt such an informal policy and mindset?

19

The Crash of ValuJet Flight 592

A Case Study in State-Corporate Crime

RICK A. MATTHEWS
Ohio University

DAVID KAUZLARICH
Southern Illinois University at Edwardsville

The article begins with a brief review of "state-corporate crime." This concept refers to any situation in which the "mutually reinforcing interaction" between a state and corporate entity results in physical or nonphysical harm to society. The form and process of these criminal associations manifest themselves in such a way that both parties serve to improve their social capital or further organizational goals. The authors use a case study methodology to construct the events surrounding the 1996 crash of ValuJet flight 592 as an instance of state-facilitated, state-corporate crime. They point to specific events such as SabreTech's problematic removal, storage, packaging, and transportation of highly flammable oxygen generators as the most proximate cause of the tragedy. However, they also draw attention to the contradictory roles and responses of government regulators within the FAA and NTSB as distal causes of the crash. The authors produce a socio-historic

From *Sociological Focus*, Vol. 3, No. 3, pp. 281–298. Reprinted with permission.

portrait of a rogue company and absentee and/or remiss federal regulators who share collective responsibility for the loss of 110 persons onboard the flight. This analysis does well to demonstrate how political expedience and corporate profit motive can come together to produce a loosely fashioned sense of criminal intent. This situation, when coupled with criminal opportunities that result from corporate misconduct and nonresponse from regulators, produces a volatile mix.

The study of occupational and corporate crime has become widely accepted within criminology, but the study of state crime has remained on the periphery of the discipline (Tunnell, 1993a). Recently, however, a number of scholars (e.g., Barak, 1991; 1993; Friedrichs, 1996a, 1996b, 1998; Ross, 1995; Tunnell, 1993b) have attempted to articulate the nature, form, extent, and varieties of state crime. While the labels differ, most working in this area agree that governmental, political, or state crimes are illegal or socially injurious acts committed for the benefit of a state or its agencies, *not* for the personal gain of some individual agent of the state. This way of viewing crimes committed by political actors is consistent with the classic distinction made by Clinard and Quinney (1973) between occupational and corporate crime, and points to the importance of viewing governmental/state/political crime as a form of organizational crime. The threat to use and use of nuclear weapons (Kauzlarich and Kramer, 1998; Kauzlarich, 1995), the state's permission of institutionalized racism and sexism (Bohm, 1993; Caulfield and Wonders, 1993), state suppression of civil, political, and human rights (Hamm, 1991; Hazlehurst, 1991), and genocide (Friedrichs, 1996a; Green, 1990) are examples of state crime. Such crime can occur internationally or domestically (Kauzlarich, 1995), can be committed by any number of state or state-related agencies (Friedrichs, 1998), and may or may not be a violation of codified law (Barak, 1991).

While the study of state crime is still in its infancy, a promising and important development has recently been made by Kramer and Michalowski (1990) through the introduction of the concept of state-corporate crime. Traditionally, the crimes of the state and the crimes of corporations have been viewed as unique and distinct manifestations of organizational behavior. Thus, a separate body of research and theorizing developed for each of these phenomena. Kramer and Michalowski (1991) point out the linkages between state and corporate goals, be they proximal or distal, and argue that some forms of organizational deviance result from the interaction between governmental agencies and private businesses.

A revised definition of state-corporate crime expanded the concept to include harmful actions that are not directly manifested through active state involvement: "State-corporate crimes are illegal or socially injurious actions that result from a mutually reenforcing interaction between (1) policies and/or practices in pursuit of goals of one or more institutions of political governance and (2) policies and/or practices in pursuit of the goals of one or more institutions of economic production and distribution" (Kramer and Michalowski, 1991, p. 5; also see Aulette and Michalowski, 1993, p. 175).

While at least two white-collar crime textbooks (Green, 1990; Friedrichs, 1996a) discuss the concept of the state-corporate crime, there is a paucity of research and theorizing on the phenomenon; only three published case studies of state-corporate crime exist in the criminological literature. The present examination of the ValuJet crash, then, can increase understanding of state-corporate crime in two ways: (1) through exposing the varied nature and form of the relationships between the polity and corporations that may lead to injurious outcomes that violate laws, and (2) exploring the usefulness of the core theoretical concepts in the organizational crime literature by applying them to an instance of state-corporate crime.

State-corporate crime, according to Kramer and Michalowski (1991), is a distinct form of organizational deviance because it involves both vertical and horizontal relationships between business and government, which many have generally viewed as separate, discrete entities.

Kramer and Michalowski (1990; 1991, p. 6) have identified two forms of state-corporate crime, state-initiated and state-facilitated. The former occurs when corporations, employed by the government, engage in organizational deviance at the direction of, or with the tacit approval of, the government. State-initiated state-corporate crime includes cases such as the space shuttle *Challenger* explosion and the environmental and human injury caused by nuclear weapons production. In both of these instances, a government agency (NASA in the *Challenger* case and the Department of Energy in the nuclear weapons case) actively pursued a shared goal with a private corporation (Morton Thiokol and Rockwell International, respectively). The day-to-day manufacture of various parts for the space shuttle and nuclear weapons rests in the hands of private corporations. Both the state and the contracted corporation must produce a commodity in a timely and efficient way to achieve mutually held organizational goals. The illegal corporate practices (environmental contamination and the manufacture of defective products) that resulted from such contractual relationships were either strongly encouraged or otherwise explicitly supported by a state agency (Kauzlarich and Kramer, 1998; Kramer, 1992).

State-facilitated crime occurs when "governmental regulatory institutions fail to restrain deviant business activities, because of direct collusion between business and government, or because they adhere to shared goals whose attainment would be hampered by aggressive regulation" (Kramer and Michalowski, 1991, p. 6). Viewing state-corporate crime in this manner sensitizes us to the variety of ways in which the state may encourage organizational deviance, or in some other way act as a criminogenic force.

Since state-facilitated crime usually involves acts of omission rather than commission, it is one of the least recognizable forms of state involvement in crime. The utility of the concept, however, is not just in its identification of the broader structural state support of the U.S. economy and how this can be organizationally criminogenic. There are a variety of identifiable and specific actions or inactions by governmental agencies that may lead to identifiable social harms. In the case study to follow, we will highlight not only the broader structural policies which contributed to the crash, but also the very specific items marginalized or overlooked by the FAA which can be directly linked to deaths of those on ValuJet flight 592. These include ignoring two clear recommendations by the National Transportation Safety Board (NTSB) to: (1) place smoke detectors in cargo holds exactly like the area in which the fire started on flight 592, and (2) reclassify D cargo holds so that they would contain a fire and not allow it to spread to the rest of the plane. Had the FAA followed these recommendations, flight 592 could have landed safely and more than a hundred lives would have been saved. Furthermore, officials in the FAA also ignored several damning reports about the low quality and maintenance of ValuJet planes, not only from other agencies such as the U.S. Department of Defense, but also by FAA field inspectors.

In the case study to follow it will become clear that the crash of ValuJet flight 592 resulted from the "mutually reinforcing interaction" between private corporations (ValuJet and SabreTech) and a governmental agency (the Federal Aviation Administration). As such, the crash represents an example of state-facilitated state-corporate crime in which the pursuit of profit by corporations along with the failure of a state agency to effectively monitor them resulted in the violent deaths of 110 people.

EVENTS LEADING TO THE CRASH

The ValuJet corporation, founded by Robert Priddy, a former baggage handler, had overcome many obstacles and quickly developed its own niche in the airline industry. ValuJet grew from 2 to 50 aircraft (including the acquisition of 48 aircraft in 31 months), and within four years had a profit of $6.8 million dollars (Levinson, Underwood, and Turque, 1996; Hosenball and Underwood, 1996). Based in Atlanta, Georgia, ValuJet was approaching its fourth year of existence when flight 592 crashed. The early years of ValuJet were characterized by rapid growth and the development of a reputation for providing exceptionally low-priced airfares (as low as $39.00) and staying, in the words of Priddy "lean and mean" (Hosenball and Underwood, 1996). The lean and mean aspect of ValuJet meant, among other things, a non-unionized labor force, paying pilots about half of the industry average, having pilots pay for their own training, and outsourcing maintenance (Hosenball and Underwood, 1996). Like many late-20th-century corporations, ValuJet viewed outsourcing as an integral profit-making component. By 1994 ValuJet was acquiring planes as fast as they could get their hands on them, most of which were older and in need of repairs. At the time of the crash of flight 592 the average age of ValutJet aircraft was 26.4 years old (Greising, 1996). Since one of the cost cutting measured employed by ValuJet was contracting out maintenance duties, the older planes they purchased were sent to out-of-house contractors. Indeed, the only maintenance ValuJet did itself was routine inspections, and it was not equipped to do heavy maintenance. In all, ValuJet had contracts with 21 different certified maintenance facilities, including SabreTech (NTSB, 1997).

One of the maintenance tasks requested of SabreTech by ValuJet was the inspection of oxygen generators on all three planes to determine if they had exceeded their allowable service life of 12 years. One of the planes had generators that were to expire in 1998 or later. However, the other two planes had generators that had already expired or were going to expire shortly. Thus, ValuJet contracted with SabreTech to remove the generators from these planes and replace them.

Oxygen generators are cylindrical tubes that provide oxygen in emergency situations, when cabin pressure is lost. The generators, along with the oxygen masks, are mounted behind panels above or adjacent to passenger seats in the plane. The generator cannot be activated until the spring-loaded mechanism strikes a percussion cap containing a small explosive charge at the end of the generator. When struck, this cap provides the necessary energy to create an exothermic chemical reaction, which then causes the generator to expel oxygen and tremendous amounts of heat. When mounted in planes, however, the generators should not cause fires because they are mounted on top of heat shields.

The guidelines for removing and disposing of oxygen generators are quite clear. The McDonnell Douglas manual, for instance, explicitly states that "if the generator has not been expended" workers are to "install safety cap over (the) primer" (NTSB, 1997, p. 10). Furthermore, this manual states that the generators must be stored in a safe environment (i.e., noncombustible surface) where they are not exposed to high temperatures or possible damage until they are expended. Expenditure of the oxygen generators is done by securing them on a nonflammable surface in an area free of combustible substances. Once the chemical reaction has occurred, and the canister has cooled, it may be disposed of. Of the 144 canisters on the two planes, only six were expended (NTSB, 1997).

In March of 1996 SabreTech crews began removing the old oxygen generators from the ValuJet planes and replacing them with new ones. According to the mechanics from SabreTech, almost all the generators that were removed were placed in cardboard boxes and then placed on racks in the hangar near the airplanes themselves (NTSB, 1997). All the work at SabreTech was to have been completed by April 24, 1996, for the first plane, and April 30, 1996, for the second. This time line was established with an agreement between ValuJet and SabreTech, which explicitly stated that ValuJet was to be credited $2,500.00 per calendar day for each day the aircraft was delayed beyond the redelivery date (NTSB, 1997). According to the mechanics at SabreTech, there was considerable pressure to complete work on the aircraft. They reportedly worked 12-hour shifts, 7 days a week to complete the task (NTSB, 1997).

The NTSB investigation of the crash of ValuJet flight 592 revealed that the mechanic who signed the work card for ValuJet said that the canisters were placed in the cardboard boxes without packing material between them and without safety caps. He later testified that he assumed that they would not be shipped that way (NTSB, 1997). However, many mechanics asked about acquiring safety caps for the generators. Since this was the first time SabreTech had performed this sort of task, the SabreTech company had no new safety caps available (NTSB, 1997). Some mechanics inquired about placing the caps from the new generators on the old generators, but their inquiries were not followed up. The supervisor from SabreTech would later claim that no one who had worked with the oxygen generators had asked about safety caps (NTSB, 1997).

While ValuJet and other airlines are allowed to outsource maintenance and other critical support functions, they are ultimately responsible for ensuring that any work done for them is done both safely and legally. Federal Aviation Regulations (FARs), under part 121, clearly state that it is the ultimate responsibility of the contracting party to oversee and train any personnel working on their aircraft.

To oversee the tasks and quality of work done by the independent maintenance contractors, ValuJet employed its own technical representatives. Their responsibilities included ensuring the necessary maintenance services provided by contractors like SabreTech had been done satisfactorily and in accordance with FARs (NTSB, 1997).

The oxygen generators were eventually packed into five cardboard boxes and brought to SabreTech's receiving and shipping area for ValuJet. Three of the five boxes were delivered by one of the mechanics who had made earlier inquiries about the lack of safety caps. When asked if he had informed anyone in the receiving and shipping area about the specific contents of the boxes he said he had not (NTSB, 1997). Unlike other facilities that do repair maintenance for airlines, SabreTech "had no formal procedure in place that required an individual leaving items in the shipping and receiving area to inform anyone in that area of what the items were, or that they were hazardous" (NTSB, 1997, p. 118). To complicate matters, none of the SabreTech mechanics could recall seeing hazardous waste warnings on any of the boxes. After an extensive NTSB investigation, it is still unclear who brought the other two boxes to this area.

On May 9 the shipping ticket for the five boxes was prepared by a SabreTech receiving clerk. The receiving clerk was given a piece of paper by the stock clerk and was told to write "Oxygen Canisters—Empty" on the shipping tickets (NTSB, 1997, p. 19). When asked later if he knew the contents of the boxes, the receiving clerk said he did not, as the boxes were already sealed. ValuJet's Atlanta address was then placed on the boxes, and they were brought to the ValuJet loading ramp.

The ramp agents for ValuJet loaded the boxes on flight 592 headed for Atlanta, placing them in the forward cargo bin of the plane. None of the boxes were secured, and they were stacked on top of each other and around two spare airplane tires being shipped to Atlanta (NTSB, 1997). One of the ramp agents said the contents of the boxes were "loose" and he heard "clinking" noises when he moved them (NTSB, 1997).

THE CRASH OF FLIGHT 592

The NTSB used recorded radar data, cockpit voice recorder (CVR) comments and sounds, and flight data recorder (FDR) information to reconstruct the flight history of ValuJet flight 592. At 12:03 Flight 592 was cleared for takeoff. By 12:07 the plane was airborne and the pilot was instructed by air traffic controllers to turn left to begin the WINCO transition climb. Within three minutes of takeoff there was an unidentified sound that was recorded on the

CVR, and the captain asked "what was that?" (NTSB, 1997, p. 170). A few seconds later the captain remarked that they were experiencing some electrical problem. Five seconds later he said "we are losing everything," and within seconds he stated "we need, we need to go back to Miami" (NTSB, 1997, p. 171). Shortly after, a male voice is heard on the CVR stating "we are on fire, we're on fire" (NTSB, 1997, p. 171).

The plane crashed within 10 minutes of takeoff, about 17 miles northwest of Miami International Airport (NTSB, 1997). The captain had turned the plane around but flames had engulfed the plane, causing it to crash nose down into the Florida Everglades. Subsequent tests with oxygen generators indicated that the heat generated by the fire was approximately 2,000°F within 10 to 15 minutes of ignition (NTSB, 1997).

While ValuJet had a responsibility to oversee and regulate SabreTech's maintenance of its aircraft, the FAA had the ultimate responsibility of overseeing both ValuJet and SabreTech. However, we suggest that neither the FAA nor ValuJet fulfilled their responsibilities. ValuJet, for example, had outsourced its maintenance to the lowest possible bidder without ensuring the work was being done properly. It is clear that the FAA did not ensure that both ValuJet and SabreTech were following Federal Aviation Requirements (NTSB, 1997).

To understand why the FAA did not adequately enforce federal regulations that may have prevented this accident, we suggest that their contradictory roles as regulators of airline safety and promoters of the airline industry lie at the core of the problem. The reasons why the FAA has such contradictory duties are rooted in its organizational development. However, the organizational development of the FAA is, we will argue, best understood within the broader historical contexts of laissez-faire economic philosophies.

THE FEDERAL AVIATION ADMINISTRATION, DEREGULATION, AND BENIGN TOLERANCE

The federal government's regulation of civil aviation began in 1926 with the passage of the Air Commerce Act, the intent of which was to help the infant airline industry reach its full commercial potential through increased safety standards enforced by a federal regulatory agency (Schiavo, 1997). The training of pilots, air traffic rules and regulations, certification of aircraft, and the establishment of airways were all among the first responsibilities addressed by this act and were given to the Secretary of Commerce.

In 1966 President Lyndon B. Johnson created the Department of Transportation (DOT), which combined all federal transportation responsibilities in order to integrate and facilitate national interests in the distribution and transportation of goods. The DOT would become the agency under which the FAA was placed. However, CAB's accident investigation responsibilities were placed under the auspices of the newly formed National Transportation Safety

Board (NTSB). In short, the NTSB was given the responsibility of investigating accidents and making recommendations to the FAA, and the FAA, as a branch of the DOT, was given the responsibility of enforcing federal regulations within the airline industry.

Congress passed the Airline Deregulation Act of 1978 (ADA of 1978) which . . . placed oversight of the FAA on the shoulders of the NTSB. . . . The ADA of l978 also changed the entire airline industry. For example, the ADA of 1978 introduced fare and route competition, and permitted unrestricted entry into the domestic carrier marketplace.

While the ADA of 1978 was grounded in laissez-faire economics, with the intention of reducing consumer costs through supply and demand pressures, it is also important in the history of regulatory law in that it was a radical departure from previous approaches to fixing perceived shortcomings. As Brown (1987) notes:

> the legislation represents a dramatic change in the thrust of regulatory reform. Until 1978, statutory reforms served only to build upon the basic regulatory framework established by the Civil Aeronautics Act of 1938. *The 1978 legislation reflected a shift from an incremental to a decremental approach to regulatory reform in that it prescribed relaxation and eventual termination of classical regulatory controls.* Unlike previous reform efforts, deregulation was seriously considered as a policy alternative and significantly affected the substance of airline regulatory reform. (p. 2, emphasis added)

Within this context, then, the FAA attempted to promote the growth of start-ups like ValuJet while also overseeing their compliance with Federal Aviation Regulations. While success rates for most start-ups were low, ValuJet seemed to be the exception to the rule. In many ways, ValuJet justified the laissez-faire philosophy of the ADA of 1978, and was touted as a model startup company in the age of deregulation. Given that only three of the over 250 airline companies had survived since 1978, the success of ValuJet was important to the FAA (particularly in its capacity of promoting the economic success of the airline industry in the wake of deregulation) and to the several political administrations that supported it (i.e., every presidential administration from Carter to Clinton).

In terms of safety, the FAA had attempted to coax ValuJet into federal compliance rather than imposing stiff penalties (Gary, Heges, and Sieder, 1996). As former Inspector General Schiavo (1997) notes, the FAA had inspected ValuJet planes nearly 5,000 times in the three years it was in operation, and had never reported any significant problems or concerns. It has become clear that since the FAA had a vested interest in the *economic* success of the airline industry as a whole, and ValuJet in particular in the wake of deregulation, they did not adequately pursue ValuJet's violations (NTSB, 1997; Schiavo, 1997). Schiavo (1997) states that

> flight is at the core of a powerful, wealthy industry of companies worth billions of dollars. These corporate giants employ tens of thousands of people

and support the economies of entire cities, buy products and supplies from thousands of smaller businesses and import untold foreign money into the U.S. Their research labs keep the U.S. on the cutting edge of aviation, space and military technology. Their marketers satisfy millions of customers every day, racing to meet the increased demand for air travel. (p. 10)

Some FAA inspectors, however, had serious concerns about ValuJet, even though the administration of the FAA did not. Internal reports and memos indicate that there were increasing problems that should have been addressed with regard to ValuJet's rapid growth, enormous profitability, and subsequently atrocious safety record (Schiavo, 1997). However, according to Schiavo (1997), the FAA did not know what to do with ValuJet:

> the airline's safety record had deteriorated almost in direct proportion to its growth. ValuJet pilots made fifteen emergency landings in 1994, then were forced down fifty-seven times in 1995 . . . but that record would be surpassed within months with fifty-nine emergency landings from February through May of 1996 . . . an unscheduled landing almost *every other day.* (Schiavo, 1997, p. 12, emphasis original)

Also, the Department of Defense (DOD) had conducted its own review of ValuJet in consideration of a contract to transport military personnel. The DOD report on ValuJet was comprehensive and emphatic: ValuJet was so replete with safety problems that the DOD would not give ValuJet a contract to transport government employees (Schiavo, 1997). Among the problems cited in the DOD report on ValuJet was its practice of using temporary solutions to deal with major problems like breakdowns, malfunctions, and accidents.

On May 2, just nine days before the ValuJet crash, the FAA produced a nine-page report on the safety records of the various new airlines. Ordered by Anthony Broderick, who was then the FAA's associate administrator of regulation and certification, the report was prepared by Bob Matthews, an analyst with the FAA's office of Accident Investigation (Fumento, 1996). Matthews had two sets of data, one with SouthWest included in the new airline starts, and one without. Contrary to their claims, ValuJet's safety record was far from exceeding FAA standards. While the other start-ups had one accident annually, ValuJet's averaged five (Fumento, 1996). To make matters worse, ValuJet's accident rate was 14 times the major air carriers, and its serious accident rate was 32 times higher (Fumento, 1996). Additionally, other incidents uncovered by the FAA before the crash of flight 592 included planes skidding off runways, planes landing with nearly empty fuel tanks, oil and fuel leaks that were left unfixed for long periods of time, and inexperienced pilots making errors of judgment. In an internal FAA report on ValuJet, there were nearly 100 safety-related problems (Stern, 1996). However, the FAA did not officially recommend closing ValuJet down until after the crash of flight 592.

While ValuJet's failure to comply with safety regulations and the FAA's unwillingness or inability to enforce them are troubling enough, it is evident that the NTSB had made safety recommendations to the FAA long before the crash of flight 592 that could have prevented the accident. For example, in

1981 the NTSB had recommended that the FAA reevaluate the classification of class D cargo holds. The first recommendation (A-81-012) from the NTSB was that the FAA reevaluate the class D certification of the Lockheed L-1011, with the suggestion that it be changed to class C, which requires extinguishing equipment or changing the liner material to insure fire containment. The second recommendation (A-81-013) was to reevaluate class D cargo holds over 500 cubic feet to ensure that any fires would die from oxygen starvation and that the rest of the plane was properly protected. This recommendation came after a plane operated by Saudi Arabian Airlines in 1980 caught fire shortly after departure. The plane landed successfully, but all 301 occupants died. The fire on the Saudi Arabian Airlines plane started in the class D cargo hold. The FAA responded by stating that the NTSB recommendations should be addressed by making sure that class D cargo liners be made of fire-resistant materials better than the ones that were being used at the time.

In 1988 American Airlines flight 132 experienced a fire in its class D cargo hold en route to Nashville Metropolitan Airport. After investigating this accident, the NTSB urged the FAA to require smoke detectors in all class D cargo compartments, and to require fire extinguishment systems for them. Additionally, the NTSB asked the FAA to evaluate the possibility of prohibiting the transportation of oxidizers in cargo compartments without smoke detectors or extinguishing systems. After several exchanges of correspondence, the FAA informed the NTSB that its cost/benefit analysis revealed the $350 million pricetag attached to this recommendation was not feasible. The FAA took the position that it was not going to force the airline industry to make these improvements because it felt they were not cost effective in terms of the amount of money required to possibly prevent a small number of accidents.

THEORETICAL INTERPRETATION

The deaths of 110 people in the crash of ValuJet flight 592 were caused by a number of factors on the individual, institutional, and structural levels of analysis. The *proximal* cause of the crash was the failure of SabreTech and ValuJet employees to follow safety procedures regarding the preparation, identification, and storage of potentially hazardous materials. Indeed, had these workers correctly capped the oxygen generators, flight 592 might have landed safely in Atlanta. One might also say that the deaths could have been avoided if the FAA had followed the NTSB's recommendation to equip class D cargo holds with smoke detectors and fire suppression equipment. However, to stop the analysis of the crash here would be a serious error, because, like most organizational crimes, a complicated nexus of relationships enveloped the actions and omissions that facilitated the crash. As Perrow (1984) has compellingly argued, understanding what he terms "normal accidents" requires attention to the *interaction* of multiple failures within and between systems and organizations.

Organizational crime theorists have relied on three basic concepts to explain the crimes committed by corporations and governments: (1) organizational motivation or goals, (2) opportunity, and (3) social control (Braithwaite, 1992;

Coleman, 1987; Kauzlarich and Kramer, 1998; Kramer and Michalowski, 1990, 1991; Vaughan, 1992). The significance of these concepts to a structural-level explanation of state-corporate crime can be encapsulated in the proposition that organizational crime results from a coincidence of pressure for goal attainment, availability and perceived attractiveness of illegitimate means, and an absence or weakness of social control mechanisms (Braithwaite, 1989; Kauzlarich and Kramer, 1998). While each of these three core concepts can be examined on the micro and meso levels of analysis, our theoretical interpretation focuses more on how structural relationships affect organizational practice and policy. Following both state-corporate crime theory and the systems or "normal accident" theory (Perrow, 1984; Sagan, 1993), we will examine motivation, opportunity, control, and the interaction of the technical, organizational, and structural dimensions of the crash.

Motivation and Organizational Goals

Barnett (1981), Coleman (1987), Gross (1980), and Michalowski (1985) have argued that the goal of capital accumulation can be a highly criminogenic force for organizations. Oftentimes, it is posited, the motivation to secure profit can direct organizational practices and policies in a fashion injurious to consumer and employee safety.

As profit-seeking organizations, ValuJet and SabreTech employed a number of questionable techniques to maximize profit. ValuJet's radical cost-cutting procedures included using older planes in various stages of disrepair, outsourcing all its maintenance, and providing very low wages and benefits to employees. SabreTech was also experiencing a high degree of pressure for capital accumulation at the time directly preceding the crash by agreeing to complete their work on the oxygen generators quickly or incur a loss of $2,500 per day. The other organization involved in the crash, the FAA, was not a direct profit-seeking entity, but one designed to both regulate and facilitate the accumulation of capital for airline companies. The FAA's refusal (on economic grounds) to institute specific safeguards that could have prevented the catastrophe of flight 592 illustrates the injurious consequences that can result not only from pursuing capital, but also from state encouragement of capital accumulation. As Barnett (1981, p. 7) and Chambliss and Zatz (1993) have noted, a major goal of the U.S. state has been to promote capital accumulation, and the state's regulatory function "must not be so severe as to diminish substantially the contribution of large corporations to growth in output and employment." For example, while state regulatory agencies have been created to help protect workers (Occupational Safety and Health Administration), the environment (Environmental Protection Agency), and consumers (Consumer Product Safety Commission), these agencies generally do not undermine an industry's fundamental contributions to the functional requirements of the economy. In like manner, the FAA would not be expected to seriously compromise the contributions that the airline industry makes to local, community, and national economies. The difference, however, between the FAA and other regulatory agencies is its expressly stated dual mandate of both regulating the airline industry *and* promoting its economic success.

The three organizations involved in the ValuJet disaster, while distinct in many ways, interacted in such a way as to produce great social injury. Like other instances of state-facilitated state-corporate crime, the pursuit of profit was critical in the formulation of FAA, SabreTech, and ValuJet organizational policy and practice. While organizations that restrain from crime might also have a strong interest in capital accumulation, there was a very distinct set of organizational relationships which led to the crash of flight 592. This particular context was characterized by little social control over the actors and organizations and ample opportunity to commit crimes, which together helped shape organizational definitions of acceptable risk.

Opportunity and the Failure of Controls

A basic tenet of organizational crime theory is that low levels of external social control provide opportunities for organizations to engage in crime. As Vaughan (1992; 1996, p. 458) has noted, not only a competitive environment shapes organizational behavior, but also "the regulatory environment (autonomy and interdependence), which is affected by the relationship between regulators and the organizations they regulate." The symbiotic relationship between those who regulate and those being regulated may vary in both depth and breadth (Vaughan, 1983), but as we show below, FAA and ValuJet coupling resulted in an "interactive complexity" conducive to catastrophe (Perrow, 1984).

Deregulation and the contradictory role of the FAA as regulator and promoter of the airline industry provides the larger background for ValuJet's organizational genesis and persistence. We have described the deficiencies and contradictions in the structural control of the airline industry brought about by deregulation, and have argued that this is related to the FAA's organizational disregard for the unsafe nature of many of ValuJet's planes and practices. Instead of aggressively mandating that ValuJet place its fleet into compliance with applicable regulations, the FAA held up ValuJet as the poster child of deregulation—a victor among many losers in the market of air travel in the post-deregulation era. In this sense, the FAA's failure to practice its mandate to make air travel safe for consumers through the vigorous inspection of airline companies and their planes *facilitated* the crash of flight 592. Following this line of theoretical reasoning, had the FAA enforced federal airline safety regulations (i.e. had it exerted formal control over ValuJet and SabreTech), the companies may not have been so indifferent to the quality and safety of their activities and commodities. Such oversight would have created an environment where both SabreTech and ValuJet would be more likely to communicate to their employees that productivity *and* safety are important and rewardable. In other words, the "normalization" of the deviance that produced the ValuJet "accident" would not have gone unnoticed or unchecked. The series of oversights and confusions regarding the content and condition of the boxes holding the oxygen generators are related to how SabreTech and ValuJet rewarded the behavior of employees that contributed to productivity and efficiency, but not behavior that contributed to safety. Following this line of reasoning and the available data, then, the unspent and uncapped oxygen containers made it onto the airplane because employees of SabreTech and ValuJet were not adequately trained, rewarded, or encouraged to conduct careful and complete inspections of materials to be transported by air. This explanation is consistent with the findings of a number of studies that illustrate the power of organizational culture over the individual and collective actions of employees in such diverse settings as the Holocaust (Hilberg, 1985; Kelman and Hamilton, 1989), police violence (Skolnick and Fyfe, 1993), and U.S. human radiation experiments (Kauzlarich and Kramer, 1998). Our interpretation is also consistent with Vaughan's (1996) notion of "the normalization of deviance," a condition in which deviations from technical protocols gradually and routinely become defined as normative. The normalization of rule breaking is applicable to the manner in which the oxygen canisters were processed, but it is institutionally situated as well. Risky practices, which can be an outcome of or a precursor to the normalization of deviance, became defined as acceptable for capital accumulation (ValuJet) and capital facilitation (FAA). While the crash was an undesirable outcome for all of the organizations involved, a number of matters related to the causes of the crash were defined as acceptable risks in light of potential organizational mandates, missions, and gains, which is related to another social phenomenon, the *sociology of mistake*. As Vaughan (1996) found with the *Challenger* explosion, the ValuJet crash can also be interpreted as an event related to how "environmental and organizational contingencies create operational forces that shape world view, normalizing signals of potential danger, resulting in mistakes with harmful human consequences" (Vaughan, 1996, p. 409).

20

The Twisted Road to Genocide

On the Psychological Development
of Evil During the Holocaust

HENRI ZUKIER
New School for Social Research

Despite all that has been written about it, Zukier observes that the Nazi Holocaust remains one of the least understood phenomena of the twentieth century. After reviewing existing explanations, the author outlines what he calls a "developmental" theory of the Holocaust. He maps out how gradual and progressive changes took place in the minds and

From *Social Research,* Vol. 61, No. 2, excerpting from pp. 423–426, 428–450, 453–455.

behaviors of the German people. He forwards concepts such as "metamorphosis" and "soul murder" to characterize how Hitler slowly vilified the Jews in the eyes of the German citizenry. He stresses how Hitler exploited ordinary processes and sentiments to overcome people's psychological prejudice against evil. Using a slow, incremental approach to the behavioral and psychological treatment of the Jews, Zukier argues that Hitler sold the army and the Germans on murder by installments. In a few short years, the country went from disliking the Jews to subjecting them to mass murder. Zukier's depiction of a "psychological gradualism from gray transgressions to the blackest of all crimes" is meant to remind us all that the Holocaust was not an epiphany. Instead, this prolonged and brutal course of events exhibits many of the same behavioral, cognitive, and cultural dimensions that we see in other violent crimes and criminals. In this case, however, the organizational context in which it occurred allowed for a new level of precision and clarity.

A MOMENT OF SELF-DISCOVERY

We all recall Simone de Beauvoir's opening lines in *The Second Sex:* "One is not born, but rather becomes a woman . . . it is civilization as a whole that produces this creature . . ." (de Beauvoir, 1989, p. 267). Surely, we also understand these lines better today than when they were written, shortly after the Second World War. In this paper, I would like to argue for a similar and equally belated "developmental" understanding of the Nazi Holocaust.

Historical writing on the Holocaust is distinguished by a paradox. This barbaric chapter in modern Western history is at once its best documented occurrence and its least understood one. The event has transcended its outward form as a particular Jewish calamity and German crime to become a historical benchmark of modern society and a measure of its moral life. Auschwitz, Jürgen Habermas observed, "has become the signature of an entire era—and involves us all. Something happened there which no one could possibly have imagined until then . . . A veil of naiveté was torn up . . ."

In spite of its centrality, or perhaps because of it, the Holocaust remains shrouded in mystery. We know a lot about the wholesale manufacture of death, yet understand very little about the mass production of mass murderers. How did a civilized nation beget the journeymen of industrial death who contrived the living hell for our post-religious and post-Dantean age?

SELF-SOOTHING MYTHS
OF THE HOLOCAUST

Discussions of the Holocaust are often foiled by two opposing misconceptions, both of which spawn self-soothing myths and obviate the need for further psychological understanding. The myths have first to be dispelled.

A. Fluke-and-Freak Theories of the Holocaust

Fluke A pervasive process in mental life, according to Freud and contemporary psychoanalysts, is a tendency toward "splitting of the ego." The individual does not admit to full "ownership" over feelings, thoughts, or behavior that violate his sense of selfhood or the norms of society. The disowned tendencies of the self are treated as extraneous forces, "not-me" intrusions, so that they can persist side by side with ordinary life without threatening self-worth (Freud, 1964). Losers in war tend to believe in the action of "chance" in history. As Gibbon observed, the Greeks, after being subdued by the Romans, imputed Rome's victory not to the merits of the republic but to Fortune, "the inconstant goddess who so blindly distributes and resumes her favors" (Gibbon, 1962, p. 619). The Holocaust is so disquieting to modern consciousness that many have repudiated any connection with the event. They treat it as an aberrant breakdown, a historical hiccup caused by a momentary revival of archaic impulses from the Dark Ages. The Holocaust rejoins the great European witchcraze of the seventeenth century, which scholars also treated as a residue of past obscurantism and still commonly misattribute to the Middle Ages. The most poignant example of fluke historiography is Friedrich Meinecke, the eminent liberal historian of the interplay of ethics and state power in Germany and himself a victim of the Nazis. In 1946, while in his mid-'80s, he overhauled in a slim volume his lifetime historical conceptions to come to terms with "the German catastrophe." Nazism, he argued, was a "storm" which "swept over all the German people," the result of "chance" and of "a unique and unexpected intervention of some sort of extraneous factor in the course of history." There was "an uncanny gulf between his [Hitler's] demonic self and the world about him," such that, Meinecke noted with evident relief, Hitler was "foreign to us Germans" (Meinecke, 1950, pp. 35, 57–8). A similar view, the so-called "functionalist" approach, also is dominant half a century after the event. German historians such as Martin Brozat, Uwe Dietrich Adam, Ernst Nolte, Andreas Hillgruber, and others have argued (in different forms) that the Holocaust was an accidental byproduct of the war, never planned or premeditated by the Nazi regime, but improvised little by little (according to some authors by local commanders in Eastern Europe) in response to perceived threats and war pressures. In the United States, too, Arno Mayer has argued in a 1988 work that the Nazis never planned a Final Solution. The Holocaust was an improvised outgrowth of Germany's anti-Bolshevik crusade and of the economic and psychological pressures resulting from the failure of the *Blitzkrieg* (Mayer, 1988). For the "fluke" historians, the Holocaust is like a robbery gone awry, unpremeditated murder committed in the course of a felony, and no grounds for character condemnation.

Freaks The related psychological view treats the Nazis as a bunch of mad monsters. Confronted with fiendish behavior, some instantly diagnose "sadism," "psychosis," or "authoritarian personality" and believe this actually solves the psychological puzzle of the Holocaust. The "freak" proponents appeal to a tautological psychology which goes from acts to dispositions and simply equates the two. Certain "kinds" of acts are only committed by certain "types" of people. This circular reasoning echoes Molière's medical doctor in *The Imaginary Invalid*. Asked why opium induces sleep, Argan, the good doctor, hastens to explain that it is, of course, because of opium's "virtus dormitiva"—its dormitive powers (Molière, 1956, Act Three, Finale). There is a timeless temptation to explain (away) the unsettling behaviors of other people by simply treating them as "demented," "them," strangers in our midst whose actions have no implications for us. In the sixteenth century, contemporaries of El Greco, dismayed by his visionary art and flamelike portraits, dismissed his innovative paintings as the twisted products of a visual defect. Centuries later, a Louisiana doctor identified a disease called drapotomania, peculiar to Southern slaves; It was "the disease causing Negroes to run away" (Stampp, 1989, pp. 102, 109).

By all accounts of observers, psychologists, and victims, the Nazis were not crazed, bloodthirsty monsters. As H. Langbein, an Auschwitz inmate and member of the resistance, observed: "Nothing would be more misguided than to believe that the SS were a horde of sadists. . . . The few who acted [on instinct] were a decisive minority" (Langbein, 1972, p. 315). Another inmate, Dr. Ella Lingens-Reiner, put the sadists' numbers at "no more than five or ten percent." "The others," she added, "were perfectly normal people, fully cognizant of good and evil" (Höhne, 1989, p. 432). These comments are echoed by virtually all other inmates and by historians. . . . Indeed, many of the participants in the killings suffered great nervous strain. . . . There were disputes, refusals to obey orders, drunken orgies, but also serious psychological illnesses . . . " (Noakes and Pridham, 1988, no. 852). Even General of the Waffen SS Bach-Zelewski, the commanding officer in Central Russia, was hospitalized for a psychological breakdown, suffering from the traumatic reliving of the executions of Jews which he had directed. Other commanders asked to be relieved of their duties. Himmler himself, witnessing the execution of a hundred men in Minsk, nearly collapsed from shock. Soldiers were routinely given large amounts of alcohol to alleviate the stress. The gas vans, precursors of the concentration camp gas chambers, were specifically developed at Himmler's urging to provide a more "humane" and less stressful method of execution—for the executioners, that is.

Moreover, the image of a group of sadists overwhelmed by aggressive instincts just waiting to be discharged is a psychological fantasy. Animal behavior is kindled by impulses—the animal hunts when it is in need of food. Adults, though they may experience similar needs, do not spontaneously or immediately yield to desire. Raw impulses are mediated, inhibited, and transformed by their integration in a cognitive system of long-term values, goals, and intentions. There is a long way from the emergence of desire to its consummation in action (Shapiro, 1981). The Holocaust, then, was not nor could it ever have been simply one big "acting-out" party. Something else, more terrifyingly human, was going on.

The Great Man and His Handful of Followers Another self-soothing myth depicts the Holocaust as the imprint in history of one titanic figure, such as populate Hegel's and Carlyle's histories. Nazism is recast as Hitlerism, a movement animated and centered around the mad will of one dictator. Implicitly, Hitler also is cast as the leader of a large criminal gang of sorts, who carried out his atrocities without the involvement of "the rest" of German society. The myth also asserts that the *Wehrmacht* remained an apolitical, professional army, uninvolved in the SS abominations. In reality, the mass murder of the Jews and of other peoples was only possible because it could draw on the mass support of all segments of German society and the military. The Holocaust, though it was ordered by the few, was executed by the many, and it is those many followers who mostly challenge our understanding.

Barbarians Atrocities presumably are committed by barbarians, and the Nazi crimes often are conveniently attributed to the more "primitive" members of German society. Historically, the very opposite is true. At one end, Hitler garnered his early electoral support among the middle class and the elite of society. At the other end, the most murderous military units, the four *Einsatzgruppen* which operated in Russia, were manned by intellectuals. Three of its four first commanders held doctorates as did many of the lesser officers.

B. Ecumenical Theories of the Holocaust

Freak-and-fluke theories exonerate the majority of people by proposing an exclusive focus on the select few "criminals" (who themselves are considered under the influence of overwhelming, impersonal forces). In contrast, ecumenical theories of the Holocaust absolve the majority by an all-inclusive reach which encompasses all people and all causes. The hardships of everyday life become the conditions which "understandably" put most people at risk to become mass murderers. The Holocaust is, potentially, in all of us, a legacy of the human condition: "There we go, but for the grace of God." This view, which dilutes any distinctive causality—and responsibility—turns the Holocaust into the metaphor of choice for all that afflicts the modern individual: political oppression, social ills, medical diseases, and personal anguish. Little wonder that the many groups which aggressively compete these days for honorific victim status often are eager to don the mantle of the Holocaust.

Coercion The most common ecumenical myth is that the German people were, at worst, unwilling participants in the Holocaust, compelled or intimidated into submission to the regime. The newsreels of the period, featuring grinning soldiers committing crimes, and the pervasive sense that individuals routinely acted beyond the call of duty do not suggest a people acting under duress. In fact, in its inner relations to the German people, the Nazi regime was not primarily a rule of terror and often yielded when its policies aroused strong protests, even on central issues. To promote the racial hygiene of the German people and rid the nation of its "inferior" elements, Hitler had devised an extensive, and highly secret, euthanasia program which claimed some 250,000 victims. Information about the program eventually leaked out and provoked popular opposition and open protests from the Church. Cardinal Bertram and Bishop Wurm wrote strong protests to Nazi ministers, and, in August 1941, Bishop Galen of Münster bitterly denounced the program in his Sunday sermon with copies of the appeal disseminated throughout the country. Hitler, who cherished the program and abhorred the Church, ordered a halt to the project, and none of the protesters suffered serious consequences. The clergy also protested the expropriation of Church property for war purposes, and Hitler again partly put an end to it. . . .

Even in the army, enlisted soldiers and high officials often could avoid participation in the murder of unarmed civilians. . . . Several officers threatened to resign, and soldiers were court-martialled for brutalities. During the Russian campaign, the Nazi governor of White Russia, Gauleiter Wilhelm Kube, consistently blocked the liquidation of German Jews while supporting the murder of the Eastern European ones. Several commanders of the *Einsatzgruppen* in Russia (Otto Rasch, Heinz Jost) quit their command without major consequences. Other high-ranking Nazis also refused or contravened orders to arrest or to shoot Jews (Krausnick, 1989). Such options also existed within the ranks. When Reserve Police Battalion 101—a group of middle-aged men up to 48 years old—received orders to liquidate a group of Jews in Poland, the commander assembled his men, informed them of their assignment, and offered to release anyone who did not feel up to the task. Only 12 out of 500 men accepted the offer.

The myth of coercion also suggests that the German civilian population was subdued by the ruthless apparatus of the *Gestapo*. Yet a detailed study of the political police found that its numbers have been vastly overestimated. There were "far too few" agents to exercise any kind of control, even with the collaboration of outside elements. For instance, in September 1941, there were 150 *Gestapo* officials in Würtzburg in charge of a population of nearly three million people distributed over 14,115 square kilometers. *Gestapo* files reveal that most cases were initiated not by agents or paid informers but by denunciations from ordinary citizens not connected to the *Gestapo* apparatus. Uncoerced collaboration was the "key relationship" and so widespread that it not only made the police system possible but rendered the professionals' work "almost superfluous" (Gellately, 1990, pp. 6, 8, 61, 130).

Hitler and his policies remained overwhelmingly popular until the end. The only significant attempt at resistance against Hitler came from a tiny group that plotted to assassinate Hitler on July 20, 1944. Many conspirators shared the Nazi outlook, including a deep hostility to the Weimar Republic and toward the Jews and pursued German expansionist policies. In 1944, they were afraid though that Hitler was jeopardizing the achievements of the war. The conspirators were aware of the unpopularity of their insurgence, and realized that unlike, say, the French resistance, they would find no support within the German population. Consequently, they opposed a return to a parliamentary system and to free elections after the coup and the presumed fall of Hitler for fear that the Nazis would be massively swept back into power.

Ignorance The myth of unwitting German complicity in the Holocaust is an offshoot of the image of an unwilling population overcome by a small minority of criminals. For if many people are involved in mass murder, even more are bound to be in the know. Recent studies have amply documented that the general outlines of the Final Solution and the fate of the Jews deported to the East were known to most Germans. As Hans Mommsen put it, "each person could sense the burden of the crime being committed against the Jewish people, just as the sickeningly sweet odor from the chimneys at Auschwitz was noticed by those living in the vicinity . . ." (Mommsen, 1990, p. 199; Kulka, 1975; Bankier, 1992).

Propaganda If not coerced, it is argued, the Germans were at least seduced by the vast machine of Goebbels's Ministry of Popular Enlightenment and Propaganda. The argument fits neither the psychological nor the historical reality. Psychological studies of persuasion have long documented the limitations of campaigns to change people's attitudes. Typically, people are only receptive to messages that agree with their prior beliefs and tend to avoid or distort contradictory information; they do the equivalent of "switching channels" on their TV set (Pratkanis and Aronson, 1991, pp. 221–230). Not surprisingly, then, historians have found that the German population was not at all thoroughly indoctrinated by the official propaganda (Kershaw, 1991).

Economic Hardships Finally, the hold of Nazism has sometimes been attributed to the German economic and political frustrations that followed the First World War. The analysis also evokes the (falsely deterministic) psychological idea of a frustration–aggression link, whereby frustration will inevitably lead to some form of aggression. Hardships are indeed a common feature of life; the Nazi response to adversity is not. Nor was the Holocaust, historically, "provoked" by such hardship. The Nazi electoral surge occurred after the economic crisis was over, during a period of relative prosperity and stability. The Nazi electoral support came not from the working class but from the traditional middle class and the social elite. The Nazis consistently failed to attract the industrial working class. Even when unemployment soared after 1928, frustrated workers turned to the Communist Party. A study of the Nazi voters concludes that Nazi appeal was weakest among the industrial working class, and that there was a "strongly negative" relationship between Nazism and unemployment: lengthening lines of jobless workers did not add to the Nazi vote (Childers, 1983, pp. 264–268). Germany's economic troubles were, moreover, part of a worldwide crisis striking many nations. Germany's plight was no worse than that of the United States and only somewhat more severe than the conditions in Great Britain and France. The response of these countries was, of course, quite different. In the United States, the crisis led to the New Deal, and domestic reform programs also were enacted elsewhere.

No (Self) Selection Many oppressive regimes come to power, and stay in power, through extensive purges of "internal enemies"—suspected opponents to their rule. Stalin consolidated his power by purges of the elites in the party, the industry, the government, the armed forces, and the NKVD. From 1930 to 1939, between 15 and 20 million people fell victim to Stalin's purges, including most members of the Central Committee and the leading figures of the Red Army High Command. The purges emboldened Hitler to launch his campaign against Russia in the belief that the Soviet leadership had been so decimated by the purges that it could no longer endure a sustained assault (Bullock, 1991).

In contrast, the Nazi rule was genuinely all-inclusive, embracing the entire German people. Though more than half the population had voted against Hitler even after he was Chancellor, the regime never conducted political or military purges (with the sole exception of the June 30, 1934 purge of Hitler's *own* SA-Storm Troopers leadership). Hitler was confident that he could pursue his economic and foreign policies and then wage his wars with the existing apparatus of government, civil service, industry, and army. The Germans who participated in the Final Solution, and in the other undertakings of the Third Reich, were not specially selected for their "mental fitness" for the tasks, nor were they even allowed to volunteer, or "self-select," as a function of their personal preferences. The Nazis assigned people even to the most murderous duty by a routine bureaucratic process, on a jurisdictional basis, without regard for or interest in the individual's psychological profile. (Still, people were not coerced, because they often could request alternative assignments.) When Hitler was appointed Chancellor of a conservative coalition government in January 1933, only two other minor ministerial posts went to the Nazis. . . . The murder squads in the East also were contituted by administrative procedure. Members did not volunteer but often were older men judged unfit for battle duty. The case study of Reserve Police Battalion 101, assigned to murder Jews in Eastern Poland, showed that it was not composed of "men specially selected or deemed particularly suited for the task."

The absence of psychological selection is crucial for our understanding of Nazism. It indicates, again, that the participants in the Final Solution were not a select group of deviants but a genuine normal cross-section of society. Even more significantly, it reveals the Nazis' confidence in their ability to psychologically enlist and convert the average person to their objectives. The Nazis did not attempt to find the "right" people, for they believed, correctly, that they could transform ordinary personalities into murderous temperaments. Almost any individual who came down the bureaucratic pipeline could be, in due time, remolded into a mass murderer.

METAMORPHOSIS

There is abundant evidence for the progressive German slide into barbarism reflected by a profound change in attitudes. On November 9-10, 1938, the Nazis organized an Eastern-European-style *pogrom* throughout the German Reich known as *Kristallnacht*. In the orgy of violence, about 200 synagogues were destroyed, 91 Jews were murdered, and thousands of homes and businesses were set afire and looted. The violence provoked widespread dismay amongst the Germans.

Prior to the war, many Germans did condone or support the legal discrimination against the Jews but had a profound aversion to physical violence against civilians. Most Germans also voted against Hitler and his policies, even after he had been installed as Chancellor. Barely a few years later, these same people were eagerly engaged in atrocities, often going beyond their orders, and gave such overwhelming support to Hitler that his opponents were afraid to organize free elections after the presumed fall of the dictator. Similarly, military historians have documented the progressive barbarization of the German army. In Western Europe, the *Wehrmacht* acted not unlike some other occupation armies; in Poland, German generals protested the violence of the police forces, which showed a "quite incredible lack of human and moral feeling" and were an "ignoble situation."

In November 1938, Hitler explained in a secret speech how he was forced to delay his plans because of the German people's psychological unpreparedness, and he outlined the necessary psychological transformation. His main goal was, "First, the gradual preparation of the German people themselves . . . it was now necessary gradually to re-educate the German people psychologically . . . that the inner voice of the nation itself gradually began to call for the use of force" (Noakes and Pridham, 1988, p. 529). Franz Stangl, the commandant of Treblinka, also commented on how Nazi policies were only gradually implemented: "to protect the sensibilities of the population, they were going to do it very slowly, only after a great deal of psychological preparation" (Sereny, 1983, p. 51). The real achievement and persistent mystery of the Holocaust are not its technological or bureaucratic force but its psychological violence; the puzzlement is not Hitler, but the millions of ordinary people who were transformed into ardent followers and the processes of the psychological manufacture of evil. How could the Holocaust have happened in the land of Goethe, it is often asked? In one sense, it did not happen there but in a systematically altered psychological environment.

SOUL MURDER

There are, by now, many masterful histories of the Holocaust. They make it tempting to cling to the belief that genocide is about the physical extermination of entire peoples, and that the facts of war exhaust the crime. Yet, descriptions of the conveyor belt of murder alone do not capture the process of the manufacture of evil. The murders threaten to conceal even larger injuries to the human spirit and help confuse the crime with its consequences. For genocide is foremost a psychological crime, and its death toll is the monstrous aftermath of the soul murder of perpetrators, victims, and bystanders. In *John Gabriel Borkman,* Ibsen explained the ravages of the one unforgivable sin, a "mysterious . . . deadly sin" of Biblical magnitude. It is "the sin of killing love in a human soul," and Borkman is called to account for the "double murder" he committed, the murder of his "own soul" and of the soul of his lover (Ibsen, 1959). Soul murder is a crime Hitler understood far better than his later chroniclers; in the camps, for instance, the Nazis systematically inflicted psychological death upon their victims, even though the inmates were marked for certain murder soon thereafter. Thus, writing in 1940, Hermann Rauschning, Hitler's one-time close confidant, compared the Nazi leader to Ibsen's character (Rauschning, 1940, p. 270).

THE PSYCHOLOGICAL
PREJUDICE AGAINST EVIL

The dynamics of soul murder are particularly elusive because of an ancient psychological prejudice against evil. Theories of evil typically lack a conception of development, of psychological transformation from one condition to another. Psychologists have thoroughly examined the processes of moral development, knowing that the growing child does not "naturally" evolve toward moral goodness. Yet the psychology of evil is a psychology of states of *being,* not one of overcoming or becoming. Evil is (erroneously) treated as an indomitable inner force which "emanates" from the wicked individual, a scourge of nature affording little control or understanding, wicked people simply are "evil incarnate."

ORDINARY PROCESSES—
EXTRAORDINARY EVIL

Against the philosophers and the psychologists, William Blake observed long ago that "Cruelty has a human heart" (Blake, 1967). The concluding paragraph of the biography of Himmler, the architect of the Final Solution, notes, "Himmler, in short, was not a simple, bloodthirsty sadistic monster. His brutality was more learned than instinctive and emotional . . . Himmler was not a sadist" (Breitman, 1991, p. 250). More generally, the Holocaust is not the story of the forcible abduction of an entire people but rather the tale of the self-seduction of a nation. In the light of history, the evil of the Holocaust can no longer be explained psychologically as the discharge of natural wickedness. Indeed, the career of Oskar Schindler, the unprincipled and dissolute German war profiteer who gradually evolved into a rescuer of 1200 Jews, and numerous similar cases indicate that episodes of singular altruism need not reflect goodness of character either. Evil, and goodness, do not simply lurk deep in the heart, waiting for the lifting of repression or for the opportunity that calls them forth. Evil and goodness do not "spring" from inner depths; they are carefully nurtured qualities of the mind. Not only were the protagonists of the Holocaust mostly ordinary people, but so were the psychological processes which transformed them into extraordinarily bad (or good) individuals. Barbarity is not a biological curse from birth; goodness, not an extraordinary gift. Both are learned, cultivated, and taught. They evolve gradually out of human interaction. Only an esthetic preference for symmetry leads us to search for abnormal causes to explain abnormal behavior. Depravity and nobility are fashioned, like other behavior, by ordinary social forces, implicating, in many ways, perpetrators, victims, and bystanders alike. Uncommon vice and virtue evolve out of common components and a process of psychological transformation. They are, in one sense, within the reach of many individuals who might be subjected to the process of transformation. Ordinary people, cast in extreme circumstances and initially subjected to great pressures, can become unusually bad or good. Indeed, as Schindler's career also shows, people need not be transformed into good or bad in all aspects of their personality, nor for the rest of their lives. There may be, though, a differential susceptibility to the dynamics of transformation, transcending the individual and rooted in a larger psychological and historical culture. Collectivities can cultivate a heightened sensitivity to good or evil. There may have been a German *Sonderweg*—a "special path" in psychology just as some historians believe there was in politics.

A PLEA FOR GENOCIDE

Understanding the dynamics of character transformation—of "learned sadism" (this, in some way, also was the argument of Simone de Beauvoir and of Molière)—will hardly exhaust the Holocaust. But at least it would rescue its agony from the clutter of self-soothing myths and restore the Holocaust to the realm of human possibility from which it arose. In that realm, though, the event must remain, like other historical events, forever underdetermined. On his voyage of discovery to America, Alexis de Tocqueville remarked how "a new political science is needed for a world itself quite new" (de Tocqueville, 1969, p. 12). The horrors of the First World War deeply unsettled Freud and transformed his psychological thinking, leading to the famous turning point of 1920 in his writings. Yet the Holocaust, perhaps because it remains utterly implausible, has eluded the social sciences and had no significant impact on them. The focus remains on the Holocaust ravages rather than on its psychological roots. Hence, a plea for genocide: to begin taking it seriously in the social sciences. Genocide was not merely an aberration of the past; it is a threat of the future whose psychological dynamics must be elucidated.

THE PSYCHOLOGICAL SPIRAL OF EVIL

Kristallnacht, the 24-hour *pogrom* that swept through Germany and Austria in November 1938, claimed 91 victims. At that pace, rounded up to 100, and assuming it could be sustained every day of the year, it would have taken the Nazis over 150 years to murder six million Jews. In fact, most of the six million were killed in less than one year, between 1942 and 1943. Clearly, the *pogrom* technique was ill-suited for the Final Solution. As the commander of *Einsatzgruppen* A operating in the Baltic states reported in 1941: ". . . native antisemitic forces were induced to start pogroms against Jews . . . though this proved to be very difficult. . . . It was anticipated from the beginning that the Jewish problem in the Ostland would not be solved solely through pogroms" (Noakes and Pridham, 1988, no. 815). The Final solution required a new method and a new mentality. Hitler had already described the new psychology of mass murder in 1919 in his first major political statement:"antisemitism . . . acquires all too easily the character of being a manifestation of emotion. But this is wrong. Antisemitism . . . must not be . . . determined by emotional criteria . . . antisemitism stemming from purely emotional reasons will always find its expression in the form of pogroms." Instead, Hitler demanded a new antisemitism "based on reason" (Noakes and Pridham, 1988, no. 2). Accordingly, the Nazis moved forcefully against *pogrom*-style, emotional outbursts of antisemitism motivated by pleasure or interest. They restrained their own SA troops, who revelled in hotheaded violence; they replaced the first commander of Dachau for condoning personalized violence against the inmates; and they struggled against popular "excesses."

I can only sketch here the barest outlines of one aspect of the process of soul murder. Nazi psychology has commonly been described as a mobilization of murderous instincts, a discharge of pre-existing, deep-seated aggression following the lifting of inhibitions; or it is described as a split within a "hollowed out" individual such that the murderous tendencies coexist with and are disconnected from the rest of the personality. The shaping of a dispassionate murderous mentality is achieved not through desensitization but through the cultivation of inner moral conflict, leading to a transformation of attitudes in search of personal consistency. If the Nazis had been more natural murderers, without moral qualms, they would not have evolved into such efficient killers. They became murderers not by leaps and bounds but by inches, insensibly, gradually, step by step. The spiral of murder is fueled, initially, by moral anxiety at one's prior actions. The Nazis did not kill the Jews in a battlefield frenzy nor out of depraved indifference but in the inner, moral frenzy that follows the silencing of the cannons.

MURDER BY INSTALLMENTS

The shaping of the murderous mentality follows a gradual, twisted psychological path. It involves an ineluctable progression from smaller initial offenses, seemingly devoid of larger significance, through moral conflict and psychological adjustment, to the ultimate atrocities. The string of small acts that leads to great crimes facilitates the incomprehension of the victims—and of the perpetrators, who may fail to grasp their condition until it is too late. We tend to think of socialization into evil (and into heroism) as one continuous, smooth process. In fact, it consists of two contrary moments, animated by different motivations. The slide into evil is not self-starting, a simple slippery slope. But, at moment two, it is self-sustaining. The beginnings of the spiral, and the progression to new levels, require the pressure of a legitimate authority. The sequence typically is triggerd by a pivotal distressing encounter with evil (or with suffering, in the case of helpers) leading to reluctant compliance under pressure (to commit evil or to help). Progressively, the individual increases his involvement, disregarding internal and external obstacles, in a sustained flight forward. Initially, the individual sets aside his compunctions and crosses his internal red line at the urging of an authority—political, scientific, or social. After his failed Beerhall Putsch of 1923, Hitler consistently resisted the demands of his associates to seize government by force. He insisted (again, unlike Stalin) on achieving power legally, even though the legitimate road was highly uncertain and would take another ten years. Medical doctors and lawyers played key roles in the campaigns of mass murder, not because of any particular expertise but to preserve the aura of political and scientific legitimacy of the regime.

At the first transgression after the initial clash with evil, and at the small incremental steps that follow, the individual keenly feels a conflict. He acts only reluctantly, "in spite of himself," knowing that "internally" he disagrees with the objectionable actions. As Eichmann proclaimed at his trial in Jerusalem, he never was an "*Inner Schweinehund,*" an "inner swine." The progression is facilitated by the illusion of minimal change; the next step is a mere adjustment, not that different from its predecessor. Gradually, insensibly, the individual adapts and the reference point for the actions changes: the individual focuses no longer on the absolute meaning of his behavior or on its general consequences. The distant end of his actions is out-of-view, and the individual would be horrified at the foretelling of his transformation; the immediate impact of his actions also is kept out of view, for he only considers their relative positions compared to what he has done before. And that relative difference is fairly small. Thus, to quell his doubts, the individual engages in self-justification, best accomplished by escalating his commitment by one or two more degrees.

The process poses a difficult psychological dilemma. Economists have argued that in deciding future actions, one should only consider anticipated consequences and not "sunk costs," past expenditures that no longer have any bearing on current deliberations. Psychologically, the evolving perpetrator is wholly driven by sunk costs: how can he find a justification for quitting at any particular moment when he has complied so far? The process is not unlike the classic Greek paradox of the heap of sand: no one grain of sand can possibly create a heap, so one can go on adding single grains of sand to each other *ad infinitum* without ever forming a heap. Through this invisible progression, the individual passes a moral point of no return but does not realize it until several steps later. Since the steps were incremental, how could he, at that point, declare the next step immoral and not the previous one? How could he quit for moral reasons without thereby acknowledging his depravity for his previous actions? Macbeth has expressed the sheer agony of this second moment: "I am in blood steeped so far that, should I wade no more, returning were as tedious as go o'er" (Shakespeare, 1974, pp. 136–38).

From moment two on, the individual has at last overcome his temptation not of violence but of morality and pity. He has neutralized any moral motivation, silenced the internal struggle, and achieved an uneasy psychological equilibrium. Profound changes occur in his attitudes to adjust his sense of himself as an innocent perpetrator. He shifts his mental focus away from the behavior itself to his relationship with authorities, to his own changing expectations, or to the details of his undertaking. He adopts not a morality of desire but one of instrumental efficiency, casting himself as the instrument of another's will or higher purpose. Conscience, which Hitler rejected as a Jewish invention, becomes conscientiousness over the quality of performance. The fragmented focus allows a diffusion of responsibility and perpetuates a salutary ambiguity about whether his own actions are causes or consequences. So he is following orders, all right: at moment one, he still follows someone else's orders; from moment two on, he follows his own inner commands, to alleviate his moral anguish. It is a desperate flight *from* crime *into* crime.

THE CONFLICT OF MOTIVATIONS

The Nazi psychological gradualism did not aim to transform the entire personality or to "split off" a murderous part of it. On the contrary, the Nazis constantly stressed the horror of their actions. In a 1943 speech to SS leaders, Himmler noted how the Final Solution was "a very grave matter," a "most difficult duty," and it was remarkable that they "stuck it out" without injury to their "soul" and "character." He also confided to a group of generals in 1944 "how difficult it was" for him "to carry out this military order" which he only "implemented out of a sense of obedience and absolute conviction."

The shaping of the murderous mentality required moral conflict. Nazism cultivated a new philosophy of heroism; it was designed to overcome not external adversity (the helpless Jewish civilians were not the greatest of challenges, after all) but the internal psychological inhibitions against atrocities. Nazism expected the perpetrators to feel bad about their actions and harnessed these feelings to fuel the murderous course. The bad feelings came from the conflict, fostered by the Nazis, between outer behavior and inner feelings; between the public and private domains; between the violence to Jews and the tenderness to family and friends (all Germans, Himmler complained bitterly, also had their one "decent Jew"); between personal preferences and the demands of the role. In this conflict, the private, "real," good part of the individual compensated for the superficial, murderous "self." The individual was heroically performing his job, thereby doing violence to his inner humane feelings. The inner heroism was celebrated in Leni Riefenstahl's *Triumph of the Will*.

Psychological gradualism from gray transgressions to the blackest of all crimes permeated the Nazis' entire enterprise. Some of its action was captured by remarks attributed to Martin Niemöller, a German World War I submarine commander turned pastor and Nazi opponent. "At first, the Nazis came for the socialists, and I did not speak out—because I was not a socialist. Then they went after the jews, but I was not a Jew, and so I did not object. Then they came for the Catholics, but I did not stand up because I was not a Catholic. Then they came for me—and there was no one left to speak up for me."

21

Recreational Abusers and Therapeutic Self-Medicators

Two Criminal Career Trajectories among Drug Using Pharmacists

DEAN A. DABNEY
Georgia State University

RICHARD C. HOLLINGER
University of Florida

This article seeks to explain the behavioral, cognitive, and cultural processes through which pharmacists come to steal and use the very drugs that they are entrusted to dispense. The article is built around personal life-history data from fifty pharmacists, all of whom were recovering from prescription drug addiction. Study participants were gathered using a snowball sampling technique in which the authors traveled across the country to interview pharmacists from twenty-four different states. The data reveal two distinct types of illicit prescription drug users. Some pharmacists used drugs to get high. They enjoyed the euphoria of drugs in general, and viewed prescription drugs as an extension of this mindset. These users are termed "recreational abusers" and are shown to have exhibited steep, experimental drug use trajectories. Other pharmacists used drugs for medicinal reasons. Faced with physical or psychological ailments, these hard-working pharmacists decided to self-medicate themselves. Over time, drug tolerance took effect and judicious usage turned into abuse. The authors term these pharmacists "therapeutic self-medicators." The article closely examines the behavioral and cognitive twists and turns that these professionals experience as they tried to cope with their problematic drug use. In doing so, the article stresses how the socialization process associated with being and becoming a pharmacist played a large part in the drug use trajectories observed among these pharmacists.

INTRODUCTION

American pharmacists fill over 1.6 billion controlled drug/medication prescription orders annually (Wivell and Wilson, 1994). Every day, hundreds of thousands of Americans walk into their local drug stores and rely on a pharmacist to accurately dispense their medications. What the public does not realize, however, is that some

---

This essay was prepared especially for this reader.

of these pharmacists are themselves using the drugs that they are entrusted to dispense. Self-report studies (Dabney, 1997; McAuliffe, Satangelo, Gingras, Rohman, Sobol, and Magnusen, 1987; Normack, Eckel, Pfifferling, and Cocolas, 1985) reveal that somewhere between forty and sixty-five percent of all practicing pharmacists have engaged in illicit prescription drug use. Moreover, these inquiries tell us that roughly twenty percent of practicing pharmacists use drugs on a regular basis and that five to ten percent consider themselves to be drug abusers.

The present study seeks to accomplish three goals. First, we will document different behavioral and motivational patterns underlying pharmacist's illicit prescription drug use. Second, we seek to organize these behaviors and motivations along two fluid and evolving criminal career trajectories. Third, we will identify social factors associated with being and becoming a pharmacist that serve to shape and reinforce these behavioral and motivational patterns of illicit prescription drug use among pharmacists.

INTERVIEW FINDINGS

Given our specific interest in the various career aspects of deviant behavior, a significant portion of each interview was focused on the pharmacist's entry into illicit drug use. After examining the transcripts of the interviews it became apparent that the initiation and subsequent progression of pharmacists' illicit prescription drug use followed one of two criminal career trajectories: recreational abusers and therapeutic self-medicators. The characteristics of these two drug using categories are discussed in greater detail below as we will attempt to detail the ways that these motivational/behavioral variants evolve over time.

Recreational Abusers

Of the 50 pharmacists interviewed, 23 (46%) could be classified as recreational abusers. One of the defining characteristics of recreational abusers is that they all began experimenting with street drugs, such as marijuana, cocaine, alcohol, and various psychedelics, while in high school or during their early college years. They described their early drug use as exclusively recreational. The motivation behind this use was quite simple, they were adventurous and wanted to experience the euphoric, mind altering effects that the drugs offered. Because of procurement problems, these individuals reported that they engaged in little, if any prescription drug use before entering pharmacy school.

Initial Use of Prescription Drugs For the recreational abuser, the onset of the illicit prescription drug use career usually began shortly after entering pharmacy training. These respondents were quick to point to the recreational motivations behind their early prescription drug use. As one 42-year-old male pharmacist stated, "I just wanted the effect, I really just wanted the effect. I know what alcohol is. But what if you take a Quaalude and drink with it?

What happens then?" Similarly, a 36-year-old male pharmacist said:

> It was very recreational at first, yeah. It was more curiosity . . . experimental.
> I had read about all these drugs. Then I discovered I had a lot of things going
> on with me at that time and that these [drugs] solved the problem for me
> instantly. I had a lot of self-exploration issues going on at that time.

Trends in the data indicate that pharmacy school provided these individuals
with the requisite access to prescription drugs. They recalled how they
exploited their newly found access to prescription drugs in an effort to expand
or surpass the euphoric effects that they received from weaker street drugs. For
example, a 27-year-old male pharmacist said:

> It was a blast. It was fun. . . . It was experimentation. We smoked a little
> pot. And then in the "model pharmacy" [a training facility in college],
> there was stuff [prescription drugs] all over the place. "Hey this is
> nice. . . . that is pretty nice." If it was a controlled substance then I tried
> it. I had my favorites, but when that supply was exhausted, I'd move on to
> something else. I was a "garbage head!" It was the euphoria. . . . I used
> to watch Cheech and Chong [movies]. That's what it was like. I wasn't
> enslaved by them [or so I thought]. They made the world go round.

Pharmacy as a Drug-Access Career Choice Over half of the recreational
abusers claimed that they specifically chose a career in pharmacy because they
expected that it would offer them an opportunity to expand their drug use
behaviors. For example, a 37-year-old male pharmacist said: "That's one of the
main reasons I went to pharmacy school, because, I'd have access to medications if I needed them." Further evidence of this trend can be seen in the
comments of a 41-year-old male pharmacist:

> I [had to] change my major. So I [based my choice] on nothing more than:
> "well, it looks like fun and . . . gee all the pharmacy majors had drugs."
> The guys [pharmacy students] that I knew . . . every weekend when they
> came back from home, they would unpack their bags and bags of pills
> would roll out. I thought, "Whoa, I got to figure out how to do this." [I
> would ask:] "How much did you pay for this?" [They would respond:]
> "I haven't paid a thing, I just stole them. Stealing is okay. I get shit wages so
> I got to make it up somehow. So we just steal the shit." Well, I thought,
> "this is it, I want to be a pharmacist." So I went into pharmacy school.

Recreational and Experimental Prescription Drug Use While many of
these recreational abusers entered pharmacy school with prior experiences in
drug use, their pre-college drug use was usually not extensive. It was not until
they got into pharmacy school that they began to develop more pronounced
and progressive drug habits. A 41-year-old male pharmacist discusses this transition into increased usage, in the following interview excerpt:

> It [pre-college use] had been recreational type use. It was pretty consistent.
> But I was still just experimenting. I hadn't, at that point, become actively

addicted. [I was] smoking pot and drinking beer, [doing] psychedelics and Quaaludes [depressant]. Just whatever [I] would come across, if [I] came across [it], great, if I didn't, no big deal . . . That was before pharmacy school. By the time I got into pharmacy school, the recreational drug use turned into a fairly steady drug use. Certainly not more than a month to two months would go by without something . . . I really started drinking and drugging. A lot of my friends after high school said, "Oh great, you're going into pharmacy school. You can wake up on uppers and go to bed on downers," all that stuff. At first, [I said] no. The first time I ever [used prescription drugs] I thought, "no, that's not why I'm doing it. No, I'm doing it [in pharmacy school] for the noble reasons." But then after a while I thought, well, maybe they had a point there after all.

Learning by Experimentation   Once in pharmacy school, the recreational abusers consistently described how they adopted an applied approach to their studies. For example, if they read about particularly interesting drugs in pharmacy school, they wanted to try them. If they were clerking or interning in a pharmacy setting which offered them access to prescription medicines, they wanted to steal drugs and use them. If a teacher or employer told them about the unusual effects of a new drug, they recalled how they wanted to experiment with it. This meant that these individuals usually began using prescription drugs soon after entering pharmacy school or while working in a pharmacy during high school. This pattern of application-oriented learning is exemplified in the comments of a 44-year-old male pharmacist:

When we studied Valium [benzodiazepine], I had to find out what Valium was . . . If I studied a class of drugs, I had to say, "Well, I don't know that. I don't understand that. What did they mean by tranquilizer? What did they mean?" I'd have to find out. Then, of course, I found the ones that I liked and the ones I didn't . . . got worse when I got on the job. It was so fascinating to me, reading the prescriptions and going and finding the drug back there [on the shelf] . . . I would take inserts home and read about it. It was just so fascinating to me. That's when I was learning about it and reading it as much as I could . . . That's where it [the use] definitely . . . definitely started.

They explained that they wanted to experience the drug effects that they read about in pharmacy textbooks. These individuals adeptly incorporated their newly found scientific training and professional socialization in a way that allowed them to excuse and redefine their use. They began to see their own drug use as beneficial to their future patients. This adaptation strategy is illustrated in the comments of a 59-year-old male recreational abuser:

In a lot of ways, it [college drug use] was pretty scientific. [I was] seeing how these things affected me in certain situations . . . testing the waters . . . "better living through chemistry." I thought, "I'll be able to counsel my patients better the more I know about the side effects of these drugs. I'll be my own rat. I'll be my own lab rat. I can tell [patients] about the shakes and chills and the scratchy groin and your skin sloughing off. I can tell you all about that stuff."

Socially Acceptable Drug Use in Pharmacy School The recreational abusers unanimously agreed that there was no shortage of socially acceptable experimental drug use while in pharmacy school. For those who were interested, this environment provided ample opportunity to refine and expand their usage. One 48-year-old male pharmacist described the makeup of his pharmacy school cohort as follows:

> There was a third of the pharmacy students in school because Mom and Dad or Grandfather or Uncle Bill were pharmacists, and they looked up to them and wanted to be one. Good enough. They had never seen a pharmacy. A [second] third had been in the [Vietnam] war. They were a pharmacy tech in the war or had worked in a pharmacy. They had the experiential effect of what pharmacy is and found a love for it or a desire to want it . . . Then you had the other third over here, and we were just drug addicts . . . It had nothing to do with altruism. We didn't know what the practice was all about, but we did know that we got letters after our names, guaranteed income if we didn't lose our letters, and we had access to anything [drugs] we needed.

Many of the recreational abusers claimed that they specifically sought out fellow pharmacy students who were willing to use prescription drugs. The most common locus for these associations were in pharmacy-specific fraternities. The respondents said that there was usually ample drug use going on in these organizations and that they allowed them the opportunity to cautiously scout out and identify with other drug users. Once they were connected with other drug users, the prescription drug use of all involved parties increased. This type of small-group drug use allowed for access to an expanded variety of drugs, a broader pharmacological knowledge base, and even larger quantities of drugs. However, numerous respondents clearly stated that these drug-based associations were tenuous and temporary in nature. Over time, as the intensity of their drug use increased, the recreational abusers described how they became more reclusive and guarded and selective in their relationships, fearing that their heightened use of prescription drugs would come to be defined as a problem by their fellow pharmacy students. One 43-year-old male pharmacist said:

> You get the sense pretty quickly that you are operating [using] on a different level. Those of us that were busily stealing [prescription drugs] from our internship sites began to tighten our social circle. We might party a little bit with the others but when it came to heavy use, we kept it hush, hush.

Unlike other pharmacy students who were genuinely experimenting with drugs on a short-term basis, these recreational abusers noticed an added intensity associated with their own prescription drug use. While most of these recreational abusers entered pharmacy school with some prior experiences in recreational street drug use, their pre-college prescription drug use was usually not extensive. As such, it was not until they got into pharmacy school that they began to develop more pronounced street and prescription drug use habits. A 38-year-old female pharmacist discusses this transition into increased usage in the following interview excerpt:

> I went off to pharmacy school. That was a 3-year program. I had tried a few things [before that], but I would back off because it was shaming for me not to get straight A's. The descent to hell started when I got to pharmacy school. There were just so many things [prescription drugs] available and so many things that I thought I just had to try. It might be a different high; it might be a different feeling, anything to alter the way that I just felt. I was pretty much using on a daily basis by the time I got to my last year.

Pharmacy Practice Yields More Use Once the recreational abusers got into a permanent practice setting, they quickly deduced that they had free reign over the pharmacy stock. At first, they referenced other pharmacists for normative or behavioral guidance in access or using the prescription drugs. However, they soon realized that their nearly unrestricted access meant that they could now try any drugs that they wanted without guidance, and most did. More importantly, increased access allowed the young pharmacists to habitually and secretly use the drugs that they liked most. Not surprisingly the levels and frequency of their drug use usually skyrocketed shortly after entering pharmacy practice and going more solo with their use. A 41-year-old male pharmacist explained:

> By the time I got to pharmacy school in 1971, I was smoking dope probably every day or every other day, and drinking with the same frequency, but not to the point of passing out kind of stuff. Then in 1971, that was also the year that I discovered barbs [barbiturates]. I had never had barbs up until I got to pharmacy school. So it was like '75 or '76 [when I got out of pharmacy school], I was using heavy Seconals and Quaaludes and Ambutols [all barbiturates]. I withdrew and it [the heavy misuse] just took off.

At the start, the recreational abusers' drug use was openly displayed and took on an air of excitement, much like others' experimentation with street or prescription drugs. However, as it intensified over time, the majority described how they slowly shielded their use from others. They thought it important to appear as though they still had the situation under control. As physical tolerance and psychological dependence increasingly progressed, these individuals began to lose control. Virtually all of the recreational abusers eventually developed serious prescription drug use habits. Using large quantities and sometimes even multiple drug types, their prescription drug use careers were usually marked by a steep downward spiral. This trend was clearly evidenced in the hand-sketched life history timeline that was drawn by each respondent. What started out as manageable social drug experimentation persistently progressed to increasingly more secretive drug abuse. In almost every case, it took several years for the drug use to reach its peak addictive state. The intense physical and psychological effects of the drug use meant that the recreational abuser's criminal/deviant career was punctuated by a very "low bottom." Commonly identified signs of "bottoming out" included life-threatening health problems, repeated dismissals from work, having action taken against their pharmacy licenses, habitual lying, extensive cover-ups, divorces, and suicide attempts. By all accounts, the personal and professional lives of these recreational abusers suffered heavily from their drug abuse. In the end, most were reclusive and paranoid—what started out as collective experimentation ended in a painful existence of solitary addiction.

Therapeutic Self-Medicators

The criminal/deviant career paths of the remaining 27 interviewees (54 percent) fit a different substantive theme. To differentiate these individuals from the recreational abusers, we call this latter group of pharmacists "therapeutic self-medicators." One of the defining characteristics of this group was that they had little or no experience with street or prescription drug use prior to entering pharmacy school. In fact, many of these individuals did not even use alcohol. What little drug involvement they did report was usually occasional experimentation with marijuana or other "soft" drugs. If they had ever used prescription drugs, it was done legitimately under the supervision of a physician. Members of this group did not begin their illicit prescription drug use until they were well into their formal pharmacy careers.

The onset of the therapeutic self-medicators' drug use was invariably attributed to a problematic life situation, accident, medical condition, or occupationally related pain. When faced with such problems, these pharmacists turned to familiar prescription medicines for immediate relief. Rather than reporting a recreational, hedonistic, or pleasure motivation, these pharmacists simply decided to use readily available prescription drugs to treat their own medical maladies.

Therapeutic Motives for Prescription Drug Use The therapeutic self-medicators unanimously insisted that their prescription drug use was never recreational—that they never used drugs solely for the euphoric effects. Instead, their drug use was focused on specific therapeutic goals. This trend is illustrated in the comments of a 33-year-old male pharmacist:

> There was no recreation involved. I just wanted to press a button and be able to sleep during the day. I was really having a tough time with this sleeping during the day. I would say by the end of that week I was already on the road [to dependency] . . . the race had started.

Other pharmacists described how their drug use began as a way of treating insomnia, physical trauma (e.g., a car accident, sports injury, or a broken bone), or some chronic occupationally induced health problem (e.g., arthritis, migraine headaches, leg cramps, or back pain).

It is important to point out that during the earliest stages of their drug use, these individuals appeared to be "model pharmacists." Most claimed to have excelled in pharmacy school. Moreover, occupational and career success usually continued after they entered full-time pharmacy practice. Personal appraisals, as well as annual supervisory evaluations, routinely described these individuals as hard working and knowledgeable professionals.

Since they were usually treating the physical pain that resulted from the rigors of pharmacy work, all of the therapeutic self-medicators described how their prescription drug use started and progressed under seemingly innocent, or even honorable, circumstances. In many cases, they were treating the physical pain that resulted from the rigors of work. Instead of taking time off from work to see a physician, they chose to simply self-medicate their own ailments. A 50-year-old male pharmacist described this situation as follows:

> When I got to Walgreen's, the pace there was stressful. We were filling 300 to 400 scripts a day with minimal support staff and working 12,13 hours days. The physical part bothered me a lot. My feet and my back hurt. So, I just kept medicating myself until it got to the point where I was up to 6 to 8 capsules of Fiorinol-3 [narcotic analgesic] a day.

Peer Influences Without exception, the therapeutic self-medicators described how they always engaged in solitary and secretive drug use. Although they usually kept their drug use to themselves, many claimed that their initial use was shaped by their interactions with co-workers. That is, they got the idea to begin self-medicating from watching a co-worker do so or merely followed the suggestion of a concerned senior pharmacist who was seeking to help them remedy a physical malady, such as a hang over, anxiety, physical pain. For example, a 38-year-old male pharmacist described an incident that occurred soon after being introduced to his hospital supervisor:

> I remember saying one time that I had a headache. [He said] "go take some Tylenol-with-Codeine elixir [narcotic analgesic]." I would never have done that on my own. He was my supervisor at the time, and I said, "okay, if you think I should." He said, "that's what we do." I guess that started the ball rolling a little bit mentally.

Members of the therapeutic self-medicator group took notice of the drug-related behaviors and suggestions of their peers but never acted upon them in the company of others. Instead, they maintained a public front condemning illicit prescription drug use but quietly followed through on the suggestive behaviors when in private.

The Perceived Utility of Self-Medication Whereas the recreational abusers used drugs to get high, the therapeutic self-medicators saw drug use as a means to a different end. Even as their drug use intensified, they were able to convince themselves that the drugs were actually having a positive effect on their work performance. This was not all together inaccurate, since they began using the drugs to remedy some constraining health problem that was detracting from their work efficiency.

Some therapeutic self-medicators looked to their notion of professional obligation to justify their drug use. For example, in describing his daily use of Talwin, a Schedule II narcotic analgesic, a 43-year-old male pharmacist maintained: "I thought I could work better. I thought I could talk better with the nurses and patients. I thought I could socialize better with it." This type of convenient, altruistic-based explanation was quite common among the therapeutic self-medicators. That is, they were adept at convincing themselves that their patients and employers needed them to produce at a certain level. When their performance fell below this level, they turned to prescription medicines as a way of neutralizing whatever inhibiting force that was deemed responsible.

A Slippery Slope At first, the pharmacists' therapeutic self-medication behaviors seemed to work well. They remedied the problematic situation (pain, insomnia, etc.) which allowed them to return to normal functioning. However, over time, they began to develop a tolerance for the drugs and thus had to take larger quantities to achieve the same desired effects. The following interview excerpt from a 50-year-old male pharmacist offers a good overview of the life history of a therapeutic self-medicator:

> Well, I didn't have a big problem with that [early occasional self-medication behavior]. I wasn't taking that much. It was very much medicinal use. It was not an everyday thing. It really was used at that point for physical pain. But that's when I started tampering with other things and started trying other things. I would have trouble sleeping so I would think, "You know, let's see what the Dalmane [benzodiazepine] is like?" When I was having weight problems. . . . "Let's give this Tenuate [amphetamine] a try." And I just started going down the line treating the things that I wanted to treat. And none of it got out of hand. It wasn't until I came down here [to Texas] . . . that things really started to go wild.

It generally took between 5 and 10 years for these pharmacists to progress into the later stages of drug abuse. That is, they were able to control their use for a long time without it interfering with their personal or professional life.

A handful of therapeutic self-medicators were not so lucky. For them, there was less time between the onset of their use and their entry into drug treatment. Their progression was much faster. This trend is illustrated by the comments of a 49-year-old male pharmacist:

> About two or three years after I had my store, I was working long, long hours. Like 8:00 to 8:00 Monday through Saturday and some hours on Sunday. And my back hurt one day. It was really killing me and I started out with two Empirin-3 [narcotic analgesic]. Just for the back pain. I mean I hurt, my back hurt, my head hurt. I don't know why, but I just reached for that bottle and I knew it was against the law to do that, but I did it any way. Man I felt good. I was off and running. This was eureka. This was it. It progressed. I started taking more and more and then I finally . . .

The key to a self-medicator's fast-paced progressive drug use seemed to lie in the given individual's perceived need to treat a wider and growing array of physical ailments. It got to the point that many "drug thirsty" pharmacists recognize that they were actively seeking out or inventing ailments to treat in themselves. As a 40-year-old female put it, "I had a symptom for everything I took." Several other quotes illustrate this tendency for therapeutic self-medicators to invent ailments.

In all, there were 27 pharmacists who fit into the category of therapeutic self-medicators. These individuals were admittedly naive about drug abuse when they entered their pharmacy careers. They were either counseled or convinced themselves that there was no harm in the occasional therapeutic use of prescription medicines. In short, the normative and behavioral advances in their deviance were gained largely by exploiting or manipulating their professional position and knowledge. The therapeutic self-medicators always used their drugs in private and kept their use from others around them. Over time, their false confidence and denial that allowed their drug use to significantly progress. Once their facade was broken, these pharmacists awoke to the reality that they were chemically dependent on one or more of the drugs that they so confidently had been dispensing to themselves.

Common Cognitive and Behavioral Themes

We found clear evidence of two very different modes of entry among the respondents, namely recreational abusers and therapeutic self-medicators. However, it is important to note that these were *not* mutually exclusive categories of offenders. In other words, these two categories were not completely dichotomous. As is usually the case, real life seldom fits cleanly into nice, neat categories. In fact, we were able to identify a number of cognitive and behavioral themes that were common to almost all of the drug-using pharmacists interviewed. These themes were expressed by nearly all of the drug-abusing pharmacists that we interviewed, regardless of how the individual initially began their illicit drug abuse career. The existence of these common themes suggests that pharmacy-specific occupational contingencies play a central role in the onset and progression of illicit use of prescription medicines. Let us examine the three most common of these cognitive and behavioral themes in more detail.

"I'm a Pharmacist, I Know What I am Doing" Intuitively, it should not be surprising that pharmacists would steal prescription medicines as a way of treating their own physical ailments. After all, they have been exposed to years of pharmacy training that emphasized the beneficial, therapeutic potential of these medicines. Each pharmacist has dispensed the medicines to hundreds of patients and then watched the drugs usually produce the predicted beneficial results. They have all read the literature and drug inserts detailing the chemical composition of drugs and studied the often dramatic curative effects of the chemical substances. Pharmacists, more so than any other member of society, are keenly aware of how and why drugs work. There was strong evidence to suggest that both the therapeutic self-medicators and the recreational abusers actively used the years of pharmacological knowledge that they had acquired. In their eyes, it made perfect sense that they should put their pharmacy knowledge to work on themselves.

This application of knowledge can be seen in the comments of a 40-year-old female self-medicator:

> So, in 1986 I was sent to the psychologist. That was when I was forced to recognize that I had an alcohol problem. And I recognized that I had to do something. And in my brilliant analysis, I made a decision that since alcohol was a central nervous system depressant, the solution for me was to use a central nervous system stimulant. That would solve my alcohol problem. So I chose the best stimulant that I had access to, and that was [pharmaceutical grade] cocaine. I started using cocaine in 1986. I never thought that it would progress. I never thought it was going to get worse. I thought, "I'm just going to use it occasionally."

Similar trends were observed among the recreational abuser group, only here, the applied use of drugs was based upon more recreational motives.

Almost all of the therapeutic self-medicators and recreational abusers described how they became masters of quickly diagnosing their own ailments or emotional needs and then identifying the appropriate pharmacological agent that would remedy the problem. Moreover, as professionals, they were confident that they would be able to self-regulate their drug intake so as to never become addicted. All of the respondents drew upon their social status as pharmacists to convince themselves that their drug use would not progress into dependency. They recall being adamant in their view that personally they were immune from such problems, believing that only stupid, naive people became addicted to drugs. As a 40-year-old female self-medicator put it, "I'm a pharmacist, I know what I am doing." A 39-year-old male self-medicator went so far as to say: "I mean, we know more [about the effect of drugs] than doctors. We have all the package inserts. We have the knowledge. We know a lot about the drugs, so what's the big deal?" Elsewhere (Dabney and Hollinger, 1999) we refer to this denial mechanism as a "paradox of familiarity," arguing that familiarity can breed consent, not contempt toward prescription drug use.

Inadequate Training and Warnings Members of both categories of pharmacists claimed that they had never been warned about the dangers of drugs, insisting instead that their training had only stressed the positive side of prescription medicines. For example, a 48-year-old male misuser stated:

> I never had anybody come right out and tell me that [prescription drug abuse] was probably unethical and illegal because they assumed that we knew that. But nobody ever said this is something that is not done.

Left without guidance on the issue, some pharmacists assumed that self-medication was acceptable behavior. To this end, a 39-year-old female self-medicator said:

> It's [self-medication] just part of it [the pharmacy job]. It's just accepted because we know so much. I'm sure it's the same way when the doctors

do it. It wasn't a big stretch to start going "You know, I got a headache here, maybe I should try one of these Percocets [narcotic analgesic]?"

Many pharmacists spoke about their prescription drug theft/use as if it were an entitlement that went along with being a pharmacist. Much like a butcher always has fresh meat at home or a car dealer always drives a state-of-the-art automobile, pharmacists will always have the best drugs. This theme is illustrated in an exchange that occurred between the interviewer and a 45-year-old male pharmacist:

Why take plain Aspirin or plain Tylenol when you've got this [Percocet— narcotic analgesic]? It works better . . . [so] you don't even have to struggle with it. I really believed that I had license to do that . . . as a pharmacist. I mean with all that stuff sitting there, you know. Oh, my back was just killing me during that period of time and this narcotic pain reliever is sitting right there. I thought, "why should [I] suffer through back pain when I have this bottle of narcotics sitting here?"

Out-of-Control Addiction The above-mentioned themes involve cognitive dimensions of the pharmacists' drug abuse in that they speak to common motivational and justification themes that were present in all of the interviews. Perhaps more important is the fact that there was a common behavioral characteristic shared by all 50 pharmacists. In every case, occasional prescription drug abuse eventually gave way to an advanced addictive state that was marked by an enormous intake of drugs, unmistakable habituation, and the constant threat of physical withdrawal. Members of the recreational abuser and therapeutic self-medicator groups alike routinely reported daily use levels exceeding 50–100 times the recommended daily dosage. One pharmacist reported that his drug use regimen progressed to 150 Percocets [strong narcotic analgesic] per day. Another individual reported injecting up to 200 mg of Morphine each day. Still another respondent described a daily use pattern that, among other things, included 5g of cocaine.

Invariably, these advanced levels of drug use led to clear signs of habituation and the constant threat of physical withdrawal. At this point, the individuals recall growing increasingly desperate. Consider the following quote from a 44-year-old male pharmacist who was in charge of ordering the narcotics at the independent retail pharmacy where he worked:

I was ordering excessive quantities and chasing down drug tracks. That's what I used to do. I was really reaching my bottom. I would chase these delivery trucks down in the morning because I didn't come to my store until mid afternoon. I was in withdrawal in the morning and I was without drugs, so I had to have it. I was just going nuts. Many mornings I had gone to work sweating. It would be 30 degrees, it would be January, and the clerk would say, "you look sick," and I would say, "It's the flu." So I would pay the delivery guys extra money to deliver my drugs first or I would chase the delivery trucks down in the morning. I knew the trucks delivered at 6 in the morning, they came by my area, and I would get up early and chase the trucks down the highway. I would go in excess of 100 miles an hour trying to catch up with this truck and flag it down.

The advanced stages of drug addiction invariably produced traumatic physical psychological outcomes. Eventually, "out-of-control" drug use patterns along with the realization of chemical dependency left the pharmacists in a problematic mental state. It was at this point that all of the pharmacists recalled coming to grips with their addiction. This personal realization was accompanied by a shift in the way that they thought about their drug use. They no longer denied the situation by drawing upon recreational or therapeutic explanations. Instead, they finally admitted the dire nature of their situation and became more and more reclusive. In short, all of the respondents grew to realize that they had a drug problem, turning then to fear and ignorance to foster the final weeks or months of their drug addiction.

CONCLUSION

Two identifiable criminal career trajectories were observed among the pharmacists who we interviewed: recreational abusers and therapeutic self-medicators. Clearly, our discussion of the therapeutic self-medicator category goes far beyond what is present in the existing literature. However, we submit that it is our documentation of the recreational abusers that provides the more innovative findings. While McAuliffe (1984) was the first to document recreational drug use among health professionals, this empirical revelation has had minimal impact on the way that the various healthcare professions think about or address problem of substance abuse within their ranks. The pharmacy profession has been especially reluctant to address the reality of the prescription drug abuse situation. For example, existing self-reports (Baptista, Novua, and Hernandez, 1994; Coleman, Honeycutt, Ogden, McMillan, O'Sullivan, Light, and Wingfield, 1997; Gallegos, Veit, Wilson, Porter, and Talbott, 1988; Kriegler et al., 1994; McAuliffe et al., 1987; Miller and Banahan, 1990; Normack et al., 1985) and interview (Bissell, Haberman, and Williams, 1989; Sheffield, 1988) research on drug using pharmacists largely ignores the recreational origins of drug use and, instead, describes the affected individuals as having misplaced therapeutic motivations. This assumption is reinforced by published biographical accounts of recovering drug using pharmacists (Babbicke, 1991; Crawford, 1992; Reimenschneider, 1990; Starr, 1989a and 1989b; Tucker, 1985). While principally intended to raise awareness among fellow pharmacists, these confessionals consistently emphasize the well-intentioned motives behind the individuals' destructive drug use past.

CHAPTER 9

Patterns and Prospects

This book directs readers' attention to the three interdependent parts of the criminal event: offenders, victims, and a setting. Each of these elements play an important role in the interactive dynamic of criminal occurrences, thus one should be mindful of all three when pondering crime-related phenomena. This book also builds around the premise that there exists observable patterns in the structure and process of criminal events. A series of core components are set forth in Chapter 1 of the textbook to help the reader appreciate the patterned aspects of criminal events. First, one must be aware of the behavioral dimensions of the crime. Second, one must consider the cognitive or mental factors that shape the act. Third, it is necessary to ponder how cultural factors present in the immediate environment help influence the criminal outcome. Fourth, one needs to be cognizant of the pressures and reactions from the larger society that come to impact the occurrence of crime.

These four core components come together to form what is called an underlying conceptual framework that allows for an orderly discussion of the crime. Armed with this heuristic tool, it becomes possible to formulate a typology or taxonomy of crime that distills criminal offenses down into a manageable set of meaningful categories. This textbook considers seven major categories of crime: murder/assault, violent sex crime, robbery, burglary, common property crime, public order crime, and crimes that occur within complex organizations. Each of these types is said to exhibit its own unique combination of behavioral, cognitive, cultural, and societal reaction characteristics.

Too often, we think superficially about crime or choose to approach it as though it were one amorphous, unidimensional concept. The purpose of the abovementioned partitioning exercise is to delve more deeply into the subject matter and thus provoke a fuller appreciation of the similarities and differences that exist across criminal offenses. Such an appreciation allows one to think more clearly about the crime-related experiences of today. The concluding pages of this textbook seek to highlight noteworthy similarities and differences that exist across the major crime types.

BEHAVIORAL CHARACTERISTICS
ACROSS CRIME TYPES

The criminal law and its accompanying legal definitions should serve as the departure point of any crime-related discussion. Every criminal offense is comprised of a set of behavioral (*actus reus*) and mental (*mens reus*) prerequisites. These statutory provisions are clearly stated in the criminal code and establish what an individual must do and think to be in violation of the law. Each of the preceding seven chapters commenced with a discussion of legal definitions. Chapters 2 through 4 provided definitions for what are commonly referred to as crimes of violence, namely, murder, assault, rape, sexual assault, and robbery. These crimes require an act of force or threat of force against another person. However, they are set apart from one another based on the outcome of the force. Murder, the most serious of all offenses, produces a lethal outcome. An act of assault often mimics murder in its process (use of a weapon, fisticuffs, etc.) but produces a physical injury instead of a death. In the case of the violent sex crimes (rape and sexual assault), the force or threat of force is used to achieve a nonconsensual sex act. For robbery, the violence serves to facilitate a theft. The *mens reus* or guilty mind dimension of a criminal statute is often more complicated. In the case of murder, gradations of intent (purposely/knowingly, recklessly, and negligently) yield three statutory forms of criminal homicide (murder, manslaughter, and negligent homicide, respectively). The criminal assault that can be found in Chapter 2 notes that the level of intended bodily harm (i.e., serious bodily injury versus less than serious bodily injury) yields another set of offense gradations (aggravated versus simple assault). A similar trend is observed in Chapter 3 with regard to the statutory provisions for rape versus sexual assault or statutory rape.

Chapters 5 and 6 deal with property offenses. The *actus reus* criteria for these offenses target transgressions against personal property. Burglary is described as a "crime against habitation" given that the statute prohibits the unlawful entry into a building or occupied structure. The intent of the entry can be to commit a theft or any other form of felony. Conversely, the offenses contained in Chapter 6 (larceny-theft and auto theft) are more pure and simple property crimes as they specify only that the offender intended to steal from another person. The *mens reus* dimension of these property crimes is satisfied by a determined or intentional state of mind.

It is tempting to think of robbery, burglary, theft, and auto theft as constituting a single conceptual category, as they all involve offenses against property. There are important differences that justify a multifaceted treatment of these crimes.

As mentioned, auto theft and larceny-theft are pure forms of property crime that target personal possessions. However, enter force into the equation and a decidedly different criminal event emerges (i.e., robbery). The crime of burglary is different still as it involves the targeting of a structure, not a person. What's more, the burglary statute extends beyond a simple property offense to include those felonious acts (rape, assault, drug offense) that take place pursuant to an unlawful entry.

Chapter 7 tackles a different set of crimes, those against public order or *mala prohibitum* (violations of man/woman-made law) offenses. Unlike *mal in se* (inherently evil acts) offenses that produce measurable harm against a person or his or her property, these offenses yield no aggrieved party. Chapter 7 showcases two of the most prominent examples of public order crime—drug abuse offenses and prostitution or commercialized vice—and seeks to articulate the unique but murky statutory landscape that goes along with these "victimless" crimes.

The last substantive chapter (Chapter 8) explores yet another dense statutory landscape—crimes that occur within complex organizations. With a few exceptions (perjury, bribery, land use violations), the acts described herein could be subsumed under one or more of the legal definitions presented in Chapters 2 through 6. Legally speaking, a corporate homicide is little more than a murder committed by a corporate entity. Similarly, embezzlement or employee theft is little more than a theft committed within the purview of one's job. The legal definitions of these criminal events are not what warrants their separate treatment, but rather the organizational context in which they occur significantly change the behavioral, cognitive, cultural, and societal dimensions of these criminal events.

Chapter 1 identifies skills/techniques as another important behavioral feature of crime. With the exception of drug dealing and organization-based crimes, most of the offenses discussed here require low levels of skill on the part of the offender—it simply does not take a rocket scientist to inflict bodily harm on another person or deprive that person of their property. This notwithstanding, one finds that the tools of the trade can vary widely across different types of crime. For example, guns or other lethal weapons are present in a high percentage of murders, assaults, and robberies. The burglar usually relies on a hammer or crowbar. The shoplifter will often use clothing to conceal merchandise. The auto thief will usually enlist the aid of a screwdriver and coat hanger to accomplish the crime. Similarly, a prostitute, pimp, and john must be well versed in sex acts and the "lingo" that goes with them. The white-collar criminal may need to be adept in the use of deception, a calculator, or the legislative/bureaucratic process. The robber and rapist must be skilled at subduing their victims through verbal commands or intimidating physical gestures.

Criminal events transpire when offenders, victims, and audience members intersect in a given setting. These participants engage in a dynamic set of actions and counteractions to produce the criminal outcome. This text uses the term "criminal transaction" to describe this exchange process. A full discussion of the criminal transaction must consider broad-based issues such as the demographics of the actors, the environment in which the crimes occur, and the way that these events tend to play themselves out. In the case of the offender-victim relationship, it is noted that violent crimes such as murder, assault, rape, and robbery tend to take on a one-on-one offender-victim dynamic. Conversely, property offenders, public order offenders, and many organizational criminals are prone to work in small groups. What's more, robbery, burglary and common property offense are described as stranger crimes while murder, assault, rape, and white-collar crimes tend to involve a victim and perpetrator(s) who know one another.

There was not much variation observed in the demographic composition of offenders and victims across crime types. Most crimes are intra-age, intra-racial, and intra-gendered in nature. More precisely, lower class, young, minority, males are over-represented in the populations of known offenders and victims. Notable exceptions include rape, which tends to be a male-on-female crime, commercial sex crimes (mostly male pimps and johns but female prostitutes), and white-collar crimes (involve disproportionate numbers of white offenders and victims).

Setting is another important characteristic of the criminal transaction. Crimes such as rape, murder, assault, and auto theft tend to occur in or near one's place of residence. Conversely, acts of prostitution, drug dealing, robbery, and larceny-theft generally take place away from home in public spaces. With the exception of burglary, we find that the highest offending rates are observed in urban areas, followed by suburban and rural locales. Crimes can also be patterned in terms of the time of day in which they occur. For example, most residential burglaries and shoplifting cases occur in the daytime while most nonresidential burglaries and auto thefts during the nighttime.

Most criminal transactions play themselves out as intense, quick-hitting exchanges between two people. Those crimes that regularly occur in public settings are more apt to include bystanders or multiple offenders and/or victims. The transaction tends to become more protracted and complicated as additional offenders, victims, and/or audience members are added to the mix.

The criminal career of the offender is yet another important behavioral factor to consider. Research suggests that all classes of property offenders, drug offenders, members of the commercial sex market, and white-collar criminals tend to sustain their offending behaviors over long periods of time. Conversely, murderers and rapists tend to accumulate somewhat shorter criminal track records. Most offenders are willing to move across crime types, behaving as criminal generalists. Evidence of short-term specialization has been observed for rape, robbery, and select white-collar offenses.

COGNITIVE CHARACTERISTICS
ACROSS CRIME TYPES

One cannot fully appreciate crime without delving into the thought processes that go with the behaviors. This textbook breaks the cognitive dimension of crime into three component parts: motivation, planning, and normative neutralization. Criminal motivation, or the mental state of the offender, clearly varies across the types of crime outlined in this textbook. For example, murder and assault routinely take shape as a "crime of passion," whereby the offender lashes out in a rage-filled emotional state. Robbery and property crimes such as burglary, auto theft, and larceny, tend to be spurred on by financial motives. The same holds true for the suppliers in the drug and commercial sex markets. In many cases, the property offender sees fit to deprive another of their valuables as a way of subsidizing his or her own drug habit. Power or status can also serve as a motivating force for crime. This is often the case in rape, gang violence, political crime, or even some forms of inner-city robbery (e.g., carjacking, drug robbery). Self-gratification or euphoria of some sort can drive individuals to crime. This is usually the case with the clients in commercial sex and drug transactions.

Criminal planning is yet another important part of the cognitive aspects of crime. Here again, one observes variation across crime types. Crimes of passion generally come together quickly and leave little time for pre-event planning. For example, murderers and assaulters are known to simply react to what they perceive to be an infuriating situation and thus engage in little or no conscious forethought. Conversely, by virtue of their collaborative nature, we find that crimes such as drug dealing and prostitution require a higher level of pre-event coordination. In the case of robbery, burglary, and auto theft, the perpetrator must at least scan the environment looking for an attractive target. These property crimes also oblige a certain level of strategy in anticipation of security measures and/or victim resistance.

Individuals usually feel a need to justify their illicit involvements to themselves and others. Offenders must account for their perceived wrongdoing, victims must account for their perceived weakness, and audience members must account for their apathy and inaction. This textbook uses the term "normative neutralization" to describe the thought processes through which individuals excuse, justify, or rationalize their roles in a criminal event. The content of these neutralizations are shaped by the type of event as well as the individual's stock of knowledge. This yields variation across crime types. Property crimes tend to be justified in terms of necessity (i.e., "I needed the money, car, or merchandise"). Violent crimes such as rape, murder, and assault tend to take on a different flavor with the offender blaming the victim or evoking a right to vengeance. Drug offenders, white-collar criminals, and participants in the commercialized vice market tend to take a different tact; they downplay the societal harm that has been produced by their actions.

CULTURAL CHARACTERISTICS
ACROSS CRIME TYPES

Culture refers to that familiar layer of reality that exists in between individual agency and larger societal influences. It speaks to the routinized social world that most immediately surrounds a given social phenomenon. This text uses the term "criminal subculture" to refer to the normative and physical petri dish that nourishes criminal involvement. The term conjures up images of peer pressure, collegiality, mentoring activities, and criminal collaboration. Some crimes have more pronounced connections to the criminal subculture than others. In the case of "common street crimes" such as robbery, burglary, and auto theft, there tends to be clear and pronounced connections to what we know as the criminal underbelly of society. These offenders usually live in close proximity to other seasoned criminals and routinely interact with other known criminals. Some people go so far as to think of public order crimes such as prostitution and drug abuse offenses as representing the perfect union between the individual participants and the criminal subculture. A slightly different trend emerges for murder, assault, rape, and most crimes that are committed within organizational contexts. Persons who commit murder and assault associate with other physical problem-solvers but often manage to stay on the fringe of the larger criminal subculture. Sexual predators are known to be more reclusive and favor social interactions with other sexual deviants via the world of pornography and places that objectify women. White-collar offenders tend to socialize with persons inside of their chosen occupation or profession. While this usually provides distance between them and street criminals, it exposes them to a whole other set of harmful normative messages and bad examples.

It is important to think of the cultural dimension of crime as having both a structure and a process. This textbook uses Best and Luckenbill's (1994) term "organizational alignment" to describe the social organization of crime. Offenders are categorized as loners, colleagues, peers, teams, or members of formal organizations. Here again, we find variation across crime types. Most murderers, embezzlers, and shoplifters lead a solitary criminal existence as loners. Assaulters, rapists, and auto thieves tend to work alone but associate with other known offenders in a colleague-like arrangement. Robbers and burglars often move from partner to partner in a peerlike arrangement. We often see more stable criminal collaboration among prostitutes, drug offenders, and corporate/political criminals, thus taking on what Best and Luckenbill would call a team orientation.

This textbook uses the term "socialization scripts" to describe the process through which criminal learning occurs. Some offenders benefit from a more clearly defined criminal tutelage. This is often the case with drug dealers, robbers, burglars, auto thieves, professional shoplifters, and members of the commercial vice market. Conversely, most murderers, assaulters, rapists, and embezzlers are left to their own devises to put in place the behavioral and cognitive aspects of their crimes.

SOCIETAL REACTIONS
ACROSS CRIME TYPES

Social control efforts play an important role in the patterned aspects of crime. By their very definition, all crimes represent violations of the law. The law, which represents the authority of the state, prescribes a host of formal sanctions that are to be meted out against transgressors. The most visible of these formal social control efforts are carried out by members of the criminal justice system. Both officially and unofficially, the criminal justice system adopts varied levels of response to different types of crime.

Legislative mandate designates criminal offenses to be either misdemeanors or felonies. The former is punishable by a fine or jail term that must be less than 1 year while the latter carries with it a punishment of at least 1 year imprisonment. Felonies are generally broken down into three grades (class I, II, and III) to allow for graded increases in the prescribed term of imprisonment. Some of the crimes that are discussed in this book, namely, simple assault, sexual assault, petty theft, and minor drug and sex offenses, are afforded a misdemeanor designation in the criminal code. The remainder are felony offenses. In most jurisdictions, property offenses such as auto theft, burglary, and fraud will be assigned a class II or class III felony status, meaning that they are subject to 1 to 10 years in prison. Violent crimes such as robbery, murder, rape, and drug dealing tend to receive a felony I classification and carry the prospect of more lengthy prison terms or even death.

Members of law enforcement represent the front line defense in the formal social control apparatus. Police departments tend to prioritize their response to crime. There exists a more concerted effort when it comes to the investigation and apprehension of violent criminals than with property and drug crimes. Budgetary or logistical restraints lead to limited enforcement when it comes to commercialized sex crimes and forms of crime that occur within organizational settings. These efforts are reflected in differences in clearance rates that exist across the crime types.

When arrests do occur, it is up to the prosecutor and judge to shape the system's formal response to criminal cases as they move through the court system. Here again, one sees varied levels of response across crime types. Violent crimes such as murder, aggravated assault, rape, and robbery yield higher bail amounts, higher conviction rates, and more severe sentencing outcomes than do property and public order offenses. This can be vividly depicted in the differences that exist between the adjudication patterns for murder and prostitution.

Once convicted, criminals face their next dose of formal social control from agents of the correctional system. Murderers, rapists, and robbers can expect to serve more time behind bars than burglars, thieves, and prostitutes. The "war on drugs" has yielded a noticeable trend in this regard as mandatory sentencing practices have come to increase the time served for convicted drug offenders.

It is important to note that our society responds to crime in ways that extend beyond the purview of the criminal justice system. Informal social control efforts on the part of friends, family members, and other valued role models play an equally important part in the patterned aspect of criminal events. Cooney (1999) notes that third-party observers can have the potential to have a huge impact on the process of a violent confrontation; they can stand aside and simply watch the murder or assault unfold, they can mediate the dispute, or they can join in on the violence. Unfortunately, most audience members do little to stave off the violent outcomes. The same can be said about property crimes: People often stand by and do nothing as a person shoplifts or steals a car right in front of them. Violent sex crimes are another case in which we see missed opportunities for informal social control. As friends, family members, and role models, most people buy into the awkward gender norms that guide consensual sexual relations. This gives rise to a tacit reinforcement of patriarchal ideals and sets the stage for male-on-female sexual transgressions. In some cases, young men become so misguided in their view of sex and women that they embark upon protracted routines as stranger rapists. For sure, most members of the public protest against the commission of violent and property crimes. However, upon closer examination, one notes that actions do not always fall in line with the words.

Public order crimes present a different set of problems for our ongoing informal social control efforts. Given the absence of a victim, many members of society turn a blind eye to prostitution and drug offenses. Many even engage in these acts from time to time. This allows youthful offenders to tacitly reinforce their offending patterns. A slightly different pattern exists with regard to crimes in complex organizations, as most members of the public have difficulty assigning criminal responsibility to organizational actors. We think of business or political practices as somehow being immune to the possibilities of violence or theft. This ignorance and apathy provides would-be offenders with added fuel to their fires.

FUTURE PROSPECTS

Combining the abovementioned variables allows one to realize that crime is not as simple and uniform as it appears. Instead, a great deal of variation exists across different types of crime. Readers should come away from this book with two important affirmations. First, one should appreciate the merits of the typologies approach to crime. That is to say, the reader should see the utility in breaking down crime into manageable categories. Second, they should have developed a better appreciation for the behavioral, cognitive, cultural, and social control differences that exist across different crime types. This higher level of sensitivity and openness should leave the reader better prepared to combat crime-related problems.

Too often, practitioners think that there exists a silver bullet approach to crime prevention; that one can develop an all-encompassing set of prevention strategies that will work well on all forms of crime. This textbook suggests that a more flexible, situational-focused approach is in order. Each category of crime has its own unique idiosyncracies. While this text has sought to highlight trends that exist within a given crime type, reality dictates that subtypes and subpatterns will exist. To guard against the volatility of social situations, policy makers are wise to approach their crime-related problems carefully. They should take time to assess the behavioral, cognitive, cultural, and societal patterns before reacting. They should adopt a more open-minded approach to the subject matter. In short, they need to appreciate the nature of a problem before they can adequately explain or prevent it.

DISCUSSION QUESTIONS

1. Are the differences that exist across crime types really that noteworthy? Engage in a pencil-paper exercise in which the behavioral, cognitive, cultural, and social control dimensions of the seven major crime types are mapped out before you. Focus on general trends and reflect upon the differences and similarities.

2. Is it useful or counterproductive to think of the seven major crime types as being comprised of an untold number of situationally defined subtypes? Think about a crime such as rape and then consider the behavioral, cognitive, cultural, and social control variations that exist across stranger rape, date rape, gang rape, and wife rape.

3. Think about the types of prevention strategies that would be best suited for the conceptual framework outlined in this text. Devise a prevention agenda for a crime such as murder and then adapt that model to combat drug offenses.

4. Why is it so important to appreciate crime before one seeks to explain or prevent it? Try to identify specific examples in the criminology and criminal justice literature where practitioners and theorists seem to forego this observation.

References

Abbey, Antonio. (1991). Misperception as an antecedent of acquaintance rape: A consequence of ambiguity in communication between men and women. In A. Parrot & R. Warshaw (Eds.), *Acquaintance rape: The hidden crime,* pp. 96–111. New York: Wiley & Sons.

Abel, Gene, Judith Becker & Linda Skinner. (1980). Aggressive behavior and sex. *Psychiatric clinics of North America* 3, 133–151.

Action, W. (1870). *Prostitution considered in its moral, social and sanitary aspects.* London: Frank Cass.

Adler, Michael J. & Mortimer Adler. (1933). *Crime, law and social science.* New York: Harcourt Brace.

Adler, Patricia. (1993). *Wheeling and dealing: An ethnography of an upper-level drug dealing and smuggling community.* New York: Columbia University Press.

Agar, Michael. (1973). *Ripping and running: A formal ethnography of urban heroin addicts.* New York: Seminar Press.

Agnew, Robert. (1990). The origins of delinquent events: An examination of offender accounts. *Journal of Research in Crime and Delinquency* 27(3), 267–294.

Akers, Ronald L. (1973). *Deviant behavior: A social learning approach.* Belmont, Calif.: Wadsworth/West.

———. (1985). *Deviant behavior: A social learning approach,* third edition. Belmont, Calif.: Wadsworth.

Albanese, Jay S. (1995). *White collar crime in America.* Englewood Cliffs, N.J.: Prentice Hall.

Albonetti, C. A. (1994). The symbolic punishment of white-collar offenders. In G. S. Bridges & M. A. Myers (Eds.), *Inequality, crime, and social control* (pp. 269–282). Boulder, Colo: Westview Press.

Albrecht, W. Steve, Gerald W. Wernz, & Timothy L. Williams. (1995). *Fraud: Bringing light to the dark side of business.* New York: Irwin Professional Publishing.

American Law Institute. (1962). *Model penal code: Proposed official draft.* Philadelphia: American Law Institute.

Amir, Menachem. (1974). *Patterns in forcible rape.* Chicago: University of Chicago Press.

Anderson, Elijah. (1990). *Streetwise.* Chicago: University of Chicago Press.

———. (1999). *Code of the streets: Decency, violence, and the moral life of the inner city.* New York: W. W. Norton.

Anglin. M. Douglas & George Speckart. (1984). *Narcotics use and crime: A confirmatory analysis.* Unpublished Report. Los Angeles: University of California Los Angeles.

Arboleda-Florez. J., Helen Durie & John Costello. (1977). Shoplifting–An ordinary crime. *Journal of Offender Therapy and Comparative Criminology* 21(3), 201–207.

Armstrong, L. (1994). *Carjacking, District of Columbia.* Washington, D.C., Bureau of Justice Statistics.

Arnold, Bruce L. & John Hagan. (1992). Careers of misconduct: The structure of prosecuted professional deviance among lawyers. *American Sociological Review* 57(6), 771–785.

Asmussen, K. J. (1992). Weapon possession in public high school. *School safety* Fall, 28–30.

Associated Press. (1994). "State is No. 1 in Nation in Arrests Involving Pot." *The Courier-Journal* March 16, 1994: 7B.

Association of Grand Jurors of New York County. (1928). *Criminal receivers in the United States.* New York: Putnam's Sons.

Aulette, Judy R. & Raymond J. Michalowski. (1993). Fire in Hamlet: A case study of state-corporate crime. In K. Tunnell (Ed.), *Political crime in contemporary America* (pp. 171–206). New York: Garland.

Ayers, K. & James Frank. (1987). Deciding to prosecute white collar crime: A national survey of state attorney generals. *Justice Quarterly* 4, 425–440.

Babbicke, T. C. (1991). Pharmaceutical diversion and abuse: Our nation's other drug problem. *FBI law enforcement bulletin* 52(6), 1–4.

Ball John C. & Carl D. Chambers. (1970). *The epidemiology of heroin use in the United States.* Springfield, Ill.: Charles C. Thomas.

Ball, John C., Lawrence Rosen. John A. Flueck & David Nurco. (1981). The criminality of heroin addicts when addicted and when off opiates. In J. A. Inciardi (Ed.), *The drugs-crime connection,* 39–65. Beverly Hills, Calif.: Sage Publications.

Ball John C., John W. Shaffer & David Nurco. (1983). The day to day criminality of heroin addicts in Baltimore: A study of the continuity of offense rates. *Drug and alcohol dependence* 12, 119–42.

Ball, John C. & Richard W. Snarr. (1969). A test of the maturation hypothesis with respect to opiate addiction. *Narcotics* 21, 9–13.

Bamfield, Joshua. (1998). A breach of trust: Employee collusion and theft from major retailers. In M. Gill (Ed.), *Crime at work: Increasing risk for the offenders* (pp. 123–141). London: Perpetuity Press.

Banitt, Rivka, Shoshana Katznelson & Shlomit Streit. (1970). The situational aspects of violence: A research model. In S. Shoham (Ed.), *Israel studies in criminology* (pp. 241–258). Tel-Aviv: Gomeh.

Bankier, David. (1992). *The Germans and the final solution.* Oxford: Blackwell.

Baptista, Trino, Dario Novoa & Rafael Hernandez. (1994). Substance use among Venezuelan medical and pharmacy students. *Drug and alcohol dependency* 34, 121–127.

Barak, Gregg. (1991). *Crimes by the capitalist state.* Albany: State University of New York Press.

———. (1993). Crime, criminology, and human rights: Toward an understanding of state criminality. In K. Tunnell (Ed.), *Political crime in contemporary America* (pp. 207–230). New York: Garland.

Barnett, Harold. (1981). Corporate capitalism, corporate crime. *Crime and delinquency* 27, 4–23.

Barofsky, G., G. Stollak & L. Masse. (1971). Bystanders reactions to physical assault: Sex differences in socially responsible behavior. *Journal of Experimental Social Psychology* 7, 313–318.

Baron, Larry & Murray A. Strauss. (1989). *Four theories of rape in American society.* New Haven: Yale University Press.

Baron, Stephen & Timothy Hartnagel. (1997). Attributions, affect, and crime: Street youths' reactions to unemployment. *Criminology* 35, 409–434.

Bart, Pauline. (1979). Rape as a paradigm of sexism in society—Victimization and its discontents. *Women's Studies International Quarterly* 2, 347–57.

Barthes, R. (1980). An Introduction to the structural analysis of narratives. *New literary history* 6, 237–272.

Bass, Ronald & Lois Hoeffler. (1992). *Telephone based fraud: A survey of the American public.* New York: Louis Harris and Associates.

Baston, L. D. & B. M. Taylor. (1991). *School crime: A national victimization survey report.* Washington, D.C.: Department of Justice.

Battin-Pearson, Sara R., Terence P. Thornberry, J. David Hawkins & Marvin D. Krohn. (1998). *Gang membership, delinquent peers, and delinquent behavior.* Washington, D.C.: Office for Juvenile Justice and Delinquency Prevention.

Baumer, Terry L. & Dennis P. Rosenbaum. (1984). *Combating retail theft: Programs and strategies.* Boston: Butterworth.

Beccaria, Cesare. (1963). *On crimes and punishment.* New York: MacMillan.

Beck, Allen J. (2001). *Prison and jail inmates at midyear 2000.* Washington, D.C.: U.S. Department of Justice, Bureau of Justice Statistics.

Beck, Allen, Darrell Gillard, Lawrence Greenfield, Caroline Harlow, Thomas Hester, Louis Jankowski, Tracy Snell, James Stephan & Danielle Morton. (1993). *Survey of state prison inmates, 1991.* Washington, D.C.: U.S. Department of Justice, Bureau of Justice Statistics.

Beck, Allen J. & Paige M. Harrison. (2001). *Prisoners in 2000.* Washington, D.C.: U.S. Department of Justice, Bureau of Justice Statistics.

Beck, Allen J. & Bernard E. Shipley. (1989). *Recidivism of prisoners released in 1983.* Washington, D.C.: U.S. Department of Justice, Bureau of Justice Statistics.

Becker, Howard S. (1953). Becoming a marijuana user. *American Journal of Sociology* 59, 225–242.

————. (1963). *Outsiders: Studies in the sociology of deviance.* New York: Free Press.

Beckett, Katherine & Theodore Sasson. (2000). *The politics of injustice: Crime and punishment in America.* Thousand Oaks, Calif.: Pine Forge Press.

Benedict, Jeff. (1998). *Athletes and acquaintance rape.* Thousand Oaks, Calif.: Sage Publications.

Bennett, Trevor & Richard Wright. (1984). *Burglars on burglary: Prevention and the offender.* Brookfield, VT: Gower.

Benson, Michael L. (1985). Denying the guilty mind: Accounting for involvement in white collar crime. *Criminology* 23, 583–607.

————. (2001). Prosecuting corporate crime: Problems and constraints. In N. Shover & J. P. Wright (Eds.), *Crimes of privilege: Readings in white-collar crime* (pp. 281–392). New York: Oxford.

Benson, Michael L., Francis T. Cullen & William J. Maakestad. (1993). *Local prosecutors and corporate crime.* Washington, D.C.: National Institute of Justice.

Bentham, Jeremy. (1948). *An introduction to the principles of morals and legislation.* New York: Hafner Publishing.

Berdie, Ralph. (1947). Playing the dozens. *Journal of Abnormal and Social Psychology* 42, 102–121.

Bergen, R. K. (1996). Understanding women's experiences of wife rape. In

R. K. Bergen (Ed.), *Wife rape: Understanding the response of survivors and service providers.* Beverly Hills: Sage.

Berger, R. J., P. Searles, R. G. Salem & B. A. Pierce. (1986). Sexual assault in a college community. *Sociological focus* l9, 1–26.

Berk, B. (1977). Face-saving at the singles dance. *Social Problems* 24:5, 530–544.

Bernat, Jeffrey A., Karen S. Calhoun & Henry E. Adams. (1999). Sexually aggressive and nonaggressive men: Sexual arousal and judgements in response to acquaintance rape and sexual analogues. *Journal of Abnormal Psychology* 108, 662–673.

Beschner, George M. & William Brower. (1985). The scene. In G. Beschner, J. M. Walters & E. Bovelle (Eds.), *Life with heroin: Voices from the inner city* (pp. 19–29). Lexington, Mass.: Lexington Books.

Best, Joel & David F. Luckenbill. (1994). *Organizing deviance.* Englewood Cliffs, N.J.: Prentice Hall.

Beverly. (1978). Shelter resident murdered by husband. *Aegis* September/ October, 13.

Bissell, LeClair, Paul W. Haberman & Ronald L. Williams. (1989). Pharmacists recovering from alcohol and other drug addictions: An interview study. *American pharmacy* NS29(6), 19–30.

Black, Donald. (1983). Crime as social control. *American Sociological Review* 43, 34–45.

Blake, William. (1967). A divine image. In *Songs of experience.* London: Hart-Davis.

Blakely, M. K. (1984). The New Bedford verdict. *Ms.* July, 116.

Blanchard, W. H. (1959). The group process in gang rape. *Journal of Social Psychology* 49, 259–266.

Block, C. R. & R. Block. (1993). *Street gang crime in Chicago: Research in brief.* Washington, D.C.: National Institute of Justice.

Blumberg, Rae Lester. (1979). A paradigm for predicting the position of

women: Policy implications and problems. In J. Lipman-Blumen & J. Bernard (Eds.), *Sex roles and social policy* (pp. 113–125). London: Sage Studies in International Sociology.

Blumer, Herbert. (1969). *Symbolic interactionism: Perspective and method.* Englewood Cliffs, N.J.: Prentice Hall.

Bohannan, Paul (1971). *Divorce and after.* Garden City, N.Y.: Anchor.

Bohm, Robert. (1993). Social relationships that arguably should be criminal although they are not: On the politic economy of crime. In K. Tunnell (Ed.), *Political crime in contemporary America* (pp. 3–30). New York: Garland.

Boss, Maria & Barbara Crutchfied George. (2002). Challenging conventional views of white-collar crime. In D. Shicor, L. Gaines & R. Ball (Eds.), *Readings in white-collar crime* (pp. 26–47). Prospect Heights, Ill.: Waveland Press.

Bottoms, Anthony & Paul Wiles. (1992). Explanations of crime and place. In D. Evans, N. Fyfe & D. Herbert (Eds.), *Crime, policing and place: Essays in environmental criminology.* London: Routledge.

Boyum, David & Ann Marie Rocheleau. (1994). *Heroin users in New York, Chicago, and San Diego.* Washington, D.C.: Office of National Drug Control Policy.

Braithwaite, John. (1984). *Corporate crime in the pharmaceutical industry.* London: Routledge and Hagan Paul.

———. (1989). Criminological theory and organizational crime. *Justice Quarterly* 6, 333–358.

———. (1992). Poverty, power and white-collar crime: Sutherland and the paradoxes of criminological theory. In K. Schlegel & D. Weisburd (Eds.), *White collar crime reconsidered* (pp. 78–107). Boston: Northeastern University Press.

Breitman, R. (1991). *The architect of genocide.* New York: Knopf.

Briar, Scott & Irving Piliavin. (1965). Delinquency, situational inducements, and commitment to conformity. *Social Problems* 13, 35–45.

Broude, Gwen & Sarah Greene. (1976). Cross-cultural codes on twenty sexual attitudes and practices. *Ethnology* 15, 409–28.

Brown, Jodi M. & Patrick A. Langan. (1999). *Felony sentences in the United States, 1996.* Washington, D.C.: U.S. Department of Justice, Bureau of Justice Statistics.

Brown, Anthony. (1987). *The politics of airline deregulation.* Knoxville: University of Tennessee Press.

Browne, A. (1993). *Report to the Council on Scientific Affairs (I-91).* Washington, D.C.: Council on Scientific Affairs.

Brownmiller, Susan. (1975). *Against our will: Men, women, and rape.* New York: Fawcett Columbine.

Bullock, Alan. (1991). *Hitler and Stalin: Parallel lives.* New York: Vintage.

Bureau of Justice Statistics. (1987). *White collar crime.* Washington, D.C.: U.S. Department of Justice, Bureau of Justice Statistics.

———. (1994). *Carjacking: National crime victimization survey.* Washington, D.C.: U.S. Department of Justice, Bureau of Justice Statistics.

———. (1995). *Drug abuse resistance education (DARE).* Washington, D.C.: U.S. Department of Justice, Bureau of Justice Statistics.

———. (1999). *Carjacking: National crime victimization survey.* Washington, D.C.: U.S. Department of Justice, Bureau of Justice Statistics.

———. (2000). *Crime victimization in the United States, 1999 statistical tables: National crime victimization survey.* Washington, D.C.: U.S. Department of Justice, Bureau of Justice Statistics.

———. (2001a). *Federal criminal case processing, 1999.* Washington, D.C.: U.S. Department of Justice, Bureau of Justice Statistics.

———. (2001b). *Compendium of federal justice statistics, 1999.* Washington, D.C.: U.S. Department of Justice, Bureau of Justice Statistics.

———. (2001c). *Drug and crime facts.* Washington, D.C.: U.S. Department of Justice, Bureau of Justice Statistics.

———. (2001d). *Compendium of federal justice statistics, 1999.* Washington, D.C.: U.S. Department of Justice, Bureau of Justice Statistics.

———. (2002). *Compendium of federal justice statistics, 2000.* Washington, D.C.: U.S. Department of Justice, Bureau of Justice Statistics.

———. (2003). *Federal criminal case processing, 2001: With trends 1982–2001.* Washington, D.C.: U.S. Department of Justice, Bureau of Justice Statistics.

Burgess, Ann W. & Lynda Lytle Holmstrom. (1974). *Rape: Victims of crisis.* Bowie, Md: Brady.

Burt. M. R. (1980). Cultural myths and supports for rape. *Journal of Personality and Social Psychology* 38, 217–230.

Cabinet for Human Resources. (1990). *Kentucky total and nonwhite population and labor force data by county.* Frankfort: Cabinet for Human Resources.

Calavita, Kitty & Henry Pontell. (1993). Savings and loan fraud as organized crime: Towards a conceptual typology of corporate illegality. *Criminology* 31, 519–548.

Calavita, Kitty, Henry N. Pontell & Robert H. Tillman. (1997). *Big money crime: Fraud and politics in the savings and loan crisis.* Berkeley: Calif.: University of California Press.

Calhoun, Thomas C. (1992). Male street hustling: Introduction processes and stigma containment. *Sociological spectrum,* 12, 35–52.

Callahan, C. & F. Rivara. (1992). Urban high school youth and handguns. *Journal of the American Medical Association* 267, 3038–3042.

Cameron, Mary Owen. (1964). *The booster and the snitch: Department store shoplifting.* New York: Free Press.

Campbell, J. C. (1989). Women's responses to sexual abuse in intimate-relationships. *Health care for women international* 10, 335–346.

Campbell, J. C., M. Poland, J. Waller & J. Ager. (1992). Correlates of battering during pregnancy. *Research in nursing and health* 15, 219–226.

Carlen, P. (1996). *Jigsaw: A political criminology of youth homelessness.* Milton Keynes: Open University Press.

Carmody, D. (1989). Increasing rapes on campus spur colleges to fight back. *New York Times* January 1, I10.

Carpenter, Belinda J. (2000). *Re-thinking prostitution: Feminism, sex, and the self.* New York: Peter Lang.

Cary, Peter, Stephen Hedges & Jill Sieder. (1996). A start-up's struggles. *U.S. News and World Report* June 24, 50.

Caudill, H. M. (1962). *Night comes to the Cumberlands.* Boston: Little, Brown.

Caulfield, Susan & Nancy Wonders. (1993). Personal and political: Violence against women and the role of the state. In K. Tunnell (Ed.), *Political crime in contemporary America* (pp. 79–100). New York: Garland.

Centers for Disease Control and Prevention. (1995). *Vital statistics.* Atlanta: Centers for Disease Control.

Cernkovich, S. P. Giordano & M. Pugh. (1985). Chronic offenders: The missing cases in self-report in delinquency research. *Journal of Criminal Law and Criminology* 76, 705–732.

Challinger, Dennis. (1987). Car security hardware—How good is it? In *Car theft: Putting the brakes on, proceedings of seminar on car theft.* Sydney: National Roads and Motorists' Association and the Australian Institute of Criminology.

Chambers, Carl D. (1974). Narcotic addiction and crime: an empirical overview: In J. A. Inciardi & C. D. Chambers (Eds.) (pp. 125–142). *Drugs and the criminal justice system.* Beverly Hills: Sage Publications.

Chambliss, William J. & Robert Seidman. (1971). *Law, order, and power.* Reading, Mass.: Addison-Wesley.

Chambliss, William & Majorie Zatz. (1993). *Making law: The state, the law, and structural contradictions.* Bloomington: Indiana University Press.

Chancer, L. S. (1987). New Bedford, Massachusetts, March 6, 1983–March 22, 1984: The "before and after" of a group rape. *Gender and society* 1, 239–260.

Chein, Isidor, Donald L Gerard, Robert S. Lee & Eva Rosenfeld. (1964). *The road to H: Narcotics, juvenile delinquency, and social-policy.* New York: Basic Books.

Childers, Thomas. (1983). *The Nazi voter.* Chapel Hill, NC: University of North Carolina Press.

Chitwood, Dale D., James A. Inciardi, Clyde McCoy, Duane McBride, H. Virginia McCoy & Edward J. Trapido. (1991). *A community approach to AIDS intervention.* Westport, Conn.: Greenwood Press.

Clark, Colin & Trevor Pinch. (1992). The anatomy of a deception: Fraud and finesse in the mock auction sales 'con.' *Qualitative sociology* 15(2), 151–175.

Clarke, Michael. (1990). *Business crime: Its nature and control.* New York: St. Martin's Press.

Clarke, Ronald V. & Derek Cornish. (1985). Modeling offenders' decisions: a framework for research and policy. In M. Tonry & N. Morris (Eds.), *Crime and Justice: An annual review of research,* volume 6. Chicago: University of Chicago Press.

Clarke, Ronald V. & Patricia M. Harris. (1992a). Auto theft and its prevention. In M. Tonry (Ed.), *Crime and justice: An annual review of research,* volume 16 (pp. 1–54). Chicago: University of Chicago Press.

———. (1992b). A rational choice perspective on the targets of automobile theft. *Criminal Behaviour and Mental Health* 2, 25–42.

Clarke, Ronald V., Elizabeth Perkins & Danald J. Smith, Jr. (2001). Explaining repeat residential burglaries: An analysis of property stolen. In G. Farrell, & K. Pease (Eds.), *Crime prevention studies: Repeat victimization* volume 12 (pp. 119–132), Monsey, N.Y.: Criminal Justice Press.

Clinard, Marshall B. (1990). *Corporate corruption: The abuse of power.* New York: Praeger.

Clinard, Marshall B. & Peter C. Yeager. (1980). *Corporate crime: The first comprehensive account of illegal practices*

among America's top corporations.
New York: Free Press.

Clinard, Marshall B. & Richard Quinney. (1973). *Criminal behavior systems: A typology.* New York: Holt, Rinehart, and Winston.

Clinard, Marshall B., Richard Quinney & John Wildeman. (1994). *Criminal behavior systems: A typology* (3rd ed.). Cincinnati: Anderson.

Cloward, Richard A. & Lloyd E. Ohlin. (1960). *Delinquency and opportunity.* New York: Free Press.

Cohen, Albert K. (1955). *Delinquent boys.* New York: Free Press.

Cohen, Bernard. (1980). *Deviant street networks: Prostitution in New York City.* Toronto: Lexington Books.

Cohen, M. A. (1989). Corporate crime and punishment: An study of social harm and sentencing practices in federal courts, 1984–1987. *American Criminal Law Review* 26, 605–662.

Coleman, Elizabeth Ann, Grace Honeycutt, Bennie Ogden, Donald E. McMillan, Patricia O'Sullivan, Kim Light & William Wingfield. (1997). Assessing substance abuse among health care students and the efficacy of educational interventions. *Journal of Professional Nursing* 13(1), 28–37.

Coleman, James William. (1987). Toward an integrated theory of white-collar crime. *American Journal of Sociology* 93, 400–439.

———. (1998). *The criminal elite: Understanding white-collar crime* (4th ed.). New York: St. Martin's Press.

Collins, James J., Robert L. Hubbard & J. V. Rachal. (1984). *Heroin and cocaine use and illegal income.* Center for Social Research and Policy Analysis. Research Triangle Park, N.C.: Research Triangle Institute.

———. (1985). Expensive drug use and illegal income: A test of explanatory hypotheses. *Criminology* 23, 743–64.

Colquhoun, P. (1806). *A treatise on the police of the metropolis.* Montclair, N.J.: Smith, Patterson Publishing Company.

Conklin, John. (1972). *Robbery and the criminal justice system.* Philadelphia: Lippincott.

———. (1977). *Illegal but not criminal: Business crime in America.* Englewood Cliffs: N.J.: Prentice Hall.

Cook, D. (1987). Women on welfare. In P. Carlen, P. & A. Worall (Eds.), *Crime or injustice in gender, crime and justice.* Milton Keynes: The Open University Press.

———. (1989). *Rich law, poor law.* Milton Keynes: The Open University Press.

Cook, P. J. (1976). A strategic choice analysis of robbery. In W. Skogan (Ed.), *Sample surveys of the victims of crime.* Cambridge, Mass.: Ballinger.

———. (1980). Reducing injury and death rates in robbery. *Policy Analysis* 6, 21–45.

Cooney, Mark. (1998). *Warriors and peacemakers: How third parties shape violence.* New York: New York University Press.

Cordner, Gary, Jack R. Greene & Tim S. Bynum. (1983). The sooner the better: Some effects of police response time. In R. R. Bennett (Ed.), *Police at work* (pp. 145-164). Beverly Hills: Sage.

Cornish, Derek & Ronald V. Clarke. (1986). *The reasoning criminal: Rational choice perspectives on offending.* New York: Springer-Verlag.

Courier Journal. (1992). "900,000 Pot Plants Destroyed." *The Courier Journal* November 10, 7B.

Crawford, Nicole. (1992). Breaking free from addiction. *Pharmacy Student* 22(2), 10–13.

Cressey, Donald R. (1953). *Other people's money.* New York: Free Press.

———. (1972). *Criminal organization: Its elemental forms.* New York: Harper and Row.

Croall, Hazel. (2001). Who is the white-collar criminal? In N. Shover & J. P. Wright (Eds.), *Crimes of privilege: Readings in white-collar crime* (pp. 255–276). New York: Oxford.

Cromwell, Paul J., James N. Olson & D'Aunn Wester Avary. (1991). *Breaking and entering: An ethnographic analysis of burglary.* Beverly Hills, Calif.: Sage.

———. (1993). Who buys stolen property? A new look at criminal receiving. *Journal of Crime and Justice* 56(1), 75–95.

——. (1999). Decision strategies of residential burglars. In P. Cromwell (Ed.), *In their own words: Criminals on crime* (2nd ed.) (pp. 50–56). Los Angeles: Roxbury.

Cromwell, Paul J., James N. Olson, D'Aunn W. Avary & Alan Marks. (1991). How drugs affect decisions by burglars. *International Journal of Offender Therapy and Comparative Criminology* 35(4), 310–321.

Cromwell, Paul, Lee Parker & Shawna Mobley. (1999). The five-finger discount: An analysis of motivations for shoplifting. In P. Cromwell (Ed.), *In their own words: Criminals on crime* (2nd ed.) (pp. 57–70). Los Angeles: Roxbury.

Crozier, M. & E. Friedberg. (1977). *L'Acteur et le systeme.* Paris: Le Seuil.

Cullen, Francis T., William J. Maakestad & Gray Cavender. (1987). *Corporate crime under attack: The Ford Pinto case and beyond.* Cincinnati: Anderson.

Cusson, Maurice. (1983). *Why delinquency?* Toronto: University of Toronto Press.

Dabney, Dean A. (1995). Neutralization and deviance in the workplace: Theft of supplies and medicines by hospital nurses. *Deviant Behavior* 16, 313–332.

——. (1997). *A Sociological examination of illicit prescription drug use among pharmacists.* Unpublished doctoral dissertation, University of Florida, Gainesville, Fla.

——. (2001). Use of mind-altering or potentially addictive prescription drugs among pharmacists. *Journal of the American Pharmaceutical Association* 41(3), 392–400.

Dabney, Dean A., Laura Dugan & Richard C. Hollinger. (2001). *Profiling the active shoplifter.* Paper presented at the annual meetings of the Academy of Criminal Justice Sciences, Washington, D.C.

Dabney, Dean A. & Richard C. Hollinger. (1999). Illicit prescription drug use among pharmacists: Evidence of a paradox of familiarity. *Work & Occupations* 26(1), 77–106.

——. (2002). Drugged druggists: The convergence of two criminal career trajectories. *Justice Quarterly* (19)1, 201–233.

Daly, Kathleen. (1989). Gender and varieties of white-collar crime. *Criminology* 27, 769–793.

Daly, Kathleen & Meda Chesney-Lind. (1988). Feminism and criminology. *Justice Quarterly* 5, 497–538.

Davidson, Terry. (1978). *Conjugal crime.* New York: Hawthorn.

Davis, A., B. G. Gardner & M. Gardner. (1941). *Deep south.* Los Angeles: University of California, Los Angeles Press.

Davis, Peter. (1995). Interview, "If You Came This Way." All Things Considered, National Public Radio, October 12.

Davis, Nanette J. (1993). *Prostitution: An international handbook on trends, problems, and policies.* Westport, Conn.: Greenwood Press.

DeFleur, M. L. & R. Quinney. (1966). A reformulation of Sutherland's differential association theory and a strategy for empirical verification. *Journal of Research in Crime and Delinquency* 3, 1–22.

DeKeseredy, Walter S. & Martin D. Schwartz. (1994). Locating a history of some Canadian woman abuse in elementary and high school dating relationships. *Humanity and society* 18, 49–63.

De Tocqueville, Alexis. (1969). *Democracy in America.* New York: Anchor.

Della Porta, Donatella & Alberto Vannicci. (1999). *Corrupt exchanges: Actors, resources, and mechanisms of political corruption.* New York: Aldine De Gruyter.

Dembo, Richard, James A. Ciarlo & Robert W. Taylor. (1983). A model for assessing and improving drug abuse treatment resource use in inner city areas. *The International Journal of the Addictions* 18, 921–36.

Deseran, F. A., W. W. Falk & P. Jenkins. (1984). Determinants of earnings of farm families in the U.S. *Rural sociology* 49, 210–229.

Deutch, M. (1949). A theory of cooperation and competition. *Human relations* 2, 129–152.

Diana, Lewis. (1985). *The prostitute and her clients.* Springfield, Ill.: Charles C. Thomas Publishers.

Ditton, Jason. (1977). *Part-time crime: An ethnography of fiddling and pilferage.* New York: MacMillan Press.

Dobash, R. Emerson & Russell P. Dobash. (1979). *Violence against wives.* New York: Free Press.

Dobrin, Adam, Brian Wiersma, Colin Loftin & David McDowall. (1995). *Statistical handbook on violence in America.* Phoenix: Oryx Press.

Donahue, M., C. McLaughlin & L. Damm. (1994). *Accounting for carjackings: An analysis of police records in a Southeastern city.* Washington, D.C.: U.S. Department of Justice, Bureau of Justice Statistics.

Douglas, J. P. Rasmussen & C. Flanagan. (1977). *The nude beach.* Beverly Hills: Sage.

Drug Enforcement Administration. (1989). *Crack-cocaine: Overview, 1989.* Washington, D.C.: Drug Enforcement Administration.

Durose, Matthew R., David J. Levin & Patrick A. Langan. (2001). *Felony sentences in state courts, 1998.* Washington, D.C.: U.S. Department of Justice, Bureau of Justice Statistics.

Eck, John & William Spellman. (1993). Theft from vehicles in shipyard parking lots. In R. V. Clarke (Ed.), *Situational crime prevention: Successful case studies* (pp. 164–173). Guilderland, N.Y.: Harrow and Heston.

Edelhertz, Herbert. (1970). *The nature, impact, and prosecution of white collar crime.* Washington, D.C.: National Institute for Law Enforcement and Criminal Justice.

Ehrhart. J. K. & B. R. Sandler. (1985). *Campus gang rape: Party games?*

Washington, D.C.: Association of American Colleges.

Ermann, M. David & Richard J. Lundman. (1978). *Corporate and government deviance.* New York: Oxford University Press.

Ericson, Neil. (2001). *Substance abuse: The nation's number one health problem.* Washington, D.C.: Office of Juvenile Justice and Delinquency Prevention.

Fagan, J., E. Piper & M. Moore. (1986). Violent delinquents and urban youths. *Criminology* 24, 439–471.

Farr, Kathryn A. (1998). Dominance bonding through the good old boys sociability group. *Sex roles* 18, 259–277.

Farr, Kathryn A. & Don C. Gibbons. (1990). Observations on the development of crime categories. *International Journal of Offender Therapy and Comparative Criminology* 34, 223–237.

Farrell, Graham, Coretta Phillips & Ken Pease. (1995). Like taking candy: Why does repeat victimization occur? *British Journal of Criminology* 35(3), 384–399.

Farrell, R. & J. Nelson. (1976). A causal model of secondary deviance: The case of homosexuality. *Sociological Quarterly* 17, 109–120.

Farrington, David P. (1993). Motivations for conduct disorder and delinquency. *Development and psychopathology* 5, 225–241.

Faupel, Charles. (1987). Heroin use and criminal careers. *Qualitative Sociology* 10(2), 115–131.

———. (1991). *Shooting dope: Career patterns of hard-core heroin users.* Gainesville, Fla.: University of Florida Press.

Fear, R. W. G. (1974). An analysis of shoplifting. *Security gazette* July, 262–263.

Federal Bureau of Investigations. (2000). *Crime in the United States 1999: Uniform crime reports.* Washington, D.C.: U.S. Department of Justice.

———. (2002). *Crime in the United States 2001: Uniform crime reports.* Washington, D.C.: U.S. Department of Justice.

Feeney, Floyd. (1986). Robbers as decision-makers. In D. B. Cornish & R. V. Clarke (Eds.), *The reasoning criminal: Rational choice perspectives on offending.* New York: Springer-Verlag.

Feinburg, Gary. (1984). Profile of the elderly offender. In E. Newman, D. J. Newman & M. Gerwitz (Eds.), *Elderly criminals.* Cambridge, Mass.: Oelgeshlager, Gunn and Hain.

Felder, Fred & Bert Pryor. (1984). An equity theory explanation of bystanders' reactions to shoplifting. *Psychological reports* 54, 746.

Felson, Marcus. (1998). *Crime & everyday life* (2nd ed.). Thousand Oaks, Calif.: Pine Forge.

Felson, Richard, Eric Baumer & Steven Messner. (in press). Acquaintance robbery. *Justice quarterly.*

Felson, Richard & Harold J. Steadman. (1983). Situational factors in disputes leading to criminal violence. *Criminology* 21(1), 59–74.

Ferraro, Kathleen, J. (1979a). Hard love: Letting go of an abusive husband. *Frontiers* 4(2), 16–18.

———. (1979b). Physical and emotional battering: Aspects of managing hurt. *California Sociologist* 2(2), 134–149.

———. (1981a). Battered women and the shelter movement. Unpublished Ph.D. dissertation, Arizona State University.

———. (1981b). Processing battered women. *Journal of Family Issues* 2(4), 415–438.

Feucht, Thomas E. (1993). Prostitutes on crack cocaine: Addiction, utility, and marketplace economics. *Deviant Behavior* 14, 91–108.

Fields, Allen & James M. Walters. (1985). Hustling: supporting a heroin habit. In B. Hanson, G. Beschner, J. M. Walters & E. Bovelle (Eds.), *Life with heroin: Voices from the inner city.* (pp. 39–73). Lexington, Mass.: Lexington Books.

Finkelhor, D. & K. Yllo. (1985). *License to rape: Sexual abuse of wives.* New York: Holt, Rinehart & Winston.

Fisher, Bonnie, Fancis T. Cullen & Michael Turner. (2000). *The sexual victimization of college women.* Washington, D.C.: U.S. Department of Justice, Bureau of Justice Statistics.

Fisher, Gary & E. Rivlin. (1971). Psychological needs of rapists. *British Journal of Criminology* 11, 182–85.

Fisher, R. (1995). *Carjackers: A study of forcible motor vehicle thieves among new commitments.* Washington, D.C.: Bureau of Justice Statistics.

Fischl, M., T. Fayne, S. Flanagan, M. Ledan, R. Stevens, M. Fletcher, L. La Voie, & E. Trapido. (1988). Seroprevalence and Risks of HIV Infection in Spouses of Persons Infected with HIV. Paper presented at the IV International Conference on AIDS, Stockholm, Sweden.

Fitzgerald, Nora & K. Jack Riley. (2000). Drug facilitated rape: Looking for the missing pieces. *National Institute of Justice Journal* April, 8–15.

Fleisher, Mark S. (1995). *Beggars and thieves: Lives of urban street criminals.* Madison: University of Wisconsin Press.

Florida Motor Vehicle Theft Prevention Authority. (1993). *A study of motor vehicle theft in Florida.* Tallahassee, Fla.: Florida Motor Vehicle Theft Prevention Authority.

Flowers, R. Barri. (2001). *Runaway kids and teenage prostitution.* Westport, Conn.: Praeger.

Fontes, Lisa Aronso. (1995). *Sexual abuse in nine North American cultures: Treatment and prevention.* Thousand Oaks, Calif.: Sage Publications.

Fort, J. (1971). Sex and youth: Normal, hippie, radical, and Hell's Angel. *Medical aspects of human sexuality* February, 18–29.

Foucault, Michel. (1972). *The archaeology of knowledge.* London: Tavistock.

Fox, James A. & Maryln Zawitz. (2002). *Homicide trends in the United States.* Washington, D.C.: U.S. Department of Justice, Bureau of Justice Statistics.

Frank, Nancy. (1993). Maiming and killing: Occupational health crimes. *Annals of the American Academy of Political and Social Science* 525, 107–118.

Freeh, Louis. (1996). *Crime in the United States—1995.* Washington, D.C.: U.S. Department of Justice.

Freidrich, Robert J. (1980). Police use of force: Individuals, situations, and organizations. *Annals of the American Academy of Political and Social Science* 452, 82–97.

Friedrichs, David O. (1996a). *Trusted criminals: White collar crime in contemporary society.* Belmont, Calif.: Wadsworth.

———. (1996b). Governmental crime, Hitler, and white collar crime: A problematic relationship. *Caribbean Journal of Criminology and Social Psychology* 1, 44–63.

———. (1998). *State crime,* Volumes I and II. Aldershot, U.K.: Dartmouth.

———. (1998b). *Trusted criminals: White collar crime in contemporary society* (2nd ed.). Belmont, Calif.: Wadsworth.

Freud, Sigmund. (1964). Splitting of the ego in the process of defence. In J. Strachey, A. Strachey & A. Tyson (Eds.), *The standard edition of the complete psychological works of Sigmund Freud,* Volume 23 (pp. 271–278). Newark, DE: Hogarth Press.

Friday, S. & C. Wellford. (1994). *Carjacking: A descriptive analysis of carjacking in four states, preliminary report.* Washington, D.C.: U.S. Department of Justice, Bureau of Justice Statistics.

Friedman, N. L. (1974). Cookies and contests: Notes on ordinary occupational deviance and its neutralization. *Sociological Symposium Spring,* 1–9.

Frieze, I. (1983). Investigating the causes and consequences of marital rape. *Signs: Journal of Women in Culture and Society* 8, 532–553.

Frieze, I. H., & R. J. Bulman. (1983). Theoretical perspectives for understanding reactions to victimization. *Journal of Social Issues* 39, 1–17.

Fumento, Michael. (1996). Flight from reality. *The new republic* October 20, 33.

Gabor, Thomas, Micheline Baril, Maurice Cusson, Daniel Elie, Marc LeBlanc & Andre Normandeau. (1987). *Armed robbery: Cops, robbers, and victims.* Springfield, Ill.: Charles C. Thomas.

Gacquin, Deidre A. (1978) Spouse abuse: Data from the national crime survey. *Victimology* 2, 632–643.

Gage, N. (1972). *Mafia, U.S.A.* New York: Dell.

Gall, Timothy L. & Daniel M. Lucas. (1996). *Statistics on weapons & violence.* New York: Gale Research.

Gallegos, Karl V., Frederick W. Veit, Phillip O. Wilson, Thomas Porter & G. Douglas Talbott. (1988). Substance abuse among health professionals. *Maryland Medical Journal* 37(3), 191–197.

Gandossy, Robert P., Jay R. Williams, Jo Cohen & Hendrick J. Harwood. (1980). *Drugs and Crime: A Survey and Analysis of the Literature.* National Institute of Justice. Washington, D.C.: U.S. Government Printing Office.

Ganzini, Linda, Bentson McFarland & Joseph Bloom. (1990). Victims of fraud. *Bulletin of the American Academy of Psychiatry and Law* 18, 53–63.

Garcia, Dick. (1978). "Slain women lived in fear." *The times.* Erie, PA. June 14, BI.

Garrett-Gooding, J. & R. Senter. (1987). Attitudes and acts of sexual aggression on a university campus. *Sociological inquiry* 59, 348–371.

Gartell, Nanette, Judith Herman, Silvia Olarte, Michael Feldstein & Russell Localio. (1986). Psychiatrist-patient sexual contact: Results of a national survey, I: Prevalence. *American Journal of Psychiatry* 143, 1126–1131.

Geis, Gilbert. (1967). The heavy electrical equipment antitrust cases: Price-fixing techniques and rationalizations. In M. B. Clinard & R. Quinney (Eds.), *Criminal behavior systems: A typology* (pp. 140–151). New York: Holt, Reinhart and Winston.

———. (1971). Group sexual assaults. *Medical aspects of human sexuality* May 101–113.

———. (2002). White-collar crime: What is it? In D. Shicor, L. Gaines & R. Ball

(Eds.), *Readings in white-collar crime* (pp. 7–25). Prospect Heights, Ill.: Waveland Press.

Gelfand, Donna M., Donald P. Hartman, Patrice Walder & Brent Page. (1973). Who reports shoplifters? A field-experimental study. *Journal of Personality and Social Psychology* 25(2), 276–285.

Gellately, Robert. (1990). *The Gestapo and German society–Enforcing racial policy, 1933–1945.* Oxford: Clarendon Press.

Gelles, Richard J. (1974). *The violent home.* Beverly Hills: Sage.

————. (1976). Abused wives: Why do they stay? *Journal of Marriage and the Family* 38(4), 659–668.

————. (1988). Violence and pregnancy: Are pregnant women at greater risk of abuse? *Journal of Marriage and the Family* 50, 841–847.

Gianturco, D. T. & H. L. Smith. (1974). *The promiscuous teenager.* Springfield, Ill.: Thomas.

Gibbon, E. (1962). *The decline and fall of the Roman empire.* New York: Penguin.

Gibbons, Don C. (1968). *Society, crime, and criminal careers: An introduction to criminology.* Englewood Cliffs, N.J.: Prentice Hall.

————. (1975). Offender typologies— Two decades Later. *British Journal of Criminology* 15(2), 140–156.

————. (1992). *Society, crime, and criminal careers: An introduction to criminology* (6th ed.). Englewood Cliffs, N.J.: Prentice Hall.

Gibbs, John J. & Peggy L. Shelly. (1982). Life in the fast lane: A retrospective view by commercial thieves. *Journal of Research in Crime and Delinquency* 19, 299–330.

Gill, Martin & Ken Pease. (1998). Repeat robbers: Are they different? In M. Gill (Ed.), *Crime at work: Increasing the risk for offenders* Volume II, (pp. 143–155). London: Perpetuity Press,

Gillham, James R. (1992). *Preventing residential burglary: Toward more effective community programs.* New York: Springer-Verlag.

Glaser, Myron Peretz. (1996). Ten whistleblowers: What they did and how they fared. In M. D. Ermann & R. J. Lundman (Eds.), *Corporate and governmental deviance* (5th ed.). (pp. 257–279). New York: Oxford.

Glassner, Barry & Cheryl Carpenter. (1985). The feasibility of ethnographic study of adult property offenders. Unpublished report prepared for the National Institute of Justice.

Glendinning, C. & J. Millar. (1992). *Women and poverty in Britain: The 1990s.* London: Harvester Wheatsheaf.

Goff, Colin & Charles Reasons. (1978). *Corporate crime in Canada.* Scarborough, Ontario: Prentice Hall.

Goffman, Erving. (1967). *Interaction ritual: Essays on face-to-face behavior.* Garden City, N.Y.: Doubleday.

————. (1974). *Frame analysis.* Cambridge, Mass.: Harvard University Press.

Goldman, Fred. (1976). Drug markets and addict consumption behavior. In R. Shellow (Ed.), *Drug use and crime: Report of the panel on drug use and criminal behavior* (pp. 273–296). National Technical Information Service publication number PB-259 167. Springfield, Va.: U.S. Department of Commerce.

————. (1981). Drug abuse, crime and economics: the dismal limits of social choice. In J. A. Inciardi (Ed.), *The drugs-crime connection* (pp. 155–181). Beverly Hills, Calif.: Sage Publications.

Goldstein, Paul. (1981). Getting over: economic alternatives to predatory crime among street drug users. In J. A. Inciardi (Ed.), *The drugs-crime connection* (pp. 67–84). Beverly Hills: Sage Publications.

Googe, Erich. (1978). *Deviant behavior: An interactionist approach.* Englewood Cliffs, N.J.: Prentice Hall.

Gottfredson, Michael & Travis Hirschi. (1990). *A general theory of crime.* Palo Alto, Calif.: Stanford University Press.

Green, Gary S. (1990). *Occupational crime.* Chicago: Nelson-Hall.

————. (1997). *Occupational crime* (2nd ed.). Chicago: Nelson-Hall Publishers.

Greenfeld, Lawrence A. (1995). *Prison sentences and time served for violence.* Washington, D.C.: U.S. Department of Justice, Bureau of Justice Statistics.

———. (1996). *Child victimizers: Violent offenders and their victims.* Washington, D.C.: U.S. Department of Justice, Bureau of Justice Statistics.

———. (1997). *Sex offenses and offenders: An analysis of data on rape and sexual assault.* Washington, D.C.: U.S. Department of Justice, Bureau of Justice Statistics.

Greenfeld, Lawrence, Patrick A. Langan & Steven K. Smith. (1997). *Police use of force: Collection of national data.* Washington, D.C.: U.S. Department of Justice, Bureau of Justice Statistics.

Greenwood, P. W. (1980). *Rand research on criminal careers.* Santa Monica, Calif.: Rand Corporation.

Greising. David. (1996). Managing Tragedy at ValuJet. *Business World* June 3, 40.

Griffin, Roger K. (1970). Shoplifting: A statistical survey. *Security World* 7(10), 21–25.

———. (1971). Behavioral patterns in shoplifting. *Security World* 10(2), 21–25.

———. (1988). *Annual report: Shoplifting in supermarkets.* Van Nuys, Calif.: Commercial Service Systems.

Griffin, Susan. (1971). Rape: The all American crime. *Ramparts* September 10, 26–35.

Grinspoon, Lester & James B. Bakalar. (1976). *Cocaine: A drug and its social evolution.* New York: Basic Books.

Gross, Edward. (1979). Organizations as criminal actors. In P. Wilson & J. Braitwaite (Eds.) *Two faces of deviance* (pp. 199–211). Queensland, Australia: University of Queensland Press.

———. (1980). Organizational structure and organizational crime. In G. Geis & E. Stotland (Eds.), *White collar crime: Theories and research* (pp. 211–230). Beverly Hills: Sage.

Gross, H. (1977). Micro and macro level implications for a sociology of virtue—Case of draft protesters to Vietnam War. *Sociological Quarterly* 18(3), 319–339.

Groth, A. Nicholas. (1979). *Men who rape.* New York: Plenum.

Groves, W. Byron & Michael J. Lynch. (1990). Reconciling structural and subjective approaches to the study of crime. *Journal of Research in Crime and Delinquency* 27, 348–375.

Habermas, Jürgen. (1987). *Philosophical discourses of modernity.* Cambridge: Polity Press.

Hackett, G., R. Sandza, F. Gibney & R. Gareiss. (1988). Kids: Deadly force. *Newsweek* January 11, 18–19.

Hafely, Sandra Riggs & Richard Tewksbury. (1995). The rural Kentucky marijuana industry: Organization and community involvement. *Deviant Behavior* 16, 22–33.

Hagan, John & Bill McCarthy. (1992). Streetlife and delinquency. *British Journal of Sociology* 43, 533–561.

———. (1997). *Mean streets: Youth crime and homelessness.* Cambridge: Cambridge University Press.

Hagedorn, John. (1988). *People and folks.* Chicago: Lakeview Press.

———. (1991). Back in the field again: Gang research in the nineties. In R. Huffy (Ed.), *Gangs in America* (pp. 240–259). Newbury Park, Calif.: Sage.

Hall, E. K., J. A. Howard & S. L. Boezio. (1986). Tolerance of rape: A sexist or antisocial attitude? *Psychology of Women Quarterly* 10, 110–118.

Hall, J. (1968). Theft, law and society—1968. *American Bar Association Journal* 54, 960–967.

Halperin, R. (1990). *The livelihood of kin: making ends meet the Kentucky way.* Austin: University of Texas Free Press.

Hamm, Mark. (1997). *Apocalypse in Oklahoma: Waco and Ruby Ridge revenged.* Boston: Northeastern University Press.

Hammer, Emanuel & Irving Jacks. (1955). A study of Rorschack flexor and extensor human movements. *Journal of Clinical Psychology* 11, 63–67.

Hanagan, T. J. & K. M. Jamieson. (1988). *Sourcebook of criminal justice* statistics–1987. Washington, D.C.: U.S. Government Printing Office.

Hanson, Bill, George Beschner, James M. Walters & Elliot Bovelle. (1985). *Life with heroin: Voices from the inner city.* Lexington, Mass.: Lexington Books.

Harlow, Caroline Wolf. (1988). *Motor vehicle theft.* Washington, D.C.: U.S. Department of Justice, Bureau of Justice Statistics.

Harries, Keith D. (1997). *Serious violence: Patterns of homicide and assault in America* (2nd ed.). Springfield, Ill.: Charles C. Thomas Publishers.

Harrison, Paige M. & Allen J. Beck. (2003). *Prisoners in 2002.* Washington, D.C.: U.S. Department of Justice, Bureau of Justice Statistics.

Hart, Timothy C. & Brian A. Reaves. (1999). *Felony defendants in large urban counties, 1996.* Washington, D.C.: U.S. Department of Justice, Bureau of Justice Statistics.

Hayes, Read. (1993). *Shoplifting control.* Orlando: Prevention Press.

Hawkins, J. (1991). Rowers on the river Styx. *Harvard magazine* April, 43–52.

Hayano, D. (1977). The professional poker player: Career identification and the problem of respectability. *Social Problems* 24, 556–564.

Hazelhurst, Kayleen. (1991). Passion and policy: Aboriginal deaths in custody in Australia 1980–1989. In G. Barak (Ed.), *Crimes by the capitalist state* (pp. 21–48). Albany: State University of New York Press.

Heckathorn, Douglas D. (1997). Respondent-driven sampling: A new approach to the study of hidden populations. *Social Problems* 44, 174–199.

Henriquez, Mark A. (1999). IACP national database project on police use of force. In *Use of force by police: Overview of national and local data* (pp. 19–24). Washington, D.C.: National Institute of Justice.

Hepburn, John. (1984). Occasional property crime. In R. Meier (Ed.), *Major forms of crime* (pp. 73–94). Newbury Park, Calif.: Sage.

Henry, Stuart. (1978). *The hidden economy: The context and control of borderline crime.* London: M. Robertson.

Henslin, James M. (1972). Studying deviance in four settings: Research experiences with cabbies, suicides, drug users, and abortionees. In J. Douglas (Ed.), *Research on deviance.* New York: Random House.

Herbst, T. H. & R. J. Hanson. (1971). Non-farm work as a substitute for farm enterprises. *American Society of Farm Managers and Rural Appraisers* 35, 63–68.

Herman, Dianne. (1984). The rape culture. In J. Freeman (Ed.), *Women: A feminist perspective* (pp. 20–39). Palo Alto, Calif.: Maflower.

Herman, J. (1981). *Father-daughter incest.* Cambridge, Mass.: Harvard University Press.

Herzog, K. (1989). Rape trial over, sex debate isn't. *Frankfort State Journal* May 14, AI, A12.

Heyl, Barbara Sherman. (1979). *The madam as entrepreneur: Career management in house prostitution.* New Brunswick, N.J.: Transaction Books.

Higgins, Paul C. & Gary L. Albrecht. (1981). Cars and kids: A self-report study of juvenile auto theft and traffic violations. *Social science research* 66(1), 29–41.

Hilberg, Raul. (1985). *The destruction of the European Jews.* New York: Holmes & Meier.

Hilberman, Elaine. (1980). Overview: The "wife-beater's wife" reconsidered. *American Journal of Psychiatry* 137(11), 1336–1347.

Hilts, Philip J. (1996). *Smokescreen: The truth behind the tobacco industry cover up.* Reading, Mass.: Addison-Wesley.

Hindelang, Michael J., Travis Hirschi & Joseph Weis. (1981). *Measuring delinquency.* Beverly Hills, Calif.: Sage.

Hirschi, Travis (1969). *Causes of delinquency.* Berkeley, Calif.: University of California Press.

Hirschi, Travis & Michael Gottfredson. (1987). Causes of white-collar crime. *Criminology* 25, 949–971.

Hobbs, Dick. (1995). *Bad business: Professional crime in modern Britain.* New York: Oxford University Press.

Hodgson, James F. (1997). *Games pimps play: Pimps, players and wives-in-law.* Toronto: Canadian Scholars' Press.

Hoebel, E. Adamson. (1954). *The law of primitive man.* Boston: Harvard University Press.

Hoffman, R. (1986). Rape and the college athlete: Part one. *Philadelphia Daily News* March 17, 104.

Höhne, H. (1989). *The order of the death's head.* New York: Ballantine.

Hoigard, Cecilie & Liv Finstad. (1986). *Backstreets: Prostitution, money and love.* University Park, PA: Penn State University Press.

Hollinger, Richard C. (1986). Acts against the workplace: Social bonding and employee deviance. *Deviant behavior* 7, 53–75.

———. (1991). Neutralizing in the workplace: An empirical analysis of property theft and production deviance. *Deviant behavior* 12, 169–202.

Hollinger, Richard C. & John Clark. (1983). *Theft by employees.* Lexington, Mass.: Lexington Books.

Hollinger, Richard C. & Jason Davis. (2000). *2000 National retail security survey, final report.* Gainesville, Fla.: University of Florida.

Hollinger, Richard C., Karen B. Slora & William Terris. (1992). Deviance in the fast food restaurant: Correlates of employee theft, altruism, and counterproductivity. *Deviant behavior* 13, 155–184.

Holtz, J. (1975). The professional duplicate bridge player: Conflict management in a free, legal, quasi-deviant occupation. *Urban life* 4(2), 131–160.

Home Office. (2000). *Setting the boundaries.* London: HMSO.

Hope, Tim. (1987). Residential aspects of autocrime. In *Research bulletin No. 23* (pp. 28–33). London: Home Office Research and Planning Unit.

Horning, Donald. (1970). Blue-collar theft: Conceptions of property, attitudes, toward pilfering, and work group norms in a modern industrial plant. In E. O. Smigel & H. L. Ross (Eds.), *Crimes against bureaucracy* (pp. 46–64). New York: Van Nostrand Reinhold Press.

Hosenball, Mark & Anne Underwood. (1996). Seeing no evil: Did industry regulators take too long to scrutinize Atlanta's ValuJet? *Newsweek* May 27:46.

Hubbard, Philip. (1999). *Sex and the city: Geographies of prostitution in the urban West.* Brookfield, Vt.: Ashgate.

Hunt, M. (1974). *Sexual behavior in the 1970s.* New York: Dell.

Inciardi, James A. (1974). The villification of euphoria: some perspectives on an elusive issue. *Addictive diseases* 1, 241–267.

———. (1975). *Careers in Crime.* Chicago: Rand McNally College Publishing Company.

———. (1979). Heroin use and street crime. *Crime and delinquency* 25, 335–346.

———. (1993). Kingrats, chicken heads, slow necks, freaks, and blood suckers: A glimpse at the Miami sex-for-crack market. In M. S. Ratner (Ed.), *Crack pipe as pimp: An ethnographic investigation of sex-for-crack exchanges* (pp. 37–65). New York: Lexington Books.

Inciardi, James A., Ruth Horowitz & Anne E. Pottieger. (1993). *Street kids, street drugs, street crime: An examination of drug use and serious delinquency in Miami.* Belmont, Calif.: Wadsworth.

Inciardi, James A., Duane C. McBride & Hillary Suratt. (1998). The heroin street addict: Profiling a national population. In J. A. Inciardi & L. D. Harrison (Eds.), *Heroin in the age of crack-cocaine* (pp. 31–51). Thousand Oaks, Calif.: Sage.

Inciardi, James A., Dorthy Lockwood & Anne E. Pottieger. (1993). *Women and crack cocaine.* New York: Macmillan.

Inlander, Charles B., Lowell S. Levin & Ed Weiner. (1988). *Medicine on trial: The appalling story of medical ineptitude and the arrogance that overlooks it.* New York: Pantheon Books.

International Police Organization. (1999). *International crime statistics, 1998.* Paris: International Police Organization.

Jacobs, Bruce A. (1999). *Dealing crack: The social world of streetcorner selling.* Boston: Northeastern University Press.

Jacobs, Bruce A. & Richard Wright. (1999). Stick-up, street culture, and offender motivation. *Criminology* 37(1), 149–173.

Jacobs, Bruce A., Volkan Topalli & Richard Wright. (2000). Managing retaliation: The case of drug robbery. *Criminology* 38, 171–198.

Jacoby, Joseph E., Neil A. Weiner, Terence P. Thornberry & Marvin E. Wolfgang. (1973). Drug use in a birth cohort. In *National commission on marijuana and drug abuse, drug use in America: Problem in perspective,* Appendix I (pp. 300–343). Washington, D.C.: U.S. Government Printing Office.

Janis, I. L. (1982). *Groupthink* (2nd ed.). Boston: Houghton-Mifflin.

Janness, Valerie. (1993). *Making it work: The prostitutes' rights movement in perspective.* New York: Aldine de Gruyter.

Jeffrey, C. Ray. (1977). *Crime prevention through environmental design* (2nd ed.). Beverly Hills: Sage.

Jesilow, Paul, Henry N. Pontell & Gilbert Geis. (1985). Medical criminals: Physicians and white-collar offenses. *Justice Quarterly* 2, 149–165.

Joannou, M. (1995). She who would be politically free herself must strike the blow: Suffragette Autobiography and Suffragette Militancy. In J. Swindells (Ed.), *The uses of autobiography.* London: Taylor and Francis.

Joey. (1974). *Killer: Autobiography of a mafia hit man.* New York: Pocket Books.

Johnson, Allan Griswold. (1980). On the prevalence of rape in the United States. *Signs* 6, 136–146

Johnson, Bruce D., Paul J. Goldstein, Edward Preble, James Schmeidler, Douglas S. Lipton, Barry Spunt & Thomas Miller. (1985). *Taking care of business: The economics of crime by heroin abusers.* Lexington, MA: Lexington Books.

Johnson, Bruce D. & Eloise Dunlap. (1997). Crack selling in New York City. Paper presented at the 49th Annual Meeting of the American Society of Criminology, San Diego.

Johnson, J. A. & J. L. Bootman. (1995). Drug-related morbidity and mortality. *Archives of Internal Medicine* 155, 1949–1956.

Johnson, John M. (1981). Program enterprise and official cooptation of the women's shelter movement. *American behavioral scientist* 24(6), 827–841.

Johnson, Lloyd D., Jerald G. Bachman & Patrick M. O'Malley. (1995). *Monitoring the future 1995.* Ann Arbor, Mich.: Institute for Social Research, University of Michigan.

———. (1984–1995). *Monitoring the future.* Ann Arbor, Mich.: Institute for Social Research, University of Michigan. Data adapted by and cite from Bureau of Justice Statistics (1997). *Sourcebook of criminal justice statistics–1996.* Washington, D.C.: United States Department of Justice.

Jones, Del. (1997). "48% of workers admit to unethical or illegal acts." *USA Today* 3 April, 1–4.

Kalish, Carol B. (1988). *International crime rates.* Washington, D.C.: U.S. Department of Justice, Bureau of Justice Statistics.

Kanin, Eugene. (1957). Male aggression in dating-courtship relations. *American Journal of Sociology* 63, 191–204.

———. (1961). Reference groups and sex conduct norm violation. *Sociological Quarterly* 8, 495–504.

———. (1965). Male sex aggression and three psychiatric hypotheses. *Journal of Sex Research* 1, 221–229.

———. (1969). Selected dyadic aspects of male sex aggression. *Journal of Sex Research* 5, 12–28.

Kaplan, H. Roy. (1978). *Lottery winners: How they won and how winning changed their lives.* New York: Harper & Row.

Kappeler, Victor E., Richard D. Sluder & Geoffrey P. Alpert. (1998). *Forces of deviance: Understanding the dark side of policing* (2nd ed.). Prospect Heights, Ill.: Waveland Press.

Karmen, Andrew. (1980). Auto theft: Beyond victim blaming. *Victimology: An International Journal* 5, 161–174.

Kasinsky, Renee. (1975). Rape: A normal act? *Canadian forum* September, 18–22.

Kaslow, R. A. & D. P. Francis. (1989). *The epidemiology of AIDS: Expression, occurrence, and control of human immuno-deficiency virus type I infection.* New York: Oxford University Press.

Katz, Jack. (1988). *Seductions of crime: The sensual attractions of doing evil.* New York: Basic Books.

Kauzlarich, David. (1995). A criminology of the nuclear state. *Humanity and society* 19, 37–57.

Kauzlarich, David & Ronald C. Kramer. (1993). State-corporate crime in the U.S. nuclear weapons production complex. *The Journal of Human Justice* 5, 4–28.

———. (1998). *Crimes of the American nuclear state.* Boston: Northeastern University Press.

Kelly, L. (1988). *Surviving sexual violence.* Minneapolis: University of Minnesota Press.

Kelman, Herbert & Lee Hamilton. (1989). *Crimes of obedience: Toward a social psychology of authority and responsibility.* New Haven: Yale University Press

Kennedy, Leslie W. & David D. Forde. (1999). *When push comes to shove: A routine conflict approach to violence.* Albany, N.Y.: State University Press of New York.

Kentucky Agricultural Statistics Service. (1993). *1992–1993 Kentucky agricultural statistics.* Louisville: Kentucky Department of Agriculture.

Kinnell, H. (1993). *Prostitutes' exposure to rape: Implications for HIV prevention and for legal reform.* Paper presented to the seventh Social Aspects of AIDS Conference. London, England.

Kirkpatrick, Clifford & Eugene Kanin. (1957). Male sex aggression on a university campus. *American Sociological Review* 22, 52–58.

Kleck, Gary & Karen McElrath. (1991). The effects of weaponry on human violence. *Social forces* 69(3), 669–692.

Kleck, Gary & Susan Sayles. (1990). Rape and resistance. *Social Problems* 37(2), 149–162.

Kleemans, Edward R. (2001). Repeat burglary victimization: Results of empirical research in the Netherlands. In G. Farrell & K. Pease (Eds.), *Crime prevention studies: Repeat victimization* Volume 12, (pp. 53–68). Monsey, N.Y.: Criminal Justice Press.

Klein, Malcolm. (1971). *Street gangs and street workers.* Englewood Cliffs, N.J.: Prentice Hall.

Klein, Malcolm & Cheryl Maxson. (1989). Street gang violence. In N. Weiner (Ed.), *Violent crimes, violent criminals* (pp. 198–234). Beverly Hills: Sage.

Klemke, Lloyd W. (1982). Exploring juvenile shoplifting. *Sociology and social research* 67, 59–75.

———. (1992). *The sociology of shoplifting: Boosters and snitches today.* Westport, Conn.: Praeger.

Klockars, Carl B. (1974). *The professional fence.* New York: Free Press.

Knapp Commission Report on Police Corruption. (1973). New York: George Braziller.

Koss, Mary P. (1989), Hidden rape: Sexual aggression and victimization in a national sample of students in higher education. In M. A. Pirog-Good & J. E. Stets (Eds.), *Violence in dating relationships: Emerging social issues* (pp. 145–168). New York: Praeger.

Koss, Mary P. & Kenneth F. Leonard. (1984). Sexually aggressive men: Empirical findings and theoretical implications. In N. Malamuth & E. Donnerstein (Eds.), *Pornography and sexual aggression* (pp. 213–232). New York: Academic Press.

Kramer, Ronald C. (1992). The space shuttle Challenger explosion: A case study of state-corporate crime. In K. Schlegel & D. Weisburd (Eds.), *White collar crime reconsidered* (pp. 214–243). Boston: Northeastern University Press.

Kramer, Ronald & Raymond Michalowski. (1990). State-corporate crime. Paper presented at the Annual Meeting of the American Society of Criminology, Baltimore.

———. (1991). State-corporate crime: Case studies in organizational deviance. Unpublished manuscript.

Krausnick, H. (1989). *Hitler's einasatzgruppen: Die truppe des weltanschauungskrieges, 1938–1942.* Frankfurt: Fischer Taschenbuch.

Kriegler, Kathleen A., Jeffrey N. Baldwin & David M. Scott. (1994). A survey of alcohol and other drug use behaviors and risk factors in health profession students. *Journal of the American Colleges of Health* 42, 259–265.

Kulka, O. D. (1975). Public opinion in national socialist Germany and the Jewish question. *Zion* XL, 186–290.

LaFollette, Marcel C. (1992). *Stealing into print: Fraud, plagiarism, and misconduct in scientific publishing.* Berkeley, Calif.: University of California Press.

LaFree, Gary. (1982). Male power and female victimization: Towards a theory of interracial rape. *American Journal of Sociology* 88, 311–328.

Langan, Patrick A. & David J. Levin. (2002). *Recidivism of prisoners released in 1994.* Washington, D.C.: Bureau of Justice Statistics.

Langbein, H. (1972). *Menschen in Auschwitz.* Frankfurt: Europaische Verlagsanstalt.

Langenhove, L. & R. Harre. (1993). Positioning and autobiography: Telling your life. In J. Nussbaum & N. Couplan (Eds.), *Discourse and life span identity.* London: Sage.

Langer, J. (1976). Drug entrepreneurs and the dealing culture. *Australian and New Zealand Journal of Sociology* 12(2), 82–90.

Lanza-Kaduce, Lonn. (1980). Deviance among professionals: The case of unnecessary surgery. *Deviant Behavior* 1, 333–359.

Larson, D. K. (1976). Impact of off-farm income in farm family income levels. *Agricultural finance review* 36, 7–11.

Lee, Matthew T. & M. David Ermann. (1999). "Pinto madness" as a flawed landmark narrative: An organizational and network analysis. *Social Problems* 44, 30–47.

Lemert, Edwin M. (1953). An isolation and closure theory of naive check forgery. *Journal of Criminal Law and Criminology* 44, 296–307.

———. (1967). The behavior of the systematic check forger. *Social Problems* 14, 141–149.

LeMoncheck, Linda. (1999). When good sex turns bad: Rethinking a continuum model of sexual violence against women. In K. Burgess-Jackson (Ed.), *A most detestable crime: New philosophical essays on rape* (pp. 159–181). New York: Oxford University Press.

Lesieur, Henry R. & Michael Welch. (1995). Vice crimes: Individual choices and social controls. In J. Shelley (Ed.), *Criminology: A contemporary handbook* (2nd ed.) (pp. 201–229). Belmont, Calif.: Wadsworth.

Lester, D. & G. Lester. (1975). *Crime of passion: Murder and the murderer.* Chicago: Nelson Hall.

Letkeman, P. (1973). Overt crimes (victim confrontation): The technical dimensions of robbery, with special attention to bank robbery. In P. Letkeman (Ed.), *Crime as work* (pp. 90–116). Englewood Cliffs, N.J.: Prentice Hall.

Lever, Janet & Deanne Dolnick. (2000). Clients and call girls: Seeking sex and intimacy. In R. Weitzer (Ed.), *Sex for sale: Prostitution, pornography, and the sex industry* (pp. 85–100). New York: Routledge.

Leveson, Irving & Jeffrey H. Weiss. (1976). *Analysis of urban health problems.* New York: Spectrum.

Levi, Ken. (1975). *Icemen.* Ann Arbor, Mich.: University Microfilms.

Levin, David J., Patrick A. Langan & Jodi Brown. (1999). *State court sentencing of convicted felons, 1996.* Washington, D.C.: U.S. Department of Justice, Bureau of Justice Statistics.

Levi, Michael. (1998). The craft of the long-firm fraudster: Criminal skills and commercial responses. In M. Gill (Ed.), *Crime at work: Increasing the risk for offenders* (pp. 155–167). London: Perpetuity Press.

Levinson, Marc, Anne Underwood & Bill Turque. (1996). A new day at the FAA? *Newsweek* July 1, 46.

Liddy, D. T. (1987). Car theft—A strategy needed. Paper presented at the annual meeting of the Australian Automobile Association. Canberra.

Liebow, Eliot. (1967). *Tally's corner.* Boston: Little, Brown.

Light, Roy, Claire Nee & Helen Ingham. (1993). *Car theft: The offender's perspective.* Home Office Research Study No. 130. London: Home Office Research and Planning Unit.

Llewellyn, Karl N. & E. Adamson Hoebel. (1941). *The Cheyenne way: Conflict and case law in primitive jurispudence.* Norman: University of Oklahoma Press.

Lo, Lucia. (1994). Exploring teenage shoplifting behavior. *Environment and behavior* 26(5), 613–639.

Lofland, John. (1969). *Deviance and identity.* Englewood Cliffs, N.J.: Prentice-Hall.

Loftin, Colin. (1985). Assaultive violence as a contagious social process. *Bulletin of the New York Academy of Medicine* 62, 550–555.

———. (1984). Assaultive violence as contagious process. *Bulletin of the New York Academy of Medicine* 62, 550–555.

Loftquist, William S. (1993). Organizational probation and the US sentencing commission. *Annals of the American Academy of Political and Social Science* 525, 157–169.

Lombroso, Cesare. (1912). *Crime: Its causes and remedies.* Montclair, N.J.: Patterson Smith.

Luckenbill, David F. (1986). Deviant career mobility: The case of male prostitutes. *Social Problems* 33(4), 283–296.

———. (1981). Generating compliance: The case of robbery. *Urban Life* 10(1), 25–46.

Lukoff, Irving & Debra Quatrone. (1973). Heroin use and crime in a methadone maintenance program: A two year follow-up of the Addiction and Research Corporation Program: A preliminary report. In G. J. Hayim, I. Lukoff & D. Quatrone (Eds.), *Heroin use in a methadone maintenance program* (pp. 63–112). Washington, D.C.: U.S. Department of Justice, National Institute of Law Enforcement and Criminal Justice.

Lyman, Sanford M. & Marvin B. Scott. (1970). *A Sociology of the absurd.* New York: Meredith.

Lynne Duke. (1987). "The Graveyard." *Miami Herald Tropic* April 5, 12–28.

Maas, P. (1968). *The Valachi papers.* New York: G. P. Putnam.

Mack. J. (1970). Full time miscreants, delinquent neighborhoods and criminal networks. *British Journal of Sociology* 15, 38–53

Mad, J. (1970). The able criminal. Report to the current research seminar of the sixth World Criminological Congress. Madrid, Spain.

Maguire, Kathleen & Ann L. Pastore. (2000). *Sourcebook of criminal justice statistics 1999.* Washington, D.C.: U.S. Department of Justice, Bureau of Justice Statistics.

———. (2001). *Sourcebook of criminal justice statistics 2000.* Washington, D.C.: U.S. Department of Justice, Bureau of Justice Statistics.

Maguire, Mike & Trevor Bennet. (1982). *Burglary in a dwelling.* London: Heinemann.

Maher, Lisa. (1997). *Sexed work: Gender, race, and resistance in a Brooklyn drug market.* New York: Oxford.

Malamuth, Neil, Scott Haber & Seymour Feshback. (1980). Testing hypotheses regarding rape: Exposure to sexual violence, sex difference, and the "normality" of rapists. *Journal of Research in Personality* 14, 121–137.

Malamuth, Neil, Maggie Heim, and Seymour Feshback. (1980). Sexual responsiveness of college students to rape depictions: Inhibitory and disinhibitory effects. *Social Psychology* 38, 399–408.

Mancini, Alan M. & Rejendra Jain. (1987). Commuter parking lots—vandalism and deterrence. *Transportation Quarterly* 16, 539–553.

Manson, Donald A. (1986). *Tracking offenders: White-collar crime.* Washington, D.C.: Bureau of Justice Statistics.

Mars, Gerald. (1982). *Cheats at work: An anthropology of workplace crime.* London: Allen and Unwin.

Martin, Del. (1976). *Battered wives.* San Francisco: Glide.

Mativat, Francois & Pierre Tremblay. (1997). Counterfeiting credit cards: Displacement effects, suitable offenders and crime wave patterns. *British Journal of Criminology* 37(2), 165–183.

Matthews, R. (1986). Beyond Wolfenden. In J. Young & R. Matthews (Eds.), *Confronting crime.* London: Sage.

Matza, David. (1969). *Becoming deviant.* Englewood Cliffs. N.J.: Prentice Hall.

Mawby, R. I. (2001). The impact of repeat victimisation on burglary victims in east and west Europe. In G. Farrell & K. Pease (Eds.), *Crime prevention studies: Repeat victimization* Volume 12, (pp. 69–82), Monsey, N.Y.: Criminal Justice Press.

Maxson, Cheryl. (1997). *Gang members on the move.* Washington, D.C.: Office for Juvenile Justice and Delinquency Prevention.

Maxson, Cheryl, Malcolm Klein & M. Gordon. (1985). Differences between gang and nongang homicides. *Criminology* 21, 209–222.

Maxson, Cheryl & Malcolm Klein. (1990). Street gang violence: Twice as great or half as great? In R. Huff (Ed.), *Gangs in America* (pp. 71–102). Newbury Park, Calif.: Sage.

Maxwell, S. R. & C. D. Maxwell. (2000). Examining the "criminal careers" of prostitutes within the nexus of drug use, drug selling, and other illicit activities. *Criminology* 38, 787–809.

Mayer, Arno. (1988). *Why did the heavens not cry.* New York: Pantheon.

Mayhew, Patricia. (1990). Opportunity and vehicle crime. In D. Gottfredson & R. V. Clarke (Eds.), *Policy and theory in crime and justice: Contributions in honor of Leslie T. Wilkins* (pp. 28–50). Aldershot, UK: Gower.

Mayhew, Patricia, Ronald V. Clarke, Andrew Sturman & Mike Hough. (1976). *Crime as opportunity.* Home Office Research Study No. 34. London, H. M. Stationery Office.

McAuliffe, William E. (1984). Nontherapeutic opiate addiction in health professionals: A new form of impairment. *American Journal of Drug and Alcohol Abuse* 10(1), 1–22.

McAuliffe, William E., Susan L. Santangelo, Judy Gingras, Mary Rohman, Arthur Sobol & Elizabeth Magnuson. (1987). Use and abuse of controlled substances by pharmacists and pharmacy students. *American Journal of Hospital Pharmacy* 44(2), 311–317.

McCaghy, Charles H., Peggy C. Giordano & Trudy Knicely Henson. (1977). Auto theft: Offender and offense characteristics. *Criminology* 15(3), 367–385.

McCall, George. (1978). *Observing the law.* New York: Free Press.

McCarthy, Bill. (1995). Not just for the thrill of it: An instrumentalist elaboration of Katz's explanation of sneaky thrill property crimes. *Criminology* 33, 519–538.

McClusky, Kayrn & Sarah Wardle. (1999). The social structure of robbery. In D. Canter & L. Alison (Eds.), *The social psychology of crime: Groups, teams and networks* (pp. 247–285). Burlington, VT: Ashgate.

McCormick, Albert E. (1977). Rule enforcement and moral indignation: Some observations on the effects of criminal antitrust convictions upon societal reaction processes. *Social Problems* 25, 30–39.

McGlinchey, Anne. (1981). Woman battering and the church's response. In A. R. Roberts (Ed.), *Sheltering battered women* (pp. 133–140). New York: Springer.

McGlothlin, William H., M. Douglas Anglin & Bruce D. Wilson. (1978). Narcotic addiction and crime. *Criminology* 16, 293–315.

McKegany, Neil & Marina Barnard. (1996). *Sex work on the streets: Prostitutes and their clients.* Philadelphia: Open University Press.

McLeod, E. (1982). *Women working: Prostitution now.* London: Croom Helm.

McNamara, Robert P. (1994). *The Times Square hustler: Male prostitution in New York City.* Westport, Conn.: Praeger.

McPhail, C. (1991). *The myth of the madding crowd.* New York: Aldine.

———. (1993). The dark side of purpose: Individual and collective violence in riots. Presidential address, Midwest Sociological Society, Chicago.

Medea, A. & K. Thompson. (1974). *Against rape.* New York: Farrar, Straus, & Giroux.

Meinecke, Friedrich. (1950). *The German catastrophe.* Cambridge, Mass.: Harvard University Press.

Mendelson, B. (1956). The victimology. In S. Schafer (Ed.), *The victim and his criminal: A study of functional responsibility.* New York: Random House.

Merton, Robert K. (1938). Social structure and anomie. *American Sociological Review* 3, 672–682.

———. (1957). *Social theory and social structure.* Glencoe, Ill.: Free Press.

Meyer, Thomas J. (1984). "Date rape:" A serious problem that few talk about. *Chronicle of Higher Education* December 5, 10.

Miami Herald (1987). April 9, 1D, 2D, April 22, 12–28.

Michalowski, Raymond. (1985). *Order, law, and crime.* New York: Random House.

Miethe, Terrance. (1999). *Whistleblowing at work: Tough choices in exposing fraud, waste, and abuse on the job.* Boulder, Colo.: Westview.

Miethe, Terrance D. & Robert McCorkle. (1998). *Crime profiles: The anatomy of dangerous persons, places and situations,* Los Angeles: Roxbury.

———. (2001). *Crime profiles: The anatomy of dangerous persons, places and situations* (2nd ed.). Los Angeles: Roxbury.

Millar, J. (1997). Gender. In A. Walker & C. Walker (Eds.), *Britain divided: The growth of social exclusion in the 1980s and 1990s.* London: Children's Poverty Action Group.

Miller, Eleanor M., Kim Romenesko & Lisa Wondolkowski. (1993). The United States. In N. J. Davis (Ed.), *Prostitution: An international handbook on trends, problems, and policies* (pp. 300–326). Westport, Conn.: Greenwood Press.

Miller, Christina Jarvis & Benjamin F. Banahan III. (1990). A comparison of alcohol and illicit drug use between pharmacy students and the general college population. *American Journal of Pharmaceutical Education* 54(1), 27–30.

Miller, Jody. (1993). Your life is on the line every time you're on the streets. *Humanity & society* 17, 422–442.

———. (1995). Gender and power on the streets: Street prostitution in the era of crack cocaine. *Journal of Contemporary Ethnography* 23(4), 427–452.

———. (1998). Up it up: Gender and the accomplishment of street robbery. *Criminology* 36(1), 37–65.

Miller, Walter B. (1958). Lower class culture as a generating milieu of gang delinquency. *Journal of Social Issues* 14, 5–19.

Mills, C. S. & B. J. Granoff. (1992). Date and acquaintance rape among a sample of college students. *Social work* 37, 504–509.

Mills, T. (1985). The assault on the self: Stages of coping with battered husbands. *Qualitative sociology* 8, 2.

Mokhiber, Russell. (1998). *Corporate crime and violence: Big business power and the abuse of the public trust.* San Francisco: Sierra Club Books.

Molière, Jean Baptiste Poquelin. (1956). *Le malade imaginaire in Oeuvres complètes.* Paris: Gallimard.

Mommsen, Hans. (1990). Was haben die deutschen vom völkermord an den juden gewusst? In W. H. Pehle (Ed.), *Der judenpogrom 1938*. Frankfurt: Fischer.

Montell, W. L. (1986). *Killings: Folk justice in the upper South*. Lexington: University of Kentucky Press.

Monto, Martin A. (2000). Why men seek out prostitutes. In R. Weitzer (Ed.), *Sex for sale: Prostitution, pornography, and the sex industry* (pp. 67–84). New York: Routledge.

Moore, J. (1978). *Homeboys*. Philadelphia: Temple University Press.

Moore, Richard. (1983). College shoplifters: Rebuttal of Beck and McIntyre. *Psychological Reports* 53, 1111–1116.

———. (1984). Shoplifting in middle America: Patterns and motivational correlates. *International Journal of Offender Therapy and Comparative Criminology* 28(1), 53–64.

Moran, Alvin. (1971). Criminal homicide: External restraint and subculture of violence. *Criminology* 8, 357–374.

Morgan, Frank. (2001). Repeat burglary in a Perth suburb: Indicator of short-term or long-term risk? In G. Farrell & K. Pease (Eds.), *Crime prevention studies: Repeat victimization* Volume 12, (pp. 83–118). Monsey, N.Y.: Criminal Justice Press.

Morgan, Kathleen O. & Scott Morgan. (2000). *City crime rankings: Crime in metropolitan America* (7th ed.). Lawrence, Kan.: Morgan Quito Press.

Morris, Richard W. (1985). Not the cause, nor the cure: Self-image and control among inner city black male heroin users. In B. Hanson, G. Beschner, J. M. Walters & E. Bovelle (Eds.), *Life with heroin: Voices from the inner city* (pp. 135–153). Lexington, Mass.: Lexington Books.

Morgan, Robin. (1980). Theory and practice: Pornography and rape. In L. Lederer (Ed.), *Take back the night: Women on pornography* (pp. 134–140). New York: William Morrow.

Mumola, Christopher J. (1999). *Substance abuse and treatment, state and federal prisoners, 1997*. Washington, D.C.: U.S.

Department of Justice, Bureau of Justice Statistics.

Murphy, R. F. (1959). Social structure and sex antagonism. *Southwestern Journal of Anthropology* 15, 89–98.

Murphy, Sheilga, Dan Waldorf & Craig Reinarman. (1990). Drifting into dealing: Becoming a cocaine seller. *Qualitative Sociology* 13(4), 335–360.

Musto, David. (1973). *The American disease: Origins of narcotic control*. New Haven, Conn.: Yale University Press.

Nash, George. (1973). *The impact of drug abuse treatment upon criminality: A look at 19 programs*. Upper Montclair, N.J.: Montclair State College.

National crime victimization survey, 1999. (2001). Washington, D.C.: U.S. Department of Justice, Bureau of Justice Statistics.

National crime victimization survey, 2001. (2003). Washington, D.C.: U.S. Department of Justice, Bureau of Justice Statistics.

National household survey on drug abuse—population estimates, 1999. (2001) Washington, D.C.: Substance Abuse and Mental Health Services Administration.

National Institute of Drug Abuse. (2001). *NIDA news release: 33-year study emphasizes lethal consequences of heroin addiction*. Washington, D.C.: NIDA.

National Institute of Justice. (1998). *ADAM: 1997 annual report on adult and juvenile arrestees*. Washington, D.C.: National Institute of Justice.

National School Safety Center. (1989). *Safe schools overview*. Malibu, Calif.: National School Safety Center, Pepperdine University.

National Transportation Safety Board. (1997). *Aircraft accident report: In-flight fire and impact with terrain, ValuJet airlines flight 592*. Washington, D.C.: U.S. Government Printing Office.

Needleman, Martin & Carolyn Needleman. (1979). Organizational crime: Two models of criminogenesis. *The Sociological Quarterly* 20, 517–528.

New Orleans Times Picayune. (1993). "Guns get respect on mean streets of urban U.S." *New Orleans Times Picayune* January 17, A8.

Nimick, E. (1990). Juvenile court property cases. *OJJDP update on statistics.* Washington, D.C.: United States Department of Justice, November, 1–5.

Noakes, J. & G. Pridham. (1988). *Nazism: A history in documents and eyewitness accounts.* New York: Schocken.

Normack, James W., Fred M. Eckel, John-Henry Pfifferling & George Cocolas. (1985). Impairment risk in North Carolina pharmacists. *American pharmacy* NS25(6), 45–48.

NRMA Insurance, Ltd. (1987). *Car theft in New South Wales.* Sydney: NRMA Insurance, Ltd.

O'Brien. John E. (1971). Violence in divorce-prone families. *Journal of Marriage and the Family* 33(4), 692–698.

O'Donnell, John A. (1966). Narcotic addiction and crime. *Social Problems* 13, 374–85.

O'Sullivan, Chris S. (1990). *What's rape? A content analysis of coverage of the 1989 Central Park assault.* Paper presented at the meeting of the Eastern Psychological Association, Philadelphia.

Office of National Drug Control Policy. (2000a). *What America's users spent on illegal drugs 1988–1998.* Washington, D.C.: Office of National Drug Control Policy.

———. (2000b). *Drug abuse warning network (DAWN): Annual medical examiners data, 1999.* Washington, D.C.: Office of National Drug Control Policy.

———. (2001). *The economic costs of drug abuse in the United States.* Washington, D.C.: Office of National Drug Control Policy.

———. (2002). *FY2002 national drug control budget, 2001.* Washington, D.C.: Office of National Drug Control Policy.

Osgood, Wayne D., Patrick M. O'Malley, Gerald G. Bachman & Lloyd D. Johnston. (1989). Time trends and age trends in arrests and self-reported behavior. *Criminology* 27(3), 389–415.

Oster, Clinton, John Strong & Kurt Zorn. (1992). *Why airplanes crash: Aviation safety in a changing world.* New York: Oxford.

Pace, E. (1971). "Shift in crime patterns adds to 'fences' here." *New York Times* October 12, 1, 31.

Padilla, Felix. (1992). *The gang as an American enterprise.* New Brunswick, N.J.: Rutgers University Press.

Pagelow, Mildred Daley. (1981). *Woman-battering.* Beverly Hills: Sage.

———. (1992). Adult victims of domestic violence. *Journal of Interpersonal Violence* 7, 87–120.

Park, Robert E. K., Ernest W. Burgess & Roderick D. McKenzie. (1928). *The city.* Chicago: University of Chicago Press.

Parker, J. S. (1989). Criminal sentencing policy for organizations: The unifying approach for optimal penalties. *American Criminal Law Review* 26, 513–604.

Pascall, G. (1986). *Social policy: A feminist analysis.* London: Tavistock Press.

Pateman, Carole. (1988). *The sexual contract.* Stanford, Calif.: Stanford University Press.

Peacock, P. L. (1995). Marital rape. In V. Wiehe & A. Richards (Eds.), *Intimate betrayal* (pp. 55–73). Thousand Oaks, Calif.: Sage.

Pearce, J. E. (1994). *Days of darkness: The feuds of Eastern Kentucky.* Lexington: University of Kentucky Press.

Perrow, Charles. (1984). *Normal accidents: Living with high-risk technologies.* New York: Basic Books.

Person, E. (1988). *Dreams and love and fateful encounters: The power of the romantic passion.* New York: Norton.

Pescor, Michael J. (1943). A statistical analysis of the clinical records of hospitalized drug addicts. *Public health reports supplement,* 143.

Pfuhl, E. (1978). The unwed father: A non-deviant rule breaker. *Sociological Quarterly* 19, 113–128.

Phoenix, Joanna. (1999a). *Making sense of prostitution.* London: Macmillan.

————. (1999b). Prostitutes, Ponces and Poncing: Making Sense of Violence. In J. Seymour & P. Bagguley (Eds.), *Relating intimacies: Power and resistance.* London: Macmillan.

————. (2000). Prostitute identities: Men, money and violence. *British Journal of Criminology* 40, 37–55.

Pierson, D. K. (1984). Mixed bag of reactions follows rape trial verdict. *Lansing State Journal* April 1, 1B-2B.

Pittman, D. J. & W. Handy. (1964). Patterns in criminal aggravated assault. *Journal of Criminal Law, Criminology, and Police Science* 55(4), 462–470.

Pogrebin, Mark R., Eric D. Poole & Amos Martinez. (1996). Accounts of professional misdeeds: the sexual exploitation of clients by psychotherapists. *Deviant behavior* 13, 229–252.

Pokorny, Alex D. (1965). Human violence: A comparison of homicide, aggravated assault, suicide, and attempted suicide. *Journal of Criminal Law, Criminology, and Police Science* 56, 488–497.

Polk, Kenneth. (1994). *When good kids kill: Scenarios of masculine violence.* New York: Cambridge University Press.

Polsky, Ned. (1967). *Hustlers, beats, and others.* Chicago: Aldine.

Potter, Gary & Larry Gaines. (1992). Country comfort: Vice and corruption in rural settings. *Journal of Contemporary Criminal Justice* 8(1), 36–61.

Potter, Gary, Larry Gaines & B. Holbrook. (1990). Blowing smoke: An evaluation of Kentucky's marijuana eradication program. *American Journal of Police* 9, 22–34.

Potterat, John J., Richjard B. Rotenberg, Stephen Q. Muth, Wiliam W. Darrow & Lyanne Phillips-Plummer. (1998). Pathways to prostitution: The chronology of sexual and drug abuse milestones. *The Journal of Sex Research* 35(4), 333–340.

Poyner, Barry. (1991). Situational crime prevention in two parking facilities. In R. V. Clarke (Ed.), *Situational crime prevention: Successful case studies* (pp. 174–184). Guilderland, N.Y.: Harrow and Heston.

Pratkanis, A. & E. Aronson. (1991). *Age of propoganda.* New York: W. H. Freeman.

Preble, Edward & John J. Casey. (1969). Taking care of business—The heroin addict's life on the street. *International Journal of the Addictions* 4, 1–24.

President's Commission on Law Enforcement and Administration of Justice. (1967). *Task force report: Crime and its impact—an assessment.* Washington, D.C.: U.S. Government Printing Office.

Prus, Robert & Styllianoss Irini. (1980). *Hookers, rounders and desk clerks: The social organization of a hotel community.* Salem, Wisc.: Sheffield.

Pulver, G. (1986). Economic growth in rural America. In Joint Economics Committe (Ed.), *New dimensions in rural policy: Building upon our heritage.* Washington, D.C.: U.S. Government Printing Office.

Quinney, Richard. (1970). *The social reality of crime.* Boston: Little, Brown.

Rada, Richard. (1978). *Clinical aspects of rape.* New York: Grune and Stratton.

Rampart Independent Review Panel. (1999). The Los Angeles police department rampart division scandal: Exposing police misconduct and responding to it. In M. D. Ermann & R. J. Lundman (Eds.), *Corporate and governmental deviance* (6th ed.) (pp. 250–276). New York: Oxford.

Rand, Michael R. (1994). *Carjacking.* Washington, D.C.: U.S. Department of Justice, Bureau of Justice Statistics.

————. (1997). *Violence-related injuries treated in hospital emergency departments.* Washington, D.C.: U.S. Department of Justice, Bureau of Justice Statistics.

Rauschning, H. (1940). *The voice of destruction.* New York: G. P. Putnam.

Rebovich, Donald J. & Jenny Layne. (2000). *The national public survey on white collar crime.* Morgantown, W.Va.: National White Collar Crime Center.

Reiman, Jeffrey. (1998). *The rich get richer and the poor get prison: Ideology, class, and criminal justice* (5th ed.). Boston: Allyn and Bacon.

Reimenschneider, James. (1990). One more day, one more miracle. *Pharmacy update* 1(20), 1+.

Reis, S. (1976). *Crime and criminology.* Hinsdale. Ill.: Dryden Press.

Reiss, Albert J. & Michael Tonry. (2002). Organizational crime. In N. Shover & J. P. Wright (Eds.), *Crimes of privilege: Readings in white-collar crime* (pp. 32–34). New York: Oxford.

Rengert, George F. & John Wasilchick. (1989). *Space, time and crime: Ethnographic insights into residential burglary.* Washington, D.C.: National Institute of Justice.

————. (2000). *Suburban burglary: A tale of two suburbs.* Springfield, Ill.: Charles C. Thomas.

Reppetto, Thomas A. (1974). *Residential crime.* Cambridge, Mass.: Ballinger.

Ridington. Jillian. (1978). The transition process: A feminist environment as reconstitutive milieu. *Victimology* 2(3–4), 563–576.

Riley, Jack. (1997). *Crack, powder cocaine, and heroin: Drug purchase patterns and use in six U.S. cities.* Washington, D.C.: Office of National Drug Control Policy.

Ritzer, George. (1988). *Contemporary sociological theory.* New York: Knopf.

Rivera, G. F., Jr & R. M. Regoli. (1987). Sexual victimization experiences of sorority women. *Sociology and social research* 72, 39–42.

Robin, Gerald D. (1963). Patterns of department store shoplifting. *Crime and delinquency* 9, 63–172.

Robins, Lee N. & George E. Murphy. (1967). Drug use in a normal population of young Negro men. *American Journal of Public Health* 570, 1580–1596.

Rogers, J. & M. Buffalo. (1974). Neutralization techniques: Toward a simplified measurement scale. *Pacific sociological review* 17(3), 313.

Romanesko, Kim & Eleanor M. Miller. (1989). The second step in double

jeopardy: Appropriating the labor of female street hustlers. *Crime and delinquency* 35, 109–135.

Rosenfeld, Richard & Scott H. Decker. (1996). Consent to search and seize: Evaluating an innovative youth firearm suppression program. *Law and contemporary problems* 59, 197–219.

Rosenthal, Marilynn M. (1995). *The incompetent doctor: Behind closed doors.* Philadelphia: Open University Press.

Rosoff, Stephen M., Henry N. Pontell & Robert Tillman. (1998). *Profit without honor: White-collar crime and the looting of America.* Upper Saddle River, N.J.: Prentice Hall.

Ross, Jeffrey I. (1995). *Controlling state crime.* New Brunswick, N.J.: Transaction Publishers.

Rossi, Peter, Emily Waite, Christine E. Bose & Richard Berk. (1974). The seriousness of crime: Normative structure and individual differences. *American Sociological Review* 39, 224–237.

Roy, Maria. (1977). *Battered women.* New York: Van Nostrand.

Rubenstein, Jonathan. (1974). *City police.* New York: Ballantine.

Russell, Diana E. H. (1975). *The politics of rape.* Briarcliff Manor, N.Y.: Stein and Day.

————. (1982). The prevalence and incidence of forcible rape and attempted rape of females. *Victimology* 7, 81–93.

————. (1984). *Sexual exploitation: Rape, child sexual abuse, and sexual harassment.* Beverly Hills: Sage.

————. (1990). *Rape in marriage.* Bloomington: Indiana University Press.

Russell, D. H. (1973). Emotional aspects of shoplifting. *Psychiatric annals* 3, 77–79.

Sagan, Scott D. (1993). *The limits of safety: Organizations, accidents, and nuclear weapons.* Princeton, N.J.: Princeton University Press.

Samaha, Joel. (1999). *Criminal law* (6th ed.). Belmont, Calif.: Wadsworth.

Sampson, Robert J. & John H. Laub. (1992). Crime and deviance in the life course. *Annual Review of Sociology* 24, 509–525.

Sanday, Peggy Reeves. (1979). *The socio-cultural context of rape.* Washington, D.C.: United States Department of Commerce, National Technical Information Service.

———. (1981). The socio-cultural context of rape: A cross-cultural study. *Journal of Social Issues* 37, 5–27.

Sanders, W. (1993). *Drive-bys and gang bangs: Gangs and grounded culture.* Chicago: Aldine.

Saul, Leon J. (1972). Personal and social psychopathology and the primary prevention of violence. *American Journal of Psychiatry* 128(12), 1578–1581.

Sayers, J. (1986). *Sexual contradictions: Psychology, psychoanalysis and feminism.* London: Tavistock.

Scalia, John. (2001). *Federal drug offenders, 1999 with trends 1984–1999.* Washington, D.C.: U.S. Department of Justice, Bureau of Justice Statistics.

Scanzoni, John. (1972). *Sexual bargaining.* Englewood Cliffs, N.J.: Prentice Hall.

Schafer, Stephan. (1968). *The victim and his criminal.* New York: Random House.

Schiavo, Mary. (1997). *Flying blind, flying safe.* New York: Avon Books.

Schlosser, E. (1994a). Reefer madness. *The Atlantic monthly* August, 45–63.

———. (1994b). Marijuana and the Law. *The Atlantic monthly* September, 84–94.

Schlueter, Gregory R., Francis C. O'Neal, JoAnn Hickey & Gloria Seiler. (1989). Rational and nonrational shoplifter types. *International Journal of Offender Therapy and Comparative Criminology* 33(3), 227–238.

Schwendinger, Julia & Herman Schwendinger. (1983). *Rape and inequality.* Beverly Hills: Sage.

Scully, Diana. (1994). *Understanding sexual violence: A study of convicted rapists.* New York: Routledge.

Scully, Diana and Joseph Marolla. (1984). Convicted rapists' vocabulary of

motive: Excuses and justifications. *Social Problems* 31, 530–44

———. (1985). Rape and psychiatric vocabulary of motive: Alternative perspectives. In A. Wolbert Burgess (Ed.), *Rape and sexual assault: A research handbook* (pp. 294–312). New York: Garland Publishing.

———. (1985). Riding the bull at Gilley's: Convicted rapists describe the rewards of rape. *Social Problems* 32, 251–263.

Sereny, Gitta. (1983). *Into that darkness.* New York: Vintage.

Sexty, C. (1990). *Women losing out: Access to housing in Britain today.* London: Shelter.

Shakespeare, William. (1974). *Macbeth.* Boston: Houghton Mifflin.

Shapiro, D. (1981). *Autonomy and rigid character.* New York: Basic Books.

Shapiro, Susan P. (1990). Collaring the crime, not the criminal. *American Sociological Review* 55, 346–365.

Sharpe, Karen. (1998). *Red light, blue light: Prostitutes, punters and the police.* Brookfield, VT: Ashgate.

Shaw, Clifford & Henry D. McKay. (1942). *Juvenile delinquency and urban areas.* Chicago: University of Chicago Press.

Sheffield, Jean W. (1988). Establishing a rehabilitation program for impaired pharmacists. *American Journal of Hospital Pharmacy* 45(10), 2092–2098.

Sheley, J., Z. McGee & J. Wright. (1992). Gun-related violence in and around inner-city schools. *American Journal of Diseases of Children* 146, 677–682.

Sherman, Lawerence W., Patrick R. Gartin & Michael D. Bueger. (1989). Hot spots of predatory crime: Routine activities and the criminology of place. *Criminology* 27(1), 27–56.

Shibutani, Tamotsu. (1961). *Society and personality: An interactionist approach to social psychology.* Englewood Cliffs, N.J.: Prentice Hall.

Shields, N. & C. Hanneke. (1983). Battered wives' reactions to marital rape. In R. Gelles, G. Hotaling,

M. Straus & D. Finkelhor (Eds.), *The dark side of families*. Beverly Hills: Sage.

Shoham, Shlomo, Sara Ben-David, Rivka Vadmani, Joseph Atar, and Suzanne Fleming. (1973). The cycles of interaction in violence. In S. Shoham (Ed.), *Israel studies in criminology* (pp. 69–87). Jerusalem: Jerusalem Academic Press.

Short, J. (1974). Collective behavior, crime, and delinquency. In D. Glaser (Ed.), *Handbook of criminology* (pp. 403–439). New York: Rand McNally.

Short, J. & F. Strodtbeck. (1974). *Group process and gang delinquency*. Chicago: University of Chicago Press.

Shotland, R. Lance & Margret K. Straw (1976). Bystander response to an assault: When a man attacks a woman. *Journal of Personality and Social Psychology* 34(5), 990–999.

Shover, Neal (1983). The later stages of ordinary property offender careers. *Social Problems* 31(2), 208–218.

———. (1991). Burglary. In M. Tonry (Ed.), *Crime and justice: A review of research*. Chicago: University of Chicago Press.

———. (1996). Aging criminals: Change in the criminal calculus. In P. Cromwell (Ed.), *In their own words: Criminals on crime* (pp. 57–64). Los Angeles: Roxbury.

———. (1996). *Great pretenders: Pursuits and careers of persistent thieves*. Boulder, Colo.: Westview.

Shover, Neal & David Honaker. (1992). The socially-bounded decision making of persistent property offenders. *Howard Journal of Criminal Justice* 31, 276–293.

———. (1996). The socially bounded decision making of persistent property offenders. In P. Cromwell (Ed.), *In their own words: Criminals on crime* (pp. 10–22). Los Angeles: Roxbury.

Simon, David R. & Frank E. Hagan. (1999). *White-collar deviance*. Boston: Allyn and Bacon.

Simon, R. (1975). *Women and crime*. Lexington, Mass.: Lexington Books.

Simon, Thomas, James Mercy & Craig Perkins. (2001). *Injuries from violent crime, 1992–1998*. Washington, D.C.: U.S. Department of Justice, Bureau of Justice Statistics.

Skogan, Wesley. (1978). Weapon use in robbery. In J. Inciardi & A. Pottieger (Eds.), *Violent crime: Historical and contemporary issues*. Beverly Hills: Sage.

Skolnick, Jerome & James Fyfe. (1993). *Above the law: Police and the excessive use of force*. New York: Free Press.

Slobodian, Paul J. & Kevin D. Browne. (1997). Car crime as a developmental career: An analysis of young offenders in Coventry. *Psychology, Crime & the Law*, 3, 275–286.

Smigel, Erwin O. (1956). Public attitudes toward stealing as related to the size of the victim organization. In E. O. Smigel & H. L. Ross (Eds.), *Crimes against bureaucracy* (pp. 15–28). New York: Van Nostrand Reinhold Press.

Smith, Don. (1976). The social context of pornography. *Journal of Communications*, 26, 16–24.

Smith, Jean Paul. (1973). Substance in illicit drugs. In R. H. Blum et al. (Eds.), *Drug dealers-Taking action* (pp. 13–30) San Francisco: Jossey Bass.

Smith, M. D. & N. Bennett. (1985). Poverty, inequality, and theories of forcible rape. *Crime and delinquency* 31, 295–305.

Smithyman, Samuel. (1978). The undetected rapist. Unpublished Doctoral Dissertation: Claremont Graduate School.

Snell, John E., Richard Rosenwald & Ames Robey. (1964). The wifebeater's wife: A study of family interaction. *Archives of general psychiatry* 11 (August), 107–112.

Sommers, Ira & Deborah R. Baskin. (1993). The situational context of violent female offending. *Journal of Research in Crime and Delinquency* 30(2), 136–162.

Spiegel, John P. (1968). The resolution of role conflict within the family. In W. Bell & E. F. Vogel (Eds.), *A modern introduction to the family* (pp. 391–411). New York: Free Press.

Sprey, Jetse. (1971). On the management of conflict in families. *Journal of Marriage and the Family* 33(4), 699–706.

Spunt, B., P. Goldstein, H. Brownstein, M. Fendrich & S. Langley. (1994). Alcohol and homicide: Interviews with prison inmates. *Journal of Drug Issues* 24(1), 143–163.

Stampp, K. M. (1989). *The peculiar institution.* New York: Vintage.

Standing Bear, Zug G. (1994). Crime as a hobby: Taking an "involuntary discount" on expensive wines. *Deviant Behavior* 15, 111–124.

Starr, Cinthia. (1989a). Breaking out part 1: Pharmacists in recovery. *Drug topics* June 5, 29–34.

———. (1989b). Breaking out part 2: Pharmacists in galvanized. *Drug topics* June 19, 12–15.

Staub, Ervin. (1989). *The roots of evil: The origins of genocide and other group violence.* New York: Cambridge University Press.

Steffensmeier, Darrel J. (1986). *The fence: In the shadow of two worlds.* Savage, Md.: Rowman & Littlefield.

Steffensmeir, Darrell J. & Renee Hoffman Steffensmeir. (1977). Who reports shoplifters? Research continuities and further developments. *Journal of Criminology and Penology* 5, 79–95.

Steffensmeir, Darrell J. & Robert T. Terry. (1973). Deviance and respectability: An observational study of reactions to shoplifting. *Social Forces* 51, 417–426.

Stein, Michael & George McCall. (1994). Home ranges and daily rounds: Uncovering community among urban nomads. *Research in community sociology* 1, 77–94.

Steinmetz, Suzanne K. (1978). The battered husband syndrome. *Victimology* 2(3–4), 499–509.

Steinmetz, Suzanne K. & Murray A. Strauss. (1974). *Violence in the family.* New York: Harper and Row.

Stern, Willy. (1996). Has the FAA been coming clean? *Business week* June 17, 37+

Stevenson, Robert J. (1998). *The boiler room and other telephone sales scams.* Chicago: University of Illinois Press.

Stitt, B. Grant & David J. Giacopassi. (1993). Assessing victimization from corporate harms. In M. B. Blankenship (Ed.), *Understanding corporate criminality* (pp. 57–84). New York: Garland.

Stolberg, Sheryl. (1993). Mortality study finds tobacco is no. 1 culprit. *Los Angeles times* November 10, A1, A33.

Straus, Murray A. (1978). Wifebeating: How common and why? *Victimology* 2(3–4), 443–458.

———. (1979). Measuring intrafamily conflict and violence: The conflict tactics (CT) scales. *Journal of Marriage and the Family* 41(1), 75–88.

Stevens, Dennis J. (1999). *Inside the mind of a serial rapist.* San Francisco: Austin & Winfield Publishers.

Substance Abuse and Mental Health Services Administration. (2001). *Drug abuse warning network: The DAWN report.* Washington, D.C.: Substance Abuse and Mental Health Services Administration.

Substance Abuse Report. (1988). Sex for crack: How the new prostitution affects drug abuse treatment. *Substance abuse report* November 15, 1–4.

Sueling, Barbara. (1975). *More wacky laws.* New York: Scholastic.

Sullivan, Mercer L. (1989). *Getting paid: Youth crime and work in the inner city.* Ithaca, N.Y.: Cornell University Press.

Sutherland, Edwin H. (1939). *Principles of Criminology* (3rd ed.). Philadelphia: J. B. Lippincott.

———. (1940). White collar criminality. *American Sociological Review* 5, 1–12.

———. (1949). *White collar crime.* New York: Holt, Rinehart & Winston.

Sutherland, Edwin H. & Donald R. Cressey. (1945). Is "white-collar crime" crime? *American Sociological Review* 10, 132–139.

———. (1970). *Criminology* (8th ed.). Philadelphia: J. B. Lippincott.

———. (1974). *Principles of criminology* (9th ed.). Philadelphia: J. B. Lippincott.

Suttles, G. (1972). *The social construction of communities.* Chicago: University of Chicago Press.

Swazey, J. P., K. S. Louis & M. S. Anderson. (1989). University policies and ethical issues in research and graduate education: Highlights of the CGS Dean's survey. *CGS Communicator* 22, 1–8.

Sykes, Gresham & David Matza. (1957). Techniques of neutralization: A theory of delinquency. *American Sociological Review* 22, 664–670.

Szasz, Thomas. (1992). *Our right to drugs: The case for a free market.* New York: Praeger.

Szockyj, Elizabeth. (1993). Insider trading: The SEC meets Carl Karcher. *Annals of the American Academy of Political and Social Science* 525, 46–58.

Tanay, E. (1972). Psychiatric aspects of homicide prevention. *American Journal of Psychology* 128, 814–817.

Tappan, Paul. (1960). *Crime, justice and corrections.* New York: McGraw-Hill.

Tathum, Ronald L. (1974). Employee views of theft in retailing. *Journal of Retailing* 50, 49–55.

Taylor, Avril. (1993). *Women drug users: An ethnography of a female injecting community.* New York: Oxford University Press.

Teich, A. (1992). Integrity in research: The scientific community view. *Knowledge, creation, diffusion, utilization* 14, 185–192.

Terry, Charles E. & Mildred Pellens. (1928). *The opium problem.* New York: The Haddon Craftsman.

Thomas, W. I. & Florian Znaniecki. (1920). *The polish peasant in Europe and America.* Chicago: University of Chicago Press.

Thrasher, F. (1927). *The gang.* Chicago: University of Chicago Press.

Tierney, Kathleen J. (1982). The battered women movement and the creation of the wife beating problem. *Social Problems* 29(3), 207–220.

Tillman, Robert. (1998). *Broken promises: Fraud by small business health insurers.* Boston: Northeastern University Press.

Tittle, Charles R. (1995). *Control balance: Toward a general theory of deviance.* Boulder, Colo.: Westview.

Tittle, Charles R. & Raymond Patternoster. (2000). *Social deviance and crime: An organizational and theoretical approach.* Los Angeles: Roxbury.

Titus, Richard M., Fred Heinzelmann & John M. Boyle. (1995). Victimization of persons by fraud. *Crime & Delinquency* 41, 54–72.

Tjaden, Patricia & Nancy Thoennes. (2000). *Extent, nature, and consequences of intimate partner violence.* Washington, D.C.: National Institute of Justice.

Toch, Hans. (1969). *Violent men: An inquiry into the psychology of violence.* Chicago: Aldine.

Topalli, Volkan, Richard Wright & Robert Fornango. (2002). Drug dealers, robbery and retaliation: Vulnerability, deterrence, and the contagion of violence. *British Journal of Criminology* 42 (in press).

Trebach, Arnold S. & James A. Inciardi. (1993). *Legalize it? Debating American drug policy.* Washington, D.C.: American University Press.

Tremblay, Pierre, Yvan Clermont & Maurice Cusson. (1994). Jockeys and Joyriders: Changing patterns in car theft opportunity structures. *British Journal of Criminology* 34(3), 307–321.

Tucker, R. (1985). Addiction: Three stories. *American pharmacy* NS25(6), 38–43.

Tunnell, Kenneth D. (1992). *Choosing crime: The criminal calculus of property offenders.* Chicago: Nelson-Hall Publishers.

———. (1993a). *Political crime in contemporary America.* New York: Garland.

———. (1993b). Political crime and pedagogy: A content analysis of criminology and criminal justice texts. *The Journal of Criminal Justice Education* 4, 101–114.

Turk, Austin. (1982). *Political criminality.* Beverly Hills: Sage.

Turner, C. T. & S. Cashdan. (1988). Perceptions of college students motivations for shoplifting. *Psychological reports* 62, 855–862.

Tyco International. (2001 Nov. 23). New study finds that U.S. retailers losing 432 billion to theft: Losses from employees theft reach record levels. Boca Raton, Fla.: Tyco International, LTD press release.

Uniform crime reports (1997). Washington, D.C.: Federal Bureau of Investigation.

U.S. Department of Health and Human Services. (1991). *Morbidity and mortality weekly report: Weapon carrying among high school students-United States, 1991.* Washington, D.C.: Department of Health and Human Services.

U.S. Department of Labor. (l980). *Handbook of labor statistics.* Washington, D.C.: U.S. Government Printing Office.

U.S. Senate. (1975). *Criminal redistribution systems and their economic impact on small business.* Report of the Select Committee On Small Business, 95th Congress, 1st Session. Washington, D.C.: U.S. Government Printing Office.

Vaughan, Diane. (1983). *Controlling unlawful organizational behavior: Social structure and corporate misconduct.* Chicago: University of Chicago Press.

———. (1983). The macro-micro connection in "white-collar crime" theory. In K. Schlegel & D. Weisburd (Eds.), *White collar crime reconsidered* (pp. 124–145). Boston: Northeastern University Press.

———. (1985). *Controlling unlawful organizational behavior: Social structure and corporate misconduct.* Chicago: University of Chicago Press.

———. (1996). *The challenger launch decision: Risky, technology, culture and deviance at NASA.* Chicago: University of Chicago Press.

———. (2002). The *Challenger* space shuttle disaster: Conventional wisdom and a revisionist account. In M. D. Ermann & R. J. Lundman (Eds.), *Corporate and governmental deviance* (6th ed.) (pp. 306–334). New York: Oxford.

Vaughan, Sharon Rice. (1919). The last refuge: Shelter for battered women. *Victimology* 4(1), 113–150.

Veevers, J. (1975). The moral careers of voluntarily childless wives: Notes on the defense of a variant world view. *Family coordinator* 24(4), 473–487.

Verlarde, A. (1975). Becoming prostituted: The decline of the massage parlor profession and the masseuse. *British Journal of Criminology* 15(3), 251–263.

Vigil, D. (1998). *Barrio gangs.* Austin: University of Texas Press.

Voskull, J. (1993). "Prison Poverty Has No Bounds." *Louisville Courier-Journal* December 5, 1A.

Wagenaar, Willem A. (1988). *Paradoxes of gambling behavior.* Hillsdale, N.J.: Erlbaum.

Waldorf, Dan. (1993). Don't be your own best customer: Drug use of San Francisco gang drug sellers. *Crime, law, and social change* 19, 1–15.

Walker, Lenore E. (1997). *The battered woman.* New York: Harper and Row.

Walker, Samuel. (2001). *Sense and nonsense about crime and drugs* (5th ed.). Belmont, Calif.: Wadsworth.

Walklate, S. (1989). *Victimology.* London: Unwin Hyman.

Waller, Irvin & Norman Okihiro. (1978). *Burglary: The victim and the public.* Toronto: University of Toronto Press.

Wallisch, Lynn S. (1996). *Gambling in Texas: 1995 surveys of adult and adolescent gambling behavior.* Austin: Texas Commission on Alcohol and Drug Abuse.

Walsh, Dermot P. (1980). *Break-ins: Burglary from private houses.* London: Constable.

———. (1986). Victim selection procedures among economic criminals: The rational choice perspective. In D. B. Cornish & R. V. Clarke (Eds.), *The reasoning criminal: Rational choice perspectives on offending* (pp. 39–52). New York: Springer-Verlag.

Walsh, Marilyn E. (1977). *The fence: A new look at the world of property theft.* Westport, Conn.: Greenwood.

Walters, Glenn. (1990). *The criminal lifestyle.* Newbury Park, Calif.: Sage.

Walters, James M. (1985). Taking care of business' updated: A fresh look at the daily routine of the heroin user. In B. Hanson, G. Beschner, J. M. Walters & E. Bovelle (Eds.), *Life with heroin: Voices from the inner city* (pp. 31–48). Lexington, Mass.: Lexington Books.

Ward, D., M. Jackson & R. Ward. (1979). Crimes of violence by women. In F. Adler & R. Simon (Eds.) *The Criminology of deviant women* (pp. 114–38). Boston: Houghton Mifflin.

Warley, Raquel-Maria, Susan M. Crimmins, Judith A. Ryder & Herny H. Brownstein. (1998). Comparing assault and homicide offenses among adolescent male offenders. Paper presented at the Annual Meetings of the American Society of Criminology, Washington, D.C.

Warrior, Betsy. (1978). *Working on wife abuse.* Cambridge, Mass.: Betsy Warrior.

Warshaw, Robin. (1994). *I never called it rape.* New York: Harper/Perennial.

Warshaw, Robin & Andrea Parrot. (1991). The contribution of sex-role socialization to acquaintance rape. In A. Parrot & L. Bechhofer (Eds.), *Acquaintance rape: The hidden crime* (pp. 73–83). New York: John Wiley & Sons.

Watson, S. & Austerberry, H. (1986). *Housing and homelessness: A feminist perspective.* London: Routledge and Kegan Paul.

Weaver, Frances M. & John S. Carroll. (1985). Crime perceptions in a natural setting by expert and novice shoplifters. *Social Psychology Quarterly* 48(4), 349–359.

Webster, P. (1978). Politics of rape in primitive society. *Heresies* 6, 16–18, 20, 22.

Weedon, C. (1987). *Feminist practice and post-structuralist theory.* Oxford: Blackwell.

Weidner, Robert R. (2001). *"I don't do Manhattan:" Causes and consequences of a decline in street prostitution.* New York: LFB Publishers.

Weis, Carl. (1974). *Terror in the prisons: Homosexual rape and why society condones it.* Indianapolis: Bobbs-Merrill.

Weis, Kurt & Sandra Borges. (1973). Victimology and rape: The case of the legitimate victim. *Issues in criminology* 8, 71–115.

Weisburd, David & Rosann Greenspan. (2000). *Police attitudes toward abuse of authority: Findings from a national study.* Washington, D.C.: National Institute of Justice.

Weisburd, David, Elin Waring & Ellen F. Chayet. (2001). *White-collar crime and criminal careers.* New York: Cambridge University Press.

Weisburd, David, Stanton Wheeler, Elin Waring & Nancy Bode. (1991). *Crimes of the middle class.* New Haven, Conn.: Yale University Press.

Weisheit, Ralph. (1990a). *Cash crop: A study of illicit marijuana growers.* Draft of report for grant Cx-oo16. Washington, D.C. National Institute of Justice.

———. (1990b). Domestic marijuana growers: Mainstreaming deviance. *Deviant Behavior* 11(2), 107–129.

———. (1991a). Drug use among domestic marijuana growers. *Contemporary drug problems* Summer, 191–217.

———. (1991b). The intangible rewards from crime: The case of domestic marijuana cultivation. *Crime & Delinquency* 37, 506–527.

———. (1992). *Domestic marijuana: A neglected industry.* Westport, Conn.: Greenwood Press.

———. (1993). Studying drugs in rural areas: Notes from the field. *Journal of Research in Crime and Delinquency* 30, 213–232.

Weisheit, R. A., B. A. Smith & K. Johnson. (1991). Does the American experience with alcohol prohibition generalize to marijuana? *American Journal of Criminal Justice* 15(2), 13–55.

Weisheit, R. A., D. Falcone & L. Wells. (1194). *Rural crime and rural policing.*

Washington, D.C.: National Institute of Justice.

Weiss, R. D. & S. M. Marin. (1987). *Cocaine.* Washington, D.C.: American Psychiatric Press.

Weissman, James C., Paul L. Katsampes & Thomas A. Giacienti. (1947). Opiate use and criminality among a jail population. *Addictive diseases* 1, 269–81.

Wells, Joseph T. (1993). Accountancy and white-collar crime. *Annals of the American Academy of Political and Social Science* 525, 83–94.

West, Donald J. (1983). Sex offenses and offending. In M. Tonry & N. Morris (Eds.), *Crime and Justice: An annual review of research* (pp. 1–30). Chicago: University of Chicago Press.

West, D. & D. Farrington. (1977). *The delinquent way of life.* London: Heinemann.

Westley, W. (1966). The escalation of violence through legitimation. *Annals of the American Association of Political and Social Science* 364, 120–126.

Wheeler, Hollis. (1985). Pornography and rape: A feminist perspective. In A. Wolbert Burgess (Ed.), *Rape and sexual assault: A research handbook* (pp. 314–391). New York: Garland Publishing.

Whelehan, Patricia. (2001). *An anthropological perspective on prostitution.* Lewiston, N.Y.: Edwin Mellen Press.

Wilkinson, R. (1955). *Women of the streets: A sociological study of the common prostitution.* British Social and Biological Council: London.

Williams, Terry. (1989). *The cocaine kids: The inside story of a teenage drug ring.* Reading, Mass.: Addison-Wesley Publishing Co.

Wilson, J. & A. Abrahamse. (1992). Does crime pay? *Justice Quarterly* 9(3), 357–377.

Wilson, John J. (2000). *1998 national youth gang survey.* Washington, D.C.: Office for Juvenile Justice and Delinquency Prevention.

Wilson, William J. (1987). *The truly disadvantaged.* Chicago: University of Chicago Press.

Winick, Charles & Paul M. Kinsie. (1971). *The living commerce: Prostitution in the United States.* Chicago: Quadrangle Books.

Wivell, M. K & G. L. Wilson. (1994). Prescription for harm: Pharmacist liability. *Trial* 30(5), 36–39.

Wolff, C. (1989). "Youths rape and beat Central Park jogger." *New York Times* April 21, B1, B3.

Wolfgang, Marvin E. (1958). *Patterns of criminal homicide.* Philadelphia: University of Pennsylvania Press.

Won, G. & G. Yamamoto. (1968). Social structure and deviant behavior: A study of shoplifting. *Sociology and social research* 53(1), 45–55.

Worden, Robert E. & Robin L. Shepard. (1996). Demeanor, crime, and police behavior: A reexamination of the police services study data. *Criminology* 34, 83–105.

Wright, James D., Peter Rossi & Kathleen Daly. (1983). *Under the gun.* Hawthorne, N.Y.: Aldine.

Wright, Richard & Trevor Bennett. (1990). Exploring the offender's perspective: Observing and interviewing criminals. In K. Kempf (Ed.), *Measurement issues in criminology.* New York: Springer-Verlag.

Wright, Richard, Robert H. Logie & Scott Decker. (1995). Criminal expertise and offender decision making: An experimental study of the target selection process in residential burglary. *Journal of Research in Crime and Delinquency* 32(1), 39–53.

Wright, Richard & Scott H. Decker. (1994). *Burglars on the job: Streetlife and residential break-ins.* Boston: Northeastern University Press.

———. (1997). *Armed robbers in action: Stickups and street culture.* Boston: Northeastern University Press.

Wright, Richard, Scott H. Decker, Allison K. Redfern & Dietrich L. Smith. (1992). A snowball's chance in hell: Doing field work with active residential burglars. *Journal of*

Research in Crime and Delinquency 29, 148–61.

Zawitz, Marianne W. (1995). *Guns used in crime.* Washington, D.C.: U.S. Department of Justice, Bureau of Justice Statistics.

———. (1996). *Firearm injuries from crime.* Washington, D.C.: U.S. Department of Justice, Bureau of Justice Statistics.

Zawitz, Marianne W. & Kevin J. Strom. (2000). *Firearm injuries and death from crime, 1993–1997.* Washington, D.C.: U.S. Department of Justice, Bureau of Justice Statistics.

Zevitz, R. & M. Farkas. (2000). Sex offenders community notification: Examining the importance of neighborhood meetings. *Behavioral science and the law* 18, 393–406.

Zinberg, Noman E. (1984). *Drug set and setting: The basis for controlled intoxicant use.* New Haven, Conn.: Yale University Press.

Credits

This page constitutes an extension of the copyright page. We have made every effort to trace the ownership of all copyrighted material and to secure permission from copyright holders. In the event of any question arising as to the use of any material, we will be pleased to make the necessary corrections in future printings. Thanks are due to the following authors, publishers, and agents for permission to use the material indicated.